PUBLICATIONS OF THE NEWTON INSTITUTE

Higher Order Operational Techniques in Semantics

Publications of the Newton Institute

Edited by H. P. F. Swinerton-Dyer
Executive Director, Isaac Newton Institute for Mathematical Sciences

The Isaac Newton Institute of Mathematical Sciences of the University of Cambridge exists to stimulate research in all branches of the mathematical sciences, including pure mathematics, statistics, applied mathematics, theoretical physics, theoretical computer science, mathematical biology and economics. The four six-month long research programmes it runs each year bring together leading mathematical scientists from all over the world to exchange ideas through seminars, teaching and informal interaction.

Associated with the programmes are two types of publication. The first contains lecture courses, aimed at making the latest developments accessible to a wider audience and providing an entry to the area. The second contains proceedings of workshops and conferences focusing on the most topical aspects of the subjects.

Higher Order Operational Techniques in Semantics

Edited by

Andrew D. Gordon and Andrew M. Pitts

Computer Laboratory, Cambridge University

CAMBRIDGE
UNIVERSITY PRESS

CAMBRIDGE UNIVERSITY PRESS
Cambridge, New York, Melbourne, Madrid, Cape Town,
Singapore, São Paulo, Delhi, Tokyo, Mexico City

Cambridge University Press
The Edinburgh Building, Cambridge CB2 8RU, UK

Published in the United States of America by
Cambridge University Press, New York

www.cambridge.org
Information on this title: www.cambridge.org/9780521631686

First published 1998

A catalogue record for this publication is available from the British Library

ISBN 978-0-521-63168-6 Hardback

Contents

Contributors

Andrew D. Gordon Computer Laboratory, Cambridge University, Pembroke Street, Cambridge CB2 3QG, UK

Robert Harper School of Computer Science, Carnegie Mellon University, Pittsburgh, PA 15213-3891, USA

My Hoang SAP Technology, Inc., 950 Tower Lane, 16th Floor, Foster City, CA 94404, USA

Brian T. Howard Department of Mathematics and Computer Science, Bridgewater College, Bridgewater, Virginia 22812, USA

Søren B. Lassen Computer Laboratory, Cambridge University, Pembroke Street, Cambridge CB2 3QG, UK

Greg Morrisett Department of Computer Science, Cornell University, Ithaca, NY 14853-7501, USA

Alan Jeffrey School of Cognitive and Computing Sciences, University of Sussex, Falmer, Brighton BN1 9QH, UK

John C. Mitchell Department of Computer Science, Stanford University, Stanford CA 94305-9045, USA

Andrew M. Pitts Computer Laboratory, Cambridge University, Pembroke Street, Cambridge CB2 3QG, UK

David Sands Department of Computing Science, Chalmers University of Technology and University of Göteborg, S-412 96 Göteborg, Sweden

Scott F. Smith Department of Computer Science, The Johns Hopkins University, Baltimore, MD 21218-2686, USA

Ian D. B. Stark Department of Computer Science, Edinburgh University, King's Buildings, Mayfield Road, Edinburgh EH9 3JZ, UK

Carolyn Talcott Department of Computer Science, Stanford University, Stanford CA 94305-9045, USA

Preface

This is a collection of articles about recent developments in operational semantics for higher order programming languages, by some of the leading researchers in the field. The idea for the book arose at the workshop on *Higher Order Operational Techniques in Semantics* (*HOOTS*) that took place in October 1995. The workshop was organised by the editors of this volume as part of a six-month programme on *Semantics of Computation* at the Isaac Newton Institute for Mathematical Sciences, Cambridge UK, with financial assistance from the EPSRC and Harlequin Ltd.

Although international conferences and workshops on programming language semantics occur regularly, the HOOTS workshop was unusual for its focus on operational techniques across a range of high-level programming styles. These uses of operational semantics have arisen from a variety of research communities—for example, in concurrency theory, in functional programming, and in type theory—and some of the methods and techniques have emerged only recently. For these reasons the HOOTS workshop was a timely and stimulating meeting. The nine contributions to this volume are original articles which develop in depth many of the themes introduced at the workshop. Each has been refereed in the usual way. We wish to thank all the contributors and referees for their efforts.

Finally, we are grateful to Lindy Rees for drawing the HOOTS logo.

Andrew D. Gordon
Andrew M. Pitts

August 1997

Introduction

The articles in this volume concern operational semantics of higher order programming languages, mathematical techniques for developing the properties of such operational semantics, and applications of those techniques. In this Introduction we set the articles in the wider context of research into programming languages and bring out some of the themes and techniques that recur throughout the book.

Operational Semantics

The various approaches to giving meanings to programming languages fall broadly into three categories: denotational, axiomatic, and operational. In a denotational semantics, the meaning of programs is defined abstractly using elements of some suitable mathematical structure. In an axiomatic semantics, meaning is defined indirectly via the axioms and rules of some logic of program properties. In an operational semantics, the meaning of programs is defined in terms of their behaviour, for example the steps of computation they can take during program execution. Whilst the first two approaches have much in common with semantic studies in mathematical logic and linguistics, the third is distinctive of computer science. Nevertheless, operational semantics is often regarded as the 'poor relation' of the other two approaches. The reason for this has to do with the fact that it tends to be quite concrete, with important general properties of a language's various features sometimes obscured by the low-level description of how program execution takes place. Thus at its worst, an operational specification may come perilously close to committing the sin of 'definition by implementation' (which is a sin because such a definition is not particularly useful). Such a criticism was certainly pertinent in the early days of the subject and was a stimulus to the development of the more mathematically principled methods of denotational and axiomatic semantics. To quote Plotkin (1981, page 21), the early attempts at semantic definitions based on abstract machines had "a tendency to pull the syntax to pieces or at any rate to wander around the syntax creating various complex symbolic structures which do not seem particularly forced by the demands of the language itself".

This situation changed radically with the development by Kahn, Milner, Plotkin, and others of a *structural* approach to operational semantics (SOS). SOS is now very widely used and in particular features in all the contributions in this volume. Because of the seminal work on the subject by Plotkin (1981), SOS is often taken to entail the use of (labelled) transition systems to describe steps of computation. However, Milner and Kahn's uses of 'relational', 'natural', or 'big-step' semantics (of which the Definition of Standard ML by Milner, Tofte, Harper, and MacQueen (1997) is the shining example) were similar in spirit to Plotkin's development. In

(1997) is the shining example) were similar in spirit to Plotkin's development. In each case, there are two key ideas. First, inspired by their use in mathematical logic for specifying formal systems, inductive definitions are used to define relations between programs or machine configurations. These relations comprise the operational description of the language. Second, the rule schemes used in these inductive definitions are syntax-directed. This often permits a simplification of the configurations of the machine—in the best cases they become just certain phrases of the language itself. It means also that SOS has a compositional aspect more usually associated with denotational semantics and which is essential for reasoning about program properties.

Higher Order Programming Languages

By a *higher order* programming language we mean one in which the means of manipulation—be it function, or procedure, or process, or object—can itself be manipulated. Most of the papers in this volume make use of function-oriented languages based on various kinds of λ-calculi, both typed and untyped. The articles by Lassen, Mitchell-Hoang-Howard, and Sands concern pure functional languages; whereas those by Jeffrey, Morrisett-Harper, Pitts-Stark, Smith, and Talcott concern the combination of functions with various 'effects'—such as the dynamic creation and mutation of state, and the spawning of concurrent communicating threads of computation. Object-oriented languages are studied in the articles by Gordon and Smith.

Higher order languages present difficult challenges for any style of semantics, be it axiomatic, denotational, or operational. For example, an axiomatic semantics of higher order procedures which is sound, expressive and useable has proved elusive (see Reynolds (1982) and O'Hearn and Tennent (1993)). Another well-known example is the difficulty of finding mathematical structures which yield denotational semantics that are both compositional and agree with the observable behaviour of programs. The search for such 'fully abstract' denotational models has been long and hard even in the apparently simple case of pure higher order functions (Plotkin 1977), let alone for the combination of functions with local state (Meyer and Sieber 1988), or with features involving non-deterministic interaction (where even mere compositionality is a challenge). Recent developments involving mathematical games (Abramsky 1997; Hyland 1997) promise to solve many of these problems. As with the classical Scott-Plotkin denotational models based upon order-theoretic structure, a considerable mathematical investment is required to understand and apply such models.

The challenge of higher order languages for operational semantics is somewhat different. In contrast to the axiomatic and denotational approaches, it is relatively easy to give inductively defined, structural operational semantics for all of the language features mentioned above. The reader will find such definitions throughout the articles in this book. What is not so easy is to develop the mathematical properties and applications of such operational definitions. The articles in this book discuss various techniques for achieving such a development. A related problem is the syntax-dependent nature of operational methods, which makes it hard to reuse the theory developed for one language in a related language. The articles by Smith and Talcott address this issue.

Aims, Methods and Techniques

Of course, a principal aim of an operational semantics of a language is to give a mathematically precise definition of how to execute programs—for example as a guide to implementors of the language. Beyond that, the following three types of application are well represented in what follows.

Proving properties of programs. Operational semantics is frequently used to define notions of semantic equivalence of programs and to develop the theory of such notions. (Examples of this occur in the articles by Gordon, Jeffrey, Lassen, Pitts-Stark, and Talcott.)

Correctness of interpreters and compilers. Interpretations of one language in another occur throughout computer science and one naturally wishes to verify the extent to which meaning is preserved or reflected under such translations. (See the articles by Jeffrey, Morrisett-Harper, and Smith.)

Questions of efficiency. The concrete nature of an operational semantics makes it potentially[1] better suited to studying intensional questions of efficiency, use of temporary storage space, etc. (See the articles by Morrisett-Harper and Sands.)

In pursuit of the above aims, the following operational methods and techniques are employed in the articles in this volume.

Context lemmas and extensionality principles. For many languages (particularly deterministic ones), operational semantics gives rise to a natural notion of semantic equivalence variously called *contextual*, *operational*, or *observational* equivalence. Roughly speaking, two program phrases are contextually equivalent if occurrences of the phrases in any executable program, that is, in any 'context', can be interchanged without affecting the results of executing the program. Although this notion is intuitively appealing, for higher order languages it can be difficult to establish its general properties (other than the fact that it is a congruence, that is, respects the language constructs, which follows immediately from its definition). For example, for a language with higher order functions, we may hope for an extensionality result that explains contextual equivalence of functions

[1]Computational complexity for higher order languages is a rather under-developed area.

in terms of contextual equivalence of their results when applied to an argument. Milner's Context Lemma for the simply typed language PCF (Milner 1977; Plotkin 1977) is an early example of such a result: it says that one can restrict attention to simple, applicative contexts when proving contextual equivalence of PCF functions. For functional languages with effects, it seems that the best such context lemma we can hope for restricts attention to a rather more involved collection of contexts—the ones Mason and Talcott (1992) call 'closed instantiations of uses' (ciu). Various versions of this 'ciu' theorem of Mason and Talcott are treated in the articles by Talcott and Pitts-Stark.

Bisimulation. For languages involving interaction (between a program and its environment, or between concurrent threads within a program) contextual equivalence may provide a rather too coarse notion of semantic equivalence, identifying programs with rather different intermediate interactions. For this reason Milner (1989) and Park (1981) introduced a family of notions of semantic equivalence known collectively as *bisimilarities* and which have been highly influential in the development of process calculi. Such equivalences are co-inductively defined, that is, are the greatest fixed points of suitable monotone operations. Roughly speaking two processes are bisimilar if they are related by some bisimulation—a binary relation between processes with the property that whenever two processes are related and one can do an action, the other can match that action in such a way that the resulting processes remain related. Somewhat surprisingly, this notion was usefully fed back into the more traditional setting of functional programming by the work of Abramsky (1990) who obtains an extensional characterisation of contextual equivalence for his 'lazy λ-calculus' in terms of an applicative bisimilarity. In view of the results of Pitts (1994), one might expect such characterisations of contextual equivalence in cases where the denotational semantics involves reflexive domains. Indeed, the results of Howe (1996) and Gordon (1994, 1995) show that this is correct for various kinds of pure functional programming language. However, for functions with effects and for objects the situation is not so straightforward. The article of Pitts-Stark shows that such extensional characterisations of contextual equivalence cannot hold for call-by-value higher order functions with local state. Gordon's article, extending previous work of Gordon and Rees (1996), considers applicative bisimilarity for some object-based languages of Abadi and Cardelli (1996), together with a notion of *experimental equivalence* also of co-inductive character; he shows that the latter coincides with contextual equivalence whereas the former does not.

Howe's method for proving congruence. In the previous two paragraphs we have mentioned characterisations of contextual equivalence in terms of other, more extensional equivalences—'ciu' equivalence, bisimilarity, and experimental equivalence. The proof of such characterisations hinges upon showing that these other equivalences are congruences, that is, respect the various constructs of the language in question. Such congruence proofs are non-trivial for higher order languages (mainly because their operational semantics involve non-trivial instances of substitution). Howe (1996) originated a method for proving congruence that has proved to be remarkably robust, inasmuch as it has been adapted to a wide range of higher order languages. Here, Lassen provides a rather slick version of Howe's method for pure functional languages as part of his relational reasoning about contexts. Gordon applies Howe's method to both the applicative bisimilarity and the experimental equivalence he develops for the Abadi-Cardelli object calculi. And Jeffrey makes use of Howe's technique for a language of higher order functions with concurrent communication (a fragment of Reppy's CML).

Relational proof techniques. The results mentioned in the previous paragraph give useful proof methods for contextual equivalence, via the construction of suitable bisimulations. In the world of process calculi, this technique has been sharpened by the development of various auxiliary notions, such as 'bisimulation up to bisimilarity', and 'bisimulation up to context' (see particularly Sangiorgi (1994)). Lassen's article shows that, with some effort, similar techniques can be established, and are useful, for higher order functional languages. He also touches upon *improvement theory*, introduced by Sands (1995) and developed in detail in Sands' article in this volume. One functional program is an improvement of another, in Sands' sense, if its execution is more efficient (takes less steps) in any program context. This notion not only permits some reasoning about the time behaviour of recursive functional programs, but as Sands shows, it also provides a useful method for proving properties of contextual equivalence of such programs.

Analogues of domain-theoretic methods. Some of the proof techniques in this volume are direct analogues of familiar domain-theoretic techniques. Consider, for example, the familiar Tarski characterisation of the least fixed point $\mathit{fix}(f)$ of a continuous function f on a domain as the countable limit of $f^n(\bot)$. This has an operational analogue expressing a finiteness property of evaluation of recursively defined terms: see (Mason, Smith, and Talcott 1996) and the articles by Lassen and Pitts-Stark. Similarly, the calculus of finite elements in recursively defined domains (and in particular the 'minimal invariant' property of such domains) has an operational analogue which is explored in Smith's article. Such results enable one to reuse some familiar denotational methods, such as Scott's induction principle (Scott 1993). For example, the operational analogue of Scott induction is used in proving the Fundamental Property of the logical relation introduced in the article of Pitts-Stark. Birkedal and Harper (1997) provide another good example of the application of such techniques.

Methods from the λ-calculus. A glance through recent text books such as those by Gunter (1992) and Mitchell (1996) shows the extent to which the mathematics of the λ-calculus (both the typed and untyped varieties) has influenced the development of programming language theory. The Mitchell-Hoang-Howard article provides a good example of this: labelling techniques originally developed for the untyped λ-calculus are adapted to prove completeness of the usual reduction strategy for the functional language PCF and to prove a confluence result for a language with subtyping. Another example is provided by the notion of 'logical relation', originally developed for the simply typed λ-calculus by Plotkin (1973). Subsequently, versions of this notion have proved very useful in denotational semantics (the work of Reynolds (1974) is a classic example) and, more recently, in operational semantics (see Pitts (1997), for example). The article by Pitts-Stark provides an example of the use of logical relations in operational semantics, in this case for reasoning about contextual equivalence of functions with local state in an ML-like language.

References

Abadi, M. and L. Cardelli (1996). *A Theory of Objects*. Springer-Verlag, New York.

Abramsky, S. (1990). The lazy λ-calculus. In D. A. Turner (Ed.), *Research Topics in Functional Programming*, Chapter 4, pp. 65–117. Addison Wesley.

Abramsky, S. (1997). Semantics of interaction: an introduction to game semantics. In A. M. Pitts and P. Dybjer (Eds.), *Semantics and Logics of Computation*, Publications of the Newton Institute, pp. 1–31. Cambridge University Press.

Birkedal, L. and R. Harper (1997). Relational interpretation of recursive types in an operational setting (Summary). In *Proc. TACS'97*, Lecture Notes in Computer Science. Springer-Verlag, Berlin. to appear.

Gordon, A. D. (1994). *Functional Programming and Input/Output*. Distinguished Dissertations in Computer Science. Cambridge University Press.

Gordon, A. D. (1995). Bisimilarity as a theory of functional programming. In *Eleventh Conference on the Mathematical Foundations of Programming Semantics, New Orleans, 1995*, Volume 1 of *Electronic Notes in Theoretical Computer Science*. Elsevier.

Gordon, A. D. and G. D. Rees (1996, January). Bisimilarity for a first-order calculus of objects with subtyping. In *Conference Record of the 23rd ACM Symposium on Principles of Programming Languages, St Petersburg Beach, Florida*, pp. 386–395. ACM Press.

Gunter, C. A. (1992). *Semantics of Programming Languages: Structures and Techniques*. Foundations of Computing. MIT Press.

Howe, D. J. (1996, February). Proving congruence of bisimulation in functional programming languages. *Information and Computation 124*(2), 103–112.

Hyland, J. M. E. (1997). Game semantics. In A. M. Pitts and P. Dybjer (Eds.), *Semantics and Logics of Computation*, Publications of the Newton Institute, pp. 131–184. Cambridge University Press.

Mason, I. A., S. F. Smith, and C. L. Talcott (1996). From operational semantics to domain theory. *Information and Computation 128*(1), 26–47.

Mason, I. A. and C. L. Talcott (1992). References, local variables and operational reasoning. In *Proceedings of the 7th Annual Symposium on Logic in Computer Science*, pp. 186–197. IEEE Computer Society Press.

Meyer, A. and K. Sieber (1988). Towards fully abstract semantics for local variables. In *Proc. 15th Symp. on Principles of Programming Languages, San Diego*, pp. 191–203. ACM.

Milner, R. (1977). Fully abstract models of typed lambda-calculi. *Theoretical Computer Science 4*, 1–22.

Milner, R. (1989). *Communication and Concurrency*. Prentice Hall.

Milner, R., M. Tofte, R. Harper, and D. MacQueen (1997). *The Definition of Standard ML (Revised)*. MIT Press.

Mitchell, J. C. (1996). *Foundations for Programming Languages*. Foundations of Computing. MIT Press.

O'Hearn, P. W. and R. D. Tennent (1993). Semantical analysis of specification logic, 2. *Information and Computation 107*, 25–57.

Park, D. (1981). Concurrency and automata on infinite sequences. In P. Deussen (Ed.), *Proceedings of the 5th GI-Conference on Theoretical Computer Science*, Volume 104 of *Lecture Notes in Computer Science*, pp. 167–183. Springer-Verlag, Berlin.

Pitts, A. M. (1994). A co-induction principle for recursively defined domains. *Theoretical Computer Science 124*, 195–219. (A preliminary version of this work appeared as Cambridge Univ. Computer Laboratory Tech. Rept. No. 252, April 1992.).

Pitts, A. M. (1997). Reasoning about local variables with operationally-based logical relations. In P. W. O'Hearn and R. D. Tennent (Eds.), *Algol-Like Languages*, Volume 2, Chapter 17, pp. 173–193. Birkhauser. First appeared in *Proceedings Eleventh Annual IEEE Symposium on Logic in Computer Science*, Brunswick, NJ, July 1996, pp 152–163.

Plotkin, G. D. (1973, October). Lambda-definability and logical relations. Memorandum SAI-RM-4, School of Artificial Intelligence, University of Edinburgh.

Plotkin, G. D. (1977). LCF considered as a programming language. *Theoretical Computer Science 5*, 223–255.

Plotkin, G. D. (1981). A structural approach to operational semantics. Technical Report DAIMI FN-19, Aarhus University.

Reynolds, J. C. (1974). On the relation between direct and continuation semantics. In J. Loeckx (Ed.), *Automata, Languages and Programming, Proceedings 1974*, Volume 14 of *Lecture Notes in Computer Science*, pp. 141–156. Springer-Verlag, Berlin.

Reynolds, J. C. (1982). Idealized Algol and its specification logic. In D. Néel (Ed.), *Tools and Notions for Program Construction*, pp. 121–161. Cambridge University Press.

Sands, D. (1995). A naïve time analysis and its theory of cost equivalence. *Journal of Logic and Computation 5*, 495–541.

Sangiorgi, D. (1994, August). On the bisimulation proof method. Technical Report ECS-LFCS-94-299, Department of Computer Science, Edinburgh University.

Scott, D. S. (1993). A type-theoretical alternative to ISWIM, CUCH, OWHY. *Theoretical Computer Science 121*, 411–440.

Operational equivalences for untyped and polymorphic object calculi

Andrew D. Gordon

Abstract

We survey several definitions of operational equivalence from studies of the λ-calculus in the setting of the ς-calculus, Abadi and Cardelli's untyped object calculus. In particular, we study the relationship between the following: the equational theory induced by the primitive semantics; Morris-style contextual equivalence; experimental equivalence (the equivalence implicit in a Milner-style context lemma); and the form of Abramsky's applicative bisimilarity induced by Howe's format.

We repeat this study in the setting of Abadi and Cardelli's polymorphic object calculus obtained by enriching system $\mathbf{F}_{<:}$ with primitive covariant self types for objects. In particular, we obtain for the first time a co-inductive characterisation of contextual equivalence for an object calculus with subtyping, parametric polymorphism, variance annotations and structural typing rules. Soundness of the equational theory induced by the primitive semantics of the calculus has not been proved denotationally, because structural typing rules invalidate conventional denotational models. Instead, we show soundness of the equational theory using operational techniques.

In their book, Abadi and Cardelli (1996) study a series of untyped and typed object calculi—analogous to typed λ-calculi, but taking objects instead of functions as primitive—as a way of explaining a variety of features of object-oriented languages. In particular, they provide typed forms of classes, subclasses, inheritance, binary methods and Self types.

In earlier work, Gordon and Rees (1996) investigated operational equivalence for one of Abadi and Cardelli's typed object calculi, with object types, function types, subtyping and a range of first-order constructs such as records, variants and dynamic types. This paper extends the earlier study by considering, for the first time, operational equivalence for an object calculus with both subtype polymorphism and parametric polymorphism. We focus on a particular system of primitive self types, invented by Abadi and Cardelli, and used by them to represent classes and inheritance. Unlike the first-order system of the earlier study, the system of primitive self types features variance annotations, which help to establish certain typed equivalences, and structural rules, which build in certain assumptions about the set of types. These assumptions may be checked operationally, but turn out to be incompatible with standard denotational models for calculi with subtype polymorphism. See Chapter 16 of Abadi and Cardelli's book for a discussion. The operational techniques developed in this paper provide the only known soundness proof for the equational theory of primitive objects presented here. The denotational techniques used by Abadi and Cardelli (1994) to prove soundness of an equational theory for simpler calculi do not directly apply to the calculus studied here.

The paper divides into two substantial sections. In Section 1, we review the relationship between several forms of operational equivalence for the ς-calculus, a minimal, untyped object calculus analogous to the untyped λ-calculus. We use Abadi and Cardelli's Church-Rosser theorem, Melliès' standardisation theorem and Howe's general congruence theorem to show the relation between the untyped equational theory, Morris-style contextual equivalence, a Milner-style context lemma and Howe's form of applicative bisimilarity for the ς-calculus. In Section 2, we apply Howe's method to bisimilarity for $\mathbf{S}_\lambda$, an object calculus with subtyping, parametric polymorphism and structural typing rules. Without appeal to Church-Rosser or standardisation theorems, or any denotational model, we use bisimilarity to prove the soundness of a typed equational theory. Finally, we conclude in Section 3.

We illustrate both Sections 1 and 2 with simple examples of object equivalence. In separate work, Gordon, Lassen, and Hankin (1997) apply a theory of operational equivalence for an untyped imperative object calculus to verify a compiler optimisation. Similarly, we expect the techniques of this paper could be applied to typed intermediate languages used in modern compilers.

1 Equivalence of Untyped Objects

We begin, in Section 1.1, by reviewing the syntax and primitive semantics of the ς-calculus. We define a ς-theory to be an equivalence relation on terms of the ς-calculus that is preserved by all contexts of the ς-calculus and that includes the primitive reduction rules. Abadi and Cardelli's equational theory, $\leftrightarrow$, is by definition the least ς-theory. In Section 1.2, we review Abadi and Cardelli's big-step operational semantics, an interpreter that expresses a particular reduction strategy for the ς-calculus. In Section 1.3 we introduce the notion of context closure and establish some of its basic properties. In Section 1.4 we define a relation on terms to be *adequate* if whenever two closed terms are related and the interpreter terminates on one, it terminates on the other. We define *contextual equivalence* in the style of Morris' definition for the λ-calculus (Morris 1968). We show that Abadi and Cardelli's relation $\leftrightarrow$ is the least adequate ς-theory and that contextual equivalence is the greatest adequate ς-theory.

In Section 1.5 we introduce two forms of bisimilarity on closed terms of the ς-calculus: *experimental equivalence*, $\sim$, and *applicative bisimilarity*, $\approx$. Experimental equivalence is obtained by generalising Milner's context lemma (Milner 1977), and applicative bisimilarity is obtained by specialising Howe's general form of bisimilarity (Howe 1996) to the ς-calculus.

Via a variation of Howe's theorem, given in Section 1.6, we show in Sections 1.7 and 1.8 that experimental equivalence and applicative bisimilarity, respectively, are preserved by all contexts, and hence are included in contextual equivalence. We show that applicative bisimilarity makes more distinctions than contextual equivalence, but that experimental equivalence coincides with contextual equivalence. Therefore either of these relations may be used to establish contextual equivalence. In Section 1.9 we use a notion of complete adequacy to show that the equational theory is finer grained than applicative bisimilarity. Finally, we conclude this study of equivalence of untyped objects by examining various examples in Section 1.10.

We may summarise the inclusions between the various ς-theories as follows, where $\approx^\circ$ and $\sim^\circ$ are the extensions to open terms of the relations $\approx$ and $\sim$, respectively.

Hierarchy of ς-theories:

$\leftrightarrow$	Least ς-theory
$\subset \approx^\circ$	Applicative bisimilarity
$\subset \sim^\circ$	Experimental equivalence
$= \simeq$	Contextual equivalence

Many of the technical ideas in this section are known already from earlier work on object calculi with first-order object types (Gordon and Rees 1996). The purpose of this section is to consolidate the relationship between various operational techniques for object calculi in the setting of the simplest object calculus, the ς-calculus. In Section 2, we generalise our treatment of contextual and experimental equivalence of untyped objects to a second-order polymorphic calculus, $\mathbf{S}_\lambda$.

1.1 The ς-Calculus: Syntax, Reduction and Equational Theory

In this section we recall Abadi and Cardelli's untyped object calculus, the ς-calculus, which consists of a set of terms equipped with a many-step reduction relation, $\twoheadrightarrow$, and an equivalence relation, $\leftrightarrow$.

We begin with an infinite set of *variables*, ranged over by x, y, z. The set of *terms* is defined by the following grammar.

Syntax of untyped terms:

$a, b, c, d ::=$	terms
x	variable
$[\ell_i = \varsigma(x_i)b_i \;^{i \in 1..n}]$	object (ℓ_i distinct)
$a.\ell$	method select
$a.\ell \Leftarrow \varsigma(x)b$	method update

An *object* $[\ell_i = \varsigma(x_i)b_i \,^{i \in 1..n}]$ consists of a set of *components*, each of the form $\ell = \varsigma(x)b$, where $\varsigma(x)b$ is a *method* and ℓ is a *label* that names the method. In a method, $\varsigma(x)b$, the variable x is bound; its scope is b. The variable x represents self, the object in which the method is located, and term b represents the result of the method. We identify terms up to consistent renaming of bound variables and permutation of components in objects. We define $fv(a)$, the set of variables that occur free in term a, in the usual way. If $fv(a) = \varnothing$ we say that term a is closed. We write $a\{\!\{x \leftarrow b\}\!\}$ for the outcome of substituting term b for each free occurrence of variable x in term a. We write $a\{x\}$ to note that variable x may occur free in term a. We adopt the abbreviation $a\{\!\{b\}\!\}$ for $a\{\!\{x \leftarrow b\}\!\}$, when we have noted $a\{x\}$ already. We postpone examples of programs written in the ς-calculus until Section 1.10.

Before introducing the equivalence relation, $\leftrightarrow$, on terms we need some preliminary definitions. If $\mathcal{R}$ is a relation on terms, let its *compatible refinement*, $\widehat{\mathcal{R}}$, be the least relation on terms closed under the following rules.

Compatible refinement:

(Comp x) $\dfrac{}{x \,\widehat{\mathcal{R}}\, x}$

(Comp Object) (ℓ_i distinct)
$$\frac{b_i \,\mathcal{R}\, b_i' \quad \forall i \in 1..n}{[\ell_i = \varsigma(x_i)b_i \,^{i \in 1..n}] \,\widehat{\mathcal{R}}\, [\ell_i = \varsigma(x_i)b_i' \,^{i \in 1..n}]}$$

(Comp Select)
$$\frac{a \,\mathcal{R}\, a'}{a.\ell \,\widehat{\mathcal{R}}\, a'.\ell}$$

(Comp Update)
$$\frac{a \,\mathcal{R}\, a' \quad b \,\mathcal{R}\, b'}{a.\ell \Leftarrow \varsigma(x)b \,\widehat{\mathcal{R}}\, a'.\ell \Leftarrow \varsigma(x)b'}$$

Intuitively, $\widehat{\mathcal{R}}$ relates two terms if they have the same outermost form, and their immediate subterms are related by $\mathcal{R}$. We say that a relation, $\mathcal{R}$, on terms is *compatible* (with the syntax) if and only if $\widehat{\mathcal{R}} \subseteq \mathcal{R}$. We define the relation, $\leftrightarrow$, on terms of the ς-calculus to be the least relation closed under the following rules.

Equational rules:

(Eq Symm)
$$\frac{b \leftrightarrow a}{a \leftrightarrow b}$$

(Eq Trans)
$$\frac{a \leftrightarrow b \quad b \leftrightarrow c}{a \leftrightarrow c}$$

(Eq Comp)
$$\frac{a \,\widehat{\leftrightarrow}\, b}{a \leftrightarrow b}$$

(Eval Select) (where $a = [\ell_i = \varsigma(x_i)b_i\{x_i\} \,^{i \in 1..n}]$)
$$\frac{j \in 1..n}{a.\ell_j \leftrightarrow b_j\{\!\{a\}\!\}}$$

(Eval Update) (where $a = [\ell_i = \varsigma(x_i)b_i\{x_i\} \,^{i \in 1..n}]$)
$$\frac{j \in 1..n}{a.\ell_j \Leftarrow \varsigma(x)b \leftrightarrow [\ell_j = \varsigma(x)b, \ell_i = \varsigma(x_i)b_i\{x_i\} \,^{i \in (1..n)-\{j\}}]}$$

We say that a relation $\mathcal{R}$ on terms is a ς-*theory* if and only if each of the rules above is satisfied with $\mathcal{R}$ instead of $\leftrightarrow$. By definition, $\leftrightarrow$ is the least ς-theory. Note that any relation $\mathcal{R}$ such that $\widehat{\mathcal{R}} \subseteq \mathcal{R}$ is reflexive. Therefore, any ς-theory is reflexive. Rules (Eval Select) and (Eval Update) represent the *primitive semantics* of the ς-calculus, the basic computation steps of the calculus; $\leftrightarrow$ is the least compatible equivalence to include the primitive semantics.

Let *many-step reduction*, $\twoheadrightarrow$, be the relation on terms such that $a \twoheadrightarrow b$ if and only if $a \leftrightarrow b$ is derivable without use of the rule (Eq Symm). From its definition, $\twoheadrightarrow$ is reflexive, transitive and compatible. We conclude this section by stating the following properties of $\twoheadrightarrow$ and $\leftrightarrow$:

Proposition 1.1

(1) *If* $a \twoheadrightarrow b$ *and* $a \twoheadrightarrow c$, *then there exists* d *such that* $b \twoheadrightarrow d$ *and* $c \twoheadrightarrow d$.

(2) $a \leftrightarrow b$ *if and only if there exists* c *such that* $a \twoheadrightarrow c$ *and* $b \twoheadrightarrow c$.

Abadi and Cardelli proved the diamond property, part (1); part (2), a Church-Rosser property, is a standard corollary.

1.2 An Operational Semantics for the ς-Calculus

In this section we recall Abadi and Cardelli's reduction strategy for the primitive semantics. Let a *result*, u, v or w, be an object $[\ell_i = \varsigma(x_i)b_i\,^{i \in 1..n}]$. A result reduces to itself. If a reduces to the result v, the method select, $a.\ell$, reduces by reducing the body of the method named ℓ in v. If a reduces to the result v, the method update, $a.\ell \Leftarrow \varsigma(x)b$, reduces to the result obtained by making a fresh copy of v, and replacing the method named ℓ with method $\varsigma(x)b$. Formally, the *reduction relation*, $a \rightsquigarrow v$, where a is a term and v is a result, is specified inductively by the rules in the following table.

Reduction rules:

(Red Object) (where $v = [\ell_i = \varsigma(x_i)b_i\,^{i \in 1..n}]$)

$$\frac{}{v \rightsquigarrow v}$$

(Red Select) (where $v' = [\ell_i = \varsigma(x_i)b_i\{\!\{x_i\}\!\}\,^{i \in 1..n}]$)

$$\frac{a \rightsquigarrow v' \quad b_j\{\!\{v'\}\!\} \rightsquigarrow v \quad j \in 1..n}{a.\ell_j \rightsquigarrow v}$$

(Red Update)

$$\frac{a \rightsquigarrow [\ell_i = \varsigma(x_i)b_i\{\!\{x_i\}\!\}\,^{i \in 1..n}] \quad j \in 1..n}{a.\ell_j \Leftarrow \varsigma(x)b \rightsquigarrow [\ell_j = \varsigma(x)b, \ell_i = \varsigma(x_i)b_i\{\!\{x_i\}\!\}\,^{i \in (1..n)-\{j\}}]}$$

The reduction relation is weak in the sense that reduction does not occur inside method bodies. The reduction relation is deterministic: one can easily show that $a \leadsto u$ and $a \leadsto v$ imply that $u = v$, for any terms a, u and v. The rules defining the reduction relation suggest an algorithm, an interpreter, for computing the result, if any, of a closed term. Given an input term a, the algorithm will terminate with result v if and only if $a \leadsto v$.

We say that a closed term a *converges*, written $a\Downarrow$, if and only if there is a result v with $a \leadsto v$. If a closed term a does not converge, we say that it *diverges*, written $a\Uparrow$. An example of a divergent term is $\Omega = [\ell = \varsigma(s)s.\ell].\ell$. Using Proposition 1.1 and a standardisation theorem proved by Melliès, Abadi and Cardelli obtain the following connection between the ς-theory $\leftrightarrow$ and the reduction relation $\leadsto$.

Proposition 1.2 *Let a be a closed term and v a closed result.*

(1) *If $a \leadsto v$ then $a \leftrightarrow v$.*

(2) *If $a \leftrightarrow v$ then $a\Downarrow$.*

1.3 The Context Closure of a Relation

We define and state properties of context closure in this section, and use it to define contextual equivalence in the next. If $\mathcal{R}$ is a relation on terms, let its *context closure*, $\mathcal{R}^{\mathcal{C}}$, be the least relation on terms closed under the following rules.[1]

Context closure:

(Context $\mathcal{R}$)
$$\frac{a\ \mathcal{R}\ b}{a\ \mathcal{R}^{\mathcal{C}}\ b}$$

(Context Comp)
$$\frac{a\ \widehat{\mathcal{R}^{\mathcal{C}}}\ b}{a\ \mathcal{R}^{\mathcal{C}}\ b}$$

Lemma 1.3

(1) *For any $\mathcal{R}$, $\mathcal{R}^{\mathcal{C}}$ is compatible, and hence reflexive.*

(2) *Both compatible refinement and context closure are monotone.*

(3) *For any $\mathcal{R}$, $\mathcal{R}$ is compatible, that is, $\widehat{\mathcal{R}} \subseteq \mathcal{R}$, if and only if $\mathcal{R}^{\mathcal{C}} \subseteq \mathcal{R}$.*

(4) *For any $\mathcal{R}$, $(\mathcal{R}^{\mathcal{C}})^{\mathcal{C}} = \mathcal{R}^{\mathcal{C}}$.*

[1] Søren Bøgh Lassen suggested the definition based on compatible refinement. Gordon and Rees (1996) use the following equivalent property, based on contexts, that is, terms containing holes: that $a'\ \mathcal{R}^{\mathcal{C}}\ b'$ if and only if there is a context $\mathcal{C}$ containing n holes $-_1, \ldots, -_n$, and a set $\{(a_1, b_1), \ldots, (a_n, b_n)\} \subseteq \mathcal{R}$ such that $a' = \mathcal{C}[a_1, \ldots, a_n]$, the outcome of filling each hole $-_i$ with a_i, and $b' = \mathcal{C}[b_1, \ldots, b_n]$, the outcome of filling each hole $-_i$ with b_i.

We shall define contextual equivalence using the context closure of a singleton relation, of the form $\{(a,b)\}^{\mathcal{C}}$. Whenever $a' \{(a,b)\}^{\mathcal{C}} b'$ is derivable, the derivation implicitly represents a context, $\mathcal{C}$, such that $a' = \mathcal{C}[a]$ and $b' = \mathcal{C}[b]$. This use of context closure enjoys the following properties, which may easily be proved by induction on derivations.

Lemma 1.4

(1) *If* $a' \{(a,a)\}^{\mathcal{C}} a''$ *then* $a' = a''$.

(2) *If* $a' \{(a,b)\}^{\mathcal{C}} b'$ *then* $b' \{(b,a)\}^{\mathcal{C}} a'$.

(3) *Suppose* $a' \{(a,c)\}^{\mathcal{C}} c'$.
For all b, *there is* b' *such that* $a' \{(a,b)\}^{\mathcal{C}} b'$ *and* $b' \{(b,c)\}^{\mathcal{C}} c'$.

(4) *If* $a' \{(a,b)\}^{\mathcal{C}} b'$ *and* $a'' \{(a',b')\}^{\mathcal{C}} b''$ *then* $a'' \{(a,b)\}^{\mathcal{C}} b''$.

Intuitively, the following asserts that for a reflexive and transitive relation, the property of being compatible is equivalent to the property of being preserved by contexts:

Lemma 1.5 *If* $\mathcal{R}$ *is reflexive and transitive, then* $\mathcal{R}$ *is compatible if and only if for all* a, b, a', b', *if* $a \mathcal{R} b$ *and* $a' \{(a,b)\}^{\mathcal{C}} b'$ *then* $a' \mathcal{R} b'$.

Proof For the left-to-right direction, suppose $\mathcal{R}$ is compatible and consider any a and b with $a \mathcal{R} b$. By Lemma 1.3(2), $\{(a,b)\} \subseteq \mathcal{R}$ implies $\{(a,b)\}^{\mathcal{C}} \subseteq \mathcal{R}^{\mathcal{C}}$. Given that $\mathcal{R}$ is compatible, Lemma 1.3(3) implies $\mathcal{R}^{\mathcal{C}} \subseteq \mathcal{R}$. By transitivity, $\{(a,b)\}^{\mathcal{C}} \subseteq \mathcal{R}$. Hence $a' \mathcal{R} b'$ whenever $a' \{(a,b)\}^{\mathcal{C}} b'$.

For the right-to-left direction, it suffices to show for any a and b that $a \widehat{\mathcal{R}} b$ implies $a \mathcal{R} b$. We proceed by a case analysis of the derivation of $a \widehat{\mathcal{R}} b$.

(Comp x) In this case, there is a variable x such that $a = b = x$. By reflexivity, $x \mathcal{R} x$.

(Comp Object) In this case $a = [\ell_i = \varsigma(x_i)a_i\ ^{i\in 1..n}]$ and $b = [\ell_i = \varsigma(x_i)b_i\ ^{i\in 1..n}]$, with $a_i \mathcal{R} b_i$ for each $i \in 1..n$. If $n = 0$, we get $a = [] \mathcal{R} [] = b$ by reflexivity of $\mathcal{R}$. Otherwise, for each $i \in 0..n$, let

$$c_i = [\ell_j = \varsigma(x_j)b_j\ ^{j\in 1..i}, \ell_k = \varsigma(x_k)a_k\ ^{k\in i+1..n}]$$

so that $c_0 = a$ and $c_n = b$. For each $i \in 1..n$, we have:

$$\begin{aligned} c_{i-1} &= [\ell_j = \varsigma(x_j)b_j\ ^{j\in 1..i-1}, \ell_i = \varsigma(x_i)a_i, \ell_k = \varsigma(x_k)a_k\ ^{k\in i+1..n}] \\ c_i &= [\ell_j = \varsigma(x_j)b_j\ ^{j\in 1..i-1}, \ell_i = \varsigma(x_i)b_i, \ell_k = \varsigma(x_k)a_k\ ^{k\in i+1..n}] \end{aligned}$$

Therefore $c_{i-1} \{(a_i,b_i)\}^{\mathcal{C}} c_i$. By assumption, this and $a_i \mathcal{R} b_i$ imply $c_{i-1} \mathcal{R} c_i$. Hence we have $a = c_0 \mathcal{R} c_1 \mathcal{R} \cdots \mathcal{R} c_{n-1} \mathcal{R} c_n = b$. By transitivity of $\mathcal{R}$, we get $a \mathcal{R} b$.

Cases (Comp Select) and (Comp Update) are no harder. □

1.4 Adequacy and Contextual Equivalence for the ς-Calculus

In general, let a relation $\mathcal{R}$ on terms be *adequate* if and only if for all closed terms a and b, $a \mathcal{R} b$ implies $a\Downarrow \Leftrightarrow b\Downarrow$. Given any ς-theory $\mathcal{R}$, a little calculation shows that part (2) of Proposition 1.2, with $\mathcal{R}$ instead of $\leftrightarrow$, is equivalent to $\mathcal{R}$ being adequate, but we omit the details. In particular, of course, $\leftrightarrow$ is adequate. Therefore, since it is the least ς-theory, it is moreover the least adequate ς-theory. Not all ς-theories are adequate; the universal relation on terms is a ς-theory, but is not adequate. Adequacy guarantees that a relation is *consistent* in the sense that not all equations are instances of the relation; pick a term that converges and one that does not.

We now introduce Morris-style contextual equivalence, which equates terms provided they may be interchanged in a larger term, the context, without affecting whether it converges or not. Let Morris' *contextual equivalence*, $\simeq$, be the relation on terms such that $a \simeq b$ if and only if $\{(a,b)\}^{\mathcal{C}}$ is adequate, that is, for any closed terms a' and b', $a' \{(a,b)\}^{\mathcal{C}} b'$ implies $a'\Downarrow \Leftrightarrow b'\Downarrow$.[2]

Proposition 1.6 *Contextual equivalence is reflexive, transitive and symmetric.*

Proof Reflexivity and symmetry follow from Lemma 1.4, parts (1) and (2). As in the λ-calculus, transitivity "requires a little proof" (Plotkin 1977). Suppose that $a \simeq b$ and $b \simeq c$. We shall show that $a \simeq c$. Consider any closed a' and c' such that $a' \{(a,c)\}^{\mathcal{C}} c'$. Given $a'\Downarrow$ we shall prove that $c'\Downarrow$. By Lemma 1.4(3), there is b' such that $a' \{(a,b)\}^{\mathcal{C}} b'$ and $b' \{(b,c)\}^{\mathcal{C}} c'$. Although a' and c' are closed, it need not be that b' is closed. Let $\{x_1,\ldots,x_n\} = fv(b')$. For any term d, define $bind\ (x_1,\ldots,x_i)\ in\ d$, where $i \in 1..n$, by:

$$\begin{aligned} bind\ (x_1)\ in\ d &\triangleq [\ell = \varsigma(x_1)d] \\ bind\ (x_1,\ldots,x_i,x_{i+1})\ in\ d &\triangleq [\ell = \varsigma(x_{i+1})(bind\ (x_1,\ldots,x_i)\ in\ d).\ell] \end{aligned}$$

Observe that if $fv(d) = \{x_1,\ldots,x_n\}$ then $fv(bind\ (x_1,\ldots,x_n)\ in\ d) = \varnothing$. Moreover, if $fv(d) = \varnothing$ then $(bind\ (x_1,\ldots,x_n)\ in\ d).\ell\Downarrow \Leftrightarrow d\Downarrow$. We make the following definitions.

$$\begin{aligned} a'' &\triangleq (bind\ (x_1,\ldots,x_n)\ in\ a').\ell \\ b'' &\triangleq (bind\ (x_1,\ldots,x_n)\ in\ b').\ell \\ c'' &\triangleq (bind\ (x_1,\ldots,x_n)\ in\ c').\ell \end{aligned}$$

[2] This style of equivalence was introduced in the setting of the λ-calculus by Morris (1968). We may recast Morris' extensional equivalence in the setting of the ς-calculus as follows. Let a term a be *normal* if and only if for all b, $a \twoheadrightarrow b$ implies that $a = b$. Let $a\downarrow$ mean there is c such that $a \twoheadrightarrow c$ and c is normal. Let a relation $\mathcal{R}$ be *normal* if and only if for all terms a and b, $a \mathcal{R} b$ implies $a\downarrow \Leftrightarrow b\downarrow$. Let two terms a and b be *extensionally equivalent* if and only if $\{(a,b)\}^{\mathcal{C}}$ is normal. Morris gives definitions equivalent to these for the λ-calculus. He proves that extensional equivalence is the greatest compatible equivalence relation that is normal and includes $\alpha\beta\eta$-conversion. It is now accepted practice (Plotkin 1975) to modify Morris' definition by replacing the predicate $\downarrow$, based on reduction of a possibly open term to a normal term, with the predicate $\Downarrow$, based on weak reduction of a closed term to a result. It is much more efficient to implement weak reduction of closed terms than reduction of possibly open terms.

Now, $a' \ \{(a,b)\}^{\mathcal{C}}\ b'$ implies that $a'' \ \{(a,b)\}^{\mathcal{C}}\ b''$, and $b' \ \{(b,c)\}^{\mathcal{C}}\ c'$ implies that $b''\{(b,c)\}^{\mathcal{C}}c''$. Since a' is closed, $a'\Downarrow$ implies that $a''\Downarrow$. Since $a \simeq b$ and b'' is closed, $b''\Downarrow$. Then $b \simeq c$ and $b''\Downarrow$ imply that $c''\Downarrow$. Since c' is closed, it follows that $c'\Downarrow$, as required. A symmetric argument establishes that $c'\Downarrow$ implies $a'\Downarrow$. Therefore, $a \simeq c$, which completes the proof of transitivity. □

Given the standardisation and Church-Rosser theorems for the ς-calculus, it follows that $\simeq$ includes $\leftrightarrow$:

Proposition 1.7 *For all terms a and b, $a \leftrightarrow b$ implies $a \simeq b$.*

Proof Suppose $a \leftrightarrow b$. Consider any closed terms a' and b' such that $a' \ \{(a,b)\}^{\mathcal{C}}\ b'$. Using (Eq Comp) we obtain $a' \leftrightarrow b'$. Now suppose that $a'\Downarrow$, that is, that there is u such that $a' \leadsto u$. By Proposition 1.2(1), we have $a' \leftrightarrow u$. By symmetry and transitivity, $u \leftrightarrow b'$. By Proposition 1.2(2), $b'\Downarrow$. By symmetric reasoning, $b'\Downarrow$ implies $a'\Downarrow$. Therefore, $a'\Downarrow \Leftrightarrow b'\Downarrow$, as required to establish that $a \simeq b$. □

Morris advocated contextual equivalence on the basis of its privileged position in the set of relations on terms:

Proposition 1.8 *Contextual equivalence is the greatest relation on terms that is compatible and adequate.*

Proof To see that contextual equivalence is compatible, by Lemma 1.5 and Proposition 1.6 it suffices to show for any a, b, a', b', that $a \simeq b$ and $a' \ \{(a,b)\}^{\mathcal{C}}\ b'$ imply $a' \simeq b'$. For any a'' and b'' with $a'' \ \{(a',b')\}^{\mathcal{C}}\ b''$, we need to establish that $a''\Downarrow \Leftrightarrow b''\Downarrow$. By Lemma 1.4(4), $a' \ \{(a,b)\}^{\mathcal{C}}\ b'$ and $a'' \ \{(a',b')\}^{\mathcal{C}}\ b''$ imply that $a'' \ \{(a,b)\}^{\mathcal{C}}\ b''$. But then $a \simeq b$ implies that $a''\Downarrow \Leftrightarrow b''\Downarrow$. It follows that contextual equivalence is compatible, and it is clearly adequate.

To see that it is the greatest such relation on terms, consider any terms a and b, such that $a\,\mathcal{R}\,b$ for some relation $\mathcal{R}$ that is compatible and adequate. Consider any terms a' and b' such that $a' \ \{(a,b)\}^{\mathcal{C}}\ b'$. Since $\mathcal{R}$ is compatible, we have $a'\,\mathcal{R}\,b'$. Since it is adequate, $a'\Downarrow \Leftrightarrow b'\Downarrow$. So $a \simeq b$. Therefore, $\mathcal{R} \subseteq \simeq$ for any $\mathcal{R}$ that is compatible and adequate. □

Combining Propositions 1.6, 1.7 and 1.8 we obtain that contextual equivalence is an adequate ς-theory. Moreover it is the greatest such relation.

1.5 Two Forms of Bisimilarity for the ς-Calculus

Neither the definition of contextual equivalence, nor its characterisation as the greatest adequate ς-theory, are particularly amenable ways of proving particular contextual equivalences. The next few sections are devoted to two forms of bisimilarity defined on closed terms of the ς-calculus, which allow co-inductive proofs of contextual equivalence.

We first need some auxiliary notions. Let an *experiment*, ϵ, be one of the following kinds of term fragment: either a select, $.\ell$, or an update, $.\ell \Leftarrow \varsigma(x)b$, where at most x is free in b. We write $a\epsilon$ for the term obtained by inserting term a into the implicit hole at the beginning of the term fragment ϵ. If $\mathcal{R}$ is a relation on closed terms, let its *open extension*, $\mathcal{R}^\circ$, be the relation such that for any terms a and b, $a \mathcal{R}^\circ b$ if and only if $a\sigma \mathcal{R} b\sigma$ for all substitutions σ with $dom(\sigma) = fv(a) \cup fv(b)$ and such that $\sigma(x)$ is a closed result for each $x \in dom(\sigma)$. Note that if a and b are closed terms, $a \mathcal{R} b$ if and only if $a \mathcal{R}^\circ b$. Finally, let *Kleene equivalence*, $\approx^{kl}$, be the relation on closed terms such that let $a \approx^{kl} b$ if and only if for all closed results v, $a \rightsquigarrow v \Leftrightarrow b \rightsquigarrow v$. Given that reduction is deterministic, two terms are Kleene equivalent just if both diverge or both converge to the same result. Kleene equivalence is not a ς-theory, as it does not satisfy (Eq Comp) with $\approx^{kl}$ instead of $\leftrightarrow$. For a counterexample, consider any terms a and b with $a \neq b$; $a \approx^{kl} b$ does not imply $[\ell = \varsigma(x)a] \approx^{kl} [\ell = \varsigma(x)b]$.

We will later use the following properties of Kleene equivalence and experiments:

Lemma 1.9

(1) $\approx^{kl}$ *is reflexive, symmetric and transitive.*

(2) *For closed* a *and* u, $a \rightsquigarrow u$ *implies* $a \approx^{kl} u$.

(3) $a\epsilon \rightsquigarrow u$ *if and only if there is* v *with* $a \rightsquigarrow v$ *and* $v\epsilon \rightsquigarrow u$.

(4) $a \approx^{kl} b$ *implies* $a\epsilon \approx^{kl} b\epsilon$.

Proof (1) is obvious. (2) depends on reduction being deterministic. (3) follows by inspection of the reduction rules. (4) follows from (3). □

Now we introduce two co-inductive forms of operational equivalence.

- Let *experimental equivalence*, $\sim$, be the greatest relation on closed terms such that $a \sim b$ if and only if
  (1) whenever $a \rightsquigarrow u$ there is a result v such that $b \rightsquigarrow v$ and, for all experiments ϵ, $u\epsilon \sim v\epsilon$;
  (2) whenever $b \rightsquigarrow v$ there is a result u such that $a \rightsquigarrow u$ and, for all experiments ϵ, $u\epsilon \sim v\epsilon$.

  Experimental equivalence relates two terms if they can be interchanged without affecting convergence in contexts built up simply from method selects and method updates. This is the equivalence implicit in Milner's context lemma. In Section 1.7, we shall prove that $\sim^\circ = \simeq$.

- Let *applicative bisimilarity*, $\approx$, be the greatest relation on closed terms such that $a \approx b$ if and only if

(1) whenever $a \rightsquigarrow [\ell_i = \varsigma(x_i)a_i\{x_i\}^{i \in 1..n}]$ there is a result v such that $b \rightsquigarrow v$, $v = [\ell_i = \varsigma(x_i)b_i\{x_i\}^{i \in 1..n}]$ and $a_i\{\!\{w\}\!\} \approx b_i\{\!\{w\}\!\}$ for each $i \in 1..n$ and all closed results w;

(2) whenever $b \rightsquigarrow [\ell_i = \varsigma(x_i)b_i\{x_i\}^{i \in 1..n}]$ there is a result u such that $a \rightsquigarrow u$, $u = [\ell_i = \varsigma(x_i)a_i\{x_i\}^{i \in 1..n}]$ and $a_i\{\!\{w\}\!\} \approx b_i\{\!\{w\}\!\}$ for each $i \in 1..n$ and all closed results w.

This is the specialisation to the ς-calculus of a general form of equivalence introduced by Howe (1996), which generalises the applicative bisimulation of Abramsky and Ong (1993). In Sections 1.8 and 1.9, we shall prove that $\approx^\circ \subset \simeq$.

Gordon and Rees (1996) consider but reject various alternative forms of operational equivalence for primitive objects.[3]

In the next section, we state a general theorem, inspired by Howe, that will be used to show that both experimental equivalence and applicative bisimilarity are compatible. We close this section with the following proposition.

Proposition 1.10 *Suppose $\mathcal{R}$ is an equivalence relation on closed terms that includes Kleene equivalence. Then (Eval Select) and (Eval Update) hold with $\mathcal{R}^\circ$ instead of $\leftrightarrow$.*

Proof Since the rules (Eval Select) and (Eval Update) are closed under substitutions of results for variables, it suffices to show that they hold for $\mathcal{R}$; they then hold for $\mathcal{R}^\circ$ too.

For (Eval Select), we show that $a.\ell_j \mathrel{\mathcal{R}} b_j\{\!\{a\}\!\}$ where $a = [\ell_i = \varsigma(x_i)b_i\{x_i\}^{i \in 1..n}]$ and $j \in 1..n$. We argue that $a.\ell_j \approx^{kl} b_j\{\!\{a\}\!\}$. Suppose that $a.\ell_j \rightsquigarrow v$. Only (Red Select) can derive this reduction, so it must be that $b_j\{\!\{a\}\!\} \rightsquigarrow v$. Conversely, suppose that $b_j\{\!\{a\}\!\} \rightsquigarrow v$. By (Red Select), we can derive $a.\ell_j \rightsquigarrow v$. Therefore $a.\ell_j \approx^{kl} b_j\{\!\{a\}\!\}$. Hence $a.\ell_j \mathcal{R} b_j\{\!\{a\}\!\}$, given that $\mathcal{R}$ includes Kleene equivalence. A similar argument shows (Eval Update) to hold for $\mathcal{R}$. □

We will use this proposition, together with the tools in the next section, to show that both $\sim^\circ$ and $\approx^\circ$ are σ-theories.

1.6 Howe's Method for the ς-Calculus

The fact that applicative bisimilarity in the ς-calculus is compatible is a corollary of a general result of Howe (1996). Unfortunately Howe's general theorem

[3]For instance, by restricting the definition of experimental equivalence so that the experiments, ϵ, can only be selects, we obtain a variant equivalence in which objects are treated like records. This equivalence is not contained in contextual equivalence, and therefore is uninteresting. To see this, consider the objects $a = [\ell_1 = \varsigma(s)v, \ell_2 = \varsigma(s)v]$ and $b = [\ell_1 = \varsigma(s)v, \ell_2 = \varsigma(s)s.\ell_1]$, where v is some closed result. Let $a' = (a.\ell_1 \Leftarrow \varsigma(s)\Omega).\ell_2$ and $b' = (b.\ell_1 \Leftarrow \varsigma(s)\Omega).\ell_2$. Although $a'\{(a,b)\}^{\mathcal{C}} b'$, we have $a'\Downarrow$ but $b'\Uparrow$. Therefore a and b are contextually distinct, but they are equated by the variant equivalence.

does not imply that experimental equivalence is compatible. In this section we use Howe's method, though not his theorem, to prove a general property, Proposition 1.12, from which it is easy to prove that both these operational equivalences are compatible.

Given a relation $\mathcal{R}$ on closed terms, to prove that $\mathcal{R}^\circ$ is compatible, Howe's method is to construct an auxiliary relation, $\mathcal{R}^\bullet$, that by definition is compatible, and to prove that $\mathcal{R}^\circ = \mathcal{R}^\bullet$. For any relation $\mathcal{R}$ on closed terms, we begin by defining its *compatible extension*, $\mathcal{R}^\bullet$, to be the least relation on terms closed under the following rule.

Compatible extension, $\mathcal{R}^\bullet$:

($\mathcal{R}^\bullet$ Def)

$$\frac{a \, \widehat{\mathcal{R}^\bullet} \, c \quad c \, \mathcal{R}^\circ \, b}{a \, \mathcal{R}^\bullet \, b}$$

Lemma 1.11 *Whenever $\mathcal{R}$ is a reflexive and transitive relation on closed terms, its compatible extension $\mathcal{R}^\bullet$ enjoys the following properties:*

($\mathcal{R}^\bullet$ Refl) $\dfrac{}{a \, \mathcal{R}^\bullet \, a}$ *($\mathcal{R}^\bullet$ Right)* $\dfrac{a \, \mathcal{R}^\bullet \, b \quad b \, \mathcal{R}^\circ \, c}{a \, \mathcal{R}^\bullet \, c}$ *($\mathcal{R}^\bullet$ Comp)* $\dfrac{a \, \widehat{\mathcal{R}^\bullet} \, b}{a \, \mathcal{R}^\bullet \, b}$ *($\mathcal{R}^\bullet$ Sound)* $\dfrac{a \, \mathcal{R}^\circ \, b}{a \, \mathcal{R}^\bullet \, b}$ *($\mathcal{R}^\bullet$ Subst)* $\dfrac{a\{x\} \, \mathcal{R}^\bullet \, b\{x\} \quad u \, \mathcal{R}^\bullet \, v}{a\{\!\{u\}\!\} \, \mathcal{R}^\bullet \, b\{\!\{v\}\!\}}$

The following proposition is the crucial property of $\mathcal{R}^\bullet$, which we use in Sections 1.7 and 1.8 to prove that $\mathcal{R}^\circ = \mathcal{R}^\bullet$ and hence complete the application of Howe's method, where $\mathcal{R}$ is the preorder form of experimental equivalence and applicative bisimilarity, respectively. Let a relation $\mathcal{R}$ on closed terms be *pre-adequate* if and only if $a \, \mathcal{R} \, b$ and $a\Downarrow$ implies that $b\Downarrow$.

Proposition 1.12 *Assume that $\mathcal{R}$ is a reflexive and transitive relation on closed terms, that is pre-adequate, includes Kleene equivalence, and possesses either one or the other of the following properties:*

- *($\mathcal{R}$ Exp) For all closed a and b and all experiments ϵ, $a \, \mathcal{R} \, b$ implies $a\epsilon \, \mathcal{R} \, b\epsilon$.*
- *($\mathcal{R}$ Result Freedom) For closed u and v, $u \, \mathcal{R}^\bullet \, v$ implies $u \, \widehat{\mathcal{R}^\bullet} \, v$.*

Then, for any closed terms a, b and u, $a \, \mathcal{R}^\bullet \, b$ and $a \rightsquigarrow u$ imply there is v with $u \, \mathcal{R}^\bullet \, v$ and $b \rightsquigarrow v$.

We omit the proof. The case depending on ($\mathcal{R}$ Result Freedom) corresponds to the theorem of Howe (1996). The case depending on ($\mathcal{R}$ Exp) corresponds to the typed proof we give for Proposition 2.19 in Appendix B.

1.7 Properties of Experimental Equivalence

We begin with a co-inductive definition of experimental equivalence, and the corresponding preorder, experimental order:

- Let a relation on closed terms, $\mathcal{S}$, be an *experimental simulation* if and only if $a\ \mathcal{S}\ b$ and $a \leadsto u$ implies there is a result v such that $b \leadsto v$ and, for all experiments ϵ, $u\epsilon\ \mathcal{S}\ v\epsilon$.
- Let a relation on closed terms, $\mathcal{S}$, be an *experimental bisimulation* if and only if both $\mathcal{S}$ and $\mathcal{S}^{-1}$ are experimental simulations.
- Let *experimental order*, $\lesssim$, be the union of all experimental simulations, and let *experimental equivalence*, $\sim$, be the union of all experimental bisimulations.

By standard considerations (Milner 1989), $\lesssim$ is itself an experimental simulation, and $\sim$ is an experimental bisimulation. Moreover, $\lesssim$ is the greatest experimental simulation and $\sim$ is the greatest experimental bisimulation (which is how $\sim$ was introduced in Section 1.5). Hence, to prove $a \lesssim b$ it is enough to exhibit an experimental simulation $\mathcal{S}$ such that $a\ \mathcal{S}\ b$. A little calculation, using the fact that reduction is deterministic, shows that $a \sim b$ if and only if $a \lesssim b$ and $b \lesssim a$.

We show that $\lesssim^{\circ}$ is compatible by Howe's method:

Proposition 1.13

(1) *Relation $\lesssim$ is reflexive and transitive.*

(2) *Relation $\lesssim$ includes Kleene equivalence.*

(3) *Relation $\lesssim$ is pre-adequate.*

(4) *($\lesssim$ Exp) holds, that is, $a\epsilon \lesssim b\epsilon$ whenever $a \lesssim b$.*

(5) $\lesssim^{\circ} = \lesssim^{\bullet}$.

Proof

(1) Reflexivity and transitivity follow easily from the definition of $\lesssim$.

(2) It suffices to show that $\mathcal{S} = \{(a, b) \mid a \approx^{kl} b\}$ is an experimental simulation. Suppose that $a\ \mathcal{S}\ b$ and that $a \leadsto u$. By definition of $a \approx^{kl} b$ it follows that $b \leadsto u$ too. Since $\mathcal{S}$ is reflexive, we have $u\epsilon\ \mathcal{S}\ u\epsilon$ for any experiment ϵ. Therefore $\mathcal{S}$ is an experimental simulation.

(3) Suppose $a \lesssim b$ and $a\Downarrow$, that is, there is u with $a \leadsto u$. By definition of $\lesssim$, there is v with $b \leadsto v$, that is, $b\Downarrow$.

(4) Suppose that $a \lesssim b$ and consider any experiment ϵ. We must show that $a\epsilon \lesssim b\epsilon$. Suppose then that $a\epsilon \rightsquigarrow u$. To conclude $a\epsilon \lesssim b\epsilon$ we must exhibit v such that $b\epsilon \rightsquigarrow v$, and for all ϵ', $u\epsilon' \lesssim v\epsilon'$. By Lemma 1.9(3), there is u' such that $a \rightsquigarrow u'$ and $u'\epsilon \rightsquigarrow u$. Since $a \lesssim b$, there is v' such that $b \rightsquigarrow v'$ and moreover that $u'\epsilon \lesssim v'\epsilon$. Since $u'\epsilon \rightsquigarrow u$ there is v such that $v'\epsilon \rightsquigarrow v$, and for all ϵ', $u\epsilon' \lesssim v\epsilon'$, as required.

(5) Consider the compatible extension, $\lesssim^\bullet$, of $\lesssim$. By ($\lesssim^\bullet$ Sound), $\lesssim^\circ \subseteq \lesssim^\bullet$. For the reverse inclusion, let $\mathcal{S} = \{(a, b) \mid a \lesssim^\bullet b \;\&\; a, b \text{ closed}\}$. We show that $\mathcal{S}$ is an experimental simulation. Suppose that $a \lesssim^\bullet b$ for any closed terms a and b. Whenever $a \rightsquigarrow u$ we must exhibit v such that $b \rightsquigarrow v$ and for all experiments ϵ, $u\epsilon \; \mathcal{S} \; v\epsilon$. Given $a \rightsquigarrow u$, Proposition 1.12 asserts there is a result v such that $b \rightsquigarrow v$ and $u \lesssim^\bullet v$. For any ϵ, $u\epsilon \lesssim^\bullet v\epsilon$, by ($\lesssim^\bullet$ Comp). Hence we have $u\epsilon \; \mathcal{S} \; v\epsilon$, as required for $\mathcal{S}$ to be an experimental simulation. Suppose then that $a \lesssim^\bullet b$ where terms a and b may have free variables. Consider any substitution σ sending variables to closed results such that $dom(\sigma) = fv(a) \cup fv(b)$. To show $a \lesssim^\circ b$ we must prove that $a\sigma \lesssim b\sigma$. By ($\lesssim^\bullet$ Subst), $a \lesssim^\bullet b$ implies $a\sigma \lesssim^\bullet b\sigma$. Since $a\sigma$ and $b\sigma$ are closed, $a\sigma \; \mathcal{S} \; b\sigma$. Since $\mathcal{S}$ is an experimental simulation, $\mathcal{S} \subseteq \lesssim$. It follows that $a\sigma \lesssim b\sigma$; hence $\lesssim^\bullet \subseteq \lesssim^\circ$. □

Now we have:

Proposition 1.14 *Relation $\sim^\circ$ is an adequate ς-theory.*

Proof Since $\lesssim$ is pre-adequate, $\sim$ is adequate. Since $\sim$ is $\sim^\circ$ restricted to closed terms, $\sim^\circ$ is adequate. By the previous proposition, $\lesssim^\circ$ is compatible. Since $\sim$ is the symmetrisation of $\lesssim$ it follows that $\sim^\circ$ is compatible. Property $\approx^{kl} \subseteq \lesssim$ implies $\approx^{kl} \subseteq \sim$. Therefore, since $\sim$ is an equivalence it follows by Proposition 1.10 that rules (Eval Select) and (Eval Update) hold with $\sim^\circ$ instead of $\leftrightarrow$. So $\sim^\circ$ satisfies all the rules of $\leftrightarrow$, and therefore is a ς-theory. □

Next, we verify our observation from Section 1.5 that experimental equivalence relates two terms if they can be interchanged without affecting convergence in contexts built up simply from method selects and method updates.

Proposition 1.15 *For all closed a and b, $a \sim b$ if and only if for all experiments $\epsilon_1, \ldots, \epsilon_n$, $a\epsilon_1 \cdots \epsilon_n\Downarrow \Leftrightarrow b\epsilon_1 \cdots \epsilon_n\Downarrow$.*

Proof For the left-to-right direction, since a and b are closed we have $a \sim^\circ b$. Since $\sim^\circ$ is compatible, $a\epsilon_1 \cdots \epsilon_n \sim^\circ b\epsilon_1 \cdots \epsilon_n$. Since the ϵ_i are experiments, $a\epsilon_1 \cdots \epsilon_n$ and $b\epsilon_1 \cdots \epsilon_n$ are closed, so we have $a\epsilon_1 \cdots \epsilon_n \sim b\epsilon_1 \cdots \epsilon_n$. Therefore $a\epsilon_1 \cdots \epsilon_n\Downarrow \Leftrightarrow b\epsilon_1 \cdots \epsilon_n\Downarrow$.

For the right-to-left direction, let $\mathcal{S}$ be the following relation on closed terms:

$$\mathcal{S} \triangleq \{(a, b) \mid a\epsilon_1 \cdots \epsilon_n\Downarrow \Leftrightarrow b\epsilon_1 \cdots \epsilon_n\Downarrow \text{ for all experiments } \epsilon_1, \ldots, \epsilon_n\}$$

Since $\mathcal{S}$ is symmetric, if we can show it to be an experimental simulation, it will follow that $a \mathcal{S} b$ implies $a \sim b$, which establishes the right-to-left direction of the proposition. Suppose, then, that $a \mathcal{S} b$. Consider any u such that $a \rightsquigarrow u$. Since $a \mathcal{S} b$ it follows there must be a result v such that $b \rightsquigarrow v$. Now consider any experiment ϵ; it suffices to show that $u\epsilon \mathcal{S} v\epsilon$. To show this consider any experiments $\vec{\epsilon} = \epsilon_1, \ldots, \epsilon_n$. We must prove that $u\epsilon\vec{\epsilon}\Downarrow$ implies $v\epsilon\vec{\epsilon}\Downarrow$. Suppose that $u\epsilon\vec{\epsilon}\Downarrow$. By Lemma 1.9, $u\epsilon\vec{\epsilon} \approx^{kl} a\epsilon\vec{\epsilon}$, and therefore $a\epsilon\vec{\epsilon}\Downarrow$. By definition, $a \mathcal{S} b$ implies that $b\epsilon\vec{\epsilon}\Downarrow$. By Lemma 1.9, $b\epsilon\vec{\epsilon} \approx^{kl} v\epsilon\vec{\epsilon}$, and therefore $v\epsilon\vec{\epsilon}\Downarrow$, as desired. □

Given the following lemma, we prove that the open extension of experimental equivalence coincides with contextual equivalence.

Lemma 1.16 *$a\{x\} \simeq b\{x\}$ implies that for all closed v, $a\{\!\{v\}\!\} \simeq b\{\!\{v\}\!\}$.*

Proof See Appendix A. □

Proposition 1.17 $\simeq \, = \, \sim^\circ$.

Proof Since $\sim^\circ$ is both compatible and adequate, Proposition 1.8 implies that $\sim^\circ \subseteq \simeq$. To show the reverse direction, suppose that $a \simeq b$. Let $\{x_1, \ldots, x_n\} = fv(a) \cup fv(b)$. Consider any substitution $\sigma = \{\!\{x_1 \leftarrow v_1\}\!\} \cdots \{\!\{x_n \leftarrow v_n\}\!\}$ for arbitrary closed results $v_1, \ldots, v_n$. By Lemma 1.16, $a\sigma \simeq b\sigma$. By Proposition 1.15, this implies that $a\sigma \sim b\sigma$. Since σ is arbitrary, it follows that $a \sim^\circ b$. This proves that $\simeq \subseteq \sim^\circ$. □

Milner (1977) proves a context lemma for the combinatory logic form of PCF: two closed terms a and b are contextually equivalent if and only if $a\, c_1 \ldots c_n\Downarrow \Leftrightarrow b\, c_1 \ldots c_n\Downarrow$ for all lists of terms $c_1, \ldots, c_n$. It is often easier to establish the latter property than to prove contextual equivalence directly. Mason and Talcott have proved similar theorems (named "CIU" theorems after the phrase "Closed Instances of Use") for a range of λ-calculi with state (Talcott 1997). By combining Proposition 1.15 and Proposition 1.17 we obtain that any terms a and b are contextually equivalent if and only if all their closed instances are experimentally equivalent, that is, for all closing substitutions σ and all lists of experiments $\epsilon_1, \ldots, \epsilon_n$, that $(a\sigma)\epsilon_1 \cdots \epsilon_n\Downarrow \Leftrightarrow (b\sigma)\epsilon_1 \cdots \epsilon_n\Downarrow$. So experimental equivalence for the ς-calculus is both a generalisation of the equivalence implicit in Milner's context lemma, and a specialisation to a stateless calculus of CIU equivalence. Moreover, experimental equivalence corresponds to the typed bisimilarity studied by Gordon and Rees (1996), although the latter is defined rather differently via a labelled transition system.

1.8 Properties of Applicative Bisimilarity

We begin with a co-inductive definition of applicative bisimilarity and the corresponding preorder, applicative similarity:

- Let a relation on closed terms, $\mathcal{S}$, be an *applicative simulation* if and only if $a \mathrel{\mathcal{S}} b$ and $a \leadsto [\ell_i = \varsigma(x_i)a_i\{x_i\}^{\,i\in 1..n}]$ imply there is a result v such that $b \leadsto v$, $v = [\ell_i = \varsigma(x_i)b_i\{x_i\}^{\,i\in 1..n}]$ and $a_i\{\!\{w\}\!\} \mathrel{\mathcal{S}} b_i\{\!\{w\}\!\}$ for each $i \in 1..n$ and all closed results w.

- Let a relation on closed terms, $\mathcal{S}$, be an *applicative bisimulation* if and only if both $\mathcal{S}$ and $\mathcal{S}^{-1}$ are applicative simulations.

- Let *applicative similarity*, $\lessapprox$, be the union of all applicative simulations, and let *applicative bisimilarity*, $\approx$, be the union of all applicative bisimulations.

This is equivalent to the definition of applicative bisimilarity in Section 1.5 since, by standard considerations, $\lessapprox$ and $\approx$ are the greatest applicative simulation and the greatest applicative bisimulation respectively. A little calculation, using the fact that reduction is deterministic, shows that $a \approx b$ if and only if $a \lessapprox b$ and $b \lessapprox a$.

We show that $\lessapprox^{\circ}$ is compatible by Howe's method:

Proposition 1.18

(1) *Relation* $\lessapprox$ *is reflexive and transitive.*

(2) *Relation* $\lessapprox$ *includes Kleene equivalence.*

(3) *Relation* $\lessapprox$ *is pre-adequate.*

(4) *Property* ($\lessapprox$ *Result Freedom*) *holds, that is,* $u \mathrel{\widehat{\lessapprox^{\bullet}}} v$ *whenever* $u \lessapprox^{\bullet} v$.

(5) $\lessapprox^{\circ} = \lessapprox^{\bullet}$.

Proof We only sketch the proof, as it is a special case of Howe's general theorem. The proofs of parts (1) to (3) are similar to the proofs of those parts of Proposition 1.13. The proof of (4) is routine. We prove part (5) as follows. By ($\lessapprox^{\bullet}$ Sound), $\lessapprox^{\circ} \subseteq \lessapprox^{\bullet}$. For the reverse inclusion, let $\mathcal{S} = \{(a,b) \mid a \lessapprox^{\bullet} b \,\&\, a, b \text{ closed}\}$. We show that $\mathcal{S}$ is a simulation. Suppose that $a \lessapprox^{\bullet} b$ for any closed terms a and b. Whenever $a \leadsto u$ we must exhibit v such that $b \leadsto v$ and $u \mathrel{\widehat{\mathcal{S}^{\circ}}} v$. Given $a \leadsto u$, Proposition 1.12 asserts there is result v such that $b \leadsto v$ and $u \lessapprox^{\bullet} v$. By ($\lessapprox$ Result Freedom), $u \mathrel{\widehat{\lessapprox^{\bullet}}} v$. By ($\lessapprox^{\bullet}$ Subst), $\lessapprox^{\bullet} \subseteq \mathcal{S}^{\circ}$. Hence $u \mathrel{\widehat{\mathcal{S}^{\circ}}} v$. □

By a proof similar to that of Proposition 1.14, we get:

Proposition 1.19 *Relation* $\approx^{\circ}$ *is an adequate* ς*-theory.*

1.9 Complete Adequacy and the Hierarchy of ς-Theories

We say a ς-theory $\mathcal{R}$ is *completely adequate* if and only if $\mathcal{R}$ is adequate and for all closed a and b, $a\Uparrow$ and $b\Uparrow$ imply $a \mathrel{\mathcal{R}} b$. A little calculation shows this to be equivalent to the definition of complete adequacy given by Meyer and Cosmadakis (1988): a ς-theory is completely adequate if and only if for all closed a, $a\Uparrow$ if and only if $a \mathrel{\mathcal{R}} \Omega$. Completely adequate ς-theories enjoy the following relationship with convergence and divergence:

Lemma 1.20 *For any completely adequate ς-theory $\mathcal{R}$ and any closed a,*

- *$a\Downarrow$ if and only if there is a result v with $a \mathrel{\mathcal{R}} v$, and*
- *$a\Uparrow$ if and only if $a \mathrel{\mathcal{R}} \Omega$.*

Some—but not all—adequate ς-theories are completely adequate:

Lemma 1.21 *Relations $\approx^\circ$, $\sim^\circ$ and $\simeq$ are completely adequate, but $\leftrightarrow$ is not.*

Proof Relation $\{(a, b) \mid a\Uparrow \;\&\; b\Uparrow\}$ is both an experimental bisimulation and an applicative bisimulation, so $\approx^\circ$ and $\sim^\circ$ are completely adequate. Since $\simeq$ is the greatest adequate ς-theory, it includes both $\approx^\circ$ and $\sim^\circ$. Therefore $\simeq$ must itself be completely adequate. Given Lemma 1.20, no completely adequate ς-theory can be recursively enumerable, or else convergence would be decidable. So $\leftrightarrow$, being recursively enumerable, cannot be completely adequate. □

We use Lemma 1.21 in the proof of the following theorem. It asserts that the open extension of applicative bisimilarity is an adequate ς-theory that lies between the least such, the equational theory, $\leftrightarrow$, and the greatest such, contextual equivalence, $\simeq$, in the strict subset ordering. Moreover, the open extension of experimental equivalence coincides with contextual equivalence.

Theorem 1.22 $\leftrightarrow \subset \approx^\circ \subset \sim^\circ = \simeq$.

Proof The equation is simply Proposition 1.17. To see that $\leftrightarrow \subset \approx^\circ$, first note that since $\approx^\circ$ is a ς-theory, $\leftrightarrow \subseteq \approx^\circ$. Since $\approx^\circ$ but not $\leftrightarrow$ is completely adequate, $\leftrightarrow \subset \approx^\circ$. It remains to show $\approx^\circ \subset \simeq$. Since $\approx^\circ$ is adequate, is compatible and is an equivalence, $\approx^\circ \subseteq \simeq$. To show the inclusion is strict, we exhibit terms u and v with $u \simeq v$ but not $u \approx^\circ v$.

Let $u = [\ell = \varsigma(x)x.\ell]$ and $v = [\ell = \varsigma(x)\Omega]$. If $u \approx v$, it follows that $x.\ell\{\!\{x \leftarrow w\}\!\} \approx \Omega\{\!\{x \leftarrow w\}\!\}$, for all closed results w. But consider the result $w = [\ell = \varsigma(s)[]]$. We have $x.\ell\{\!\{x \leftarrow w\}\!\}\Downarrow$ but $\Omega\{\!\{x \leftarrow w\}\!\}\Uparrow$, so $x.\ell\{\!\{x \leftarrow w\}\!\} \approx \Omega\{\!\{x \leftarrow w\}\!\}$ is false. Hence u and v are not applicatively bisimilar.

To see that $u \simeq v$, we appeal to Proposition 1.17, and show that $u \sim v$. Since u and v are results (which reduce only to themselves) it is enough to show that

$u\epsilon \sim v\epsilon$ for any experiment ϵ. We proceed by a case analysis of ϵ. If $\epsilon = .\ell$, $u\epsilon\Uparrow$ and $v\epsilon\Uparrow$, and therefore $u\epsilon \sim v\epsilon$. If $\epsilon = .\ell \Leftarrow \varsigma(x)b$ then $u\epsilon \leftrightarrow [\ell = \varsigma(x)b]$ and $v\epsilon \leftrightarrow [\ell = \varsigma(x)b]$. Therefore $u\epsilon \sim v\epsilon$, since $\leftrightarrow \subseteq \sim^\circ$ and $u\epsilon$ and $v\epsilon$ are closed. If ϵ is neither $.\ell$ nor $.\ell \Leftarrow \varsigma(x)b$, for any b, both $u\epsilon$ and $v\epsilon$ are stuck. So $u\epsilon\Uparrow$ and $v\epsilon\Uparrow$. Therefore $u\epsilon \sim v\epsilon$. In any case, it follows that $u \sim v$ and therefore $u \simeq v$. □

Since Kleene equivalence relates any two divergent closed terms, but $\leftrightarrow$ does not, it follows that $\leftrightarrow$ does not include Kleene equivalence. On the other hand, it follows from Propositions 1.13 and 1.18 that both experimental equivalence and applicative bisimilarity include Kleene equivalence; in fact we have the following:

Proposition 1.23 *Any completely adequate ς-theory includes Kleene equivalence.*

Proof Suppose $\mathcal{R}$ is a completely adequate ς-theory. To show that $\mathcal{R}$ includes Kleene equivalence, consider any closed terms a and b such that $a \approx^{kl} b$, that is, for all closed results v, $a \rightsquigarrow v \Leftrightarrow b \rightsquigarrow v$. Given determinacy of reduction, either $a\Uparrow$ or there is a result v such that $a \rightsquigarrow v$. In the first case, $a \approx^{kl} b$ implies that $b\Uparrow$. Since $\mathcal{R}$ is completely adequate, $a\Uparrow$ and $b\Uparrow$ imply $a \mathcal{R} b$. In the second case, $a \rightsquigarrow v$ and $a \approx^{kl} b$ imply $b \rightsquigarrow v$ too. Since $\leftrightarrow$ includes reduction, we have $a \leftrightarrow v$, $b \leftrightarrow v$ and hence $a \leftrightarrow b$. Since $\mathcal{R}$ is a ς-theory, $a \mathcal{R} b$. In all, this shows that $a \mathcal{R} b$ whenever $a \approx^{kl} b$. Therefore $\mathcal{R}$ includes Kleene equivalence. □

1.10 Untyped Examples

In this section, we exercise our development in the setting of encodings of functions and numbers within the ς-calculus.

When writing examples it is convenient to augment our notation with fields, that is, constant components of an object with no dependence on self. Abadi and Cardelli encode fields as methods as follows. Let a *field* be a method $\varsigma(x)b$ such that the self parameter $x \notin fv(b)$. We write $[\ell = a, \ldots]$ short for $[\ell = \varsigma(x)a, \ldots]$ for some variable $x \notin fv(a)$. We write $a.\ell := b$ short for $a.\ell \Leftarrow \varsigma(x)b$, for some variable $x \notin fv(b)$. Also, when we don't care what result a method ℓ returns, we write $[\ell = \uparrow, \ldots]$, short for $[\ell = \varsigma(s)s.\ell, \ldots]$.

Functions as Objects

The λ-calculus may be encoded in the ς-calculus as follows:

$$\lambda(x)(b\{\!\{x\}\!\}) \triangleq [arg = \uparrow, val = \varsigma(x)b\{\!\{x.arg\}\!\}]$$
$$b(a) \triangleq (b.arg := a).val$$

(Unlike elsewhere, the substitution in the term $b\{\!\{x.arg\}\!\}$ replaces the variable x with a term, $x.arg$, that is not an object.)

We can derive β-conversion in any ς-theory:

$$\begin{aligned}
&(\lambda(x)b\{x\})(a) \\
&\quad\leftrightarrow \ [arg = a,\ val = \varsigma(x)b\{\!\{x.arg\}\!\}].val \\
&\quad\leftrightarrow \ b\{\!\{[arg = a,\ val = \varsigma(x)b\{\!\{x.arg\}\!\}].arg\}\!\} \\
&\quad\leftrightarrow \ b\{\!\{a\}\!\}
\end{aligned}$$

On the other hand, η-conversion cannot be included in any adequate ς-theory. Although Ω diverges, $\lambda(x)(\Omega(x))$ converges. A relation that included η-conversion would equate $\lambda(x)(\Omega(x))$ and Ω. But no adequate relation may equate a term that converges with one that does not.

Numbers as Objects

The following term is an object-oriented numeral for 0:

$$\begin{aligned}
zero \ \triangleq \ [&case = \lambda(z)\lambda(f)z, \\
&succ = \varsigma(n)n.case \Leftarrow \varsigma(x)\lambda(z)\lambda(f)f(n)]
\end{aligned}$$

Hence we can define an object-oriented numeral, $\underline{n}$, for each n by induction: let $\underline{0} = zero$ and $\underline{n+1} = \underline{n}.succ$.

The $succ$ method generates numeral $\underline{n+1}$ from $\underline{n}$. The $case$ method allows testing for whether a numeral is for 0 or not:

$$\begin{aligned}
\underline{0}.case(a)(b) &\leftrightarrow a \\
\underline{n+1}.case(a)(b) &\leftrightarrow b(\underline{n})
\end{aligned}$$

Here is a function intended to compute the addition of two numerals.

$$add \ \triangleq \ [arg = \uparrow,\ val = \varsigma(s)\lambda(x)x.case(s.arg)(s(s.arg.succ))]$$

In the subterm $s(s.arg.succ)$, self parameter s is used to achieve self-application.

Proposition 1.24 *For all n and m, $add(\underline{m})(\underline{n}) \leftrightarrow \underline{m+n}$.*

Proof First, note that for any a:

$$\begin{aligned}
add(a) &\leftrightarrow (add.arg := a).val \\
&\leftrightarrow [arg = a,\ val = \varsigma(s)\lambda(x)x.case(s.arg)(s(s.arg.succ))].val \\
&\leftrightarrow \lambda(x)x.case(a)((add.arg := a)(a.succ)) \\
&\leftrightarrow \lambda(x)x.case(a)(add(a.succ))
\end{aligned}$$

The last step is justified by the fact that $(v.\ell := a).\ell := b \leftrightarrow v.\ell := b$ for any closed result v and terms a and b.

We prove by induction on n that for all m, $add(\underline{m})(\underline{n}) \leftrightarrow \underline{m+n}$. Here is the base case:

$$\begin{aligned} add(\underline{m})(\underline{0}) &\leftrightarrow \underline{0}.case(\underline{m})(add(\underline{m}.succ)) \\ &\leftrightarrow \underline{m} = \underline{m+0} \end{aligned}$$

Assuming the induction hypothesis for n, we prove it for $n+1$:

$$\begin{aligned} add(\underline{m})(\underline{n+1}) &\leftrightarrow \underline{n+1}.case(\underline{m})(add(\underline{m}.succ)) \\ &\leftrightarrow add(\underline{m+1})(\underline{n}) \\ &\leftrightarrow \underline{(m+1)+n} = \underline{m+(n+1)} \end{aligned}$$

Hence the proposition holds for all n and m. □

1.11 Discussion

This completes our development of operational equivalence in the ς-calculus. We proved that contextual equivalence is the greatest adequate ς-theory, and via experimental equivalence we obtained a useful principle of co-induction for contextual equivalence. We demonstrated the new idea of using context closure to define contextual equivalence, without needing to define contexts explicitly. Our examples showed that $\leftrightarrow$, the least adequate ς-theory, is enough for certain calculations. (We will make more use of co-induction in the typed setting of the next section.)

Most of the properties of operational equivalences for the ς-calculus are analogous to properties of operational equivalences on the λ-calculus. One notable exception is the fact that Howe's applicative bisimilarity is finer grained than contextual equivalence (see the proof of Theorem 1.22).

2 Equivalence of Polymorphically Typed Objects

In this section, we study contextual equivalence for a polymorphic object calculus, $\mathbf{S}_\lambda$, characterise it co-inductively by generalising experimental equivalence from Section 1 and validate a typed equational theory. We refrain from investigating Church-Rosser or standardisation properties as they are unnecessary for validating the equational theory. We refrain from investigating Howe-style applicative bisimilarity because, just as in the ς-calculus, it is finer grained than contextual equivalence.

We introduce the syntax, type system and equational theory of $\mathbf{S}_\lambda$ in Section 2.1 and its operational semantics in Section 2.2. Sections 2.3, 2.4 and 2.5 introduce typed forms of context closure, contextual equivalence and open extension, respectively. We define a typed form of experimental equivalence in Section 2.6, prove it to be compatible in Section 2.7 and show it equals contextual equivalence in Section 2.8. Section 2.9 illustrates how co-induction may be used to prove two objects equivalent. We discuss related work and variants of this work in Section 2.10.

2.1 $\mathbf{S}_\lambda$: Syntax, Type System and Equational Theory

Our subject, $\mathbf{S}_\lambda$, is Abadi and Cardelli's calculus $\mathbf{S}_\forall$ plus first-order (that is, simply typed) functions. The object calculus $\mathbf{S}_\forall$ has covariant self types, second-order (that is, polymorphic) functions and subtyping. The fragment of $\mathbf{S}_\lambda$ consisting of first-order and second-order functions corresponds to the calculus $\mathbf{F}_{<:}$ (Cardelli, Martini, Mitchell, and Scedrov 1994). Abadi and Cardelli use $\mathbf{S}_\forall$ as a metalanguage to interpret a typed class-based language with inheritance.

The types of $\mathbf{S}_\lambda$ are given as follows, where X ranges over an infinite collection of type variables, and ν ranges over the set $\{^-, ^o, ^+\}$ of variance annotations.

Syntax of $\mathbf{S}_\lambda$ types:

$A, B ::=$	types
X	type variable
Top	the biggest type
$Obj(X)[\ell_i \nu_i{:}B_i\ ^{i \in 1..n}]$	object type (ℓ_i distinct, $\nu_i \in \{^-, ^o, ^+\}$)
$A \to B$	function type
$\forall(X{<:}A)B$	polymorphic type

In $Obj(X)[\ell_i \nu_i{:}B_i\ ^{i \in 1..n}]$, the type variable X is bound in each type B_i. In $\forall(X{<:}A)B$, the type variable X is bound in type B. We identify types up to consistent renaming of bound type variables and permutation of components of object types. Let $fv(A)$ be the set of type variables that occur free in type A. Intuitively, terms of type $A = Obj(X)[\ell_i \nu_i{:}B_i\{X\}\ ^{i \in 1..n}]$ are objects, such that for each $i \in 1..n$ there is a method labelled ℓ_i returning a result of type $B_i\{\!\{A\}\!\}$. The annotation ν_i determines the external operations on method ℓ_i. Annotation $^+$ allows select but not update. Annotation $^-$ allows update but not select. Annotation ^{o} allows both select and update. The variable X, bound in the type of each method, is the type of self, the whole object.

Informally, let a positive or negative occurrence of X in A be one for which the path to X never goes under a nonvariant annotation, and goes under a contravariant annotation or through the bound of a polymorphic type an even or odd number of times, respectively. We write $A\{X^+\}$ and $A\{X^-\}$ to mean that X occurs at most positively and negatively, respectively, in A. See Abadi and Cardelli's book for a formal definition of these predicates.

Syntax of typed terms:

$a, b ::=$	terms
x	variable
$obj(X{=}A)[\ell_i = \varsigma(x_i{:}X)b_i\ ^{i \in 1..n}]$	object (ℓ_i distinct)
$a.\ell$	method select
$a.\ell \Leftarrow (Y{<:}A, y{:}Y)\varsigma(x{:}Y)b$	method update

$\lambda(x{:}A)b$	abstraction
$b(a)$	application
$\lambda(X{<:}A)b$	type abstraction
$b(A)$	type application

In $obj(X{=}A)[\ell_i = \varsigma(x_i{:}X)b_i\ ^{i\in 1..n}]$, the type variable X and the variable x_i are bound in b_i, for each $i \in 1..n$. The type variable X is not bound in A. In $a.\ell \Leftarrow (Y{<:}A, y{:}Y)\varsigma(x{:}Y)b$, the type variable Y is bound in $y{:}Y$ and $\varsigma(x{:}Y)b$, the variable y is bound in $\varsigma(x{:}Y)b$, and the variable x is bound in b. In $\lambda(x{:}A)b$, the variable x is bound in b. In $\lambda(X{<:}A)b$, the type variable X is bound in b. As in the untyped calculus, we identify terms up to consistent renaming of bound variables and type variables, and permutation of components in objects. An update $a.\ell \Leftarrow (Y{<:}A, y{:}Y)\varsigma(x{:}Y)b$ updates the method labelled ℓ with $\varsigma(x{:}Y)b$, where $a{:}A$, Y is a type variable representing the type of self, and $y{:}Y$ is bound to the result of evaluating a. The "old self" parameter, y, is useful in situations where the updated method returns a result of self type. For an example, see the object-oriented *zero* in Section 2.9, or Abadi and Cardelli's work.

Let v range over ***results***, objects, abstractions or type abstractions, that is, terms of the form $obj(X{=}A)[\ell_i = \varsigma(x_i{:}X)b_i\ ^{1\in 1..n}]$, $\lambda(x{:}A)b$ or $\lambda(X{<:}A)b$.

If phrase ϕ is a type or a term, we write $\phi\{\!\{X \leftarrow B\}\!\}$ for the outcome of substituting type B for each free occurrence of type variable X in ϕ. As in the untyped calculus, we write $a\{\!\{x \leftarrow b\}\!\}$ for the outcome of substituting term b for each free occurrence of variable x in a. We write $\phi\{X\}$ and $a\{x\}$, respectively, to note that type variable X may occur free in phrase ϕ, either a type or a term, and that variable x may occur free in term a. Having already noted $\phi\{X\}$ and $a\{x\}$, respectively, we usually write $\phi\{\!\{B\}\!\}$ for $\phi\{\!\{x \leftarrow B\}\!\}$ and $a\{\!\{b\}\!\}$ for $a\{\!\{x \leftarrow b\}\!\}$.

Let an *environment*, E, consist of a sequence of declarations: $X{<:}A$ declares that type variable X has bound A; $x{:}A$ declares that variable x has type A. The empty environment is $\varnothing$. If E is an environment, let $dom(E)$ be the set of type variables and variables declared in E. The type system is based on the following five judgments.

Judgments:

$E \vdash \diamond$	well formed environment judgment
$E \vdash A$	type judgment
$E \vdash A{<:}B$	subtyping judgment
$E \vdash \nu A{<:}\nu' B$	subtyping judgment with variance
$E \vdash a : A$	value typing judgment

The following rules determine the well formed environments and types; (Type Object) requires that the self parameter occurs positively in primitive object types.

Environments and types:

(Env $\varnothing$) $$\frac{}{\varnothing \vdash \diamond}$$

(Env x) $$\frac{E \vdash A \quad x \notin dom(E)}{E, x{:}A \vdash \diamond}$$

(Env $X{<:}$) $$\frac{E \vdash A \quad X \notin dom(E)}{E, X{<:}A \vdash \diamond}$$

(Type $X{<:}$) $$\frac{E', X{<:}A, E'' \vdash \diamond}{E', X{<:}A, E'' \vdash X}$$

(Type Top) $$\frac{E \vdash \diamond}{E \vdash \mathit{Top}}$$

(Type Object) (ℓ_i distinct, $\nu_i \in \{^-, ^o, ^+\}$) $$\frac{E, X{<:}\mathit{Top} \vdash B_i \quad B_i\{X^+\} \quad \forall i \in 1..n}{E \vdash \mathit{Obj}(X)[\ell_i \nu_i{:}B_i \,^{i \in 1..n}]}$$

(Type Arrow) $$\frac{E \vdash A \quad E \vdash B}{E \vdash A \rightarrow B}$$

(Type All<:) $$\frac{E, X{<:}A \vdash B}{E \vdash \forall(X{<:}A)B}$$

The following rules define the subtyping judgment. (Sub Object) uses the auxiliary judgment, $E \vdash \nu A{<:}\nu' B$, to relate the method types according to their annotations.

Subtyping:

(Sub Refl) $$\frac{E \vdash A}{E \vdash A{<:}A}$$

(Sub Trans) $$\frac{E \vdash A{<:}B \quad E \vdash B{<:}C}{E \vdash A{<:}C}$$

(Sub X) $$\frac{E', X{<:}A, E'' \vdash \diamond}{E', X{<:}A, E'' \vdash X{<:}A}$$

(Sub Top) $$\frac{E \vdash A}{E \vdash A{<:}\mathit{Top}}$$

(Sub Object) (where $A = \mathit{Obj}(X)[\ell_i \nu_i{:}B_i\{X\} \,^{i \in 1..n+m}]$ and $A' = \mathit{Obj}(X)[\ell_i \nu_i'{:}B_i'\{X\} \,^{i \in 1..n}]$) $$\frac{E \vdash A' \quad E, Y{<:}A \vdash \nu_i B_i\{\!\{Y\}\!\}{<:}\nu_i' B_i'\{\!\{Y\}\!\} \quad \forall i \in 1..n}{E \vdash A{<:}A'}$$

(Sub Arrow) $$\frac{E \vdash A'{<:}A \quad E \vdash B{<:}B'}{E \vdash (A \rightarrow B){<:}(A' \rightarrow B')}$$

(Sub All) $$\frac{E \vdash A'{<:}A \quad E, X{<:}A' \vdash B{<:}B'}{E \vdash \forall(X{<:}A)B{<:}\forall(X{<:}A')B'}$$

(Sub Invariant) $$\frac{E \vdash B}{E \vdash {}^oB{<:}{}^oB}$$

(Sub Covariant) $$\frac{E \vdash B{<:}B' \quad \nu \in \{^o, ^+\}}{E \vdash \nu B{<:}{}^+B'}$$

(Sub Contravariant) $$\frac{E \vdash B'{<:}B \quad \nu \in \{^o, ^-\}}{E \vdash \nu B{<:}{}^-B'}$$

The following rules determine types for terms. (Val Select) and (Val Update) are structural rules that incorporate the assumption that a term a whose type A is a subtype of an object type A' is in fact an object.

Typing rules for terms:

(Val Subsumption)

$$\frac{E \vdash a : A \quad E \vdash A <: B}{E \vdash a : B}$$

(Val x)

$$\frac{E', x{:}A, E'' \vdash \diamond}{E', x{:}A, E'' \vdash x : A}$$

(Val Object) (where $A = Obj(X)[\ell_i \nu_i{:}B_i\{X\}^{\ i \in 1..n}]$)

$$\frac{E, x_i{:}A \vdash b_i\{\!\{A\}\!\} : B_i\{\!\{A\}\!\} \quad \forall i \in 1..n}{E \vdash obj(X{=}A)[\ell_i = \varsigma(x_i{:}X)b_i\{X\}^{\ i \in 1..n}] : A}$$

(Val Select) (where $A' = Obj(X)[\ell_i \nu_i{:}B_i\{X\}^{\ i \in 1..n}]$)

$$\frac{E \vdash a : A \quad E \vdash A <: A' \quad \nu_j \in \{^o, ^+\} \quad j \in 1..n}{E \vdash a.\ell_j : B_j\{\!\{A\}\!\}}$$

(Val Update) (where $A' = Obj(X)[\ell_i \nu_i{:}B_i\{X\}^{\ i \in 1..n}]$)

$$\frac{\begin{array}{c} E \vdash a : A \quad E \vdash A <: A' \\ E, Y <: A, y{:}Y, x{:}Y \vdash b : B_j\{\!\{Y\}\!\} \quad \nu_j \in \{^o, ^-\} \quad j \in 1..n \end{array}}{E \vdash a.\ell_j \Leftarrow (Y <: A, y{:}Y)\varsigma(x{:}Y)b : A}$$

(Val Fun)

$$\frac{E, x{:}A \vdash b : B}{E \vdash \lambda(x{:}A)b : A \to B}$$

(Val Appl)

$$\frac{E \vdash b : A \to B \quad E \vdash a : A}{E \vdash b(a) : B}$$

(Val Fun2<:)

$$\frac{E, X <: A \vdash b : B}{E \vdash \lambda(X <: A)b : \forall(X <: A)B}$$

(Val Appl2<:)

$$\frac{E \vdash b : \forall(X <: A)B\{X\} \quad E \vdash A' <: A}{E \vdash b(A') : B\{\!\{A'\}\!\}}$$

The type system enjoys the following standard properties.

Proposition 2.1

(1) *Weakening:*
If $E, E' \vdash \mathcal{J}$ *and* $E, F \vdash \diamond$ *and* $dom(E') \cap dom(F) = \varnothing$ *then* $E, F, E' \vdash \mathcal{J}$.

(2) *Type substitution:*
If $E, X <: B, E'\{X\} \vdash \mathcal{J}\{X\}$ *and* $E \vdash A <: B$ *then* $E, E'\{\!\{A\}\!\} \vdash \mathcal{J}\{\!\{A\}\!\}$.

(3) *Result substitution:*
If $E, x{:}A, E' \vdash \mathcal{J}\{x\}$ *and* $E \vdash v : A$ *then* $E, E' \vdash \mathcal{J}\{\!\{v\}\!\}$.

(4) *Bound weakening:*
If $E, X <: B, E' \vdash \mathcal{J}$ *then* $E \vdash A <: B$ *imply* $E, X <: A, E' \vdash \mathcal{J}$.

We now generalise the untyped notion of a ς-theory to $\mathbf{S}_\lambda$. Let a *relation on typed terms* be a set of quadruples of the form (E, a, a', A), where E is an environment, a and a' are terms and A is a type. If $\mathcal{R}$ is a relation on typed terms, we write

$E \vdash a \mathcal{R} a' : A$ to mean that $(E, a, a', A) \in \mathcal{R}$. If $\mathcal{R}$ is a relation on typed terms, let us say that $\mathcal{R}$ is *well formed* if and only if $E \vdash a \mathcal{R} a' : A$ implies $E \vdash a : A$ and $E \vdash a' : A$.

If $\mathcal{R}$ is a relation on typed terms, let its *compatible refinement*, $\widehat{\mathcal{R}}$, be the least relation on typed terms closed under the following rules. These rules are simply binary versions of the typing rules for terms, except that subsumption is omitted.

Compatible refinement:

(Comp x)

$$\frac{E', x{:}A, E'' \vdash \diamond}{E', x{:}A, E'' \vdash x \,\widehat{\mathcal{R}}\, x : A}$$

(Comp Object) (where $A = Obj(X)[\ell_i \nu_i{:}B_i\{X\}^{\,i \in 1..n}]$)

$$\frac{E, x_i{:}A \vdash b_i\{\!\{A\}\!\} \,\mathcal{R}\, b_i'\{\!\{A\}\!\} : B_i\{\!\{A\}\!\} \quad \forall i \in 1..n}{\begin{array}{l} E \vdash obj(X{=}A)[\ell_i = \varsigma(x_i{:}X)b_i\{X\}^{\,i \in 1..n}] \,\widehat{\mathcal{R}} \\ \qquad obj(X{=}A)[\ell_i = \varsigma(x_i{:}X)b_i'\{X\}^{\,i \in 1..n}] : A \end{array}}$$

(Comp Select) (where $A' = Obj(X)[\ell_i \nu_i{:}B_i\{X\}^{\,i \in 1..n}]$)

$$\frac{E \vdash a \,\mathcal{R}\, a' : A \quad E \vdash A <: A' \quad \nu_j \in \{^{o}, ^{+}\} \quad j \in 1..n}{E \vdash a.\ell_j \,\mathcal{R}\, a'.\ell_j : B_j\{\!\{A\}\!\}}$$

(Comp Update) (where $A' = Obj(X)[\ell_i \nu_i{:}B_i\{X\}^{\,i \in 1..n}]$)

$$\frac{\begin{array}{c} E \vdash a \,\mathcal{R}\, a' : A \quad E \vdash A <: A' \\ E, Y <: A, y{:}Y, x{:}Y \vdash b \,\mathcal{R}\, b' : B_j\{\!\{Y\}\!\} \quad \nu_j \in \{^{o}, ^{-}\} \quad j \in 1..n \end{array}}{E \vdash a.\ell_j \Leftarrow (Y <: A, y{:}Y)\varsigma(x{:}Y)b \,\widehat{\mathcal{R}}\, a'.\ell_j \Leftarrow (Y <: A, y{:}Y)\varsigma(x{:}Y)b' : A}$$

(Comp Fun)

$$\frac{E, x{:}A \vdash b \,\mathcal{R}\, b' : B}{E \vdash \lambda(x{:}A)b \,\widehat{\mathcal{R}}\, \lambda(x{:}A)b' : A \to B}$$

(Comp Appl)

$$\frac{E \vdash b \,\mathcal{R}\, b' : A \to B \quad E \vdash a \,\mathcal{R}\, a' : A}{E \vdash b(a) \,\widehat{\mathcal{R}}\, b'(a') : B}$$

(Comp Fun2<:)

$$\frac{E, X <: A \vdash b \,\mathcal{R}\, b' : B}{E \vdash \lambda(X <: A)b \,\widehat{\mathcal{R}}\, \lambda(X <: A)b' : \forall(X <: A)B}$$

(Comp Appl2<:)

$$\frac{E \vdash b \,\mathcal{R}\, b' : \forall(X <: A)B\{X\} \quad E \vdash A' <: A}{E \vdash b(A') \,\widehat{\mathcal{R}}\, b'(A') : B\{\!\{A'\}\!\}}$$

Lemma 2.2 *If $\mathcal{R}$ is a well formed relation on typed terms, so is $\widehat{\mathcal{R}}$.*

Now we introduce a typed equational theory by generalising the theory $\leftrightarrow$ defined on the ς-calculus. In $\mathbf{S}_\lambda$, we define $\leftrightarrow$ to be the least relation on typed terms closed under the following rules.

Equational rules:

(Eval Select) (where $A = Obj(X)[\ell_i \nu_i{:}B_i\{X\}\ ^{i \in 1..n}]$
and $u = obj(X{=}A)[\ell_i = \varsigma(x_i{:}X)b_i\{X, x_i\}\ ^{i \in 1..n}]$)

$$\frac{E \vdash u : A \quad \nu_j \in \{^o, ^+\} \quad j \in 1..n}{E \vdash u.\ell_j \leftrightarrow b_j\{\!\{A, u\}\!\} : B_j\{\!\{A\}\!\}}$$

(Eval Update) (where $A = Obj(X)[\ell_i \nu_i{:}B_i\{X\}\ ^{i \in 1..n}]$)
$u = obj(X{=}A)[\ell_i = \varsigma(x_i{:}X)b_i\ ^{i \in 1..n}]$
$v = obj(X{=}A)[\ell_j = \varsigma(x{:}X)b\{\!\{X, u\}\!\}, \ell_i = \varsigma(x_i{:}X)b_i\ ^{i \in (1..n)-\{j\}}]$

$$\frac{E \vdash a : A \quad E, Y{<:}A, y{:}Y, x{:}Y \vdash b\{Y, y\} : B_j\{\!\{Y\}\!\} \quad \nu_j \in \{^o, ^-\} \quad j \in 1..n}{E \vdash u.\ell_j \Leftarrow (Y{<:}A, y{:}Y)\varsigma(x{:}Y)b\{Y, y\} \leftrightarrow v : A}$$

(Eval Beta Result)

$$\frac{E \vdash \lambda(x{:}A)b\{x\} : A \to B \quad E \vdash v : A}{E \vdash (\lambda(x{:}A)b\{x\})(v) \leftrightarrow b\{\!\{v\}\!\} : B}$$

(Eval Beta2<:)

$$\frac{E \vdash \lambda(X{<:}A)b\{X\} : \forall(X{<:}A)B\{X\} \quad E \vdash C{<:}A}{E \vdash (\lambda(X{<:}A)b\{X\})(C) \leftrightarrow b\{\!\{C\}\!\} : B\{\!\{C\}\!\}}$$

(Eq Symm)

$$\frac{E \vdash b \leftrightarrow a : A}{E \vdash a \leftrightarrow b : A}$$

(Eq Trans)

$$\frac{E \vdash a \leftrightarrow b : A \quad E \vdash b \leftrightarrow c : A}{E \vdash a \leftrightarrow c : A}$$

(Eq Comp)

$$\frac{E \vdash a \mathrel{\widehat{\leftrightarrow}} b : A}{E \vdash a \leftrightarrow b : A}$$

(Eq Subsumption)

$$\frac{E \vdash a \leftrightarrow a' : A \quad E \vdash A <: B}{E \vdash a \leftrightarrow a' : B}$$

Rule (Eq Comp) is a structural rule—because of the structural assumptions in rules (Comp Select) and (Comp Update)—and indeed is the only such rule in the definition of the equational theory. Within the equational theory, one can derive versions of (Eval Select) and (Eval Update) that incorporate structural assumptions, but we omit the details.

As usual, we say that a relation on typed terms, $\mathcal{R}$, is *symmetric* or *transitive* if and only if it satisfies rules (Eq Symm) or (Eq Trans), respectively, with $\mathcal{R}$ instead of $\leftrightarrow$. We say $\mathcal{R}$ is *reflexive* if and only if $E \vdash a \mathrel{\mathcal{R}} a : A$ whenever $E \vdash a : A$. We say $\mathcal{R}$ is *compatible* if and only if $\widehat{\mathcal{R}} \subseteq \mathcal{R}$. Moreover, we say that $\mathcal{R}$ *allows subsumption* if and only if $E \vdash a \mathrel{\mathcal{R}} b : A$ and $E \vdash A{<:}B$ imply $E \vdash a \mathrel{\mathcal{R}} b : B$. Note that any relation $\mathcal{R}$ is reflexive if it is compatible and allows subsumption.

The relation $\leftrightarrow$ is well formed:

Proposition 2.3 *$E \vdash a \leftrightarrow a' : A$ implies $E \vdash a : A$ and $E \vdash a' : A$.*

Let us say that a relation on typed terms, $\mathcal{R}$, is an $\mathbf{S}_\lambda$-theory if and only if it is well formed and each of the rules defining $\leftrightarrow$ is sound with $\mathcal{R}$ instead of $\leftrightarrow$. Hence $\leftrightarrow$ is the least $\mathbf{S}_\lambda$-theory.

2.2 An Operational Semantics for $\mathbf{S}_\lambda$

We modify the operational semantics of the ς-calculus to apply to typed terms, and to reduce applications and type applications. We adopt a call-by-value reduction strategy for applications. The *reduction relation*, $a \leadsto v$, where a is a term and v is a result, is given by the following.

Reduction rules:

(Red Result) (where v is a result)

$$\frac{}{v \leadsto v}$$

(Red Select) (where $v' = obj(X{=}A)[\ell_i = \varsigma(x_i{:}X)b_i\{X, x_i\}\ ^{i \in 1..n}]$)

$$\frac{a \leadsto v' \quad b_j\{\!\{A, v'\}\!\} \leadsto v \quad j \in 1..n}{a.\ell_j \leadsto v}$$

(Red Update) (where $v' = obj(X{=}A)[\ell_i = \varsigma(x_i{:}X)b_i\ ^{i \in 1..n}]$ and $v = obj(X{=}A)[\ell_j = \varsigma(x{:}X)b\{\!\{X, v'\}\!\}, \ell_i = \varsigma(x_i{:}X)b_i\ ^{i \in (1..n)-\{j\}}]$)

$$\frac{a \leadsto v' \quad j \in 1..n}{a.\ell_j \Leftarrow (Y{<:}A', y{:}Y)\varsigma(x{:}Y)b\{Y, y\} \leadsto v}$$

(Red Appl)

$$\frac{b \leadsto \lambda(x{:}A)c\{x\} \quad a \leadsto u \quad c\{\!\{u\}\!\} \leadsto v}{b(a) \leadsto v}$$

(Red Appl2)

$$\frac{b \leadsto \lambda(X{<:}A)c\{X\} \quad c\{\!\{A'\}\!\} \leadsto v}{b(A') \leadsto v}$$

Reduction is deterministic: $u = v$ whenever $a \leadsto u$ and $a \leadsto v$. Let a term a *converge*, written $a\Downarrow$, if and only if there is a result v such that $a \leadsto v$. Reduction preserves types. (This is proved in detail for $\mathbf{S}_\forall$ by Abadi and Cardelli.)

Proposition 2.4 (Subject Reduction) *If $\varnothing \vdash a : A$ and $a \leadsto v$ then $\varnothing \vdash v : A$ too.*

2.3 The Context Closure of a Relation

Before defining contextual equivalence in the next section, we introduce in this section a typed form of context closure. If $\mathcal{R}$ is a relation on typed terms, let its *context closure*, $\mathcal{R}^{\mathcal{C}}$, be the least relation on typed terms closed under the following rules.

Context closure:

$$\text{(Context } \mathcal{R}) \quad \frac{E \vdash a\,\mathcal{R}\,b : A}{E \vdash a\,\mathcal{R}^{\mathcal{C}}\,b : A} \qquad \text{(Context Comp)} \quad \frac{E \vdash a\,\widehat{\mathcal{R}^{\mathcal{C}}}\,b : A}{E \vdash a\,\mathcal{R}^{\mathcal{C}}\,b : A} \qquad \text{(Context Subsumption)} \quad \frac{E \vdash a\,\mathcal{R}^{\mathcal{C}}\,b : A \quad E \vdash A <: B}{E \vdash a\,\mathcal{R}^{\mathcal{C}}\,b : B}$$

Lemma 2.5 *For any relation on typed terms, $\mathcal{R}$:*

(1) *If $\mathcal{R}$ is well formed, so is $\mathcal{R}^{\mathcal{C}}$.*

(2) *$\mathcal{R}^{\mathcal{C}}$ is compatible and allows subsumption, and hence is reflexive.*

(3) *Both compatible refinement and context closure are monotone.*

(4) *$\mathcal{R}$ is compatible and allows subsumption if and only if $\mathcal{R}^{\mathcal{C}} \subseteq \mathcal{R}$.*

(5) $(\mathcal{R}^{\mathcal{C}})^{\mathcal{C}} = \mathcal{R}^{\mathcal{C}}$.

Much as in the untyped case, we shall define contextual equivalence using the context closure of a singleton relation, this time of the form $\{(E, a, b, A)\}^{\mathcal{C}}$. This use of context closure enjoys the following properties, which may easily be proved by induction on derivations.

Lemma 2.6

(1) *If $E' \vdash a' \; \{(E, a, a, A)\}^{\mathcal{C}} \; a'' : A'$ then $a' = a''$.*

(2) *If $E' \vdash a' \; \{(E, a, b, A)\}^{\mathcal{C}} \; b' : A'$ then $E' \vdash b' \; \{(E, b, a, A)\}^{\mathcal{C}} \; a' : A'$.*

(3) *Suppose $E' \vdash a' \; \{(E, a, c, A)\}^{\mathcal{C}} \; c' : A'$. For all b, there is b' such that $E' \vdash a' \; \{(E, a, b, A)\}^{\mathcal{C}} \; b' : A'$ and $E' \vdash b' \; \{(E, b, c, A)\}^{\mathcal{C}} \; c' : A'$.*

(4) *If $E' \vdash a' \; \{(E, a, b, A)\}^{\mathcal{C}} \; b' : A'$ and $E'' \vdash a'' \; \{(E', a', b', A')\}^{\mathcal{C}} \; b'' : A''$ then $E'' \vdash a'' \; \{(E, a, b, A)\}^{\mathcal{C}} \; b'' : A''$.*

(5) *If $E' \vdash a' \; \{(E, a, b, A)\}^{\mathcal{C}} \; b' : A'$ then $E = E', E''$ for some environment E''.*

Context closure allows an alternative characterisation of when a reflexive and transitive relation is compatible and allows subsumption. The proof is a generalisation of the proof of the corresponding untyped property.

Lemma 2.7 *If $\mathcal{R}$ is reflexive and transitive, then $\mathcal{R}$ is compatible and allows subsumption if and only if $\mathcal{R}$ satisfies the property that $E' \vdash a' \; \mathcal{R} \; b' : A'$ whenever $E \vdash a \; \mathcal{R} \; b : A$ and $E' \vdash a' \; \{(E, a, b, A)\}^{\mathcal{C}} \; b' : A'$.*

2.4 Adequacy and Contextual Equivalence for $\mathbf{S}_\lambda$

Let a relation on typed terms, $\mathcal{R}$, be *adequate* if and only if for all terms a and b and all types B, $\varnothing \vdash a \mathrel{\mathcal{R}} b : B$ implies $a\Downarrow \Leftrightarrow b\Downarrow$.

Much as in the untyped calculus, we define *contextual equivalence*, $\simeq$, to be the relation on typed terms such that $E \vdash a \simeq b : A$ if and only if $E \vdash a : A$, $E \vdash b : A$, and $\{(E, a, b, A)\}^{\mathcal{C}}$ is adequate. The latter condition, that $\{(E, a, b, A)\}^{\mathcal{C}}$ is adequate, says that for all terms a' and b', and all types A', that $\varnothing \vdash a' \; \{(E, a, b, A)\}^{\mathcal{C}} \; b' : A'$ implies $a'\Downarrow \Leftrightarrow b'\Downarrow$.

Proposition 2.8 *Contextual equivalence is reflexive, transitive and symmetric.*

Proof Reflexivity and symmetry follow from Lemma 2.6, parts (1) and (2), respectively. The presence of environments makes the following proof of transitivity simpler than in the untyped setting. Assume that $E \vdash a \simeq b : A$ and $E \vdash b \simeq c : A$; we will show that $E \vdash a \simeq c : A$. We have $E \vdash a : A$ and $E \vdash c : A$ from our two assumptions. It remains to show that $\varnothing \vdash a' \; \{(E, a, c, A)\}^{\mathcal{C}} \; c' : A'$ implies that $a'\Downarrow \Leftrightarrow c'\Downarrow$. Suppose then that $a'\Downarrow$; we must prove that $c'\Downarrow$. We have $E \vdash b : A$ by either assumption. By Lemma 2.6(3) there is a term b' such that $\varnothing \vdash a' \; \{(E, a, b, A)\}^{\mathcal{C}} \; b' : A'$ and $\varnothing \vdash b' \; \{(E, b, c, A)\}^{\mathcal{C}} \; c' : A'$. We deduce that $b'\Downarrow$ from $E \vdash a \simeq b : A$ and $a'\Downarrow$. We deduce that $c'\Downarrow$ from $E \vdash b \simeq c : A$ and $b'\Downarrow$. A symmetric argument establishes that $c'\Downarrow$ implies $a'\Downarrow$. Therefore $E \vdash a \simeq c : A$, as required. □

Proposition 2.9 *Contextual equivalence is the greatest relation on typed terms that is well formed, compatible, adequate and allows subsumption.*

Proof By definition, contextual equivalence is clearly well formed and adequate. To show that contextual equivalence is compatible and allows subsumption, by Lemma 2.7, given that it is reflexive and transitive, it suffices to show the property that $E' \vdash a' \simeq b' : A'$ whenever $E \vdash a \simeq b : A$ and $E' \vdash a' \; \{(E, a, b, A)\}^{\mathcal{C}} \; b' : A'$. We need to show $E' \vdash a' : A'$, $E' \vdash b' : A'$ and that $\{(E', a', b', A')\}^{\mathcal{C}}$ is adequate. By definition, $E \vdash a \simeq b : A$ implies that $\{(E, a, b, A)\}$ is a well formed relation on typed terms. By Lemma 2.5(1), $\{(E, a, b, A)\}^{\mathcal{C}}$ is also well formed, hence $E' \vdash a' : A'$ and $E' \vdash b' : A'$. Now, suppose $\varnothing \vdash a'' \; \{(E', a', b', A')\}^{\mathcal{C}} \; b'' : A''$. By Lemma 2.6(4), this and $E' \vdash a' \; \{(E, a, b, A)\}^{\mathcal{C}} \; b' : A'$ imply $\varnothing \vdash a'' \; \{(E, a, b, A)\}^{\mathcal{C}} \; b'' : A''$. Therefore $E \vdash a \simeq b : A$ implies that $a''\Downarrow \Leftrightarrow b''\Downarrow$. Hence $\{(E', a', b', A')\}^{\mathcal{C}}$ is adequate.

Suppose $\mathcal{R}$ is well formed, compatible, adequate and allows subsumption. To see that contextual equivalence is the greatest such relation, we pick any quadruple $(E, a, b, A) \in \mathcal{R}$, and show that $(E, a, b, A) \in {\simeq}$, that is, that $E \vdash a : A$, $E \vdash b : A$ and that $\{(E, a, b, A)\}^{\mathcal{C}}$ is adequate. The type assignments follow from the fact that $\mathcal{R}$ is well formed. Since $\mathcal{R}$ is compatible and allows subsumption, $\mathcal{R}^{\mathcal{C}} \subseteq \mathcal{R}$. Since contextual closure is monotone, $\{(E, a, b, A)\}^{\mathcal{C}} \subseteq \mathcal{R}^{\mathcal{C}}$. We deduce $\{(E, a, b, A)\}^{\mathcal{C}} \subseteq \mathcal{R}$, which, with the fact that $\mathcal{R}$ is adequate, implies that the relation $\{(E, a, b, A)\}^{\mathcal{C}}$ is adequate. The proposition follows. □

However, as in the untyped case, it is not immediately clear that contextual equivalence is a $\mathbf{S}_\lambda$-theory. To prove this, we turn in Section 2.6 to a notion of bisimilarity for $\mathbf{S}_\lambda$. We pave the way in the next section by introducing a typed form of open extension.

2.5 Open Extension

In this section, we generalise the untyped notion of open extension to relations on typed terms. First, we need the notion of an iterated substitution. We allow σ to range over finite sequences of substitutions for type variables or variables. We define $\phi\{\!\{\sigma\}\!\}$ to be the outcome of applying the substitution σ to phrase ϕ:

$$\begin{aligned} \phi\{\!\{\varnothing\}\!\} &\triangleq \phi \\ \phi\{\!\{\sigma, X \leftarrow A\}\!\} &\triangleq (\phi\{\!\{\sigma\}\!\})\{\!\{X \leftarrow A\}\!\} \\ \phi\{\!\{\sigma, x \leftarrow v\}\!\} &\triangleq (\phi\{\!\{\sigma\}\!\})\{\!\{x \leftarrow v\}\!\} \end{aligned}$$

Second, we define E-closure, a substitution that fixes the type variables and variables declared in environment E to be particular closed types and results, respectively. We define the judgment $E \vdash \sigma$, that σ is an *E-closure*, by the following rules.

Rules for E-closure:

$$\begin{array}{lll} \text{(Closure } \varnothing) & \text{(Closure } X) & \text{(Closure } x) \\ \dfrac{}{\varnothing \vdash \varnothing} & \dfrac{E \vdash \sigma \quad \varnothing \vdash A{<:}B\{\!\{\sigma\}\!\}}{E, X{<:}B \vdash \sigma, X \leftarrow A} & \dfrac{E \vdash \sigma \quad \varnothing \vdash v : B\{\!\{\sigma\}\!\}}{E, x{:}B \vdash \sigma, x \leftarrow v} \end{array}$$

Now, if $\mathcal{R}$ is a closed relation on typed terms, let its *open extension*, $\mathcal{R}^\circ$, be the relation on typed terms such that $E \vdash a\ \mathcal{R}^\circ\ b : A$ if and only if $\varnothing \vdash a\{\!\{\sigma\}\!\}\ \mathcal{R}\ b\{\!\{\sigma\}\!\} : A\{\!\{\sigma\}\!\}$ for all substitutions σ such that $E \vdash \sigma$. We will often use the fact that $\varnothing \vdash a\ \mathcal{R}^\circ\ b : A$ if and only if $\varnothing \vdash a\ \mathcal{R}\ b : A$.

We may easily show the following:

Lemma 2.10 *Suppose $\mathcal{R}$ is a well formed relation on typed terms. Then $\mathcal{R}^\circ$ possesses the weakening, type substitution, result substitution and bound weakening properties stated in Proposition 2.1.*

We can represent an E-closure within the syntax of $\mathbf{S}_\lambda$ as follows. For any environment E and any substitution σ, and any terms b and a, we define the terms $\lambda(E)b$ and $a(\sigma)$ as follows.

$$\begin{aligned} \lambda(\varnothing)b &\triangleq b \\ \lambda(E, X{<:}A)b &\triangleq \lambda(E)\lambda(X{<:}A)b \end{aligned}$$

$$\begin{aligned}
\lambda(E, x{:}A)b &\triangleq \lambda(E)\lambda(x{:}A)b \\
a(\varnothing) &\triangleq a \\
a(\sigma, X \leftarrow A) &\triangleq a(\sigma)(A) \\
a(\sigma, x \leftarrow v) &\triangleq a(\sigma)(v)
\end{aligned}$$

The following is proved by induction on the derivation of $E \vdash \sigma$.

Proposition 2.11 *If* $E \vdash a : A$ *and* $E \vdash \sigma$ *then* $\varnothing \vdash (\lambda(E)a)(\sigma) \leftrightarrow a\{\!\{\sigma\}\!\} : A\{\!\{\sigma\}\!\}$.

2.6 Bisimilarity for $\mathbf{S}_\lambda$

We introduce a typed form of bisimilarity for $\mathbf{S}_\lambda$, by generalising the definition of experimental equivalence for the ς-calculus. Let an (A, B)*-action*, α, be a term fragment given by one of the rules:

- (Action Select) $.\ell_j$ is an $(A, B_j\{\!\{A\}\!\})$-action, if $A = Obj(X)[\ell_i\nu_i{:}B_i\{X\}\ ^{i\in 1..n}]$, $j \in 1..n$, $\nu_j \in \{^o, ^+\}$ and $\varnothing \vdash A$.
- (Action Update) $.\ell_j \Leftarrow (Y{<:}A, y{:}Y)\varsigma(x{:}Y)b$ is an (A, A)-action, if $A = Obj(X)[\ell_i\nu_i{:}B_i\{X\}\ ^{i\in 1..n}]$, $j \in 1..n$, $\nu_j \in \{^o, ^-\}$, $\varnothing \vdash A$ and we have $\varnothing, Y{<:}A, y{:}Y, x{:}Y \vdash b : B_j\{\!\{Y\}\!\}$.
- (Action Appl) (v) is an $(A \to B, B)$-action, if $\varnothing \vdash v : A$ and $\varnothing \vdash B$.
- (Action Appl2) (A') is a $(\forall(X{<:}A)B\{X\}, B\{\!\{A'\}\!\})$-action, if $\varnothing \vdash A'{<:}A$ and $\varnothing \vdash \forall(X{<:}A)B\{X\}$.

This definition is such that if α is an (A, B)-action both $\varnothing \vdash A$ and $\varnothing \vdash B$ are derivable. We may attach an action to a term, to yield another term:

Lemma 2.12 *If* $\varnothing \vdash a : A$ *and* α *is an* (A, B)*-action, then* $\varnothing \vdash a\alpha : B$.

Next we introduce similarity and bisimilarity:

- Let a relation on typed terms, $\mathcal{R}$, be *closed* if and only if $E = \varnothing$ whenever $E \vdash a\,\mathcal{R}\,b : A$.
- Let a well formed closed relation on typed terms, $\mathcal{S}$, be a *simulation* if and only if $\varnothing \vdash a\ \mathcal{S}\ b : A$ implies that whenever $a \leadsto u$ there is a result v such that $b \leadsto v$ and, for all types B, and all (A, B)-actions α, $\varnothing \vdash u\alpha\ \mathcal{S}\ v\alpha : B$.
- Let a well formed closed relation on typed terms, $\mathcal{R}$, be a *bisimulation* if and only if both $\mathcal{S}$ and $\mathcal{S}^{-1}$ are simulations.
- Let *similarity*, $\lesssim$, be the union of all simulations and let *bisimilarity*, $\sim$, be the union of all bisimulations.

By standard considerations, similarity is the greatest simulation and bisimilarity is the greatest bisimulation.

Proposition 2.13

(1) *Similarity is reflexive and transitive.*

(2) $\varnothing \vdash a \sim b : A$ *if and only if* $\varnothing \vdash a \lesssim b : A$ *and* $\varnothing \vdash b \lesssim a : A$.

(3) *Bisimilarity is reflexive, transitive and symmetric.*

A corollary is that $\varnothing \vdash a \sim b : A$ if and only if

(1) whenever $a \rightsquigarrow u$ there is a result v such that $b \rightsquigarrow v$ and, for all types B, and all (A, B)-actions α, $\varnothing \vdash u\alpha \sim v\alpha : B$;

(2) whenever $b \rightsquigarrow v$ there is a result u such that $a \rightsquigarrow u$ and, for all types B, and all (A, B)-actions α, $\varnothing \vdash u\alpha \sim v\alpha : B$.

Here are some basic facts about similarity.

Proposition 2.14

(1) *If* α *is an* (A, B)*-action,* $\varnothing \vdash a \lesssim b : A$ *implies* $\varnothing \vdash a\alpha \lesssim b\alpha : B$.

(2) *If* $\varnothing \vdash a \lesssim b : A$ *and* $\varnothing \vdash A <: A'$ *then* $\varnothing \vdash a \lesssim b : A'$.

(3) *If* $\varnothing \vdash a \lesssim b : A$ *and* $a \rightsquigarrow u$ *there is* v *such that* $b \rightsquigarrow v$ *and* $\varnothing \vdash u \lesssim v : A$.

Bisimilarity satisfies the following context lemma:

Proposition 2.15 *Suppose* $\varnothing \vdash a : A_0$ *and* $\varnothing \vdash b : A_0$. *Then* $\varnothing \vdash a \sim b : A_0$ *if and only if for all types* $A_1, \ldots, A_n$*, and all* $\alpha_1, \ldots, \alpha_n$ *where each* α_i *is an* (A_{i-1}, A_i)*-action,* $a\alpha_1 \cdots \alpha_n\Downarrow \Leftrightarrow b\alpha_1 \cdots \alpha_n\Downarrow$.

The analogous result from Section 1, Proposition 1.15, asserts that two terms of the ς-calculus are experimentally equivalent if and only if they cannot be distinguished by contexts of the form $-\epsilon_1 \cdots \epsilon_n$. Such contexts are usually known as evaluation contexts and are used to define small step semantics. As explained in Section 1.7, experimental equivalence corresponds to a stateless form of CIU equivalence, since CIU equivalence is based on evaluation contexts. On the other hand, Proposition 2.15 asserts that two terms of $\mathbf{S}_\lambda$ are bisimilar if and only if they cannot be distinguished by contexts, built up from actions, taking the form $-\alpha_1 \cdots \alpha_n$. Due to the presence of call-by-value functions, contexts of this form constitute a proper subset of the evaluation contexts for $\mathbf{S}_\lambda$, since evaluation contexts of the form $(\lambda(x{:}A)b)(-)$ are excluded. Since fewer contexts need to be considered, this property of bisimilarity for $\mathbf{S}_\lambda$ is stronger than the corresponding property of CIU equivalence, were it to be specialised to $\mathbf{S}_\lambda$.

Let *Kleene equivalence*, $\approx^{kl}$, be the closed relation on typed terms such that $\varnothing \vdash a \approx^{kl} b : A$ if and only if $\varnothing \vdash a : A$ and $\varnothing \vdash b : A$ and for all results v, $a \rightsquigarrow v \Leftrightarrow b \rightsquigarrow v$.

Proposition 2.16

(1) *If* $\varnothing \vdash a : A$ *and* $a \leadsto u$ *then* $\varnothing \vdash a \approx^{kl} u : A$.

(2) *If* $\varnothing \vdash a \approx^{kl} b : A$ *then* $\varnothing \vdash a \lesssim b : A$.

Having enumerated some basic facts about bisimilarity, we turn in the next section to proving that similarity, and hence bisimilarity, is compatible.

2.7 Howe's Method for $\mathbf{S}_\lambda$

We begin by defining the compatible extension, $\lesssim^\bullet$, of similarity, and stating some easily proved facts about it.

Compatible extension:

(Cand Def)

$$\frac{E \vdash a \mathrel{\widehat{\lesssim^\bullet}} b : A \quad E \vdash A <: B \quad E \vdash b \lesssim^\circ c : B}{E \vdash a \lesssim^\bullet c : B}$$

Lemma 2.17 *The following rules are sound.*

(Cand Refl)

$$\frac{E \vdash a : A}{E \vdash a \lesssim^\bullet a : A}$$

(Cand Right)

$$\frac{E \vdash a \lesssim^\bullet b : A \quad E \vdash A <: B \quad E \vdash b \lesssim^\circ c : B}{E \vdash a \lesssim^\bullet c : B}$$

(Cand Comp)

$$\frac{E \vdash a \mathrel{\widehat{\lesssim^\bullet}} b : A}{E \vdash a \lesssim^\bullet b : A}$$

(Cand Subsumption)

$$\frac{E \vdash a \lesssim^\bullet b : A \quad E \vdash A <: B}{E \vdash a \lesssim^\bullet b : B}$$

(Cand Sound)

$$\frac{E \vdash a \lesssim^\circ b : A}{E \vdash a \lesssim^\bullet b : A}$$

(Cand Subst)

$$\frac{E, x{:}A, E' \vdash a\{x\} \lesssim^\bullet a'\{x\} : B \quad E \vdash u \lesssim^\bullet u' : A}{E, E' \vdash a\{\!\{u\}\!\} \lesssim^\bullet a'\{\!\{u'\}\!\} : B}$$

Moreover, $\lesssim^\bullet$ *possesses the weakening, type substitution and bound weakening properties stated in Proposition 2.1.*

Any closed instance of $\lesssim^\bullet$ may be decomposed as follows:

Lemma 2.18 *Whenever* $\varnothing \vdash a \lesssim^\bullet c : C$ *there is a type* B *and a term* b *such that* $\varnothing \vdash a \mathrel{\widehat{\lesssim^\bullet}} b : B$, $\varnothing \vdash B <: C$ *and* $\varnothing \vdash b \lesssim c : C$.

The following is the central property of $\lesssim^\bullet$:

Proposition 2.19 *Whenever* $\varnothing \vdash a \lesssim^\bullet b : A$ *and* $a \leadsto u$ *there is* v *with* $b \leadsto v$ *and* $\varnothing \vdash u \lesssim^\bullet v : A$.

Proof See Appendix B. □

Lemma 2.20 *Let* $\mathcal{S} = \{(\varnothing, a, b, A) \mid \varnothing \vdash a \lesssim^\bullet b : A\}$. *Then* $\mathcal{S}$ *is a simulation.*

Proof Suppose that $\varnothing \vdash a \lesssim^\bullet b : A$. Pick any result u such that $a \leadsto u$. By Proposition 2.19, there is a result v such that $b \leadsto v$ and $\varnothing \vdash u \lesssim^\bullet v : A$. Now, consider any type B and any (A, B)-action α. By (Cand Comp), $\varnothing \vdash u\alpha \lesssim^\bullet v\alpha : B$. Therefore $\mathcal{S}$ is a simulation. □

Proposition 2.21 $\lesssim^\circ = \lesssim^\bullet$.

Proof By (Cand Sound), $\lesssim^\circ \subseteq \lesssim^\bullet$. For the other direction, suppose that $E \vdash a \lesssim^\bullet b : A$. By Lemma 2.20, it is enough to show that $\varnothing \vdash a\{\!\{\sigma\}\!\} \lesssim^\bullet b\{\!\{\sigma\}\!\} : A\{\!\{\sigma\}\!\}$ for any substitution σ such that $E \vdash \sigma$. But this follows from the properties (Cand Refl), (Cand Subst) and type substitution, proved for $\lesssim^\bullet$ in Lemma 2.17. □

Since $\lesssim^\bullet$ is compatible, a corollary is that $\lesssim^\circ$ is compatible.

2.8 Properties of Bisimilarity

We can now relate bisimilarity and contextual equivalence.

Proposition 2.22 *Relation* $\sim^\circ$ *is an adequate* $\mathbf{S}_\lambda$*-theory.*

Proof Relation $\sim^\circ$ is well formed by definition. For adequacy, suppose $\varnothing \vdash a \sim^\circ b : B$ for any a, b and B. By definition of open extension, this is equivalent to $\varnothing \vdash a \sim b : B$. By definition of bisimilarity, $a\Downarrow \Leftrightarrow b\Downarrow$. Hence $\sim^\circ$ is adequate. By Proposition 2.21, $\lesssim^\circ$ is compatible and allows subsumption. Hence, given Proposition 2.13, $\sim^\circ$ satisfies rules (Eq Symm), (Eq Trans), (Eq Comp) and (Eq Subsumption). Moreover, $\sim$ satisfies the axioms (Eval Select), (Eval Update), (Eval Beta2<:) and (Eval Beta Result), when restricted to closed terms, since each is an instance of Kleene equivalence, and bisimilarity includes Kleene equivalence by Proposition 2.16. Therefore $\sim^\circ$ satisfies these rules, as they are preserved by substitutions. □

For the ς-calculus, adequacy of $\leftrightarrow$ follows from a standardisation theorem. We have not proved a standardisation theorem for $\mathbf{S}_\lambda$ but instead can derive adequacy of $\leftrightarrow$ from the previous proposition:

Proposition 2.23 *Relation* $\leftrightarrow$ *is the least adequate* $\mathbf{S}_\lambda$*-theory. Hence* $\leftrightarrow \subseteq \simeq$.

Proof Since $\leftrightarrow$ is by definition the least $\mathbf{S}_\lambda$-theory, it suffices to show that $\leftrightarrow$ is adequate. Suppose $\varnothing \vdash a \leftrightarrow b : A$. By Proposition 2.22 this implies $\varnothing \vdash a \sim^\circ b : A$, that is, $\varnothing \vdash a \sim b : A$. Therefore $a\Downarrow \Leftrightarrow b\Downarrow$. We have that $\leftrightarrow$ is well formed, compatible, adequate and allows subsumption; so $\leftrightarrow \subseteq \simeq$ by Proposition 2.9. □

Theorem 2.24 $\simeq = \sim^\circ$.

Proof It suffices to prove the following facts.

(1) $E \vdash a \sim^\circ b : A$ implies $E \vdash a \simeq b : A$.

(2) $\varnothing \vdash a \simeq b : A$ implies $\varnothing \vdash a \sim b : A$.

(3) $E \vdash a \simeq b : A$ implies $E \vdash a \sim^\circ b : A$.

Parts (1) and (3) prove the proposition. (2) is needed to prove (3).

(1) Since $\sim^\circ$ is well formed, compatible, adequate and allows subsumption, Proposition 2.9 implies that $\sim^\circ \subseteq \simeq$.

(2) From Proposition 2.15.

(3) We are given $E \vdash a \simeq b : A$. To show $E \vdash a \sim^\circ b : A$, we need to consider any substitution σ such that $E \vdash \sigma$, and prove that $\varnothing \vdash a\{\!\{\sigma\}\!\} \sim b\{\!\{\sigma\}\!\} : A\{\!\{\sigma\}\!\}$. By Proposition 2.11,

$$\varnothing \vdash (\lambda(E)a)(\sigma) \leftrightarrow a\{\!\{\sigma\}\!\} : A\{\!\{\sigma\}\!\}$$
$$\varnothing \vdash (\lambda(E)b)(\sigma) \leftrightarrow b\{\!\{\sigma\}\!\} : A\{\!\{\sigma\}\!\}$$

Since $\simeq$ is compatible, $E \vdash a \simeq b : A$ implies:

$$\varnothing \vdash (\lambda(E)a)(\sigma) \simeq (\lambda(E)b)(\sigma) : A\{\!\{\sigma\}\!\}$$

Hence, by Proposition 2.23, and the fact that $\simeq$ is an equivalence, we get that $\varnothing \vdash a\{\!\{\sigma\}\!\} \simeq b\{\!\{\sigma\}\!\} : A\{\!\{\sigma\}\!\}$. By (2), $\varnothing \vdash a\{\!\{\sigma\}\!\} \sim b\{\!\{\sigma\}\!\} : A\{\!\{\sigma\}\!\}$, as desired. □

In summary, we have shown that $\leftrightarrow$ is the least adequate $\mathbf{S}_\lambda$-theory and that $\simeq$ is the greatest adequate $\mathbf{S}_\lambda$-theory. As in the ς-calculus, we can show that $\leftrightarrow \subset \simeq$, but we omit the details.

2.9 A Typed Example

In this section we give an example proof by bisimulation that two objects are contextually equivalent. The example illustrates that the types at which two terms are considered affects whether they are equivalent or not.

We extensively use the following notation for typed field update, given that $E \vdash a : A$ where E is an environment determined by context, and that $\{Y, y, s\} \cap fv(b) = \varnothing$.

$$a_A.\ell := b \;\triangleq\; a.\ell \Leftarrow (Y{<:}A, y{:}Y)\varsigma(s{:}Y)b$$

We write $obj(X{=}A)[\ell = \uparrow, \ldots]$ short for $obj(X{=}A)[\ell = \varsigma(s{:}X)s.\ell, \ldots]$.

We use the following encoding of Booleans as polymorphic objects:

$$\begin{aligned}
Bool(A) &\triangleq Obj(Y)[then^o{:}A, else^o{:}A, val^o{:}A] \quad \text{where } Y \notin fv(A)\\
Bool &\triangleq \forall(X{<:}Top)Bool(X)\\
true &\triangleq \lambda(X{<:}Top)obj(Y{=}Bool(X))\\
&\qquad [then = \uparrow, else = \uparrow, val = \varsigma(s{:}Y)s.then]\\
false &\triangleq \lambda(X{<:}Top)obj(Y{=}Bool(X))\\
&\qquad [then = \uparrow, else = \uparrow, val = \varsigma(s{:}Y)s.else]\\
if_A\ a\ then\ a'\ else\ a'' &\triangleq ((a(A)_{Bool(A)}.then := a')_{Bool(A)}.else := a'').val
\end{aligned}$$

We encode natural numbers using Booleans, rather than using functions as in Section 1.10.[4]

$$\begin{aligned}
Nat &\triangleq Obj(X)[iszero^o{:}Bool, succ^o{:}X, pred^o{:}X]\\
zero &\triangleq obj(X{=}Nat)\\
&\quad [iszero = true,\\
&\quad succ = \varsigma(s{:}X)(s.pred \Leftarrow (Y{<:}X, y{:}Y)\varsigma(x{:}Y)y)_X.iszero := false,\\
&\quad pred = \uparrow]
\end{aligned}$$

For each number n we define the numeral $\underline{n}{:}Nat$ by induction: let $\underline{0} = zero$ and $\underline{n+1} = \underline{n}.succ$.

Our example is a proof of equivalence of two parity checkers coded as objects. A parity checker is an object with methods T, F and $even$. The parity checker receives bits represented by selects on methods T and F. A select on $even$ yields either $true$ or $false$, indicating whether or not the checker has received an even number of T bits. We program this behaviour as the object $parity$ as follows.

$$\begin{aligned}
Parity &\triangleq Obj(X)[T^o{:}X, F^o{:}X, even^o{:}Bool]\\
parity(b) &\triangleq obj(X{=}Parity)\\
&\quad [T = \varsigma(s{:}X)s_X.even := (if_{Bool}\ s.even\ then\ false\ else\ true),\\
&\quad F = \varsigma(s{:}X)s,\\
&\quad even = b]\\
parity &\triangleq parity(true)
\end{aligned}$$

[4]In the $succ$ method of $zero$, we need to write $s.pred \Leftarrow (Y{<:}X, y{:}Y)\varsigma(x{:}Y)y$, exploiting the "old self" parameter $y{:}Y$, because (Val Update) dictates that the updated method return a result of type Y. The simpler code $s_X.pred := s$, which would be operationally equivalent, does not type check.

(The term b in $parity(b)$ is expected to be either *true* or *false*.)

Here is a fancier parity checker, $numParity$, that enriches the behaviour of the previous checker by providing a num method that returns a count of the number of T bits received so far. The following code assumes it may be tested whether or not a numeral is even; in particular, it appeals to an operation $isEven(a)$ with the properties $\varnothing \vdash isEven(\underline{2n}) \leftrightarrow true{:}Bool$ and $\varnothing \vdash isEven(\underline{2n+1}) \leftrightarrow false{:}Bool$. This operation may easily be programmed in $\mathbf{S}_\lambda$ but we omit the details.

$$\begin{array}{rcl} NumParity & \triangleq & Obj(X)[T^o{:}X, F^o{:}X, even^o{:}Bool, num^o{:}Nat] \\ numParity(n) & \triangleq & obj(X{=}NumParity) \\ & & \quad [T = \varsigma(s{:}X)s_X.num := (s.num.succ), \\ & & \quad F = \varsigma(s{:}X)s, \\ & & \quad even = \varsigma(s{:}X)isEven(s.num), \\ & & \quad num = \underline{n}] \\ numParity & \triangleq & numParity(0) \end{array}$$

Since $\varnothing \vdash numParity{<:}Parity$ we might hope that $\varnothing \vdash parity \simeq numParity$: $Parity$, but in fact this is false. Let term $c\{x\} = (x_{Parity}.even{:=}true).T.even$. We have $\varnothing \vdash c\{\!\{parity\}\!\} \leftrightarrow false : Bool$ whereas $\varnothing \vdash c\{\!\{numParity\}\!\} \leftrightarrow true : Bool$. Since contextual equivalence is compatible and includes $\leftrightarrow$, it cannot be that $\varnothing \vdash parity \simeq numParity : Parity$.

The problem is that the type *Parity* allows updates of its three methods. Hence the behaviour of *parity* and *numParity* may be distinguished, even though method update is not part of the intended behaviour of a parity checker. We can disallow method updates by observing the objects at the following type, obtained by decorating *Parity* with positive variance annotations.

$$Parity^+ \triangleq Obj(X)[T^+{:}X, F^+{:}X, even^+{:}Bool]$$

We have $\varnothing \vdash Parity{<:}Parity^+$. The only operations on objects of the type $Parity^+$ are selects on the three methods, so *parity* and *numParity* ought to be equivalent at this type.

To prove this equivalence we first need to relax the notion of simulation in a standard way. Let a well formed closed relation on typed terms, $\mathcal{S}$, be a *simulation up to* $\sim$ if and only if $\varnothing \vdash a\,\mathcal{S}\,b : A$ implies that whenever $a \rightsquigarrow u$ there is a result v such that $b \rightsquigarrow v$ and, for all types B, and all (A, B)-actions α, $\varnothing \vdash u\alpha{\sim}\mathcal{S}{\sim}v\alpha{:}B$. Let $\mathcal{S}$ be a *bisimulation up to* $\sim$ if and only if both $\mathcal{S}$ and $\mathcal{S}^{-1}$ are simulations up to $\sim$. The following lemma may be proved by standard techniques (Milner 1989).

Lemma 2.25 *If $\mathcal{S}$ is a bisimulation up to $\sim$, then $\mathcal{S} \subseteq \sim$.*

Proposition 2.26 $\varnothing \vdash parity \simeq numParity : Parity^+$.

Proof Let $\mathcal{S}$ and Δ be the following relations on typed terms.

$$\begin{aligned}\mathcal{S} &\triangleq \{(\varnothing, \mathit{parity}(\mathit{true}), \mathit{numParity}(2n), \mathit{Parity}^+),\\ &\qquad (\varnothing, \mathit{parity}(\mathit{false}), \mathit{numParity}(2n+1), \mathit{Parity}^+) \mid n \geq 0\}\\ \Delta &\triangleq \{(\varnothing, a, a, A) \mid \varnothing \vdash a : A\}\end{aligned}$$

We shall show that $\mathcal{S} \cup \Delta$ is a bisimulation up to $\sim$. Given the forms of $\mathcal{S}$ and Δ, and the fact that $\leftrightarrow\ \subseteq\ \sim^\circ$ (combine Proposition 2.23 and Theorem 2.24) it suffices to prove that $\varnothing \vdash a\,\mathcal{S}\,b : \mathit{Parity}^+$ implies:

(1) whenever $a \rightsquigarrow u$ there is a result v such that $b \rightsquigarrow v$ and, for all types B, and all (Parity^+, B)-actions α, $\varnothing \vdash u\alpha \leftrightarrow(\mathcal{S} \cup \Delta)\leftrightarrow v\alpha : B$;

(2) whenever $b \rightsquigarrow v$ there is a result u such that $a \rightsquigarrow u$ and, for all types B, and all (Parity^+, B)-actions α, $\varnothing \vdash u\alpha \leftrightarrow(\mathcal{S} \cup \Delta)\leftrightarrow v\alpha : B$.

Given $\varnothing \vdash a\,\mathcal{S}\,b : \mathit{Parity}^+$, the terms a and b must take one of two forms:

- First, $a = \mathit{parity}(\mathit{true})$ and $b = \mathit{numParity}(2n)$ for some $n \geq 0$. We have $a \rightsquigarrow a$ and $b \rightsquigarrow b$. There are three ways of choosing α so that α is a (Parity^+, B)-action for some B, all using the rule (Action Select).

  (1) In this case, $\alpha = .T$ and $B = \mathit{Parity}^+$. We may calculate:

  $$\begin{aligned}\varnothing &\vdash \mathit{parity}(\mathit{true}).T \leftrightarrow \mathit{parity}(\mathit{false}) : \mathit{Parity}^+\\ \varnothing &\vdash \mathit{parity}(2n).T \leftrightarrow \mathit{parity}(2n+1) : \mathit{Parity}^+\end{aligned}$$

  Therefore, $\varnothing \vdash \mathit{parity}(\mathit{true}).T\ (\leftrightarrow\mathcal{S}\leftrightarrow)\ \mathit{numParity}(2n).T : \mathit{Parity}^+$.

  (2) In this case, $\alpha = .F$ and $B = \mathit{Parity}^+$. We may calculate:

  $$\begin{aligned}\varnothing &\vdash \mathit{parity}(\mathit{true}).F \leftrightarrow \mathit{parity}(\mathit{true}) : \mathit{Parity}^+\\ \varnothing &\vdash \mathit{parity}(2n).F \leftrightarrow \mathit{parity}(2n) : \mathit{Parity}^+\end{aligned}$$

  Therefore, $\varnothing \vdash \mathit{parity}(\mathit{true}).F\ (\leftrightarrow\mathcal{S}\leftrightarrow)\ \mathit{numParity}(2n).F : \mathit{Parity}^+$.

  (3) In this case, $\alpha = .\mathit{even}$ and $B = \mathit{Bool}$. We may calculate:

  $$\begin{aligned}\varnothing &\vdash \mathit{parity}(\mathit{true}).\mathit{even} \leftrightarrow \mathit{true} : \mathit{Bool}\\ \varnothing &\vdash \mathit{parity}(2n).\mathit{even} \leftrightarrow \mathit{true} : \mathit{Bool}\end{aligned}$$

  Therefore, $\varnothing \vdash \mathit{parity}(\mathit{true}).\mathit{even}\ (\leftrightarrow\Delta\leftrightarrow)\ \mathit{numParity}(2n).\mathit{even} : \mathit{Bool}$.

- Second, $a = \mathit{parity}(\mathit{false})$ and $b = \mathit{numParity}(2n+1)$ for some $n \geq 0$. This case follows by a symmetric argument.

This proves that $\mathcal{S} \cup \Delta$ is a bisimulation up to $\sim$. Lemma 2.25 implies $\mathcal{S} \cup \Delta \subseteq \sim$. Hence by Theorem 2.24, we obtain $\varnothing \vdash \mathit{parity} \simeq \mathit{numParity} : \mathit{Parity}^+$. □

This proof illustrates how variance annotations may usefully limit the observations that need to be considered in a bisimulation proof.

2.10 Discussion

Our calculus, $\mathbf{S}_\lambda$, consists of Abadi and Cardelli's $\mathbf{S}_\forall$ augmented with first-order functions, $\lambda(x{:}A)b$. Without first-order functions, Theorem 2.24, that $\simeq \; = \; \sim^\circ$, would fail. Without first-order functions, ς is the only binder for variables, and ς only binds variables of object type. Therefore contextual equivalence for $\mathbf{S}_\forall$ would have the pathological property that $E \vdash a \simeq b : A$ would hold whenever E includes a declaration binding a variable to a polymorphic type.

Reduction rule (Red Appl) confers a call-by-value evaluation strategy on the calculus. Hence Abadi and Cardelli's rule (Eq Top), which asserts the equivalence of all terms at type *Top*, is false, since no convergent term may equal a divergent term. Instead, use of a call-by-name evaluation strategy, as in the work of Gordon and Rees (1996) for first-order object calculi, would allow validation of (Eq Top).

Our equational theory for $\mathbf{S}_\lambda$ is fairly weak; for instance, we have not included any version of Abadi and Cardelli's rule (Eq Sub Object), that allows hidden methods to be deleted from an object. We leave as further work the task of formulating a version of (Eq Sub Object) for $\mathbf{S}_\lambda$ and adapting the operational proof of soundness due to Gordon and Rees.

3 Conclusions

The main contribution of this paper is the development of earlier work on operational equivalence of untyped and first-order languages to deal with an object calculus, $\mathbf{S}_\lambda$, with polymorphic types, subtyping, primitive covariant self types, structural typing rules and variance annotations. Section 1 recast a variety of untyped operational techniques originating with the λ-calculus in the setting of the ς-calculus. The main results of Section 2—that bisimilarity for $\mathbf{S}_\lambda$ is compatible, equals contextual equivalence and justifies an equational theory—parallel those in the earlier study of first-order objects by Gordon and Rees (1996). The proof techniques smoothly scale to the richer type system of $\mathbf{S}_\lambda$. Our equational theory is similar to others put forward by Abadi and Cardelli (1996), but their denotational techniques are not applicable to $\mathbf{S}_\lambda$.

Our work follows on from many earlier studies of contextual equivalence and applicative bisimulation, cited in Section 1. The most closely related work is a recent unpublished paper by Dami (1997), who proposes an ideal model for polymorphism and subtyping, in the presence of structural typing rules. His work is based on a notion of operational subsumption rather than bisimilarity. Our approach is to develop bisimulation directly from the operational semantics of object calculi; instead, both Sangiorgi (1996) and Hüttel and Kleist (1996) obtain approximations to contextual equivalence by mapping object calculi into the π-calculus. In an unpublished report, Rees (1994) proves for a call-by-value form of the polymorphic λ-calculus that contextual equivalence equals a form of applicative bisimulation. To the best of my knowledge, Rees' paper and the study by

Pierce and Sangiorgi (1997) of bisimulation for a polymorphic π-calculus are the only other works on bisimulation for polymorphic calculi. The results of this paper are just the beginning; for instance, it would be worthwhile to investigate richer equational theories for polymorphic calculi, and whether parametricity principles (Reynolds 1983) may be derived operationally.

Acknowledgements Søren Bøgh Lassen suggested the basic idea for the proof in Appendix A. Luca Cardelli, Roy Crole, Søren Bøgh Lassen, Paul Hankin, Benjamin Pierce and two anonymous referees commented on a draft. This paper grew out of work in collaboration with Gareth Rees. This paper was written with the support of a University Research Fellowship awarded by the Royal Society.

A Proof of Lemma 1.16

Our goal is to prove Lemma 1.16, that $a\{x\} \simeq b\{x\}$ implies that for all closed results v, $a\{\!\{v\}\!\} \simeq b\{\!\{v\}\!\}$. Consider any closed result $v = [\ell_i = \varsigma(x_i)b_i\ ^{i\in 1..n}]$. The idea for our proof is to extend v with an additional method labelled ℓ, where ℓ is fresh, to obtain results v_a and v_b below.

$$\begin{aligned} v_a &\triangleq [\ell_i = \varsigma(x_i)b_i\ ^{i\in 1..n}, \ell = \varsigma(x)a\{x\}] \\ v_b &\triangleq [\ell_i = \varsigma(x_i)b_i\ ^{i\in 1..n}, \ell = \varsigma(x)b\{x\}] \end{aligned}$$

By (Eval Select), $v_a.\ell \leftrightarrow a\{\!\{v_a\}\!\}$ and $v_b.\ell \leftrightarrow b\{\!\{v_b\}\!\}$. Now, the results v, v_a and v_b are all distinct up to contextual equivalence, because observing contexts can examine the ℓ method. But in contexts not containing the label ℓ, these three results would be equivalent; and the facts $v_a.\ell \leftrightarrow a\{\!\{v_a\}\!\}$ and $v_b.\ell \leftrightarrow b\{\!\{v_b\}\!\}$ would imply that $a\{\!\{v\}\!\}$ would be equivalent to $b\{\!\{v\}\!\}$ also.

To formalise this proof sketch we develop a notion of contextual equivalence indexed by the set of labels that may occur in observing contexts. For any term a, let $\mathcal{L}(a)$ be the set of labels that occur in a. If $\mathcal{R}$ is a relation on terms and $\mathcal{L}$ is a set of labels, let the *$\mathcal{L}$-indexed context closure* of $\mathcal{R}$ be the relation $\mathcal{R}^{\mathcal{C}}_{\mathcal{L}}$ given by the following rules.

Indexed context closure:

(Indexed $\mathcal{R}$) $\dfrac{a\,\mathcal{R}\,b}{a\,\mathcal{R}^{\mathcal{C}}_{\mathcal{L}}\,b}$ (Indexed x) $\dfrac{}{x\,\mathcal{R}^{\mathcal{C}}_{\mathcal{L}}\,x}$ (Indexed Select) $\dfrac{a\,\mathcal{R}^{\mathcal{C}}_{\mathcal{L}}\,b \quad \ell\in\mathcal{L}}{a.\ell\,\mathcal{R}^{\mathcal{C}}_{\mathcal{L}}\,b.\ell}$ (Indexed Update) $\dfrac{a_1\,\mathcal{R}^{\mathcal{C}}_{\mathcal{L}}\,b_1 \quad \ell\in\mathcal{L} \quad a_2\,\mathcal{R}^{\mathcal{C}}_{\mathcal{L}}\,b_2}{a_1.\ell \Leftarrow \varsigma(x)a_2\,\mathcal{R}^{\mathcal{C}}_{\mathcal{L}}\,b_1.\ell \Leftarrow \varsigma(x)b_2}$

(Indexed Object)
$$\frac{\ell_i\in\mathcal{L} \quad a_i\,\mathcal{R}^{\mathcal{C}}_{\mathcal{L}}\,b_i \quad \forall i\in 1..n}{[\ell_i = \varsigma(x_i)a_i\ ^{i\in 1..n}]\,\mathcal{R}^{\mathcal{C}}_{\mathcal{L}}\,[\ell_i = \varsigma(x_i)b_i\ ^{i\in 1..n}]}$$

Lemma A.1 *For all $\mathcal{R}$, $\mathcal{L}$ and $\mathcal{L}'$:*

(1) *For all a and b, $a\ \mathcal{R}^{\mathcal{C}}_{\mathcal{L}}\ b$ implies $a\ \mathcal{R}^{\mathcal{C}}\ b$.*

(2) *For all a and b, $a\ \mathcal{R}^{\mathcal{C}}\ b$ implies there is a finite set of labels $\mathcal{L}$, such that $a\ \mathcal{R}^{\mathcal{C}}_{\mathcal{L}}\ b$.*

(3) *For all a and b, $a\ \mathcal{R}^{\mathcal{C}}_{\mathcal{L}}\ b$ and $\mathcal{L} \subseteq \mathcal{L}'$ imply that $a\ \mathcal{R}^{\mathcal{C}}_{\mathcal{L}'}\ b$.*

Proof By inductions on derivations. For (2), let $\mathcal{L}$ be the set $\mathcal{L}(a) \cup \mathcal{L}(b)$, which is finite. □

For any set of labels $\mathcal{L}$, and any terms a and b, let $a \simeq_{\mathcal{L}} b$ if and only if for all closed a' and b', $a'\ \{(a,b)\}^{\mathcal{C}}_{\mathcal{L}}\ b'$ implies that $a' \Downarrow \Leftrightarrow b' \Downarrow$. It follows that $\simeq_{\varnothing}$ is the universal relation on terms and that if $\mathcal{L}$ is the set of all labels that $\simeq_{\mathcal{L}} = \simeq$. We can easily prove the following basic facts about $\simeq_{\mathcal{L}}$.

Lemma A.2

(1) *For all a and b, $a \simeq b$ if and only if for all finite sets of labels $\mathcal{L}$, $a \simeq_{\mathcal{L}} b$.*

(2) *$a \simeq_{\mathcal{L}} b$ and $\mathcal{L}' \subseteq \mathcal{L}$ imply $a \simeq_{\mathcal{L}'} b$.*

(3) *For each $\mathcal{L}$, $\simeq_{\mathcal{L}}$ is symmetric and transitive.*

(4) *If $a \simeq_{\mathcal{L}} b$ and $a'\ \{(a,b)\}^{\mathcal{C}}_{\mathcal{L}}\ b'$ then $a' \simeq_{\mathcal{L}} b'$.*

The following—the crucial lemma of this development—lets us augment an object with a freshly labelled method whilst preserving equivalence.

Lemma A.3 *Consider any closed result $w = [\ell_i = \varsigma(z_i)c_i\ ^{i\in 1..p}]$ and any set of labels $\mathcal{L}$ such that $\mathcal{L}(w) \subseteq \mathcal{L}$. Then for any $\ell \notin \mathcal{L}$ and any term c and variable z:*

$$w \ \simeq_{\mathcal{L}}\ [\ell_i = \varsigma(z_i)c_i\ ^{i\in 1..p}, \ell = \varsigma(z)c]$$

Proof Let $\mathcal{R}$ be the following relation on terms:

$$\mathcal{R} \ \triangleq\ \{(w, [\ell_i = \varsigma(z_i)c_i\ ^{i\in 1..p}, \ell = \varsigma(z)d]) \mid d \text{ is any term}\}$$

Since the result w is closed, the indexed context closure of $\mathcal{R}$ has the following property, which we refer to as ($\mathcal{R}^{\mathcal{C}}_{\mathcal{L}}$ Sub): for all terms $a\{\!\{x\}\!\}$, $b\{\!\{x\}\!\}$, and all results u and v, $a\{\!\{x\}\!\}\ \mathcal{R}^{\mathcal{C}}_{\mathcal{L}}\ b\{\!\{x\}\!\}$ and $u\ \mathcal{R}^{\mathcal{C}}_{\mathcal{L}}\ v$ imply $a\{\!\{u\}\!\}\ \mathcal{R}^{\mathcal{C}}_{\mathcal{L}}\ b\{\!\{v\}\!\}$.

For the lemma to follow, it suffices to prove the following two properties:

(1) $a\ \mathcal{R}^{\mathcal{C}}_{\mathcal{L}}\ b$ and $a \rightsquigarrow u$ implies there is v with $u\ \mathcal{R}^{\mathcal{C}}_{\mathcal{L}}\ v$ and $b \rightsquigarrow v$.

(2) $a\ \mathcal{R}^{\mathcal{C}}_{\mathcal{L}}\ b$ and $b \rightsquigarrow v$ implies there is u with $u\ \mathcal{R}^{\mathcal{C}}_{\mathcal{L}}\ v$ and $a \rightsquigarrow u$.

We prove (1) by induction on the derivation of $a \rightsquigarrow u$:

(Red Object) In this case, $a = u$. Only (Indexed $\mathcal{R}$) or (Indexed Object) can derive $u \mathcal{R}^{\mathcal{C}}_{\mathcal{L}} b$; in either case b must be an object. Let $v = b$ to obtain $u \mathcal{R}^{\mathcal{C}}_{\mathcal{L}} v$ and $b \rightsquigarrow v$.

(Red Select) In this case, $a = a'.\ell_j$, $a' \rightsquigarrow u'$, $u' = [\ell_i = \varsigma(x_i)a_i\{x_i\}^{i \in I}]$, $a_j\{\!\{u'\}\!\} \rightsquigarrow u$ and $j \in I$. Only (Indexed Select) can derive $a'.\ell_j \mathcal{R}^{\mathcal{C}}_{\mathcal{L}} b$. Therefore $\ell_j \in \mathcal{L}$ and there is b' such that $b = b'.\ell_j$ and $a' \mathcal{R}^{\mathcal{C}}_{\mathcal{L}} b'$. By induction hypothesis, $a' \rightsquigarrow u'$ implies there is v' with $u' \mathcal{R}^{\mathcal{C}}_{\mathcal{L}} v'$ and $b' \rightsquigarrow v'$. Only (Indexed $\mathcal{R}$) or (Indexed Object) can derive $u' \mathcal{R}^{\mathcal{C}}_{\mathcal{L}} v'$.

(Indexed $\mathcal{R}$) Here $u' = w$ and $v' = [\ell_i = \varsigma(x_i)a_i\{x_i\}\ ^{i \in I}, \ell = \varsigma(z)d]$ for some term d, and $I = 1..p$. Since $\mathcal{L}(a_j\{x_j\}) \subseteq \mathcal{L}$ we have $a_j\{x_j\} \mathcal{R}^{\mathcal{C}}_{\mathcal{L}} a_j\{x_j\}$. This with $u' \mathcal{R}^{\mathcal{C}}_{\mathcal{L}} v'$ implies by ($\mathcal{R}^{\mathcal{C}}_{\mathcal{L}}$ Sub) that $a_j\{\!\{u'\}\!\} \mathcal{R}^{\mathcal{C}}_{\mathcal{L}} a_j\{\!\{v'\}\!\}$. By induction hypothesis, $a_j\{\!\{u'\}\!\} \rightsquigarrow u$ implies there is v such that $u \mathcal{R}^{\mathcal{C}}_{\mathcal{L}} v$ and $a_j\{\!\{v'\}\!\} \rightsquigarrow v$. By (Red Select), $b' \rightsquigarrow v'$ and $a_j\{\!\{v'\}\!\} \rightsquigarrow v$ imply that $b \rightsquigarrow v$.

(Indexed Object) Here $v' = [\ell_i = \varsigma(x_i)b_i\{x_i\}\ ^{i \in I}]$ with $a_i\{x_i\} \mathcal{R}^{\mathcal{C}}_{\mathcal{L}} b_i\{x_i\}$ for each $i \in I$. Given ($\mathcal{R}^{\mathcal{C}}_{\mathcal{L}}$ Sub), $u' \mathcal{R}^{\mathcal{C}}_{\mathcal{L}} v'$ implies $a_j\{\!\{u'\}\!\} \mathcal{R}^{\mathcal{C}}_{\mathcal{L}} b_j\{\!\{v'\}\!\}$. By induction hypothesis, $a_j\{\!\{u'\}\!\} \rightsquigarrow u$ implies there is v such that $u \mathcal{R}^{\mathcal{C}}_{\mathcal{L}} v$ and $b_j\{\!\{v'\}\!\} \rightsquigarrow v$. By (Red Select), $b' \rightsquigarrow v'$ and $b_j\{\!\{v'\}\!\} \rightsquigarrow v$ imply that $b \rightsquigarrow v$.

Case (Red Update) follows by similar reasoning to (Red Select). Part (2) follows by a similar induction. □

Proposition A.4 *For all finite sets of labels $\mathcal{L}$, all terms $a\{x\}$ and $b\{x\}$, $a\{x\} \simeq b\{x\}$ implies that for all closed v, $a\{\!\{v\}\!\} \simeq_{\mathcal{L}} b\{\!\{v\}\!\}$.*

Proof Consider any finite set of labels, $\mathcal{L}$, and any $a\{x\}$ and $b\{x\}$ such that $a\{x\} \simeq b\{x\}$. Consider any closed $v = [\ell_i = \varsigma(x_i)b_i{}^{i \in 1..n}]$. Let $\mathcal{L}' = \mathcal{L} \cup \mathcal{L}(a\{x\}) \cup \mathcal{L}(b\{x\}) \cup \mathcal{L}(v)$. Since $\mathcal{L}'$ is finite we may choose some label $\ell \notin \mathcal{L}'$. Define the objects v_a and v_b as follows.

$$v_a \triangleq [\ell_i = \varsigma(x_i)b_i\ ^{i \in 1..n}, \ell = \varsigma(x)a\{x\}]$$
$$v_b \triangleq [\ell_i = \varsigma(x_i)b_i\ ^{i \in 1..n}, \ell = \varsigma(x)b\{x\}]$$

By Lemma A.3, $v \simeq_{\mathcal{L}'} v_a$ and $v \simeq_{\mathcal{L}'} v_b$. By Lemma A.2(4), these facts and $\mathcal{L}(a\{x\}) \cup \mathcal{L}(b\{x\}) \subseteq \mathcal{L}'$ imply $a\{\!\{v\}\!\} \simeq_{\mathcal{L}'} a\{\!\{v_a\}\!\}$ and $b\{\!\{v\}\!\} \simeq_{\mathcal{L}'} b\{\!\{v_b\}\!\}$. Since $\simeq$ is compatible, $v_a.\ell \simeq v_b.\ell$. By Proposition 1.7, $\leftrightarrow \subseteq \simeq$, so $v_a.\ell \simeq a\{\!\{v_a\}\!\}$ and $v_b.\ell \simeq b\{\!\{v_b\}\!\}$. Therefore $a\{\!\{v_a\}\!\} \simeq b\{\!\{v_b\}\!\}$. By Lemma A.2(1), $a\{\!\{v_a\}\!\} \simeq_{\mathcal{L}'} b\{\!\{v_b\}\!\}$. By Lemma A.2(3), the latter, $a\{\!\{v\}\!\} \simeq_{\mathcal{L}'} a\{\!\{v_a\}\!\}$ and $b\{\!\{v\}\!\} \simeq_{\mathcal{L}'} b\{\!\{v_b\}\!\}$ imply that $a\{\!\{v\}\!\} \simeq_{\mathcal{L}'} b\{\!\{v\}\!\}$. By Lemma A.2(2), $\mathcal{L} \subseteq \mathcal{L}'$ implies $a\{\!\{v\}\!\} \simeq_{\mathcal{L}} b\{\!\{v\}\!\}$. □

By Lemma A.2(1), Lemma 1.16 is a corollary: $a\{x\} \simeq b\{x\}$ implies that for all closed v, $a\{\!\{v\}\!\} \simeq b\{\!\{v\}\!\}$.

B Proof of Proposition 2.19

Here we prove the central property of the compatible extension of similarity, $\lesssim^\bullet$, that it is preserved by reduction. First, we need a couple of lemmas about the type system of $\mathbf{S}_\lambda$.

Lemma B.1

(1) *If* $\varnothing \vdash A{<:}Obj(X)[\ell_i \nu'_i{:}B_i\ ^{i \in I}]$ *then* $A = Obj(X)[\ell_i \nu_i{:}A_i\ ^{i \in J}]$ *with* $I \subseteq J$, *and for each* $i \in I$ *we have* $\varnothing, X{<:}A \vdash \nu_i A_i {<:} \nu'_i B_i$.

(2) *If* $\varnothing \vdash \forall(X{<:}A)B\{X\}{<:}\forall(X{<:}A')B'\{X\}$, *then both* $\varnothing \vdash A'{<:}A$ *and* $\varnothing, X{<:}A' \vdash B\{X\}{<:}B'\{X\}$.

(3) *If* $\varnothing \vdash (A \to B){<:}(A' \to B')$, *both* $\varnothing \vdash A'{<:}A$ *and* $\varnothing \vdash B{<:}B'$.

Lemma B.2 *Assume* $A\{X^+\}$, $A'\{X^+\}$. *Suppose* $\varnothing, X{<:}B'' \vdash \nu A\{X\}{<:}\nu' A'\{X\}$, $\varnothing \vdash B{<:}B'$ *and* $\varnothing \vdash B'{<:}B''$.

(1) *If* $\nu' \in \{^o, ^+\}$ *then* $\nu \in \{^o, ^+\}$ *and* $\varnothing \vdash A\{\!\{B\}\!\}{<:}A'\{\!\{B'\}\!\}$.

(2) *If* $\nu' \in \{^o, ^-\}$ *then* $\nu \in \{^o, ^-\}$ *and* $\varnothing \vdash A'\{\!\{B\}\!\}{<:}A\{\!\{B'\}\!\}$.

Proof of Proposition 2.19 *Whenever* $\varnothing \vdash a \lesssim^\bullet b : A$ *and* $a \rightsquigarrow u$ *there is* v *with* $b \rightsquigarrow v$ *and* $\varnothing \vdash u \lesssim^\bullet v : A$.

Proof By induction on the derivation of $a \rightsquigarrow u$. By Lemma 2.18, there is a type A' and a term c such that $\varnothing \vdash a \mathrel{\widehat{\lesssim^\bullet}} c : A'$, $\varnothing \vdash A'{<:}A$ and $\varnothing \vdash c \lesssim b : A$. We examine each reduction rule in turn.

(Red Result) In this case, $a = u$. Therefore a is a result. From $\varnothing \vdash u \mathrel{\widehat{\lesssim^\bullet}} c : A'$, it follows that c too is a result. Since c is a result, $\varnothing \vdash c \lesssim b : A$ implies there is a result v such that $b \rightsquigarrow v$ and $\varnothing \vdash c \lesssim v : A$. By (Cand Def), $\varnothing \vdash u \mathrel{\widehat{\lesssim^\bullet}} c : A'$, $\varnothing \vdash A'{<:}A$ and $\varnothing \vdash c \lesssim v : A$ imply that $\varnothing \vdash u \lesssim^\bullet v : A$.

(Red Select) In this case, $a = a'.\ell_j$, $a' \rightsquigarrow u'$, $a_j\{\!\{C, u'\}\!\} \rightsquigarrow u$ and $j \in 1..n$, where $u' = obj(X{=}C)[\ell_i = \varsigma(x_i{:}X)a_i\{X, x_i\}\ ^{i \in 1..n}]$.

Only (Comp Select) can be responsible for $\varnothing \vdash a'.\ell_j \mathrel{\widehat{\lesssim^\bullet}} c : A'$. Therefore there is a type $D' = Obj(X)[\ell_i \nu'_i{:}D'_i\{X\}\ ^{i \in I}]$, a type D and a term c' such that $c = c'.\ell_j$ where $\varnothing \vdash a' \lesssim^\bullet c' : D$, $\varnothing \vdash D{<:}D'$, $\nu'_j \in \{^o, ^+\}$, $j \in I$ and $A' = D'_j\{\!\{D\}\!\}$. By Lemma B.1(1), $\varnothing \vdash D{<:}D'$ implies that $D = Obj(X)[\ell_i \nu_i{:}D_i\{X\}\ ^{i \in J}]$ with $I \subseteq J$ and $\varnothing, X{<:}D \vdash \nu_i D_i\{X\}{<:}\nu'_i D'_i\{X\}$ for each $i \in I$. The latter and $\nu'_j \in \{^o, ^+\}$ imply that $\nu_j \in \{^o, ^+\}$.

By induction hypothesis, $\varnothing \vdash a' \lesssim^\bullet c' : D$ plus $a' \rightsquigarrow u'$ imply there is a result w' such that $c' \rightsquigarrow w'$ and $\varnothing \vdash u' \lesssim^\bullet w' : D$.

By Lemma 2.18, there is a type D'' and a result w'' such that $\varnothing \vdash u' \widehat{\lesssim^\bullet} w'' : D''$, $\varnothing \vdash D''{<:}D$ and $\varnothing \vdash w'' \lesssim w' : D$. Since only (Comp Object) may derive $\varnothing \vdash u' \widehat{\lesssim^\bullet} w'' : D''$, it must be that $D'' = C$, that $C = Obj(X)[\ell_i \nu_i'':C_i\{X\}^{\,i\in 1..n}]$, $w'' = obj(X{=}C)[\ell_i = \varsigma(x_i{:}X)b_i\{X, x_i\}^{\,i\in 1..n}]$ and $\varnothing, x_i{:}C \vdash a_i\{\!\{C, x_i\}\!\} \lesssim^\bullet b_i\{\!\{C, x_i\}\!\} : C_i\{\!\{C\}\!\}$ for each $i \in 1..n$.

By Proposition 2.16, $\varnothing \vdash b_j\{\!\{C, w''\}\!\} \sim w''.\ell_j : C_j\{\!\{C\}\!\}$. By (Cand Comp), we have $\varnothing \vdash u' \lesssim^\bullet w'' : C$. By (Cand Subst), $\varnothing \vdash a_j\{\!\{C, u'\}\!\} \lesssim^\bullet b_j\{\!\{C, w''\}\!\} : C_j\{\!\{C\}\!\}$. By induction hypothesis, the latter and $a_j\{\!\{C, u'\}\!\} \rightsquigarrow u$ imply there is w such that $\varnothing \vdash u \lesssim^\bullet w : C_j\{\!\{C\}\!\}$ and $b_j\{\!\{C, w''\}\!\} \rightsquigarrow w$.

By Proposition 2.16, $c' \rightsquigarrow w'$, $\varnothing \vdash c'{:}D$ and $\varnothing \vdash w'{:}D$ imply $\varnothing \vdash w' \lesssim c'{:}D$. The latter and $\varnothing \vdash w'' \lesssim w' : D$ imply $\varnothing \vdash w'' \lesssim c' : D$, by transitivity.

Given that $\nu_j \in \{^o, ^+\}$, fragment $.\ell_j$ is a $(D, D_j\{\!\{D\}\!\})$-action. Therefore, Proposition 2.14(1) and $\varnothing \vdash w'' \lesssim c' : D$ imply that $\varnothing \vdash w''.\ell_j \lesssim c'.\ell_j : D_j\{\!\{D\}\!\}$.

Since $\varnothing \vdash C{<:}D$, Lemma B.1(1) implies $\varnothing, X{<:}C \vdash \nu_j'' C_j\{X\}{<:}\nu_j D_j\{X\}$. Since $\nu_j \in \{^o, ^+\}$, Lemma B.2 implies that $\varnothing \vdash C_j\{\!\{C\}\!\}{<:}D_j\{\!\{C\}\!\}$. Since $\nu_j' \in \{^o, ^+\}$, Lemma B.2, $\varnothing, X{<:}D \vdash \nu_j D_j\{X\}{<:}\nu_j' D_j'\{X\}$ and $\varnothing \vdash C{<:}D$ imply that $\varnothing \vdash D_j\{\!\{C\}\!\}{<:}D_j'\{\!\{D\}\!\} = A'$. By transitivity, we get $\varnothing \vdash C_j\{\!\{C\}\!\}{<:}A$. Similarly, we get $\varnothing \vdash D_j\{\!\{D\}\!\}{<:}A$. Hence, Proposition 2.14(2) implies that from $\varnothing \vdash b_j\{\!\{C, w_j''\}\!\} \sim w''.\ell_j{:}C_j\{\!\{C\}\!\}$ we have $\varnothing \vdash b_j\{\!\{C, w_j''\}\!\} \sim w''.\ell_j{:}A$, and from $\varnothing \vdash w''.\ell_j \lesssim c'.\ell_j{:}D_j\{\!\{D\}\!\}$ we have $\varnothing \vdash w''.\ell_j \lesssim c'.\ell_j{:}A$. Combining these with $\varnothing \vdash c = c'.\ell_j \lesssim b : A$, we obtain $\varnothing \vdash b_j\{\!\{C, w_j''\}\!\} \lesssim b : A$ by transitivity.

From $\varnothing \vdash b_j\{\!\{C, w_j''\}\!\} \lesssim b : A$ and $b_j\{\!\{C, w''\}\!\} \rightsquigarrow w$ there is v with $b \rightsquigarrow v$ and $\varnothing \vdash w \lesssim v : A$. By (Cand Right), $\varnothing \vdash u \lesssim^\bullet w : C_j\{\!\{C\}\!\}$, $\varnothing \vdash C_j\{\!\{C\}\!\}{<:}A$ and $\varnothing \vdash w \lesssim v : A$ imply that $\varnothing \vdash u \lesssim^\bullet v : A$.

(Red Update) In this case, $a = a'.\ell_j \Leftarrow (Y{<:}C', y{:}Y)\varsigma(x{:}Y)a_j'\{Y, y\}$, $a' \rightsquigarrow u'$ where $u' = obj(X{=}C)[\ell_i = \varsigma(x_i{:}X)a_i\{X\}^{\,i\in I}]$, $j \in I$, and

$$u = obj(X{=}C)[\ell_j = \varsigma(x{:}X)a_j'\{\!\{X, u'\}\!\}, \ell_i = \varsigma(x_i{:}X)a_i\{X\}^{\,i\in I-\{j\}}].$$

Only (Comp Update) can yield

$$\varnothing \vdash a'.\ell_j \Leftarrow (Y{<:}C', y{:}Y)\varsigma(x{:}Y)a_j'\{Y, y\} \widehat{\lesssim^\bullet} c : A'$$

so it must be that $C' = A'$ and c must take the form

$$c'.\ell_j \Leftarrow (Y{<:}A', y{:}Y)\varsigma(x{:}Y)c_j'\{Y, y\}$$

and there is a type $D' = Obj(X)[\ell_k \nu_k'{:}D_k'\{X\}^{\,k\in K}]$ such that $\varnothing \vdash a' \lesssim^\bullet c' : A'$, $\varnothing \vdash A'{<:}D'$, $\varnothing, Y{<:}A', y{:}Y, x{:}Y \vdash a_j'\{Y, y\} \lesssim^\bullet c_j'\{Y, y\} : D_j'\{\!\{Y\}\!\}$, $\nu_j' \in \{^o, ^-\}$ and $j \in K$.

By induction hypothesis, $\varnothing \vdash a' \lesssim^\bullet c' : A'$ and $a' \rightsquigarrow u'$ imply there is w' with $\varnothing \vdash u' \lesssim^\bullet w' : A'$ and $c' \rightsquigarrow w'$. By Lemma 2.18, there is a type A'' and a result w'' such that $\varnothing \vdash u' \widehat{\lesssim^\bullet} w'' : A''$, $\varnothing \vdash A'' <: A'$ and $\varnothing \vdash w'' \lesssim w' : A'$. Since only (Comp Object) may derive $\varnothing \vdash u' \widehat{\lesssim^\bullet} w'' : A''$, it must be that $A'' = C$, that $C = Obj(X)[\ell_i \nu_i{:}C_i\{X\}^{\,i \in I}]$, $w'' = obj(X{=}C)[\ell_i = \varsigma(x_i{:}X)b_i\{X\}^{\,i \in I}]$ and $\varnothing, x_i{:}C \vdash a_i\{\!\{C\}\!\} \lesssim^\bullet b_i\{\!\{C\}\!\} : C_i\{\!\{C\}\!\}$ for each $i \in I$.

Let $w = obj(X{=}C)[\ell_j = \varsigma(x{:}X)c'_j\{\!\{X, w''\}\!\}, \ell_i = \varsigma(x_i{:}X)b_i\{X\}^{\,i \in I - \{j\}}]$. By type substitution, $\varnothing, Y{<:}A', y{:}Y, x{:}Y \vdash a'_j\{Y, y\} \lesssim^\bullet c'_j\{Y, y\} : D'_j\{\!\{Y\}\!\}$ and $\varnothing \vdash C{<:}A'$ imply $\varnothing, y{:}C, x{:}C \vdash a'_j\{\!\{C, y\}\!\} \lesssim^\bullet c'_j\{\!\{C, y\}\!\} : D'_j\{\!\{C\}\!\}$. By (Cand Comp), $\varnothing \vdash u' \widehat{\lesssim^\bullet} w'' : C$ implies $\varnothing \vdash u' \lesssim^\bullet w'' : C$. By (Cand Subst), this implies $\varnothing, x{:}C \vdash a'_j\{\!\{C, u'\}\!\} \lesssim^\bullet c'_j\{\!\{C, w''\}\!\} : D'_j\{\!\{C\}\!\}$. By Lemma B.1(1), $\varnothing \vdash C{<:}D'$ implies $\varnothing, X{<:}C \vdash \nu_j C_j\{X\}{<:}\nu'_j D'_j\{X\}$. By Lemma B.2, this, $\nu'_j \in \{^\circ, ^-\}$ and $\varnothing \vdash C{<:}C$ imply $\varnothing \vdash D'_j\{\!\{C\}\!\}{<:}C_j\{\!\{C\}\!\}$. By (Cand Subsumption), $\varnothing, x{:}C \vdash a'_j\{\!\{C, u'\}\!\} \lesssim^\bullet c'_j\{\!\{C, w''\}\!\} : D'_j\{\!\{C\}\!\}$ implies that $\varnothing, x{:}C \vdash a'_j\{\!\{C, u'\}\!\} \lesssim^\bullet c'_j\{\!\{C, w''\}\!\} : C_j\{\!\{C\}\!\}$. From this, and $\varnothing, x_i{:}C \vdash a_i\{\!\{C\}\!\} \lesssim^\bullet b_i\{\!\{C\}\!\} : C_i\{\!\{C\}\!\}$ for each $i \in I - \{j\}$ we obtain $\varnothing \vdash u \widehat{\lesssim^\bullet} w : C$ by (Comp Object).

If we define $\alpha = .\ell_j \Leftarrow (Y{<:}A', y{:}Y)\varsigma(x{:}Y)c'_j\{Y, y\}$, then α is an (A', A')-action. By Proposition 2.16, $\varnothing \vdash w \sim w''\alpha : A'$. By Proposition 2.16, $\varnothing \vdash c' : A'$, $\varnothing \vdash w' : A'$ and $c' \rightsquigarrow w'$ imply that $\varnothing \vdash w' \sim c' : A'$. By transitivity, $\varnothing \vdash w'' \lesssim w' : A'$ implies $\varnothing \vdash w'' \lesssim c' : A'$. By Proposition 2.14(1), $\varnothing \vdash w'' \lesssim c' : A'$ implies $\varnothing \vdash w''\alpha \lesssim c'\alpha : A'$, that is, $\varnothing \vdash w''\alpha \lesssim c : A'$. From this, $\varnothing \vdash w \lesssim w''\alpha : A'$, $\varnothing \vdash A'{<:}A$ and $\varnothing \vdash c \lesssim b : A$, we obtain $\varnothing \vdash w \lesssim b : A$. By Proposition 2.14(3), there is v such that $b \rightsquigarrow v$ and $\varnothing \vdash w \lesssim v : A$. Now, $\varnothing \vdash C{<:}A'$ and $\varnothing \vdash A'{<:}A$ imply $\varnothing \vdash C{<:}A$. Given $\varnothing \vdash u \lesssim^\bullet w : C$ and $\varnothing \vdash C{<:}A$, (Cand Def) implies $\varnothing \vdash u \lesssim^\bullet v : A$.

The cases for (Red Appl) and (Red Appl2) follow similarly. □

This proof was obtained by modifying the proof of the corresponding property for experimental order for the ς-calculus. The presence of structural typing rules complicates the argument, but leaves the structure of the proof unchanged.

References

Abadi, M. and L. Cardelli (1994, June). A semantics of object types. In *Proceedings LICS'94*, pp. 332–341.

Abadi, M. and L. Cardelli (1996). *A Theory of Objects*. Springer-Verlag.

Abramsky, S. and L. Ong (1993). Full abstraction in the lazy lambda calculus. *Information and Computation 105*, 159–267.

Cardelli, L., S. Martini, J. C. Mitchell, and A. Scedrov (1994). An extension of system F with subtyping. *Information and Computation 109*(1/2), 4–56.

Dami, L. (1997). Operational subsumption: an ideal model of subtyping. Unpublished draft. University of Geneva.

Gordon, A. D., S. B. Lassen, and P. D. Hankin (1997). Compilation and equivalence of imperative objects. Technical Report 429, University of Cambridge Computer Laboratory. Short version in *Proceedings FST&TCS'97*.

Gordon, A. D. and G. D. Rees (1996). Bisimilarity for a first-order calculus of objects with subtyping. Technical Report 386, University of Cambridge Computer Laboratory. Short version in *Proceedings POPL'96*, pp. 386–395 .

Howe, D. J. (1996). Proving congruence of bisimulation in functional programming languages. *Information and Computation 124*(2), 103–112.

Hüttel, H. and J. Kleist (1996). Objects as mobile processes. In *Proceedings MFPS'96*.

Meyer, A. R. and S. S. Cosmadakis (1988, July). Semantical paradigms: Notes for an invited lecture. In *Proceedings LICS'88*, pp. 236–253.

Milner, R. (1977). Fully abstract models of typed lambda-calculi. *Theoretical Computer Science 4*, 1–23.

Milner, R. (1989). *Communication and Concurrency*. Prentice-Hall.

Morris, J. H. (1968, December). *Lambda-Calculus Models of Programming Languages*. Ph. D. thesis, MIT.

Pierce, B. and D. Sangiorgi (1997). Behavioral equivalence in the polymorphic pi-calculus. In *Proceedings POPL'97*.

Plotkin, G. D. (1975). Call-by-name, call-by-value and the λ-calculus. *Theoretical Computer Science 1*, 125–159.

Plotkin, G. D. (1977). LCF considered as a programming language. *Theoretical Computer Science 5*, 223–255.

Rees, G. (1994, April). Observational equivalence for a polymorphic lambda calculus. University of Cambridge Computer Laboratory.

Reynolds, J. C. (1983). Types, abstraction and parametric polymorphism. In *Information Processing 83*, pp. 513–523. North-Holland.

Sangiorgi, D. (1996). An interpretation of typed objects into typed π-calculus. In *Proceedings FOOL 3, New Brunswick*.

Talcott, C. (1997). Reasoning about functions with effects. In this volume, pp. 347–390.

Semantics for core Concurrent ML using computation types

Alan Jeffrey

Abstract

This paper presents two typed higher-order concurrent functional programming languages, based on Reppy's Concurrent ML. The first is a simplified, monomorphic variant of CML, which allows reduction of terms of any type. The second uses an explicit type constructor for computation, in the style of Moggi's monadic metalanguage. Each of these languages is given an operational semantics, which can be used as the basis of bisimulation equivalence. We show how Moggi's translation of the call-by-value lambda-calculus into the monadic metalanguage can be extended to these concurrent languages, and that this translation is correct up to weak bisimulation.

1 Introduction

Reppy's (1991a, 1992) Concurrent ML is an extension of New Jersey ML with features for spawning threads, which can communicate by one-to-one synchronous handshake in the style of Milner's (1989) CCS.

There are (at least) two approaches to giving the operational semantics to CML. The 'functional language definition' tradition (Milner, Tofte, and Harper 1990, for example) is to define unlabelled reductions between entire programs, and to use this semantics to prove properties such as type-safety. Reppy uses this approach to give a reduction semantics to CML based on *evaluation contexts* $E[\_]$, for example giving the semantics of if-expressions as:

$$\overline{E[\text{if true then } e \text{ else } f] \longrightarrow E[e]} \quad \overline{E[\text{if false then } e \text{ else } f] \longrightarrow E[f]}$$

The 'concurrency semantics' tradition (Milner 1989, for example) is to define labelled reductions between program fragments, and to use this semantics as the basis of equivalences (such as bisimulation) between program fragments. Ferreira, Hennessy and Jeffrey (1995) use this approach to give a labelled transition system semantics to CML including *silent transitions* $\xrightarrow{\tau}$ and *value transitions* $\xrightarrow{\checkmark v}$, for example giving the semantics of if-expressions as:

$$\frac{e \xrightarrow{\checkmark \text{true}} e'}{\text{if } e \text{ then } f \text{ else } g \xrightarrow{\tau} e' \parallel f} \quad \frac{e \xrightarrow{\checkmark \text{false}} e'}{\text{if } e \text{ then } f \text{ else } g \xrightarrow{\tau} e' \parallel g}$$

$$\frac{e \xrightarrow{\alpha} e'}{\text{if } e \text{ then } f \text{ else } g \xrightarrow{\alpha} \text{if } e' \text{ then } f \text{ else } g}$$

The resulting labelled transition system can be used as the basis of an equational theory of CML expressions, using *bisimulation* as equivalence.

Unfortunately, there are some problems with this semantics:

- It is complex, due to having to allow expressions in any evaluation context to reduce (for example requiring three rules for if-expressions rather than Reppy's two axiom schemas).
- It produces very long reductions, due to large numbers of 'book-keeping' steps (for example the long reduction in Table 9).
- The resulting equational theory does not have pleasant mathematical properties (for example neither β- nor η-conversion hold for the language).

In this paper we present a variant of CML using *computation types*. These provide an explicit type constructor $\_\,\mathsf{comp}$ for computation, which means that the type system can distinguish between expressions which can perform computation (those of type $A\,\mathsf{comp}$) and those which are guaranteed to be in normal form (anything else). Differentiating by type between expressions which can and cannot perform reductions makes the operational semantics much simpler, for example the much shorter reduction in Table 16 and the simpler operational rules for if-expressions:

$$\frac{}{\mathsf{if\ true\ then}\ f\ \mathsf{else}\ g \xrightarrow{\tau} f} \qquad \frac{}{\mathsf{if\ false\ then}\ f\ \mathsf{else}\ g \xrightarrow{\tau} g}$$

Computation types were originally proposed by Moggi (1991) in a denotational setting to provide models of non-trivial computation (such as CML communication) without losing pleasant mathematical properties (such as β- and η-reduction). Moggi provided a translation from the call-by-value λ-calculus into the language with computation types, which we can adapt for CML and prove to be correct up to weak bisimulation.

We can also use equational reasoning to transform inefficient programs (such as the translation of the long reduction in Table 9) into efficient ones (such as the short reduction in Table 16). We conjecture that such optimisations may make languages with explicit computation types simpler to optimise.

In section 2 we present a cut-down version of the operational semantics for CML presented in (Ferreira, Hennessy, and Jeffrey 1995), including a suitable definition of bisimulation for CML programs.

In section 3 we present the variant of CML with explicit computation types, and show that the resulting equational theory of bisimulation has better mathematical properties than that of CML. This is a variant of the language presented in (Jeffrey 1995a).

In section 4 we provide a translation from the first language into the second, and show that it is correct up to bisimulation.

In section 5 we briefly discuss some related work.

2 Concurrent ML

In this section, we introduce a subset of Concurrent ML (CML), and provide a labelled transition system semantics for it. This provides weak bisimulation as an equivalence on programs.

This section is based on joint work with Ferreira and Hennessy, and is discussed in more detail in (Ferreira, Hennessy, and Jeffrey 1995).

2.1 Syntax

Concurrent ML (CML) is an extension to New Jersey ML which allows for the implementation of concurrent programs. Communication takes place along channels, and is a one-to-one handshake similar to Milner's (1989) CCS. For example, the process which transmits value v of type A along channel a and then returns the canonical value `()` of type `unit` is:

$$\texttt{send}\,(\texttt{a}, v)$$

In this paper, we use monomorphically typed channels, so for each type A we assume a type A chan of channels which can carry values of type A. We will not consider channel generation in this paper, and instead assume fixed disjoint sets K_A of channels for each type A ranged over by a, b... The type of `send` is then:

$$\texttt{send} : (A\ \texttt{chan} * A) \texttt{ -> unit}$$

The process which accepts value v of type A along channel a and returns v is:

$$\texttt{accept a}$$

This has type:

$$\texttt{accept} : A\ \texttt{chan -> } A$$

Evaluation proceeds as in ML, with left-to-right call-by-value evaluation, so a process which accepts values v then w along channel a and returns the pair (v, w) is:

$$(\texttt{accept a}, \texttt{accept a})$$

We can define the sequential composition of `e` and `f` to be a term which evaluates `e`, discards the result, then evaluates `f` to be (for fresh `x`):

$$\texttt{e}; \texttt{f} = \texttt{let x = e in f}$$

A thunked process can be forked off for concurrent evaluation using spawn. For example the concurrent passing of v along a can be given:

```
spawn (fn x => send (a, v)); accept a
```

This spawns `send (a, v)` off for concurrent execution, then evaluates `accept a`. These two processes can then communicate. In this paper, we are ignoring CML's *threads* so spawn has type:

```
spawn : (unit -> A) -> unit
```

CML does *not* provide a general 'external choice' operator such as CCS $+$. Instead, guarded choice is provided, and the type mechanism is used to ensure that choice is only ever used on guarded computation. The type A event is used as the type of guarded processes of type A, and CML allows for the creation of guarded input and output:

```
transmit : (A chan * A) -> unit event        receive : A chan -> A event
```

and for guarded sequential computation:

```
wrap : (A event * (A -> B)) -> B event
```

For example the guarded process which inputs a value on a and outputs it on b is given:

```
wrap (receive a, fn x => send (b, x)) : unit event
```

CML provides choice between guarded processes using choose. In CML this is defined on lists, but for simplicity we shall give it only for pairs:

```
choose : (A event * A event) -> A event
```

For example the guarded process which chooses between receiving a signal on a or b is:

```
choose (receive a, receive b) : A event
```

Guarded processes can be treated as any other process, using the function sync:

```
sync : A event -> A
```

For example, we can execute the above guarded process by saying:

```
sync (choose (receive a, receive b)) : A
```

In fact, accept and send are not primitives in CML, and are defined:

$$\texttt{accept} \stackrel{\text{def}}{=} \texttt{fn}\ x\ \texttt{=> sync (receive}\ x\texttt{)}$$
$$\texttt{send} \stackrel{\text{def}}{=} \texttt{fn}\ x\ \texttt{=> sync (transmit}\ x\texttt{)}$$

This paper cannot provide a full introduction to CML, and the interested reader is referred to Reppy's papers (Reppy 1991a; Reppy 1992) for further explanation.

The fragment of CML we will consider here is missing much of CML's functionality, notably polymorphism, guards and thread identifiers. It is similar to the fragment of CML considered in (Ferreira, Hennessy, and Jeffrey 1995) except that for simplicity we do not consider the `always` command. We will call this subset 'core τ-free CML', or μCML for short.

For simplicity, we will only use `unit`, `bool`, `int` and A `chan` as base types, although other types such as lists could easily be added.

The *integer values* are given by the grammar:

$$n ::= \cdots \mid \texttt{-1} \mid \texttt{0} \mid \texttt{1} \mid \cdots$$

The *channel values* are given by the grammar:

$$k ::= \texttt{a} \mid \texttt{b} \mid \cdots$$

The *values* are given by the grammar:

$$v ::= \texttt{true} \mid \texttt{false} \mid n \mid k \mid \texttt{()} \mid \texttt{rec}\, x = \texttt{fn}\, x \texttt{=>}\, e \mid x$$

The *expressions* are given by the grammar:

$$e ::= v \mid ce \mid \texttt{if}\, e\, \texttt{then}\, e\, \texttt{else}\, e \mid \texttt{(}e\texttt{,}e\texttt{)} \mid \texttt{let}\, x = e\, \texttt{in}\, e \mid ee$$

Finally, the *basic functions* are given by the grammar:

$$\begin{aligned} c \;::=\;& \texttt{fst} \mid \texttt{snd} \mid \texttt{add} \mid \texttt{mul} \mid \texttt{leq} \mid \texttt{transmit} \mid \texttt{receive} \\ & \mid \texttt{choose} \mid \texttt{spawn} \mid \texttt{sync} \mid \texttt{wrap} \mid \texttt{never} \end{aligned}$$

μCML is a typed language, with a type system given by the grammar:

$$A \;::=\; \texttt{unit} \mid \texttt{bool} \mid \texttt{int} \mid A\,\texttt{chan} \mid A \,\texttt{*}\, A \mid A \,\texttt{->}\, A \mid A\,\texttt{event}$$

The type judgements for expressions are given as judgements $\Gamma \vdash e : A$, where Γ ranges over contexts of the form $x_1 : A_1, \ldots, x_n : A_n$. The type system is in Tables 1 and 2.

We can define syntactic sugar for μCML definitions, writing $\texttt{fn}\, x \texttt{=>}\, e$ for $\texttt{rec}\, y = \texttt{fn}\, x \texttt{=>}\, e$ when y is not free in e, using pattern-matching on pairs as shorthand for projections, and using $\stackrel{\text{def}}{=}$ as shorthand for recursive function declaration. For example, a one-place buffer can be defined:

$$\begin{aligned} \texttt{cell} \quad &: \quad A\,\texttt{chan} \,\texttt{*}\, A\,\texttt{chan} \,\texttt{->}\, B \\ \texttt{cell}\,\texttt{(}x\texttt{,}y\texttt{)} \quad &\stackrel{\text{def}}{=} \quad \texttt{cell}\,\texttt{(}\,\texttt{snd}\,\texttt{(send}\,\texttt{(}y\texttt{,}\,\texttt{accept}\,x\texttt{)}\texttt{,}\texttt{(}x\texttt{,}y\texttt{)))} \end{aligned}$$

$$\frac{\Gamma \vdash \mathtt{e} : A}{\Gamma \vdash \mathtt{ce} : B}[c : A \to B] \qquad \frac{\Gamma \vdash \mathtt{e} : \mathtt{bool} \quad \Gamma \vdash f : A \quad \Gamma \vdash g : A}{\Gamma \vdash \mathtt{if}\, e\, \mathtt{then}\, f\, \mathtt{else}\, g : A}$$

$$\frac{\Gamma \vdash \mathtt{e} : A \quad \Gamma \vdash f : B}{\Gamma \vdash (\mathtt{e},f) : A * B} \qquad \frac{\Gamma \vdash \mathtt{e} : A \quad \Gamma, \mathtt{x} : A \vdash f : B}{\Gamma \vdash \mathtt{let}\, x = \mathtt{e}\, \mathtt{in}\, f : B}$$

$$\frac{\Gamma \vdash f : A \mathtt{->} B \quad \Gamma \vdash \mathtt{e} : A}{\Gamma \vdash f\mathtt{e} : B} \qquad \frac{}{\Gamma, \mathtt{x} : A \vdash \mathtt{x} : A} \qquad \frac{\Gamma \vdash \mathtt{x} : A}{\Gamma, y : B \vdash \mathtt{x} : A}[x \neq y]$$

$$\frac{}{\Gamma \vdash \mathtt{true} : \mathtt{bool}} \qquad \frac{}{\Gamma \vdash \mathtt{false} : \mathtt{bool}}$$

$$\frac{}{\Gamma \vdash n : \mathtt{int}} \qquad \frac{}{\Gamma \vdash k : A\, \mathtt{chan}}[k \in K_A]$$

$$\frac{}{\Gamma \vdash \mathtt{()} : \mathtt{unit}} \qquad \frac{\Gamma, \mathtt{x} : A \mathtt{->} B, y : A \vdash \mathtt{e} : B}{\Gamma \vdash \mathtt{rec}\, x = \mathtt{fn}\, y \mathtt{=>} \mathtt{e} : A \mathtt{->} B}$$

Table 1: Types for μCML expressions

2.2 Operational semantics

The semantics we will use here is based on the 'semantics of concurrency' tradition: we extend the programming language with enough syntactic constructs that it is possible to give a transition system semantics between program fragments. A comparison of this semantics with Reppy's (1992) reduction semantics is given in (Ferreira, Hennessy, and Jeffrey 1995).

The semantics we provide has four transitions: reduction (τ), returning a value ($\checkmark v$), input on a channel ($k?x$), and output on a channel ($k!v$).

A transition $e \xrightarrow{\tau} e'$ represents a single-step reduction, for example[1]:

$$\mathtt{if\ true\ then\ 0\ else\ 1} \xrightarrow{\tau} 0$$

We will often write $e \Longrightarrow e'$ for $e \xrightarrow{\tau} \cdots \xrightarrow{\tau} e'$, for example:

$$\mathtt{if\ true\ then\ add(1,-1)\ else\ 1} \Longrightarrow 0$$

A transition $e \xrightarrow{\checkmark v} e'$ represents a process returning a value v, for example:

$$0 \xrightarrow{\checkmark 0} \delta$$

We will often write $e \stackrel{l}{\Longrightarrow} e'$ for $e \Longrightarrow\xrightarrow{l} e'$, for example:

$$\mathtt{if\ true\ then\ add(1,-1)\ else\ 1} \stackrel{\checkmark 0}{\Longrightarrow} \delta$$

In this case the computation is sequential, so the remaining computation after returning the value '0' is the empty computation 'δ'. CML allows processes to

[1]In this example, and in others, we have 'garbage collected' some empty processes by treating $\|$ as an associative operation with left unit δ. These equivalences are correct up to strong bisimulation.

$$
\begin{aligned}
\texttt{fst} &: A * B \to A \\
\texttt{snd} &: A * B \to B \\
\texttt{add} &: \texttt{int} * \texttt{int} \to \texttt{int} \\
\texttt{mul} &: \texttt{int} * \texttt{int} \to \texttt{int} \\
\texttt{leq} &: \texttt{int} * \texttt{int} \to \texttt{bool} \\
\texttt{transmit} &: A\ \texttt{chan} * A \to \texttt{unit event} \\
\texttt{receive} &: A\ \texttt{chan} \to A\ \texttt{event} \\
\texttt{choose} &: A\ \texttt{event} * A\ \texttt{event} \to A\ \texttt{event} \\
\texttt{spawn} &: \texttt{unit -> unit} \to \texttt{unit} \\
\texttt{sync} &: A\ \texttt{event} \to A \\
\texttt{wrap} &: A\ \texttt{event} * (A\ \texttt{->}\ B) \to B\ \texttt{event} \\
\texttt{never} &: \texttt{unit} \to A\ \texttt{event}
\end{aligned}
$$

Table 2: Types for μCML basic functions

spawn threads which can continue after their parent has terminated, so there are cases when the remaining computation is non-trivial, such as:

$$\texttt{spawn (fn () => send (a,0))} \xrightarrow{\checkmark()} \texttt{send (a,0)} \parallel \delta$$

Here '$\parallel$' represents the parallel composition of two processes, with the rightmost process being the main thread of computation, for example:

$$\texttt{spawn (fn () => send (a,0)); accept a} \Longrightarrow \texttt{send (a,0)} \parallel \texttt{accept a}$$

A transition $e \xrightarrow{k?x} e'$ represents an input on channel k, where e' has a free variable x, for example:

$$\texttt{accept a} \xrightarrow{\texttt{a?x}} x$$

Similarly, a transition $e \xrightarrow{k!v} e'$ represents an output of value v on channel k, for example:

$$\texttt{send (a,0)} \xrightarrow{\texttt{a!0}} ()$$

Input and output transitions can be synchronised to produce reductions, for example:

$$\texttt{send (a,0)} \parallel \texttt{accept a} \Longrightarrow () \parallel 0$$

Since the rightmost process in a concurrent expression is the 'main thread' this means there is an asymmetry in the operational semantics for $\checkmark$-actions: only the rightmost process may return a value. For example:

$$() \parallel 0 \xrightarrow{\checkmark 0} () \parallel \delta \qquad () \parallel 0 \not\xrightarrow{\checkmark()} \delta \parallel 0$$

In μCML there are no normal forms for pairs—such a normal form is needed for the operational semantics, so we will extend the language of values with pairs $\langle v, w \rangle$. This allows pairs of values to be communicated, for example since:

$$\texttt{(1,-1)} \xrightarrow{\checkmark\texttt{(1,-1)}} \delta$$

we have:

$$\texttt{send (b, (1,-1))} \xrightarrow{\texttt{b!(1,-1)}} \texttt{()}$$

and so we have the communication:

$$\texttt{send (b, (1,-1))} \parallel \texttt{add (accept b)} \Longrightarrow \texttt{()} \parallel \texttt{add}\langle\texttt{-1, 1}\rangle$$

So far we have only considered first-order processes, but CML is a higher-order language which can communicate values of any type, for example since **send** is defined to be a λ-abstraction:

$$\texttt{send} \xrightarrow{\checkmark\,\texttt{send}} \delta$$

so we have:

$$\texttt{send (b, send)} \xrightarrow{\texttt{b! send}} \texttt{()}$$

and so we have the higher-order communication:

$$\texttt{send (b, send)} \parallel \texttt{accept b(a,0)} \Longrightarrow \texttt{()} \parallel \texttt{send (a,0)}$$

CML also allows communications of events, so we need to extend the language in a similar fashion to Reppy (1992) to include values of event type. These values are of the form [*ge*] where *ge* is a CCS-style ***guarded sum***, for example:

$$\begin{aligned}
\texttt{transmit (a,0)} &\Longrightarrow [\texttt{a!0}] \\
\texttt{receive a} &\Longrightarrow [\texttt{a?}] \\
\texttt{choose (transmit (a,0) , receive a)} &\Longrightarrow [\texttt{a!0} \oplus \texttt{a?}] \\
\texttt{wrap (receive a, fn } x \texttt{ => e)} &\Longrightarrow [\texttt{a?} \Rightarrow \texttt{fn } x \texttt{ => e}]
\end{aligned}$$

This syntax is based on Reppy's, and is slightly different from that normally associated with process calculi, for example:

- we write $\texttt{a!0} \oplus \texttt{a?}$ rather than $\texttt{a!0} + \texttt{a?}$, and
- we write $\texttt{a?} \Rightarrow \texttt{fn } x \texttt{ => } e$ rather than $\texttt{a?}x.e$.

By extending the syntax of μCML expressions to include guarded expressions, we get a particularly simple semantics for sync as just removing the outermost level of [_], for example:

$$\begin{aligned}
&\texttt{send (a,0)} \\
&\quad \Longrightarrow \texttt{sync (transmit (a,0))}
\end{aligned}$$

$$\frac{\Gamma \vdash \mathtt{e} : A \quad \Gamma \vdash \mathtt{f} : B}{\Gamma \vdash \mathtt{e} \parallel \mathtt{f} : B} \qquad \frac{}{\Gamma \vdash \delta : A}$$

$$\frac{\Gamma \vdash \mathtt{v} : A \quad \Gamma \vdash \mathtt{w} : B}{\Gamma \vdash \langle \mathtt{v}, \mathtt{w} \rangle : A * B} \qquad \frac{\Gamma \vdash \mathtt{e} : A}{\Gamma \vdash [\mathtt{e}] : A\ \mathtt{event}}$$

$$\frac{\Gamma \vdash \mathtt{v} : A\ \mathtt{chan} \quad \Gamma \vdash \mathtt{w} : A}{\Gamma \vdash \mathtt{v!w} : \mathtt{unit}} \qquad \frac{\Gamma \vdash \mathtt{v} : A\ \mathtt{chan}}{\Gamma \vdash \mathtt{v?} : A}$$

$$\frac{\Gamma \vdash ge_1 : A \quad \Gamma \vdash ge_2 : A}{\Gamma \vdash ge_1 \oplus ge_2 : A} \qquad \frac{\Gamma \vdash ge : A \quad \Gamma \vdash \mathtt{v} : A \to B}{\Gamma \vdash ge \Rightarrow \mathtt{v} : B}$$

Table 3: Types for μCML$^+$ expressions

$$\begin{aligned} &\Longrightarrow \ \mathtt{sync\ [a!0]} \\ &\Longrightarrow \ \mathtt{a!0} \\ &\xrightarrow{\mathtt{a!0}} \ () \end{aligned}$$

In summary, we give the operational semantics for μCML by first extending it to μCML$^+$ by adding expressions:

$$\mathtt{e} ::= \cdots \mid \mathtt{e} \parallel \mathtt{e} \mid ge$$

adding values:

$$\mathtt{v} ::= \cdots \mid \langle \mathtt{v}, \mathtt{v} \rangle \mid [ge]$$

and adding guarded expressions:

$$ge ::= k? \mid k!\mathtt{v} \mid \delta \mid ge \oplus ge \mid ge \Rightarrow \mathtt{v}$$

The typing for μCML$^+$ extends that of μCML with the rules in Table 3.

The extended language μCML$^+$ has a semantics as a labelled transition system with labels:

$$\mu ::= k!\mathtt{v} \mid k?x \qquad \alpha ::= \tau \mid \mu \qquad l ::= \alpha \mid \checkmark \mathtt{v}$$

The operational semantics is given in Tables 4–8.

This operational semantics is very fine-grained, and is designed to mimic the execution of a CML program very closely. As a result, derivations of fairly simple computations can be surprisingly long. For example, one reduction of $\mathtt{cell}\langle i, o\rangle$ is given in Table 9.

2.3 Bisimulation

As we mentioned above, one reason for choosing a labelled transition system semantics over a reduction semantics is that we can define *bisimulation* as an

$$\frac{e \xrightarrow{\alpha} e'}{ce \xrightarrow{\alpha} ce'} \quad \frac{e \xrightarrow{\alpha} e'}{\texttt{if}\ e\ \texttt{then}\ f\ \texttt{else}\ g \xrightarrow{\alpha} \texttt{if}\ e'\ \texttt{then}\ f\ \texttt{else}\ g}$$

$$\frac{e \xrightarrow{\alpha} e'}{(e,f) \xrightarrow{\alpha} (e',f)} \quad \frac{e \xrightarrow{\alpha} e'}{\texttt{let}\ x = e\ \texttt{in}\ f \xrightarrow{\alpha} \texttt{let}\ x = e'\ \texttt{in}\ f}$$

$$\frac{f \xrightarrow{\alpha} f'}{fe \xrightarrow{\alpha} f'e} \quad \frac{e \xrightarrow{\alpha} e'}{e \parallel f \xrightarrow{\alpha} e' \parallel f} \quad \frac{f \xrightarrow{l} f'}{e \parallel f \xrightarrow{l} e \parallel f'}$$

Table 4: CML operational semantics: static rules

$$\frac{ge_1 \xrightarrow{\alpha} e}{ge_1 \oplus ge_2 \xrightarrow{\alpha} e} \quad \frac{ge_2 \xrightarrow{\alpha} e}{ge_1 \oplus ge_2 \xrightarrow{\alpha} e} \quad \frac{ge \xrightarrow{\alpha} e}{ge \Rightarrow v \xrightarrow{\alpha} ve}$$

Table 5: CML operational semantics: dynamic rules

$$\frac{f \xrightarrow{\checkmark v} f'}{fe \xrightarrow{\tau} f' \parallel \texttt{let}\ y = e\ \texttt{in}\ g[v/x]} [v = \texttt{rec}\ x = \texttt{fn}\ y \texttt{=>}\ g]$$

$$\frac{e \xrightarrow{\checkmark v} e'}{ce \xrightarrow{\tau} e' \parallel \delta(c, v)}$$

$$\frac{e \xrightarrow{\checkmark \texttt{true}} e'}{\texttt{if}\ e\ \texttt{then}\ f\ \texttt{else}\ g \xrightarrow{\tau} e' \parallel f} \quad \frac{e \xrightarrow{\checkmark \texttt{false}} e'}{\texttt{if}\ e\ \texttt{then}\ f\ \texttt{else}\ g \xrightarrow{\tau} e' \parallel g}$$

$$\frac{e \xrightarrow{\checkmark v} e'}{(e,f) \xrightarrow{\tau} e' \parallel \texttt{let}\ x = f\ \texttt{in}\ \langle v, x\rangle} \quad \frac{e \xrightarrow{\checkmark v} e'}{\texttt{let}\ x = e\ \texttt{in}\ f \xrightarrow{\tau} e' \parallel f[v/x]}$$

$$\frac{e \xrightarrow{k!v} e' \quad f \xrightarrow{k?x} f'}{e \parallel f \xrightarrow{\tau} e' \parallel f'[v/x]} \quad \frac{e \xrightarrow{k?x} e' \quad f \xrightarrow{k!v} f'}{e \parallel f \xrightarrow{\tau} e'[v/x] \parallel f'}$$

Table 6: CML operational semantics: silent reductions

$$\frac{}{v \xrightarrow{\checkmark v} \delta} \quad \frac{}{k!v \xrightarrow{k!v} ()} \quad \frac{}{k? \xrightarrow{k?x} x}$$

Table 7: CML operational semantics: axioms

$$
\begin{array}{rclrcl}
\delta(\mathtt{fst}, \langle v, w \rangle) & = & v & \delta(\mathtt{transmit}, \langle k, v \rangle) & = & [k!v] \\
\delta(\mathtt{snd}, \langle v, w \rangle) & = & w & \delta(\mathtt{receive}, k) & = & [k?] \\
\delta(\mathtt{add}, \langle m, n \rangle) & = & m + n & \delta(\mathtt{choose}, \langle [ge_1], [ge_2] \rangle) & = & [ge_1 \oplus ge_2] \\
\delta(\mathtt{mul}, \langle m, n \rangle) & = & m \times n & \delta(\mathtt{wrap}, \langle [ge], v \rangle) & = & [ge \Rightarrow v] \\
\delta(\mathtt{leq}, \langle m, n \rangle) & = & m \leq n & \delta(\mathtt{spawn}, v) & = & v() \parallel () \\
\delta(\mathtt{sync}, [ge]) & = & ge & \delta(\mathtt{never}, ()) & = & [\delta]
\end{array}
$$

Table 8: CML operational semantics: basic functions

equivalence on programs. This is discussed at length in (Ferreira, Hennessy, and Jeffrey 1995), and is summarised here. We will use notation adapted from Gordon's (1995) presentation of Howe's (1989) proof technique.

Let an *open type-indexed* relation $\mathcal{R}$ be a family of relations $\mathcal{R}_{\Gamma,A}$ such that if $e\ \mathcal{R}_{\Gamma,A}\ f$ then $\Gamma \vdash e : A$ and $\Gamma \vdash f : A$. We will often elide the subscripts from relations, for example writing $e\ \mathcal{R}\ f$ for $e\ \mathcal{R}_{\Gamma,A}\ f$ when context makes the type obvious.

Let a *closed type-indexed* relation $\mathcal{R}$ be an open type-indexed relation where Γ is everywhere the empty context, and can therefore be elided.

For any closed type-indexed relation $\mathcal{R}$, let its *open extension* $\mathcal{R}^\circ$ be defined as:

$$e\ \mathcal{R}^\circ_{\vec{x}:\vec{A},B}\ f \text{ iff } e[\vec{v}/\vec{x}]\ \mathcal{R}_B\ f[\vec{v}/\vec{x}] \text{ for all } \vdash \vec{v} : \vec{A}.$$

A closed type-indexed relation $\mathcal{R}$ is *structure preserving* iff:

- if $v\ \mathcal{R}_A\ w$ and A is a base type then $v = w$,
- if $\langle v_1, v_2 \rangle\ \mathcal{R}_{A_1 * A_2}\ \langle w_1, w_2 \rangle$ then $v_i\ \mathcal{R}_{A_i}\ w_i$,
- if $[ge_1]\ \mathcal{R}_{A\ \mathtt{event}}\ [ge_2]$ then $ge_1\ \mathcal{R}_A\ ge_2$, and
- if $v\ \mathcal{R}_{A \text{->} B}\ v'$ then for all $\vdash w : A$ we have $vw\ \mathcal{R}_B\ v'w$.

A closed type-indexed relation $\mathcal{R}$ is a *first-order strong simulation* iff it is structure preserving and the following diagram can be completed:

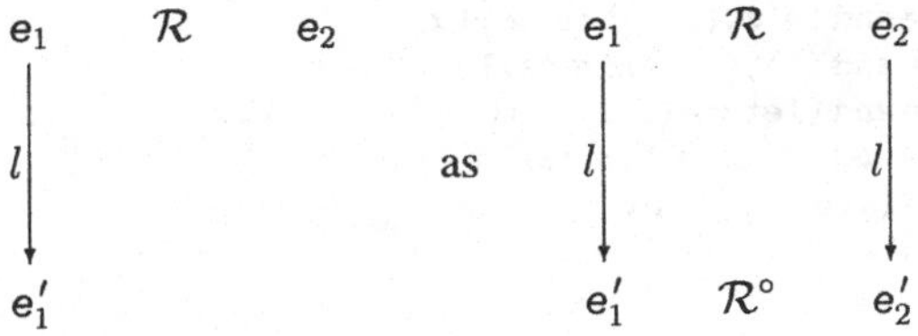

Note the use of the open extension $\mathcal{R}^\circ$. This means, for example, that if $e_1\ \mathcal{R}\ e_2$ we require that the move $e_1 \xrightarrow{k?x} f_1$ be matched by a move $e_2 \xrightarrow{k?x} f_2$ where

```
cell⟨i,o⟩
   ─τ→  let x = ⟨i,o⟩ in cell ( snd (send ( snd x, accept ( fst x)),x))
   ─τ→  cell ( snd (send ( snd ⟨i,o⟩, accept ( fst ⟨i,o⟩)),⟨i,o⟩))
   ─τ→  let x = snd (send ( snd ⟨i,o⟩, accept ( fst ⟨i,o⟩)),⟨i,o⟩)
        in cell x
   ─τ→  let x = snd (let y = ( snd ⟨i,o⟩, accept ( fst ⟨i,o⟩))
                     in sync ( transmit y)
                    ,⟨i,o⟩)
        in cell x
   ─τ→  let x = snd (let y = (o, accept ( fst ⟨i,o⟩))
                     in sync ( transmit y)
                    ,⟨i,o⟩)
        in cell x
   ─τ→  let x = snd (let y = let z = accept ( fst ⟨i,o⟩) in ⟨o,z⟩
                     in sync ( transmit y)
                    ,⟨i,o⟩)
        in cell x
   ─τ→  let x = snd (let y = let z = let x' = fst ⟨i,o⟩ in sync ( receive x') in ⟨o,z⟩
                     in sync ( transmit y)
                    ,⟨i,o⟩)
        in cell x
   ─τ→  let x = snd (let y = let z = let x' = i in sync ( receive x') in ⟨o,z⟩
                     in sync ( transmit y)
                    ,⟨i,o⟩)
        in cell x
   ─τ→  let x = snd (let y = let z = sync ( receive i) in ⟨o,z⟩
                     in sync ( transmit y)
                    ,⟨i,o⟩)
        in cell x
   ─τ→  let x = snd (let y = let z = sync [i?] in ⟨o,z⟩ in sync ( transmit y),⟨i,o⟩)
        in cell x
   ─τ→  let x = snd (let y = let z = i? in ⟨o,z⟩ in sync ( transmit y),⟨i,o⟩)
        in cell x
  ─i?v→ let x = snd (let y = let z = v in ⟨o,z⟩ in sync ( transmit y),⟨i,o⟩)
        in cell x
   ─τ→  let x = snd (let y = ⟨o,v⟩ in sync ( transmit y),⟨i,o⟩)
        in cell x
   ─τ→  let x = snd ( sync ( transmit⟨o,v⟩),⟨i,o⟩) in cell x
   ─τ→  let x = snd ( sync [o!v],⟨i,o⟩) in cell x
   ─τ→  let x = snd (o!v,⟨i,o⟩) in cell x
  ─o!v→ let x = snd ((),⟨i,o⟩) in cell x
   ─τ→  let x = snd (let y = ⟨i,o⟩ in ((),y)) in cell x
   ─τ→  let x = snd⟨(),⟨i,o⟩⟩ in cell x
   ─τ→  let x = ⟨i,o⟩ in cell x
   ─τ→  cell ⟨i,o⟩
```

Table 9: CML operational semantics: example reduction

f_2 is such that for all values $\vdash v : B$ we have $f_1[v/x] \; \mathcal{R} \; f_2[v/x]$. Thus in the terminology of (Milner, Parrow, and Walker 1992) our definition corresponds to the *late* version of bisimulation.

$\mathcal{R}$ is a *first-order strong bisimulation* iff $\mathcal{R}$ and $\mathcal{R}^{-1}$ are first-order strong simulations. Let $\sim^1$ be the largest first-order strong bisimulation.

Proposition 1 $\sim^1$ *is an equivalence.*

Proof Use diagram chases to show that if $\mathcal{R}$ is a first-order strong simulation then so are I and $\mathcal{R}\mathcal{R}$. The result follows. $\qquad\square$

Unfortunately, $\sim^1$ is not a congruence for μCML^+, since we have:

$$\text{add } (1,-1) \sim^1 \text{add } (-1,1)$$

however, sending the thunked expressions on channel a we get:

$$\text{transmit } (\text{a,fn } x \Rightarrow \text{add } (1,-1)) \not\sim^1 \text{transmit } (\text{a,fn } x \Rightarrow \text{add } (-1,1))$$

since the left hand side can perform the move:

$$\text{transmit } (\text{a,fn } x \Rightarrow \text{add } (1,-1)) \xrightarrow{\text{a!fn } x \;\Rightarrow\; \text{add } (1,-1)} ()$$

but this can only be matched by the right hand side up to strong bisimulation:

$$\text{transmit } (\text{a,fn } x \Rightarrow \text{add } (-1,1)) \xrightarrow{\text{a!fn } x \;\Rightarrow\; \text{add } (-1,1)} ()$$

The problem is that the definition of strong bisimulation demands that the actions performed by expressions match up to syntactic identity, rather than up to strong bisimulation. In fact, it is easy to verify that the only first-order strong bisimulation which is a congruence for μCML is the identity relation.

To find a satisfactory treatment of bisimulation for μCML, we need to look to *higher-order bisimulation*, where the structure of the labels is accounted for. To this end, given a closed type-indexed relation $\mathcal{R}$, define its *extension to labels* $\mathcal{R}^l$ as:

$$\frac{}{\tau \; \mathcal{R}_A^l \; \tau} \qquad \frac{v \; \mathcal{R}_A \; w}{\checkmark v \; \mathcal{R}_A^l \; \checkmark w} \qquad \frac{}{kx \; \mathcal{R}_A^l \; k?x} \qquad \frac{v \; \mathcal{R}_B \; w}{k!v \; \mathcal{R}_A^l \; k!w}[k \in K_B]$$

Then $\mathcal{R}$ is a *higher-order strong simulation* iff it is structure preserving and the following diagram can be completed:

$$
\begin{array}{ccc}
e_1 & \mathcal{R} & e_2 \\
\Big\downarrow{\scriptstyle l_1} & & \\
e_1' & &
\end{array}
\qquad \text{as} \qquad
\begin{array}{ccc}
e_1 & \mathcal{R} & e_2 \\
\Big\downarrow{\scriptstyle l_1} & & \Big\downarrow{\scriptstyle l_2} \\
e_1' & \mathcal{R}^\circ & e_2'
\end{array}
\quad \text{where } l_1 \; \mathcal{R}^l \; l_2
$$

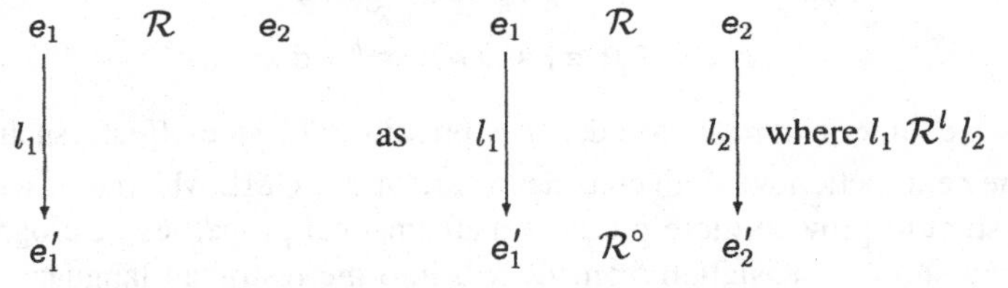

Let $\sim^h$ be the largest higher-order strong bisimulation.

Proposition 2 *$\sim^h$ is a congruence.*

Proof Use a similar technique to the proof of Proposition 1 to show that $\sim^h$ is an equivalence. To show that $\sim^h$ is a congruence, define $\mathcal{R}$ as:

$$\mathcal{R} = \{(C[e], C[f]) \mid e \sim^h f\}$$

and then show by induction on C that $\mathcal{R}$ is a simulation. The result follows. □

For many purposes, strong bisimulation is too fine an equivalence as it is sensitive to the number of reductions performed by expressions. This means it will not even validate elementary properties such as β-reduction. We require the looser *weak bisimulation* which allows τ reductions to be ignored.

Let $\stackrel{\hat{l}}{\Longrightarrow}$ be $\Longrightarrow$ if $l = \tau$ and $\stackrel{l}{\Longrightarrow}$ otherwise. Then $\mathcal{R}$ is a *higher-order weak simulation* iff it is structure preserving and the following diagram can be completed:

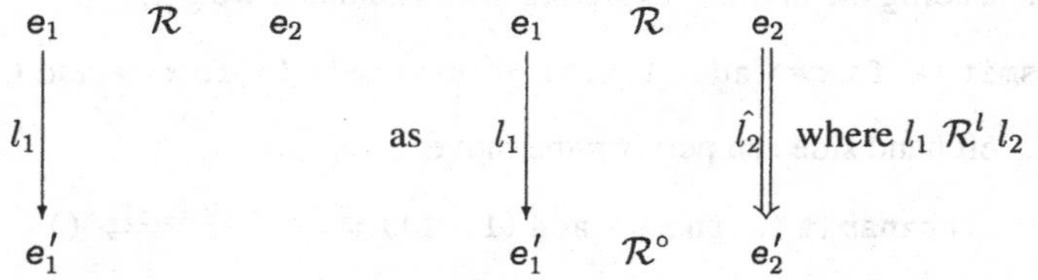

A *higher-order weak bisimulation* is a higher-order weak simulation whose inverse is also a higher-order weak simulation. Let $\approx^h$ be the largest higher-order weak bisimulation.

Proposition 3 *$\approx^h$ is a congruence.*

Proof Given in (Ferreira, Hennessy, and Jeffrey 1995), using a variant of Gordon's (1995) presentation Howe's (1989) proof technique. Note that this proof relies on the fact that we are considering the subset of μCML without `always`, and hence do not have to consider initial τ-actions in summations, which present the same problems as in the first-order case (Milner 1989). □

Unfortunately, this equivalence does not have many pleasant mathematical properties. For example none of the usual equations for products are true:

$$\texttt{fst (e,f)} \not\approx^h \texttt{e}$$
$$\texttt{snd (e,f)} \not\approx^h \texttt{f}$$
$$\texttt{(fst e, snd e)} \not\approx^h \texttt{e}$$

(For each counter-example consider an expression with side-effects, such as `cell`.)

In the next section we shall consider a variant of μCML which uses a restrictive type system to provide more pleasant mathematical properties of programs. We shall then show a translation from μCML into the restricted language, which is correct up to weak bisimulation.

3 Concurrent monadic ML

In the previous section, we showed how to define an operational semantics for CML which can be used as the basis of a bisimulation equivalence between programs. Unfortunately, this equivalence does not have pleasant mathematical properties. For example β-conversion does not hold:

$$\texttt{(fn x => (x,x))(cell (a,b))} \not\approx^h \texttt{(cell (a,b), cell (a,b))}$$

Because CML computations are non-trivial (CML processes may diverge, and can have side-effects) we cannot use the standard mathematical models of typed λ-calculi such as cartesian closed categories (Lambek and Scott 1986).

In this section, we present a *Concurrent Monadic ML* (*CMML*) a variant of CML with a type system based on Moggi's (1991) computation types. Such type systems have proved popular in giving an elegant treatment to functional languages with non-trivial computation, such as Concurrent Haskell (Peyton Jones, Gordon, and Finne 1996).

CMML can be provided with an operational semantics similar to that given to CML in the previous section, although the semantics is much simpler, and has pleasant properties such as forming a category with finite products and a restricted class of exponentials.

The language presented here (μCMML) is a subset of the language presented in (Jeffrey 1995a).

3.1 Syntax

The main difference between CMML and CML is that the distinction between values and expressions is handled by the CMML type system rather than as a separate syntactic category. For example, in CML we have:

$$\vdash \texttt{0} : \texttt{int} \text{ (a value)} \qquad \vdash \texttt{add (-1,1)} : \texttt{int} \text{ (an expression)}$$

whereas in CMML we have:

$$\vdash 0 : \mathsf{int} \text{ (an expression)} \qquad \vdash \mathsf{add}\langle -1, 1\rangle : \mathsf{int\,comp} \text{ (an expression)}$$

This uses an explicit type constructor $A\,\mathsf{comp}$ to represent computations which return results of type A. For example $\mathsf{add}\langle -1, 1\rangle$ returns the result 0, so it has the type $\mathsf{int\,comp}$.

Moggi (1991) proposed two syntactic constructions for manipulating computation types:

- the expression $[e]$ which immediately returns e, and
- the expression $\mathsf{let}\ x \Leftarrow e\ \mathsf{in}\ f$ which evaluates e, binds the result to x and then evaluates f.

For example $(1+1)+(1+1)$ can be calculated as:

$$\begin{aligned}&\mathsf{let}\, x \Leftarrow [1]\\&\mathsf{in\,let}\, y \Leftarrow \mathsf{add}\langle x, x\rangle\\&\quad\mathsf{in\,add}\langle y, y\rangle\end{aligned}$$

Note that expressions written in μCMML tend to be more long-winded than their μCML equivalents: this is because the flow of execution through a μCMML program is made explicit by the use of let-expressions. Such an explicit language may seem overly verbose to functional programmers used to programming in the SML style, where execution order is implicit in the left-to-right evaluation order. However, as we shall see, making execution order explicit has the benefit of a simpler semantics and better equational properties.

Using an explicit type constructor for computation has the advantage that the only terms which perform computation are those of type $A\,\mathsf{comp}$, and that an expression of any other type is guaranteed to be in normal form. This gives us the normal form results (Proposition 4 below):

- the only closed term of type unit is (),
- the only closed terms of type bool are true and false,
- the only closed terms of type int are $\ldots, -1, 0, 1, \ldots$,
- the only closed terms of type $A\,\mathsf{chan}$ are a, b, ...,
- the only closed terms of type $A * B$ are of the form $\langle e, f\rangle$, and
- the only closed terms of type $A \to B\,\mathsf{comp}$ are of the form $\mathsf{rec}\, x = \mathsf{fn}\, y \Rightarrow e$.

These results make the operational semantics much simpler to define, for example rather than two rules for function application:

$$\frac{e \xrightarrow{\alpha} e'}{ef \xrightarrow{\alpha} e'f} \qquad \frac{e \xrightarrow{\surd v} e'}{ef \xrightarrow{\tau} e' \parallel \mathtt{let}\; y = f\; \mathtt{in}\; g[v/x]}[v = \mathtt{rec}\; x = \mathtt{fn}\; y \Rightarrow g]$$

we only need one simple β-reduction rule:

$$\frac{}{f\, e \xrightarrow{\tau} g[e/y][f/x]}[f = (\mathsf{rec}\, x = \mathsf{fn}\, y \Rightarrow g)]$$

The simplicity of the operational semantics rests on the normal form result described above, but this requires a somewhat non-standard treatment of projections on pairs. In μCML projections are given using `fst` and `snd`, for example a function to swap a pair is:

$$\vdash \mathtt{fn}\, x \Rightarrow (\mathtt{snd}\, x, \mathtt{fst}\, x) : A * B \to B * A$$

If we were to allow `fst` and snd in CMML we would no longer have the normal form result described above. However, projections on pairs are useful both practically and as the categorical basis of products. In CMML we use a restricted form of projections which maintains the normal form result: we use Pascal-style record field selection on *selector expressions* rather than ML-style selection functions. If x is a variable of type $A * B$ then $x.\mathsf{l}$ is a selector expression of type A, and $x.\mathsf{r}$ is a selector expression of type B. For example a CMML function to swap a pair is:

$$\vdash \mathsf{fn}\, x \Rightarrow [\langle x.\mathsf{r}, x.\mathsf{l}\rangle] : A * B \to (B * A)\,\mathsf{comp}$$

Similarly, we need to use a restricted form of function space, since the result of any function application should be a computation. This means that rather than the CML function type:

$$\frac{\Gamma, x : A \texttt{->} B, y : A \vdash e : B}{\Gamma \vdash \texttt{rec}\, x \texttt{=} \texttt{fn}\, y \texttt{=>} e : A \texttt{->} B} \qquad \frac{\Gamma \vdash e : A \texttt{->} B \quad \Gamma \vdash f : A}{\Gamma \vdash ef : B}$$

we have the restricted CMML function type:

$$\frac{\Gamma, x : A \to B\,\mathsf{comp}, y : A \vdash e : B\,\mathsf{comp}}{\Gamma \vdash \mathsf{rec}\, x = \mathsf{fn}\, y \Rightarrow e : A \to B\,\mathsf{comp}} \qquad \frac{\Gamma \vdash f : A \to B\,\mathsf{comp} \quad \Gamma \vdash e : A}{\Gamma \vdash f\, e : B\,\mathsf{comp}}$$

For example there is no CMML projection function with type $A * B \to A$, instead we have:

$$\vdash \mathsf{fn}\, x \Rightarrow [x.\mathsf{l}] : A * B \to A\,\mathsf{comp}$$

The concurrent features of μCMML are similar to those of μCML$^+$, for example a concurrent communication is given by:

$$k!0 \parallel k? \xrightarrow{\tau} [()] \parallel [0]$$

We will now give the grammar and type system for μCMML.

Integers and channels are given as for μCML:

$$\begin{aligned} n &::= \cdots \mid -1 \mid 0 \mid 1 \mid \cdots \\ k &::= \mathsf{a} \mid \mathsf{b} \mid \cdots \end{aligned}$$

Basic functions are given by the grammar:

$$c ::= \mathsf{add} \mid \mathsf{mul} \mid \mathsf{leq}$$

Expressions are given by the grammar:

$$\begin{aligned} e ::= {} & \mathsf{true} \mid \mathsf{false} \mid n \mid k \mid () \mid \mathsf{rec}\, x = \mathsf{fn}\, x \Rightarrow e \mid c\, e \\ & \mid \mathsf{if}\, e\, \mathsf{then}\, e\, \mathsf{else}\, e \mid \mathsf{let}\, x \Leftarrow e\, \mathsf{in}\, e \mid e\, e \mid lv \mid [e] \mid \langle e, e\rangle \\ & \mid \delta \mid e \parallel e \mid e \,\square\, e \mid e!e \mid e? \end{aligned}$$

$$\frac{}{\Gamma \vdash \mathsf{true} : \mathsf{bool}} \quad \frac{}{\Gamma \vdash \mathsf{false} : \mathsf{bool}} \quad \frac{}{\Gamma \vdash n : \mathsf{int}}$$

$$\frac{}{\Gamma \vdash k : A\,\mathsf{chan}}[k \in K_A] \quad \frac{}{\Gamma \vdash () : \mathsf{unit}}$$

$$\frac{\Gamma \vdash e : A}{\Gamma \vdash c\,e : B\,\mathsf{comp}}[c : A \to B\,\mathsf{comp}] \quad \frac{\Gamma, x : A \to B\,\mathsf{comp}, y : A \vdash e : B\,\mathsf{comp}}{\Gamma \vdash \mathsf{rec}\,x = \mathsf{fn}\,y \Rightarrow e : A \to B\,\mathsf{comp}}$$

$$\frac{\Gamma \vdash e : \mathsf{bool} \quad \Gamma \vdash f : A\,\mathsf{comp} \quad \Gamma \vdash g : A\,\mathsf{comp}}{\Gamma \vdash \mathsf{if}\,e\,\mathsf{then}\,f\,\mathsf{else}\,g : A\,\mathsf{comp}}$$

$$\frac{\Gamma \vdash e : A\,\mathsf{comp} \quad \Gamma, x : A \vdash f : B\,\mathsf{comp}}{\Gamma \vdash \mathsf{let}\,x \Leftarrow e\,\mathsf{in}\,f : B\,\mathsf{comp}} \quad \frac{\Gamma \vdash f : A \to B\,\mathsf{comp} \quad \Gamma \vdash e : A}{\Gamma \vdash f\,e : B\,\mathsf{comp}}$$

$$\frac{}{\Gamma, x : A \vdash x : A} \quad \frac{\Gamma \vdash x : A}{\Gamma, y : B \vdash x : A}[x \neq y] \quad \frac{\Gamma \vdash lv : A * B}{\Gamma \vdash lv.\mathsf{l} : A} \quad \frac{\Gamma \vdash lv : A * B}{\Gamma \vdash lv.\mathsf{r} : B}$$

$$\frac{\Gamma \vdash e : A}{\Gamma \vdash [e] : A\,\mathsf{comp}} \quad \frac{\Gamma \vdash e : A \quad \Gamma \vdash f : B}{\Gamma \vdash \langle e, f \rangle : A * B}$$

$$\frac{}{\Gamma \vdash \delta : A\,\mathsf{comp}} \quad \frac{\Gamma \vdash e : A\,\mathsf{comp} \quad \Gamma \vdash f : B\,\mathsf{comp}}{\Gamma \vdash e \parallel f : B\,\mathsf{comp}}$$

$$\frac{\Gamma \vdash e : A\,\mathsf{comp} \quad \Gamma \vdash f : A\,\mathsf{comp}}{\Gamma \vdash e \,\Box\, f : A\,\mathsf{comp}} \quad \frac{\Gamma \vdash e : A\,\mathsf{chan} \quad \Gamma \vdash f : A}{\Gamma \vdash e!f : \mathsf{unit}\,\mathsf{comp}} \quad \frac{\Gamma \vdash e : A\,\mathsf{chan}}{\Gamma \vdash e? : A\,\mathsf{comp}}$$

Table 10: Types for μCMML expressions

$$\begin{aligned} \mathsf{add} &: \mathsf{int} * \mathsf{int} \to \mathsf{int}\,\mathsf{comp} \\ \mathsf{mul} &: \mathsf{int} * \mathsf{int} \to \mathsf{int}\,\mathsf{comp} \\ \mathsf{leq} &: \mathsf{int} * \mathsf{int} \to \mathsf{bool}\,\mathsf{comp} \end{aligned}$$

Table 11: Types for μCMML basic functions

Selector expressions are given by the grammar:

$$lv ::= x \mid lv.\mathsf{l} \mid lv.\mathsf{r}$$

Types are given by the grammar:

$$A ::= \mathsf{unit} \mid \mathsf{bool} \mid \mathsf{int} \mid A\,\mathsf{chan} \mid A * A \mid A \to A\,\mathsf{comp} \mid A\,\mathsf{comp}$$

Typing is given by Tables 10 and 11.

Proposition 4 *We have the following normal form results:*

1. *If* $\Gamma \vdash e : \mathsf{unit}$ *then* e *is an selector or* $e = ()$.

2. *If* $\Gamma \vdash \mathsf{e} : \mathsf{bool}$ *then* e *is an selector or* $\mathsf{e} = \mathsf{true}$ *or* $\mathsf{e} = \mathsf{false}$.

3. *If* $\Gamma \vdash \mathsf{e} : \mathsf{int}$ *then* e *is an selector or* $\mathsf{e} = n$.

4. *If* $\Gamma \vdash \mathsf{e} : A\,\mathsf{chan}$ *then* e *is an selector or* $\mathsf{e} = k$.

5. *If* $\Gamma \vdash \mathsf{e} : A * B$ *then* e *is an selector or* $\mathsf{e} = \langle f, g \rangle$.

6. *If* $\Gamma \vdash \mathsf{e} : A \to B\,\mathsf{comp}$ *then* e *is an selector or* $\mathsf{e} = (\mathsf{rec}\, x = \mathsf{fn}\, y \Rightarrow f)$.

Proof A case analysis on the proof of $\Gamma \vdash \mathsf{e} : A$. □

When $\Gamma \vdash e : A$ and $\Gamma, x : A \vdash f : B$, define the substitution $\Gamma \vdash f[e/x] : B$ as normal, except that:

$$lv.\mathsf{l}[e/x] = \pi(lv[e/x]) \qquad lv.\mathsf{r}[e/x] = \pi'(lv[e/x])$$

where:

$$\pi\langle e, f \rangle = e \quad \pi lv = lv.\mathsf{l} \quad \pi'\langle e, f \rangle = f \quad \pi' lv = lv.\mathsf{r}$$

Note that this is well-defined because of Proposition 4.5.

As an example μCMML program, consider a one-place buffer:

$$\begin{aligned} \mathsf{cell} &: A\,\mathsf{chan} * A\,\mathsf{chan} \to B\,\mathsf{comp} \\ \mathsf{cell}\langle i, o \rangle &\stackrel{\mathsf{def}}{=} \mathsf{let}\, x \Leftarrow i?\, \mathsf{in}\, \mathsf{let}\, y \Leftarrow o!x\, \mathsf{in}\, \mathsf{cell}\langle i, o \rangle \end{aligned}$$

Comparing this definition with its μCML equivalent is instructive, so we shall repeat the definition here:

```
       cell   :  A chan * A chan -> B
cell (x,y)  def=  cell ( snd (send (y, accept x), (x,y)))
```

Writing programs in μCMML can be repetitive, because of the number of let-expressions required. However, the let-expressions are precisely what controls the flow of execution through a μCMML program, so it is easier to recognise the behaviour of a μCMML program. In the above example, it requires some thought to realise that `cell(a, b)` will input on a before outputting the result on b, and that the process does not just simply diverge, whereas the execution of the μCMML equivalent is much more obvious.

In Section 4 we shall see that μCML programs can be translated into μCMML, and that in particular we can perform some simple equational reasoning to transform `cell` into cell.

3.2 Operational semantics

The operational semantics for μCMML is given in Tables 12–15. It is similar to that of μCML, except that it is simpler, due to the normal form results in Proposition 4. For example, since any closed term of type bool must be either true or false, the only two rules required for if-statements in μCMML are:

$$\frac{}{\mathsf{if\ true\ then}\ f\ \mathsf{else}\ g \xrightarrow{\tau} f} \qquad \frac{}{\mathsf{if\ false\ then}\ f\ \mathsf{else}\ g \xrightarrow{\tau} g}$$

This can be compared with the more complex three rules required for μCML:

$$\frac{e \xrightarrow{\surd \mathtt{true}} e'}{\mathtt{if}\ e\ \mathtt{then}\ f\ \mathtt{else}\ g \xrightarrow{\tau} e' \parallel f} \qquad \frac{e \xrightarrow{\surd \mathtt{false}} e'}{\mathtt{if}\ e\ \mathtt{then}\ f\ \mathtt{else}\ g \xrightarrow{\tau} e' \parallel g}$$

$$\frac{e \xrightarrow{\alpha} e'}{\mathtt{if}\ e\ \mathtt{then}\ f\ \mathtt{else}\ g \xrightarrow{\alpha} \mathtt{if}\ e'\ \mathtt{then}\ f\ \mathtt{else}\ g}$$

In the operational semantics of μCML, terms in many contexts can reduce, whereas there are far fewer reduction contexts in μCMML. In fact, looking at the sequential sub-language of μCMML (without $\parallel$ or $\square$) the only reduction context is let:

$$\frac{e \xrightarrow{\alpha} e'}{\mathsf{let}\ x \Leftarrow e\ \mathsf{in}\ f \xrightarrow{\alpha} \mathsf{let}\ x \Leftarrow e'\ \mathsf{in}\ f}$$

Many of the operational rules in μCML require spawning off concurrent processes, whereas in μCMML the main rule which produces extra concurrent processes is β-reduction for let-expressions:

$$\frac{e \xrightarrow{\surd g} e'}{\mathsf{let}\ x \Leftarrow e\ \mathsf{in}\ f \xrightarrow{\tau} e' \parallel f[g/x]}$$

The other significant difference between the operational semantics for μCML and μCMML is the treatment of summation. In μCML choice is only allowed between guarded expressions $ge_1 \oplus ge_2$, whereas in μCMML choice is allowed between arbitrary expressions $e \square f$. In particular, this means we need operational rules for when processes in a choice can perform silent reductions:

$$\frac{e \xrightarrow{\tau} e'}{e \square f \xrightarrow{\tau} e' \square f} \qquad \frac{f \xrightarrow{\tau} f'}{e \square f \xrightarrow{\tau} e \square f'}$$

and when processes in a choice can return a value:

$$\frac{e \xrightarrow{\surd g} e'}{e \square f \xrightarrow{\tau} e' \parallel [g]} \qquad \frac{f \xrightarrow{\surd g} f'}{e \square f \xrightarrow{\tau} f' \parallel [g]}$$

Note that we are using rules for choice based on CSP (Hoare 1985) external choice rather than CCS (Milner 1989) summation. This is because we will be using $\approx^h$ as our equivalence on programs, and CCS summation does not preserve weak bisimulation. We have used slightly different termination rules for choice from

$$\frac{e \xrightarrow{\alpha} e'}{\text{let}\, x \Leftarrow e \,\text{in}\, f \xrightarrow{\alpha} \text{let}\, x \Leftarrow e' \,\text{in}\, f}$$

$$\frac{e \xrightarrow{\alpha} e'}{e \parallel f \xrightarrow{\alpha} e' \parallel f} \quad \frac{f \xrightarrow{l} f'}{e \parallel f \xrightarrow{l} e \parallel f'} \quad \frac{e \xrightarrow{\tau} e'}{e \,\Box\, f \xrightarrow{\tau} e' \,\Box\, f} \quad \frac{f \xrightarrow{\tau} f'}{e \,\Box\, f \xrightarrow{\tau} e \,\Box\, f'}$$

Table 12: CMML operational semantics: static rules

$$\frac{e \xrightarrow{\mu} e'}{e \,\Box\, f \xrightarrow{\mu} e'} \quad \frac{f \xrightarrow{\mu} f'}{e \,\Box\, f \xrightarrow{\mu} f'}$$

Table 13: CMML operational semantics: dynamic rules

$$\frac{}{f\, e \xrightarrow{\tau} g[e/y][f/x]}[f = (\text{rec}\, x = \text{fn}\, y \Rightarrow g)] \quad \frac{}{c\, e \xrightarrow{\tau} [\delta(c, e)]}$$

$$\frac{}{\text{if true then}\, f \,\text{else}\, g \xrightarrow{\tau} f} \quad \frac{}{\text{if false then}\, f \,\text{else}\, g \xrightarrow{\tau} g}$$

$$\frac{e \xrightarrow{\surd g} e'}{\text{let}\, x \Leftarrow e \,\text{in}\, f \xrightarrow{\tau} e' \parallel f[g/x]}$$

$$\frac{e \xrightarrow{k!g} e' \quad f \xrightarrow{k?x} f'}{e \parallel f \xrightarrow{\tau} e' \parallel f'[g/x]} \quad \frac{e \xrightarrow{k?x} e' \quad f \xrightarrow{k!g} f'}{e \parallel f \xrightarrow{\tau} e'[g/x] \parallel f'}$$

$$\frac{e \xrightarrow{\surd g} e'}{e \,\Box\, f \xrightarrow{\tau} e' \parallel [g]} \quad \frac{f \xrightarrow{\surd g} f'}{e \,\Box\, f \xrightarrow{\tau} f' \parallel [g]}$$

Table 14: CMML operational semantics: silent reductions

$$\frac{}{[e] \xrightarrow{\surd e} \delta} \quad \frac{}{k!e \xrightarrow{k!e} [()]} \quad \frac{}{k? \xrightarrow{k?x} [x]}$$

Table 15: CMML operational semantics: axioms

$$\begin{array}{ll} \text{cell}\langle i, o\rangle & \\ \xrightarrow{\tau} & \text{let}\, x \Leftarrow i? \,\text{in let}\, y \Leftarrow o!x \,\text{in cell}\langle i, o\rangle \\ \xrightarrow{i?e} & \text{let}\, x \Leftarrow [e] \,\text{in let}\, y \Leftarrow o!x \,\text{in cell}\langle i, o\rangle \\ \xrightarrow{\tau} & \text{let}\, y \Leftarrow o!e \,\text{in cell}\langle i, o\rangle \\ \xrightarrow{o!e} & \text{let}\, y \Leftarrow [()] \,\text{in cell}\langle i, o\rangle \\ \xrightarrow{\tau} & \text{cell}\langle i, o\rangle \end{array}$$

Table 16: CMML operational semantics: example reduction

CSP, in order to ensure *forward commutativity* of the resulting transition system (see Section 3.3 below for why this is important).

As an example of a μCMML program execution, one possible run of the one-place buffer is given in Table 16, which can be compared to the equivalent μCML execution in Table 9. The extra complexity of the μCML execution is due to the book-keeping work that μCML has to do because an expression of any type has the capability of computation, so the operational semantics has to allow computation at any point in evaluation. For example, in the evaluation of send (e,f), both e and f have to terminate before the communication can happen, so if $e \stackrel{\surd k}{\Longrightarrow} \delta$ and $f \stackrel{\surd v}{\Longrightarrow} \delta$ then:

$$
\begin{array}{ll}
\multicolumn{2}{l}{\texttt{send}\,(e,f)} \\
\quad \stackrel{\tau}{\longrightarrow} & \texttt{let}\,x = (e,f)\,\texttt{in sync}\,(\texttt{transmit}\,x) \\
\quad \Longrightarrow & \texttt{let}\,x = \texttt{let}\,y = f\,\texttt{in}\,\langle k, y\rangle\,\texttt{in sync}\,(\texttt{transmit}\,x) \\
\quad \Longrightarrow & \texttt{let}\,x = \langle k, v\rangle\,\texttt{in sync}\,(\texttt{transmit}\,x) \\
\quad \longrightarrow & \texttt{sync}\,(\texttt{transmit}\langle k, v\rangle) \\
\quad \longrightarrow & \texttt{sync}\,[k!v] \\
\quad \longrightarrow & k!v \\
\quad \stackrel{k!v}{\longrightarrow} & ()
\end{array}
$$

whereas the type system for μCMML ensures that e and f do not have to be evaluated before $e!f$ can communicate.

3.3 Bisimulation

We can define 'structure-preserving' and 'bisimulation' for μCMML in the same way as for μCML.

Proposition 5 $\approx^h$ *is a congruence for* μCMML.

Proof Similar to the proof of Proposition 3. □

In comparison to μCML, this equivalence has some pleasant mathematical properties. In particular we can define a category of μCML terms, where:

- objects are μCML types,
- morphisms from A to B are expressions with one free variable $x : A \vdash e : B$ viewed up to higher-order weak bisimulation $\approx^{h^\circ}$,
- the identity morphism is $x : A \vdash x : A$, and
- morphism composition is substitution: $(x : A \vdash e : B); (y : B \vdash f : C)$ is $x : A \vdash f[e/y] : C$.

This category has binary products $A * B$ with projections:

$$x : A * B \vdash x.\mathsf{l} : A \qquad x : A * B \vdash x.\mathsf{r} : B$$

and mediating morphism:

$$\frac{x : A \vdash e : B \quad x : A \vdash f : C}{x : A \vdash \langle e, f \rangle : B * C}$$

To verify that these satisfy the defining property for products we have to show that (whenever $\Gamma \vdash g : A * B$):

$$\begin{aligned} \pi\langle e, f\rangle &\approx^h e \\ \pi'\langle e, f\rangle &\approx^h f \\ g &\approx^h \langle \pi g, \pi' g\rangle \end{aligned}$$

The category has an initial object unit with mediating morphism:

$$x : A \vdash () : \mathsf{unit}$$

since (whenever $\Gamma \vdash e : \mathsf{unit}$):

$$e \approx^h ()$$

The category has monad given by the _comp type constructor with action on morphisms given by:

$$\frac{x : A \vdash e : B}{y : A\,\mathsf{comp} \vdash \mathsf{let}\, x \Leftarrow y\, \mathsf{in}\, [e] : B\,\mathsf{comp}}$$

and strict monadic structure given by natural transformations:

$$\begin{gathered} x : A \vdash [x] : A\,\mathsf{comp} \\ x : A\,\mathsf{comp}\,\mathsf{comp} \vdash \mathsf{let}\, y \Leftarrow x\, \mathsf{in}\, y : A\,\mathsf{comp} \\ x : A * (B\,\mathsf{comp}) \vdash \mathsf{let}\, y \Leftarrow x.\mathsf{r}\, \mathsf{in}\, [\langle x.\mathsf{l}, y\rangle] : (A * B)\,\mathsf{comp} \end{gathered}$$

since (whenever $\Gamma \vdash e : A\,\mathsf{comp}$, $\Gamma, x : A \vdash f : B\,\mathsf{comp}$, $\Gamma, y : B \vdash g : C\,\mathsf{comp}$ and $x, y \notin \Gamma$):

$$\begin{aligned} \mathsf{let}\, x \Leftarrow [e]\, \mathsf{in}\, f &\approx^h f[e/x] \\ \mathsf{let}\, x \Leftarrow e\, \mathsf{in}\, [x] &\approx^h e \\ \mathsf{let}\, y \Leftarrow \mathsf{let}\, x \Leftarrow e\, \mathsf{in}\, f\, \mathsf{in}\, g &\approx^h \mathsf{let}\, x \Leftarrow e\, \mathsf{in}\, \mathsf{let}\, y \Leftarrow f\, \mathsf{in}\, g \end{aligned}$$

This category has all _comp exponentials given by $A \to B\,\mathsf{comp}$ with the currying adjunction given by:

$$\frac{x : A * B \vdash e : C\,\mathsf{comp}}{y : A \vdash \mathsf{fn}\, z \Rightarrow \mathsf{let}\, x \Leftarrow [\langle y, z\rangle]\, \mathsf{in}\, e : B \to C\,\mathsf{comp}}$$

$$\frac{x : A \vdash e : B \to C\,\mathsf{comp}}{y : A * B \vdash \mathsf{let}\, x \Leftarrow [y.\mathsf{l}]\, \mathsf{in}\, e(y.\mathsf{r}) : C}$$

since (whenever $\Gamma, x : A \vdash e : B\,\mathsf{comp}$, $\Gamma \vdash f : A$ and $\Gamma \vdash g : A \to B\,\mathsf{comp}$):

$$\begin{array}{rcl} (\mathsf{fn}\, x \Rightarrow e)f & \approx^h & e[x/f] \\ \mathsf{fn}\, x \Rightarrow (g\, x) & \approx^h & g \end{array}$$

The categorical structure of μCMML is based on Moggi's (1991) general theory of computation types, and is discussed further in (Jeffrey 1995a; Jeffrey 1995b).

In order to prove the above bisimulations, we need to show some properties about the labelled transition systems produced by μCMML programs. In particular we require the labelled transition system to be *value deterministic*:

$$\text{if} \quad \begin{array}{ccc} e & \xrightarrow{\checkmark f} & e' \\ {\scriptstyle \checkmark g}\downarrow & & \\ e'' & & \end{array} \quad \text{then } f = g \text{ and } e' = e''$$

single-valued:

$$\text{if } e \xrightarrow{\checkmark f} e' \xrightarrow{\;l\;} e'' \text{ then } l \neq \checkmark g$$

forward commutative:

$$\text{if} \quad \begin{array}{ccc} e & \xrightarrow{\checkmark f} & e' \\ {\scriptstyle \alpha}\downarrow & & \\ e'' & & \end{array} \quad \text{then} \quad \begin{array}{ccc} e & \xrightarrow{\checkmark f} & e' \\ {\scriptstyle \alpha}\downarrow & & \downarrow{\scriptstyle \alpha} \\ e'' & \xrightarrow{\checkmark f} & \circ e''' \end{array}$$

and *backward commutative*:

$$\text{if} \quad \begin{array}{ccc} e & \xrightarrow{\checkmark f} & e' \\ & & \downarrow{\scriptstyle \alpha} \\ & & e''' \end{array} \quad \text{then} \quad \begin{array}{ccc} e & \xrightarrow{\checkmark f} & e' \\ {\scriptstyle \alpha}\downarrow & & \downarrow{\scriptstyle \alpha} \\ e'' & \xrightarrow{\checkmark f} & \circ e''' \end{array}$$

From these properties we can show that:

$$\text{if } e \xrightarrow{\checkmark f} e' \text{ then } e \approx^h e' \parallel [f]$$

which is used in proving the above bisimulations.

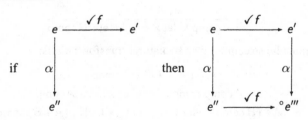

4 Translating CML to CMML

As we have seen, the operational semantics for μCML is more complex than that of μCMML, since terms of any type can reduce. However, in this section we shall show that there is a translation from μCML^+ into μCMML, and that the translation is correct up to weak bisimulation.

4.1 The translation

This translation is based on Moggi's (1991) translation of the call-by-value λ-calculus into the computational λ-calculus.

First, we translate each μCML^+ type A into an μCMML type $T[\![A]\!]$. The only tricky question is how to translate the function space `A -> B`. Moggi has proposed $A\,\mathsf{comp} \rightarrow B\,\mathsf{comp}$ for the *call-by-name* translation (where functions take computations as arguments) and $A \rightarrow B\,\mathsf{comp}$ for the *call-by-value* translation (where functions take canonical forms as arguments). Since μCML is a call-by-value language, we shall use the latter translation. This is given in Table 17, and can be extended to contexts:

$$T[\![x_1 : A_1, \ldots, x_n : A_n]\!] \;=\; x_1 : T[\![A_1]\!], \ldots, x_n : T[\![A_n]\!]$$

The trick for translating μCML^+ terms into μCMML terms is to provide two translations:

- translate μCML^+ values $\Gamma \vdash v : A$
  into μCMML expressions $T[\![\Gamma]\!] \vdash V[\![v]\!] : T[\![A]\!]$, and
- translate μCML^+ expressions $\Gamma \vdash e : A$
  into μCMML computations $T[\![\Gamma]\!] \vdash E[\![e]\!] : T[\![A]\!]\,\mathsf{comp}$.

This reflects the intuition that any expression in μCML^+ can perform computation, whereas in μCMML only terms of type $A\,\mathsf{comp}$ can compute. The two translations are given in Tables 18 and 19, assuming that $K_A = K_{T[\![A]\!]}$.

Note that most of the μCML^+ expressions have the same form, which is to evaluate their argument in a let-expression before continuing. This corresponds to the notion that μCML^+ is a call-by-value language, where expressions are evaluated to canonical form before being manipulated.

For example, the translation of `cell` is given in Table 20, where to save space we have used the fact that:

$$\begin{aligned} E[\![\mathsf{send}\ e]\!] &\approx^h \mathsf{let}\ x \Leftarrow E[\![e]\!]\ \mathsf{in}\ x.\mathsf{l}!x.\mathsf{r} \\ E[\![\mathsf{accept}\ e]\!] &\approx^h \mathsf{let}\ x \Leftarrow E[\![e]\!]\ \mathsf{in}\ x? \end{aligned}$$

$$\begin{array}{rcl} \mathcal{T}[\![\mathtt{bool}]\!] & = & \mathsf{bool} \\ \mathcal{T}[\![A\ \mathtt{chan}]\!] & = & \mathcal{T}[\![A]\!]\ \mathsf{chan} \\ \mathcal{T}[\![\mathtt{int}]\!] & = & \mathsf{int} \\ \mathcal{T}[\![\mathtt{unit}]\!] & = & \mathsf{unit} \\ \mathcal{T}[\![A * B]\!] & = & \mathcal{T}[\![A]\!] * \mathcal{T}[\![B]\!] \\ \mathcal{T}[\![A\ \texttt{->}\ B]\!] & = & \mathcal{T}[\![A]\!] \to \mathcal{T}[\![B]\!]\ \mathsf{comp} \\ \mathcal{T}[\![A\ \mathtt{event}]\!] & = & \mathcal{T}[\![A]\!]\ \mathsf{comp} \end{array}$$

Table 17: Translation of μCML$^+$ types into μCML

$$\begin{array}{rcl} \mathcal{V}[\![\mathtt{true}]\!] & = & \mathsf{true} \\ \mathcal{V}[\![\mathtt{false}]\!] & = & \mathsf{false} \\ \mathcal{V}[\![n]\!] & = & n \\ \mathcal{V}[\![k]\!] & = & k \\ \mathcal{V}[\![()]\!] & = & () \\ \mathcal{V}[\![\langle v, w\rangle]\!] & = & \langle \mathcal{V}[\![v]\!], \mathcal{V}[\![w]\!]\rangle \\ \mathcal{V}[\![\mathtt{rec}\ x = \mathtt{fn}\ y \texttt{=>}\ e]\!] & = & \mathsf{rec}\ x = \mathsf{fn}\ y \Rightarrow \mathcal{E}[\![e]\!] \\ \mathcal{V}[\![x]\!] & = & x \\ \mathcal{V}[\![\mathtt{[}ge\mathtt{]}]\!] & = & \mathcal{E}[\![ge]\!] \end{array}$$

Table 18: Translation of μCML$^+$ values into μCML

This translation is almost unreadable, and very inefficient, but we can use β-reduction to remove some extraneous lets:

$$\begin{array}{l} \mathcal{V}[\![\mathtt{cell}]\!] \approx^h \mathsf{rec}\ x_1 = \mathsf{fn}\ x_2 \Rightarrow \\ \quad \mathsf{let}\ x_4 \Leftarrow \mathsf{let}\ x_5 \Leftarrow \mathsf{let}\ x_6 \Leftarrow \mathsf{let}\ x_8 \Leftarrow \mathsf{let}\ x_{10} \Leftarrow x_2.\mathsf{l?}\ \mathsf{in}\ [\langle x_2.\mathsf{r}, x_{10}\rangle] \\ \qquad\qquad\qquad\qquad \mathsf{in}\ x_8.\mathsf{l!}x_8.\mathsf{r} \\ \qquad\qquad\qquad \mathsf{in}\ [\langle x_6, x_2\rangle] \\ \qquad\qquad \mathsf{in}\ [x_5.\mathsf{r}] \\ \quad \mathsf{in}\ x_1\ x_4 \end{array}$$

$$
\begin{array}{rcl}
E[\![\texttt{v}]\!] & = & [V[\![\texttt{v}]\!]] \\
E[\![\texttt{fst e}]\!] & = & \mathsf{let}\, x \Leftarrow E[\![\texttt{e}]\!]\, \mathsf{in}\, [x.\mathsf{l}] \\
E[\![\texttt{snd e}]\!] & = & \mathsf{let}\, x \Leftarrow E[\![\texttt{e}]\!]\, \mathsf{in}\, [x.\mathsf{r}] \\
E[\![\texttt{add e}]\!] & = & \mathsf{let}\, x \Leftarrow E[\![\texttt{e}]\!]\, \mathsf{in}\, \mathsf{add}\, x \\
E[\![\texttt{mul e}]\!] & = & \mathsf{let}\, x \Leftarrow E[\![\texttt{e}]\!]\, \mathsf{in}\, \mathsf{mul}\, x \\
E[\![\texttt{leq e}]\!] & = & \mathsf{let}\, x \Leftarrow E[\![\texttt{e}]\!]\, \mathsf{in}\, \mathsf{leq}\, x \\
E[\![\texttt{transmit e}]\!] & = & \mathsf{let}\, x \Leftarrow E[\![\texttt{e}]\!]\, \mathsf{in}\, [x.\mathsf{l}!x.\mathsf{r}] \\
E[\![\texttt{receive e}]\!] & = & \mathsf{let}\, x \Leftarrow E[\![\texttt{e}]\!]\, \mathsf{in}\, [x?] \\
E[\![\texttt{choose e}]\!] & = & \mathsf{let}\, x \Leftarrow E[\![\texttt{e}]\!]\, \mathsf{in}\, [x.\mathsf{l} \,\square\, x.\mathsf{r}] \\
E[\![\texttt{spawn e}]\!] & = & \mathsf{let}\, x \Leftarrow E[\![\texttt{e}]\!]\, \mathsf{in}\, x\,() \parallel [()] \\
E[\![\texttt{sync e}]\!] & = & \mathsf{let}\, x \Leftarrow E[\![\texttt{e}]\!]\, \mathsf{in}\, x \\
E[\![\texttt{wrap e}]\!] & = & \mathsf{let}\, x \Leftarrow E[\![\texttt{e}]\!]\, \mathsf{in}\, [\mathsf{let}\, y \Leftarrow x.\mathsf{l}\, \mathsf{in}\, x.\mathsf{r}\, y] \\
E[\![\texttt{never e}]\!] & = & \mathsf{let}\, x \Leftarrow E[\![\texttt{e}]\!]\, \mathsf{in}\, [\delta] \\
E[\![\texttt{if e then f else g}]\!] & = & \mathsf{let}\, x \Leftarrow E[\![\texttt{e}]\!]\, \mathsf{in}\, \mathsf{if}\, x\, \mathsf{then}\, E[\![\texttt{f}]\!]\, \mathsf{else}\, E[\![\texttt{g}]\!] \\
E[\![\texttt{(e,f)}]\!] & = & \mathsf{let}\, x \Leftarrow E[\![\texttt{e}]\!]\, \mathsf{in}\, \mathsf{let}\, y \Leftarrow E[\![\texttt{f}]\!]\, \mathsf{in}\, [\langle x, y\rangle] \\
E[\![\texttt{let x = e in f}]\!] & = & \mathsf{let}\, x \Leftarrow E[\![\texttt{e}]\!]\, \mathsf{in}\, E[\![\texttt{f}]\!] \\
E[\![\texttt{fe}]\!] & = & \mathsf{let}\, x \Leftarrow E[\![\texttt{f}]\!]\, \mathsf{in}\, \mathsf{let}\, y \Leftarrow E[\![\texttt{e}]\!]\, \mathsf{in}\, x\, y \\
E[\![\texttt{e} \parallel \texttt{f}]\!] & = & E[\![\texttt{e}]\!] \parallel E[\![\texttt{f}]\!] \\
E[\![\texttt{v?}]\!] & = & V[\![\texttt{v}]\!]? \\
E[\![\texttt{v!w}]\!] & = & V[\![\texttt{v}]\!]!V[\![\texttt{w}]\!] \\
E[\![\delta]\!] & = & \delta \\
E[\![\mathsf{ge}_1 \oplus \mathsf{ge}_2]\!] & = & E[\![\mathsf{ge}_1]\!] \,\square\, E[\![\mathsf{ge}_2]\!] \\
E[\![\mathsf{ge} \Rightarrow \texttt{v}]\!] & = & \mathsf{let}\, x \Leftarrow E[\![\mathsf{ge}]\!]\, \mathsf{in}\, V[\![\texttt{v}]\!] x
\end{array}
$$

Table 19: Translation of μCML$^+$ expressions into μCML

Then associativity gives:

$$
\begin{array}{l}
V[\![\texttt{cell}]\!] \approx^h \mathsf{rec}\, x_1 = \mathsf{fn}\, x_2 \Rightarrow \\
\quad \mathsf{let}\, x_{10} \Leftarrow x_2.\mathsf{l}? \\
\quad \mathsf{in}\, \mathsf{let}\, x_8 \Leftarrow [\langle x_2.\mathsf{r}, x_{10}\rangle] \\
\quad\quad \mathsf{in}\, \mathsf{let}\, x_6 \Leftarrow x_8.\mathsf{l}!x_8.\mathsf{r} \\
\quad\quad\quad \mathsf{in}\, \mathsf{let}\, x_5 \Leftarrow [\langle x_6, x_2\rangle] \\
\quad\quad\quad\quad \mathsf{in}\, \mathsf{let}\, x_4 \Leftarrow [x_5.\mathsf{r}]\, \mathsf{in}\, x_1\, x_4
\end{array}
$$

$$
\begin{array}{ll}
V[\![\texttt{cell}]\!] \approx^h & \mathsf{rec}\, x_1 = \mathsf{fn}\, x_2 \Rightarrow \\
& \mathsf{let}\, x_3 \Leftarrow [x_1] \\
& \mathsf{in}\ \mathsf{let}\, x_4 \Leftarrow \mathsf{let}\, x_5 \Leftarrow \mathsf{let}\, x_6 \Leftarrow \mathsf{let}\, x_8 \Leftarrow \mathsf{let}\, x_9 \Leftarrow \mathsf{let}\, x_{11} \Leftarrow [x_2] \\
& \qquad\qquad\qquad\qquad\qquad\qquad\qquad\qquad\qquad\quad \mathsf{in}\, [x_{11}.\mathsf{r}] \\
& \qquad\qquad\qquad\qquad\qquad\qquad\qquad\qquad \mathsf{in}\ \mathsf{let}\, x_{10} \Leftarrow \mathsf{let}\, x_{12} \Leftarrow \mathsf{let}\, x_{13} \Leftarrow [x_2] \\
& \qquad\qquad\qquad\qquad\qquad\qquad\qquad\qquad\qquad\qquad\qquad\qquad\quad \mathsf{in}\, [x_{13}.\mathsf{l}] \\
& \qquad\qquad\qquad\qquad\qquad\qquad\qquad\qquad\qquad\qquad \mathsf{in}\, x_{12}? \\
& \qquad\qquad\qquad\qquad\qquad\qquad\qquad\qquad\quad \mathsf{in}\, [\langle x_9, x_{10}\rangle] \\
& \qquad\qquad\qquad\qquad\qquad\quad \mathsf{in}\, x_8.\mathsf{l}!x_8.\mathsf{r} \\
& \qquad\qquad\qquad \mathsf{in}\ \mathsf{let}\, x_7 \Leftarrow [x_2] \\
& \qquad\qquad\qquad\quad \mathsf{in}\, [\langle x_6, x_7\rangle] \\
& \qquad\qquad \mathsf{in}\, [x_5.\mathsf{r}] \\
& \quad \mathsf{in}\, x_3\, x_4
\end{array}
$$

Table 20: Example translation of μCML$^+$ into μCMML

So further use of β-reduction gives:

$$
\begin{array}{ll}
V[\![\texttt{cell}]\!] \approx^h & \mathsf{rec}\, x_1 = \mathsf{fn}\, x_2 \Rightarrow \\
& \mathsf{let}\, x_{10} \Leftarrow x_2.\mathsf{l}? \\
& \mathsf{in}\ \mathsf{let}\, x_6 \Leftarrow x_2.\mathsf{r}!x_{10} \\
& \quad \mathsf{in}\, x_1\, x_2
\end{array}
$$

and since (up to α-conversion) this is the definition of cell, we have:

$$V[\![\texttt{cell}]\!] \approx^h \mathsf{cell}$$

This example shows that it is easy to perform syntactic manipulations on the expressions of μCMMLto drastically reduce them in size, and improve their efficiency. This suggests that μCMML may be a suitable intermediate language for a μCML compiler, where verifiable optimisations can be performed.

4.2 Correctness of the translation

We will now show that the translation of μCML$^+$ into μCMML is correct up to bisimulation. We will do this by defining an appropriate notion of weak bisimulation between μCML and μCMML programs. This proof uses Milner and Sangiorgi's (1992) technique of 'bisimulation up to'.

A *closed type-indexed relation between* μCML *and* μCMML is a family of relations:

$$
\begin{array}{lcl}
\mathcal{R}^e_A & \subseteq & \{(e, e) \mid \vdash e : A, \vdash e : T[\![A]\!]\,\mathsf{comp}\} \\
\mathcal{R}^v_A & \subseteq & \{(v, e) \mid \vdash v : A, \vdash e : T[\![A]\!]\}
\end{array}
$$

For any closed type-indexed relation $\mathcal{R}$, let its *open extension* $\mathcal{R}^{eo}$ be defined as:

$$\mathsf{e}\ \mathcal{R}^{eo}_{\vec{x}:\vec{A},B}\ \mathsf{e} \text{ iff } \mathsf{e}[\vec{v}/\vec{x}]\ \mathcal{R}^{e}_{B}\ \mathsf{e}[V[\![\vec{v}]\!]/\vec{x}] \text{ for all } \vdash \vec{v} : \vec{A}.$$

A closed type-indexed relation $\mathcal{R}$ is structure-preserving iff:

- if $v\ \mathcal{R}^{v}_{A}\ \mathsf{e}$ and A is a base type then $v = \mathsf{e}$,
- if $\langle v_1, v_2 \rangle\ \mathcal{R}^{v}_{A_1 * A_2}\ \langle \mathsf{e}_1, \mathsf{e}_2 \rangle$ then $v_i\ \mathcal{R}^{v}_{A_i}\ \mathsf{e}_i$,
- if $[ge]\ \mathcal{R}^{v}_{A\ \mathtt{event}}\ \mathsf{e}$ then $ge\ \mathcal{R}^{e}_{A}\ \mathsf{e}$, and
- if $v\ \mathcal{R}^{v}_{A\to B}\ \mathsf{e}$ then for all $\vdash w : A$ we have $vw\ \mathcal{R}^{e}_{B}\ \mathsf{e}(V[\![w]\!])$.

A closed type-indexed relation can be extended to labels as:

$$\frac{}{\tau\ \mathcal{R}^{l}_{A}\ \tau} \qquad \frac{v\ \mathcal{R}^{v}_{A}\ \mathsf{e}}{\surd v\ \mathcal{R}^{l}_{A}\ \surd \mathsf{e}} \qquad \frac{}{k?x\ \mathcal{R}^{l}_{A}\ k?x} \qquad \frac{v\ \mathcal{R}^{v}_{B}\ \mathsf{e}}{k!v\ \mathcal{R}^{l}_{A}\ k!\mathsf{e}}[k \in K_B]$$

A closed type-indexed relation between μCML and μCMML is a *higher-order weak bisimulation* iff it is structure preserving and we can complete the following diagrams:

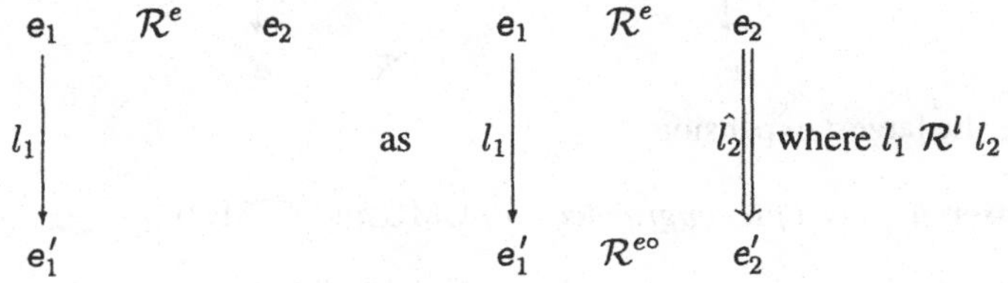

and:

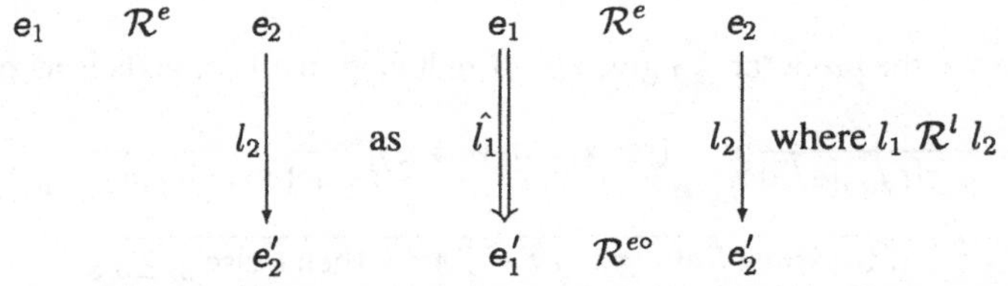

A closed type-indexed relation between μCML and μCMML is a *higher-order strong bisimulation up to* $(\leq, \sqsubseteq)$ iff it is structure preserving and we can complete the following diagrams:

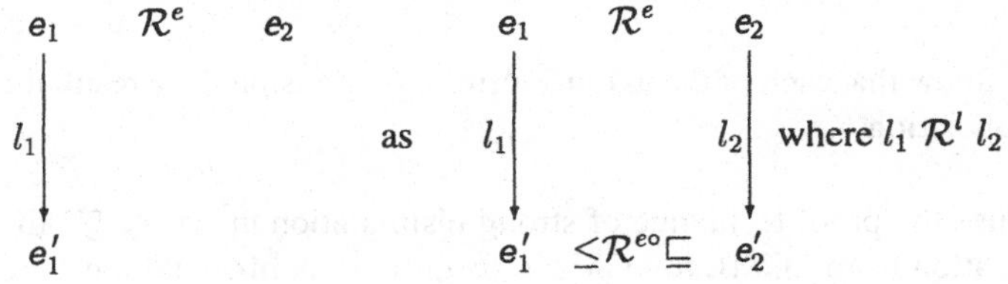

and:

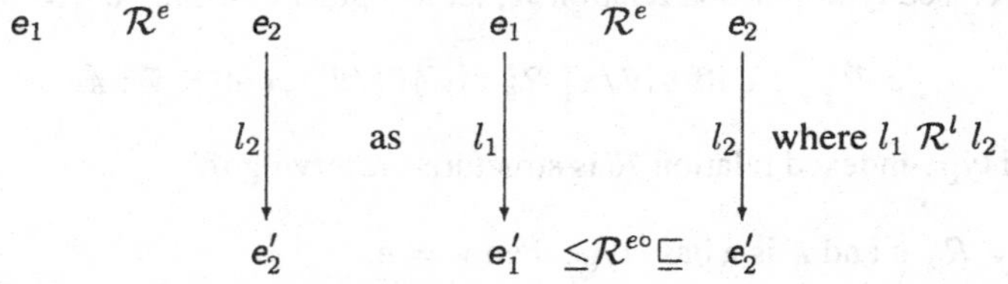

An *expansion* on μCMML (and similarly on μCML) is a weak bisimulation $\mathcal{R}$ such that the following diagrams can be completed:

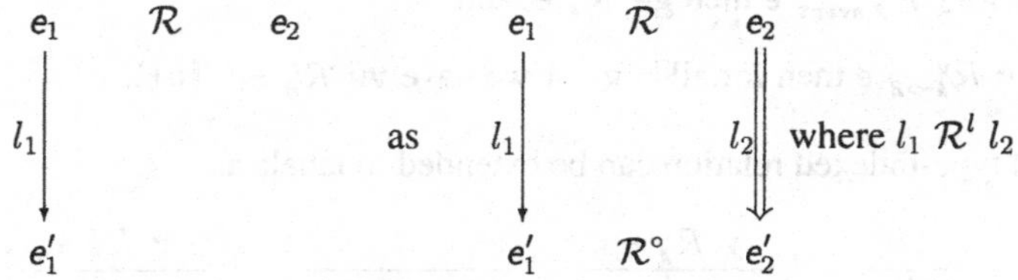

and:

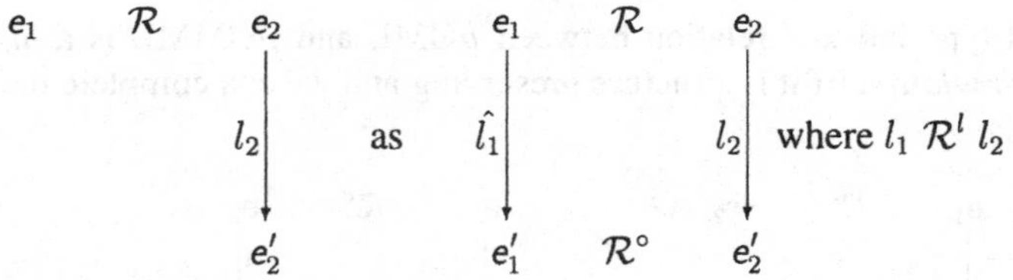

Let $\lesssim$ be the largest expansion.

Proposition 6 *$\lesssim$ is a precongruence on μCML and μCMML.*

Proof Similar to Proposition 3. □

For example, the preorder $\leq_\beta$ given by β-reducing in all contexts is an expansion:

$$\frac{}{e\,f \geq_\beta g[f/y][e/x]}[e = (\mathsf{rec}\,x = \mathsf{fn}\,y \Rightarrow g)] \qquad \frac{}{\mathsf{let}\,x \Leftarrow [e]\,\mathsf{in}\,f \geq_\beta f[e/x]}$$

$$\frac{}{\mathsf{if\ true\ then}\ f\ \mathsf{else}\ g \geq_\beta f} \qquad \frac{}{\mathsf{if\ false\ then}\ f\ \mathsf{else}\ g \geq_\beta g}$$

$$\frac{}{e \geq_\beta e} \qquad \frac{e \geq_\beta f \geq_\beta g}{e \geq_\beta g} \qquad \frac{e \geq_\beta f}{C[e] \geq_\beta C[f]}$$

Proposition 7 *If $e \leq_\beta f$ then $e \lesssim f$.*

Proof Show that each of the axioms forms an expansion. The result then follows from Proposition 6. □

We can use the proof technique of strong bisimulation up to $(\lesssim, \sqsubseteq)$ to show that the translation from μCML to μCMML forms a weak bisimulation.

Proposition 8 *Any strong bisimulation up to* $(\gtrsim, \lesssim)$ *is a weak bisimulation.*

Proof An adaptation of the results in (Sangiorgi and Milner 1992). □

Proposition 9 *The translation of* μCML$^+$ *into* μCMML *is a strong bisimulation up to* $(\geq_\beta, \leq_\beta)$.

Proof Let $\mathcal{R}$ be:

$$\mathcal{R}^e_A = \{(\mathtt{e}, E[\![\mathtt{e}]\!]) \mid \vdash \mathtt{e} : A\} \qquad \mathcal{R}^v_A = \{(\mathtt{v}, V[\![\mathtt{v}]\!]) \mid \vdash \mathtt{v} : A\}$$

and let $L[\![l]\!]$ be the extension of the translation to labels:

$$\begin{array}{rclrcl} L[\![\tau]\!] & = & \tau & L[\![\checkmark \mathtt{v}]\!] & = & \checkmark V[\![\mathtt{v}]\!] \\ L[\![\mathtt{k!v}]\!] & = & k!V[\![\mathtt{v}]\!] & L[\![\mathtt{k?x}]\!] & = & k?x \end{array}$$

First show that the translation respects substitution of values, that is:

$$E[\![(\mathtt{e}[\mathtt{v}/\mathtt{x}])]\!] = E[\![\mathtt{e}]\!][V[\![\mathtt{v}]\!]/x]$$

Next show by induction on *ge* that if $ge \xrightarrow{l} \mathtt{e}$ then l is an input or output label.

Then show that for any $\vdash \mathtt{e} : A$, if $\mathtt{e} \xrightarrow{l} \mathtt{e}'$ then $E[\![\mathtt{e}]\!] \xrightarrow{L[\![l]\!]} \geq_\beta E[\![\mathtt{f}']\!]$ and $\mathtt{e}' \geq_\beta \mathtt{f}'$. This is an induction on the proof of reduction, for example if:

$$\frac{ge \xrightarrow{\alpha} \mathtt{e}'}{ge \Rightarrow \mathtt{v} \xrightarrow{\alpha} \mathtt{ve}'}$$

where $\mathtt{v} = \mathtt{rec}\ y = \mathtt{fn}\ z \Rightarrow g$ then by induction:

$$E[\![ge]\!] \xrightarrow{L[\![\alpha]\!]} \geq_\beta E[\![\mathtt{f}']\!] \qquad \mathtt{e}' \geq_\beta \mathtt{f}'$$

and so:

$$\begin{array}{ll} E[\![ge \Rightarrow \mathtt{v}]\!] & \\ \quad = & \mathsf{let}\ x \Leftarrow E[\![ge]\!]\ \mathsf{in}\ V[\![\mathtt{v}]\!]\ x \\ \quad \xrightarrow{L[\![\alpha]\!]} \geq_\beta & \mathsf{let}\ x \Leftarrow E[\![\mathtt{f}']\!]\ \mathsf{in}\ V[\![\mathtt{v}]\!]\ x \\ \quad \geq_\beta & \mathsf{let}\ x \Leftarrow E[\![\mathtt{f}']\!]\ \mathsf{in}\ E[\![g]\!][x/z][V[\![\mathtt{v}]\!]/y] \\ \quad = & E[\![\mathtt{let}\ z = \mathtt{f}'\ \mathtt{in}\ g[\mathtt{v}/y]]\!] \end{array}$$

and:

$$\begin{array}{ll} \mathtt{ve}' & \\ \quad \geq_\beta & \mathtt{vf}' \\ \quad \geq_\beta & \mathtt{let}\ z = \mathtt{f}'\ \mathtt{in}\ g[\mathtt{v}/y] \end{array}$$

The other cases are similar.

Then show that for any $\vdash \mathsf{e} : A$, if $E[\![\mathsf{e}]\!] \xrightarrow{l_2} \mathsf{e}'$ then $\mathsf{e} \xrightarrow{l_1} \geq_\beta \mathsf{e}'$, $L[\![l_1]\!] = l_2$ and $\mathsf{e}' \geq_\beta E[\![\mathsf{e}']\!]$. This is an induction on e, for example if:

$$\frac{E[\![ge]\!] \xrightarrow{\alpha_1} e'}{E[\![ge \Rightarrow v]\!] \xrightarrow{\alpha_2} \mathsf{let}\, x \Leftarrow e' \,\mathsf{in}\, V[\![v]\!]\, x}$$

where $v = \mathtt{rec}\, y = \mathtt{fn}\, z \Rightarrow g$ then by induction:

$$ge \xrightarrow{\alpha_1} \geq_\beta \mathsf{e}' \qquad L[\![\alpha_1]\!] = \alpha_2 \qquad \mathsf{e}' \geq_\beta E[\![\mathsf{e}']\!]$$

and so:

$$\begin{aligned} & ge \Rightarrow v \\ & \quad \xrightarrow{\alpha_1} \geq_\beta \ \mathsf{v}\mathsf{e}' \\ & \quad \geq_\beta \ \mathtt{let}\, z = \mathsf{e}' \,\mathtt{in}\, g[v/y] \end{aligned}$$

and:

$$\begin{aligned} & \mathsf{let}\, x \Leftarrow e' \,\mathsf{in}\, V[\![v]\!]\, x \\ & \quad \geq_\beta \ \mathsf{let}\, x \Leftarrow E[\![\mathsf{e}']\!] \,\mathsf{in}\, V[\![v]\!]\, x \\ & \quad \geq_\beta \ \mathsf{let}\, x \Leftarrow E[\![\mathsf{e}']\!] \,\mathsf{in}\, E[\![g]\!][x/z][V[\![v]\!]/y] \\ & \quad = \ E[\![\mathtt{let}\, z = \mathsf{e}' \,\mathtt{in}\, g[v/y]]\!] \end{aligned}$$

The other cases are similar. □

Proposition 10 *e is weakly bisimilar to $E[\![\mathsf{e}]\!]$.*

Proof Follows from Propositions 7, 8 and 9. □

It follows from this that weak bisimulation for μCMML is at least as fine as weak bisimulation for μCML^+.

Proposition 11 *If $E[\![\mathsf{e}]\!] \approx^h E[\![\mathtt{f}]\!]$ then $\mathsf{e} \approx^h \mathtt{f}$.*

Proof Follows immediately from Proposition 10. □

However, note that the translation is *not* necessarily fully abstract, in that we have not shown that this implication is an 'if and only if'. This is because the bisimulation is higher-order, and the clause for bisimulation between functions requires the functions to agree on all arguments, not just ones which are the image of $E[\![\_]\!]$.

5 Related work

In this paper we have defined an operational semantics for a subset of CML, and defined a notion of higher-order bisimulation for the language. This has then been translated into a metalanguage based on Moggi's translation of the call-by-value λ-calculus.

Much research remains to be done. In particular, the treatment of channels in this paper is very simplistic, in that we do not treat channel generation or polymorphism. Defining an operational semantics for higher-order processes with channel generation would not be difficult (the semantics of the Higher-Order π-calculus (Sangiorgi 1992) could be adapted) but the corresponding definition of bisimulation is trickier to use. It may be possible to modify Sangiorgi's *context bisimulation* for CML, but this remains work to be done.

There has already been a considerable amount of research into the foundations of CML and related languages. Much of this is concerned with developing more detailed type systems, where types contain information on the behaviour of expressions as they evolve, (Nielson and Nielson 1993).

The semantics of CML is presented by Reppy (1991b, 1992) and has been shown (Ferreira, Hennessy, and Jeffrey 1995) to be first-order weakly bisimilar to ours.

In (Bolignano and Debabi 1994; Debabi 1994) there are a number of different semantics given to languages related to CML. A denotational semantics is given using the concept of "dynamic types" but it has not yet been related to any operationally based equivalence. An operational semantics is also given for a language called *FPI*. This contains many CML features but the author notes that accommodating any *spawn* or *fork* operator would be difficult.

In (Havelund 1994; Baeten and Vaandrager 1992) the *spawn* operator is studied within the context of process algebras. The former gives a two-level operational semantics for a simple "pure" process algebra with *fork* and uses this to develop a semantic equivalence based on strong bisimulation; an axiomatisation is also given using an auxiliary operator called *forked*. The latter shows how the various algebraic theories of *ACP* can be adapted to support the addition of a *spawn* operator. This contains a labelled transition system based operational semantics for *ACP* + *spawn* and their treatment of *spawn* has been used in (Ferreira and Hennessy 1995) to give an operational semantics of a language which can be considered to be an untyped version of μCML. However bisimulation based equivalences are not developed in (Ferreira and Hennessy 1995); instead a testing equivalence is defined (Hennessy 1988) and a fully-abstract denotational semantics based on Acceptance Trees is given.

The implementation of concurrency most similar to that presented here is Concurrent Haskell (Peyton Jones, Gordon, and Finne 1996). This uses a monadic type system to separate the functional behaviour of terms from the concurrent behaviour, in a similar fashion to CMML. The main differences are that Concurrent

Haskell is a call-by-need language, and that communication is by shared mutable variables rather than by synchronous handshake. It should be possible to extend the results about bisimulation to Concurrent Haskell, although the treatment of name generation remains a stumbling block, and the semantics would be for reduction to *weak head normal form* rather than *head normal form*.

Crole and Gordon (1994) have provided a very similar translation for a λ-calculus with I/O primitives, and have shown that the translation preserves weak bisimulation. Their proof is simpler than that provided here, because the reduction semantics for their calculus is deterministic.

References

Baeten, J. C. M. and F. W. Vaandrager (1992). An algebra for process creation. *Acta Informatica 29*(4), 303–334.

Bolignano, D. and M. Debabi (1994). A semantic theory for concurrent ML. In *Proc. TACS '94*.

Debabi, M. (1994). *Integration de Paradigmes de Programmation Paralle, Fonctionnelle et Imperative*. Ph.D thesis, Universite D'Orsay.

Ferreira, W. and M. Hennessy (1995). Towards a semantic theory of CML. Technical report 95:02, COGS, Sussex Univ.

Ferreira, W., M. Hennessy, and A. Jeffrey (1995). A theory of weak bisimulation for core CML. COGS Comp. Sci. Tech. Report 05/95, Univ. Sussex.

Gordon, A. (1995). Bisimilarity as a theory of functional programming. In *Proc. MFPS 95*, Number 1 in Electronic Notes in Comp. Sci. Springer-Verlag.

Gordon, A. D. and R. L. Crole (1994). A sound metalogical semantics for input/output effects. In *Proc. Computer Science Logic*, Volume 933 of *LNCS*, pp. 339–353. Springer Verlag.

Havelund, K. (1994). *The Fork Calculus: Towards a Logic for Concurrent ML*. Ph.D thesis, École Normale Superieur, Paris.

Hennessy, M. (1988). *Algebraic Theory of Processes*. MIT Press.

Hoare, C. A. R. (1985). *Communicating Sequential Processes*. Prentice-Hall.

Howe, D. (1989). Equality in lazy computation systems. In *Proc. LICS 89*, pp. 198–203.

Jeffrey, A. (1995a). A fully abstract semantics for a concurrent functional language with monadic types. In *Proc. LICS 95*, pp. 255–264.

Jeffrey, A. (1995b). A fully abstract semantics for a nondeterministic functional language with monadic types. In *Proc. MFPS 95*, Electronic Notes in Comput. Sci. Elsevier.

Peyton Jones, S., A. Gordon, and S. Finne (1996). Concurrent Haskell. In *Proc. 23rd ACM SIGPLAN-SIGACT Symp. Principles of Programming Languages (POPL'96)*, pp. 295–308. ACM Press.

Lambek, J. and P. J. Scott (1986). *Introduction to Higher Order Categorical Logic*. Cambridge University Press.

Milner, R. (1989). *Communication and Concurrency*. Prentice-Hall.

Milner, R., J. Parrow, and D. Walker (1992). A calculus of mobile proceses. *Inform. and Comput. 100*(1), 1–77.

Milner, R., M. Tofte, and R. Harper (1990). *The Definition of Standard ML*. MIT Press.

Moggi, E. (1991). Notions of computation and monad. *Inform. and Comput. 93*, 55–92.

Nielson, F. and H. R. Nielson (1993). From CML to process algebras. Report DAIMI FN-19, Dept. Comp. Sci., Aarhus University.

Reppy, J. (1991a). A higher-order concurrent langauge. In *Proc. SIGPLAN 91*, pp. 294–305.

Reppy, J. (1991b). An operational semantics of first-class synchronous operations. Technical report TR 91-1232, Dept. Comp. Sci., Cornell Univ.

Reppy, J. (1992). *Higher-Order Concurrency*. Ph.D thesis, Cornell Univ.

Sangiorgi, D. (1992). *Expressing Mobility in Process Algebras: First-order and Higher-order Paradigms*. Ph.D thesis, LFCS, Edinburgh Univ.

Sangiorgi, D. and R. Milner (1992). Techniques of 'weak bisimulation up to'. In *Proc. CONCUR 92*. Springer Verlag. LNCS 630.

Relational reasoning about contexts

S. B. Lassen

1 Introduction

The syntactic nature of operational reasoning requires techniques to deal with term contexts, especially for reasoning about recursion. In this paper we study applicative bisimulation and a variant of Sands' improvement theory for a small call-by-value functional language. We explore an indirect, relational approach for reasoning about contexts. It is inspired by Howe's precise method for proving congruence of simulation orderings and by Pitts' extension thereof for proving applicative bisimulation up to context. We illustrate this approach with proofs of the unwinding theorem and syntactic continuity and, more importantly, we establish analogues of Sangiorgi's bisimulation up to context for applicative bisimulation and for improvement. Using these powerful bisimulation up to context techniques, we give concise operational proofs of recursion induction, the improvement theorem, and syntactic minimal invariance. Previous operational proofs of these results involve complex, explicit reasoning about contexts.

Related work

Applicative bisimulation (Abramsky 1990) is an operational theory for higher-order languages, inspired by bisimulation theories for concurrency (Park 1981; Milner 1989). It excels in reasoning about infinite data structures. These exist in every higher-order language but are particularly relevant in lazy functional languages (Gordon 1995; Pitts 1997) and functional object-oriented languages (Gordon and Rees 1996). But applicative bisimulation is not very helpful for reasoning about recursive control structures. There are more 'intensional' operational theories (Talcott 1997; Sands 1997b) which address recursion effectively by counting computation steps. But even they are of limited use for proving results such as the validity of the fundamental induction rules for recursion: recursion induction (also known as Park induction), syntactic continuity (ω induction), syntactic minimal invariance (syntactic projections), and the improvement theorem. Existing operational proofs are complex and involve explicit reasoning about term contexts.

Intuitively, a context is a term containing a hole, that may be filled by another term. This is an evocative idea, but for formal arguments contexts are difficult to work with, both technically and notationally. For this reason, Howe deals only indirectly with contexts in his influential congruence proof for applicative bisimilarity (Howe 1989; Howe 1996). Instead the proof is 'relational': a larger relation which is closed under contexts is constructed and is shown to coincide with applicative bisimilarity by bisimulation and induction on the evaluation relation. This relational approach yields a formally and notationally very precise proof. Moreover, Howe's congruence proof applies to many different typed and untyped higher-order languages and operational orderings; see, e.g., Sands (1991, Ong (1992, Ferreira, Hennessy, and Jeffrey (1995, Lassen (1997, Gordon (1997).

Pitts (1995) extends Howe's congruence proof for applicative bisimilarity to also establish an up to context rule for applicative bisimulation. The proof is also 'relational' and illustrates the versatility of Howe's implicit, relational approach to reasoning about term contexts. Specifically it shows how to use this proof method to establish applicative bisimulation up to context results. (We present the proof in Section 5.2.) The results we present in this paper stem from the study of this work.

Sangiorgi's bisimulation up to context is a powerful refined bisimulation proof rule for process calculi (Sangiorgi and Milner 1992; Sangiorgi 1994). Bisimulation up to context allows you to disregard a common term context when relating terms in bisimulation proofs. Unfortunately, his correctness proofs do not carry over to applicative bisimulation for higher-order languages. Gordon (1995) and Sands (1997b) present restricted applicative bisimulation up to context rules. They demonstrate the power of this approach to produce concise proofs of equivalences which are difficult to derive by other operational methods. Both Sangiorgi (1996, 1995) and Sands couple bisimulation up to context with efficiency preorders, called 'expansion' and 'improvement', respectively. As suggested by Pitts (1995), we also introduce an improvement preorder. The problem which we address in this fashion leads us to adopt an improvement theory based on a different cost measure than that of Sands (1997b).

Overview

Section 2 defines the syntax and operational semantics of the untyped, functional ML fragment which we study below. Section 3 introduces an algebra of relations on terms. This is essential for the calculations with relations in later sections. A substantial example is the proof of the unwinding theorem in Section 4. Applicative (bi)simulation is defined in Section 5. Preliminary applicative simulation up to context results are established and applicative bisimilarity is shown to be a congruence by Howe's and Pitts' techniques. A deficiency of applicative simulation up to context is discovered which leads us to introduce an improvement preorder in Section 6. Improvement enjoys a strong up to context rule from which congruence and the improvement theorem follow. Section 7 uses improvement to strengthen the applicative simulation up to context rule from Section 5. Finally, Section 8 concludes. An appendix contains proofs from Sections 6 and 7.

2 A functional ML fragment

We operate with a small call-by-value functional language with lists, an untyped fragment of ML (Milner, Tofte, and Harper 1990).

Syntax

Let f, g, x, y, z range over an infinite set of variables. The syntax of expressions is:

$$\begin{array}{llll} (\mathit{Exp}) & d, e & ::= & x \mid \texttt{fn}\, x \texttt{ => } e \mid \texttt{nil} \mid e_1 \texttt{ :: } e_2 \mid e_1\, e_2 \\ & & \mid & \texttt{let fun}\, f\, x = d \,\texttt{in}\, e \,\texttt{end} \mid \texttt{let val}\, x = d \,\texttt{in}\, e \,\texttt{end} \\ & & \mid & (\texttt{case}\, d \,\texttt{of nil => }\, e_1 \mid x_1 \texttt{ :: } x_2 \texttt{ => } e_2 \mid f \texttt{ => } e_3). \end{array}$$

Expressions are identified up to α-renaming of bound variables.

In let val $x = d$ in e end and fn x => e, x is bound in e.

In let fun $f\,x = d$ in e end, f and x are bound in d, and f is bound in e.

In case d of nil => e_1 | x_1 : : x_2 => e_2 | f => e_3, x_1 and x_2 are bound in e_2, and f is bound in e_3.

Terms are parsed as in ML. The scope of fn and case extends as far to the right as possible. Application associates to the left and has higher precedence than : : which associates to the right. For instance, the term fn x => x : : y : : $x\,y\,z$ parses as fn x => $(x :: (y :: ((x\,y)\,z)))$.

The set of values is given by the grammar:

$$(\mathit{Val}) \qquad u, v, w \quad ::= \quad x \mid \texttt{fn}\, x \texttt{ => } e \mid \texttt{nil} \mid v_1 \texttt{ :: } v_2.$$

Let $e\{\vec{v}/\vec{x}\} = e\{v_1/x_1, \ldots, v_n/x_n\}$ be the result of simultaneous, capture free substitution of values $\vec{v} = v_1 \ldots v_n$ for free occurrences of $\vec{x} = x_1 \ldots x_n$ in e. (See Stoughton (1988) for a precise definition of simultaneous substitution.) By $\vec{x}$ we always mean an ordered list of pairwise distinct variables. We write $x \in \vec{x}$ to mean variable x occurs in $\vec{x}$.

Let $\mathit{Exp}_{\vec{x}}$ and $\mathit{Val}_{\vec{x}}$ be the set of expressions and values, respectively, with free variables contained in $\vec{x}$. Notice $\mathit{Val}_{\vec{x}} \subseteq \mathit{Exp}_{\vec{x}}$. We call expressions $p, q \in \mathit{Exp}_{\emptyset}$ closed.

A closed value is either the empty list nil, 'cons' of two closed values $v_1 :: v_2$, or a function fn x => e with $e \in \mathit{Exp}_x$. The case construct has three corresponding branches. This allows both decomposition of lists and dynamic dispatch on the 'type' of values. (The latter would not be well-typed in ML but is common in untyped languages, e.g., Scheme (Clinger and Rees (editors) 1991) has a proc? predicate that tells whether a value is a closure; this feature is necessary for the formulation of syntactic minimal invariance in Proposition 11 but otherwise our results are unaffected by the exact choice of language constructs for accessing values—as long as application is the only means of 'destructing' functions.)

We take `let val` $x = d$ `in` e `end` as a language primitive instead of encoding it as (`fn` x `=>` e) d, because the encoding introduces a function application step. This difference affects the improvement theory of Section 6 and will be important later in the proof of Proposition 11.

We define Ω to be a divergent expression:

$$\Omega \stackrel{\text{def}}{=} \texttt{let fun } f\, x = f\, f \texttt{ in } f\, f \texttt{ end}.$$

We write `rec` $f\ x$ `=>` d for the recursive function,

$$\texttt{rec } f\ x \texttt{ => } d \stackrel{\text{def}}{=} \texttt{fn } x \texttt{ => let fun } f\ x = d \texttt{ in } d \texttt{ end}.$$

For example, `fn` x `=>` Ω = `rec` $f\ x$ `=>` $f\ f$.

A call-by-value fixed point combinator, Yv, can be expressed as:

$$\texttt{Yv} \stackrel{\text{def}}{=} \texttt{fn } f \texttt{ => (fn } g \texttt{ => fn } x \texttt{ => } f\,(g\,g)\,x) \texttt{ (fn } g \texttt{ => fn } x \texttt{ => } f\,(g\,g)\,x).$$

So explicit recursion is redundant; later on we prove `rec` $f\ x$ `=>` e is semantically equivalent to `Yv` (`fn` f `=>` `fn` x `=>` e).

Evaluation semantics

We define the operational semantics of closed expressions by an evaluation relation $\Downarrow \subseteq Exp_\emptyset \times Val_\emptyset$ between expressions and values. An important measure of 'computational cost' which we shall use extensively is the number of function applications ('computation steps') in evaluations. Therefore we introduce a family of evaluation relations indexed by this measure, $\Downarrow_N \subseteq Exp_\emptyset \times Val_\emptyset$ for $N \geq 0$, inductively defined by the rules in Table 1.

'Plain' evaluation is just $\Downarrow \stackrel{\text{def}}{=} \bigcup_{N \geq 0} \Downarrow_N$, i.e., $p \Downarrow v$ iff $\exists N \geq 0.\ p \Downarrow_N v$. It is also given inductively by Table 1 with all N subscripts erased from the rules.

Note that $v \Downarrow_0 v$ for all $v \in Val_\emptyset$. Moreover, evaluation is deterministic:

Proposition 1 (Determinacy) *If* $p \Downarrow_N v$ *and* $p \Downarrow_{N'} v'$, $N = N'$ *and* $v = v'$.

Examples

1. Let `I` be the identity function, `I` $\stackrel{\text{def}}{=}$ `fn` x `=>` x, then

$$\texttt{I}\ p \Downarrow_{N+1} v \quad \text{iff} \quad p \Downarrow_N v,$$

for all $p \in Exp_\emptyset$, $v \in Val_\emptyset$ and $N \geq 0$. (Therefore we shall use applications of `I` as syntactic representations of function application steps in analogy with Sands' 'ticks' (1997b).)

$$\text{(Eval fn)}\ \ \mathtt{fn}\ x\ \mathtt{=>}\ e\ \Downarrow_0\ \mathtt{fn}\ x\ \mathtt{=>}\ e$$

$$\text{(Eval nil)}\ \ \mathtt{nil}\ \Downarrow_0\ \mathtt{nil}$$

$$\text{(Eval cons)}\ \ \frac{e_1 \Downarrow_{N_1} v_1 \quad e_2 \Downarrow_{N_2} v_2}{e_1\ \mathtt{::}\ e_2\ \Downarrow_{N_1+N_2}\ v_1\ \mathtt{::}\ v_2}$$

$$\text{(Eval apply)}\ \ \frac{e_1 \Downarrow_{N_1} \mathtt{fn}\ x\ \mathtt{=>}\ e \quad e_2 \Downarrow_{N_2} v_2 \quad e\{v_2/x\} \Downarrow_{N_3} v}{e_1\ e_2\ \Downarrow_{N_1+N_2+N_3+1}\ v}$$

$$\text{(Eval let fun)}\ \ \frac{e\{(\mathtt{rec}\ f\ x\ \mathtt{=>}\ d)/f\} \Downarrow_N v}{\mathtt{let\ fun}\ f\ x = d\ \mathtt{in}\ e\ \mathtt{end}\ \Downarrow_N\ v}$$

$$\text{(Eval let val)}\ \ \frac{d \Downarrow_{N_1} u \quad e\{u/x\} \Downarrow_{N_2} v}{\mathtt{let\ val}\ x = d\ \mathtt{in}\ e\ \mathtt{end}\ \Downarrow_{N_1+N_2}\ v}$$

$$\text{(Eval case)}\ \ \frac{e_0 \Downarrow_{N_1} v_0 \quad e \Downarrow_{N_2} v \quad e = \begin{cases} e_1 & \text{if } v_0 = \mathtt{nil} \\ e_2\{v_1/x_1, v_2/x_2\} & \text{if } v_0 = v_1\ \mathtt{::}\ v_2 \\ e_3\{v_0/f\} & \text{if } v_0 = \mathtt{fn}\ x\ \mathtt{=>}\ d \end{cases}}{\begin{pmatrix} \mathtt{case}\ e_0\ \mathtt{of\ nil\ =>}\ e_1 \\ \quad \mid x_1\ \mathtt{::}\ x_2\ \mathtt{=>}\ e_2 \\ \quad \mid f\ \mathtt{=>}\ e_3 \end{pmatrix} \Downarrow_{N_1+N_2}\ v}$$

Table 1: Evaluation relation

2. The divergent expression Ω does not evaluate to anything. Any derivation $\Omega \Downarrow_N v$ would have $\Omega \Downarrow_{N-1} v$ as premise, and this is impossible because of determinacy.

3. Let $e^\infty \stackrel{\text{def}}{=} (\texttt{fn}\ g\ \texttt{=>}\ \texttt{fn}\ x\ \texttt{=>}\ e(g\,g)x)\ (\texttt{fn}\ g\ \texttt{=>}\ \texttt{fn}\ x\ \texttt{=>}\ e(g\,g)x)$, so that $\texttt{Yv} = \texttt{fn}\ f\ \texttt{=>}\ f^\infty$. Then

$$\texttt{Yv}\ u \Downarrow_2 \texttt{fn}\ x\ \texttt{=>}\ u\,u^\infty\,x \quad \text{because} \quad u^\infty \Downarrow_1 \texttt{fn}\ x\ \texttt{=>}\ u\,u^\infty\,x,$$

for $u \in \mathit{Val}_\emptyset$.

Let an *evaluation context*, E, be a term with a hole, $-$, at redex position (Felleisen and Friedman 1987). They are given by the grammar:

$$(\textit{Ev. ctx.}) \qquad E ::= - \mid E :: e \mid e :: E \mid E\,e \mid e\,E \\ \mid \texttt{let val}\ x = E\ \texttt{in}\ e\ \texttt{end} \\ \mid (\texttt{case}\ E\ \texttt{of nil =>}\ e_1 \mid x_1 :: x_2\ \texttt{=>}\ e_2 \mid f\ \texttt{=>}\ e_3).$$

We write $E[e]$ for the term obtained from E by filling in e for the hole $-$. (We adopt a liberal definition of redex position which does not suggest an evaluation order in 'cons' expressions, $e_1 :: e_2$, and function applications, $e_1\ e_2$. One can indicate a left-to-right evaluation order by excluding evaluation contexts of the form $e :: E$ and $e\ E$ where e is not a value. But evaluation order is immaterial here as we do not consider small-step reductions of terms and our language has no side effects.)

Evaluation contexts satisfy

$$E[p] \Downarrow_N v \quad \text{iff} \quad \exists M, u.\, p \Downarrow_M u \ \&\ E[u] \Downarrow_{N-M} v. \tag{2.1}$$

Combined with the examples above, we see that $E[\Omega]$ diverges and

$$E[\texttt{I}\ p] \Downarrow_{N+1} v \quad \text{iff} \quad \texttt{I}\ E[p] \Downarrow_{N+1} v \quad \text{iff} \quad E[p] \Downarrow_N v. \tag{2.2}$$

3 Relations

This section introduces our notation for relations and operations on them. Compatible refinement and context closure are of particular importance. Their precise definitions are key to the relational proofs in later sections. The relational algebra given here is quite general and language independent, except that only value substitutions are considered as our language is call-by-value.

Open and closed relations

A binary relation R is a set of pairs. We use infix notation, $a\ R\ b$, to mean $(a, b) \in R$.

Let Rel be the universal relation on closed expressions,

$$Rel = \{(p, p') \mid p, p' \in Exp_\emptyset\}.$$

We call every $R \subseteq Rel$ a *closed* relation. For instance, $Id = \{(p, p) \mid p \in Exp_\emptyset\}$ is the closed identity relation.

Moreover, we define

$$Rel^\circ = \{((\vec{x})e, (\vec{x})e') \mid e, e' \in Exp_{\vec{x}}\},$$

where $(\vec{x})e$ is a 'meta-abstraction' of $e \in Exp_{\vec{x}}$; the $(\vec{x})$ prefix is a binder and $\vec{x}$ is subject to α-renaming. We call all $R \subseteq Rel^\circ$ *open* relations and write $\vec{x} \vdash e\ R\ e'$ whenever $(\vec{x})e\ R\ (\vec{x})e'$. By identifying every $p \in Exp_\emptyset$ with the 0-ary abstraction $()p$, we have $Rel \subseteq Rel^\circ$ and closed relations are special cases of open ones.

We call Rel° the *open extension* of Rel. Generally, given any closed relation R, its open extension, $R^\circ \subseteq Rel^\circ$, is given by

$$\frac{\forall v_1, \ldots, v_n \in Val_\emptyset.\ e\{v_1 \cdots v_n/x_1 \ldots x_n\}\ R\ e'\{v_1 \cdots v_n/x_1 \ldots x_n\}}{x_1 \ldots x_n \vdash e\ R^\circ\ e'}$$

For example, Id° is the open identity relation.

Both Rel and Rel° are closed under relation composition, which we write by juxtaposition, $a\ R\,S\ b \overset{\text{def}}{\Leftrightarrow} \exists c.\ a\ R\ c \wedge c\ S\ b$. Open extension satisfies

$$R^\circ\, S^\circ \subseteq (R\,S)^\circ. \tag{3.1}$$

Relation Substitution

For $R, S \subseteq Rel^\circ$, the *relation substitution* of S into R, written $R\{S\} \subseteq Rel^\circ$, relates expressions obtained by simultaneous substitution of S related values into R related expressions,

$$\frac{\vec{x} \vdash e\ R\ e' \quad \vec{y} \vdash \vec{v}\ S\ \vec{v}'}{\vec{y} \vdash e\{\vec{v}/\vec{x}\}\ R\{S\}\ e'\{\vec{v}'/\vec{x}\}}$$

where $\vec{y} \vdash \vec{v}\ S\ \vec{v}'$ is shorthand for $\vec{y} \vdash v_i\ S\ v_i'$, for all $i = 1 \ldots n$, if $\vec{v} = v_1 \ldots v_n$ and $\vec{v}' = v_1' \ldots v_n'$. Relation substitution is associative. Note that $R\{S\} \subseteq Rel$ if $S \subseteq Rel$. As a drill in the notation let us show

$$R \subseteq S^\circ \quad \text{iff} \quad R\{Id\} \subseteq S. \tag{3.2}$$

For the forward implication, suppose $R \subseteq S^\circ$ and $e\{\vec{v}/\vec{x}\}\ R\{Id\}\ e'\{\vec{v}/\vec{x}\}$ because $\vec{x} \vdash e\ R\ e'$ and $v_1, \ldots, v_n \in Val_\emptyset$. Then $\vec{x} \vdash e\ S^\circ\ e'$ and, by definition of open extension, $e\{\vec{v}/\vec{x}\}\ S\ e'\{\vec{v}/\vec{x}\}$. Conversely, if $R\{Id\} \subseteq S$ and $\vec{x} \vdash e\ R\ e'$ then $e\{\vec{v}/\vec{x}\}\ R\{Id\}\ e'\{\vec{v}/\vec{x}\}$ and $e\{\vec{v}/\vec{x}\}\ S\ e'\{\vec{v}/\vec{x}\}$, for all $v_1, \ldots, v_n \in Val_\emptyset$. From the definition of open extension we get $\vec{x} \vdash e\ S^\circ\ e'$, as required.

$$\text{(Comp } x\text{)}\ \vec{x}x\vec{y} \vdash x\ \widehat{R}\ x$$

$$\text{(Comp fn)}\ \frac{\vec{x}x \vdash e\ R\ e'}{\vec{x} \vdash \texttt{fn}\ x\ \texttt{=>}\ e\ \ \widehat{R}\ \ \texttt{fn}\ x\ \texttt{=>}\ e'}$$

$$\text{(Comp nil)}\ \vec{x} \vdash \texttt{nil}\ \widehat{R}\ \texttt{nil}$$

$$\text{(Comp cons)}\ \frac{\vec{x} \vdash e_1\ R\ e_1' \quad \vec{x} \vdash e_2\ R\ e_2'}{\vec{x} \vdash e_1\ \texttt{::}\ e_2\ \ \widehat{R}\ \ e_1'\ \texttt{::}\ e_2'}$$

$$\text{(Comp apply)}\ \frac{\vec{x} \vdash e_1\ R\ e_1' \quad \vec{x} \vdash e_2\ R\ e_2'}{\vec{x} \vdash e_1\ e_2\ \ \widehat{R}\ \ e_1'\ e_2'}$$

$$\text{(Comp let fun)}\ \frac{\vec{x}fx \vdash d\ R\ d' \quad \vec{x}f \vdash e\ R\ e'}{\vec{x} \vdash \texttt{let fun}\ f\ x = d\ \texttt{in}\ e\ \texttt{end}\ \ \widehat{R}\ \ \texttt{let fun}\ f\ x = d'\ \texttt{in}\ e'\ \texttt{end}}$$

$$\text{(Comp let val)}\ \frac{\vec{x} \vdash d\ R\ d' \quad \vec{x}x \vdash e\ R\ e'}{\vec{x} \vdash \texttt{let val}\ x = d\ \texttt{in}\ e\ \texttt{end}\ \ \widehat{R}\ \ \texttt{let val}\ x = d'\ \texttt{in}\ e'\ \texttt{end}}$$

$$\text{(Comp case)}\ \frac{\vec{x} \vdash d\ R\ d' \quad \vec{x} \vdash e_1\ R\ e_1' \quad \vec{x}x_1x_2 \vdash e_2\ R\ e_2' \quad \vec{x}f \vdash e_3\ R\ e_3'}{\vec{x} \vdash \begin{pmatrix} \texttt{case}\ d\ \texttt{of nil =>}\ e_1 \\ \quad \mid x_1\ \texttt{::}\ x_2\ \texttt{=>}\ e_2 \\ \quad \mid f\ \texttt{=>}\ e_3 \end{pmatrix} \widehat{R} \begin{pmatrix} \texttt{case}\ d'\ \texttt{of nil =>}\ e_1' \\ \quad \mid x_1\ \texttt{::}\ x_2\ \texttt{=>}\ e_2' \\ \quad \mid f\ \texttt{=>}\ e_3' \end{pmatrix}}$$

Table 2: Compatible refinement

For any open relation R, we say R satisfies *weakening* if

$$\vec{x}\vec{y} \vdash e\ R\ e' \ \Rightarrow\ \vec{x}x\vec{y} \vdash e\ R\ e',\ \text{if } x \notin \vec{x}\vec{y}.$$

We call R *substitutive* if $R\{R\} \subseteq R$, and we say that R is *closed under substitutions* if $R\{Id^\circ\} \subseteq R$. In the latter case $R\{Id\} = R \cap Rel$. Every open extension, R°, satisfies weakening and is closed under substitutions. Any substitutive and reflexive open relation also satisfies weakening and closure under substitutions. Each of these properties is preserved by relation composition.

Compatible refinement

For every open relation R, its *compatible refinement* (Gordon 1994) $\widehat{R} \subseteq Rel^\circ$ relates expressions with identical outermost syntactic constructor and immediate subterms pairwise related by R. Table 2 makes this definition precise for our language. Compatible refinement is monotone, preserves weakening, and commutes with relation composition, $\widehat{RS} = \widehat{R}\,\widehat{S}$.

An open relation R is *compatible* if $\widehat{R} \subseteq R$. Every compatible relation is reflexive, as can be shown by structural induction on expressions.

Compatibility can also be expressed in terms of contexts. A *context* C is an expression with 'holes'. If C has n holes, $C[e_1, \ldots, e_n]$ denotes the expression obtained by filling expressions $e_1 \ldots e_n$ into the holes in C, possibly involving capture of free variables of e_i if the i'th hole occurs in the scope of binders in C, for $i = 1, \ldots, n$. A relation R is compatible if whenever e_i and e'_i are related by R, for $i = 1, \ldots, n$, so are $C[e_1, \ldots, e_n]$ and $C[e'_1, \ldots, e'_n]$, for all contexts C. But a precise formulation of this which accounts for free variables and variable capture becomes complicated. The formalisation above, $\widehat{R} \subseteq R$, is easier to work with.

Throughout, we exploit compatible refinement as a tractable, indirect notation for contexts.

Lemma 1 *Any compatible and transitive relation which is closed under substitutions is substitutive.*

Proof Suppose R is compatible, transitive and closed under substitutions. If $\vec{x} \vdash e\ R\ e'$ and $\vec{y} \vdash \vec{u}\ R\ \vec{u}'$, then $\vec{y} \vdash e\{\vec{u}/\vec{x}\}\ Id^{\circ}\{R\}\ e\{\vec{u}'/\vec{x}\}$ and $\vec{y} \vdash e\{\vec{u}'/\vec{x}\}\ R\{Id^{\circ}\}\ e'\{\vec{u}'/\vec{x}\}$. Since R is compatible, $\vec{y} \vdash e\{\vec{u}/\vec{x}\}\ R\ e\{\vec{u}'/\vec{x}\}$ follows by easy structural induction on e; in general, $Id^{\circ}\{R\} \subseteq R$ for any compatible relation R. Moreover, $\vec{y} \vdash e\{\vec{u}'/\vec{x}\}\ R\ e'\{\vec{u}'/\vec{x}\}$ since R is closed under substitutions. By transitivity we conclude $\vec{y} \vdash e\{\vec{u}/\vec{x}\}\ R\ e'\{\vec{u}'/\vec{x}\}$, as required. □

Context closure

For any relation R, its *context closure*, $R^{\mathsf{C}} \subseteq Rel^{\circ}$, relates expressions e, e' with matching outermost context C,

$$e = C[d_1, \ldots, d_n], \quad e' = C[d'_1, \ldots, d'_n],$$

and subterms d_i, d'_i related by R. This can be defined inductively by means of compatible refinement,

$$(\text{Ctx } R)\ \frac{\vec{y} \vdash e\ R\ e'}{\vec{x} \vdash e\ R^{\mathsf{C}}\ e'} \text{ if } \vec{y} \subseteq \vec{x} \qquad (\text{Ctx Comp})\ \frac{\vec{x} \vdash e\ \widehat{R^{\mathsf{C}}}\ e'}{\vec{x} \vdash e\ R^{\mathsf{C}}\ e'}$$

where $\vec{y} \subseteq \vec{x}$ means that all variables in $\vec{y}$ occur in $\vec{x}$, in any order. The side condition $\vec{y} \subseteq \vec{x}$ ensures that R^{C} satisfies weakening, even if R does not. Furthermore, context closure is monotone, idempotent $(R^{\mathsf{C}})^{\mathsf{C}} = R^{\mathsf{C}}$, and R^{C} is compatible, by (Ctx Comp).

Lemma 2 *If R is closed then R^{C} is substitutive.*

Proof (Sketch) Whenever $\vec{x} \vdash e\ R^{\mathsf{C}}\ e'$ and $\vec{y} \vdash \vec{v}\ R^{\mathsf{C}}\ \vec{v}'$, we can prove $\vec{y} \vdash e\{\vec{v}/\vec{x}\}\ R^{\mathsf{C}}\ e'\{\vec{v}'/\vec{x}\}$ by induction on the derivation of $\vec{x} \vdash e\ R^{\mathsf{C}}\ e'$.

Weakening is used as we enter the scope of binders. For example, if $\vec{x} \vdash e\ R^{\mathsf{C}}\ e'$ is derived by (Ctx Comp) and (Comp fn), then $e = \texttt{fn}\ z\ \texttt{=>}\ d$, $e' = \texttt{fn}\ z\ \texttt{=>}\ d'$, and $\vec{x}z \vdash d\ R^{\mathsf{C}}\ d'$. By weakening, $\vec{y}z \vdash \vec{v}\ R^{\mathsf{C}}\ \vec{v}'$ holds. Furthermore, $\vec{y}z \vdash z\ R^{\mathsf{C}}\ z$, by (Comp x) and (Ctx Comp). We calculate

$$\begin{array}{lll} & \vec{x}z \vdash d\ R^{\mathsf{C}}\ d' \ \&\ \vec{y}z \vdash \vec{v}z\ R^{\mathsf{C}}\ \vec{v}'z & \\ \Rightarrow & \vec{y}z \vdash d\{\vec{v}z/\vec{x}z\}\ R^{\mathsf{C}}\ d'\{\vec{v}'z/\vec{x}z\} & \text{by induction hypothesis} \\ \Rightarrow & \vec{y}z \vdash d\{\vec{v}/\vec{x}\}\ R^{\mathsf{C}}\ d'\{\vec{v}'/\vec{x}\} & \\ \Rightarrow & \vec{y} \vdash (\texttt{fn}\ z\ \texttt{=>}\ d\{\vec{v}/\vec{x}\})\ \widehat{R^{\mathsf{C}}}\ (\texttt{fn}\ z\ \texttt{=>}\ d'\{\vec{v}'/\vec{x}\}) & \text{by (Comp fn)} \\ \Rightarrow & \vec{y} \vdash e\{\vec{v}/\vec{x}\}\ R^{\mathsf{C}}\ e'\{\vec{v}'/\vec{x}\} & \text{by (Ctx Comp).} \end{array}$$

□

Substitutive context closure, R^{SC}, is a substitutive extension of ordinary context closure, R^{C}. Each R^{SC} relates expressions e, e' with matching outermost context C,

$$e = C[d_1\{\vec{v_1}/\vec{x}\}, \ldots, d_n\{\vec{v_n}/\vec{x}\}], \quad e' = C[d_1'\{\vec{v_1}'/\vec{x}\}, \ldots, d_n'\{\vec{v_n}'/\vec{x}\}],$$

subterms d_i', d_i' related by R, and substitutions with values $\vec{v_i}, \vec{v_i}'$ inductively related by R^{SC}. It is important that R^{SC} has a succinct inductive definition,

$$\text{(SC Subst)}\ \frac{\vec{x} \vdash e\ R\{R^{\mathsf{SC}}\}\ e'}{\vec{x} \vdash e\ R^{\mathsf{SC}}\ e'} \qquad \text{(SC Comp)}\ \frac{\vec{x} \vdash e\ \widehat{R^{\mathsf{SC}}}\ e'}{\vec{x} \vdash e\ R^{\mathsf{SC}}\ e'}$$

Clearly $R^{\mathsf{C}} \subseteq R^{\mathsf{SC}}$ and if R is closed they coincide. The advantage of R^{SC} is that it is always substitutive. Substitutive context closure is monotone, idempotent, and R^{SC} is compatible, substitutive, and satisfies weakening. Compatibility is direct from (SC Comp). Weakening and substitutivity follow by induction on derivations. Since R^{SC} is compatible and substitutive, it is also reflexive and closed under substitutions.

Readers familiar with 'meta-terms' (Klop, van Oostrom, and van Raamsdonk 1993) will notice that substitutive context closure corresponds to closure under substitution of related meta-abstractions for meta-variables in meta-terms, whereas ordinary context closure is the closure under conventional variable capturing contexts. In fact, Pitts (1994b) advocates meta-terms, called 'extended expressions', as a generalised notion of contexts in place of conventional variable capturing contexts because the latter cannot be identified up to α-renaming of bound variables. However, our relational representation of contexts allows us to reason about conventional variable capturing contexts up to α-equivalence.

4 The unwinding theorem

As a first illustration of our relational approach to reasoning about contexts, we give a relational proof of the unwinding theorem. It says that a recursive function in a context converges if and only if one of its finite approximants does. The *finite approximants* of $\texttt{rec}\ f\ x\ \texttt{=>}\ d$ are given inductively by

$$\begin{array}{lll} \texttt{rec}^{(0)}\ f\ x\ \texttt{=>}\ d & \stackrel{\text{def}}{=} & \texttt{fn}\ x\ \texttt{=>}\ \Omega, \\ \texttt{rec}^{(n+1)}\ f\ x\ \texttt{=>}\ d & \stackrel{\text{def}}{=} & \texttt{fn}\ x\ \texttt{=>}\ \texttt{let val}\ f\ \texttt{=}\ (\texttt{rec}^{(n)}\ f\ x\ \texttt{=>}\ d)\ \texttt{in}\ d\ \texttt{end}. \end{array}$$

We say p *converges* iff $\exists v.\ p \Downarrow v$.

Theorem 1 (Unwinding) *For every recursive function* $\texttt{rec}\ f\ x \texttt{ => } d$ *and every context* C, $C[\texttt{rec}\ f\ x \texttt{ => } d]$ *converges if and only if there exists* $n \geq 0$ *such that* $C[\texttt{rec}^{(n)}\ f\ x \texttt{ => } d]$ *converges.*

Our proof below shows how the relational notation offers a tractable formulation of a complex syntactic argument. For instance, the proof is not complicated by the fact that we prove the theorem for arbitrary recursive functions, possibly with free variables.

First we construct a family of relations $\{R_n\}_{n\geq 0}$ with each R_n given by

$$\vec{x} \vdash \texttt{rec}\ f\ x \texttt{ => } d\ \ R_n\ \ \texttt{rec}^{(n)}\ f\ x \texttt{ => } d,$$

$$\vec{x} \vdash \texttt{let fun}\ f\ x = d\ \texttt{in}\ d\ \texttt{end}\ \ R_n\ \ \texttt{let val}\ f = (\texttt{rec}^{(n)}\ f\ x \texttt{ => } d)\ \texttt{in}\ d\ \texttt{end},$$

if $d \in \mathit{Exp}_{\vec{x}fx}$. For each $n \geq 0$, we construct a relation U_n which satisfies

$$\vdash C[\texttt{rec}\ f\ x \texttt{ => } d]\ \ U_n\ \ C[\texttt{rec}^{(n)}\ f\ x \texttt{ => } d], \tag{4.1}$$

for arbitrary contexts C. In the course of the proof of the main lemma below, U_n must be preserved by evaluation in an appropriate sense. Therefore we cannot take U_n to be the context closure of R_n. We are going to strengthen the induction hypothesis by taking U_n to be the larger relation

$$U_n \stackrel{\text{def}}{=} \left(\bigcup_{m\geq n} R_m\right)^{\mathsf{SC}}.$$

By this definition, U_n satisfies (4.1), it is substitutive, and $U_n \subseteq U_{n'}$ whenever $n' \leq n$. These are key properties for the proof that are easier to formulate precisely in terms of relations rather than contexts. The inductive definition of substitutive context closure is also convenient for formal reasoning. By the construction of U_n, whenever $\vec{x} \vdash e\ U_n\ e'$, we can argue by cases on the derivation: either $\vec{x} \vdash e\ R_m\{U_n\}\ e'$ for some $m \geq n$, by (SC Subst), and we can decompose e and e' into expressions related by R_m and substitutions of values related by U_n; or $\vec{x} \vdash e\ \widehat{U_n}\ e'$, by (SC Comp), and we may proceed by analysis of the derivation by the rules for compatible refinement in Table 2. For instance, we can deduce, for all values v and v',

$$\vec{x} \vdash v\ U_{n+1}\ v' \quad \text{implies} \quad \vec{x} \vdash v\ \widehat{U_n}\ v', \tag{4.2}$$

since $U_{n+1} \subseteq U_n$ and $\vec{x} \vdash \texttt{rec}\ f\ x \texttt{ => } d\ \ \widehat{R_m}\ \ \texttt{rec}^{(m+1)}\ f\ x \texttt{ => } d$, for all m.

Lemma 3

(1) If $\vdash p\ U_{n+N}\ p'$ *and* $p \Downarrow_N v$, *also* $p' \Downarrow_N v'$ *and* $\vdash v\ U_n\ v'$, *for some* v'.

(2) If $\vdash p\ U_0\ p'$ *and* $p' \Downarrow_N v'$*, also* $p \Downarrow_N v$ *and* $\vdash v\ U_0\ v'$*, for some* v.

Proof In outline, the proof argument for (1) is that any occurrence of `rec` in p is "unfolded" (evaluated recursively) at most N times in the evaluation $p \Downarrow_N v$ and evaluates in "lock-step" with any $\mathtt{rec}^{(m+N)}$ in p' ($m \geq n$). In the end, each residual occurrence of `rec` in v is matched by some $\mathtt{rec}^{(m')}$ in v' ($m' \geq n$). The proof of (2) is similar; evaluation of $\mathtt{rec}^{(m)}$ in p' is matched by evaluation of `rec` in p such that any residual occurrence $\mathtt{rec}^{(m')}$ in v' is matched by `rec` in v.

We spell out the proof of (1) in detail as illustration of the relational proof technique explored in this paper. By induction on the derivation of $p \Downarrow_N v$, we inductively construct a related derivation $p' \Downarrow_N v'$. Consider the derivation of $\vdash p\ U_{n+N}\ p'$. There are two cases:

(SC Subst) $\vdash p\ R_m\{U_{n+N}\}\ p'$, for some $m \geq n + N$, and $p = r\{\vec{u}/\vec{x}\}$, $p' = r_m\{\vec{u}'/\vec{x}\}$, where $\vec{x} \vdash r\ R_m\ r_m$ and $\vdash \vec{u}\ U_{n+N}\ \vec{u}'$.

If $r = \mathtt{rec}\ f\ x \Rightarrow d$, $r_m = \mathtt{rec}^{(m)}\ f\ x \Rightarrow d$, then p, p' are values, $N = 0$, $v = p$, $p' \Downarrow_0 v' = p'$, and $\vdash v = p\ U_n\ p' = v'$.

If $r = \mathtt{let\ fun}\ f\ x = d\ \mathtt{in}\ e\ \mathtt{end}$, $r_m = \mathtt{let\ fun}^{(m)}\ f\ x = d\ \mathtt{in}\ e\ \mathtt{end}$, then $p \Downarrow_N v$ must be derived by rule (Eval let fun) from $e\{\vec{u}t/\vec{x}f\} \Downarrow_N v$, where $t = (\mathtt{rec}\ f\ x \Rightarrow d)\{\vec{u}/\vec{x}\}$. We let $t' = (\mathtt{rec}^{(m)}\ f\ x \Rightarrow d)\{\vec{u}'/\vec{x}\}$ and observe that $\vdash t\ U_{n+N}\ t'$ and $\vdash e\{\vec{u}t/\vec{x}f\}\ U_{n+N}\ e\{\vec{u}'t'/\vec{x}f\}$. By induction hypothesis $e\{\vec{u}'t'/\vec{x}f\} \Downarrow_N v'$ with $\vdash v\ U_n\ v'$. And from the definition of r_m and by (Eval let val), also $p' \Downarrow_N v'$.

(SC Comp) $\vdash p\ \widehat{U_{n+N}}\ p'$. We proceed by analysis of the derivation of $p \Downarrow_N v$.

Case (Eval apply) $p = p_1\, p_2$, $p_1 \Downarrow_{N_1} v_1 = \mathtt{fn}\ x \Rightarrow e$, $p_2 \Downarrow_{N_2} v_2$, $e\{v_2/x\} \Downarrow_{N_3} v$, and $N = N_1 + N_2 + N_3 + 1$. By (Comp apply), $p' = p_1'\, p_2'$ with $\vdash p_i\ U_{n+N}\ p_i'$ and by the induction hypothesis $p_i' \Downarrow_{N_i} v_i'$ with $\vdash v_i\ U_{n+N-N_i}\ v_i'$. Notice that $n + N - N_i > n + N_3 + 1$, for $i = 1, 2$. Therefore $\vdash v_2\ U_{n+N_3}\ v_2'$ and from (4.2) follows $v_1' = \mathtt{fn}\ x \Rightarrow e'$ such that $x \vdash e\ U_{n+N_3}\ e'$. So $\vdash e\{v_2/x\}\ U_{n+N_3}\ e'\{v_2'/x\}$, by substitutivity, and $e'\{v_2'/x\} \Downarrow_{N_3} v'$ with $\vdash v\ U_n\ v'$, by induction hypothesis. By (Eval apply), we conclude $p' \Downarrow_N v'$.

Case (Eval let fun) $p = \mathtt{let\ fun}\ f\ x = e_1\ \mathtt{in}\ e_2\ \mathtt{end}$ and $e_2\{(\mathtt{rec}\ f\ x \Rightarrow e_1)/f\} \Downarrow_N v$. We have $p' = \mathtt{let\ fun}\ f\ x = e_1'\ \mathtt{in}\ e_2'\ \mathtt{end}$, with $fx \vdash e_1\ U_{n+N}\ e_1'$ and $f \vdash e_2\ U_{n+N}\ e_2'$. Then also $\vdash \mathtt{rec}\ f\ x \Rightarrow e_1\ U_{n+N}\ \mathtt{rec}\ f\ x \Rightarrow e_1'$ and $\vdash e_2\{(\mathtt{rec}\ f\ x \Rightarrow e_1)/f\}\ U_{n+N}\ e_2'\{(\mathtt{rec}\ f\ x \Rightarrow e_1')/f\}$ by compatibility and substitutivity of U_{n+N}. By the induction hypothesis $e_2'\{(\mathtt{rec}\ f\ x \Rightarrow e_1')/f\} \Downarrow_N v'$ such that $\vdash v\ U_n\ v'$. By (Eval let fun), we conclude $p' \Downarrow_N v'$.

Case (Eval case) $p = \texttt{case}\ p_0\ \texttt{of nil => } e_1 \mid x_1\ \texttt{::}\ x_2\ \texttt{=>}\ e_2 \mid f\ \texttt{=>}\ e_3$, $p_0 \Downarrow_{N_1} u$, $q \Downarrow_{N_2} v$, $N = N_1 + N_2$, where

$$q = \begin{cases} e_1 & \text{if } u = \texttt{nil} \\ e_2\{u_1/x_1, u_2/x_2\} & \text{if } u = u_1\ \texttt{::}\ u_2 \\ e_3\{u/f\} & \text{if } u = \texttt{fn}\ x\ \texttt{=>}\ e. \end{cases}$$

By (Comp case), $p' = \texttt{case}\ p_0'\ \texttt{of nil => } e_1' \mid x_1\ \texttt{::}\ x_2\ \texttt{=>}\ e_2' \mid f\ \texttt{=>}\ e_3'$, with $\vdash p_0\ U_{n+N}\ p_0'$, $\vdash e_1\ U_{n+N}\ e_1'$, $x_1x_2 \vdash e_2\ U_{n+N}\ e_2'$, $f \vdash e_3\ U_{n+N}\ e_3'$. By induction hypothesis $p_0' \Downarrow_{N_1} u'$ such that $\vdash u\ U_{n+N_2}\ u'$, since $n + N = (n+N_2)+N_1$. By analysis of the derivation of $\vdash u\ U_{n+N_2}\ u'$ we see that they have matching outermost constructor and, if this is not function abstraction, also $\vdash u\ \widehat{U_{n+N_2}}\ u'$. Accordingly, let

$$q' = \begin{cases} e_1' & \text{if } u = \texttt{nil} = u' \\ e_2'\{u_1'/x_1, u_2'/x_2\} & \text{if } u = u_1\ \texttt{::}\ u_2, u' = u_1'\ \texttt{::}\ u_2' \text{ with } \vdash u_i\ U_{n+N_2}\ u_i' \\ e_3'\{u'/f\} & \text{if } u = \texttt{fn}\ x\ \texttt{=>}\ e, u' = \texttt{fn}\ x\ \texttt{=>}\ e'. \end{cases}$$

Since $N_2 \leq N$, $U_{n+N} \subseteq U_{n+N_2}$ and, by substitutivity of U_{n+N_2}, $\vdash q\ U_{n+N_2}\ q'$. By induction hypothesis $q' \Downarrow_{N_2} v'$ with $\vdash v\ U_n\ v'$ and we conclude $p' \Downarrow_N v'$ by (Eval case).

The remaining cases are simpler. This completes the proof of (1).

The proof of (2) is very similar and proceeds by induction on the derivation of $p' \Downarrow_N v'$. The (Eval apply) case exploits that the applied function cannot be $\texttt{rec}^{(0)}\ f\ x\ \texttt{=>}\ e$ as this would diverge. □

Proof of The Unwinding Theorem If $C[\texttt{rec}\ f\ x\ \texttt{=>}\ d] \Downarrow_N v$, from (4.1) and Lemma 3(1) follows, for all $n \geq N$, $\exists v'.\ C[\texttt{rec}^{(n)}\ f\ x\ \texttt{=>}\ d] \Downarrow_N v'$. Conversely, if $C[\texttt{rec}^{(n)}\ f\ x\ \texttt{=>}\ d] \Downarrow_N v'$, also $\exists v.\ C[\texttt{rec}\ f\ x\ \texttt{=>}\ d] \Downarrow_N v$, by (4.1) and Lemma 3(2) because $U_n \subseteq U_0$. □

The backward direction of the proof can also be derived from the (computationally adequate) theory of applicative bisimulation below, instead of Lemma 3(2).

An important consequence of the unwinding theorem is a 'syntactic continuity' property of contextual equivalence (Pitts 1997). In Sections 5.4 and 6.3 we see how Lemma 3 entails syntactic continuity for applicative similarity and improvement. Syntactic continuity is a 'domain-theoretic' property that holds in all computationally adequate continuous models; see Pitts (1996a) and Braüner (1996).

There exist a number of operational proofs of these results, both for small-step reduction semantics (Mason, Smith, and Talcott 1996; Sands 1997a) and big-step evaluation semantics like ours (Pitts 1997). But note that our proof holds for *open* recursive terms r and that Lemma 3 gives very precise information about the operational relationship between r and its finite approximants. Our relational notation makes it feasible to express and reason about the details of contexts and substitutions. A characteristic of such relational proofs is that operational issues are dealt with in one sweeping induction on the derivation of evaluations and syntactic issues are dealt with in terms of the general algebra of relations. No auxiliary lemmas about evaluation and contexts are needed.

In the remainder of the paper we apply the relational technique used in the proof above to the study of operational preorders and equivalences.

5 Similarity

The primary operational relation we study is Abramsky's applicative bisimulation (Abramsky 1990). It is the basis for a co-inductive generalisation of Milner's context lemma (Milner 1977) to untyped functional languages. The basic idea is that higher-order functions are infinite data structures, built from the 'lazy' function abstraction data constructor, and are related co-inductively by applicative bisimulation in analogy with bisimulation of infinite behaviours in process calculi.

In this section we develop the theory of applicative (bi)simulation for our language, including preliminary simulation up to context results based on Howe's and Pitts' congruence proof techniques. This part is mainly a presentation of unpublished work by Pitts (1995) and serves as a basis for our further developments of this idea in Sections 6 and 7. Our aim is to develop techniques for reasoning about recursion. We shall see that simulation up to context is particularly useful for this purpose. In order to complete the discussion of proof rules for recursion we also prove a syntactic continuity property.

We consider an applicative bisimulation preorder, $\lesssim \subseteq Rel$, which we call *similarity*. Expressions are similar if they evaluate to similar values.

$$p \lesssim p' \quad \text{iff} \quad \forall v.\, p \Downarrow v \Rightarrow \exists v'.\, p' \Downarrow v' \;\&\; v \lesssim v'. \tag{5.1}$$

Functions are similar if they are similar on all arguments; by definition of open extension this may be expressed as

$$\texttt{fn}\, x \texttt{ => } e \;\lesssim\; \texttt{fn}\, x \texttt{ => } e' \quad \text{iff} \quad x \vdash e \lesssim^{\circ} e'. \tag{5.2}$$

Following Howe (1996) we extend similarity to arbitrary values with matching outermost constructor and immediate subterms pairwise similar.

$$\texttt{nil} \;\lesssim\; \texttt{nil}. \tag{5.3}$$

$$v_1 \texttt{ :: } v_2 \;\lesssim\; v_1' \texttt{ :: } v_2' \quad \text{iff} \quad v_1 \lesssim v_1' \quad \text{and} \quad v_2 \lesssim v_2'. \tag{5.4}$$

We regard (5.2)–(5.4) as a definition of similarity on values by structural induction. We formalise this by means of a variant of compatible refinement on values, akin to Gordon's 'matching values' (Gordon 1995). For every open relation R, let $\overline{R}$ relate 'matching' values built from identical value constructors and with function

$$\text{(Match } x\text{)}\ \vec{x}x\vec{y} \vdash x\ \overline{R}\ x$$

$$\text{(Match fn)}\ \frac{\vec{x}x \vdash e\ R\ e'}{\vec{x} \vdash \texttt{fn}\ x\ \texttt{=>}\ e\ \overline{R}\ \texttt{fn}\ x\ \texttt{=>}\ e'}$$

$$\text{(Match nil)}\ \vec{x} \vdash \texttt{nil}\ \overline{R}\ \texttt{nil}$$

$$\text{(Match cons)}\ \frac{\vec{x} \vdash v_1\ \overline{R}\ v_1' \quad \vec{x} \vdash v_2\ \overline{R}\ v_2'}{\vec{x} \vdash v_1\ \texttt{::}\ v_2\ \overline{R}\ v_1'\ \texttt{::}\ v_2'}$$

Table 3: Matching values

bodies pairwise related by R. This is defined inductively by the rules in Table 3. Now (5.2)–(5.4) can be expressed by

$$v \lesssim v' \quad \text{iff} \quad \vdash v\ \overline{\lesssim^{\circ}}\ v'. \tag{5.5}$$

We take the mutually recursive equations (5.1) and (5.5) as a co-inductive definition of similarity. To make this definition precise, we define a monotone simulation operator on relations, $\langle\_\rangle$, which maps any open relation $R \subseteq \mathit{Rel}^{\circ}$ to the closed relation $\langle R\rangle \subseteq \mathit{Rel}$ given by

$$p\ \langle R\rangle\ p' \overset{\text{def}}{\Leftrightarrow} \forall v.\, p \Downarrow v \ \Rightarrow\ \exists v'.\, p' \Downarrow v' \ \&\ \vdash v\ \overline{R}\ v'.$$

We define similarity co-inductively as the greatest fixed point of $\langle\_^{\circ}\rangle$,

$$\lesssim \ \overset{\text{def}}{=}\ \nu R.\langle R^{\circ}\rangle, \tag{5.6}$$

and *bisimilarity*, $\sim$, as the greatest symmetric fixed point, definable as

$$\sim \ \overset{\text{def}}{=}\ \nu R.\langle R^{\circ}\rangle \cap \langle (R^{\circ})^{\text{op}}\rangle^{\text{op}},$$

where $a\ S^{\text{op}}\ b \overset{\text{def}}{\Leftrightarrow} b\ S\ a$, for every relation S. Closed relations form a complete lattice, ordered by subset inclusion, and $\langle\_^{\circ}\rangle$ and $\langle\_^{\circ}\rangle \cap \langle(\_^{\circ})^{\text{op}}\rangle^{\text{op}}$ are monotone operations with respect to this ordering. The Tarski-Knaster fixed point theorem asserts that their greatest fixed points exist and are also greatest post-fixed points.

Since evaluation is deterministic, $\sim$ is the largest symmetric relation contained in $\lesssim$,

$$\sim \ \overset{\text{def}}{=}\ \lesssim \cap \lesssim^{\text{op}}.$$

Therefore it suffices to focus attention on the more primitive relation $\lesssim$. In particular, we shall only formulate simulation proof rules for $\lesssim$ and omit the obvious analogues for $\sim$.

Equations (5.1)–(5.4) hold because $\lesssim$ is a fixed point, $\lesssim \; = \langle \lesssim^\circ \rangle$. An immediate consequence of (5.1) is *computational adequacy* with respect to termination behaviour,

$$p \not\lesssim \Omega \quad \text{iff} \quad \exists v.\ p \Downarrow v. \tag{5.7}$$

We shall call $R \subseteq \mathit{Rel}$ a *simulation* if it is a post-fixed point of $\langle \_^\circ \rangle$, that is, $R \subseteq \langle R^\circ \rangle$. By the co-inductive definition (5.6), $\lesssim$ is the largest simulation, and we have the co-induction simulation rule:

$$\frac{R \subseteq \langle R^\circ \rangle}{R \subseteq \lesssim}$$

Simulation is a powerful proof technique. To prove two expressions similar, we exhibit a simulation containing them. For example, $\lesssim$ is reflexive because the identity relation is a simulation, $\mathit{Id} \subseteq \langle \mathit{Id}^\circ \rangle$, and $\lesssim$ is transitive because $\lesssim \lesssim$ is a simulation, $\lesssim \lesssim \; = \langle \lesssim^\circ \rangle \langle \lesssim^\circ \rangle \subseteq \langle \lesssim^\circ \lesssim^\circ \rangle \subseteq \langle (\lesssim \lesssim)^\circ \rangle$, where we use the fact that $\langle \_ \rangle$ satisfies

$$\langle R \rangle \langle S \rangle \subseteq \langle R\, S \rangle, \text{ for all } R, S \subseteq \mathit{Rel}^\circ. \tag{5.8}$$

Hence $\lesssim$ is a preorder and $\sim$ is an equivalence relation.

We call expressions p and p' *Kleene equivalent* if they both diverge or both evaluate to the same value (because of determinacy, each expression can evaluate to at most one value). Kleene equivalence is easily seen to be a symmetric simulation and hence is included in $\sim$. An immediate consequence is *soundness* of evaluation with respect to bisimilarity,

$$p \Downarrow v \quad \text{implies} \quad p \sim v. \tag{5.9}$$

Many useful program laws are instances of Kleene equivalence. For instance, beta laws such as

$$(\texttt{fn}\ x\ \texttt{=>}\ e)\ v \ \sim\ e\{v/x\}.$$

$$\texttt{let fun}\ f\ x = d\ \texttt{in}\ e\ \texttt{end} \ \sim\ e\{(\texttt{rec}\ f\ x\ \texttt{=>}\ d)/f\}.$$

These also hold for open expressions and $\sim^\circ$, by definition of open extension. From the beta law for recursive function declarations follows a fixed point law for recursive functions,

$$\texttt{rec}\ f\ x\ \texttt{=>}\ d \ \sim\ \texttt{fn}\ x\ \texttt{=>}\ d\{(\texttt{rec}\ f\ x\ \texttt{=>}\ d)/f\},$$

by (5.2) and the definition of $\texttt{rec}\ f\ x\ \texttt{=>}\ d$.

As an example of a co-inductive argument about recursive data, consider

$$u \stackrel{\text{def}}{=} \texttt{rec}\ f\ x\ \texttt{=>}\ f, \quad v \stackrel{\text{def}}{=} \texttt{rec}\ f\ x\ \texttt{=>}\ \texttt{fn}\ y\ \texttt{=>}\ f. \tag{5.10}$$

By definition of recursive functions, $u = \texttt{fn}\ x\ \texttt{=>}\ p$ and $v = \texttt{fn}\ x\ \texttt{=>}\ q$, where

$$p \stackrel{\text{def}}{=} \texttt{let fun}\ f\ x = f\ \texttt{in}\ f\ \texttt{end},$$

$$q \stackrel{\text{def}}{=} \texttt{let fun}\ f\ x = (\texttt{fn}\ y\ \texttt{=>}\ f)\ \texttt{in}\ (\texttt{fn}\ y\ \texttt{=>}\ f)\ \texttt{end}.$$

Observe that $p \Downarrow u$ and $q \Downarrow \texttt{fn}\ y$ `=>` v. Both u and v perpetually return a function no matter how many arguments they are applied to. To see that they are bisimilar, we construct the relation $R = \{(p,q),(p,v)\}$ satisfying $u\ \langle R^\circ\rangle\ v$ and $v\ \langle (R^\circ)^{\text{op}}\rangle\ u$. Both R and R^{op} are simulations, hence $R \subseteq \sim$, and $u \sim v$ follows by definition of $\sim$ because $\langle \_ \rangle$ is monotone.

Similarity extends to open expressions by open extension, $\lesssim^\circ$. A manipulation of fixed points and monotone operators yields $\lesssim^\circ = \nu R.\langle R\rangle^\circ$. We call R an *open simulation* if $R \subseteq \langle R\rangle^\circ$, in which case $R \subseteq \lesssim^\circ$, by co-induction.

$$\frac{R \subseteq \langle R\rangle^\circ}{R \subseteq \lesssim^\circ} \tag{5.11}$$

By (3.2), $R \subseteq \langle R\rangle^\circ$ iff $R\{\mathit{Id}\} \subseteq \langle R\rangle$. If R is closed under substitutions then $R\{\mathit{Id}\} = R \cap \mathit{Rel}$ and R is an open simulation if $R \cap \mathit{Rel} \subseteq \langle R\rangle$.

5.1 Simulation up to context

Often when one wants to prove that a relation R is contained in similarity, $R \subseteq \lesssim$, either R is not itself a simulation or it is not possible to show this directly. The solution is to extend R to a larger relation S which is a simulation and thus $S \subseteq \lesssim$ and $R \subseteq \lesssim$. In fact, this is the co-inductive dual of "strengthening the induction hypothesis" in induction arguments. The proofs of syntactic continuity and precongruence are examples of this. In both cases the constructed relations are tailored to the respective problems. However, often the process of 'completing' R follows a common pattern. We shall investigate refined simulation rules which implicitly extend R so as to become a simulation. Gordon (1995) presents a number of such refinements of bisimulation for a typed, call-by-name functional language. One of these is Milner's *bisimulation up to bisimilarity* (Milner 1989). For $\lesssim$ this says:

Proposition 2 (Simulation up to $\lesssim$) $$\frac{R \subseteq \langle \lesssim^\circ\ R^\circ\ \lesssim^\circ\rangle}{R \subseteq \lesssim}$$

Proof If $R \subseteq \langle \lesssim^\circ\ R^\circ\ \lesssim^\circ\rangle$, then $\lesssim R \lesssim$ is a simulation:

$$\begin{array}{rcll} \lesssim R \lesssim & \subseteq & \langle \lesssim^\circ\rangle\,\langle \lesssim^\circ\ R^\circ\ \lesssim^\circ\rangle\,\langle \lesssim^\circ\rangle & \text{as } \lesssim \text{ is a fixed point for } \langle \_^\circ\rangle \\ & \subseteq & \langle \lesssim^\circ\ \lesssim^\circ\ R^\circ\ \lesssim^\circ\ \lesssim^\circ\rangle & \text{by (5.8)} \\ & \subseteq & \langle \lesssim^\circ\ R^\circ\ \lesssim^\circ\rangle & \lesssim^\circ \text{ is transitive} \\ & \subseteq & \langle (\lesssim R \lesssim)^\circ\rangle & \text{(3.1).} \end{array}$$

Therefore $\lesssim R \lesssim\ \subseteq\ \lesssim$ and, since $\lesssim$ is reflexive, $R \subseteq \lesssim$. □

It is possible to derive an 'equational' simulation rule which does not involve the simulation operator, $\langle \_ \rangle$, nor the evaluation relation.

Proposition 3 $\dfrac{R \subseteq \lesssim \overline{R^\circ} \lesssim}{R \subseteq \lesssim}$

Proof The inclusion $\lesssim \overline{R^\circ} \lesssim \; \subseteq \langle \lesssim^\circ R^\circ \lesssim^\circ \rangle$ follows easily from the definitions of $\lesssim$ and $\langle \_ \rangle$, and the rule is an immediate consequence of Proposition 2. □

Recall the example (5.10), where

$$u = \texttt{rec}\ f\ x \texttt{ => } f, \quad v = \texttt{rec}\ f\ x \texttt{ => } \texttt{fn}\ y \texttt{ => } f.$$

An 'equational' proof of $u \sim v$ using Proposition 3 looks as follows. Let $R = \{(u, v), (u, \texttt{fn}\ y \texttt{ => } v)\}$. By the fixed point law for `rec` we calculate

$$\begin{array}{lllllll} u & \sim & \texttt{fn}\ x \texttt{ => } u & \overline{R^\circ} & \texttt{fn}\ x \texttt{ => fn}\ y \texttt{ => } v & \sim & v, \\ u & \sim & \texttt{fn}\ x \texttt{ => } u & \overline{R^\circ} & \texttt{fn}\ y \texttt{ => } v, & & \end{array}$$

hence $R \subseteq \lesssim$ and $R^{\mathrm{op}} \subseteq \lesssim$, by symmetrical applications of Proposition 3. Therefore $R \subseteq \sim$ and $u \sim v$.

Proposition 3 is not a complete proof rule because it can only relate expressions p and p' where p' converges: if $p \lesssim \overline{R^\circ} \lesssim p'$, there exist values v and v' such that $p \lesssim v\ \overline{R^\circ}\ v' \lesssim p'$, and then p' converges, by (5.1). This prevents us from relating two diverging expressions. We can repair this deficiency as in Gordon (1994), by throwing in the singleton relation $\{(\Omega, \Omega)\}$,

$$\frac{R \subseteq \lesssim (\overline{R^\circ} \cup \{(\Omega, \Omega)\}) \lesssim}{R \subseteq \lesssim} \tag{5.12}$$

Another refinement of bisimulation known from process calculi is Sangiorgi's powerful *bisimulation up to context* (Sangiorgi 1994). Here and in ensuing sections we study variants of this proof principle for similarity and improvement.

As a first formulation of simulation up to context we have the following result for closed relations and context closure. The proof is adapted from Pitts (1995).

Proposition 4 (Simulation up to context) $\dfrac{R \subseteq \langle R^{\mathsf{C}} \rangle}{R \subseteq \lesssim}$

Proof Assume $R \subseteq \langle R^{\mathsf{C}} \rangle$. We shall prove

$$R^{\mathsf{C}} \cap \mathit{Rel} \subseteq \langle R^{\mathsf{C}} \rangle. \tag{5.13}$$

Since R is closed, R^{C} is substitutive, by Lemma 2. As R^{C} is also reflexive, it is closed under substitutions. Therefore (5.13) implies that R^{C} is an open simulation, $R^{\mathsf{C}} \subseteq \langle R^{\mathsf{C}} \rangle^\circ$, and then $R^{\mathsf{C}} \subseteq \lesssim^\circ$, by the open simulation rule (5.11). As $R \subseteq R^{\mathsf{C}}$, the result follows.

By definition of $\langle \_ \rangle$, (5.13) means that whenever $\vdash p\ R^{\mathsf{C}}\ p'$ and $p \Downarrow v$, there exists v' such that $p' \Downarrow v'$ and $\vdash v\ \overline{R^{\mathsf{C}}}\ v'$. The proof is by induction on the derivation of $p \Downarrow v$.

(Ctx R) If $\vdash p\ R\ p'$, then $p\ \langle R^{\mathsf{C}}\rangle\ p'$ is immediate from assumption $R \subseteq \langle R^{\mathsf{C}}\rangle$.

(Ctx Comp) Otherwise $\vdash p\ \widehat{R^{\mathsf{C}}}\ p'$ and we proceed by analysis of the derivation of $p \Downarrow v$. Each case is as in the proof of Lemma 3, except that we omit the arithmetic on N subscripts exercised there and we observe that the results are matching values. We show three representative cases:

Case (Eval cons) $p = p_1 :: p_2$, $p_i \Downarrow v_i$, and $v = v_1 :: v_2$. Since $\vdash p\ \widehat{R^{\mathsf{C}}}\ p'$, we have $p' = p'_1 :: p'_2$ with $\vdash p_i\ R^{\mathsf{C}}\ p'_i$. By induction hypothesis $p'_i \Downarrow v'_i$ such that $\vdash v_i\ \overline{R^{\mathsf{C}}}\ v'_i$, for $i = 1, 2$, so $p' \Downarrow v'_1 :: v'_2$ and $\vdash v_1 :: v_2\ \overline{R^{\mathsf{C}}}\ v'_1 :: v'_2$, by (Eval cons) and (Match cons).

Case (Eval apply) $p = p_1\,p_2$, $p_1 \Downarrow v_1 = \mathtt{fn}\ x \Rightarrow e$, $p_2 \Downarrow v_2$, and $e\{v_2/x\} \Downarrow v$. Since $\vdash p\ \widehat{R^{\mathsf{C}}}\ p'$, also $p' = p'_1\,p'_2$ with $\vdash p_i\ R^{\mathsf{C}}\ p'_i$. By the induction hypothesis $p'_i \Downarrow v'_i$ with $\vdash v_i\ \overline{R^{\mathsf{C}}}\ v'_i$, for $i = 1, 2$. Then $v'_1 = \mathtt{fn}\ x \Rightarrow e'$ with $x \vdash e\ R^{\mathsf{C}}\ e'$ and, by compatibility, $\vdash v_2\ R^{\mathsf{C}}\ v'_2$. By substitutivity and induction hypothesis, $\vdash e\{v_2/x\}\ R^{\mathsf{C}}\ e'\{v'_2/x\}$ and $e'\{v'_2/x\} \Downarrow v'$ with $\vdash v\ \overline{R^{\mathsf{C}}}\ v'$. We conclude $p' \Downarrow v'$ by (Eval apply).

Case (Eval case) $p = \mathtt{case}\ p_0\ \mathtt{of\ nil} \Rightarrow e_1 \mid x_1 :: x_2 \Rightarrow e_2 \mid f \Rightarrow e_3$, $p_0 \Downarrow u$ and $q \Downarrow v$, where

$$q = \begin{cases} e_1 & \text{if } u = \mathtt{nil} \\ e_2\{u_1/x_1, u_2/x_2\} & \text{if } u = u_1 :: u_2 \\ e_3\{u/f\} & \text{if } u = \mathtt{fn}\ x \Rightarrow d. \end{cases}$$

By (Comp case), $p' = \mathtt{case}\ p'_0\ \mathtt{of\ nil} \Rightarrow e'_1 \mid x_1 :: x_2 \Rightarrow e'_2 \mid f \Rightarrow e'_3$, with $\vdash p_0\ R^{\mathsf{C}}\ p'_0$, $\vdash e_1\ R^{\mathsf{C}}\ e'_1$, $x_1 x_2 \vdash e_2\ R^{\mathsf{C}}\ e'_2$, $f \vdash e_3\ R^{\mathsf{C}}\ e'_3$. By induction hypothesis $p'_0 \Downarrow u'$ such that $\vdash u\ \overline{R^{\mathsf{C}}}\ u'$. By analysis of the derivation of the latter, we construct

$$q' = \begin{cases} e'_1 & \text{if } u = \mathtt{nil} = u' \\ e'_2\{u'_1/x_1, u'_2/x_2\} & \text{if } u = u_1 :: u_2, u' = u'_1 :: u'_2 \text{ with } \vdash u_i\ \overline{R^{\mathsf{C}}}\ u'_i \\ e'_3\{u'/f\} & \text{if } u = \mathtt{fn}\ x \Rightarrow d, u' = \mathtt{fn}\ x \Rightarrow d', \end{cases}$$

where $\vdash q\ R^{\mathsf{C}}\{\overline{R^{\mathsf{C}}}\}\ q'$. By compatibility and substitutivity, $\overline{R^{\mathsf{C}}} \subseteq R^{\mathsf{C}}$ and $R^{\mathsf{C}}\{\overline{R^{\mathsf{C}}}\} \subseteq R^{\mathsf{C}}$. By induction hypothesis $q' \Downarrow v'$ with $\vdash v\ \overline{R^{\mathsf{C}}}\ v'$ and we conclude $p' \Downarrow v'$ by (Eval case).

We conclude (5.13), so R^{C} is an open simulation contained in $\lesssim^{\circ}$. □

Proposition 4 is not a complete proof rule. For example, $\mathtt{fn}\ x \Rightarrow x$ and $\mathtt{fn}\ x \Rightarrow \mathtt{I}\ x$ are bisimilar but they are not related by any closed relation R such that $x \vdash x\ R^{\mathsf{C}}\ \mathtt{I}\ x$, because x and $\mathtt{I}\ x$ have no common context and R relates only closed expressions.

A more satisfactory and complete rule for simulation up to context would be

$$\frac{R \subseteq \langle (R^\circ)^{\mathsf{C}} \rangle}{R \subseteq \lesssim} \tag{5.14}$$

Unfortunately, our attempts to prove (or refute) this have failed and we leave it as an open problem. A simple calculation, using (3.2), shows that (5.14) is equivalent to the 'open' rule:

$$\frac{R \subseteq \langle R^{\mathsf{C}} \rangle^\circ}{R \subseteq \lesssim^\circ}$$

It differs from Proposition 4 in that R may be open so that R^{C} may capture free variables in expressions related by R. The premise is equivalent to $R\{Id\} \subseteq \langle R^{\mathsf{C}} \rangle$, by (3.2). In Section 7 we prove a weaker version where we require that the premise holds not only for identical instantiations, $R\{Id\}$, but also for $\overline{R^{\mathsf{C}}}$ related instantiations, $R\{\overline{R^{\mathsf{C}}}\}$,

$$\frac{R\{\overline{R^{\mathsf{C}}}\} \cap Rel \subseteq \langle R^{\mathsf{C}} \rangle}{R \subseteq \lesssim^\circ} \tag{5.15}$$

If R is closed then $R\{\overline{R^{\mathsf{C}}}\} = R$ and (5.15) reduces to Proposition 4.

We have found neither simulation up to $\lesssim$ nor up to context to be particularly useful in themselves. It seems that their potential is only realised when combined. In connection with the precongruence proof for similarity below, we will show a stronger version of Proposition 4.

Proposition 5 (Simulation up to context and $\lesssim$) $\dfrac{R \subseteq \langle R^{\mathsf{C}} \lesssim^\circ \rangle}{R \subseteq \lesssim}$

This can be used to show that the Yv fixed point combinator enjoys a least pre-fixed point induction rule:

Proposition 6 $\texttt{fn}\ x \texttt{ => } e\{v/f\} \lesssim v$ *implies* $\texttt{Yv}\ (\texttt{fn}\ f \texttt{ => fn}\ x \texttt{ => } e) \lesssim v$.

Proof Let $u \stackrel{\text{def}}{=} \texttt{fn}\ f \texttt{ => fn}\ x \texttt{ => } e$, $w \stackrel{\text{def}}{=} \texttt{fn}\ x \texttt{ => } u\ u^\infty\ x$. Recall $u^\infty = (\texttt{fn}\ f \texttt{ => fn}\ x \texttt{ => } u(f\ f)x)\ (\texttt{fn}\ f \texttt{ => fn}\ x \texttt{ => } u(f\ f)x)$. We have $\texttt{Yv}\ u \Downarrow_2 w$, $u^\infty \Downarrow_1 w$, and $\texttt{Yv}\ u \sim u^\infty$.

Now assume the premise holds. It suffices to show $u^\infty \lesssim v$. We proceed by simulation up to context and $\lesssim$. Let $R \stackrel{\text{def}}{=} \{(u^\infty, v)\}$, then $R \subseteq \langle R^{\mathsf{C}} \lesssim^\circ \rangle$ holds because $u^\infty \Downarrow w = \texttt{fn}\ x \texttt{ => } u\ u^\infty\ x$ and we have

$$\begin{aligned} \vdash \texttt{fn}\ x \texttt{ => } u\ u^\infty\ x \quad & \overline{R^{\mathsf{C}}} \quad \texttt{fn}\ x \texttt{ => } u\ v\ x \\ & \overline{\sim^\circ} \quad \texttt{fn}\ x \texttt{ => } e\{v/f\} \\ & \overline{\lesssim^\circ} \quad v, \end{aligned}$$

by Kleene equivalence, assumption, and (5.5). Bisimulation up to context and $\lesssim$ yields $R \subseteq \lesssim$. Hence $u^\infty \lesssim v$ and we conclude $\texttt{Yv}\ u \lesssim v$, as required. □

For example, by the fixed point law for `rec`, we get

$$\texttt{Yv}\,(\texttt{fn}\ f\ \texttt{=>}\ \texttt{fn}\ x\ \texttt{=>}\ e) \lesssim \texttt{rec}\ f\ x\ \texttt{=>}\ e. \tag{5.16}$$

Proposition 5 is still too restrictive for many purposes. For instance, it is not clear how to prove the converse of (5.16) and the least pre-fixed point induction rule for `rec`. One might expect simulation up to $\lesssim$ and simulation up to context to combine as follows:

$$\frac{R \subseteq \langle \lesssim^\circ R^{\mathsf{C}} \lesssim^\circ \rangle}{R \subseteq \lesssim} \tag{5.17}$$

But this fails. As a counterexample (due to Andrew Gordon) take

$$R \stackrel{\text{def}}{=} \{(\texttt{fn}\ x\ \texttt{=>}\ \texttt{nil}, \texttt{fn}\ x\ \texttt{=>}\ \Omega)\}. \tag{5.18}$$

Clearly $x \vdash \texttt{nil} \not\lesssim^\circ \Omega$ and $\texttt{fn}\ x\ \texttt{=>}\ \texttt{nil} \not\lesssim \texttt{fn}\ x\ \texttt{=>}\ \Omega$. But $R \subseteq \langle \sim^\circ R^{\mathsf{C}} \sim^\circ \rangle$ because

$$x \vdash \texttt{nil} \sim^\circ (\texttt{fn}\ x\ \texttt{=>}\ \texttt{nil})\,\texttt{nil}\ R^{\mathsf{C}}\ (\texttt{fn}\ x\ \texttt{=>}\ \Omega)\,\texttt{nil} \sim^\circ \Omega. \tag{5.19}$$

This failure corresponds to the situation for process calculi, where a symmetric rule for weak bisimulation up to context and weak bisimulation also fails (Sangiorgi 1996). There the rule is repaired by introducing a more fine-grained efficiency preorder, called expansion. In Section 6 we develop a corresponding improvement relation for our language. Then we repair (5.17) by replacing the left occurrence of similarity in the premise with improvement (Proposition 10).

5.2 Precongruence

A *precongruence* is a compatible preorder, that is, a preorder which is preserved by all language constructs. Precongruence is an important property of similarity because it allows compositional (in)equational reasoning. Moreover, it shows that bisimilarity coincides with conventional contextual equivalence (an issue which we shall not address in this paper, however). We shall now prove that similarity is a precongruence by means of Howe's general method for proving congruence of simulation orderings (Howe 1996). We employ an extension of the method, due to Pitts (1995), which also establishes the simulation up to context results of the previous section.

Recall that $\lesssim^\circ$ is a preorder. It is a precongruence if it is also compatible, $\widehat{\lesssim^\circ} \subseteq \lesssim^\circ$. Howe proves this by simulation but since $\lesssim^\circ$ is not itself a simulation he constructs a larger 'candidate relation' which is. Pitts parameterises the candidate relation by a closed relation R. For every $R \subseteq \mathit{Rel}$, the parameterised candidate relation, $R^\sharp$, is defined inductively by

$$(\text{Cand } R)\ \frac{p\ R\ p' \quad \vec{x} \vdash p' \lesssim^\circ e''}{\vec{x} \vdash p\ R^\sharp\ e''} \qquad (\text{Cand Comp})\ \frac{\vec{x} \vdash e\ \widehat{R^\sharp}\ e' \quad \vec{x} \vdash e' \lesssim^\circ e''}{\vec{x} \vdash e\ R^\sharp\ e''}$$

Each $R^\sharp$ satisfies all the properties of Howe's candidate relation:

Lemma 4 *(1)* $R^\sharp$ *is reflexive, compatible, and substitutive.*

(2) $R^\sharp$ *contains similarity,* $\lesssim^\circ \subseteq R^\sharp$.

(3) $R^\sharp$ *contains its composition with similarity,* $R^\sharp \lesssim^\circ \subseteq R^\sharp$.

Proof Compatibility, $\widehat{R^\sharp} \subseteq R^\sharp$, is immediate from (Cand Comp) because $\lesssim^\circ$ is reflexive. Every compatible relation is reflexive, so $R^\sharp$ and $\widehat{R^\sharp}$ are reflexive. Again by (Cand Comp) follows (2). Since $\lesssim^\circ$ is transitive, (3) is also immediate from the definition of $R^\sharp$. Weakening,

$$\vec{x}\vec{y} \vdash e\ R^\sharp\ e' \quad \Rightarrow \quad \vec{x}x\vec{y} \vdash e\ R^\sharp\ e',$$

can be shown by induction on the derivation of $\vec{x}\vec{y} \vdash e\ R^\sharp\ e'$, using the fact that $\lesssim^\circ$ satisfies weakening, being an open extension. Finally, substitutivity,

$$\vec{x} \vdash e\ R^\sharp\ e' \ \&\ \vec{y} \vdash \vec{u}\ R^\sharp\ \vec{u'} \quad \Rightarrow \quad \vec{y} \vdash e\{\vec{u}/\vec{x}\}\ R^\sharp\ e'\{\vec{u'}/\vec{x}\},$$

is proved by induction on the derivation of $\vec{x} \vdash e\ R^\sharp\ e'$, using (3), weakening, and the fact that $\lesssim^\circ$ is closed under substitutions. □

Lemma 5 $\dfrac{R \subseteq \langle R^\sharp \rangle}{R^\sharp \subseteq \lesssim^\circ}$

Proof As in the proof of Proposition 4, it suffices to prove $R^\sharp \cap Rel \subseteq \langle R^\sharp \rangle$, then $R^\sharp$ will be an open simulation and $R^\sharp \subseteq \lesssim^\circ$.

We assume $\vdash p\ R^\sharp\ p''$ and $p \Downarrow v$, and we will prove that there exists v'' such that $p'' \Downarrow v''$ and $\vdash v\ \overline{R^\sharp}\ v''$. The proof is by induction on the derivation of $p \Downarrow v$.

First consider the derivation of $\vdash p\ R^\sharp\ p''$. We see that there exists p' such that $p' \lesssim p''$ and either $p\ R\ p'$ or $p\ \widehat{R^\sharp}\ p'$. In either case we argue exactly as in the proof of Proposition 4 to get that $p' \Downarrow v'$, for some v' such that $\vdash v\ \overline{R^\sharp}\ v'$. Then, by definition of $\lesssim$, there exists v'' such that $p'' \Downarrow v''$ and $\vdash v'\ \overline{\lesssim^\circ}\ v''$. Since $\overline{R^\sharp}\ \overline{\lesssim^\circ} \subseteq \overline{R^\sharp \lesssim^\circ}$ and $R^\sharp \lesssim^\circ \subseteq R^\sharp$, $\vdash v\ \overline{R^\sharp}\ v''$ follows, as required. □

Howe's candidate relation is just $\emptyset^\sharp$, for which the premise of the lemma holds trivially and thus establishes $\emptyset^\sharp \subseteq \lesssim^\circ$. We have the reverse inclusion from above, so $\lesssim^\circ$ and $\emptyset^\sharp$ coincide. Since $\emptyset^\sharp$ is substitutive and compatible, so is $\lesssim^\circ$. As $\lesssim^\circ$ is also a preorder, it is a precongruence.

Proposition 7 $\lesssim^\circ$ *is substitutive and a precongruence.*

Consequently, $\sim^\circ$ is also substitutive and is a congruence, that is, a compatible equivalence relation.

Lemma 5 also entails Proposition 4: since $\lesssim^\circ$ is reflexive we see that $R^{\mathsf{C}} \subseteq R^\sharp$; therefore $R \subseteq \langle R^{\mathsf{C}} \rangle$ implies $R \subseteq \langle R^\sharp \rangle$ and Lemma 5 gives $R^\sharp \subseteq \lesssim^\circ$ and thus $R \subseteq \lesssim$. Moreover, since $R^\sharp \lesssim^\circ \subseteq R^\sharp$, also $R^{\mathsf{C}} \lesssim^\circ \subseteq R^\sharp$, so Lemma 5 entails Proposition 5 too.

5.3 Equational theory

Let us summarise our results about bisimilarity from above. We supplement some equational laws that follow directly from (5.1)–(5.4) by inspection of evaluations.

Extensionality

$$v \sim v' \quad \text{iff} \quad \vdash v \overline{\sim^\circ} v' \quad \text{iff} \quad \vdash v \widehat{\sim^\circ} v'.$$

$$\vec{x} \vdash e \sim^\circ e' \quad \text{iff} \quad \forall u_1, \ldots, u_n \in Val_\emptyset.\ e\{\vec{u}/\vec{x}\} \sim e'\{\vec{u}/\vec{x}\}.$$

The latter is just the definition of open extension.

Congruence and substitutivity

$$p \sim p.$$

$$p \sim p' \quad \text{and} \quad p' \sim p'' \quad \text{imply} \quad p \sim p''.$$

$$p \sim p' \quad \text{implies} \quad p' \sim p.$$

$$\vdash p \widehat{\sim^\circ} p' \quad \text{implies} \quad p \sim p'.$$

$$x \vdash e \sim^\circ e' \quad \text{and} \quad v \sim v' \quad \text{imply} \quad e\{v/x\} \sim e'\{v'/x\}.$$

Strachey's property (Gordon 1994)

$$\text{either} \quad p \sim \Omega \quad \text{or} \quad \exists v.\, p \sim v.$$

Functions

$$(\texttt{fn}\ x \texttt{ => } e)\ v \ \sim\ e\{v/x\}.$$

Combined with the extensionality laws we get:

$$\texttt{fn}\ x \texttt{ => } e \sim \texttt{fn}\ x \texttt{ => } e' \quad \text{iff} \quad \forall v.\ (\texttt{fn}\ x \texttt{ => } e)\ v \sim (\texttt{fn}\ x \texttt{ => } e')\ v.$$

Let We have laws corresponding to those of Moggi's computational lambda calculus (Moggi 1989), here presented as in Talcott (1997).

$$\texttt{let val}\ x = v\ \texttt{in}\ e\ \texttt{end} \ \sim\ e\{v/x\}.$$

$$\texttt{let val}\ x = p\ \texttt{in}\ E[x]\ \texttt{end} \ \sim\ E[p],$$

where E is any closed evaluation context.

Actually, these laws follow from the laws for `case` below because `let` can be encoded by means of `case`,

$$\begin{pmatrix}\texttt{let val}\ x = p \\ \texttt{in}\ e\ \texttt{end}\end{pmatrix} \sim \begin{pmatrix}\texttt{case}\ p\ \texttt{of nil => } e\{\texttt{nil}/x\} \\ \quad \mid x_1 \texttt{ :: } x_2 \texttt{ => } e\{x_1 \texttt{ :: } x_2/x\} \\ \quad \mid f \texttt{ => } e\{f/x\}\end{pmatrix}.$$

Case

$$\begin{pmatrix}\texttt{case}\ v\ \texttt{of nil => } e_1 \\ \quad\mid x_1\ \texttt{: :}\ x_2\ \texttt{=>}\ e_2 \\ \quad\mid f\ \texttt{=>}\ e_3\end{pmatrix} \sim \begin{cases} e_1 & \text{if } v = \texttt{nil} \\ e_2\{v_1/x_1, v_2/x_2\} & \text{if } v = v_1\ \texttt{: :}\ v_2 \\ e_3\{v/f\} & \text{if } v = \texttt{fn}\ x\ \texttt{=>}\ e. \end{cases}$$

$$\begin{pmatrix}\texttt{case}\ p\ \texttt{of nil => } E[\texttt{nil}] \\ \quad\mid x_1\ \texttt{: :}\ x_2\ \texttt{=>}\ E[x_1\ \texttt{: :}\ x_2] \\ \quad\mid f\ \texttt{=>}\ E[f]\end{pmatrix} \sim E[p].$$

Fixed point `rec` is a fixed point operator:

$$\texttt{rec}\ f\ x\ \texttt{=>}\ d \sim \texttt{fn}\ x\ \texttt{=>}\ d\{(\texttt{rec}\ f\ x\ \texttt{=>}\ d)/f\}.$$

Furthermore, `rec` is rationally open (Braüner 1996):

$$C[\texttt{rec}\ f\ x\ \texttt{=>}\ d] \sim \Omega \quad \text{iff} \quad \forall n \geq 0.\ C[\texttt{rec}^{(n)}\ f\ x\ \texttt{=>}\ d] \sim \Omega.$$

This rule is useful for equational reasoning about divergence, without direct reference to the evaluation relation. Rational openness and the unwinding theorem are easily derived from each other using adequacy (5.7). (Rational openness also follows from syntactic continuity and syntactic bottom below.)

5.4 Inequational theory

We also list some order-theoretic properties of similarity, taken from Pitts (1997), in order to complete our discussion about proof rules for recursion.

Extensionality, precongruence, and substitutivity As for $\sim$ above, except symmetry.

Syntactic bottom Ω is least with respect to $\lesssim$,

$$\Omega \lesssim p.$$

This is direct from (5.1).

Recursion induction $\texttt{rec}\ f\ x\ \texttt{=>}\ e$ is the least pre-fixed point of the functional $\texttt{fn}\ x\ \texttt{=>}\ e\{-/f\}$,

$$\texttt{fn}\ x\ \texttt{=>}\ e\{v/f\} \lesssim v \quad \text{implies} \quad \texttt{rec}\ f\ x\ \texttt{=>}\ e \lesssim v.$$

In Section 5.1 we proved this result for the Yv combinator, Proposition 6. The recursion induction rule for `rec` follows from syntactic continuity below; see Pitts (1997). In the following sections we shall discuss other proofs of recursion induction using improvement and simulation up to context.

Syntactic continuity Every recursive function is the least upper bound of its finite approximants and all language constructs are continuous with respect to this least upper bound,

$$C[\texttt{rec}\ f\ x\ \texttt{=>}\ e] \lesssim q \quad \text{iff} \quad \forall n \geq 0.\, C[\texttt{rec}^{(n)}\ f\ x\ \texttt{=>}\ e] \lesssim q.$$

Proof We employ Lemma 3 from the proof of the unwinding theorem in Section 4 to give a co-inductive proof. A similar proof is outlined in Pitts (1997). Here we can use the relations from the formulation of Lemma 3 to construct the appropriate simulations. Note that we do not require that $\texttt{rec}\ f\ x\ \texttt{=>}\ e$ is closed.

First consider the backward implication (which is the most interesting). Recall the relations U_n from Lemma 3(1). We construct the relation

$$T \stackrel{\text{def}}{=} \bigcap_{n \geq 0} (U_n \lesssim^{\circ}).$$

Observe that $\forall n \geq 0.\, C[\texttt{rec}^{(n)}\ f\ x\ \texttt{=>}\ e] \lesssim q$ implies $\vdash C[\texttt{rec}\ f\ x\ \texttt{=>}\ e]\ T\ q$. We show that T is an open simulation, then $T \subseteq \lesssim^{\circ}$ and the result follows. So suppose $\vdash p\ T\ p'$ and $p \Downarrow_N v$. By definition of T, for all $n \geq 0$, $\vdash p\ U_{n+1+N}\ p_n$, for some $p_n \lesssim p'$. From Lemma 3(1) we get $p_n \Downarrow_N v_n$ with $\vdash v\ U_{n+1}\ v_n$. By the same argument as for (4.2) holds

$$\vdash u\ U_{n+1}\ u' \quad \text{implies} \quad \vdash u\ \overline{U_n}\ u', \tag{5.20}$$

so we get $\vdash v\ \overline{U_n}\ v_n$. Since $p_n \lesssim p'$ also $p' \Downarrow v'_n$ with $\vdash v_n\ \overline{\lesssim^{\circ}}\ v'_n$, hence $\vdash v\ \overline{U_n \lesssim^{\circ}}\ v'_n$. Evaluation is deterministic so all v'_n are identical. Therefore $\vdash v\ \overline{U_n \lesssim^{\circ}}\ v'_0$, for all $n \geq 0$, and we conclude $\vdash v\ \overline{T}\ v'_0$ and $p\ \langle T \rangle\ p'$, hence T is an open simulation as it is closed under substitutions.

The forward implication holds if $C[\texttt{rec}^{(n)}\ f\ x\ \texttt{=>}\ e] \lesssim C[\texttt{rec}\ f\ x\ \texttt{=>}\ e]$ for all n. This is derivable from syntactic bottom and precongruence, by induction on n. It also follows from Lemma 3(2). To see this we first extend (5.20) with

$$\vdash v\ U_0^{\text{op}}\ v' \quad \text{implies} \quad \vdash v\ \overline{U_0^{\text{op}} \cup \lesssim^{\circ}}\ v'. \tag{5.21}$$

This holds because $\vdash \texttt{rec}^{(0)}\ f\ x\ \texttt{=>}\ e\ \overline{\lesssim^{\circ}}\ \texttt{rec}\ f\ x\ \texttt{=>}\ e$, by syntactic bottom. Lemma 3(2) gives $U_0^{\text{op}} \cap \mathit{Rel} \subseteq \langle U_0^{\text{op}} \cup \lesssim^{\circ} \rangle$ and we deduce $U_0^{\text{op}} \cup \lesssim^{\circ}$ is an open simulation and $U_0^{\text{op}} \subseteq \lesssim^{\circ}$. From (4.1) we get $C[\texttt{rec}^{(n)}\ f\ x\ \texttt{=>}\ e] \lesssim C[\texttt{rec}\ f\ x\ \texttt{=>}\ e]$ as required. □

Determinacy of evaluation plays a key role in the above proof of syntactic continuity. One can add nondeterminism to the language such that the operational semantics and theory of applicative bisimulation still satisfy the unwinding theorem, rational openness, and recursion induction, but syntactic continuity fails. Braüner (1996) uses this example to illustrate that syntactic continuity is a strictly stronger property than rational openness.

6 Improvement

Following Sands (1997b) we introduce a stricter operational ordering and equivalence that takes computational cost into account, in our case the number of function applications in evaluations. Improvement theory has independent interest as a formal approach to the study of program efficiency but Sands has also demonstrated that it is a powerful tool for reasoning about conventional operational equivalence and recursion. Here we are interested in the latter use of improvement.

We study the theory in some detail as its scope goes far beyond repairing the rule for simulation up to context and $\lesssim$ of the previous section. Our relational approach is instrumental in establishing a rule for improvement simulation up to variable capturing contexts. This is interesting in its own right, especially in the absence of a satisfactory counterpart for similarity, and it entails Sands' improvement theorem.

As motivation for our definition of improvement below, recall that (5.19),

$$x \vdash \texttt{nil} \sim^{\circ} (\texttt{fn}\; x \texttt{ => nil})\,\texttt{nil}\; R^{\mathsf{C}}\; (\texttt{fn}\; x \texttt{ =>}\; \Omega)\,\texttt{nil} \sim^{\circ} \Omega,$$

was used to prove $R \subseteq \langle \lesssim^{\circ} R^{\mathsf{C}} \lesssim^{\circ} \rangle$ and thus invalidated the symmetric up to context and $\lesssim$ rule (5.17),

$$\frac{R \subseteq \langle \lesssim^{\circ} R^{\mathsf{C}} \lesssim^{\circ} \rangle}{R \subseteq \lesssim}$$

Here nil is bisimilar to (fn x => nil) nil but the latter is more "expensive" as it takes one more function application step to compute. So nil is not "improved" by (fn x => nil) nil. This will be the requirement by which we shall repair (5.17) in Section 7.

We measure the number of function applications in evaluations, essentially because applications 'destruct' function abstractions. In fact, the counterexample to (5.17) can be constructed with any 'lazy' value constructor and associated destructors, but function abstraction and application happen to be the only lazy value constructor and destructor in ML. In general the cost measure must count every destruction of any lazy constructor. We should mention that this is tailored to support reasoning about applicative similarity and it is not meant as a contribution to the discussion of what constitutes a good measure of program efficiency for functional languages (Lawall and Mairson 1996).

We define an improvement preorder, $\trianglerighteq$, and a cost equivalence relation, $\triangleleft\!\triangleright$, co-inductively like similarity and bisimilarity but with the additional requirement that $p \trianglerighteq q$ implies that q evaluates in less function application steps than p. The definitions and the basic theory are quite analogous to those of Section 4.

Let the improvement simulation operator, $\langle \_ \rangle_I$, be given by

$$p\,\langle R\rangle_I\, p' \;\stackrel{\mathrm{def}}{\Leftrightarrow}\; \forall N.\forall v.\, p \Downarrow_N v \;\Rightarrow\; \exists v'.\, p' \Downarrow_{\leq N} v' \;\&\; \vdash v\, \overline{R}\, v',$$

for $R \subseteq \mathit{Rel}^{\circ}$, $p, p' \in \mathit{Exp}_{\emptyset}$. Notation $p' \Downarrow_{\leq N} v'$ means $\exists N' \leq N.\, p' \Downarrow_{N'} v'$. The compound operator $\langle \_^{\circ} \rangle_I$ is monotone and we define *improvement*, $\trianglerighteq$, as the greatest fixed point

$$\trianglerighteq \stackrel{\text{def}}{=} \nu R.\langle R^\circ\rangle_I, \tag{6.1}$$

Cost equivalence, $\gtrless$, is the greatest symmetric fixed point and is also the largest symmetric relation contained in improvement,

$$\gtrless \;=\; \trianglerighteq \cap \trianglerighteq^{\text{op}}.$$

Cost equivalence is computationally adequate, (5.7). But the evaluation relation is not sound, (5.9), with respect to cost equivalence; instead we have a more detailed correspondence between evaluation and cost equivalence:

$$p \Downarrow_N v \quad \text{implies} \quad p \gtrless \mathtt{I}^N v.$$

Application of the identity function $\mathtt{I}$ is used as syntactic representation of function application steps. $\mathtt{I}^N v$ means N-fold application of $\mathtt{I}$ to v.

We call post-fixed points of $\langle\_^\circ\rangle_I$ *improvement simulations* and we have co-induction improvement simulation rules:

$$\frac{R \subseteq \langle R^\circ\rangle_I}{R \subseteq \trianglerighteq} \qquad \frac{R \subseteq \langle R\rangle_I^\circ}{R \subseteq \trianglerighteq^\circ} \tag{6.2}$$

We call R an *improvement simulation* if $R \subseteq \langle R^\circ\rangle_I$ and R is an *open improvement simulation* if $R \subseteq \langle R\rangle_I^\circ$.

Improvement refines similarity, $\trianglerighteq \subseteq \lesssim$, because

$$\langle R\rangle_I \subseteq \langle R\rangle, \text{ for all } R \subseteq Rel^\circ, \tag{6.3}$$

so every improvement simulation is also an (applicative) simulation.

6.1 Improvement simulation up to context

Refined simulation rules are equally important for improvement as they are for applicative simulation. It turns out that we are able to prove stronger refinements of improvement simulation than was the case for applicative simulation. In the process we will also derive that improvement is a precongruence.

Lemma 6 $\dfrac{R \subseteq \langle S^+\rangle_I}{S^+ \subseteq \trianglerighteq^\circ}$, *where* $S \stackrel{\text{def}}{=} (R^\circ)^{\mathsf{C}}$ *and* S^+ *is the transitive closure.*

The proof is postponed to Appendix A.

Proposition 8 $\trianglerighteq^\circ$ *is substitutive and a precongruence.*

Proof As $\trianglerighteq$ itself satisfies the premise of the lemma, we get $(\gtrsim^{\circ})^{\mathsf{C}+} \subseteq \gtrsim^{\circ}$. Therefore $\gtrsim^{\circ}$ is compatible and transitive, and hence a precongruence. Since $\gtrsim^{\circ}$ is closed under substitutions, it is also substitutive by Lemma 1. □

Another consequence of Lemma 6 is a full symmetric rule for improvement simulation up to context and improvement.

Proposition 9 (Improvement simulation up to context and $\gtrsim$)

$$\frac{R \subseteq \langle \gtrsim^{\circ} (R^{\circ})^{\mathsf{C}} \gtrsim^{\circ} \rangle_I}{R \subseteq \gtrsim}$$

Proof From $R \subseteq \langle \gtrsim^{\circ} (R^{\circ})^{\mathsf{C}} \gtrsim^{\circ} \rangle_I$ we get that $R \cup \gtrsim \subseteq \langle ((R \cup \gtrsim)^{\circ})^{\mathsf{C}+} \rangle_I$. Hence $((R \cup \gtrsim)^{\circ})^{\mathsf{C}+} \subseteq \gtrsim^{\circ}$ and $R \subseteq \gtrsim$. □

6.2 Equational theory

The equational theory of cost equivalence is analogous to that of bisimilarity, except for some applications of the identity function, I, to account for computational cost. Since these 'syntactic computation steps' can be erased up to bisimilarity, the cost equivalence theory here entails the corresponding theory of bisimilarity in Section 4.

The cost equivalence version of Strachey's property accounts for the cost of computing a value:

$$\text{either} \quad p \mathrel{\lessgtr} \Omega \quad \text{or} \quad \exists! N. \exists v.\, p \mathrel{\lessgtr} \mathtt{I}^N v.$$

The beta law for function application records the computation step:

$$(\mathtt{fn}\ x \Rightarrow e)\ v \mathrel{\lessgtr} \mathtt{I}\ e\{v/x\}.$$

Notice that `let val` $x = d$ `in` e `end` is one step 'cheaper' than the conventional encoding (`fn` x `=>` e) d. This will be important in the proof of Proposition 11.

The remaining equational laws for bisimilarity in Section 5.3 carry over to cost equivalence unchanged.

The laws can be used to move around syntactic computation steps. For instance, the evaluation context law for `case` yields

$$\mathtt{I}\left(\begin{array}{l}\mathtt{case}\ p\ \mathtt{of}\ \mathtt{nil} \Rightarrow e_1 \\ \qquad\quad \mid x_1 :: x_2 \Rightarrow e_2 \\ \qquad\quad \mid f \Rightarrow e_3\end{array}\right) \sim \begin{array}{l}\mathtt{case}\ p\ \mathtt{of}\ \mathtt{nil} \Rightarrow \mathtt{I}\ e_1 \\ \qquad\quad \mid x_1 :: x_2 \Rightarrow \mathtt{I}\ e_2 \\ \qquad\quad \mid f \Rightarrow \mathtt{I}\ e_3,\end{array}$$

because (`I`−) is an evaluation context. A further law of this kind,

$$E[\mathtt{I}\ p] \mathrel{\lessgtr} \mathtt{I}\ E[p],$$

moves $\texttt{I}$ across evaluation contexts; it is direct from (2.2). Such laws form a useful 'tick algebra' (Sands 1997b) for equational reasoning about computation steps.

Cost equivalence satisfies a unique fixed point rule:

$$\texttt{fn}\, x \;\texttt{=>}\; e\{^{v}/_{f}\} \;\underset{\sim}{\triangleleft\!\triangleright}\; v \quad \text{implies} \quad \texttt{rec}\; f\; x \;\texttt{=>}\; e \;\underset{\sim}{\triangleleft\!\triangleright}\; v.$$

This rule follows from recursion induction and co-induction rules below. For illustration, we can use it to prove the following correspondence between explicit recursion and the $\texttt{Yv}$ fixed point combinator.

$$\texttt{I}^2\; (\texttt{rec}\; f\; x \;\texttt{=>}\; \texttt{I}^3\, e) \;\underset{\sim}{\triangleleft\!\triangleright}\; \texttt{Yv}\; u, \quad \text{where } u = (\texttt{fn}\; f \;\texttt{=>}\; \texttt{fn}\; x \;\texttt{=>}\; e),$$

by calculating $\texttt{Yv}\; u \underset{\sim}{\triangleleft\!\triangleright} \texttt{I}^2\; \texttt{fn}\; x \;\texttt{=>}\; u\; u^{\infty}\, x$ and $x \vdash \texttt{I}^3\, e\{^{(\texttt{fn}\, x \,\texttt{=>}\, u\, u^{\infty}\, x)}/_{f}\} \underset{\sim}{\triangleleft\!\triangleright}^{\circ}$ $u\; u^{\infty}\, x$. As usual, a corresponding result for bisimilarity, $\texttt{rec}\; f\; x \;\texttt{=>}\; e \sim \texttt{Yv}\; u$, follows as a corollary. This and Proposition 6 constitute a proof of recursion induction for similarity.

6.3 Inequational theory

All the inequational theory for similarity in Section 5.4 also holds for improvement.

The proofs of syntactic bottom and syntactic continuity for improvement are again analogous to those for similarity above. The lemmas from the proof of the unwinding theorem in Section 4 were carefully phrased to also account for computational cost and the syntactic continuity proof for similarity is easily extended with this bookkeeping.

We supplement recursion induction,

$$\texttt{fn}\, x \;\texttt{=>}\; e\{^{v}/_{f}\} \;\underset{\sim}{\triangleright}\; v \quad \text{implies} \quad \texttt{rec}\; f\; x \;\texttt{=>}\; e \;\underset{\sim}{\triangleright}\; v,$$

with recursion co-induction,

$$v \;\underset{\sim}{\triangleright}\; \texttt{fn}\, x \;\texttt{=>}\; e\{^{v}/_{f}\} \quad \text{implies} \quad v \;\underset{\sim}{\triangleright}\; \texttt{rec}\; f\; x \;\texttt{=>}\; e,$$

which says that recursive functions are also greatest post-fixed points with respect to improvement. We can use improvement simulation up to context and $\underset{\sim}{\triangleright}$ to prove the recursion (co-)induction rules.

Proof of recursion (co-)induction We only prove the first (induction) rule. The second (co-induction) rule follows by a symmetric argument because the improvement simulation up to context and $\underset{\sim}{\triangleright}$ rule, Proposition 9, is symmetric.

Assume $\texttt{fn}\, x \;\texttt{=>}\; e\{^{v}/_{f}\} \underset{\sim}{\triangleright} v$. By extensionality, $\vdash \texttt{fn}\, x \;\texttt{=>}\; e\{^{v}/_{f}\} \;\overline{\underset{\sim}{\triangleright}^{\circ}}\; v$. Let R be the singleton relation, $r\; R\; v$, where $r = \texttt{rec}\; f\; x \;\texttt{=>}\; e$. Then r is a fixed point, $r \underset{\sim}{\triangleleft\!\triangleright} \texttt{fn}\, x \;\texttt{=>}\; e\{^{r}/_{f}\}$, and $\vdash r \;\overline{\underset{\sim}{\triangleleft\!\triangleright}^{\circ}}\; \texttt{fn}\, x \;\texttt{=>}\; e\{^{r}/_{f}\}$. Now $r\; \langle \underset{\sim}{\triangleleft\!\triangleright}^{\circ}\; (R^{\circ})^{\mathsf{C}}\; \underset{\sim}{\triangleright}^{\circ} \rangle_{I}\; v$ because $r \Downarrow_0 r$, $v \Downarrow_0 v$, and

$$\vdash r \;\overline{\underset{\sim}{\triangleleft\!\triangleright}^{\circ}}\; \texttt{fn}\, x \;\texttt{=>}\; e\{^{r}/_{f}\} \;\overline{(R^{\circ})^{\mathsf{C}}}\; \texttt{fn}\, x \;\texttt{=>}\; e\{^{v}/_{f}\} \;\overline{\underset{\sim}{\triangleright}^{\circ}}\; v.$$

Hence $R \subseteq \langle \mathrel{\underset{\sim}{\Diamond}}^{\circ} \, (R^{\circ})^{\mathsf{C}} \, \mathrel{\underset{\sim}{\trianglerighteq}}^{\circ} \rangle_I$. By Proposition 9, we conclude $R \subseteq \mathrel{\underset{\sim}{\trianglerighteq}}$, i.e., $r \mathrel{\underset{\sim}{\trianglerighteq}} v$. □

Recursion co-induction and the unique fixed point rule are call-by-value versions of Sands' improvement theorem. This is apparent from the following reformulation, derived by means of equational laws for $\mathrel{\underset{\sim}{\Diamond}}$.

$$x \vdash \texttt{let fun}\ f\ x = d_0\ \texttt{in}\ d_0\ \texttt{end} \ \mathrel{\underset{\sim}{\trianglerighteq}}^{\circ}\ \texttt{let fun}\ f\ x = d_0\ \texttt{in}\ d_1\ \texttt{end}$$
$$\Rightarrow\ \texttt{let fun}\ f\ x = d_0\ \texttt{in}\ e\ \texttt{end} \ \mathrel{\underset{\sim}{\trianglerighteq}}\ \texttt{let fun}\ f\ x = d_1\ \texttt{in}\ e\ \texttt{end},$$

for $d_0, d_1 \in \mathit{Exp}_{fx}$ and $e \in \mathit{Exp}_f$. The same holds for $\mathrel{\underset{\sim}{\Diamond}}$.

It should be noted that a reason why our improvement theory satisfies the improvement theorem is that recursion is bound up with function abstraction in ML, that is, recursive unfoldings require a function application step (cf. the general version of the improvement theorem in Sands (1997a)). Hence our cost measure is actually more fine-grained than Sands' count of unfoldings of recursion in Sands (1997b). In languages where recursion is not coupled with function abstraction, the two cost measures are incomparable and the two resulting improvement theories will be complementary.

7 Applicative simulation up to improvement

A motivation for introducing improvement is its use in refining applicative simulation. We can extend Proposition 5 as follows.

Proposition 10 (Applicative simulation up to $\mathrel{\underset{\sim}{\trianglerighteq}}$ and context and $\lesssim$)

$$\frac{R \subseteq \langle \mathrel{\underset{\sim}{\trianglerighteq}}^{\circ} \, R^{\mathsf{C}} \, \lesssim^{\circ} \rangle}{R \subseteq \lesssim}$$

This rule allows us to give a direct proof of recursion induction for similarity, analogous to the proof for improvement above: suppose $\texttt{fn}\ x\ \texttt{=>}\ e\{v/f\} \lesssim v$ and let $R = \{(\texttt{rec}\ f\ x\ \texttt{=>}\ e, v)\}$, then

$$\texttt{rec}\ f\ x\ \texttt{=>}\ e \mathrel{\underset{\sim}{\Diamond}} \texttt{fn}\ x\ \texttt{=>}\ e\{(\texttt{rec}\ f\ x\ \texttt{=>}\ e)/f\}\ \overline{R^{\mathsf{C}}}\ \texttt{fn}\ x\ \texttt{=>}\ e\{v/f\} \lesssim v,$$

and we deduce $R \subseteq \langle \mathrel{\underset{\sim}{\Diamond}}^{\circ} \ R^{\mathsf{C}} \ \lesssim^{\circ} \rangle$; hence $R \subseteq \lesssim$, by Proposition 10, and $\texttt{rec}\ f\ x\ \texttt{=>}\ e \lesssim v$, as required.

In analogy with Proposition 9 we would like to have a stronger rule:

$$\frac{R \subseteq \langle \mathrel{\underset{\sim}{\trianglerighteq}}^{\circ} \, (R^{\circ})^{\mathsf{C}} \, \lesssim^{\circ} \rangle}{R \subseteq \lesssim} \tag{7.1}$$

But we do not know if this holds. It would entail (5.14) which we left as an open problem. In Appendix A we prove a weaker version:

Lemma 7 $\dfrac{R\{\overline{R^{\mathsf{C}}}\} \cap \mathit{Rel} \subseteq \langle \gtrsim^{\circ}\, R^{\mathsf{C}} \lesssim^{\circ} \rangle}{R \subseteq \lesssim^{\circ}}$

It extends the open rule for simulation up to context (5.15) which we discussed in Section 5.1 as an approximation to (5.14).

When R is closed, Lemma 7 reduces to Proposition 10 above. But the utility of the lemma goes beyond that of Proposition 10 as we will now demonstrate by proving a syntactic minimal invariance property and by deriving equational rules for reasoning about open expressions.

7.1 Syntactic minimal invariance

As a non-trivial example, we consider a syntactic version of the domain-theoretic minimal invariance property for our language (Pitts 1994a).

Let π be the recursive function

$$\begin{aligned}\pi \stackrel{\text{def}}{=} \texttt{rec}\ f\ x \texttt{ => case}\ x\ \texttt{of nil => nil}\\ \mid x_1 \texttt{ :: } x_2 \texttt{ => } f\ x_1 \texttt{ :: } f\ x_2\\ \mid g \texttt{ => fn}\ y \texttt{ => } f(g(f\ y)).\end{aligned}$$

(This would not be well-typed in ML where one would define a corresponding type-indexed family of functions instead.)

Minimal invariance says that π is the identity function, $\pi \sim \texttt{I}$. We can prove this by means of Lemma 7.

Proposition 11 (Syntactic minimal invariance) $\pi \sim \texttt{I}$.

Proof $\pi \lesssim \texttt{I}$ follows by recursion induction from

$$x \vdash \begin{array}{l}\texttt{case}\ x\ \texttt{of nil => nil}\\ \quad\mid x_1 \texttt{ :: } x_2 \texttt{ => I}\ x_1 \texttt{ :: I}\ x_2\\ \quad\mid g \texttt{ => fn}\ y \texttt{ => I}(g(\texttt{I}\ y))\end{array} \sim^{\circ} x,$$

which is easily verified by case analysis on the value of x.

We invoke Lemma 7 to prove $\texttt{I} \lesssim \pi$. Let $R \subseteq \mathit{Rel}^{\circ}$ be given by

$$y \vdash y\ R\ \pi\ y,$$

and $S = \gtrsim^{\circ} R^{\mathsf{C}} \lesssim^{\circ}$. We prove $R\{\overline{R^{\mathsf{C}}}\} \cap \mathit{Rel} \subseteq \langle S \rangle$, i.e.,

$$\vdash v\ \overline{R^{\mathsf{C}}}\ v' \quad \text{implies} \quad \pi\ v' \Downarrow v'' \quad \text{with} \quad \vdash v\ \overline{S}\ v'',$$

by induction on the derivation of $\vdash v\ \overline{R^{\mathsf{C}}}\ v'$.

(Match nil) $v = \texttt{nil}$, $v' = \texttt{nil}$. Then $\pi\ v' \Downarrow \texttt{nil}$. Clearly $\vdash v\ \overline{S}\ \texttt{nil}$.

(Match cons) $v = v_1 :: v_2$, $v' = v'_1 :: v'_2$, and $\vdash v_i\ \overline{R^{\mathsf{C}}}\ v'_i$. By induction hypothesis $\pi\ v'_i \Downarrow v''_i$ with $\vdash v_i\ \overline{S}\ v''_i$. So $\pi\ v' \Downarrow v'' = v''_1 :: v''_2$ and $\vdash v\ \overline{S}\ v''$.

(Match fn) $v = \texttt{fn}\ y \texttt{ => } e$, $v' = \texttt{fn}\ y \texttt{ => } e'$, and $y \vdash e\ R^{\mathsf{C}}\ e'$. Then $\pi\ v' \Downarrow v'' = \texttt{fn}\ y \texttt{ => } \pi(v'(\pi\ y))$ and $\vdash v\ \overline{S}\ v''$ because

$$\begin{aligned} y \vdash e \ & \gtrsim\!\!\!\!\lessdot^{\circ} \ \texttt{let val}\ y = y\ \texttt{in let val}\ y = e\ \texttt{in}\ y\ \texttt{end end} \\ & R^{\mathsf{C}} \ \texttt{let val}\ y = \pi\ y\ \texttt{in let val}\ y = e'\ \texttt{in}\ \pi\ y\ \texttt{end end} \\ & \sim^{\circ} \ \pi(v'(\pi\ y)), \end{aligned}$$

and $\gtrsim\!\!\!\!\lessdot^{\circ}\ R^{\mathsf{C}} \sim^{\circ}\ \subseteq S$.

We conclude $R \subseteq \lesssim^{\circ}$ by Lemma 7. Therefore $v \lesssim \pi\, v$, for all closed values v, and $\mathtt{I} \lesssim \pi$ holds by extensionality. □

Simulation up to $\gtrsim\!\!\!\!\rhd$ and context and $\lesssim$, Lemma 7, substantially simplifies the proof. Mason, Smith, and Talcott (1996) give a direct operational proof of this result. It is also possible to recast their proof in the relational proof style used throughout this paper.

The finite approximants of π (as defined in Section 4) are 'syntactic projections'. Syntactic minimal invariance and syntactic continuity entail that their least upper bound is the identity function and thus:

$$p \lesssim q \quad \text{iff} \quad \forall n \geq 0.\ \pi_n\, p \lesssim q, \tag{7.2}$$

where π_n is the n'th finite approximant of the recursive function π.

In Milner's construction of the fully abstract continuous model of PCF (Milner 1977) and in the operational model constructions for a call-by-value language like ours in Mason, Smith, and Talcott (1996), syntactic projections are used to address domain-theoretic notions of finite elements and ω-algebraicity syntactically.

Viewed as a proof rule, (7.2) is a sort of generalised Take Lemma (Bird and Wadler 1987) or higher-order structural induction principle; see Smith (1997). Pitts (1996b, 1994a) has also developed this idea and its domain-theoretic background and he has studied various applications.

7.2 Equational rules

From Lemma 7 we can derive an 'equational' version akin to Proposition 3.

Proposition 12 $\dfrac{R \subseteq \gtrsim\!\!\!\!\rhd^{\circ}\ \overline{R^{\mathsf{C}}} \lesssim^{\circ}}{R \subseteq \lesssim^{\circ}}$

Proof If $R \subseteq \gtrsim\!\!\!\!\rhd^{\circ}\ \overline{R^{\mathsf{C}}} \lesssim^{\circ}$ then

$$\begin{aligned} R\{\overline{R^{\mathsf{C}}}\} & \subseteq (\gtrsim\!\!\!\!\rhd^{\circ}\ \overline{R^{\mathsf{C}}} \lesssim^{\circ})\{\overline{R^{\mathsf{C}}}\} \\ & \subseteq (\gtrsim\!\!\!\!\rhd^{\circ}\{\overline{Id^{\mathsf{C}}}\})(\overline{R^{\mathsf{C}}}\{\overline{R^{\mathsf{C}}}\})(\lesssim^{\circ}\{\overline{Id^{\mathsf{C}}}\}) \\ & \subseteq \gtrsim\!\!\!\!\rhd^{\circ}\ (\overline{R^{\mathsf{C}}}\{\overline{R^{\mathsf{C}}}\}) \lesssim^{\circ}, \end{aligned} \tag{7.3}$$

because $\gtrsim^\circ$ and $\lesssim^\circ$ are closed under substitutions.

Moreover, we can show $\overline{R^C}\{\overline{R^C}\} \subseteq \ \gtrsim\!\!\lesssim^\circ \overline{R^C} \gtrsim\!\!\lesssim^\circ$, i.e.,

$$\vec{x} \vdash u\ \overline{R^C}\ u' \quad \text{and} \quad \vec{y} \vdash \vec{v}\ \overline{R^C}\ \vec{v}' \quad \text{imply} \quad \vec{y} \vdash u\{\vec{v}/\vec{x}\} \gtrsim\!\!\lesssim^\circ \overline{R^C} \gtrsim\!\!\lesssim^\circ u'\{\vec{v}'/\vec{x}\},$$

by induction on the derivation of $\vec{x} \vdash u\ \overline{R^C}\ u'$. In the (Match fn) case the substitutions of u and u' into the function bodies can be replaced by let bindings up to cost equivalence.

Therefore $\gtrsim^\circ (\overline{R^C}\{\overline{R^C}\}) \lesssim^\circ \ \subseteq\ \gtrsim^\circ \overline{R^C} \lesssim^\circ$ and

$$\begin{array}{rcll} R\{\overline{R^C}\} \cap Rel & \subseteq & \gtrsim \overline{R^C} \lesssim & \text{from (7.3)} \\ & \subseteq & \gtrsim \langle R^C \rangle \lesssim & \text{by definition of } \langle\_\rangle \\ & \subseteq & \langle \gtrsim^\circ \rangle \langle R^C \rangle \langle \lesssim^\circ \rangle & \gtrsim \text{ and } \lesssim \text{ are simulations} \\ & \subseteq & \langle \gtrsim^\circ R^C \lesssim^\circ \rangle & \text{by (5.8),} \end{array}$$

and we conclude $R \subseteq \ \gtrsim^\circ$, by Lemma 7. □

Proposition 12 is a useful proof rule in itself—for instance, the proof of recursion induction using Proposition 10 above is more directly an instance of the equational proof rule of Proposition 12. Furthermore, from it we can derive a version of a proof rule by Sands (1997b), called 'bisimulation up to context and improvement': let relation $\rhd \subseteq Rel$ be given by

$$p \rhd q \quad \text{iff} \quad p \gtrsim \mathrm{I}\ q.$$

Proposition 13 $\dfrac{R \subseteq \ \rhd^\circ R^C \lesssim^\circ}{R \subseteq \ \lesssim^\circ}$

Proof Suppose $R \subseteq \ \rhd^\circ R^C \lesssim^\circ$. We construct $S \subseteq Rel^\circ$ by

$$\vec{x} \vdash (\texttt{fn}\ z\ \texttt{=>}\ e) \quad S \quad (\texttt{fn}\ z\ \texttt{=>}\ e'),$$

whenever $z \notin \vec{x}$ and there exist d and d' such that

$$\vec{x} \vdash d\ R\ d' \quad \text{and} \quad \vec{x} \vdash d \rhd^\circ e\ R^C\ e' \lesssim^\circ d'.$$

Observe that

$$\vec{x} \vdash d \gtrsim^\circ (\texttt{fn}\ z\ \texttt{=>}\ e)\,\texttt{nil} \quad \text{and} \quad \vec{x} \vdash (\texttt{fn}\ z\ \texttt{=>}\ e')\,\texttt{nil} \lesssim^\circ d'.$$

Therefore $R \subseteq \ \gtrsim^\circ S^C \lesssim^\circ$. We have $S \subseteq \ \gtrsim^\circ \overline{S^C} \lesssim^\circ$ because

$$\vec{x} \vdash (\texttt{fn}\ z\ \texttt{=>}\ e) \quad \overline{R^C} \quad (\texttt{fn}\ z\ \texttt{=>}\ e'),$$

and

$$\overline{R^C} \subseteq \overline{(\gtrsim^\circ S^C \lesssim^\circ)^C} \subseteq \overline{(\gtrsim^\circ)^C}\,\overline{(S^C)^C}\,\overline{(\lesssim^\circ)^C} \subseteq \ \gtrsim^\circ \overline{S^C} \lesssim^\circ.$$

Hence $S \subseteq \ \lesssim^\circ$, by Proposition 12, and $R \subseteq \ \gtrsim^\circ S^C \lesssim^\circ$ implies $R \subseteq \ \lesssim^\circ$, because $\lesssim^\circ$ is a precongruence and contains $\gtrsim^\circ$. □

Sands (1997b) has demonstrated how (versions of) this rule allows simple calculational proofs of many functional program equivalences from the literature. It is particularly useful for call-by-value languages with inductively defined data types for which conventional applicative simulation is of little use.

For illustration, we solve Exercise 10.20 from Winskel (1993). Let

$$\begin{array}{lll} f & \stackrel{\text{def}}{=} & \texttt{rec}\ f\ x \texttt{ => fn } y \texttt{ => case } x \texttt{ of nil => } y \\ & & \qquad\qquad\qquad\qquad\qquad \mid x_1 \texttt{ :: } x_2 \texttt{ => } f(\text{append}(rx_1y)x_2)(sx_1y) \\ & & \qquad\qquad\qquad\qquad\qquad \mid h \texttt{ => } \Omega, \end{array}$$

$$\begin{array}{lll} g & \stackrel{\text{def}}{=} & \texttt{rec}\ g\ x \texttt{ => fn } y \texttt{ => case } x \texttt{ of nil => } y \\ & & \qquad\qquad\qquad\qquad\qquad \mid x_1 \texttt{ :: } x_2 \texttt{ => } gx_2(g(rx_1y)(sx_1y)) \\ & & \qquad\qquad\qquad\qquad\qquad \mid h \texttt{ => } \Omega, \end{array}$$

where $r, s \in Val_\emptyset$ (presumably they are functions but we need not require that) and append is the list concatenation function,

$$\begin{array}{lll} \text{append} & \stackrel{\text{def}}{=} & \texttt{rec}\ a\ x \texttt{ => fn } y \texttt{ => case } x \texttt{ of nil => } y \\ & & \qquad\qquad\qquad\qquad\qquad \mid x_1 \texttt{ :: } x_2 \texttt{ => } x_1 \texttt{ :: } a\,x_2\,y \\ & & \qquad\qquad\qquad\qquad\qquad \mid g \texttt{ => } \Omega. \end{array}$$

We will now prove that f and g are bisimilar by means of Sands' proof rule. As a first attempt, let relation R be given by

$$\vec{x} \vdash (f\,u_0\,v)\ R\ (g\,u_0\,v),$$

whenever $u_0, v \in Val_{\vec{x}}$. By extensionality, $f \sim g$ if $R \subseteq \sim^\circ$.

By means of the equational laws for cost equivalence, we calculate

$$\begin{array}{lll} \vec{x} \vdash f\,u_0\,v & \gtrsim\!\!\!\!\!\lesssim^\circ & \mathrm{I}^2 \texttt{ case } u_0 \texttt{ of nil => } v \\ & & \qquad\qquad \mid x_1 \texttt{ :: } x_2 \texttt{ => let val } x = r\,x_1\,v \\ & & \qquad\qquad\qquad\qquad\qquad \texttt{in let val } y = s\,x_1\,v \\ & & \qquad\qquad\qquad\qquad\qquad\quad \texttt{in } f(\text{append}\,x\,x_2)\,y \\ & & \qquad\qquad\qquad\qquad\qquad\quad \texttt{end} \\ & & \qquad\qquad\qquad\qquad\qquad \texttt{end} \\ & & \qquad\qquad \mid h \texttt{ => } \Omega, \end{array}$$

$$\begin{array}{lll} \vec{x} \vdash g\,u_0\,v & \gtrsim\!\!\!\!\!\lesssim^\circ & \mathrm{I}^2 \texttt{ case } u_0 \texttt{ of nil => } v \\ & & \qquad\qquad \mid x_1 \texttt{ :: } x_2 \texttt{ => let val } x = r\,x_1\,v \\ & & \qquad\qquad\qquad\qquad\qquad \texttt{in let val } y = s\,x_1\,v \\ & & \qquad\qquad\qquad\qquad\qquad\quad \texttt{in } g\,x_2(g\,x\,y) \\ & & \qquad\qquad\qquad\qquad\qquad\quad \texttt{end} \\ & & \qquad\qquad\qquad\qquad\qquad \texttt{end} \\ & & \qquad\qquad \mid h \texttt{ => } \Omega. \end{array}$$

The resulting expressions are identical except for the subterms $f(\text{append}\,x\,x_2)\,y$ and $g\,x_2(g\,x\,y)$. We need to extend R to also relate these. Let $@(u_n,\ldots,u_0)$ abbreviate append $u_n(\text{append}\,u_{n-1}(\ldots(\text{append}\,u_1\,u_0)\ldots))$. Now, let R be given by

$$\vec{x} \vdash (f\,@(u_n,\ldots,u_0)\,v)\ R\ (g\,u_0(\ldots(g\,u_n\,v)\ldots)),$$

for all $n \geq 0$ and $u_0, \ldots, u_n, v \in Val_{\vec{x}}$. From the calculations above we see that

$$\vec{x} \vdash (f\,@(u_0)\,v) = (f\,u_0\,v) \rhd^{\circ} R^{\mathsf{C}} \sim^{\circ} (g\,u_0\,v),$$

because $\vec{x}x_1x_2xy \vdash (f(\mathbf{append}\,x\,x_2)\,y) = (f\,@(x,x_2)\,y)\ R\ (g\,x_2(g\,x\,y))$. If $n \geq 1$ we calculate

$$\begin{array}{lll}
\vec{x} \vdash f\,@(u_n, u_{n-1}, \ldots, u_0)\,v & & \\
\quad \underset{\sim}{\bowtie}^{\circ} & \mathtt{I}^2\,\mathtt{case}\ u_n\ \mathtt{of\ nil} \Rightarrow f\,@(u_{n-1},\ldots,u_0)\,v & \\
& \mid x_1 :: x_2 \Rightarrow \mathtt{let\ val}\ x = r\,x_1\,v & \\
& \qquad \mathtt{in\ let\ val}\ y = s\,x_1\,v & \\
& \qquad\quad \mathtt{in}\ \mathtt{I}^2\,f\,@(x, x_2, u_{n-1},\ldots,u_0)\,y & \\
& \qquad\quad \mathtt{end} & \\
& \qquad \mathtt{end} & \\
& \mid h \Rightarrow \Omega, & \\
\quad \underset{\sim}{\rhd}^{\circ} & \mathtt{I}^2\,\mathtt{case}\ u_n\ \mathtt{of\ nil} \Rightarrow f\,@(u_{n-1},\ldots,u_0)\,v & \\
& \mid x_1 :: x_2 \Rightarrow \mathtt{let\ val}\ x = r\,x_1\,v & \\
& \qquad \mathtt{in\ let\ val}\ y = s\,x_1\,v & \\
& \qquad\quad \mathtt{in}\ f\,@(x, x_2, u_{n-1},\ldots,u_0)\,y & \\
& \qquad\quad \mathtt{end} & \\
& \qquad \mathtt{end} & \\
& \mid h \Rightarrow \Omega, & \\
\vec{x} \vdash g\,u_0(\ldots(g\,u_{n-1}(g\,u_n\,v))\ldots) & & \\
\quad \underset{\sim}{\bowtie}^{\circ} & \mathtt{I}^2\,\mathtt{case}\ u_0\ \mathtt{of\ nil} \Rightarrow g\,u_0(\ldots(g\,u_{n-1}\,v)\ldots) & \\
& \mid x_1 :: x_2 \Rightarrow \mathtt{let\ val}\ x = r\,x_1\,v & \\
& \qquad \mathtt{in\ let\ val}\ y = s\,x_1\,v & \\
& \qquad\quad \mathtt{in}\ g\,u_0(\ldots(g\,u_{n-1}(g\,x_2(g\,x\,y)))\ldots) & \\
& \qquad\quad \mathtt{end} & \\
& \qquad \mathtt{end} & \\
& \mid h \Rightarrow \Omega. &
\end{array}$$

Since $\vec{x}x_1x_2xy \vdash (f\,@(x, x_2, u_{n-1},\ldots,u_0)\,y)\ R\ (g\,u_0(\ldots(g\,u_{n-1}(g\,x_2(g\,x\,y)))\ldots))$ and $\vec{x} \vdash (f\,@(u_{n-1},\ldots,u_0)\,v)\ R\ (g\,u_0(\ldots(g\,u_{n-1}\,v)\ldots))$, we get that

$$\vec{x} \vdash (f\,@(u_n, u_{n-1},\ldots,u_0)\,v) \rhd^{\circ} R^{\mathsf{C}} \sim^{\circ} (g\,u_0(\ldots(g\,u_{n-1}(g\,u_n\,v))\ldots)).$$

Hence $R \subseteq \rhd^{\circ} R^{\mathsf{C}} \sim^{\circ}$ and thus $R \subseteq \lesssim^{\circ}$ by Proposition 13. From the calculations above it is easy to obtain $R^{\mathrm{op}} \subseteq \rhd^{\circ} (R^{\mathrm{op}})^{\mathsf{C}} \sim^{\circ}$ too, and hence $R^{\mathrm{op}} \subseteq \lesssim^{\circ}$, again by Proposition 13. We conclude that $R \subseteq \sim^{\circ}$ and $f \sim g$.

The shortcoming of Lemma 7, compared to (7.1), is less apparent in the derived equational rules of Propositions 12 and 13. But note that they work for *open* relations, in contrast to the 'closed' equational rule for simulation up to similarity of Proposition 3. We do not know if stronger, closed versions hold:

$$(i)\ \frac{R \subseteq \underset{\sim}{\rhd}\ \overline{(R^{\circ})^{\mathsf{C}}} \lesssim}{R \subseteq \lesssim} \qquad\qquad (ii)\ \frac{R \subseteq \rhd\ (R^{\circ})^{\mathsf{C}} \lesssim}{R \subseteq \lesssim} \qquad\qquad (7.4)$$

They are consequences of (7.1) because $\underset{\sim}{\triangleright}\ \overline{(R^\circ)^{\mathsf{C}}} \lesssim\ \subseteq \langle \underset{\sim}{\triangleright}^\circ\ (R^\circ)^{\mathsf{C}} \lesssim^\circ \rangle$ and (ii) follows from (i) as in the proof of Proposition 13. Propositions 12 and 13 are weaker than (7.4): sometimes reasoning about open terms does not suffice as it may be necessary to argue by cases on the values of the free variables. One such example is syntactic minimal invariance, Proposition 11. It would follow from (7.4)(i), by structural induction on closed values, but not from Proposition 12.

8 Conclusion

The 'relational' proof style of Howe (1996) and Pitts (1995) has been used throughout this paper. It is a rather low-level approach but is precise and tractable and applies to a wide range of problems involving term contexts and evaluation. Our proofs of the unfolding theorem and various simulation up to context results substantiate this. The algebra of relations in Section 3 and, in particular, context closure facilitate the construction of relations for this style of proofs. Our results are stated for an untyped ML fragment but should carry over to other typed and untyped higher-order languages.

Simulation up to context is a proof technique with a great practical potential for applicative bisimulation and improvement. This is witnessed by our proofs of recursion induction, the improvement theorem, syntactic minimal invariance, and Exercise 10.20 from Winskel (1993), as well as by the examples of Gordon (1995) and Sands (1997b). But an important problem is left open, namely the validity of (5.14) and (7.1),

$$\frac{R \subseteq \langle (R^\circ)^{\mathsf{C}} \rangle}{R \subseteq \lesssim} \qquad\qquad \frac{R \subseteq \langle \underset{\sim}{\triangleright}^\circ\ (R^\circ)^{\mathsf{C}} \lesssim^\circ \rangle}{R \subseteq \lesssim}$$

The significance of the gap between these and the weaker rule of Lemma 7,

$$\frac{R\{\overline{R^{\mathsf{C}}}\} \cap \mathit{Rel} \subseteq \langle \underset{\sim}{\triangleright}^\circ\ R^{\mathsf{C}} \lesssim^\circ \rangle}{R \subseteq \lesssim^\circ}$$

is unclear. In Section 7 we demonstrated how Lemma 7 allows us to prove a range of non-trivial results.

Acknowledgements After some time of fruitless investigations into applicative bisimulation up to context, this work got under way when Andrew Pitts showed me his notes on the subject (Pitts 1995). I am grateful for his encouragement and valuable guidance in this project. I wish to thank David Sands for discussions; his work has been influential in every aspect of this research. Finally, I am indebted to Andrew Gordon, Peter Ørbæk and an anonymous referee for detailed comments and helpful suggestions. I am supported by a grant from the Danish Natural Science Research Council.

A Proofs

This appendix contains the rather delicate proofs of Lemmas 6 and 7. The first of these uses the following lemma.

Lemma 8 *Compatibility is preserved by transitive closure.*

Proof First observe that compatibility is preserved by relation composition: if R and S are compatible, so is their composition $R\,S$,

$$\widehat{RS} = \widehat{R}\,\widehat{S} \subseteq R\,S.$$

Next, suppose R is compatible. If $\vec{x} \vdash e\ \widehat{R^+}\ e'$, each immediate subterm e_i of e is related to a corresponding subterm e_i' of e', $\vec{x}\vec{y_i} \vdash e_i\ R^+\ e_i'$, for some $\vec{y_i}$. This means that there exists $m_i \geq 1$ such that $\vec{x}\vec{y_i} \vdash e_i\ R^{m_i}\ e_i'$, where R^{m_i} is the m_i-fold composition of R with itself. Let m be the greatest of these m_i, for all pairs of subterms. Since R is compatible it is also reflexive. Hence $\vec{x}\vec{y_i} \vdash e_i\ R^{m-m_i}\ e_i$ and then $\vec{x}\vec{y_i} \vdash e_i\ R^m\ e_i'$, for all corresponding subterms e_i and e_i'. Hence $\vec{x} \vdash e\ \widehat{R^m}\ e'$, by definition of compatible refinement, and then $\vec{x} \vdash e\ R^m\ e'$ because compatibility is preserved by relation composition. So $\vec{x} \vdash e\ R^+\ e'$ and we conclude that R^+ is compatible. □

Proof of Lemma 6 $\dfrac{R \subseteq \langle S^+\rangle_I}{S^+ \subseteq \gtrsim^\circ}$, where $S \stackrel{\text{def}}{=} (R^\circ)^{\mathsf{C}}$.

Proof Assume $R \subseteq \langle S^+\rangle_I$. We are going to prove that S^+ is an open improvement simulation,

$$S^+ \subseteq \langle S^+\rangle_I^\circ.$$

Then $S^+ \subseteq \gtrsim^\circ$, by the improvement simulation rule (6.2).

First we need some properties of S^+.

By definition of context closure, S is compatible. Compatibility is preserved by transitive closure, Lemma 8, so S^+ is also compatible.

Open extension, R°, is closed under substitutions and so is S because closure under substitutions is preserved by context closure. It is also preserved by relation composition and, consequently, by transitive closure. Therefore S^+ is closed under substitutions.

By Lemma 1, S^+ is substitutive because it is compatible, transitive and closed under substitutions.

We proceed to prove $S^+ \subseteq \langle S^+\rangle_I^\circ$. Since S^+ is closed under substitutions, it suffices to show $S^+ \cap Rel \subseteq \langle S^+\rangle_I$. This is equivalent to asserting that predicate $\mathcal{P}(N)$, defined by

$$\mathcal{P}(N) \stackrel{\text{def}}{\Leftrightarrow} \begin{array}{l}\forall p, p', v.\ \vdash p\ S^+\ p'\ \&\ p \Downarrow_N v \Rightarrow \\ \qquad \exists v'.\ p' \Downarrow_{\leq N} v'\ \&\ \vdash v\ \overline{S^+}\ v',\end{array}$$

holds for all N. The proof is by a series of nested inductions on N, on the derivation of $\vdash p\ S^+\ p'$, and on the derivation of $p \Downarrow_N v$.

The outer induction hypothesis is

(I.H.1) $\mathcal{P}(N)$ *for all* $N < N_0$.

Then we must show $\mathcal{P}(N_0)$. This follows if

$$\forall p, p', v.\ \vdash p\ S\ p' \ \&\ p \Downarrow_{\leq N_0} v \Rightarrow \exists v'.\ p' \Downarrow_{\leq N_0} v' \ \&\ \vdash v\ \overline{S^+}\ v', \qquad \text{(A.1)}$$

because, supposing $\vdash p\ S^+\ p'$,

$$\vdash p = p_0\ S\ p_1\ S \cdots S\ p_m = p',$$

and $p \Downarrow_{N_0} v$, by repeatedly applying (A.1) to $\vdash p_i\ S\ p_{i+1}$, we get $p' \Downarrow_{\leq N_0} v'$ with

$$\vdash v = v_0\ \overline{S^+} \cdots \overline{S^+}\ v_m = v',$$

and we can conclude $\vdash v\ \overline{S^+}\ v'$ because $\overline{S^+}$ is transitive,

$$\overline{S^+} \cdots \overline{S^+} = \overline{S^+ \cdots S^+} \subseteq \overline{S^+}.$$

We strengthen (A.1) slightly and prove that predicate $\mathcal{Q}(p, M, v)$,

$$\mathcal{Q}(p, M, v) \ \stackrel{\text{def}}{\Leftrightarrow}\ \begin{array}{l} p \Downarrow_M v \ \&\ M \leq N_0 \Rightarrow \\ \quad \forall p'.\ \vdash p\ S\{\overline{S^+}\}\ p' \Rightarrow \\ \quad\quad \exists v'.\ p' \Downarrow_{\leq M} v' \ \&\ \vdash v\ \overline{S^+}\ v', \end{array}$$

holds for all p, M, v. This entails (A.1) because $\vdash p\ S\ p'$ clearly implies $\vdash p\ S\{\overline{S^+}\}\ p'$ with empty substitution of $\overline{S^+}$. Observe also that $S\{\overline{S^+}\} \subseteq S^+$ because $\overline{S^+} \subseteq S^+$, by compatibility, and $S\{S^+\} \subseteq S^+$, since $S \subseteq S^+$ and S^+ is substitutive. In fact, $\mathcal{Q}(p, M, v)$ follows from (I.H.1) whenever $M < N_0$.

We prove $\mathcal{Q}(p, M, v)$, for all p, M, v, by induction on the derivation of $p \Downarrow_M v$. For any derivation $p_0 \Downarrow_{M_0} v_0$, the induction hypothesis is

(I.H.2) $\mathcal{Q}(p, M, v)$ *for all premises* $p \Downarrow_M v$ *in the derivation of* $p_0 \Downarrow_{M_0} v_0$,

and we must show $\mathcal{Q}(p_0, M_0, v_0)$. We assume $p_0 \Downarrow_{M_0} v_0$ and $M_0 \leq N_0$, where $p_0 = e\{\vec{u}/\vec{x}\}$, $\vec{x} \vdash e\ S\ e'$ and $\vdash \vec{u}\ \overline{S^+}\ \vec{u}'$ such that $\vdash e\{\vec{u}/\vec{x}\}\ S\{\overline{S^+}\}\ e'\{\vec{u}'/\vec{x}\}$. We will show $e'\{\vec{u}'/\vec{x}\} \Downarrow_{\leq M_0} v_0'$, for some v_0' such that $\vdash v_0\ \overline{S^+}\ v_0'$.

The strategy is to exploit the assumption $\vec{x} \vdash e\ S\ e'$ to build the derivation $e'\{\vec{u}'/\vec{x}\} \Downarrow_{\leq M_0} v_0'$. The substitutions of $\vec{u}$ and $\vec{u}'$ are separated out in the induction on the derivation of $e\{\vec{u}/\vec{x}\} \Downarrow_{M_0} v_0$. If it is derived by means of the (Eval apply) rule, we need to perform these substitutions and we end up with terms related by S^+ rather than $S\{\overline{S^+}\}$. Then we invoke the stronger induction hypothesis (I.H.1). It applies because the premises of the (Eval apply) rule will all have cost-indexes smaller than M_0 and N_0.

Recall $S = (R^\circ)^{\mathsf{C}}$ and consider the derivation of $\vec{x} \vdash e\ S\ e'$. There are two cases.

(Ctx R) Suppose $\vec{y} \vdash e\ R^\circ\ e'$ with $\vec{y} \subseteq \vec{x}$. Note that $\vec{x} \vdash e\ \widehat{S}\ e$ because S and $\widehat{S}$ are reflexive. Therefore $\vdash e\{\vec{u}/\vec{x}\}\ \widehat{S}\{\overline{S^+}\}\ e\{\vec{u}'/\vec{x}\}$. From the (Ctx Comp) case below we get $e\{\vec{u}'/\vec{x}\} \Downarrow_{\leq M_0} v_0''$ with $\vdash v_0\ \overline{S^+}\ v_0''$. Moreover, $\vdash e\{\vec{u}'/\vec{x}\}\ R\ e'\{\vec{u}'/\vec{x}\}$. The assumption $R \subseteq \langle S^+ \rangle_I$ implies $e'\{\vec{u}'/\vec{x}\} \Downarrow_{\leq M_0} v_0'$ with $\vdash v_0''\ \overline{S^+}\ v_0'$. Since $\overline{S^+}$ is transitive, we obtain $\vdash v_0\ \overline{S^+}\ v_0'$, as required.

(Ctx Comp) Suppose $\vec{x} \vdash e\ \widehat{S}\ e'$. If this is derived by the (Comp x) rule, then $e = e' = x_i$, for some $x_i \in \vec{x}$, and the result is immediate because $e\{\vec{u}/\vec{x}\} \Downarrow_0 u_i$, $e'\{\vec{u}'/\vec{x}\} \Downarrow_0 u_i'$ and, by assumption, $\vdash u_i\ \overline{S^+}\ u_i'$. Otherwise e and e' are not variables, and we proceed by analysis of the derivation of $e\{\vec{u}/\vec{x}\} \Downarrow_{M_0} v_0$.

Case (Eval fn) $e\{\vec{u}/\vec{x}\}$ is a function, $e\{\vec{u}/\vec{x}\} = v_0$, and $M_0 = 0$. Since e is not a variable, it is itself a function, $e = \mathtt{fn}\ y\ \mathtt{=>}\ d$ for some $d \in Exp_{\vec{x}y}$. Then $\vec{x} \vdash e\ \widehat{S}\ e'$ must be derived by (Comp fn) so that $e' = \mathtt{fn}\ y\ \mathtt{=>}\ d'$ where $\vec{x}y \vdash d\ S\ d'$. Hence $e'\{\vec{u}'/\vec{x}\} \Downarrow_0 e'\{\vec{u}'/\vec{x}\}$ and $\vdash e\{\vec{u}/\vec{x}\}\ \overline{S^+}\ e'\{\vec{u}'/\vec{x}\}$, by (Eval fn) and (Match fn) because $y \vdash d\{\vec{u}/\vec{x}\}\ S\{\overline{S^+}\}\ d'\{\vec{u}'/\vec{x}\}$ and $S\{\overline{S^+}\} \subseteq S^+$.

Case (Eval nil) By reasoning similar to the previous case, we see e and e' are both `nil`. Hence $e'\{\vec{u}'/\vec{x}\} \Downarrow_0 e'\{\vec{u}'/\vec{x}\}$ and $\vdash e\{\vec{u}/\vec{x}\}\ \overline{S^+}\ e'\{\vec{u}'/\vec{x}\}$, by (Eval nil) and (Match nil).

Case (Eval cons) Since e is not a variable, it must be of the form $e = e_1 :: e_2$, and $e_i\{\vec{u}/\vec{x}\} \Downarrow_{M_i} v_i$, for $i = 1, 2$, such that $M_0 = M_1 + M_2$ and $v_0 = v_1 :: v_2$. Then $\vec{x} \vdash e\ \widehat{S}\ e'$ implies $e' = e_1' :: e_2'$ and $\vec{x} \vdash e_i\ S\ e_i'$. Observe that $M_i \leq N_0$ because $M_i \leq M_0$ and $M_0 \leq N_0$. Induction hypothesis (I.H.2) and $e_i\{\vec{u}/\vec{x}\} \Downarrow_{M_i} v_i$ imply $e_i'\{\vec{u}'/\vec{x}\} \Downarrow_{\leq M_i} v_i'$ with $\vdash v_i\ \overline{S^+}\ v_i'$. Hence $e'\{\vec{u}'/\vec{x}\} \Downarrow_{\leq M_0} v_0'$ with $\vdash v_0 = v_1 :: v_2\ \overline{S^+}\ v_1' :: v_2'$, by (Eval Cons) and (Match Cons).

Case (Eval apply) $e = e_1 e_2$, $e_1\{\vec{u}/\vec{x}\} \Downarrow_{M_1} v_1 = \mathtt{fn}\ y\ \mathtt{=>}\ d$, $e_2\{\vec{u}/\vec{x}\} \Downarrow_{M_2} v_2$, $d\{v_2/y\} \Downarrow_{M_3} v_0$, and $M_0 = M_1 + M_2 + M_3 + 1$. Since $\vec{x} \vdash e\ \widehat{S}\ e'$, $e' = e_1' e_2'$ with $\vec{x} \vdash e_i\ S\ e_i'$. We observe that $M_i < N_0$ because $M_i < M$ and $M \leq N_0$, for $i = 1, 2, 3$. By induction hypothesis (I.H.2), $e_i\{\vec{u}/\vec{x}\} \Downarrow_{M_i} v_i$ implies $e_i'\{\vec{u}'/\vec{x}\} \Downarrow_{\leq M_i} v_i'$ with $\vdash v_i\ \overline{S^+}\ v_i'$, for $i = 1, 2$. So $v_1' = \mathtt{fn}\ y\ \mathtt{=>}\ d'$ where $y \vdash d\ S^+\ d'$. Hence $\vdash d\{v_2/y\}\ S^+\ d'\{v_2'/y\}$, because S^+ is substitutive. Since $M_3 < N_0$, induction hypothesis (I.H.1) and $d\{v_2/y\} \Downarrow_{M_3} v_0$ imply $d'\{v_2'/y\} \Downarrow_{\leq M_3} v_0'$ with $\vdash v_0\ \overline{S^+}\ v_0'$. By (Eval apply), we conclude $e'\{\vec{u}'/\vec{x}\} \Downarrow_{\leq M_0} v_0'$.

Case (Eval let fun) $e = \mathtt{let\ fun}\ f\ y = e_1\ \mathtt{in}\ e_2\ \mathtt{end}$, $e_2\{\vec{u}w/\vec{x}f\} \Downarrow_{M_0} v_0$, where $w = \mathtt{rec}\ f\ y\ \mathtt{=>}\ e_1$. Since $\vec{x} \vdash e\ \widehat{S}\ e'$, $e' = \mathtt{let\ fun}\ f\ y{=}e_1'\ \mathtt{in}\ e_2'\ \mathtt{end}$ with $\vec{x}fy \vdash e_1\ S\ e_1'$ and $\vec{x}f \vdash e_2\ S\ e_2'$. Let $w' = \mathtt{rec}\ f\ y\ \mathtt{=>}\ e_1'$, then $\vec{x} \vdash w\ \overline{S}\ w'$ because S is compatible. Consequently, $\vec{x} \vdash w\ \overline{S^+}\ w'$ and $\vdash e_2\{\vec{u}w/\vec{x}f\}\ S\{\overline{S^+}\}\ e_2'\{\vec{u}'w'/\vec{x}f\}$. By induction hypothesis (I.H.2), $e_2\{\vec{u}w/\vec{x}f\} \Downarrow_{M_0} v_0$ implies $e_2'\{\vec{u}'w'/\vec{x}f\} \Downarrow_{\leq M_0} v_0'$ with $\vdash v_0\ \overline{S^+}\ v_0'$. By (Eval let fun), we conclude $e'\{\vec{u}'/\vec{x}\} \Downarrow_{\leq M_0} v_0'$.

Case (Eval case) $e = \texttt{case}\ e_0\ \texttt{of nil => } e_1 \mid y_1\ \texttt{::}\ y_2\ \texttt{=>}\ e_2 \mid f\ \texttt{=>}\ e_3$, $e_0\{\vec{u}/\vec{x}\} \Downarrow_{M_1} v$, $q \Downarrow_{M_2} v_0$, and $M_0 = M_1 + M_2$, where

$$q = \begin{cases} e_1\{\vec{u}/\vec{x}\} & \text{if } v = \texttt{nil} \\ e_2\{\vec{u}v_1v_2/\vec{x}y_1y_2\} & \text{if } v = v_1\ \texttt{::}\ v_2 \\ e_3\{\vec{u}v/\vec{x}f\} & \text{if } v = \texttt{fn}\ y\ \texttt{=>}\ d. \end{cases}$$

Since $\vec{x} \vdash e\ \widehat{S}\ e'$, $e' = \texttt{case}\ e_0'\ \texttt{of nil => } e_1' \mid y_1\ \texttt{::}\ y_2\ \texttt{=>}\ e_2' \mid f\ \texttt{=>}\ e_3'$, with $\vec{x} \vdash e_0\ S\ e_0'$, $\vec{x} \vdash e_1\ S\ e_1'$, $\vec{x}y_1y_2 \vdash e_2\ S\ e_2'$, and $\vec{x}f \vdash e_3\ S\ e_3'$. Observe that $M_i \leq N_0$ because $M_i \leq M_0$ and $M_0 \leq N_0$. Induction hypothesis (I.H.2) and $e_0\{\vec{u}/\vec{x}\} \Downarrow_{M_1} v$ imply $e_0'\{\vec{u}'/\vec{x}\} \Downarrow_{\leq M_1} v'$ with $\vdash v\ \overline{S^+}\ v'$. According to the derivation of $\vdash v\ \overline{S^+}\ v'$, let

$$q' = \begin{cases} e_1'\{\vec{u}'/\vec{x}\} & \text{if } v = \texttt{nil} = v' \\ e_2'\{\vec{u}'v_1'v_2'/\vec{x}y_1y_2\} & \text{if } v = v_1\ \texttt{::}\ v_2, v' = v_1'\ \texttt{::}\ v_2', \vdash v_i\ \overline{S^+}\ v_i' \\ e_3'\{\vec{u}'v'/\vec{x}f\} & \text{if } \vdash v = \texttt{fn}\ y\ \texttt{=>}\ d\ \overline{S^+}\ \texttt{fn}\ y\ \texttt{=>}\ d' = v'. \end{cases}$$

By inspection of the definitions of q and q', we see that $\vdash q\ S\{\overline{S^+}\}\ q'$. Induction hypothesis (I.H.2) and $q \Downarrow_{M_2} v_0$ imply $q' \Downarrow_{\leq M_2} v_0'$ with $\vdash v_0\ \overline{S^+}\ v_0'$. By (Eval case), we conclude $e'\{\vec{u}'/\vec{x}\} \Downarrow_{\leq M_0} v_0'$.

Case (Eval let val) Similar to the previous case.

All cases considered, we conclude $\mathcal{Q}(p_0, M_0, v_0)$, as required. This completes the induction step for $\mathcal{Q}$ and we have $\mathcal{Q}(p, M, v)$ for all p, M, v.

Therefore (A.1) and $\mathcal{P}(N_0)$ hold. This completes the induction step for $\mathcal{P}$, so $\mathcal{P}(N)$ holds for all N.

Then $S^+ \cap \mathit{Rel} \subseteq \langle S^+\rangle_I$ and S^+ is an open improvement simulation, $S^+ \subseteq \langle S^+\rangle_I^\circ$. The conclusion, $S^+ \subseteq \gtrsim^\circ$, follows co-inductively by the improvement simulation rule (6.2). □

Lemma 6 is invalid for similarity (i.e., with $\langle \_ \rangle$ and $\lesssim^\circ$ in place of $\langle \_ \rangle_I$ and $\gtrsim^\circ$). The proof above uses the improvement aspect of $\langle \_ \rangle_I$ to assert that $p' \Downarrow v'$ computes no slower than $p \Downarrow v$ when $\vdash p\ S\ p'$. If there is no bound on the cost of $p' \Downarrow v'$, the transitivity argument, why (A.1) implies $\mathcal{P}(N_0)$, breaks down.

The proof of Lemma 6 makes use of the transitive closure of S in two ways.

(*i*) S^+ is substitutive. This is used in the (Eval fn) and (Eval apply) cases of the induction step.

(*ii*) In the (Ctx R) case transitivity is used to avoid substitution of values related by $\overline{S^+}$ into expressions related by R°.

Lemma 7 is essentially a weaker version of Lemma 6 for similarity. The proof is similar to that of Lemma 6 but solves (*i*) and (*ii*) without transitive closure.

(i) Substitutions can be replaced by let bindings up to cost equivalence; thereby the compatibility of R^{C} suffices and substitutivity is not necessary.

(ii) The requirement that the premise of Lemma 7 holds for $R\{\overline{R^{\mathsf{C}}}\}$ rather than just R circumvents the problem of substitution into expressions related by R.

Proof of Lemma 7 $\dfrac{R\{\overline{R^{\mathsf{C}}}\} \cap \mathit{Rel} \subseteq \langle \underset{\sim}{\triangleright}^{\circ}\ R^{\mathsf{C}} \lesssim^{\circ}\rangle}{R \subseteq \lesssim^{\circ}}$

Proof Assume $R\{\overline{R^{\mathsf{C}}} \cap \mathit{Rel}\} \subseteq \langle \underset{\sim}{\triangleright}^{\circ}\ R^{\mathsf{C}} \lesssim^{\circ}\rangle$. We are going to prove

$$R^{\mathsf{C}}\{\mathit{Id}\} \subseteq \langle S\rangle, \quad \text{where } S = \underset{\sim}{\triangleright}^{\circ}\ R^{\mathsf{C}} \lesssim^{\circ}. \tag{A.2}$$

Observe that $S \subseteq \lesssim^{\circ} R^{\mathsf{C}}\{\mathit{Id}\}^{\circ} \lesssim^{\circ}$, because $\underset{\sim}{\triangleright}^{\circ} \subseteq \lesssim^{\circ}$ and $R^{\mathsf{C}} \subseteq R^{\mathsf{C}}\{\mathit{Id}\}^{\circ}$, by (3.2). By simulation up to similarity, Proposition 2, we get that (A.2) implies $R^{\mathsf{C}}\{\mathit{Id}\} \subseteq \lesssim$. Hence $R^{\mathsf{C}} \subseteq \lesssim^{\circ}$, by (3.2), and the conclusion, $R \subseteq \lesssim^{\circ}$, follows because $R \subseteq R^{\mathsf{C}}$,

S is compatible because $\underset{\sim}{\triangleright}^{\circ}$, R^{C}, and $\lesssim^{\circ}$ are and compatibility is preserved by relation composition. Therefore S is reflexive and $\overline{S}$ is a reflexive relation on values. Hence $R^{\mathsf{C}}\{\mathit{Id}\} \subseteq R^{\mathsf{C}}\{\overline{S}\}$, and (A.2) holds if $R^{\mathsf{C}}\{\overline{S}\} \subseteq \langle S\rangle$. The latter is equivalent to the predicate $\mathcal{P}(N)$ holding for all N, where

$$\mathcal{P}(N) \overset{\text{def}}{\Leftrightarrow} \begin{array}{l} \forall p, p', v.\ \vdash p\ R^{\mathsf{C}}\{\overline{S}\}\ p'\ \&\ p \Downarrow_N v \Rightarrow \\ \qquad \exists v'.\ p' \Downarrow v'\ \&\ \vdash v\ \overline{S}\ v', \end{array}$$

We proceed by induction on N. The induction hypothesis is

(I.H.1) $\mathcal{P}(N)$ *for all* $N < N_0$.

Then we must show $\mathcal{P}(N_0)$. This follows if $\mathcal{Q}(p, M, v)$,

$$\mathcal{Q}(p, M, v) \overset{\text{def}}{\Leftrightarrow} \begin{array}{l} p \Downarrow_M v\ \&\ M \leq N_0 \Rightarrow \\ \qquad \forall p'.\ \vdash p\ R^{\mathsf{C}}\{\overline{S}\}\ p' \Rightarrow \\ \qquad\qquad \exists v'.\ p' \Downarrow v'\ \&\ \vdash v\ \overline{S}\ v', \end{array}$$

holds for all p, M, v. We prove $\mathcal{Q}(p, M, v)$, for all p, M, v, by induction on the derivation of $p \Downarrow_M v$. For any derivation $p_0 \Downarrow_{M_0} v_0$, the induction hypothesis is

(I.H.2) $\mathcal{Q}(p, M, v)$ *for all premises* $p \Downarrow_M v$ *in the derivation of* $p_0 \Downarrow_{M_0} v_0$,

and we must show $\mathcal{Q}(p_0, M_0, v_0)$. We assume $p_0 \Downarrow_{M_0} v_0$ and $M_0 \leq N_0$, where $p_0 = e\{\vec{u}/\vec{x}\}$, $\vec{x} \vdash e\ R^{\mathsf{C}}\ e'$ and $\vdash \vec{u}\ \overline{S}\ \vec{u}'$ such that $\vdash e\{\vec{u}/\vec{x}\}\ R^{\mathsf{C}}\{\overline{S}\}\ e'\{\vec{u}'/\vec{x}\}$. We will show $e'\{\vec{u}'/\vec{x}\} \Downarrow v_0'$, for some v_0' such that $\vdash v_0\ \overline{S}\ v_0'$.

Consider the derivation of $\vec{x} \vdash e\ R^{\mathsf{C}}\ e'$. There are two cases.

(Ctx R) Suppose $\vec{x} \vdash e\ R\ e'$. Since $\vdash \vec{u}\ \overline{S}\ \vec{u}'$, there exist $\vec{w}$ and $\vec{w}'$ such that $\vdash \vec{u}\ \overline{\underset{\sim}{\rhd}^{\circ}}\ \vec{w}\ \overline{R^{\mathsf{C}}}\ \vec{w}'\ \overline{\lesssim^{\circ}}\ \vec{u}'$. As $\underset{\sim}{\rhd}^{\circ}$ and $\lesssim^{\circ}$ are precongruences, we get

$$e\{\vec{u}/\vec{x}\} \underset{\sim}{\rhd} e\{\vec{w}/\vec{x}\}\ R\{\overline{R^{\mathsf{C}}}\}\ e'\{\vec{w}'/\vec{x}\} \lesssim e'\{\vec{u}'/\vec{x}\}$$

Since $e\{\vec{u}/\vec{x}\} \Downarrow v_0$, also $e\{\vec{w}/\vec{x}\} \Downarrow v$ with $\vdash v_0\ \overline{\underset{\sim}{\rhd}^{\circ}}\ v$. From assumption $R\{\overline{R^{\mathsf{C}}}\} \cap Rel \subseteq \langle S \rangle$ follows $e'\{\vec{w}'/\vec{x}\} \Downarrow v'$ with $\vdash v\ \overline{S}\ v'$. Finally, $e'\{\vec{u}'/\vec{x}\} \Downarrow v_0'$ with $\vdash v'\ \overline{\lesssim^{\circ}}\ v_0'$, and $\vdash v_0\ \overline{\underset{\sim}{\rhd}^{\circ}}\ v\ \overline{S}\ v'\ \overline{\lesssim^{\circ}}\ v_0'$ implies $\vdash v_0\ \overline{S}\ v_0'$ because $\underset{\sim}{\rhd}^{\circ}\ S \lesssim^{\circ} \subseteq S$ by transitivity of $\underset{\sim}{\rhd}^{\circ}$ and $\lesssim^{\circ}$.

(Ctx Comp) If $\vec{x} \vdash e\ \widehat{R^{\mathsf{C}}}\ e'$, we argue as in the proof of Lemma 6 above (with R^{C} and $\overline{S}$ in place of S and $\overline{S^{+}}$), except that here we do not keep track of the cost of the evaluation $e'\{\vec{u}'/\vec{x}\} \Downarrow v_0'$. Again the result is immediate if e is a variable. Otherwise we proceed by analysis of the derivation of $e\{\vec{u}/\vec{x}\} \Downarrow_{M_0} v_0$. Only the cases when this is derived by (Eval fn) or (Eval apply) are different from those in the proof of Lemma 6.

Case (Eval fn) $e\{\vec{u}/\vec{x}\}$ is a function and $e\{\vec{u}/\vec{x}\} = v_0$. Since e is not a variable, it is itself a function, $e = \texttt{fn}\ y\ \texttt{=>}\ d$ for some $d \in Exp_{\vec{x}y}$. Then $\vec{x} \vdash e\ \widehat{R^{\mathsf{C}}}\ e'$ must be derived by (Comp fn) so that $e' = \texttt{fn}\ y\ \texttt{=>}\ d'$ where $\vec{x}y \vdash d\ R^{\mathsf{C}}\ d'$. Since $\vdash \vec{u}\ \overline{S}\ \vec{u}'$, there exist $\vec{w}$ and $\vec{w}'$ such that $\vdash \vec{u}\ \underset{\sim}{\rhd}^{\circ}\ \vec{w}\ \overline{R^{\mathsf{C}}}\ \vec{w}'\ \overline{\lesssim^{\circ}}\ \vec{u}'$. As $\underset{\sim}{\rhd}^{\circ}$, R^{C}, and $\lesssim^{\circ}$ are compatible, we get

$$y \vdash d\{\vec{u}/\vec{x}\} \underset{\sim}{\rhd}^{\circ} d\{\vec{w}/\vec{x}\}\ R^{\mathsf{C}}\{R^{\mathsf{C}}\}\ d'\{\vec{w}'/\vec{x}\} \lesssim^{\circ} d'\{\vec{u}'/\vec{x}\}.$$

Let $(let\ \vec{x} = \vec{v}\ in\ e)$ abbreviate a suitable `let` construction which beta reduces to $e\{\vec{v}/\vec{x}\}$. Then

$$y \vdash d\{\vec{w}/\vec{x}\} \underset{\sim}{\bowtie}^{\circ} (let\ \vec{x} = \vec{w}\ in\ d)\ R^{\mathsf{C}}\ (let\ \vec{x} = \vec{w}'\ in\ d') \underset{\sim}{\bowtie}^{\circ} d'\{\vec{w}'/\vec{x}\}.$$

Since $\underset{\sim}{\rhd}$ and $\lesssim$ contain $\underset{\sim}{\bowtie}$ and are transitive,

$$y \vdash d\{\vec{u}/\vec{x}\}\ S\ d'\{\vec{u}'/\vec{x}\},$$

Hence $\vdash e\{\vec{u}/\vec{x}\}\ \overline{S}\ e'\{\vec{u}'/\vec{x}\}$, as required.

Case (Eval apply) $e = e_1 e_2$, $e_1\{\vec{u}/\vec{x}\} \Downarrow_{M_1} v_1 = \texttt{fn}\ y\ \texttt{=>}\ d_1$, $e_2\{\vec{u}/\vec{x}\} \Downarrow_{M_2} v_2$, $d_1\{v_2/y\} \Downarrow_{M_3} v_0$, and $M_0 = M_1 + M_2 + M_3 + 1$. Since $\vec{x} \vdash e\ \widehat{R^{\mathsf{C}}}\ e'$, $e' = e_1' e_2'$ with $\vec{x} \vdash e_i\ R^{\mathsf{C}}\ e_i'$. We observe that $M_i < N_0$ because $M_i < M$ and $M \leq N_0$, for $i = 1, 2, 3$. By induction hypothesis (I.H.2), $e_i\{\vec{u}/\vec{x}\} \Downarrow_{M_i} v_i$ implies $e_i'\{\vec{u}'/\vec{x}\} \Downarrow v_i'$ with $\vdash v_i\ \overline{S}\ v_i'$, for $i = 1, 2$. So $v_1' = \texttt{fn}\ y\ \texttt{=>}\ d_1'$ where $y \vdash d_1\ S\ d_1'$, that is, there exist $d, d' \in Exp_y$ such that $y \vdash d_1 \underset{\sim}{\rhd}^{\circ} d\ R^{\mathsf{C}}\ d' \lesssim^{\circ} d_1'$. Since $\underset{\sim}{\rhd}^{\circ}$ and $\lesssim^{\circ}$ are closed under substitutions, $d_1\{v_2/y\} \underset{\sim}{\rhd} d\{v_2/y\}$ and $d'\{v_2'/y\} \lesssim d_1'\{v_2'/y\}$. From the former and $d_1\{v_2/y\} \Downarrow_{M_3} v_0$, we get $d\{v_2/y\} \Downarrow_{\leq M_3} v$ with $\vdash v_0\ \overline{\underset{\sim}{\rhd}^{\circ}}\ v$. Since $M_3 < N_0$ and $\vdash d\{v_2/y\}\ R^{\mathsf{C}}\{\overline{S}\}$

$d'\{{}^{v_2'}\!/_y\}$, induction hypothesis (I.H.1) and $d\{{}^{v_2}\!/_y\} \Downarrow_{\leq M_3} v$ imply $\overline{d'\{{}^{v_2'}\!/_y\} \Downarrow v'}$ with $\vdash v\ \overline{S}\ v'$. Since $d'\{{}^{v_2'}\!/_y\} \lesssim d_1'\{{}^{v_2'}\!/_y\}$, $d_1'\{{}^{v_2'}\!/_y\} \Downarrow v_0'$ with $\vdash v'\ \overline{\lesssim^\circ}\ v_0'$. Then $\vdash v_0\ \overline{S}\ v_0'$ because $\overline{\gtrsim^\circ}\ \overline{S}\ \overline{\lesssim^\circ} = \overline{\gtrsim^\circ S \lesssim^\circ}$ and $\gtrsim^\circ S \lesssim^\circ \subseteq S$. By (Eval apply), we conclude $e'\{{}^{\vec{u}'}\!/_{\vec{x}}\} \Downarrow v_0'$.

This establishes $R^{\mathsf{C}}\{\overline{S}\} \subseteq \langle S\rangle$ and then (A.2) follows, as required. □

References

Abramsky, S. (1990). The lazy lambda calculus. In D. Turner (Ed.), *Research topics in functional programming*, pp. 65–116. Addison-Wesley.

Bird, R. and P. Wadler (1987). *Introduction to Functional Programming*. International Series in Computer Science. Prentice-Hall.

Braüner, T. (1996, November). An axiomatic approach to adequacy. Technical Report DS-96-4, BRICS, Department of Computer Science, University of Aarhus. Ph.D. thesis.

Clinger, W. and J. Rees (editors) (1991, July-September). Revised[4] report on the algorithmic language scheme. *LISP Pointers IV*(3), 1–55.

Felleisen, M. and D. P. Friedman (1987). Control operators, the SECD-machine, and the λ-calculus. In M. Wirsing (Ed.), *Formal Description of Programming Concepts III*. IFIP.

Ferreira, W., M. Hennessy, and A. Jeffrey (1995, September). A theory of weak bisimulation for core CML. Technical Report 05/95, COGS, University of Sussex.

Gordon, A. D. (1994). *Functional Programming and Input/Output*. Cambridge University Press.

Gordon, A. D. (1995, July). Bisimilarity as a theory of functional programming. Minicourse. BRICS Notes Series NS-95-3, BRICS, Department of Computer Science, University of Aarhus.

Gordon, A. D. (1997). Operational equivalences for untyped and polymorphic object calculi. In this volume, pp. 9–54.

Gordon, A. D. and G. D. Rees (1996). Bisimilarity for a first-order calculus of objects with subtyping. In *POPL'96 Symposium on Principles of Programming Languages*. ACM.

Howe, D. J. (1989). Equality in lazy computation systems. In *4th Annual Symposium on logic in computer science*. IEEE.

Howe, D. J. (1996). Proving congruence of bisimulation in functional programming languages. *Information and Computation 124*(2), 103–112.

Klop, J. W., V. van Oostrom, and F. van Raamsdonk (1993). Combinatory reduction systems: introduction and survey. *Theoretical Computer Science 121*, 279–308.

Lassen, S. B. (1997). Action semantics reasoning about functional programs. *Mathematical Structures in Computer Science*. Special issue dedicated to the Workshop on Logic, Domains, and Programming Languages (Darmstadt, May 1995). To appear.

Lawall, J. L. and H. G. Mairson (1996). Optimality and inefficiency: what isn't a cost model of the lambda calculus. In *ICFP'96 International Conference on Functional Programming*, pp. 92–101. ACM.

Mason, I. A., S. F. Smith, and C. L. Talcott (1996). From operational semantics to domain theory. *Information and Computation 128*(1), 26–47.

Milner, R. (1977). Fully abstract models of typed lambda-calculi. *Theoretical Computer Science 4*, 1–23.

Milner, R. (1989). *Communication and Concurrency*. Prentice-Hall.

Milner, R., M. Tofte, and R. Harper (1990). *The Definition of Standard ML*. Cambridge, Mass.: MIT Press.

Moggi, E. (1989). Computational lambda-calculus and monads. In *4th Annual Symposium on logic in computer science*, pp. 14–23. IEEE.

Ong, C.-H. L. (1992, August 7). Concurrent lambda calculus and a general precongruence theorem for applicative bisimulation (preliminary version). Unpublished.

Park, D. M. (1981). Concurrency and automata on infinite sequences. In P. Deussen (Ed.), *Conference on Theoretical Computer Science*, Volume 104 of *Lecture Notes in Computer Science*, pp. 167–183. Springer-Verlag.

Pitts, A. M. (1994a, November). Inductive and co-inductive techniques in the semantics of functional programs. Course held at BRICS, Department of Computer Science, University of Aarhus.

Pitts, A. M. (1994b, December). Some notes on inductive and co-inductive techniques in the semantics of functional programs (draft version). BRICS Notes Series NS-94-5, BRICS, Department of Computer Science, University of Aarhus.

Pitts, A. M. (1995, March). An extension of Howe's construction to yield simulation-up-to-context results. Unpublished Manuscript.

Pitts, A. M. (1996a). A note on logical relations between semantics and syntax. Submitted to the Journal of the Interest Group in Pure and Applied Logics, Special Issue for 3rd Workshop on Logic, Language, Information and Computation (WoLLIC'96) May, 1996. Salvador (Bahia), Brazil.

Pitts, A. M. (1996b). Relational properties of domains. *Information and Computation 127*, 66–90.

Pitts, A. M. (1997). Operationally-based theories of program equivalence. In P. Dybjer and A. M. Pitts (Eds.), *Semantics and Logics of Computation*. Cambridge University Press.

Sands, D. (1991). Operational theories of improvement in functional languages (extended abstract). In *Proceedings of the Fourth Glasgow Workshop on Functional Programming*, Workshops in Computing Series, pp. 298–311. Springer-Verlag.

Sands, D. (1997a). From SOS rules to proof principles: An operational metatheory for functional languages. In *POPL'97 Symposium on Principles of Programming Languages*. ACM.

Sands, D. (1997b). Improvement theory and its applications. In this volume, pp. 275–306.

Sangiorgi, D. (1994, August). On the bisimulation proof method. Technical Report LFCS-94-299, University of Edinburgh.

Sangiorgi, D. (1995, April). Lazy functions and mobile processes. Technical Report RR-2515, INRIA-Sophia Antipolis.

Sangiorgi, D. (1996). Locality and interleaving semantics in calculi for mobile processes. *Theoretical Computer Science 155*(1), 39–83.

Sangiorgi, D. and R. Milner (1992). The problem of "weak bisimulation up to". In W. R. Cleveland (Ed.), *CONCUR '92*, Volume 630 of *Lecture Notes in Computer Science*. Springer-Verlag.

Smith, S. F. (1997). The coverage of operational semantics. In this volume, pp. 307–346.

Stoughton, A. (1988). Substitution revisited. *Theoretical Computer Science 59*, 317–325.

Talcott, C. (1997). Reasoning about functions with effects. In this volume, pp. 347–390.

Winskel, G. (1993). *The Formal Semantics of Programming Languages*. Cambridge, Mass.: MIT Press.

Labelling techniques and typed fixed-point operators

J. C. Mitchell, M. Hoang and B. T. Howard

Abstract

Labelling techniques for untyped lambda calculus were developed by Lévy, Hyland, Wadsworth and others in the 1970's. A typical application is the proof of confluence from finiteness of developments: by labelling each subterm with a natural number indicating the maximum number of times this term may participate in a reduction step, we obtain a strongly-normalising approximation of β, η-reduction. Confluence then follows by a syntactic "compactness" argument (repeated in the introduction of this paper).

This paper presents applications of labelling to typed lambda calculi with fixed-point operators, including confluence and completeness of leftmost reduction for PCF (an "applied" lambda calculus with fixed-point operators and numeric and boolean operations) and a confluence proof for a variant of typed lambda calculus with subtyping. Labelling is simpler for typed calculi than untyped calculi because the fixed-point operator is the only source of nontermination. We can also use the method of logical relations for the labelled typed calculus, extended with basic operations like addition and conditional. This method would not apply to untyped lambda calculus.

1 Introduction

This paper presents a proof method for extensions of typed lambda calculus with fixed-point operators that is based on labelled reduction. The main idea, in brief, is that we may prove properties of a typed functional language by first labelling every occurrence of the fixed-point operator with a non-negative integer giving the maximum number of times this operator may be used in computation. This produces a language with "bounded recursion." We may prove confluence (the Church-Rosser property) and termination of reduction with bounded recursion, for example, using the same techniques that would apply for pure typed lambda calculus. While some properties, such as termination, may fail when labels are removed, others, such as confluence, may be preserved. Although this paper (prepared in connection with the first author's invited talk at the Higher-Order Operational Techniques workshop) is primarily concerned with operational techniques, there are also applications of labelling in denotational semantics.

We develop two sets of results. The first are for typed lambda calculus extended with fixed-point operators and any set of additional operations satisfying certain conditions. The second are for typed lambda calculus with subtyping. In the first case, we prove confluence and termination of labelled calculus, then use these to show confluence for the unlabelled calculus and completeness of leftmost reduction. While many readers may have assumed that these properties of lambda calculus also hold when types, recursion and operations such as integer arithmetic are added, we were unable to find any prior proofs of these properties in the literature. For the second system, we observe that confluence fails for β, η-reduction in the presence of subtyping. This problem is repaired by adding an intuitive but unusual reduction rule. We then use the labelling technique to extend our confluence proof to typed lambda calculus with subtyping and fixed-point operators. This use of labelling is technically interesting since the confluence proof for typed lambda calculus with subtyping relies on termination.

The inspiration for our use of labelling comes from the untyped lambda calculus, where labelling techniques were developed by Lévy, Hyland, Wadsworth and others in the 1970's (Barendregt 1984; Hyland 1976; Lévy 1975; Wadsworth 1976). A good illustrative example is the proof of confluence from finiteness of developments: by labelling each subterm with a natural number indicating the maximum number of times this term may participate in a reduction step, we obtain a strongly-normalizing approximation of β, η-reduction. Confluence then follows by a syntactic "compactness" argument. While the techniques for proving properties of labelled systems differ between typed and untyped systems, the transfer from labelled to unlabelled versions are similar. Since this argument provides the basis for the unifying technique of this paper, we illustrate it briefly using untyped lambda calculus. Since this description is meant only to provide intuition, we will not be concerned with the details. The main properties used here will be proved later for typed systems.

The main reduction (symbolic evaluation) rule of untyped lambda calculus is β-reduction,

$$(\beta) \qquad (\lambda x.\, U)V \rightarrow [V/x]U$$

where $[V/x]U$ is the result of substituting expression V for all free occurrences of variable x in U. (See Barendregt 1984 for full presentation and discussion.) It is easy to find untyped lambda terms that may be reduced indefinitely without reaching a *normal form,* a term that cannot be further reduced. For example, we have

$$(\lambda x.\, xx)(\lambda x.\, xx) \rightarrow [(\lambda x.\, xx)/x]xx \equiv (\lambda x.\, xx)(\lambda x.\, xx)$$

However, we can eliminate infinite sequences of reduction by labelling each term with a natural number and limiting reduction to positive numbers as follows:

$$(\beta_{n+1}) \qquad (\lambda x.\, U)^{n+1}V \rightarrow ([V^n/x]U)^n$$

where V^n is result of replacing each label ℓ in V by the minimum of ℓ and n. For example, we have

$$(\lambda x.\, xx)^{n+1}(\lambda x.\, xx)^{n+m} \rightarrow [(\lambda x.\, xx)^n/x]xx \equiv (\lambda x.\, xx)^n(\lambda x.\, xx)^n$$

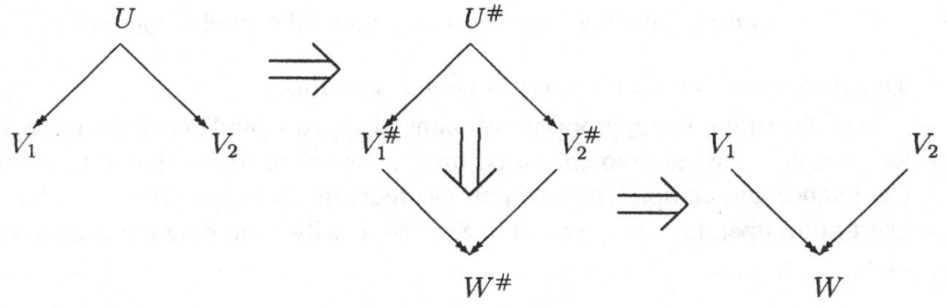

Figure 1: Confluence proof using labelling.

For this example, it is easy to see that since the labels decrease, repeated labelled reduction must eventually halt. In fact, labelled reduction is confluent and terminating on untyped lambda terms (Barendregt 1984).

The main properties connecting labelled and unlabelled reduction are given below, using $U^\#$ for an arbitrary labelling of U and $\natural(L)$ for the result of erasing labels from L:

> **Projection**: If $U^\# \twoheadrightarrow L$, for unlabelled term U and labelled term L, then $U \twoheadrightarrow \natural(L)$.
>
> **Lifting**: If $U \twoheadrightarrow V_i$, for unlabelled terms $U, V_1, \ldots, V_k$, then there exist labelings $U^\#, V_1^\#, \ldots, V_k^\#$ of these terms such that $U^\# \twoheadrightarrow V_i^\#$ for $1 \leq i \leq k$

We will use analogous properties of typed labelling in each of our labelling proofs. Intuitively, lifting and projection are very natural properties if we think of labelling as restricting the use of some computational resource and erasing the label as dropping this restriction. For example, we can consider projection as a formal statement of the intuitive property that if a program computes a result when we allocate at most n computation steps to the program, then the program will compute the same result if we run it without any such limit.

Using lifting and projection, along with confluence of labelled reduction, we can prove confluence of untyped lambda calculus as follows. Assume that untyped term U reduces to terms V_1 and V_2. We must show that there exists some term W with $V_1 \twoheadrightarrow W$ and $V_2 \twoheadrightarrow W$. The argument has three steps, also shown diagrammatically in Figure 1.

(a) Lift both reductions to obtain labelled reductions from some $U^\#$ to some $V_1^\#$ and $V_2^\#$.

(b) By confluence of labelled reduction, $V_1^\#$ and $V_2^\#$ must reduce to some common (labelled) term $W^\#$.

(c) Project these labelled reductions to obtain unlabelled reductions as desired.

This proves confluence for untyped lambda calculus.

After defining the appropriate versions of typed lambda calculus in Section 2, we review a general theorem based on the logical relation method in Section 3. Confluence and completeness of leftmost reduction for typed lambda calculi with fixed-point operators are covered in Section 4, with subtyping considered in Section 5.

2 Syntax, equations and reduction rules

2.1 Typed lambda terms

Typed lambda calculus may be defined with a wide variety of types, including function, product, disjoint union, unit, and empty types. For simplicity, we will work only with function types in this paper. The type expressions of typed lambda calculus with function types, $\lambda^{\rightarrow}$, are given by the grammar

$$\sigma ::= b \quad | \quad \sigma \rightarrow \sigma$$

where b may be any type constant. The extension of certain properties to product types appears in (Mitchell 1996), along with some discussion of the failure of confluence with terminal (one-element) types.

The compound expressions and their types are defined using inference rules. The rules use typing assertions of the form

$$\Gamma \triangleright M : \tau,$$

where Γ is a *type assignment* of the form

$$\Gamma = \{x_1 : \sigma_1, \ldots, x_k : \sigma_k\},$$

with no x_i occurring twice. Intuitively, the assertion $\Gamma \triangleright M : \tau$ says that if variables $x_1, \ldots, x_k$ have types $\sigma_1, \ldots, \sigma_k$ (respectively), then M is a well-formed term of type τ. If Γ is any type assignment, we will write $\Gamma, x : \sigma$ for the type assignment

$$\Gamma, x : \sigma \;=\; \Gamma \cup \{x : \sigma\}.$$

In doing so, we always assume that x does not appear in Γ.

The syntax of terms depends on the choice of type and term constants. A $\lambda^{\rightarrow}$ *signature* $\Sigma = \langle B, C \rangle$ consists of

- A set B whose elements are called *base types* or *type constants.*
- A collection C of pairs of the form $\langle c, \sigma \rangle$, where σ is a $\lambda^{\rightarrow}$ type expression over B and no c occurs in two distinct pairs.

A symbol c occurring in some pair $\langle c, \sigma\rangle \in C$ is called a *term constant of type* σ. We generally write $c{:}\,\sigma$ if $\langle c, \sigma\rangle \in C$. Note that the type and term constants must be consistent, in that the type of each term constant may only contain the given type constants.

Example 2.1 An example $\lambda^{\rightarrow}$ signature is Σ_{PCF}, which gives us the language PCF (without cartesian products). This signature provides symbols for natural number and boolean operations, together with fixed-point operators at all types.

type constants: $nat, bool$
term constants: $0, 1, 2, 3, 4, \ldots : nat$
$true, false: bool$
$plus: nat \rightarrow nat \rightarrow nat$
$Eq?: nat \rightarrow nat \rightarrow bool$
$cond_\sigma: bool \rightarrow \sigma \rightarrow \sigma \rightarrow \sigma$ each type σ
$fix_\sigma: (\sigma \rightarrow \sigma) \rightarrow \sigma$ each type σ

We may write terms over this signature in a more familiar form using syntactic sugar such as

$$M + N \stackrel{def}{=} plus\ M\ N$$
$$\texttt{if } M \texttt{ then } N \texttt{ else } P \stackrel{def}{=} cond_\sigma\ M\ N\ P$$

where the type subscript on $cond$ is determined by the types of N and P. ■

The $\lambda^{\rightarrow}$ terms over signature Σ and their types are defined simultaneously using axioms and inference rules. For each term constant c of type σ, we have the axiom

$$(cst) \qquad \emptyset \triangleright c : \sigma$$

We assume some countably infinite set *Var* of variables $\{v_0, v_1, \ldots\}$. Variables are given types by the axiom

$$(var) \qquad x{:}\,\sigma \triangleright x : \sigma$$

where σ must be a $\lambda^{\rightarrow}$ type over Σ. The rule

$$(add\ var) \qquad \frac{\Gamma \triangleright M : \sigma}{\Gamma, x{:}\,\tau \triangleright M : \sigma}$$

allows us to add an additional hypothesis to the typing context. For lambda abstraction, we have

$$(\rightarrow Intro) \qquad \frac{\Gamma, x{:}\,\sigma \triangleright M : \tau}{\Gamma \triangleright (\lambda x{:}\,\sigma.\, M) : \sigma \rightarrow \tau}$$

Intuitively, this rule says that if M specifies a result of type τ for every $x{:}\,\sigma$, then the expression $\lambda x{:}\,\sigma.\,M$ defines a function of type $\sigma \to \tau$. Function applications are written according to the rule

$$(\to \mathit{Elim}) \qquad \frac{\Gamma \rhd M : \sigma \to \tau,\ \Gamma \rhd N : \sigma}{\Gamma \rhd MN : \tau}$$

which says that we may apply any function with type $\sigma \to \tau$ to an argument of type σ to produce a result of type τ.

We say *M is a $\lambda^{\to}$ term over signature Σ with type τ in context Γ* if $\Gamma \rhd M : \tau$ is either a typing axiom for Σ, or follows from axioms by rules $(\mathit{add\ var})$, $(\to \mathit{Intro})$ and $(\to \mathit{Elim})$. As an expository convenience, we will often write $\Gamma \rhd M : \tau$ to mean that "$\Gamma \rhd M : \tau$ is derivable," in much the same way as one often writes a formula $\forall x.\, P(x)$, in logic, as a way of saying "$\forall x.\, P(x)$ is true." A proof of a typing assertion is called a *typing derivation.*

2.2 Equations

We write equations between typed lambda terms in a form that includes the assignment of types to variables. Since the types of terms will be used in the equational proof system, we also include the types of terms. Specifically, a typed equation has the form

$$\Gamma \rhd M = N : \tau$$

where we assume that M and N have type τ in context Γ. Intuitively, the equation

$$\{x_1{:}\,\sigma_1, \ldots, x_k{:}\,\sigma_k\} \rhd M = N : \tau$$

means that for all type-correct values of the variables $x_1{:}\,\sigma_1, \ldots, x_k{:}\,\sigma_k$, expressions M and N denote the same element of type τ. Another way of writing this equation might be

$$\forall x_1{:}\,\sigma_1 \ldots \forall x_k{:}\,\sigma_k.\, M = N{:}\,\tau.$$

A "structural" rule for equations is

$$(\mathit{add\ var}) \qquad \frac{\Gamma \rhd M = N : \sigma}{\Gamma, x{:}\,\tau \rhd M = N : \sigma}$$

which lets us add variables to the type assignment. We also have an axiom and inference rules making provable equality an equivalence relation and a congruence.

$$(\mathit{ref}) \qquad \Gamma \rhd M = M : \sigma$$

$$(\mathit{sym}) \qquad \frac{\Gamma \rhd M = N : \sigma}{\Gamma \rhd N = M : \sigma}$$

$$(\mathit{trans}) \qquad \frac{\Gamma \rhd M = N : \sigma,\ \Gamma \rhd N = P : \sigma}{\Gamma \rhd M = P : \sigma}$$

$$(\xi) \qquad \frac{\Gamma, x{:}\,\sigma \triangleright M = N : \tau}{\Gamma \triangleright \lambda x{:}\,\sigma.\, M = \lambda x{:}\,\sigma.\, N : \sigma \to \tau}$$

$$(\nu) \qquad \frac{\Gamma \triangleright M_1 = M_2 : \sigma \to \tau,\ \Gamma \triangleright N_1 = N_2 : \sigma}{\Gamma \triangleright M_1 N_1 = M_2 N_2 : \tau}$$

For $\lambda^{\to}$, three axioms remain. The first describes renaming of bound variables, while the other two specify that the introduction and elimination rules are "inverses" of each other. The axiom for renaming bound variables is

$$(\alpha) \qquad \Gamma \triangleright \lambda x{:}\,\sigma.\, M = \lambda y{:}\,\sigma.[y/x]M : \sigma \to \tau, \text{ provided } y \notin FV(M)$$

The second axiom, (β), shows how to evaluate a function application using substitution.

$$(\beta) \qquad \Gamma \triangleright (\lambda x{:}\,\sigma.\, M)N = [N/x]M : \tau$$

Finally, we have an axiom for equating extensionally equivalent function expressions,

$$(\eta) \qquad \Gamma \triangleright \lambda x{:}\,\sigma.(Mx) = M : \sigma \to \tau, \text{ provided } x \notin FV(M)$$

It is easy to see that if $x \notin FV(M)$, then by (β) we have $(\lambda x{:}\,\sigma.\, Mx)y = My$ for any argument $y{:}\,\sigma$. Therefore M and $\lambda x{:}\,\sigma.\, Mx$ define the same function.

For PCF, we add several "non-logical" axioms. (These are "non-logical" in the sense that they are specific axioms about term constants, not "logical" axioms that apply to all languages based on typed lambda calculus.) For natural numbers and conditional, we have infinitely many equational axioms:

$$0+0=0 \quad 0+1=1 \quad 1+0=1 \quad \ldots \quad 3+2=5 \quad \ldots$$
$$\mathit{Eq?}\,0\,0 = \mathit{true} \quad \mathit{Eq?}\,0\,1 = \mathit{false} \quad \mathit{Eq?}\,1\,0 = \mathit{false} \quad \mathit{Eq?}\,1\,1 = \mathit{true} \quad \ldots$$
$$\texttt{if } \mathit{true} \texttt{ then } M \texttt{ else } N = M \qquad \texttt{if } \mathit{false} \texttt{ then } M \texttt{ else } N = N$$

The axiom for fix is

$$(\mathit{fix}) \qquad \mathit{fix}_\sigma = \lambda f{:}\,\sigma \to \sigma.\, f(\mathit{fix}_\sigma f)$$

from which it is easy to derive equations such as $\mathit{fix}_\sigma M = M(\mathit{fix}_\sigma M)$.

2.3 Reduction, convertibility and confluence

Reduction is a "directed" form of equational reasoning that corresponds to symbolic evaluation of programs. In simply-typed lambda calculus, we orient each of the equational axioms except (α) and (ref). Reductions for term forms associated with products, sums and other simple types may be found in (Gunter 1992; Mitchell 1996) and elsewhere. We discuss PCF reduction below.

While we are only interested in reducing typed terms, we may define reduction on simply-typed terms without mentioning types. Since reduction models program evaluation, this is a way of emphasising that $\lambda^{\rightarrow}$ evaluation may be done without examining the types of terms. We will also see that the type of a term does not change as it is reduced. However, the connections between typed and untyped reduction may become more subtle in the presence of subtyping.

For clarity, we repeat the equational axioms in their reduction form.

$$(\beta)_{red} \qquad (\lambda x{:}\,\sigma.\, M)N \rightarrow [N/x]M,$$

$$(\eta)_{red} \qquad \lambda x{:}\,\sigma.\, Mx \rightarrow M, \text{ provided } x \notin FV(M).$$

A term of the form $(\lambda x{:}\,\sigma.\, M)N$ is called a *β-redex* and $\lambda x{:}\,\sigma.\, Mx$ (where $x \notin FV(M)$) an *η-redex*. We say *M β,η-reduces to N in one step*, written $M \rightarrow_{\beta,\eta} N$, if N can be obtained by applying (β) or (η) to some subterm of M. The reduction relation $\twoheadrightarrow_{\beta,\eta}$ is the reflexive and transitive closure of one-step β,η-reduction.

It can be shown that one-step reduction preserves type.

Lemma 2.2 *If $\Gamma \triangleright M : \sigma$, and $M \rightarrow_{\beta,\eta} N$, then $\Gamma \triangleright N : \sigma$.*

It follows by an easy induction that $\twoheadrightarrow_{\beta,\eta}$ also preserves type. This is often called the ***subject reduction property,*** based on terminology that regards $M{:}\,\sigma$ as a "sentence" whose subject is M and predicate is σ.

It is useful to write $\Gamma \triangleright M \twoheadrightarrow N : \sigma$ when $\Gamma \triangleright M : \sigma$ is well-typed and $M \twoheadrightarrow N$. We know by the Lemma above that in this case, we also have $\Gamma \triangleright N : \sigma$. A term M is in *β,η-normal form* if there is no N with $M \rightarrow_{\beta,\eta} N$.

The main theorems about β,η-reduction are confluence and strong normalization. These may be proved using the technique of logical relations (summarised in Section 3).

Confluence: β,η-Reduction is confluent on $\lambda^{\rightarrow}$ terms.

Strong Normalization: There is no infinite sequence $M_0 \rightarrow_{\beta,\eta} M_1 \rightarrow_{\beta,\eta} M_2 \rightarrow_{\beta,\eta} \ldots$ of β,η-reductions on $\lambda^{\rightarrow}$ terms.

The second property is called "normalization" since it states that every term may be reduced to a normal form (a term that cannot be reduced further). The "strong" part of the statement is that a normal form is reached by *any* sequence of reductions. In contrast, weak normalization is the property that every term may be reduced to a normal form by some sequence of reductions, but not necessarily all.

For PCF, we adopt several "non-logical" reductions based on the corresponding equational axioms. Orienting the equations above in the intuitively plausible direction gives us

$$\begin{array}{llll} 0+0 \to 0 \quad 0+1 \to 1 & 1+0 \to 1 \quad \ldots & 3+2 \to 5 \quad \ldots & \\ \mathit{Eq}?\,0\,0 \to \mathit{true} & \mathit{Eq}?\,0\,1 \to \mathit{false} & \mathit{Eq}?\,1\,0 \to \mathit{false} & \mathit{Eq}?\,1\,1 \to \mathit{true} \quad \ldots \\ \mathtt{if}\ \mathit{true}\ \mathtt{then}\ M\ \mathtt{else}\ N \to M & & \mathtt{if}\ \mathit{false}\ \mathtt{then}\ M\ \mathtt{else}\ N \to N & \end{array}$$

The reduction axiom for *fix* is

$$(\mathit{fix}) \qquad \mathit{fix}_\sigma \to \lambda f\colon \sigma \to \sigma.\, f\,(\mathit{fix}_\sigma\, f)$$

from which it is easy to derive reductions such as $\mathit{fix}_\sigma\, M \twoheadrightarrow M(\mathit{fix}_\sigma\, M)$. It is easy to see that *fix*-reduction destroys strong normalization. However, it may be shown using the techniques given in this paper that various versions of PCF with arithmetic, boolean operations and fixed-point operators are confluent. (See Mitchell 1996 for further information.)

It is worth noting that β, η-reduction is not confluent on *pre-terms,* strings that look like terms but are not necessarily well-typed. To see this, consider the pre-term

$$\lambda x\colon \sigma.(\lambda y\colon \tau.\, y)\, x$$

Using β-reduction, we may simplify this to $\lambda x\colon \sigma.\, x$, while η-reduction gives us $\lambda y\colon \tau.\, y$. Since these normal forms differ by more than names of bound variables when $\sigma \not\equiv \tau$, confluence fails for pre-terms.

One consequence of this example, which is taken from (van Dalen 1980; Nederpelt 1973), is that confluence for typed lambda calculus does not follow immediately from the confluence of untyped lambda calculus, even though the typed terms could be considered as a subset of the untyped terms (*cf.* Barendregt 1984, Appendix A). The reason is that the simple "proof" of confluence for typed lambda calculus by appeal to the Church-Rosser theorem for untyped lambda calculus applies to pre-terms as well as typed terms. Since this leads to an incorrect conclusion for pre-terms, it is not a correct proof for typed terms. The reader familiar with other presentations of typed lambda calculus may wonder whether this is still the case if we do not write type expressions in typed terms, but use variables that are each given a fixed type. In this alternate presentation of $\lambda^\to$, α-conversion must be restricted so that we only replace one bound variable by another with the same type. With this restriction on α-conversion, the example demonstrating failure of confluence still applies. Thus confluence for $\lambda^\to$ does not seem to follow from the Church-Rosser theorem for untyped β, η-reduction directly. It is worth noting, however, that if we drop η-reduction, then we *do* have confluence for β-reduction on $\lambda^\to$ pre-terms.

The convertibility relation $\leftrightarrow_{\beta,\eta}$ on typed terms is the least type-respecting equivalence relation containing reduction $\twoheadrightarrow_{\beta,\eta}$. For typographical simplicity, we will drop the β, η subscripts for the rest of this paragraph. Conversion can be visualized by saying that $\Gamma \triangleright M \leftrightarrow N : \sigma$ iff there is a sequence of terms $M_0, \ldots, M_k$ with $\Gamma \triangleright M_i : \sigma$ such that

$$M \equiv M_0 \twoheadrightarrow M_1 \twoheadleftarrow \ldots \twoheadrightarrow M_k \equiv N.$$

In this picture, the directions of $\twoheadrightarrow$ and $\twoheadleftarrow$ need not be regarded as significant. However, by reflexivity and transitivity of $\twoheadrightarrow$, this order of reduction and "backward reduction" is completely general.

A consequence of confluence is the following connection between reduction and provable equality.

Corollary 2.3 *An equation $\Gamma \triangleright M = N : \tau$ is provable from the axioms of $\lambda^{\rightarrow}$ iff $\Gamma \triangleright M \leftrightarrow N : \tau$ iff there is some term P with $M \twoheadrightarrow_{\beta,\eta} P$ and $N \twoheadrightarrow_{\beta,\eta} P$.*

This illustrates one of the general interests in confluence, namely, confluence implies a connection between reduction and equational reasoning. This connection may be used to prove the consistency of the equational proof system or, more generally, to show that certain equations are not provable from a set of equational axioms. The other general reason for studying confluence is that when we regard reduction as a model of program execution, confluence implies that the result of a computation is independent of evaluation order.

2.4 Subtyping

2.4.1 Programming language motivation

Subtyping appears in a variety of programming languages. An early form of subtyping appears in the Fortran treatment of "mixed mode" arithmetic: arithmetic expressions may be written using combinations of integer and real (floating point) expressions, with integers converted to real numbers as needed. The conversion of integers to reals has some of the properties that are typical of subtyping, since we generally think of the mathematical integers as a subset of the real numbers. However, conversion in programs involves changing the representation of a number, which is not typical of subtyping with records or objects. Fortran mixed mode arithmetic also goes beyond basic subtyping since (i) Fortran provides implicit conversion from reals to integers by truncation, which is different since this operation changes the value of the number that is represented, and (ii) Fortran also provides overloaded operations, such as $+$: $int \times int \rightarrow int$ and $+$: $real \times real \rightarrow real$.

A cleaner example of subtyping appears in Pascal subranges or the closely related range constraints of Ada (see Horowitz 1984, for example). The Pascal subrange $[1..10]$ containing the integers between 1 and 10 is a subtype of the integers. If x is a variable of type $[1..10]$, and y of type integer, then we can assign y the value of x since every integer between 1 and 10 is an integer. More powerful examples of subtyping appear in typed object-oriented languages such as Eiffel

(Meyer 1992) and C++ (Ellis and Stroustrop 1990). In these languages, a class of objects, which may be regarded for the moment as a form of type, is placed in a subtype hierarchy. An object of a subtype may be used in place of one of any supertype, since the subtype relation guarantees that all required operations are implemented. Moreover, although the representation of objects of one type may differ from the representation of objects of a subtype, the representations are generally compatible in a way that eliminates the need for conversion from one to another.

2.4.2 Typed lambda calculus with subtyping

The notation $A <: B$ is commonly used to indicate that A is a subtype of B, since $<:$ provides a rough ASCII approximation of the subset symbol "$\subseteq$". We use $\lambda^{\rightarrow}_{<:}$ to denote the extension of $\lambda^{\rightarrow}$ with subtyping. Surprisingly, reduction for $\lambda^{\rightarrow}_{<:}$ is substantially more complicated than for $\lambda^{\rightarrow}$.

Like $\lambda^{\rightarrow}$, the definition of $\lambda^{\rightarrow}_{<:}$ terms depends on a signature, which now includes subtype assumptions about the type symbols. Formally, a $\lambda^{\rightarrow}_{<:}$ *signature* is a triple $\Sigma = \langle B, \mathit{Sub}, C\rangle$ with B a set of type constants, *Sub* a set of subtyping assertions $b <: b'$ between type constants $b, b' \in B$, and C a set of term constants, each with a unique specified type written using $\rightarrow$ and type constants from B.

The $\lambda^{\rightarrow}_{<:}$ type expressions over signature $\langle B, \mathit{Sub}, C\rangle$ are the same as the $\lambda^{\rightarrow}$ type expressions over signature $\langle B, C\rangle$. Note that we only consider subtype assumptions between atomic type names. A consequence of this property is given in Lemma 2.4 below.

The distinguishing feature of $\lambda^{\rightarrow}_{<:}$ is the subtype relation, defined from the signature by the following axiom and inference rules.

$$(\mathit{ref}\ <:) \qquad \tau <: \tau$$

$$(\mathit{trans}\ <:) \qquad \frac{\rho <: \sigma,\ \sigma <: \tau}{\rho <: \tau}$$

$$(\rightarrow\ <:) \qquad \frac{\rho <: \tau,\ \tau' <: \rho'}{\tau \rightarrow \tau' <: \rho \rightarrow \rho'}$$

If we think of subtyping as an ordering, the last rule "says" that $\rightarrow$ is monotonic in its second argument, but antimonotonic in its first.

We write $\Sigma \vdash \sigma <: \tau$ if the subtype assertion $\sigma <: \tau$ is provable from assertions in *Sub* using the axiom and inference rules given above. It is easy to show that if $\Sigma \vdash \sigma <: \tau$, then the type expressions σ and τ must contain the same number and parenthesization of $\rightarrow$'s. To state this precisely, we let the *matching* relation on types be the least relation satisfying the following conditions:

$$\begin{array}{rcll} b & \text{matches} & b' & \text{for any type constants } b, b' \\ \sigma_1 \rightarrow \sigma_2 & \text{matches} & \tau_1 \rightarrow \tau_2 & \text{whenever } \sigma_i \text{ matches } \tau_i \ (i = 1, 2) \end{array}$$

Lemma 2.4 *For any $\lambda^{\rightarrow}_{<:}$ signature Σ, if $\Sigma \vdash \sigma <: \tau$ then σ matches τ.*

2.4.3 Terms

The terms of $\lambda^{\rightarrow}_{<:}$ are given by the same typing rules as in $\lambda^{\rightarrow}$, namely (cst), (var), $(\rightarrow \textit{Intro})$, $(\rightarrow \textit{Elim})$, and $(add\ var)$, plus the additional rule:

$$(subsumption) \qquad \frac{\Gamma \triangleright M : \sigma,\ \Sigma \vdash \sigma <: \tau}{\Gamma \triangleright M : \tau}$$

2.4.4 Equations

The equational proof system of $\lambda^{\rightarrow}_{<:}$ consists of exactly the same axioms and proof rules as $\lambda^{\rightarrow}$ without subtyping. Specifically, we have (ref), (sym) and $(trans)$ making provable equality an equivalence relation, the technical rule $(addvar)$ for adding variables to the type assignment, axioms (α), (β) and (η) for lambda abstraction and application, and (ξ) and (ν) making provable equality a congruence relation.

There is a common typing confusion associated with the extensionality axiom, (η), that illustrates the importance of writing types as part of equations. The extensionality axiom has the form

$$\Gamma \triangleright \lambda x{:}\, \tau.(Mx) = M, \quad x \text{ not free in } M$$

but it is not clear that the two terms involved necessarily have the same type. For example, suppose M has the form $\lambda y{:}\, \tau'.\, N$ with $\tau <: \tau'$. Then M has type $\tau' \rightarrow \rho$ but $\lambda x{:}\, \tau.(Mx)$ does not. Thus, in writing $\lambda x{:}\, \tau.(Mx) = M$, it could appear that we are equating terms with different types. However, since $\tau' \rightarrow \rho <: \tau \rightarrow \rho$, both have type $\tau \rightarrow \rho$. Our axiom scheme

$$\Gamma \triangleright \lambda x{:}\, \tau.(Mx) = M : \tau \rightarrow \rho, \quad x \text{ not free in } M,$$

applies whenever $\Gamma \triangleright \lambda x{:}\, \tau.(Mx) : \tau \rightarrow \rho$ and $\Gamma \triangleright M : \tau \rightarrow \rho$ are both derivable, which will be the case whenever $\Gamma \triangleright M : \tau \rightarrow \rho$ is derivable.

A derived rule. A general principle about subtyping and equality is given by the inference rule

$$(subsumption\ eq) \qquad \frac{\Gamma \triangleright M = N : \tau,\ \Sigma \vdash \tau <: \rho}{\Gamma \triangleright M = N : \rho}$$

which we do *not* need to add to the proof system since it is derivable from congruence and (β). More specifically, if $\tau <: \rho$, then we have the typing

$$\Gamma \triangleright \lambda x{:}\, \tau.\, x : \tau \rightarrow \rho$$

and so by reflexivity, the equation

$$\Gamma \triangleright \lambda x{:}\, \tau.\, x = \lambda x{:}\, \tau.\, x : \tau \rightarrow \rho.$$

If $\Gamma \triangleright M = N : \tau$, then by applying the identity to each side (using (ν)), we may prove

$$\Gamma \triangleright (\lambda x{:}\,\tau.\, x)M = (\lambda x{:}\,\tau.\, x)N : \rho$$

which gives us the conclusion of $(\mathit{subsumption\ eq})$ by (β) and transitivity.

Failure of Confluence. For any $\lambda^{\rightarrow}_{<:}$ term $\Gamma \triangleright \lambda x{:}\,\sigma.\, M : \sigma \rightarrow \tau$, with $\rho <: \sigma$, we can prove the equation

$$\Gamma \triangleright \lambda x{:}\,\sigma.\, M = \lambda x{:}\,\rho.\, M : \rho \rightarrow \tau$$

One way to develop some intuition for this equation is to suppose that we give the lambda abstraction $\Gamma \triangleright \lambda x{:}\,\sigma.\, M : \sigma \rightarrow \tau$ type $\rho \rightarrow \tau$ by subsumption. If we then apply this function to an argument $\Gamma \triangleright N : \rho$ and β-reduce the resulting term,

$$(\lambda x{:}\,\sigma.\, M)N \rightarrow [N/x]M,$$

we will substitute a term of type ρ for the bound variable of type σ. This suggests that if we change the type of $\lambda x{:}\,\sigma.\, M$ by subsumption, then we have a term that is "functionally equivalent" to the term $\lambda x{:}\,\rho.\, M$ with the formal parameter x given type ρ instead of σ. In other words, subsumption effectively changes the types of lambda-bound variables.

We can prove the equation above by applying $\lambda x{:}\,\sigma.\, M$ to a free variable $x{:}\,\rho$ and then lambda-abstracting x. We begin with the typing derivation

$\Gamma \triangleright \lambda x{:}\,\sigma.\, M : \sigma \rightarrow \tau$	by assumption
$\Gamma, x{:}\,\rho \triangleright \lambda x{:}\,\sigma.\, M : \sigma \rightarrow \tau$	by $(\mathit{add\ var})$
$\Gamma, x{:}\,\rho \triangleright x : \sigma$	by (var), $(\mathit{subsumption})$, $(\mathit{add\ var})$
$\Gamma, x{:}\,\rho \triangleright (\lambda x{:}\,\sigma.\, M)x : \tau$	by ($\rightarrow$ *Elim*)
$\Gamma \triangleright \lambda x{:}\,\rho.(\lambda x{:}\,\sigma.\, M)x : \rho \rightarrow \tau$	by ($\rightarrow$ *Intro*)

At this point, we apply a "trick," using (β) to show

$$\Gamma \triangleright \lambda x{:}\,\rho.(\lambda x{:}\,\sigma.\, M)x = \lambda x{:}\,\rho.\, M : \rho \rightarrow \tau$$

and (η) to show

$$\Gamma \triangleright \lambda x{:}\,\rho.(\lambda x{:}\,\sigma.\, M)x = \lambda x{:}\,\sigma.\, M : \rho \rightarrow \tau$$

giving us the desired equation by symmetry and transitivity. Since both of these terms would be in normal form when M is a normal form, the last few steps also show that confluence fails for β,η-reduction on $\lambda^{\rightarrow}_{<:}$ terms. We return to confluence for $\lambda^{\rightarrow}_{<:}$ in Section 5.

3 Reduction properties of typed lambda terms

Confluence, normalization and other properties of typed reduction may be proved using logical relations. It will be useful to review a general theorem from (Mitchell 1996) that has these two properties as corollaries. The reason for considering the general theorem is that we are interested in both confluence (since labelled confluence implies unlabelled confluence) and termination (since this is used for completeness of leftmost reduction). Since the proof of the main theorem in this section requires substantial machinery that is not related to labelling, we simply state the results in this section without proof.

A *property of typed lambda terms,* or *predicate on terms* is a type-indexed family of sets of typed lambda terms. If $\mathcal{S} = \{\mathcal{S}^\sigma\}$ is a predicate, with $\mathcal{S}^\sigma$ the set of all terms of type σ with property $\mathcal{S}$, then we write $\mathcal{S}(M)$ to indicate that $M{:}\,\sigma$ and $M \in \mathcal{S}^\sigma$ for some type σ. When we want to specify the type of M, we write $\mathcal{S}^\sigma(M)$.

A predicate $\mathcal{S}$ is *type-closed* if the following three conditions are satisfied.

(a) If $\mathcal{S}(M_1), \ldots, \mathcal{S}(M_k)$, then $\mathcal{S}(xM_1 \ldots M_k)$, where x is any variable of the appropriate type,

(b) If $\mathcal{S}^\tau(Mx)$ holds for every variable x of type σ, then $\mathcal{S}^{\sigma\to\tau}(M)$,

(c) If $\mathcal{S}^\sigma(N)$ and $\mathcal{S}^b(([N/x]M)N_1 \ldots N_k)$, then $\mathcal{S}^b((\lambda x{:}\,\sigma.\, M)NN_1 \ldots N_k)$ for each base type b.

In verifying that a particular predicate satisfies (b), we generally assume $\mathcal{S}(Mx)$ for some x not free in M and show $\mathcal{S}(M)$.

Theorem 3.1 *If $\mathcal{S}$ is any type-closed property of typed $\lambda^\to$ terms, then $\mathcal{S}(M)$ for every term $\Gamma \triangleright M : \sigma$.*

Strong normalization is the predicate *SN* defined by

$$SN(M) \text{ iff there is no infinite sequence of reductions from } M.$$

We may regard confluence as a predicate on typed $\lambda^\to$ terms by defining

$$CR(M) \text{ iff } \forall M_1, M_2[\ M \twoheadrightarrow M_1 \wedge M \twoheadrightarrow M_2 \supset \exists N.\, M_1 \twoheadrightarrow N \wedge M_2 \twoheadrightarrow N].$$

In verifying that *CR* is type-closed, the most difficult condition is (b). While it is easy to see that $SN(Mx) \supset SN(M)$, it is not immediate that $CR(Mx) \supset CR(M)$, since there may be reductions of Mx that do not apply to M.

Lemma 3.2 *The predicate CR is type-closed.*

Combining Lemma 3.2 with Theorem 3.1, we have confluence of β, η-reduction.

Theorem 3.3 (Confluence) *β, η-Reduction is confluent on typed lambda terms.*

3.1 Extending the type-closed method to constants

We prove properties of labelled and other reduction by extending the "type-closed" method to $\lambda^{\rightarrow}$ terms with constants. With constants that may have associated reduction rules, the proof that every term has a type-closed property $\mathcal{S}$ has four main parts:

1. Define a predicate $\mathcal{P}$ on the applicative structure of terms, from $\mathcal{S}$, by

$$
\begin{array}{ll}
P^{b}(M) & \text{iff } \mathcal{S}(M) \\
P^{\sigma\rightarrow\tau}(M) & \text{iff } \forall N.\, P^{\sigma}(N) \text{ implies } P^{\tau}(MN)
\end{array}
$$

2. Show that $P^{\sigma}(M)$ implies $\mathcal{S}(M)$.

2′. Show that $P^{\sigma}(c)$ for each term constant $c\colon\sigma$.

3. Show that $\mathcal{P}$ is admissible, a technical property defined in (Mitchell 1996). This allows us to conclude that $P^{\sigma}(M)$ holds for every well-typed term $\Gamma \rhd M : \sigma$.

Theorem 3.1 above is proved using steps 1, 2 and 3. If there are no reduction rules for constants, then we can treat constants just like variables. However, with reduction rules, condition (a) of the definition of type-closed may fail for constant c in place of variable x. (For example, M may be strongly normalizing and $\mathit{fix}\ M$ not strongly normalizing.) Therefore, we must treat constants by some other means.

The main idea in extending Theorem 3.1 is that in treating constant c, we may need some properties of $\mathcal{P}$ in proving $P^{\sigma}(c)$. We therefore insert an extra step (2′) in the middle of the proof. (The arguments in steps 1, 2 and 3 are essentially the same with or without term constants.) Rather that try to identify a sufficient condition for step 2′ to succeed, we simply state a theorem that says the method works when it works. We will use this for labelled fixed points and other operations.

Theorem 3.4 *Let $\mathcal{S}$ be a type-closed property of $\lambda^{\rightarrow}$ terms and let $\mathcal{P}$ be the predicate on terms defined from $\mathcal{S}$ as above. If $\mathcal{P}(c_1), \ldots, \mathcal{P}(c_k)$, for term constants $c_1, \ldots, c_k$, then $\mathcal{P}(M)$ and therefore $\mathcal{S}(M)$ holds for every well-typed $\lambda^{\rightarrow}$ term M over $c_1, \ldots, c_k$.*

4 Reduction with *fix* and additional operations

In this section, we analyse reduction for typed lambda calculus with *fix* and other operations. An important idea for handling *fix* is to label each occurrence of a fixed-point operator in a term with a bound on the number of reductions that may be applied. This produces a confluent and terminating reduction relation.

4.1 Labelled reduction

There are two versions of labelled reduction, one used to prove semantic results such as the Approximation Theorem and Computational Adequacy (see Mitchell 1996), and the other used to prove reduction properties. After defining both forms of reduction, we will focus on the simpler version used for reduction properties.

If we begin with simply-typed lambda calculus over signature Σ, containing fixed-point constants at some types, then the labelled terms over Σ are defined using the extended signature $\Sigma_{lab} \supseteq \Sigma$ obtained by adding a constant, fix_σ^n, for each type σ that has a fixed-point operator in Σ and for each natural number $n \geq 0$. The constant fix_σ^n is called the *labelled fixed-point operator with label* n. For semantic results, it is common to also add a constant $\perp_\sigma$ for each type σ that has a fixed-point operator. We use the notation $\Sigma_{lab,\perp}$ for the signature $\Sigma_{lab,\perp} \supseteq \Sigma_{lab} \supseteq \Sigma$ with labelled fixed-point operators and constants $\perp_\sigma$ at appropriate types. We say M is a *labelled term (over* Σ*)* if M is a well-typed term over $\Sigma_{lab,\perp}$ and M does not contain any fix without a label. We write $lab(M)$ for the set of labelled terms that become syntactically identical to M when we replace each fix_σ^n by fix_σ.

The two forms of reduction for labelled fixed-point operators are:

$$(lab_+) \qquad \mathit{fix}_\sigma^{n+1} \to \lambda f\colon \sigma \to \sigma.\, f(\mathit{fix}_\sigma^n\, f)$$

$$(lab_0) \qquad \mathit{fix}_\sigma^{0} \to \lambda f\colon \sigma \to \sigma.\, \perp_\sigma$$

We will call reduction using the first reduction axiom *positive labelled reduction*, or simply *labelled reduction* for short, and refer to this using the symbol lab_+. The second reduction will be indicated by lab_0. Reduction with both reduction axioms will be denoted $lab_{+,0}$. We use $lab_{+(0)}$ for either lab_+ or $lab_{+,0}$. It is also possible to add reduction rules for $\perp$, such as $(\perp_{\sigma\to\tau} M) \to \perp_\tau$, but we will not consider this.

In semantic analysis, we may wish to treat fix_σ as one of its approximants, $\lambda f\colon \sigma \to \sigma.\, f^n(\perp)$. This is precisely what happens if we label an occurrence of fix_σ with the number n and use $lab_{+,0}$ reduction. The problem with full $lab_{+,0}$ reduction, for the purpose of analysing reduction without labels, is that the reduction of $\mathit{fix}_\sigma^0\, M$ to $(\lambda f\colon \sigma \to \sigma.\, \perp_\sigma)\, M$ allows us to discard the subterm M on subsequent β-reduction. This makes it impossible to use confluence of $\beta, lab_{+,0}$-reduction to prove confluence of β, fix-reduction, for example, in any direct way. Therefore, both forms reduction are useful. Since this paper is primarily concerned with reduction properties, we will be primarily concerned with lab_+.

We develop some general connections between labelled reduction and unlabelled reduction below, in a setting that allows for a set $\mathcal{R}$ of additional rewrite axioms. Like the common rewrite axioms for addition and conditional, for example, these must be *left-linear.* This means that if $L \to R$ is a reduction, then no term variable may occur more than once in the left-hand side, L. Just to clarify notation, we write $\mathcal{R}, \beta, lab_+$ for the combination of reduction given by a set $\mathcal{R}$

of reduction axioms, β-reduction and positive labelled reduction lab_+. Two basic and useful connections are given in the following lemmas.

Lemma 4.1 (Lifting) *Suppose $\mathcal{R}$ is left-linear and $M \xrightarrow{\mathcal{R},\beta,fix}\!\!\!\!\rightarrow N$. There is a natural number k such that if $M^\# \in lab(M)$, with each label in $M^\#$ at least k, then $M^\# \xrightarrow{\mathcal{R},\beta,lab_+}\!\!\!\!\rightarrow N^\#$ for some $N^\# \in lab(N)$.*

Lemma 4.2 (Projection) *If $M^\# \xrightarrow{\mathcal{R},\beta,lab_+}\!\!\!\!\rightarrow N^\#$, where $M^\# \in lab(M)$ and $N^\# \in lab(N)$, then $M \xrightarrow{\mathcal{R},\beta,fix}\!\!\!\!\rightarrow N$.*

Both are proved by easy inductions on the length of reduction sequences. In Lemma 4.1, the number k is essentially the length of the reduction sequence from M to N, since any single reduction could be carried out by labelling any fix that is reduced with any number at least 1. The importance of assuming that $\mathcal{R}$ is left-linear is discussed below. Since $lab_{+,0}$ contains lab_+, the first lemma also holds for $\mathcal{R}, \beta, proj, lab_{+,0}$. However, Lemma 4.2 fails for $lab_{+,0}$, since the rule for fix^0 cannot be simulated using unlabelled fix. These two lemmas are used to prove the basic connection between confluence of labelled and unlabelled reduction.

Proposition 4.3 *If $\mathcal{R}, \beta, lab_+$-reduction is confluent on labelled terms, and $\mathcal{R}$ is left-linear, then $\mathcal{R}, \beta, fix$-reduction is confluent on unlabelled terms.*

Proof Suppose $N \twoheadleftarrow^{\mathcal{R},\beta,fix} M \xrightarrow{\mathcal{R},\beta,fix}\!\!\!\!\rightarrow P$. By Lemma 4.1, there are labellings $M^\#$, $N^\#$, and $P^\#$ of these terms (respectively) such that $N^\# \twoheadleftarrow^{\mathcal{R},\beta,lab_+} M^\# \xrightarrow{\mathcal{R},\beta,lab_+}\!\!\!\!\rightarrow P^\#$. Since $\mathcal{R}, \beta, lab_+$-reduction is confluent, $N^\#$ and $P^\#$ must have a common reduct $Q^\#$. By Lemma 4.2, we may erase labels to obtain

$$N \xrightarrow{\mathcal{R},\beta,fix}\!\!\!\!\rightarrow Q \twoheadleftarrow^{\mathcal{R},\beta,fix} P.$$

This shows that $\mathcal{R}, \beta, fix$-reduction is confluent. ∎

It is important to understand how left-linearity is used in the proof of Lemma 4.1. The critical step is the base case for a reduction from $\mathcal{R}$. The property that we may choose labels arbitrarily, as long as they are all big enough, may fail if we have a non-linear rule, since some reduction rule may be applicable only if two subterms have the same label. For example, consider the following algebraic rewrite rules for $Eq?$: $nat \to nat \to bool$, $succ$: $nat \to nat$ and $true, false$: $bool$.

$$\begin{array}{lcl} Eq?\,x\,x & \to & true \\ Eq?\,x\,(succ\,x) & \to & false \end{array}$$

Lemma 4.1 fails if $\mathcal{R}$ consists solely of either one of these rules, or both of them. These rules, together, also provide a counter-example to Proposition 4.3, if we drop the assumption that $\mathcal{R}$ is left-linear, since we may reduce $Eq?\ (fix\ succ)\ (fix\ succ)$

to both *true* and *false*. The first reduction is immediate, while the second proceeds by

$$Eq?\,(fix\ succ)\,(fix\ succ) \twoheadrightarrow Eq?\,(fix\ succ)\,(succ\,(fix\ succ)).$$

If we label $Eq?\,(fix\ succ)\,(fix\ succ)$ in any way, then at most one of these reductions will be possible.

4.2 Termination and confluence of labelled reduction

As an application of Theorem 3.4, we show that labelled PCF reduction is strongly normalizing. We use pcf to indicate reduction using the axioms of PCF, and pcf_+ for PCF reduction with lab_+ replacing fix-reduction. It is a simple matter to extend the argument to show that $pcf_{+,0}$-reduction, with lab_0 added, is terminating.

We begin by defining the property we wish to establish, namely

$$\mathcal{S}(M) \text{ iff } pcf_+\text{-reduction is terminating from } M$$

where M may be any labelled PCF term, *i.e.*, any $\lambda^{\rightarrow}$ term over the signature with type constants nat and $bool$, numerals, boolean constants $true$ and $false$, addition, equality test $Eq?$ on nat, conditional on each type, and labelled fixed-point constants fix_σ^n for each type σ and all $n \geq 0$. Let $\mathcal{T}$ be the set of typed terms over this signature, constructed using infinitely many variables at each type.

Let $\mathcal{P} \subseteq \mathcal{T}$ be the typed predicate defined from $\mathcal{S}$ as above. We must show $\mathcal{P}(c)$ for each constant of the signature. The numerals and boolean constants are covered by the fact that $P^b(c)$ iff $\mathcal{S}(c)$, since all of these constants are normal forms. It remains to show that $\mathcal{P}$ holds for each of the remaining constants.

We will use the subsidiary notion of *elimination context*, given by the following grammar:

$$\mathcal{E} ::= [\,] \mid \mathcal{E}M$$

Note that, for $\lambda^{\rightarrow}$, every elimination context has the form $\mathcal{E} \equiv [\,]M_1 \ldots M_k$ for some sequence of terms, with $\mathcal{E}[N] \equiv NM_1 \ldots M_k$. This form of context is often called an "applicative context" since it applies a term to a series of arguments. However, we use the phrase "elimination context" since the generalization to other types involves the elimination term forms. For example, an elimination context for $\lambda^{\times,\rightarrow}$ would allow us to apply projection functions (but not to form pairs, since pairing is the introduction form for products). We say $\mathcal{E}$ is a σ,τ-elimination context if $\mathcal{E}[M]$ has type τ whenever M has type σ. We write $\mathcal{P}(\mathcal{E})$ if $\mathcal{E} \equiv [\,]M_1 \ldots M_k$ and $\mathcal{P}(M_i)$ holds for $1 \leq i \leq k$.

A useful fact to notice is that by Theorem 3.4, we have $\mathcal{P}(M)$ for every term without constants. A consequence is that for every type σ and every type constant $b \in \{nat, bool\}$, there is a σ,b-elimination context $\mathcal{E}$ with $\mathcal{P}(\mathcal{E})$ and therefore $\mathcal{S}(\mathcal{E})$. This is easily verified by induction on types, using a variable wherever we need a term M with $P^\sigma(M)$.

The following lemma will be useful in reasoning about constants. The first two parts do not depend on the choice of $\mathcal{S}$, only the definition of $\mathcal{P}$ from $\mathcal{S}$. Part (iii) relies only on the fact that $\mathcal{S}$ is closed under reduction.

Lemma 4.4 *Let $M \in T^\sigma$ and let b be nat or bool.*

(i) If $P^b(\mathcal{E}[M])$ for every σ, b-context $\mathcal{E}$ with $\mathcal{P}(\mathcal{E})$, then $P^\sigma(M)$.

(ii) If $P^\sigma(M)$ and $\mathcal{E}$ is a σ, b-context with $\mathcal{P}(\mathcal{E})$, then $P^b(\mathcal{E}[M])$.

(iii) If $P^\sigma(M)$ and $M \xrightarrow{pcf_+}\!\!\!\!\rightarrow N$, then $P^\sigma(N)$.

Proof We prove (i) by induction on the type of M. If $M\colon b$, then the only b, b-elimination context is $\mathcal{E} = [\;]$ and the lemma clearly holds. If $M\colon \sigma \to \tau$, then every relevant $\sigma \to \tau, b$-elimination context has the form $\mathcal{E}[[\;]N_0]$, where $P^\sigma(N_0)$ and $\mathcal{E}$ is a τ, b-elimination context with $\mathcal{P}(\mathcal{E})$. Let $N \in T^\sigma$ be any term with $P^\sigma(N)$, and consider any τ, b-elimination context $\mathcal{E}$ with $\mathcal{P}(\mathcal{E})$. By the inductive hypothesis for $MN \in T^\tau$, we have $P^\tau(MN)$. Since N was chosen arbitrarily, it follows that $P^{\sigma\to\tau}(M)$. This proves (i). Part (ii) may be proved by an easy induction on types.

We prove part (iii) from (i) and (ii) using the fact that if $\mathcal{S}(M)$ and $M \xrightarrow{pcf_+}\!\!\!\!\rightarrow N$, then $\mathcal{S}(N)$. More specifically, suppose that $P^\sigma(M)$ holds and let $\mathcal{E}$ be any σ, b-elimination context with $\mathcal{P}(\mathcal{E})$. By (ii), we have $P^b(\mathcal{E}[M])$. If $M \xrightarrow{pcf_+}\!\!\!\!\rightarrow N$, then $\mathcal{E}[M] \xrightarrow{pcf_+}\!\!\!\!\rightarrow \mathcal{E}[N]$. Since $P^b(Q)$ iff $\mathcal{S}(Q)$, we therefore have $P^b(\mathcal{E}[N])$. Since this is true for every σ, b-context $\mathcal{E}$ with $\mathcal{P}(\mathcal{E})$, we have $P^\sigma(N)$ by (i). This proves the lemma. ∎

Lemma 4.5 *When $\mathcal{P}$ is defined from strong normalization of pcf_+-reduction, we have $\mathcal{P}(plus)$, $\mathcal{P}(Eq?)$, $\mathcal{P}(cond_\sigma)$, and $\mathcal{P}(fix_\sigma^n)$ for each type σ and natural number $n \geq 0$.*

Proof For addition, we assume $P^{nat}(M)$ and $P^{nat}(N)$ hold and demonstrate $P^{nat}(M + N)$. It suffices to show that $M + N$ is strongly normalizing. However, this follows immediately since M and N are both strongly normalizing and the reduction axioms for $+$ only produce a numeral from two numerals. The proof for equality test, *Eq?*, is essentially the same.

For conditional, we assume $P^{bool}(B)$, $P^\sigma(M)$, and $P^\sigma(N)$ and show that $P^\sigma(\texttt{if } B \texttt{ then } M \texttt{ else } N)$ holds. By (i) of Lemma 4.4, it suffices to show that if $\mathcal{E}[\texttt{if } B \texttt{ then } M \texttt{ else } N] \in T^b$, for $\mathcal{P}(\mathcal{E})$ and $b \equiv nat$ or $b \equiv bool$, then $\mathcal{E}[\texttt{if } B \texttt{ then } M \texttt{ else } N]$ is strongly normalizing. However, this is an easy case analysis, according to whether $B \xrightarrow{pcf_+}\!\!\!\!\rightarrow true$, $B \xrightarrow{pcf_+}\!\!\!\!\rightarrow false$, or neither, using (ii) of Lemma 4.4.

The remaining case is a labelled fixed-point constant fix_σ^n. For this, we proceed by induction on the label. The base case, for fix_σ^0, is easy since there is no associated reduction. For $\mathit{fix}_\sigma^{n+1}$, we assume $P^{\sigma\to\sigma}(M)$ and let $\mathcal{E}$ be any elimination context with $\mathcal{P}(\mathcal{E})$ and $\mathcal{E}[\mathit{fix}_\sigma^{n+1}\, M] \in T^b$. We prove the lemma by showing that $\mathcal{E}[\mathit{fix}_\sigma^{n+1}\, M]$ is strongly normalizing. If there is an infinite reduction sequence from this term, then there must also be an infinite reduction sequence from $\mathcal{E}[M(\mathit{fix}_\sigma^n\, M)]$, since every step of the first may be mimicked by one or two steps of the second (except for the inevitable lab_+-reduction and subsequent β-reduction, which merely serve to synchronise the two sequences). However, by the induction hypothesis and Lemma 4.4, we have $P^\sigma(\mathit{fix}_\sigma^n\, M)$; together with $P^{\sigma\to\sigma}(M)$ and $\mathcal{P}(\mathcal{E})$, this implies $P^b(\mathcal{E}[M(\mathit{fix}_\sigma^n\, M)])$, hence there is no such infinite reduction sequence from $\mathcal{E}[M(\mathit{fix}_\sigma^n\, M)]$. This completes the induction step and proves the lemma. ∎

Since Lemma 4.5 is easily extended to $pcf_{+,0}$, we have the following corollary of Theorem 3.4.

Theorem 4.6 *Both pcf_+ and $pcf_{+,0}$-reduction are strongly normalizing on labelled PCF terms.*

Confluence. We also wish to show that both forms of labelled PCF reduction are confluent. A general theorem that could be applied, if we did not have conditional at all types, is given in (Breazu-Tannen 1988; Breazu-Tannen and Gallier 1989). The general theorem is that if typed lambda calculus is extended with a confluent, algebraic rewrite system, the result is confluent. The proof of this is nontrivial, but is substantially simplified if we assume that $\mathcal{R}$ is left-linear. That is in fact the case we are interested in, since left-linearity is essential to Proposition 4.3 anyway. An adaptation of this proof to typed lambda calculus with labelled fixed-point operators has been carried out in (Howard and Mitchell 1990; Howard 1992). For the purposes of proving our desired results as simply as possible, however, it suffices to prove weak confluence, since confluence then follows by Newman's Lemma (Barendregt 1984; Mitchell 1996). To emphasise the fact that the argument does not depend heavily on the exact natural number and boolean operations of PCF, we show that adding β, $lab_{+(0)}$ to any weakly confluent reduction system preserves weak confluence, as long as there are no symbols in common between $\mathcal{R}$ and the reduction axioms of β, $lab_{+(0)}$. This is essentially an instance of *orthogonal rewrite systems,* as they are called in the literature on algebraic rewrite systems (Toyama 1987), except that application is shared. A related confluence property of untyped lambda calculus is Mitschke's δ-reduction theorem (Barendregt 1984), which shows that under certain syntactic conditions on $\mathcal{R}$, untyped $\mathcal{R}, \beta$-reduction is confluent.

Lemma 4.7 *Let $\mathcal{R}$ be a set of reduction axioms of the form $L \to R$, where L and R are lambda terms of the same type and L does not contain an application xM of a variable to an argument or any of the symbols λ, fix or any fix_σ^n. If $\mathcal{R}$ is weakly confluent, then $\mathcal{R}, \beta, lab_{+(0)}$ is weakly confluent.*

Proof The proof is a case analysis on pairs of redexes. We show two cases involving β-reduction and reduction from $\mathcal{R}$. The significance of the assumptions on the form of L is that these guarantee that if a subterm of a substitution instance $[M_1, \ldots, M_k/x_1, \ldots, x_k]L$ of some left-hand-side contains a β, $lab_{+(0)}$ redex, then this redex must be entirely within one of $M_1, \ldots, M_k$. The lemma would also hold with any other hypotheses guaranteeing this property.

The first case is an $\mathcal{R}$-redex inside a β-redex. This gives a term of the form

$$(\lambda y{:}\,\sigma.(\ldots [M_1, \ldots, M_k/x_1, \ldots, x_k]L \ldots))N$$

reducing to either of the terms

$$(\ldots [N/y][M_1, \ldots, M_k/x_1, \ldots, x_k]L \ldots)$$
$$(\lambda y{:}\,\sigma.(\ldots [M_1, \ldots, M_k/x_1, \ldots, x_k]R \ldots))N$$

the first by β-reduction and the second by an axiom $L \to R$ from $\mathcal{R}$. It is easy to see that both reduce in one step to

$$(\ldots [N/y][M_1, \ldots, M_k/x_1, \ldots, x_k]R \ldots)$$

The other possible interaction between β-reduction and $\mathcal{R}$ begins with a term of the form

$$(\ldots [M_1, \ldots, M_k/x_1, \ldots, x_k]L \ldots)$$

where one of $M_1, \ldots, M_k$ contains a β-redex. If $M_i \to M_i'$, then this term reduces to either of the two terms

$$(\ldots [M_1, \ldots, M_i', \ldots, M_k/x_1, \ldots, x_k]L \ldots)$$
$$(\ldots [M_1, \ldots, M_i, \ldots, M_k/x_1, \ldots, x_k]R \ldots)$$

in one step. We can easily reduce the first to

$$(\ldots [M_1, \ldots, M_i', \ldots, M_k/x_1, \ldots, x_k]R \ldots)$$

by one $\mathcal{R}$ step. Since we can also reach this term by some number of β-reductions, one for each occurrence of x_i in R, local confluence holds. The cases for other reductions in a substitution instance of the left-hand-side of an $\mathcal{R}$ axiom are very similar. ∎

By Newman's Lemma (Barendregt 1984; Mitchell 1996), it follows that pcf_+ and $pcf_{+,0}$ are confluent. We may use Proposition 4.3 to derive confluence of pcf-reduction from confluence of pcf_+. This gives us the following theorem.

Theorem 4.8 *The reductions pcf_+ and $pcf_{+,0}$ are confluent on labelled PCF terms and pcf-reduction is confluent on ordinary (unlabelled) PCF terms.*

4.3 Completeness of leftmost reduction

The final result in this section is that if $\mathcal{R}$ is a set of "left-normal" rules (defined below), and $\mathcal{R}, \beta, lab_+$ is confluent and terminating, then the leftmost reduction strategy is complete for finding $\mathcal{R}, \beta, \mathit{fix}$-normal forms. Since the PCF rules are left-normal, leftmost reduction is complete for finding normal forms of PCF programs.

A reduction axiom is *left-normal* if all the variables in the left-hand side of the rule appear to the right of all the term constants. For example, all of the PCF rules for natural numbers and booleans are left-normal. If we permute the arguments of conditional, however, putting the boolean argument at the end, then we would have reduction axioms

$$\begin{aligned} \mathit{cond}\; x\; y\; \mathit{true} &\longrightarrow x, \\ \mathit{cond}\; x\; y\; \mathit{false} &\longrightarrow y. \end{aligned}$$

These are not left-normal since x and y appear to the left of the constants *true* and *false*. Intuitively, if we have left-normal rules, then we may safely evaluate the arguments of a function from left to right. In many cases, it is possible to replace a set of rules with essentially equivalent left-normal ones by either permuting arguments or introducing auxiliary function symbols (see Mitchell 1996). However, this is not possible for inherently "non-sequential" functions such as parallel-or.

We will prove the completeness of leftmost reduction using strong normalization and confluence of positive labelled reduction, and the correspondence between labelled and unlabelled reduction. Since labelled fix reduction may terminate with fix^0 where unlabelled fix reduction could continue, our main lemma is that any fix^0 occurring to the left of the leftmost redex will remain after reducing the leftmost redex.

Lemma 4.9 *Let $\mathcal{R}$ be a set of left-normal reduction axioms with no left-hand-side containing fix^0. If $M \xrightarrow{\mathcal{R},\beta,lab_+} N$ by the leftmost reduction step, and fix^0 occurs to the left of the leftmost redex of M, then fix^0 must also occur in N, to the left of the leftmost redex if N is not in normal form.*

Proof Suppose $M \equiv \mathcal{C}[L] \rightarrow \mathcal{C}[R] \equiv N$ by contracting the leftmost $\mathcal{R}, \beta, lab_+$-redex and assume fix^0 occurs in context $\mathcal{C}[\,]$ to the left of $[\,]$. If $N \equiv \mathcal{C}[R]$ is in normal form, then fix^0 occurs in N since fix^0 occurs in $\mathcal{C}[\,]$. We therefore assume N is not in normal form and show that fix^0 occurs to the left of the leftmost redex in N.

Suppose, for the sake of deriving a contradiction, that fix^0 occurs within, or to the right of, the leftmost redex of N. Since a term beginning with fix^0 is not a redex, the leftmost redex of N must begin with some symbol to the left of fix^0, which is to the left of R when we write N as $\mathcal{C}[R]$. The proof proceeds by considering each possible form of redex.

Suppose the leftmost redex in N is $(\lambda x{:}\,\sigma.\,N_1)N_2$, with fix^0 and therefore R occurring to the right of this λ. Since fix^0 must occur between λ and R, R cannot be $(\lambda x{:}\,\sigma.\,N_1)N_2$, and so a redex of the form $(\lambda x{:}\,\sigma.\,N_1')N_2'$ must occur in M to the left of L. This contradicts the assumption that L is the leftmost redex in M. The analogous case for fix is straightforward.

It remains to consider a redex SL' with S some substitution and $L' \to R'$ in $\mathcal{R}$. We assume fix^0 and therefore R occur to the right of the first symbol of SL'. Since fix^0 is not in L', by hypothesis, and the rule is left-normal, all symbols to the right of fix^0, including R if it occurs within L', must be the result of substituting terms for variables in L'. It follows that we have a redex in M to the left of L, again a contradiction. This proves the lemma. ∎

Theorem 4.10 *Suppose $\mathcal{R}, \beta, \mathit{lab}_+$ is confluent and terminating, with $\mathcal{R}$ both left-linear and left-normal. If $M \xrightarrow{\mathcal{R},\beta,\mathit{fix}}\!\!\!\!\to N$ and N is a normal form, then there is a $\mathcal{R}, \beta, \mathit{fix}$-reduction from M to N that contracts the leftmost redex at each step.*

Proof If $M \xrightarrow{\mathcal{R},\beta,\mathit{fix}}\!\!\!\!\to N$ then, by Lemma 4.1 there exist labelings $M^\#$ and $N^\#$ of these terms such that $M^\# \xrightarrow{\mathcal{R},\beta,\mathit{lab}_+}\!\!\!\!\to N^\#$. Since $\mathcal{R}, \beta, \mathit{lab}_+$-reduction is confluent and terminating, we may reduce $M^\#$ to $N^\#$ by reducing the leftmost redex at each step.

We show that the leftmost $\mathcal{R}, \beta, \mathit{lab}_+$-reduction of $M^\#$ to $N^\#$ is also the leftmost $\mathcal{R}, \beta, \mathit{fix}$-reduction of M to N (when labels are removed). It is easy to see that this is the case if no term in the reduction sequence has fix^0 to the left of the leftmost redex, since this is the only term that would be an unlabelled redex without being a labelled one. Therefore, we assume that the final k steps of the reduction have the form

$$M_k^\# \equiv \mathcal{C}[L] \to \mathcal{C}[R] \equiv M_{k-1}^\# \to M_{k-2}^\# \to \ldots \to N^\#,$$

where fix^0 occurs to the left of L in M_k. But by Lemma 4.9 and induction on k, fix^0 must also be present in $N^\#$, which contradicts the fact that N is a $\mathcal{R}, \beta, \mathit{fix}$-normal form. It follows from Lemma 4.1 that by erasing labels we obtain a leftmost reduction from M to N. ∎

A related theorem in (Klop 1980) shows that leftmost reduction is normalizing for the untyped lambda calculus extended with any left-normal, linear and non-overlapping term rewriting system. Our proof is simpler since we assume termination, and since type restrictions make fix the only source of potential non-termination.

5 Confluence for lambda calculi with subtyping

5.1 Failures of confluence with subtyping

As noted in Section 2.4, β, η reduction fails to be confluent in the presence of subtyping. Specifically, if $\sigma <: \tau$ and $M \equiv \lambda y{:}\,\sigma.(\lambda x{:}\,\tau.\,N)\,y$, then

$$M \twoheadrightarrow \lambda x{:}\,\sigma.\,N$$

by β-reduction and

$$M \twoheadrightarrow \lambda x{:}\,\tau.\,N$$

by η-reduction. If N is a closed normal form, then both $\lambda x{:}\,\sigma.\,N$ and $\lambda x{:}\,\tau.\,N$ will be distinct normal forms. Since these two distinct normal forms differ only in the type annotations of λ-bound variables, one possible solution could be to add a reduction rule that allows us to change the type-tags of variables.

Based on this example, we consider the following reduction:

$$(\mathit{subtype}) \qquad \lambda x{:}\,\tau.\,M \rightarrow \lambda x{:}\,\sigma.\,M \qquad \text{if } \sigma <: \tau$$

Although $(\mathit{subtype})$ restores confluence for the counter-example considered above, confluence can still fail. Specifically, let N be a normal-form term and consider any types σ_1, σ_2, τ such that $\sigma_1 <: \tau$ and $\sigma_2 <: \tau$ and there is no type ρ such that $\rho <: \sigma_1$, $\rho <: \sigma_2$. Then, by $(\mathit{subtype})$ $\lambda x{:}\,\tau.\,N$ can be reduced to both $\lambda x{:}\,\sigma_1.\,N$ and $\lambda x{:}\,\sigma_2.\,N$ but there is no common term to which the latter two terms can be reduced.

5.2 Reduction system for $\lambda^{\rightarrow}_{<:}$

To understand our formulation of a confluent reduction system in the presence of subtyping, it is useful to recall the connection between the equational theory of a calculus and its reduction system, stated as Corollary 2.3. Specifically, we take equality as given by the proof system and formulate a confluent reduction system so that convertibility will coincide with provable equality. From this point of view, it is appropriate to look to provable equality for inspiration.

In the presence of subtyping, there are are interesting subtleties in the way one needs to think about equality. In $\lambda^{\rightarrow}$ without subtyping, we include the context Γ and type σ in equations $\Gamma \triangleright M = N : \sigma$ simply to indicate the common typing of both terms and to facilitate writing "well-typed" inference rules for axiomatising the true equations. Since the $\lambda^{\rightarrow}$ type σ is uniquely determined from Γ and M or N, the type does not have much to do with *how* M and N might be equal. With subtyping, however, terms M and N may have many different types (under the same assumptions about free variables) and so it is *a priori* possible for them to be equal at one type but different at another type.

This dependence of equality on the context and type implies that reduction would also need to be dependent on the context and type if there is to be the natural connection between equations and reduction. With this in mind, we formulate reduction for $\lambda^{\rightarrow}_{<:}$ in the form $\Gamma \triangleright M \xrightarrow{\sigma} N$, with the dependence of the reduction on the context Γ and the type σ at which M and N are being considered made explicit. It would be possible in our reduction system that $\Gamma \rhd M \xrightarrow{\sigma} N$ but that $\Gamma \rhd M \not\xrightarrow{\tau} N$ for a different type τ, *i.e.*, redexes strongly depend on the type. Intuitively, we take as basic redexes β, η and the rule $(subtype)$ with the restriction that $\Gamma \rhd M \xrightarrow{\sigma} N$ only if both M and N have type σ in the context Γ. The individual reduction relations $\Gamma \rhd \cdot \xrightarrow{\sigma} \cdot$ for each context Γ and type σ can then be shown to be confluent. In particular, suppose $\sigma_1 <: \tau$ and $\sigma_2 <: \tau$ and there is no type ρ such that $\rho <: \sigma_1$, $\rho <: \sigma_2$, as above. If N has type δ, we would have

$$\lambda x{:}\,\tau.\,N \xrightarrow{\sigma_1 \to \delta} \lambda x{:}\,\sigma_1.\,N$$

and

$$\lambda x{:}\,\tau.\,N \xrightarrow{\sigma_2 \to \delta} \lambda x{:}\,\sigma_2.\,N$$

but not $\lambda x{:}\,\tau.\,N \xrightarrow{\sigma_1 \to \delta} \lambda x{:}\,\sigma_2.\,N$, thus blocking the failure of confluence with the untyped version of $(subtype)$ above.

However, defining the reduction rules to depend on the type σ leads to a problem in applying the reduction rules to subterms that are redexes, since it is not clear at what type to consider the redexes. In more detail, consider a term $N \equiv (\cdots M \cdots)$ with a subterm M, and suppose that we wish to reduce N at type σ. The type σ of the whole term does not determine the type at which reductions on the subterm M can be performed and one therefore needs to specify which *typed* redexes can be simplified inside terms. Our solution is that we can consider M to be a redex of type τ, if the whole term $(\cdots M \cdots)$ can be given type σ assuming that the subterm M is of type τ. Thus, the types at which we can apply the reductions for M are not all types of M but only those with which we can give the enclosing term the indicated type. These ideas are formalized in a proof system for $\Gamma \rhd M \xrightarrow{\sigma} N$ defined below.

The reduction relation $\Gamma \rhd M \xrightarrow{\sigma} N$, where Γ is a context and σ a type, is given by the following rules.

$$(\beta) \qquad \frac{\Gamma \rhd (\lambda x{:}\,\sigma.\,M)\,N : \tau}{\Gamma \rhd (\lambda x{:}\,\sigma.\,M)\,N \xrightarrow{\tau} [N/x]\,M}$$

$$(\eta) \qquad \frac{\Gamma \rhd M : \sigma \to \tau \qquad x \notin FV(M)}{\Gamma \rhd (\lambda x{:}\,\sigma.\,M\,x) \xrightarrow{\sigma \to \tau} M}$$

$$(<:) \qquad \frac{\Gamma \rhd \lambda x{:}\,\tau.\,M : \sigma \to \delta \qquad \sigma <: \tau,\ \sigma \not\equiv \tau}{\Gamma \rhd (\lambda x{:}\,\tau.\,M) \xrightarrow{\sigma \to \delta} (\lambda x{:}\,\sigma.\,M)}$$

$$(app1) \qquad \frac{\Gamma \rhd M \xrightarrow{\sigma \to \tau} N \qquad \Gamma \rhd P : \sigma}{\Gamma \rhd M\,P \xrightarrow{\tau} N\,P}$$

$$(app2)\quad \frac{\Gamma \triangleright M : \sigma \to \tau \qquad \Gamma \triangleright P_1 \xrightarrow{\sigma} P_2}{\Gamma \triangleright M\, P_1 \xrightarrow{\tau} M\, P_2}$$

$$(abs)\quad \frac{\Gamma, x{:}\,\sigma \triangleright M \xrightarrow{\tau} N \qquad \sigma_1 <: \sigma}{\Gamma \triangleright \lambda x{:}\,\sigma.\, M \xrightarrow{\sigma_1 \to \tau} \lambda x{:}\,\sigma.\, N}$$

5.3 Confluence of reduction system

Confluence of $\lambda^{\to}_{<:}$ is proved using confluence of β, η-reduction for untyped λ-calculus. In broad outline, we consider the untyped term resulting from erasing the types of λ-bound variables in $\lambda^{\to}_{<:}$ terms and use the common reduct given by confluence of untyped λ-calculus to extract the common reduct for the reduction in $\lambda^{\to}_{<:}$.

The *type erasure*, $Erase(M)$, of a term, M, is defined by

$$\begin{aligned} Erase(x) &= x \\ Erase(M\,N) &= Erase(M)\; Erase(N) \\ Erase(\lambda x{:}\,\sigma.\, M) &= \lambda x.\, Erase(M) \end{aligned}$$

We can also reconstruct a typed $\lambda^{\to}_{<:}$ term from the erasure of any $\lambda^{\to}_{<:}$ term. We may identify such erasures using the following inference system for assigning types to untyped terms.

$$(var)\quad \Gamma \triangleright x : \sigma \qquad \text{if } x{:}\,\sigma \in \Gamma$$

$$(add\ var)\quad \frac{\Gamma \triangleright U : \tau}{\Gamma, x{:}\,\sigma \triangleright U : \tau} \qquad \text{if } x \notin Dom(\Gamma)$$

$$(\to Intro)\quad \frac{\Gamma, x{:}\,\sigma \triangleright U : \tau}{\Gamma \triangleright \lambda x.\, U : \sigma \to \tau}$$

$$(\to Elim)\quad \frac{\Gamma \triangleright U : \sigma \to \tau \qquad \Gamma \triangleright V : \sigma}{\Gamma \triangleright U\,V : \tau}$$

$$(subsump)\quad \frac{\Gamma \triangleright U : \sigma \qquad \Sigma \vdash \sigma <: \tau}{\Gamma \triangleright U : \tau}$$

With these definitions, we can now state and prove the various lemmas needed to establish the confluence of the reduction system for $\lambda^{\to}_{<:}$.

Our first lemma shows that the type-erasure of a term of $\lambda^{\to}_{<:}$ can be given the same type in the type system for untyped λ-terms.

Lemma 5.1 *If* $\Gamma \rhd M : \sigma$ *then* $\Gamma \rhd Erase(M) : \sigma$.

Proof By induction on the proof of $\Gamma \rhd M : \sigma$. ■

The next lemma states that the typed reduction rules can be mimicked as β, η-reductions on the untyped terms resulting from their type-erasure.

Lemma 5.2 *If* $\Gamma \rhd M \xrightarrow{\sigma} N$ *then* $Erase(M) \xrightarrow{\beta,\eta}\!\!\!\!\rightarrow Erase(N)$.

Proof By induction on the proof of $\Gamma \rhd M \xrightarrow{\sigma} N$. ■

We next establish the converse, *i.e.*, that β, η-reductions on untyped terms can be mimicked as typed reductions on the corresponding terms. To prove this, we need two technical propositions stating some obvious properties of substitutions.

Proposition 5.3 *If* $\Gamma, x{:}\,\sigma \rhd M : \tau$ *and* $\Gamma \rhd N : \sigma$ *then* $\Gamma \rhd [N/x]M : \tau$.

Proof By induction on the proof of $\Gamma, x{:}\,\sigma \rhd M : \tau$. ■

Proposition 5.4 $Erase([N/x]\,M) \equiv [Erase(N)/x]Erase(M)$.

Proof By induction on the structure of M. ■

Lemma 5.5 *If* $\Gamma \rhd M : \sigma$ *and* $Erase(M) \xrightarrow{\beta,\eta} U$ *then* $\exists N$ *such that* $\Gamma \rhd N : \sigma$, $\Gamma \rhd M \xrightarrow{\sigma} N$, *and* $Erase(N) \equiv U$.

Proof By induction on the structure of M.

Case $M \equiv x$**:** Vacuously true, since $Erase(M) = x$ and $x \not\xrightarrow{\beta,\eta} U$, for any term U.

Case $M \equiv M_1\, M_2$**:** Since $\Gamma \rhd M : \sigma$, we have that

$$\begin{array}{ll} \Gamma \rhd M_1 : \tau \rightarrow \rho & \text{where } \rho <: \sigma \\ \Gamma \rhd M_2 : \tau & \end{array} \tag{5.1}$$

Hence $\tau \rightarrow \rho <: \tau \rightarrow \sigma$ and by $(subsump)$,

$$\Gamma \rhd M_1 : \tau \rightarrow \sigma \tag{5.2}$$

Suppose that $Erase(M) \xrightarrow{\beta,\eta} U$. Since

$$Erase(M) = Erase(M_1)\, Erase(M_2),$$

the reduction to U could be because $Erase(M)$ itself is a β-redex, or we perform a β, η-reduction inside $Erase(M_1)$ or $Erase(M_2)$. We consider each of these cases separately.

Case I: Suppose that $Erase(M_1) \equiv \lambda x.\, V$ and $U \equiv [Erase(M_2)/x]V$. Since $Erase(M_1) \equiv \lambda x.\, V$, it follows that M_1 is of the form $\lambda x{:}\,\tau'.\, M_1'$ with $Erase(M_1') = V$. From (5.2), it follows that

$$\Gamma, x{:}\,\tau' \rhd M_1' : \sigma \tag{5.3}$$

with $\tau <: \tau'$. Using (5.1) with $\tau <: \tau'$, we get that

$$\Gamma \rhd M_2 : \tau' \tag{5.4}$$

Take N to be the term $[M_2/x]M_1'$. From judgements (5.3), (5.4), using Proposition 5.3, it follows that $\Gamma \rhd N : \sigma$. Since $M \equiv (\lambda x{:}\,\tau'.\, M_1')\, M_2$, we can use (β) to get that $\Gamma \rhd M \xrightarrow{\sigma} N$. Finally,

$$\begin{aligned} Erase(N) &\equiv Erase([M_2/x]M_1') \\ &\equiv [Erase(M_2)/x]Erase(M_1') \end{aligned}$$

by Proposition 5.4, and we thus get that $Erase(N) \equiv U$.

Case II: Suppose that $Erase(M_1) \xrightarrow{\beta,\eta} V_1'$ and $U \equiv V_1'\, Erase(M_2)$. By (5.2), we can use induction hypothesis on M_1 to get that there is a term N' such that $\Gamma \rhd N' : \tau \to \sigma$, $\Gamma \rhd M_1 \xrightarrow{\tau\to\sigma} N'$ and $Erase(N') \equiv V_1'$.

Take $N \equiv N'\, M_2$. From (5.1), we get that $\Gamma \rhd N : \sigma$. Using $(\mathit{app1})$, we get that $\Gamma \rhd M \xrightarrow{\sigma} N$. Finally,

$$\begin{aligned} Erase(N) &\equiv Erase(N')\, Erase(M_2) \\ &\equiv V_1'\, Erase(M_2) \\ &\equiv U \end{aligned}$$

Case III: The only possibility remaining is that $Erase(M_2) \xrightarrow{\beta,\eta} V_2'$ and $U \equiv Erase(M_1)\, V_2'$. This case is dealt similarly as Case II.

Case $M \equiv \lambda x{:}\,\sigma_1.\, M_1$: Since $\Gamma \rhd M : \sigma$, we have that $\sigma \equiv \sigma_2 \to \tau$, and

$$\Gamma, x{:}\,\sigma_1 \rhd M_1 : \tau' \quad \text{where } \sigma_2 <: \sigma_1 \text{ and } \tau' <: \tau, \tag{5.5}$$

By $(\mathit{subsump})$,

$$\Gamma, x{:}\,\sigma_1 \rhd M_1 : \tau \tag{5.6}$$

Suppose that $Erase(M) \xrightarrow{\beta,\eta} U$. Since $Erase(M) = \lambda x.\, Erase(M_1)$, the reduction to U could be because $Erase(M)$ itself is an η-redex, or we perform a β,η-reduction inside $Erase(M_1)$. We consider each of these cases separately.

Case I: Suppose $Erase(M_1) \equiv V\,x$ for some term V, then $Erase(M) \equiv \lambda x.\,V\,x$ and $Erase(M) \xrightarrow{\eta} V$, *i.e.*, $U \equiv V$. Since $Erase(M_1) \equiv V\,x$, we have that $M_1 \equiv M_1'\,x$ where $Erase(M_1') \equiv V$. By judgement (5.6), $\Gamma, x{:}\,\sigma_1 \rhd M_1'\,x : \tau$, *i.e.*, $\Gamma \rhd M_1' : \sigma_1' \to \tau'$ where $\sigma_1 <: \sigma_1'$ and $\tau' <: \tau$. By (5.5), $\sigma_2 <: \sigma_1$, hence $\Gamma \rhd M_1' : \sigma_2 \to \tau$, *i.e.*, $\Gamma \rhd M_1' : \sigma$.
Take $N \equiv M_1'$, we have that $\Gamma \rhd N : \sigma$.
Since $\Gamma \rhd M : \sigma$ where $\sigma \equiv \sigma_2 \to \tau$ and $M \equiv \lambda x{:}\,\sigma_1.\,M_1'\,x$, we have the type judgement $\Gamma \rhd \lambda x{:}\,\sigma_1.\,M_1'\,x : \sigma_2 \to \tau$.
By $(<:)$, and (5.5), $\Gamma \rhd \lambda x{:}\,\sigma_1.\,M_1'\,x \xrightarrow{\sigma_2\to\tau} \lambda x{:}\,\sigma_2.\,M_1'\,x$.
Hence, by (η), $\Gamma \rhd \lambda x{:}\,\sigma_2.\,M_1'\,x \xrightarrow{\sigma_2\to\tau} M_1'$, *i.e.*, $\Gamma \rhd M \xrightarrow{\sigma} N$.
Finally,

$$\begin{aligned} Erase(N) &\equiv Erase(M_1') \\ &\equiv V \\ &\equiv U \end{aligned}$$

Case II: Suppose that $Erase(M_1) \xrightarrow{\beta,\eta} V$. We have $U \equiv \lambda x.\,V$. By (5.6), we can use the induction hypothesis on M_1 to get that there is a term N_1 such that $\Gamma, x{:}\,\sigma_1 \rhd N_1 : \tau$, $\Gamma, x{:}\,\sigma_1 \rhd M_1 \xrightarrow{\tau} N_1$, and $Erase(N_1) \equiv V$.
Take $N \equiv \lambda x{:}\,\sigma_1.\,N_1$.
Using (abs) on $\Gamma, x{:}\,\sigma_1 \rhd N_1 : \tau$, we get $\Gamma \rhd \lambda x{:}\,\sigma_1.\,N_1 : \sigma_1 \to \tau$.
Since $\sigma_2 <: \sigma_1$, by $(<:)$, we have that $\Gamma \rhd \lambda x{:}\,\sigma_1.\,N_1 : \sigma_2 \to \tau$, *i.e.*, $\Gamma \rhd N : \sigma$.
Now, using (abs), we get that $\Gamma \rhd \lambda x{:}\,\sigma_1.\,M_1 \xrightarrow{\sigma_2\to\tau} \lambda x{:}\,\sigma_1.\,N_1$, *i.e.*, $\Gamma \rhd M \xrightarrow{\sigma} N$.
Finally,

$$\begin{aligned} Erase(N) &\equiv \lambda x.\,Erase(N_1) \\ &\equiv \lambda x.\,V \\ &\equiv U \end{aligned}$$

■

Corollary 5.6 *If* $\Gamma \rhd M : \sigma$ *and* $Erase(M) \xrightarrow{\beta,\eta}\!\!\!\!\to U$ *then* $\exists N$ *such that* $\Gamma \rhd N : \sigma$, $\Gamma \rhd M \xrightarrow{\sigma}\!\!\!\!\to N$, *and* $Erase(N) \equiv U$.

Proof By induction on the number of reduction steps of $Erase(M) \xrightarrow{\beta,\eta}\!\!\!\!\to U$ and Lemma 5.5. ■

Lemma 5.7 *If* U *is a* $\beta,\eta-$*normal form then*

$$U \equiv \lambda x_1.\ldots\lambda x_n.\,y\,V_1\ldots V_k$$

where $n \geq 0, k \geq 0$, y *is a variable, and* $V_1, \ldots, V_k$ *are* $\beta,\eta-$*normal forms.*

Proof By induction on the structure of U. ∎

Lemma 5.8 *If U is an untyped $\beta,\eta-$normal form and $\Gamma \rhd U : \sigma$, then there exists a term N such that $\Gamma \rhd N : \sigma$, $Erase(N) \equiv U$, and for any term P such that $\Gamma \rhd P : \sigma$*
and $Erase(P) \equiv U$, we have that $\Gamma \rhd P \xrightarrow{\sigma}\!\!\!\!\rightarrow N$.

Proof Let U be a β,η-normal form. By Lemma 5.7,

$$U \equiv \lambda x_1.\ldots\lambda x_n.\, y\, V_1 \ldots V_k, \qquad n \geq 0, k \geq 0$$

We proceed by induction on the length of U. Suppose $\Gamma \rhd U : \sigma$, then

$$\sigma \equiv \sigma_1 \to \sigma_2 \to \cdots \to \sigma_n \to \rho \tag{5.7}$$
$$\Gamma' \rhd y\, V_1 \ldots V_k : \rho \qquad \text{where} \quad \Gamma' \equiv \Gamma, x_i\colon \sigma_i, \quad i = 1, \ldots, n \tag{5.8}$$

By (5.8), we have

$$y\colon \rho_1 \to \cdots \to \rho_k \to \rho' \in \Gamma' \tag{5.9}$$
$$\Gamma' \rhd V_i : \rho_i', \qquad \text{where} \quad \rho_i' <: \rho_i, \quad i = 1, \ldots, k \tag{5.10}$$
$$\rho' <: \rho \tag{5.11}$$

Hence, $\Gamma' \rhd V_i : \rho_i$.
By induction hypothesis applied to the shorter terms V_i, there exist terms $\Gamma' \rhd N_i : \rho_i$ with the stated property.
Take $N \equiv \lambda x_1\colon\sigma_1.\ldots\lambda x_n\colon\sigma_n.\, y\, N_1 \ldots N_k$.
Since $\Gamma' \rhd N_i : \rho_i$ and $y\colon \rho_1 \to \cdots \to \rho_k \to \rho' \in \Gamma'$, using ($\to$ *Elim*) k times, we get that

$$\Gamma' \rhd y\, N_1 \ldots N_k : \rho',$$

and by (5.11),

$$\Gamma' \rhd y\, N_1 \ldots N_k : \rho.$$

Using ($\to$ *Intro*) n times, we get

$$\Gamma \rhd \lambda x_1\colon\sigma_1.\ldots\lambda x_n\colon\sigma_n.\, y\, N_1 \ldots N_k : \sigma_1 \to \sigma_2 \to \cdots \to \sigma_n \to \rho,$$

i.e.,

$$\Gamma \rhd N : \sigma.$$

Clearly, $Erase(N) \equiv U$.
Now, suppose $\Gamma \rhd P : \sigma$ and $Erase(P) \equiv U$.
Then, $P \equiv \lambda x_1\colon\sigma_1'.\ldots\lambda x_n\colon\sigma_n'.\, y\, P_1 \ldots P_k$ with $Erase(P_i) \equiv V_i$, $i = 1, \ldots, k$.
From $\Gamma \rhd P : \sigma$, we have Γ, $x_1\colon\sigma_1', \ldots, x_n\colon\sigma_n' \rhd y\, P_1 \ldots P_k : \tau'$ and $\sigma_1' \to \cdots \to \sigma_n' \to \tau' <: \sigma$, *i.e.*, $\sigma_i <: \sigma_i'$ for $i = 1, \ldots, n$ and $\tau' <: \rho$.
Hence, Γ, $x_1\colon\sigma_1, \ldots, x_n\colon\sigma_n \rhd y\, P_1 \ldots P_k : \rho$.

Since $y\colon \rho_1 \to \cdots \to \rho_k \to \rho' \in \Gamma'$ and $\Gamma' \rhd P_i : \rho_i''$ with $\rho_i'' <: \rho_i$, we have $\Gamma' \rhd P_i : \rho_i$.
By induction hypothesis, $\Gamma' \rhd P_i \xrightarrow{\rho_i}\!\!\!\!\!\!\rightarrow N_i$. By repeated use of rule $(app2)$ and the fact that $\Gamma' \rhd y : \rho_1 \to \cdots \to \rho_k \to \rho$, we have $\Gamma' \rhd y\, P_1 \ldots P_k \xrightarrow{\rho}\!\!\!\!\!\!\rightarrow y\, N_1 \ldots N_k$.
By repeated use of rule (abs), we get

$$\begin{aligned}&\Gamma \rhd \lambda x_1\colon \sigma_1. \ldots \lambda x_n\colon \sigma_n. y\, P_1 \ldots P_k \\ &\quad \xrightarrow{\sigma_1 \to \cdots \to \sigma_n \to \rho}\!\!\!\!\!\!\rightarrow \lambda x_1\colon \sigma_1. \ldots \lambda x_n\colon \sigma_n. y\, N_1 \ldots N_k \end{aligned} \tag{5.12}$$

Now, since $\sigma_n <: \sigma_n'$, by $(<:)$

$$\begin{aligned}&\Gamma,\, x_1\colon \sigma_1, \ldots, x_{n-1}\colon \sigma_{n-1} \rhd \lambda x_n\colon \sigma_n'. y\, P_1 \ldots P_k \\ &\qquad \xrightarrow{\sigma_n \to \rho} \lambda x_n\colon \sigma_n. y\, P_1 \ldots P_k\end{aligned}$$

By repeating this argument, we get

$$\begin{aligned}&\Gamma \rhd \lambda x_1\colon \sigma_1'. \ldots \lambda x_n\colon \sigma_n'. y\, P_1 \ldots P_k \\ &\quad \xrightarrow{\sigma_1 \to \cdots \to \sigma_n \to \rho} \lambda x_1\colon \sigma_1. \ldots \lambda x_n\colon \sigma_n. y\, P_1 \ldots P_k \end{aligned} \tag{5.13}$$

Using the reduction (5.13) followed by (5.12), we get that

$$\Gamma \rhd P \xrightarrow{\sigma}\!\!\!\!\!\!\rightarrow N$$

■

Lemma 5.9 *Let U be any untyped term such that $\Gamma \rhd U : \sigma$ for some context Γ and type σ. Then, U is strongly-normalizing under β, η-reduction.*

Proof By Corollary 22 of (Mitchell 1991), it follows that U is the erasure of a simply-typed λ-term. Since simply-typed λ-calculus is strongly normalizing under β, η-reduction, the result follows. ■

Theorem 5.10 *Suppose that for $\Gamma \rhd M : \sigma$, both $\Gamma \rhd M \xrightarrow{\sigma}\!\!\!\!\!\!\rightarrow N_1$ and $\Gamma \rhd M \xrightarrow{\sigma}\!\!\!\!\!\!\rightarrow N_2$, then there is a term $\Gamma \rhd P : \sigma$ such that $\Gamma \rhd N_1 \xrightarrow{\sigma}\!\!\!\!\!\!\rightarrow P$ and $\Gamma \rhd N_2 \xrightarrow{\sigma}\!\!\!\!\!\!\rightarrow P$.*

Proof Suppose $\Gamma \rhd M \xrightarrow{\sigma}\!\!\!\!\!\!\rightarrow N_1,\ \Gamma \rhd M \xrightarrow{\sigma}\!\!\!\!\!\!\rightarrow N_2$.
By Lemmas 5.2 and 5.1, we have $\Gamma \rhd \mathit{Erase}(M) \xrightarrow{\beta,\eta}\!\!\!\!\!\!\rightarrow \mathit{Erase}(N_1)$,
$\Gamma \rhd \mathit{Erase}(M) \xrightarrow{\beta,\eta}\!\!\!\!\!\!\rightarrow \mathit{Erase}(N_2)$, and $\Gamma \rhd \mathit{Erase}(N_1) : \sigma$, $\Gamma \rhd \mathit{Erase}(N_2) : \sigma$.
By confluence of β, η-reduction for untyped $\lambda-$calculus, there exists a term U' such that both $\mathit{Erase}(N_1) \xrightarrow{\beta,\eta}\!\!\!\!\!\!\rightarrow U'$ and $\mathit{Erase}(N_2) \xrightarrow{\beta,\eta}\!\!\!\!\!\!\rightarrow U'$.
By Corollary 5.6, there exist P_1', P_2' such that $\Gamma \rhd P_1' : \sigma$, $\Gamma \rhd P_2' : \sigma$, $\Gamma \rhd N_1 \xrightarrow{\sigma}\!\!\!\!\!\!\rightarrow P_1'$,
$\Gamma \rhd N_2 \xrightarrow{\sigma}\!\!\!\!\!\!\rightarrow P_2'$, and $\mathit{Erase}(P_1') \equiv U'$, $\mathit{Erase}(P_2') \equiv U'$.

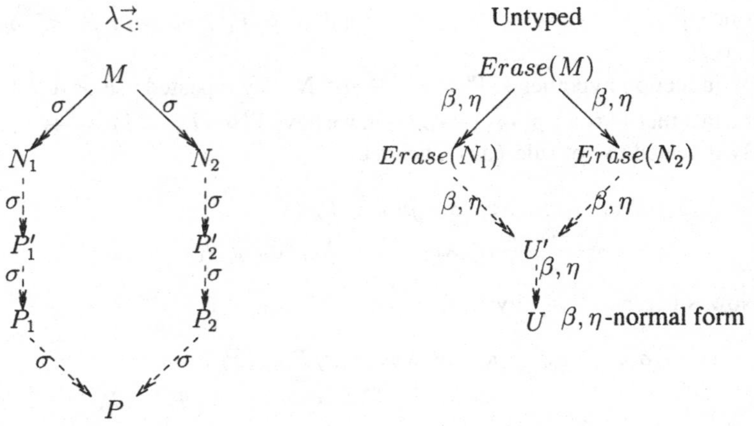

Figure 2: Proof of Theorem 5.10

Thus, by Lemma 5.1 $\Gamma \rhd U' : \sigma$. By Lemma 5.9, there exists a term U of $\beta, \eta-$normal form such that $\Gamma \rhd U : \sigma$ and $U' \xrightarrow{\beta,\eta}\!\!\!\!\rightarrow U$.
By Corollary 5.6, there exists P_1, P_2 such that $\Gamma \rhd P_1 : \sigma$, $\Gamma \rhd P_2 : \sigma$, $\Gamma \rhd P_1' \xrightarrow{\sigma}\!\!\!\!\rightarrow P_1$,
$\Gamma \rhd P_2' \xrightarrow{\sigma}\!\!\!\!\rightarrow P_2$, and $Erase(P_1) \equiv U$, $Erase(P_2) \equiv U$.
Now, by Lemma 5.8 there exists a term P such that $\Gamma \rhd P : \sigma$, and $\Gamma \rhd P_1 \xrightarrow{\sigma}\!\!\!\!\rightarrow P$,
$\Gamma \rhd P_2 \xrightarrow{\sigma}\!\!\!\!\rightarrow P$, *i.e.*, there exists P such that $\Gamma \rhd N_1 \xrightarrow{\sigma}\!\!\!\!\rightarrow P$, $\Gamma \rhd N_2 \xrightarrow{\sigma}\!\!\!\!\rightarrow P$.
This can be illustrated as in Figure 2.

■

5.4 Reduction with subtyping and recursion

In the last part of this paper, we consider reduction for $\lambda^{\rightarrow, fix}_{<:}$, the language obtained by adding fixed-point operators to $\lambda^{\rightarrow}_{<:}$. One reason this system deserves separate consideration is that our confluence proof for $\lambda^{\rightarrow}_{<:}$ relies heavily on the strong-normalization property. Since strong normalization fails for $\lambda^{\rightarrow, fix}_{<:}$, it is therefore not easy to see, *a priori*, whether reduction for $\lambda^{\rightarrow, fix}_{<:}$ is likely to be confluent.

We prove confluence of the reduction system for $\lambda^{\rightarrow, fix}_{<:}$ by using the corresponding calculus $\lambda^{\rightarrow, lab}_{<:}$ with all fixed-point operators labelled. The reduction relation $\Gamma \rhd M \xrightarrow{\sigma}_{lab} N$ on $\lambda^{\rightarrow, lab}_{<:}$ is the same as reduction for $\lambda^{\rightarrow}_{<:}$, plus the expected rule for labelled fixed points,

$$(fix_{lab}) \qquad \Gamma \rhd fix^{n+1}_{\sigma} \xrightarrow{\tau}_{lab} \lambda f\colon \sigma \rightarrow \sigma.\, f\,(fix^{n}_{\sigma}\, f) \qquad \text{if } \Gamma \rhd fix^{n+1}_{\sigma} : \tau$$

It is relatively straightforward to verify the lifting and projection properties of labelling for $\lambda_{<:}^{\rightarrow,fix}$. These may be stated as follows, writing $L \in lab(M)$ if L is a labelled term with $\natural(L) = M$.

Lemma 5.11 *Suppose that* $\Gamma \rhd M \overset{\sigma}{\twoheadrightarrow} N$. *Then there exists a natural number* k *such that if* $M^{\#} \in lab(M)$ *with each label in* M *at least* k *then* $\Gamma \rhd M^{\#} \overset{\sigma}{\twoheadrightarrow}_{lab} N^{\#}$.

Proof If $\Gamma \rhd M \overset{\sigma}{\twoheadrightarrow} N$ then there exist terms $M_1, \ldots, M_k$, $k \geq 0$ such that $M \equiv M_0$, $\Gamma \rhd M_i \overset{\sigma}{\longrightarrow} M_{i+1}$, and $M_k \equiv N$. Proof by induction on the length of the reduction sequence. ∎

Lemma 5.12 *If* $\Gamma \rhd M^{\#} \overset{\sigma}{\longrightarrow}_{lab} N^{\#}$ *then* $\Gamma \rhd M \overset{\sigma}{\longrightarrow} N$, *where* $M^{\#} \in lab(M)$, $N^{\#} \in lab(N)$.

Proof By induction on the proof of $\Gamma \rhd M^{\#} \overset{\sigma}{\longrightarrow}_{lab} N^{\#}$. ∎

Corollary 5.13 *Confluence of* $\overset{\sigma}{\twoheadrightarrow}_{lab}$ *implies confluence of* $\overset{\sigma}{\twoheadrightarrow}$.

5.5 Confluence proof using labelled reduction

As shown in the previous section, confluence of the reduction system for $\lambda_{<:}^{\rightarrow,fix}$ follows from the confluence of labelled reduction. In this section we establish the confluence of the reduction system for $\lambda_{<:}^{\rightarrow,lab}$, thereby proving confluence for λ-calculus with subtyping and fixed points.

Just as in Section 5.3, we prove the confluence of labelled reduction by considering untyped λ-terms and using confluence properties of β,η-reduction on them. However, there is one main step in extending the ideas from the proof for $\lambda_{<:}^{\rightarrow}$ to that for $\lambda_{<:}^{\rightarrow,lab}$. In $\lambda_{<:}^{\rightarrow}$ the only additional basic reduction rule besides β and η was $(<:)$, which could be easily mimicked in the untyped λ-calculus (as a 0-step reduction!). However, in $\lambda_{<:}^{\rightarrow,lab}$, we have an additional set of reduction rules, namely those of labelled fixed points, that need to be suitably mimicked as reduction on untyped terms. One possibility is to introduce labelled fixed-point constants in the target untyped calculus and include their reduction rules in the untyped calculus. However, this introduces some extraneous complication, since we would have to establish confluence of untyped lambda calculus with labelled fixed-point reduction. A simpler solution is to take the target untyped λ-calculus with only β,η-reductions and to mimic labelled fixed-point reductions through the definition of the erasure function. More specifically, we translate labelled fixed points by performing their bounded number of unwindings completely and erasing the type-annotations of the λ-bound variables from the resulting term. This reduces all labelled fixed points to terms involving fix_{σ}^{0}, which we include as constants in the untyped λ-calculus. The inclusion of these constants does not interfere with the confluence of the system since there are no associated reduction rules with these constants, and thus the reduction system is still only β,η on untyped terms.

5.5.1 Type system for untyped terms

We consider untyped terms which may include constants of the form fix^0_σ. Thus, the typing rules for untyped terms are those given in Section 5.3 together with the following additional axiom.

$$(\mathit{fix}) \qquad \phi \rhd \mathit{fix}^0_\sigma : (\sigma \to \sigma) \to \sigma$$

5.5.2 Type erasure

The *type erasure* of a term M, written $\mathit{Erase}(M)$, is defined as follows.

$$\begin{array}{rcl} \mathit{Erase}(x) & = & x \\ \mathit{Erase}(\mathit{fix}^0_\sigma) & = & \mathit{fix}^0_\sigma \\ \mathit{Erase}(\mathit{fix}^{n+1}_\sigma) & = & \lambda f.\, f\,((\mathit{Erase}(\mathit{fix}^n_\sigma))\, f) \\ \mathit{Erase}(M\,N) & = & \mathit{Erase}(M)\, \mathit{Erase}(N) \\ \mathit{Erase}(\lambda x{:}\,\sigma.\, M) & = & \lambda x.\, \mathit{Erase}(M) \end{array}$$

5.5.3 Proof of confluence

Lemma 5.14 *If* $\Gamma \rhd M : \sigma$ *then* $\Gamma \rhd \mathit{Erase}(M) : \sigma$.

Proof By induction on the proof of $\Gamma \rhd M : \sigma$. ∎

Lemma 5.15 *If* $\Gamma \rhd M \xrightarrow{\sigma}_{lab} N$ *then* $\mathit{Erase}(M) \xrightarrow{\beta,\eta}\!\!\!\!\rightarrow \mathit{Erase}(N)$

Proof By induction on the proof of $\Gamma \rhd M \xrightarrow{\sigma}_{lab} N$. ∎

Lemma 5.16 *If* $\Gamma \rhd M : \sigma$ *and* $\mathit{Erase}(M) \xrightarrow{\beta,\eta} U$ *then* $\exists N$ *such that* $\Gamma \rhd N : \sigma$, $\Gamma \rhd M \xrightarrow{\sigma}\!\!\!\!\rightarrow_{lab} N$, *and* $\mathit{Erase}(N) \equiv U$.

Proof By induction on the structure of M. We need to prove for the case where $M \equiv \mathit{fix}^n_\tau$; for the other cases the proof is the same as that of Lemma 5.5.

Case $M \equiv \mathit{fix}^n_\tau$**:** We have that $\Gamma \rhd \mathit{fix}^n_\tau : \sigma$ where $(\tau \to \tau) \to \tau <: \sigma$.
Proof by induction on n.

$n = 0$: Vacuously true, since $M \equiv \mathit{fix}^0_\tau$ and $\mathit{fix}^0_\tau \not\xrightarrow{\beta,\eta} U$ for any term U.

$n = k + 1$: Suppose $\Gamma \rhd \mathit{fix}^{k+1}_\tau : \sigma$ and $\mathit{Erase}(\mathit{fix}^{k+1}_\tau) \xrightarrow{\beta,\eta} U$.
By definition of Erase, we have $\lambda f.\, f\,((\mathit{Erase}(\mathit{fix}^k_\tau))\, f) \xrightarrow{\beta,\eta} U$.
We proceed by examining possible reductions.

Case I: $U \equiv \lambda f.\, f\,(V\, f)$ and $Erase(\mathit{fix}_\tau^k) \xrightarrow{\beta,\eta} V$.
By induction hypothesis, $\exists\, N_k$ such that

$$\Gamma \triangleright N_k : (\tau \to \tau) \to \tau, \qquad \text{since } \Gamma \triangleright \mathit{fix}_\tau^k : (\tau \to \tau) \to \tau,$$

$$\Gamma \triangleright \mathit{fix}_\tau^k \xrightarrow{(\tau\to\tau)\to\tau}\!\!\!\twoheadrightarrow_{lab} N_k, \tag{5.14}$$

$$Erase(N_k) = V. \tag{5.15}$$

Take

$$N_{k+1} = \lambda f{:}\,\tau \to \tau.\, f\,(N_k\, f)$$

Since $\Gamma \triangleright N_{k+1} : (\tau \to \tau) \to \tau$ and $(\tau \to \tau) \to \tau <: \sigma$, we have $\Gamma \triangleright N_{k+1} : \sigma$
We also have, since $(\tau \to \tau) \to \tau <: \sigma$,

$$\sigma \equiv (\sigma_1 \to \sigma_2) \to \sigma_3, \qquad \text{where } \sigma_2 <: \tau,\ \tau <: \sigma_1, \text{ and } \tau <: \sigma_3$$

By (fix_{lab}), $\Gamma \triangleright \mathit{fix}_\tau^{k+1} \xrightarrow{\sigma}_{lab} \lambda f{:}\,\tau \to \tau.\, f\,(\mathit{fix}_\tau^k\, f)$, *i.e.*, we need to prove that

$$\Gamma \triangleright \lambda f{:}\,\tau \to \tau.\, f\,(\mathit{fix}_\tau^k\, f) \xrightarrow{\sigma}\!\!\!\twoheadrightarrow_{lab} \lambda f{:}\,\tau \to \tau.\, f\,(N_k\, f)$$

From (5.14), we can get that

$$\Gamma, f{:}\,\tau \to \tau \triangleright \mathit{fix}_\tau^k \xrightarrow{(\tau\to\tau)\to\tau}\!\!\!\twoheadrightarrow_{lab} N_k, \tag{5.16}$$

Using $(app1)$ on (5.16) and $\Gamma, f{:}\,\tau \to \tau \triangleright f : \tau \to \tau$, we get

$$\Gamma, f{:}\,\tau \to \tau \triangleright (\mathit{fix}_\tau^k\, f) \xrightarrow{\tau}\!\!\!\twoheadrightarrow_{lab} N_k\, f, \tag{5.17}$$

Since $\tau <: \sigma_3$, we have $\Gamma, f{:}\,\tau\to\tau \triangleright f : \tau\to\sigma_3$; applying $(app2)$ on this judgement and (5.17), we have

$$\Gamma, f{:}\,\tau \to \tau \triangleright f\,(\mathit{fix}_\tau^k\, f) \xrightarrow{\sigma_3}\!\!\!\twoheadrightarrow_{lab} f\,(N_k\, f), \tag{5.18}$$

Now, since $\sigma_1 \to \sigma_2 <: \tau \to \tau$, using (abs) on (5.18), we get

$$\Gamma \triangleright \lambda f{:}\,\tau \to \tau.\, f\,(\mathit{fix}_\tau^k\, f) \xrightarrow{(\sigma_1\to\sigma_2)\to\sigma_3}\!\!\!\twoheadrightarrow_{lab} \lambda f{:}\,\tau \to \tau.\, f\,(N_k\, f),$$

Thus,

$$\Gamma \triangleright \lambda f{:}\,\tau \to \tau.\, f\,(\mathit{fix}_\tau^k\, f) \xrightarrow{\sigma}\!\!\!\twoheadrightarrow_{lab} \lambda f{:}\,\tau \to \tau.\, f\,(N_k\, f), \ \textit{i.e.},$$
$$\Gamma \triangleright \mathit{fix}_\tau^{k+1} \xrightarrow{\sigma}\!\!\!\twoheadrightarrow_{lab} N_{k+1}$$

From (5.15), we have

$$\begin{aligned} Erase(N_{k+1}) &= \lambda f.\, f\,((Erase(N_k))\, f) \\ &= U \end{aligned}$$

Case II: If $k \geq 1$, then by the definition of *Erase*, we have

$$\lambda f.\, f\,((\lambda g.\, g\,((Erase(fix_\tau^{k-1}))\, g))\, f) \xrightarrow{\beta,\eta} U$$

Thus, $U \equiv \lambda f.\, f\,(f\,((Erase(fix_\tau^{k-1}))\, f))$.
Take

$$N_{k+1} = \lambda f{:}\tau \to \tau.\, f\,(f\,(fix_\tau^{k-1}\ f))$$

Then, $\Gamma \rhd N_{k+1} : (\tau \to \tau) \to \tau$; since $(\tau \to \tau) \to \tau <: \sigma$, we have that
$\Gamma \rhd N_{k+1} : \sigma$.
Now, since $\Gamma \rhd fix_\tau^{k+1} : \sigma$ we have that

$$\begin{array}{lll} \Gamma \rhd fix_\tau^{k+1} & \xrightarrow{\sigma}_{lab} & \lambda f{:}\tau \to \tau.\, f\,(fix_\tau^k\, f) \\ & \xrightarrow{\sigma}_{lab} & \lambda f{:}\tau \to \tau.\, f\,((\lambda g{:}\tau \to \tau.\, g\,(fix_\tau^{k-1}\, g))\, f) \\ & \xrightarrow{\sigma}_{lab} & \lambda f{:}\tau \to \tau.\, f\,(f\,(fix_\tau^{k-1}\, f)) = N_{k+1} \end{array}$$

Thus, $\Gamma \rhd fix_\tau^{k+1} \xrightarrow{\sigma}\!\!\!\!\rightarrow_{lab} N_{k+1}$.
We also have that

$$\begin{array}{rcl} Erase(N_{k+1}) & = & \lambda f.\, f\,(f\,((Erase(fix_\tau^{k-1}))\, f)) \\ & = & U \end{array}$$

■

Corollary 5.17 *If* $\Gamma \rhd M : \sigma$ *and* $Erase(M) \xrightarrow{\beta,\eta}\!\!\!\!\rightarrow U$ *then* $\exists N$ *such that* $\Gamma \rhd N : \sigma$, $\Gamma \rhd M \xrightarrow{\sigma}\!\!\!\!\rightarrow_{lab} N$, *and* $Erase(N) \equiv U$.

Proof By induction on the number of reduction steps of $Erase(M) \xrightarrow{\beta,\eta}\!\!\!\!\rightarrow U$ and Lemma 5.16. ■

Lemma 5.18 *If* U *is a* $\beta,\eta-$*normal form then*

$$U \equiv \lambda x_1. \ldots \lambda x_n.\, h\, V_1 \ldots V_k$$

where $n \geq 0$, $k \geq 0$, h *is a variable or* fix_σ^0, *and* $V_1, \ldots, V_k$ *are* $\beta,\eta-$*normal forms.*

Proof By induction on the structure of U. ■

Lemma 5.19 *If* U *is a* $\beta,\eta-$*normal form and* $\Gamma \rhd U : \sigma$, *then there exists a term* N *such that* $\Gamma \rhd N : \sigma$, $Erase(N) \equiv U$, *and for any term* P *such that* $\Gamma \rhd P : \sigma$ *and* $Erase(P) \equiv U$, *we have that* $\Gamma \rhd P \xrightarrow{\sigma}\!\!\!\!\rightarrow_{lab} N$.

Proof Analogous to Lemma 5.8. The only significant extra case to consider is when U looks like $\lambda x_1 \ldots \lambda x_{n-1}. \lambda x_n. x_n(\mathit{fix}^0_\tau\, x_n)$, so that P could take the form $\lambda x_1{:}\sigma_1 \ldots \lambda x_{n-1}{:}\sigma_{n-1}. \mathit{fix}^1_\tau$. But we have $\Gamma \triangleright P \xrightarrow{\sigma}_{lab} P'$, where the term $P' \equiv \lambda x_1{:}\sigma_1 \ldots \lambda x_{n-1}{:}\sigma_{n-1}. \lambda x_n{:}\tau \to \tau. x_n(\mathit{fix}^0_\tau\, x_n)$ will reduce to N by the earlier argument. ∎

Theorem 5.20 *Suppose that* $\Gamma \triangleright M : \sigma$ *and* $\Gamma \triangleright M \xrightarrow{\sigma}\!\!\!\!\!\rightarrow_{lab} N_1, \Gamma \triangleright M \xrightarrow{\sigma}\!\!\!\!\!\rightarrow_{lab} N_2$, *then there is a term* $\Gamma \triangleright P : \sigma$ *such that* $\Gamma \triangleright N_1 \xrightarrow{\sigma}\!\!\!\!\!\rightarrow_{lab} P$ *and* $\Gamma \triangleright N_2 \xrightarrow{\sigma}\!\!\!\!\!\rightarrow_{lab} P$.

Proof Same as proof of Theorem 5.10. ∎

6 Conclusion

Using a proof method for extensions of typed lambda calculus with fixed-point operators that is based on labelled reduction, we have proved a series of results. For typed lambda calculus extended with fixed-point operators and additional operations satisfying certain conditions, we have proved confluence and completeness of leftmost reduction, as corollaries of the confluence and termination of labelled reduction. While these two results might have been considered "folk theorems," we were unable to find any "folk proofs," either in the literature or by word-of-mouth (except for our prior paper on the topic, Howard and Mitchell 1990). For typed lambda calculus with subtyping, we observe that confluence fails for β, η-reduction in the presence of subtyping. This problem is repaired by adding an intuitive but unusual reduction system, proved confluent using termination of β, η-reduction for typed lambda calculus. We then use the labelling technique to extend this confluence proof to typed lambda calculus with subtyping and fixed-point operators. Further discussion of types, subtyping and reduction may be found in (Hoang 1995). For a more recent, modular approach to confluence proofs for systems with fixed-point operators and *expansive* extensional rules, see (Di Cosmo and Kesner 1994).

Acknowledgments Thanks to Andrew Gordon and Andrew Pitts for inviting us to submit this paper and their encouragement while the paper was in preparation. The authors were sponsored, in part, by NSF Grants CCR-9303099-001, an NSF Presidential Young Investigator Award to J. Mitchell and an NSF Graduate Fellowship to B. Howard.

References

H.P. Barendregt. *The Lambda Calculus: Its Syntax and Semantics*. North-Holland, Amsterdam, 1984. Second edition.

V. Breazu-Tannen. Combining algebra and higher-order types. In *Proc. IEEE Symp. on Logic in Computer Science*, pages 82–90, 1988.

V. Breazu-Tannen and J.H. Gallier. Polymorphic rewriting conserves algebraic strong normalization and confluence. In *16th Int'l Colloq. on Automata, Languages and Programming*, pages 137–159, Berlin, 1989. Springer LNCS 372. A revised version appears in *Information and Computation*, 114:1–29, 1994.

R. Di Cosmo and D. Kesner. Combining first order algebraic rewriting systems, recursion and extensional lambda calculi. In *21st Int'l Colloq. on Automata, Languages and Programming*, pages 462–472, Berlin, 1994. Springer LNCS 820.

M. Ellis and B. Stroustrop. *The Annotated C++ Reference Manual*. Addison-Wesley, 1990.

C.A. Gunter. *Semantics of Programming Languages: Structures and Techniques*. MIT Press, Cambridge, MA, 1992.

B.T. Howard and J.C. Mitchell. Operational and axiomatic semantics of PCF. In *ACM Conference on LISP and Functional Programming*, pages 298–306, 1990.

M. Hoang. *Type Inference and Program Evaluation in the Presence of Subtyping*. PhD thesis, Stanford University, 1995.

E. Horowitz. *Fundamentals of Programming Languages*. Computer Science Press, 1984.

B.T. Howard. *Fixed points and extensionality in typed functional programming languages*. PhD thesis, Stanford University, 1992.

J.M.E. Hyland. A syntactic characterization of the equality in some models of the lambda calculus. *J. London Math. Society*, 2(12):361–370, 1976.

J.W. Klop. *Combinatory Reduction Systems*. PhD thesis, University of Utrecht, 1980. Published as Mathematical Center Tract 129.

J.-J. Lévy. An algebraic interpretation of the λ-β-k-calculus and a labeled λ-calculus. In C. Böhm, editor, *Proc. Lambda calculus and computer science theory*, pages 147–165. Springer LNCS 37, 1975.

B. Meyer. *Eiffel: The Language*. Prentice-Hall, 1992.

J.C. Mitchell. Type inference with simple subtypes. *J. Functional Programming*, 1(3):245–286, 1991.

J.C. Mitchell. *Foundations for Programming Languages*. MIT Press, 1996.

R.P. Nederpelt. *Strong Normalization in a typed lambda calculus with lambda structured types*. PhD thesis, Technological Univ. Eindhoven, 1973.

Y. Toyama. On the Church-Rosser property for the direct sum of term rewriting systems. *J. Assoc. Computing Machinery*, 34:128–143, 1987.

D.T. van Dalen. *The language theory of Automath*. PhD thesis, Technological Univ. Eindhoven, 1980.

C. Wadsworth. The relation between computational and denotational properties for Scott's D^∞ models. *Siam J. Comput.*, 5(3):488–521, 1976.

Semantics of memory management for polymorphic languages

Greg Morrisett and Robert Harper

Abstract

We present a static and dynamic semantics for an abstract machine that evaluates expressions of a polymorphic programming language. Unlike traditional semantics, our abstract machine exposes many important issues of memory management, such as value sharing and control representation. We prove the soundness of the static semantics with respect to the dynamic semantics using traditional techniques. We then show how these same techniques may be used to establish the soundness of various memory management strategies, including type-based, tag-free garbage collection; tail-call elimination; and environment strengthening.

1 Introduction

Type theory and operational semantics are remarkably effective tools for programming language design and implementation (Milner, Tofte, and Harper 1990; Cardelli 1989). An important and influential example is provided by *The Definition of Standard ML* (SML) (Milner, Tofte, and Harper 1990). The *static semantics* of SML is specified as a collection of *elaboration rules* that defines the context-sensitive constraints on the formation of programs. The *dynamic semantics* is specified as a collection of *evaluation rules* that defines the operational semantics of a program. The static and dynamic semantics are related by a *type soundness* theorem stating that certain forms of run-time error cannot arise in the evaluation of a well-formed program. The methodology of *The Definition of Standard ML* has been refined in a number of subsequent studies of the type theory and operational semantics of SML and related languages.

Of particular interest for the purposes of this paper is the variety of methods for defining the operational semantics of deterministic, sequential languages. Two main approaches have emerged, one based on *evaluation relations*, the other based on *transition systems*. The evaluation-based approach is typified by Kahn's *natural semantics* (Clément, Despeyroux, Despeyroux, Hascoet, and Kahn 1985) and is used extensively in *The Definition of Standard ML*. The transition-based approach is typified by Plotkin's *structured operational semantics* (Plotkin 1981), but also includes approaches based on abstract machines (Cousineau, Curien, and Mauny 1985) and program rewriting (Felleisen and Hieb 1992; Wright and Felleisen 1994). Both approaches share the goal of formulating a semantics that suppresses irrelevant details, avoids over-specification, and facilitates reasoning about programs. But experience has shown that these goals are difficult to achieve in a single framework.

As a case in point, we consider the memory allocation behaviour of programs. A significant advantage of high-level programming languages, such as SML, is that the details of memory management are inaccessible to the programmer. For example, in SML it is impossible to determine whether or not a pair of values is allocated in the heap or in registers. This is not an oversight! Rather, the intention is to free the programmer from the details of memory management, and to allow the compiler to make representation choices based on contingencies not entirely within the programmer's control[1].

Applying the abstraction criterion discussed above, the operational semantics of such languages should abstract the details of memory management from the definition of the language. Indeed, the dynamic semantics given in *The Definition of Standard ML* avoids explicit treatment of memory allocation except inasmuch as it is observable through the use of reference types. The semantics freely forms tuples, environments, closures, and recursive data structures without regard to their representation in memory. Consequently, no accounting of memory sharing is provided by the semantics.

For many purposes, such as reasoning about the extensional behaviour of programs, this approach is ideal. Yet issues of memory management cannot be entirely overlooked. For example, an important use of operational semantics is to serve as a guide to the compiler writer, who must make data structure representation decisions that critically affect the performance of compiled code. In this case it is essential to make storage allocation decisions explicit in the semantics. Otherwise, important notions, such as space safety (Appel 1992a; Shao and Appel 1994), tail recursion (Clinger and Rees 1991), and garbage collection (Wilson 1995), remain vague notions outside of the scope of a rigorous semantics.

In this paper we explore the use of operational semantics to define not only the high-level execution behaviour of programs, but also their low-level allocation behaviour. We consider as a case study an explicitly-typed, polymorphic programming language with unbounded recursion, nullary and binary product types, and lists. This language is sufficiently rich to encompass important issues, including allocation of types at run-time, allocation of aggregate data structures, inductively defined data structures, and the representation of types as data structures. Yet it is sufficiently simple that it is possible to give a rigorous treatment of its memory allocation behaviour and sharing of storage among complex values. To do so, we give an operational semantics for the language formulated as a transition system between states of an abstract machine. The machine state includes a *heap*, containing allocated types and data; an *environment*, containing types and bindings for variables; a *stack*, containing control information; and an *expression* to be evaluated. The operational semantics is related to the type system by a soundness

[1] See Appel's critique for a discussion of this and related points (Appel 1992b).

theorem characterizing the shapes of values of each type. We prefer a transition system to an evaluation relation because it is necessary for the development to make the control stack explicit in the semantics, rather than leave it implicit in the relational metatheory, as is customary in evaluation semantics.

To illustrate the use of the framework, we consider in detail several critical storage management problems. We give a detailed treatment of *tag-free copying garbage collection*. The collector is presented as a transition system that faithfully captures the behaviour of a copying garbage collector, including the use of type information to "parse" and "trace" heap values during collection. We provide the first proof of correctness for such a collector, a significant advance on current practice. In addition, we discuss two other forms of garbage collection: *tail recursion elimination*, which reduces the space required by the control stack, and *black holing*, which reduces the space required by environments. All of these memory management techniques are used within the TIL/ML compiler (Tarditi, Morrisett, Cheng, Stone, Harper, and Lee 1996), and thus the material presented here provides a faithful model of this particular implementation. Nevertheless, the framework we propose is general enough to model a variety of language implementations.

The rest of this paper is organized as follows. In Section 2, we present the syntax and static semantics of our core polymorphic language, $\lambda_{gc}^{\rightarrow\forall}$. In Section 3, we present an abstract machine for evaluating $\lambda_{gc}^{\rightarrow\forall}$ expressions. The section provides both a static and dynamic semantics for the abstract machine and a proof of type soundness.

In Section 4, we consider the issue of heap garbage and a specification for a general-purpose heap-garbage collector. We show the soundness of a particular class of collectors, namely those based on inaccessibility of heap objects. In Section 5, we show how to implement a particular heap-garbage collection algorithm, namely the *type-based, tag-free* garbage collector used by Tolmach (Tolmach 1994), which is closely related to the *mostly tag-free* collector used by the TIL/ML compiler. We prove the correctness of the algorithm using syntactic techniques similar to those used to prove type soundness for the abstract machine.

In Section 6, we consider other kinds of garbage in the abstract machine, notably stack garbage and environment garbage. We show how the addition of a tail-call facility can be used to eliminate a certain class of stack garbage, and how the addition of environment strengthening rules can be used to eliminate a certain class of environment garbage. Again, correctness of these memory management techniques can be shown through the syntactic methods employed in previous sections.

Finally, we discuss related work in Section 7, and we summarize and conclude in Section 8.

2 The $\lambda_{gc}^{\rightarrow\forall}$ Language

In this section, we present $\lambda_{gc}^{\rightarrow\forall}$, a call-by-value variant of the Girard-Reynolds polymorphic λ-calculus (Girard 1972; Reynolds 1974). In the following section, we define an abstract machine for evaluating $\lambda_{gc}^{\rightarrow\forall}$ expressions. The abstract machine makes explicit many operational details that are pertinent to memory management, such as the heap, the control stack, and the environment.

Perhaps the most novel aspect of $\lambda_{gc}^{\rightarrow\forall}$ is that, unlike traditional models of typed-languages, type information is maintained throughout evaluation in order to support type-based, tag-free garbage collection. Run-time type information can also be used to support tag-free polymorphic equality, unboxed data constructors, and unboxed function arguments, as in the TIL/ML compiler. Together, these representation optimizations result in a reduction of over 50% in allocation and 42% in running times over conventional representations(Morrisett 1995; Harper and Morrisett 1995). Therefore, modelling allocation, sharing, and garbage collection of run-time representations of *types* is just as important as modelling memory management for *values*.

To simplify the abstract machine, the expressions and types of $\lambda_{gc}^{\rightarrow\forall}$ are restricted to *named form*, also known as *A Normal Form* (Sabry and Felleisen 1992). The restriction to named form amounts to the requirement that the result of every step of evaluation or allocation be bound to a variable, which is then used to refer to the result of this computation. Every expression and every type of the second-order λ-calculus can be put into named form by simply introducing `let` and `type` expressions appropriately. For example, one named form representation of the expression $(\lambda x{:}\text{list[unit]}.\,\texttt{cons}(\langle\rangle, x))\,\texttt{nil}$ is:

$$
\begin{array}{l}
\texttt{type}\ t = \text{unit}\ \texttt{in} \\
\texttt{type}\ t_1 = \text{list}[t]\ \texttt{in} \\
\texttt{type}\ t_2 = t_1 \rightarrow t_1\ \texttt{in} \\
\texttt{let}\ x_1{:}t_2 = \lambda x{:}t_1.\,(\texttt{let}\ x_2{:}t = \langle\rangle\ \texttt{in} \\
\qquad\qquad\qquad\qquad\quad \texttt{let}\ x_3{:}t_1 = \texttt{cons}(x_2, x)\ \texttt{in} \\
\qquad\qquad\qquad\qquad\quad x_3)\ \texttt{in} \\
\texttt{let}\ x_4{:}t_1 = \texttt{nil}\ \texttt{in} \\
\texttt{let}\ x_5{:}t_1 = x_1\, x_4 \\
\texttt{in}\ x_5
\end{array}
$$

The restriction to named form is largely a matter of technical convenience; it ensures that every allocation site is named by an identifier. The penalty is that the typing rules are somewhat more complicated since we must expand bindings of type variables during type checking (see Section 2.2). The advantage is that we can easily recover the type of an expression from the types attached to the bindings of its sub-expressions.

(type variable)	t		
(type)	σ	::=	$t \mid \text{unit} \mid \sigma_1 \times \sigma_2 \mid \sigma_1 \to \sigma_2 \mid \text{list}[\sigma] \mid \forall t.\sigma$
(named form type)	τ	::=	$t \mid \text{let } t = \nu \text{ in } \tau$
(type binding)	ν	::=	$\text{unit} \mid t_1 \times t_2 \mid t_1 \to t_2 \mid \text{list}[t] \mid \forall t.\tau$
(value variable)	x		
(named form expr.)	e	::=	$x \mid \texttt{let}\, x{:}t = b\, \texttt{in}\, e \mid \texttt{type}\, t = \nu\, \texttt{in}\, e$
(expr. binding)	b	::=	$a \mid c$
(allocation)	a	::=	$\langle\rangle \mid \langle x_1, x_2\rangle \mid \texttt{fix}\ x{:}t(x_1{:}t_1).e \mid$ $\texttt{nil} \mid \texttt{cons}(x_1, x_2) \mid \Lambda t.\, e$
(computation)	c	::=	$\pi_1\, x \mid \pi_2\, x \mid x_1\, x_2 \mid$ $\texttt{case}(x, e_0, \lambda[x_1{:}t_1, x_2{:}t_2].e_1) \mid x\,[t]$

Figure 1: Syntax of the $\lambda_{\text{gc}}^{\to\forall}$Language

2.1 Syntax of $\lambda_{\text{gc}}^{\to\forall}$

The syntax of the $\lambda_{\text{gc}}^{\to\forall}$ language is defined in Figure 1. Types include type variables, unit, binary products, arrow types, list types, and type abstractions. Instead of using types directly to decorate $\lambda_{\text{gc}}^{\to\forall}$ terms, we use a named form representation of types in order to make allocation and sharing of type information explicit. A named form type is either a type variable or a let that binds a named form type *binding* (ν) to a variable in the scope of a named form type. Named form type bindings include primitive constructors (e.g., unit), compound constructors where the components are type variables (e.g., $t_1 \times t_2$, $t_1 \to t_2$, and $\text{list}[t]$), or a type abstraction where the body of the abstraction is a named form type.

The expressions of $\lambda_{\text{gc}}^{\to\forall}$ are also required to be in named form. They are variables, `let` expressions binding a named form binding to a variable in the scope of a named form expression, and `type` expressions binding a named form type binding to a type variable in the scope of a named form expression.

A named form expression binding is either an allocation binding or a computation binding. Allocation bindings correspond to values that will be allocated on the heap. These consist of primitive values (e.g., $\langle\rangle$, `nil`), compound values where the components are variables (e.g., $\langle x_1, x_2\rangle$, $\texttt{cons}(x_1, x_2)$), recursive value abstractions ($\texttt{fix}\ x{:}t(x_1{:}t_1).e$), and type abstractions ($\Lambda t.\, e$). We use $\lambda x_1{:}t_1.e$ to abbreviate a recursive value abstraction $\texttt{fix}\ x{:}t(x_1{:}t_1).e$ where x does not occur free in e. Computation bindings correspond to computational steps to be taken during evaluation. These consist of a `case` expression for testing and deconstructing lists, projection for pairs, and application for both term and type abstractions.

We have chosen to allocate all values to simplify the presentation. However, it is straightforward to modify the language to support unallocated values by defining a syntactic class of "small" values and by allowing small values to occur within bindings. For instance, both $\langle\rangle$ and `nil` would be suitable small values. This corresponds to the use of machine registers, rather than memory locations, to store values.

The binding conventions for the language are familiar: in $\forall t.\sigma$, type variable t is bound within σ; in let $t = \nu$ in τ and $\forall t.\tau$ type variable t is bound within τ; in $\texttt{type}\, t = \nu \;\texttt{in}\, e$ and $\Lambda t.\, e$, type variable t is bound within e; in $\texttt{let}\, x{:}t = b\, \texttt{in}\, e$, value variable x is bound within e; and in $\texttt{fix}\;\; x{:}t(x_1{:}t_1).e$, both x and x_1 are bound within e.

Syntactic objects are identified up to a systematic renaming (i.e., α-conversion) of bound variables. We use $FV(X)$ to denote the free value variables of a syntactic object X, and $FTV(X)$ to denote the free type variables of X. Capture-avoiding substitution of a type σ_1 for the free occurrences of a type variable t within a type σ_2, denoted $\{\sigma_1/t\}\sigma_2$, is defined as usual, given the binding conventions listed above.

2.2 Typing Rules for $\lambda_{\mathrm{gc}}^{\rightarrow\forall}$

The typing rules for $\lambda_{\mathrm{gc}}^{\rightarrow\forall}$ are defined relative to contexts declaring type variables and value variables.

$$\begin{array}{lrcl} \text{(variable type assignment)} & \Gamma & ::= & \emptyset \mid \Gamma[x{:}\sigma] \\ \text{(type variable context)} & \Delta & ::= & \emptyset \mid \Delta[t] \mid \Delta[t = \sigma] \end{array}$$

We consider type assignments as finite maps from value variables to types. Hence, the order of bindings in a type assignment is considered irrelevant, and a variable may not be declared more than once in a single type assignment.

There are two forms of type variable declarations, *abstract* declarations ($[t]$) and *transparent* declarations ($[t = \sigma]$). Abstract declarations are used when processing a polymorphic abstraction (e.g., $\Lambda t.\, e$), whereas transparent declarations are used when processing a `type` binding (e.g., let $t = \nu$ in τ and $\texttt{type}\, t = \nu\; \texttt{in}\, e$). We define $\mathit{Abstr}(\Delta)$ to be the set of abstract bindings in the context Δ, $\mathit{Transp}(\Delta)$ to be the domain of the set of transparent bindings in Δ, and $\mathit{Dom}(\Delta) = \mathit{Abstr}(\Delta) \cup \mathit{Transp}(\Delta)$.

The empty context ($\emptyset$) is always well-formed. The context $\Delta[t]$ is well-formed iff Δ is well-formed and $t \notin \mathit{Dom}(\Delta)$; The context $\Delta[t = \sigma]$ is well-formed iff Δ is well-formed, $t \notin \mathit{Dom}(\Delta)$, and the free type variables of σ are a subset of $\mathit{Abstr}(\Delta)$. Hence, a free type variable occurring in a transparent binding must be previously declared as an abstract type variable. A type assignment Γ is well-formed with respect to a context Δ iff $FTV(\Gamma) \subseteq \mathit{Abstr}(\Delta)$. Finally, we consider type variable contexts equivalent up to any re-ordering of the bindings that respects the dependencies of transparent bindings on abstract bindings.

1.	$\Delta \vdash \tau \Downarrow \sigma$	named form type τ reduces to σ	(Fig. 3)
2.	$\Delta \vdash \nu \Downarrow \sigma$	type binding ν reduces to σ	(Fig. 3)
3.	$\Delta; \Gamma \vdash e : \sigma$	expression e has type σ	(Fig. 4)
4.	$\Delta; \Gamma \vdash b : \sigma$	binding b has type σ	(Fig. 4)

Figure 2: Typing Judgements for the $\lambda_{gc}^{\rightarrow\forall}$ Language

Judgements of the typing rules are listed in Figure 2, and the axioms and inference rules that may be used to derive these judgements are given in Figures 3 and 4.

Intuitively, the first two judgements $\Delta \vdash \tau \Downarrow \sigma$ and $\Delta \vdash \nu \Downarrow \sigma$ substitute transparent type bindings in Δ for free type variables in τ and ν respectively, and eliminate any nested let-expressions within the named form type to obtain the equivalent conventional type σ. Judgements 3 and 4 are derived from conventional typing rules for the polymorphic λ-calculus.

Throughout, we assume that all judgement components are well-formed. For example, in order to derive $\Delta; \Gamma \vdash e : \sigma$, we assume that Δ is well-formed and Γ is well-formed with respect to Δ. Hence, many side-conditions, such as the requirement that a variable not be bound twice in a context, are left implicit. From the well-formedness condition and the rules, we may derive the following properties of the typing judgements.

Lemma 2.1

1. *If $\Delta \vdash \tau \Downarrow \sigma$, then $FTV(\tau) \subseteq Dom(\Delta)$ and $FTV(\sigma) \subseteq Abstr(\Delta)$.*
2. *If $\Delta \vdash \nu \Downarrow \sigma$, then $FTV(\nu) \subseteq Dom(\Delta)$ and $FTV(\sigma) \subseteq Abstr(\Delta)$.*
3. *If $\Delta; \Gamma \vdash e : \sigma$, then $FV(e) \subseteq Dom(\Gamma)$, $FTV(e) \subseteq Dom(\Delta)$, and $FTV(\sigma) \subseteq Abstr(\Delta)$.*
4. *If $\Delta; \Gamma \vdash b : \sigma$, then $FV(b) \subseteq Dom(\Gamma)$, $FTV(b) \subseteq Dom(\Delta)$, and $FTV(\sigma) \subseteq Abstr(\Delta)$.*

3 The $\lambda_{gc}^{\rightarrow\forall}$ Abstract Machine

The dynamic semantics of the $\lambda_{gc}^{\rightarrow\forall}$ language is given by a transition system between states of an abstract machine. The abstract machine is derived from the CESK machine of Felleisen and Friedman (1987). States of the machine are a

1. $\Delta \vdash \tau \Downarrow \sigma$

$$\textbf{(opaque)}\ \ \Delta[t] \vdash t \Downarrow t \qquad\qquad \textbf{(transp)}\ \ \Delta[t=\sigma] \vdash t \Downarrow \sigma$$

$$\textbf{(look-opaque)}\ \ \frac{\Delta \vdash t \Downarrow \sigma}{\Delta[t'] \vdash t \Downarrow \sigma}\ \ (t \neq t')$$

$$\textbf{(look-transp)}\ \ \frac{\Delta \vdash t \Downarrow \sigma}{\Delta[t'=\sigma'] \vdash t \Downarrow \sigma}\ \ (t \neq t')$$

$$\textbf{(type-def)}\ \ \frac{\Delta \vdash \nu \Downarrow \sigma' \qquad \Delta[t=\sigma'] \vdash \tau \Downarrow \sigma}{\Delta \vdash \text{let } t = \nu \text{ in } \tau \Downarrow \sigma}$$

2. $\Delta \vdash \nu \Downarrow \sigma$

$$\textbf{(unit)}\ \ \Delta \vdash \text{unit} \Downarrow \text{unit} \qquad\qquad \textbf{(prod)}\ \ \frac{\Delta \vdash t_1 \Downarrow \sigma_1 \qquad \Delta \vdash t_2 \Downarrow \sigma_2}{\Delta \vdash t_1 \times t_2 \Downarrow \sigma_1 \times \sigma_2}$$

$$\textbf{(arrow)}\ \ \frac{\Delta \vdash t_1 \Downarrow \sigma_1 \qquad \Delta \vdash t_2 \Downarrow \sigma_2}{\Delta \vdash t_1 \to t_2 \Downarrow \sigma_1 \to \sigma_2} \qquad\qquad \textbf{(list)}\ \ \frac{\Delta \vdash t \Downarrow \sigma}{\Delta \vdash \text{list}[t] \Downarrow \text{list}[\sigma]}$$

$$\textbf{(all)}\ \ \frac{\Delta[t] \vdash \tau \Downarrow \sigma}{\Delta \vdash \forall t.\tau \Downarrow \forall t.\sigma}$$

Figure 3: Named Form Type Reduction

3. $\Delta;\Gamma \vdash e : \sigma$

$$\textbf{(var)}\ \Delta;\Gamma[x{:}\sigma] \vdash x : \sigma \qquad \textbf{(let)}\ \frac{\Delta;\Gamma \vdash b : \sigma' \quad \Delta \vdash t \Downarrow \sigma' \quad \Delta;\Gamma[x{:}\sigma'] \vdash e : \sigma}{\Delta;\Gamma \vdash \texttt{let}\, x{:}t = b\, \texttt{in}\, e : \sigma}$$

$$\textbf{(type)}\ \frac{\Delta \vdash \nu \Downarrow \sigma' \quad \Delta[t=\sigma'];\Gamma \vdash e : \sigma}{\Delta;\Gamma \vdash \texttt{type}\, t = \nu\, \texttt{in}\, e : \sigma}$$

4. $\Delta;\Gamma \vdash b : \sigma$

$$\textbf{(unit-I)}\ \Delta;\Gamma \vdash \langle\rangle : \text{unit} \qquad \textbf{(prod-I)}\ \frac{\Delta;\Gamma \vdash x_1 : \sigma_1 \quad \Delta;\Gamma \vdash x_2 : \sigma_2}{\Delta;\Gamma \vdash \langle x_1, x_2\rangle : \sigma_1 \times \sigma_2}$$

$$\textbf{(prod-E)}\ \frac{\Delta;\Gamma \vdash x : \sigma_1 \times \sigma_2}{\Delta;\Gamma \vdash \pi_i\, x : \sigma_i \quad (i = 1,2)}$$

$$\textbf{(arrow-I)}\ \frac{\Delta \vdash t \Downarrow \sigma_1 \to \sigma_2 \quad \Delta \vdash t_1 \Downarrow \sigma_1 \quad \Delta;\Gamma[x{:}\sigma_1 \to \sigma_2, x_1{:}\sigma_1] \vdash e : \sigma_2}{\Delta;\Gamma \vdash \texttt{fix}\ \ x{:}t(x_1{:}t_1).e : \sigma_1 \to \sigma_2} \qquad \textbf{(arrow-E)}\ \frac{\Delta;\Gamma \vdash x : \sigma_1 \to \sigma \quad \Delta;\Gamma \vdash x_1 : \sigma_1}{\Delta;\Gamma \vdash x\, x_1 : \sigma}$$

$$\textbf{(list-I1)}\ \frac{FTV(\sigma) \subseteq Dom(\Delta)}{\Delta;\Gamma \vdash \texttt{nil} : \text{list}[\sigma]} \qquad \textbf{(list-I2)}\ \frac{\Delta;\Gamma \vdash x_1 : \sigma \quad \Delta;\Gamma \vdash x_2 : \text{list}[\sigma]}{\Delta;\Gamma \vdash \texttt{cons}(x_1, x_2) : \text{list}[\sigma]}$$

$$\textbf{(list-E)}\ \frac{\Delta;\Gamma \vdash x : \text{list}[\sigma'] \quad \Delta;\Gamma \vdash e_0 : \sigma \quad \Delta \vdash t_1 \Downarrow \sigma' \quad \Delta \vdash t_2 \Downarrow \text{list}[\sigma'] \quad \Delta;\Gamma[x_1{:}\sigma', x_2{:}\text{list}[\sigma']] \vdash e_1 : \sigma}{\Delta;\Gamma \vdash \texttt{case}(x, e_0, \lambda[x_1{:}t_1, x_2{:}t_2].e_1) : \sigma}$$

$$\textbf{(all-I)}\ \frac{\Delta[t];\Gamma \vdash e : \sigma}{\Delta;\Gamma \vdash \Lambda t.\, e : \forall t.\sigma} \qquad \textbf{(all-E)}\ \frac{\Delta;\Gamma \vdash x_1 : \forall t.\sigma \quad \Delta \vdash t_1 \Downarrow \sigma'}{\Delta;\Gamma \vdash x_1\,[t_1] : \{\sigma'/t\}\sigma}$$

Figure 4: Expression Typing

quadruple (H, S, E, e) where H is a *heap*, S is a *stack*, E is an *environment*, and e is an expression of the $\lambda_{\mathrm{gc}}^{\rightarrow\forall}$ language. The heap consists of a *type heap* containing allocated types, and a *value heap* containing allocated values. The environment consists of a *type environment* providing bindings for type variables, and a *value environment* providing types and values for ordinary variables. The stack consists of a composition of *frames*, each of which is a *closure* consisting of an environment and a λ-term.

In principle, we can eliminate a level of indirection by making environments map variables directly to types and values. However, this precludes sharing types and values across different environments, leading to an unrealistic model of space consumption.

This organization faithfully reflects a conventional implementation of the $\lambda_{\mathrm{gc}}^{\rightarrow\forall}$ language, except that it abstracts from the allocation of environments. (For a treatment of this topic, see Minamide, Morrisett, and Harper (1996).) In particular, this organization is a fairly accurate model of the run-time data structures used by the TIL/ML compiler (Tarditi, Morrisett, Cheng, Stone, Harper, and Lee 1996).

To establish soundness of the type system, we define a syntactic typing discipline for the states of the abstract machine, and prove progress and preservation lemmas for it. Although they do not arise in the $\lambda_{\mathrm{gc}}^{\rightarrow\forall}$ language, the syntactic typing rules for the abstract machine support cyclic data structures in the heap, following the approach suggested by Harper (1994). Hence, our abstract machine is compatible with references, arrays, and other mechanisms that may introduce cyclic data structures[2].

3.1 Syntax of the Abstract Machine

The syntax of the states of the abstract machine is given in Figure 5. We use p and l to range over *pointers* and *locations*, respectively. Heaps contain a type heap mapping pointers to heap-allocated representations of types (μ) and a value heap mapping locations to heap-allocated representations of values (h). Environments contain a type environment mapping type variables to pointers and a value environment mapping value variables to type variables and locations. Intuitively, pointers and locations correspond to machine addresses, whereas variables correspond to machine registers or stack slots.

Type heap values include base constructors; n-ary constructors, where the component types are pointers to other heap-allocated types (e.g., $p_1 \rightarrow p_2$); and type closures. Type closures contain a named form representation of a polymorphic type ($\forall t.\tau$) and a type environment mapping the free type variables of the polymorphic type to pointers bound in the type heap.

Heap values include primitive values; constructed values, where the components are locations of other allocated values (e.g., $\langle l_1, l_2 \rangle$); or value closures. Value

[2]Our syntactic approach is in contrast to the complex fixed point constructions used elsewhere (Tofte 1990).

(pointer)	p		
(type env.)	TE	$::=$	$\emptyset \mid TE[t \mapsto p]$
(type heap value)	μ	$::=$	$\text{unit} \mid p_1 \times p_2 \mid p_1 \to p_2 \mid \text{list}[p] \mid \langle\!\langle TE, \forall t.\tau \rangle\!\rangle$
(type heap)	TH	$::=$	$\emptyset \mid TH[p \mapsto \mu]$
(location)	l		
(value env.)	VE	$::=$	$\emptyset \mid VE[x{:}t \mapsto l]$
(heap value)	h	$::=$	$\langle\rangle \mid \langle l_1, l_2 \rangle \mid \langle\!\langle E, \texttt{fix}\ x{:}t(x_1{:}t_1).e \rangle\!\rangle \mid$
			$\langle\!\langle E, \Lambda t.\, e \rangle\!\rangle \mid \texttt{nil} \mid \texttt{cons}(l_1, l_2)$
(value heap)	VH	$::=$	$\emptyset \mid TH[l \mapsto h]$
(environment)	E	$::=$	(TE, VE)
(heap)	H	$::=$	(TH, VH)
(stack)	S	$::=$	$[] \mid S \circ \langle\!\langle E, \lambda x{:}t.e \rangle\!\rangle$
(program)	P	$::=$	(H, S, E, e)
(answer)	A	$::=$	$(H, [], E, x)$
(result)	r	$::=$	$\top \mid \bot \mid \texttt{*wrong*}$

Figure 5: Syntax of the $\lambda_{\text{gc}}^{\to\forall}$ Machine

closures consist of an environment and a named form representation of either a type- or value-abstraction. The environment of a closure provides bindings for the free type and value variables of the closure's abstraction.

Stacks are either empty or else a composition of a stack and a stack frame. Stack frames are represented as closures with an environment and a value abstraction. The environment provides bindings for the free type and value variables of the abstraction. Intuitively, by composing the closures that make up the stack frame, we obtain the current "continuation" for the abstract machine. If we chose to restrict $\lambda_{\text{gc}}^{\to\forall}$ expressions to continuation-passing style (CPS) as in the SML/NJ compiler (Appel and MacQueen 1991), there would be no need for a stack in the abstract machine. However, many implementations do not use a CPS representation, and memory management of the stack is a key issue for these systems. We therefore choose to work with the more general framework at the price of a slightly more complicated abstract machine. In Section 6.1 we discuss in further detail the connection between a CPS-based implementation and our abstract machine.

Answers are programs that represent terminal states of the abstract machine, and are a subset of programs where the expression component is simply a value variable and the stack is empty. Results are *semantic* tokens that represent whether programs converge, diverge, or become stuck due to a type error, respectively. To simplify the presentation, these are the only observable consequences of evaluating a program (see Definition 3.5).

The binding conventions governing these constructs are as follows:

- In the phrase $\langle\!\langle TE, \forall t.\tau \rangle\!\rangle$, all type variables in the domain of TE are bound in $\forall t.\tau$.
- In the type heap $TH[p \mapsto \mu]$, all type pointers in the domain of TH are bound in μ.
- For any closure $\langle\!\langle (TE, VE), e \rangle\!\rangle$, where e is either a fix, lambda, or type-abstraction, all type variables in the domain of TE are bound in VE and e, and all value variables in the domain of VE are bound in e.
- All locations in the domain of VH are bound in each h occurring in the co-domain of VH.
- For a program $((TH, VH), S, (TE, VE), e)$:
  1. All pointers in the domain of TH are bound in VH, S, and TE,
  2. All locations in the domain of VH are bound in S and VE,
  3. All type variables in the domain of TE are bound in VE and e,
  4. All value variables in the domain of VE are bound in e.

All syntactic forms are identified up to systematic renaming of bound variables. We write $FL(X)$ to denote the free locations of a syntactic object X, and $FP(X)$ to denote the free pointers of X.

No value variable or type variable may be bound more than once in an environment, nor may any location or pointer be bound more than once in a heap. Type environments, value environments, and value heaps are considered equivalent up to any re-ordering. Type heaps are considered equivalent up to any reordering that respects previously bound pointers. Furthermore, the typing rules preclude cycles in the type heap, but allow cycles in the value heap[3]. When convenient, we treat type environments as finite maps from type variables to pointers, value environments as finite maps from value variables to type variables and locations, type heaps as finite maps from pointers to type heap values, and value heaps as finite maps from locations to heap values.

When convenient, we use the following syntactic conventions:

- $E[t \mapsto p]$ abbreviates $(TE[t \mapsto p], VE)$ when $E = (TE, VE)$.
- $E[x{:}t \mapsto l]$ abbreviates $(TE, VE[x{:}t \mapsto l])$ when $E = (TE, VE)$.
- $E(t)$ abbreviates p when $E = (TE[t \mapsto p], VE)$.

[3]It is possible to allow cycles in the type heap to support, for instance, recursive types. We choose the simpler setting to avoid some technical difficulties in constructing closed types from allocated types in the proofs. However, the algorithms for garbage collection presented in Section 5 would continue to work even in the presence of circular type heaps.

- $E(x)$ abbreviates l when $E = (TE, VE[x{:}t \mapsto l])$.
- $H[p \mapsto \mu]$ abbreviates $(TH[p \mapsto \mu], VH)$ when $H = (TH, VH)$.
- $H[l \mapsto h]$ abbreviates $(TH, VH[l \mapsto h])$ when $H = (TH, VH)$.
- $H(p)$ abbreviates μ when $H = (TH[p \mapsto \mu], VH)$.
- $H(l)$ abbreviates h when $H = (TH, VH[l \mapsto h])$.
- $S_1 \bar{\circ} S_2$ abbreviates S_1 when $S_2 = []$.
- $S_1 \bar{\circ} S_2$ abbreviates $(S_1 \bar{\circ} S) \circ \langle\!\langle \lambda x{:}t.e \rangle\!\rangle$ when $S_2 = S \circ \langle\!\langle E, \lambda x{:}t.e \rangle\!\rangle$.
- $F_1 \uplus F_2$ abbreviates the the union of F_1 and F_2 when F_1 and F_2 are each finite maps from X to Y such that $Dom(F_1) \cap Dom(F_2) = \emptyset$.
- $H_1 \uplus H_2$ abbreviates $(TH_1 \uplus TH_2, VH_1 \uplus VH_2)$ when $H_1 = (TH_1, VH_1)$ and $H_2 = (TH_2, VH_2)$.
- $Dom(H)$ abbreviates $Dom(TH) \cup Dom(VH)$ when $H = (TH, VH)$.

3.2 Typing Rules for the Abstract Machine

The typing rules for the $\lambda_{\mathrm{gc}}^{\rightarrow\forall}$ abstract machine are defined using the following two forms of context:

$$\begin{array}{llcl}
\text{(type pointer context)} & \Phi & ::= & \emptyset \mid \Phi[p = \sigma] \\
\text{(location type assignment)} & \Psi & ::= & \emptyset \mid \Psi[l{:}\sigma]
\end{array}$$

Informally, type pointer contexts are the analogue of type variable contexts, and location type assignments are the analogue of variable type assignments. However, type pointer contexts have no dependencies, so we may consider both type pointer contexts and location type assignments as partial functions. Furthermore, the types in the image of either a location type assignment or type pointer context are required to be closed. That is, if $\Psi(l) = \sigma$ or $\Phi(p) = \sigma$, then σ has no free type variables or type pointers.

The typing judgements for the abstract machine are given in Figure 6. The axioms and inference rules for deriving these judgements are given in Figures 10 through 12 of Appendix A.

Intuitively, judgements 5 through 7 extend the reduction judgements 1 and 2 on named form types and bindings to allocated types, type environments, and type heaps. For example, the judgement $\Phi \vdash TE \Downarrow \Delta$ applies Φ (which maps pointers to types) to the range of TE (which maps type variables to pointers) to obtain a type variable context Δ (mapping type variables to types). Similarly, judgements 8 through 10 extend the typing judgements 3 and 4 for the language to value environments, heap values, and value heaps. Judgement 11 assigns an arrow type $\sigma_1 \rightarrow \sigma_2$

to a stack, meaning that the continuation of the machine is expecting the expression to evaluate to a σ_1 value, and the rest of the computation will then produce a σ_2 value. Empty stacks are assigned type unit $\rightarrow$ unit. Thus, well-typed programs always produce a unit result (see below). Finally, judgement 12 determines that a program is well-typed and is defined by the following rule:

$$(\textbf{prog})\ \frac{\begin{array}{cc} \vdash TH \Downarrow \Phi & \Phi \vdash VH : \Psi \\ \Phi; \Psi \vdash S : \sigma' \rightarrow \text{unit} & \Phi \vdash TE \Downarrow \Delta \\ \Psi; \Delta \vdash VE : \Gamma & \Delta; \Gamma \vdash e : \sigma' \end{array}}{\vdash ((TH, VH), S, (TE, VE), e) : \text{unit}}$$

The following technical lemma summarizes some properties of the type system.

Lemma 3.1

1. *If* $\Phi \vdash TE \Downarrow \Delta$ *then* $Dom(TE) = Dom(\Delta)$, $Abstr(\Delta) = \emptyset$, *and* $Rng(TE) \subseteq Dom(\Phi)$.
2. *If* $\Phi \vdash \mu \Downarrow \sigma$, *then* $FP(\mu) \subseteq Dom(\Phi)$ *and* $FTV(\sigma) = \emptyset$.
3. *If* $\vdash TH \Downarrow \Phi$, *then* $FP(TH) = \emptyset$.
4. *If* $\Psi; \Delta \vdash VE : \Gamma$, *then* $Dom(VE) = Dom(\Gamma)$, $Abstr(\Delta) = \emptyset$, *and if* $x{:}t \mapsto l$ *is in* VE, *then* t *is in* $Dom(\Delta)$, *and* $\Delta(t) = \Psi(l)$.
5. *If* $\Phi; \Psi \vdash h : \sigma$, *then* $FTV(\sigma) = \emptyset$.
6. *If* $\Phi \vdash VH : \Psi$, *then* $Dom(VH) = Dom(\Psi)$, *and* $FTV(\Psi) = \emptyset$.
7. *If* $\Phi; \Psi \vdash S : \sigma_1 \rightarrow \sigma_2$, *then* $FTV(\sigma_1) = FTV(\sigma_2) = \emptyset$.
8. *If* $\vdash P : \sigma$, *then* $FTV(\sigma) = \emptyset$.

Proof (sketch): Each part is proved by an induction on the derivation in question and an examination of the typing rules and well-formedness conditions on contexts. □

3.3 Transition System for the Abstract Machine

Execution of the abstract machine is defined by a transition system, a binary relation between machine states (programs). The individual steps of the transition system are given in Figure 8. An informal description of these rules is given below:

5.	$\Phi \vdash TE \Downarrow \Delta$	type env. TE reduces to Δ	(Fig. 10)
6.	$\Phi \vdash \mu \Downarrow \sigma$	type value μ reduces to σ	(Fig. 10)
7.	$\vdash TH \Downarrow \Phi$	type heap TH reduces to Φ	(Fig. 10)
8.	$\Psi; \Delta \vdash VE : \Gamma$	value env. VE is described by Γ	(Fig. 11)
9.	$\Phi; \Psi \vdash h : \sigma$	value h has type σ	(Fig. 11)
10.	$\Phi \vdash VH : \Psi$	value heap VH is described by Ψ	(Fig. 11)
11.	$\Phi; \Psi \vdash S : \sigma_1 \rightarrow \sigma_2$	stack S has type $\sigma_1 \rightarrow \sigma_2$	(Fig. 12)
12.	$\vdash P : \text{unit}$	program P has type unit	(Fig. 12)

Figure 6: Typing Judgements for the $\lambda_{\text{gc}}^{\rightarrow\forall}$ Abstract Machine

$$
\begin{aligned}
\hat{TE}(\text{unit}) &= \text{unit} \\
\hat{TE}(t_1 \times t_2) &= TE(t_1) \times TE(t_2) \\
\hat{TE}(t_1 \rightarrow t_2) &= TE(t_1) \rightarrow TE(t_2) \\
\hat{TE}(\text{list}[t]) &= \text{list}[TE(t)] \\
\hat{TE}(\forall t.\tau) &= \langle\!\langle TE, \forall t.\tau \rangle\!\rangle
\end{aligned}
$$

$$
\begin{aligned}
\hat{E}(\langle\rangle) &= \langle\rangle \\
\hat{E}(\langle x_1, x_2 \rangle) &= \langle E(x_1), E(x_2) \rangle \\
\hat{E}(\texttt{fix } x{:}t(x_1{:}t_1).e) &= \langle\!\langle E, \texttt{fix } x{:}t(x_1{:}t_1).e \rangle\!\rangle \\
\hat{E}(\texttt{nil}) &= \texttt{nil} \\
\hat{E}(\texttt{cons}(x_1, x_2)) &= \texttt{cons}(E(x_1), E(x_2)) \\
\hat{E}(\Lambda t.\, e) &= \langle\!\langle E, \Lambda t.\, e \rangle\!\rangle
\end{aligned}
$$

Figure 7: Environment Substitution

(return) $(H, S \circ \langle\!\langle E, \lambda x{:}t.e \rangle\!\rangle, E', x') \longmapsto (H, S, E[x{:}t \mapsto E'(x')], e)$

(talloc) $(H, S, (TE, VE), \texttt{type}\, t = \nu \;\texttt{in}\, e) \longmapsto$
$(H[p \mapsto \hat{TE}(\nu)], S, (TE[t \mapsto p], VE), e)$

(valloc) $(H, S, E, \texttt{let}\, x{:}t = a \;\texttt{in}\, e) \longmapsto (H[l \mapsto \hat{E}(a)], S, E[x{:}t \mapsto l], e)$

(proj) $$\frac{H(E(x')) = \langle l_1, l_2 \rangle}{(H, S, E, \texttt{let}\, x{:}t = \pi_i\, x' \;\texttt{in}\, e) \longmapsto (H, S, E[x{:}t \mapsto l_i], e)} (i = 1, 2)$$

(app) $$\frac{H(E(x_1)) = \langle\!\langle E', \texttt{fix}\;\; x_1'{:}t_1'(x_2'{:}t_2').e' \rangle\!\rangle}{\begin{array}{l}(H, S, E, \texttt{let}\, x{:}t = x_1\, x_2 \;\texttt{in}\, e) \longmapsto \\ \quad (H, S \circ \langle\!\langle E, \lambda x{:}t.e \rangle\!\rangle, E'[x_1'{:}t_1' \mapsto E(x_1), x_2'{:}t_2' \mapsto E(x_2)], e')\end{array}}$$

(c-nil) $$\frac{H(E(x')) = \texttt{nil}}{\begin{array}{l}(H, S, E, \texttt{let}\, x{:}t = \texttt{case}(x', e_0, \lambda[x_1{:}t_1, x_2{:}t_2].e_1) \;\texttt{in}\, e) \longmapsto \\ \quad (H, S \circ \langle\!\langle E, \lambda x{:}t.e \rangle\!\rangle, E, e_0)\end{array}}$$

(c-cons) $$\frac{H(E(x')) = \texttt{cons}(l_1, l_2)}{\begin{array}{l}(H, S, E, \texttt{let}\, x{:}t = \texttt{case}(x', e_0, \lambda[x_1{:}t_1, x_2{:}t_2].e_1) \;\texttt{in}\, e) \longmapsto \\ \quad (H, S \circ \langle\!\langle E, \lambda x{:}t.e \rangle\!\rangle, E[x_1{:}t_1 \mapsto l_1, x_2{:}t_2 \mapsto l_2], e_1)\end{array}}$$

(tapp) $$\frac{H(E(x_1)) = \langle\!\langle E', \Lambda t'.\, e' \rangle\!\rangle}{\begin{array}{l}(H, S, E, \texttt{let}\, x{:}t = x_1\, [t_1] \;\texttt{in}\, e) \longmapsto \\ \quad (H, S \circ \langle\!\langle E, \lambda x{:}t.e \rangle\!\rangle, E'[t' \mapsto E(t_1)], e')\end{array}}$$

Figure 8: Transition Rules of the Abstract Machine

- **return**: The expression is a variable x and the stack is non-empty. The right-most stack frame is popped from the stack. The frame's environment, extended with the old environment's binding for x, replaces the current environment. The body of the abstraction of the frame replaces the current expression.

- **talloc**: The expression is `type` $t = \nu$ `in` e. The type environment is substituted for the free type variables in ν, yielding a type heap value $\hat{TE}(\nu)$. This type heap value is bound in the heap to a new pointer p, and the type variable t is bound in the type environment to the pointer p. The body of the `type` replaces the current expression.

- **valloc**: The expression is `let` $x{:}t = a$ `in` e. The environment is substituted for the free type and value variables in a, yielding a heap value $\hat{E}(a)$. This heap value is bound in the heap to a new location l, and the variable x is bound in the environment to the type t and the location l. The body of the `let` replaces the current expression.

- **proj**: The expression is `let` $x{:}t = \pi_i\, x'$ `in` e, and the variable x' is bound to a location which in turn is bound to a pair $\langle l_1, l_2 \rangle$. The appropriate component (l_i) is selected, and bound to x in the environment (with the type t). The computation continues with the body of the `let`.

- **app**: The expression is `let` $x{:}t = x_1\, x_2$ `in` e, and the variable x_1 is bound to a location which in turn is bound to a `fix`-closure. The body of the `let` and the current environment are pushed onto the stack. The environment of the closure is extended to map x_1' and x_2' to the location of the closure and the argument's location respectively, and this new environment is taken as the current environment of the machine. The body of the `fix`-abstraction is taken as the current expression to be evaluated.

- **c-nil** and **c-cons**: The expression is `let` $x{:}t = b$ `in` e where b is of the form `case`$(x', e_0, \lambda[x_1{:}t_1, x_2{:}t_2].e_1)$, and the variable x' is bound to a location l in the current environment. If l is bound to `nil`, then the e_0 clause is selected as the current expression. Otherwise, if l is bound to `cons`(l_1, l_2), then the e_1 clause is selected as the current expression and the environment is extended with bindings $x_1{:}t_1 \mapsto l_1$ and $x_2{:}t_2 \mapsto l_2$. The body of the `let` and the current environment are pushed on the stack as a closure to be evaluated after evaluation of the appropriate clause is complete.

- **tapp**: The expression is `let` $x{:}t = x_1\, [t_1]$ `in` e, and the variable x_1 is bound to a location which in turn is bound to a Λ-closure. The body of the `let` and the current environment are pushed onto the stack. The type environment of the closure is extended to map the bound type variable t' to the pointer to which the argument type is bound. This new environment is taken as the current environment of the machine and the body of the Λ-abstraction is taken as the current expression to be evaluated.

We assume when adding a new binding to an environment or heap that the bound pointer (or location or variable, as appropriate) is fresh.

Two of the rules — the **talloc** and **valloc** rules — make use of the auxiliary operations, $\hat{TE}$ and $\hat{E}$, defined in Figure 7. These functions "substitute" the environment for the free variables within the binding. However, for $\forall$-types, fix, and Λ-expressions, the substitution is delayed by forming a closure consisting of the environment and the binding.

We define the relation $\overset{\mathbf{R}}{\longmapsto}$ to be the union of the relations defined by the transition rules, and write $P \overset{\mathbf{R}}{\longmapsto} P'$ if (P, P') is in $\overset{\mathbf{R}}{\longmapsto}$. That is, $P \overset{\mathbf{R}}{\longmapsto} P'$ iff $P \longmapsto P'$ via **return, talloc, valloc, c-nil, c-cons, proj, app**, or **tapp**. Since at most one rule applies for a given program, $\overset{\mathbf{R}}{\longmapsto}$ defines a partial function from closed programs to programs. We take $\overset{\mathbf{R}}{\longmapsto}^*$ to be the reflexive, transitive closure of $\overset{\mathbf{R}}{\longmapsto}$. We say a program P *diverges* if there exists an infinite sequence of programs $P_1, P_2, P_3, \cdots$ such that $P \overset{\mathbf{R}}{\longmapsto} P_1 \overset{\mathbf{R}}{\longmapsto} P_2 \overset{\mathbf{R}}{\longmapsto} P_3 \overset{\mathbf{R}}{\longmapsto} \cdots$.

Definition 3.2 (Well-Formed Answer) *An answer* $A = (H, [], E, x)$ *is well-formed if* $H(E(x)) = \langle\rangle$.

Definition 3.3 (Stuck Program) *A program P is stuck if either P is an answer and P is not well-formed, or else P is not an answer and there is no P' such that* $P \overset{\mathbf{R}}{\longmapsto} P'$.

We define evaluation as the following relation between programs and results:

Definition 3.4 (Evaluation Relation)

1. $P \Downarrow \top$ *iff there exists a well-formed A such that* $P \overset{\mathbf{R}}{\longmapsto}^* A$.
2. $P \Downarrow \bot$ *iff P diverges.*
3. $P \Downarrow$ `*wrong*` *iff there exists a stuck P' such that* $P \overset{\mathbf{R}}{\longmapsto}^* P'$.

From the fact that at most one $\overset{\mathbf{R}}{\longmapsto}$ rule can apply for a given closed program, it is clear that there is one and only one r such that $P \Downarrow r$. Hence, we treat evaluation as a total function from closed programs to results and write $eval(P) = r$ when $P \Downarrow r$.

Finally, we will need a suitable notion of observational equivalence for programs.

Definition 3.5 (Kleene Equivalence) *If* $\vdash P_1 : \text{unit}$ *and* $\vdash P_2 : \text{unit}$, *then* $P_1 \simeq P_2$ *iff* $eval(P_1) = eval(P_2)$.

Hence, two programs are equivalent iff they are both well-typed, and both converge, both diverge, or both get stuck. This equivalence is "interesting" since we can encode Turing machines using the facilities in the language. That is, determining whether $\lambda_{\text{gc}}^{\rightarrow\forall}$ programs terminate or not is in general undecidable. It is straightforward to modify the language and the abstract machine to accommodate input/output so that more interesting observations can be made. For instance, we could add an output stream as part of the state of the abstract machine and a "print" binding that appends to this stream when evaluated, and then consider programs equivalent when they produce the same output streams and have the same termination behaviour. The garbage collection techniques considered here would preserve the input/output behaviour of such a language and machine.

3.4 Type Soundness

We prove the soundness of the type system (with respect to execution by the abstract machine) by establishing that the transition system preserves typability, and that well-typed programs are either answers, or admit a further transition. (This viewpoint is inspired by Wright and Felleisen Wright and Felleisen (1994).) We state the important lemmas and give the proof of soundness here. Proofs of the most important lemmas, Preservation and Progress, may be found in Appendix B. Keep in mind that complete programs are closed expressions of type unit.

Lemma 3.6 (*TE* Substitution) *If* $\vdash TH \Downarrow \Phi$, $\Phi \vdash TE \Downarrow \Delta$, *and* $\Delta \vdash \nu \Downarrow \sigma$, *then* $\Phi \vdash \hat{TE}(\nu) \Downarrow \sigma$.

Lemma 3.7 (*E* Substitution) *If* $\vdash TH \Downarrow \Phi$, $\Phi \vdash VH : \Psi$, $\Phi \vdash TE \Downarrow \Delta$, $\Psi; \Delta \vdash VE : \Gamma$, *and* $\Delta; \Gamma \vdash a : \sigma$, *then* $\Phi; \Psi \vdash \hat{E}(a) : \sigma$ *where* $E = (TE, VE)$.

Lemma 3.8 *Let* $\Delta[t = \sigma_2](\{\sigma_2/t\}\Delta')$ *be a well-formed context.*

1. *If* $\Delta[t]\Delta' \vdash \tau \Downarrow \sigma_1$ *then* $\Delta[t = \sigma_2](\{\sigma_2/t\}\Delta') \vdash \tau \Downarrow \{\sigma_2/t\}\sigma_1$.
2. *If* $\Delta[t]\Delta' \vdash \nu \Downarrow \sigma_1$ *then* $\Delta[t = \sigma_2](\{\sigma_2/t\}\Delta') \vdash \nu \Downarrow \{\sigma_2/t\}\sigma_1$.

Proof: Simultaneously, by induction on τ and ν. □

Lemma 3.9 *Let* $\Delta[t = \sigma_2](\{\sigma_2/t\}\Delta')$ *be a well-formed context.*

1. *If* $\Delta[t]\Delta'; \Gamma \vdash e : \sigma_1$ *then* $\Delta[t = \sigma_2](\{\sigma_2/t\}\Delta'); (\{\sigma_2/t\}\Gamma) \vdash e : \{\sigma_2/t\}\sigma_1$.
2. *If* $\Delta[t]\Delta'; \Gamma \vdash b : \sigma_1$ *then* $\Delta[t = \sigma_2](\{\sigma_2/t\}\Delta'); (\{\sigma_2/t\}\Gamma) \vdash b : \{\sigma_2/t\}\sigma_1$.

Proof: Simultaneously, by induction on e and b, using Lemma 3.8. □

Lemma 3.10 (Preservation) *If* $\vdash P : \text{unit}$ *and* $P \stackrel{\mathbf{R}}{\longmapsto} P'$*, then* $\vdash P' : \text{unit}$.

Proof: See Appendix B. □

Lemma 3.11 (Canonical Forms) *If* $\Phi; \Psi \vdash h : \sigma$*, then:*

1. *if* $\sigma = \text{unit}$*, then* h *is* $\langle\rangle$.
2. *if* $\sigma = \sigma_1 \times \sigma_2$*, then* h *is* $\langle l_1, l_2 \rangle$ *for some* l_1 *and* l_2.
3. *if* $\sigma = \sigma_1 \to \sigma_2$*, then* h *is* $\langle\!\langle E, \texttt{fix } x{:}t(x_1{:}t_1).e \rangle\!\rangle$ *for some* E*,* x*,* t*,* x_1*,* t_1*, and* e.
4. *if* $\sigma = \text{list}[\sigma']$*, then* h *is either* `nil` *or* $\texttt{cons}(l_1, l_2)$ *for some* l_1 *and* l_2.
5. *if* $\sigma = \forall t.\tau$*, then* h *is* $\langle\!\langle E, \Lambda t.\, e \rangle\!\rangle$ *for some* E *and* e.

Proof: By inspection of the heap value typing rules. □

Lemma 3.12 (Progress) *If* $\vdash P : \text{unit}$*, then either* P *is an answer or else there exists a* P' *such that* $P \stackrel{\mathbf{R}}{\longmapsto} P'$.

Proof: See Appendix B. □

Lemma 3.13 *If* $\vdash A : \text{unit}$*, then* A *is well-formed.*

Proof: Since A is an answer, it is of the form $((TH, VH), [], (TE, VE), x)$. Since $\vdash A : \text{unit}$, there exists a Φ, Ψ, Δ, and Γ such that $\vdash TH \Downarrow \Phi$, $\Phi \vdash VH : \Psi$, $\Phi \vdash TE \Downarrow \Delta$, and $\Psi; \Delta \vdash VE : \Gamma$, and $\Delta; \Gamma \vdash x : \text{unit}$. From the **var** rule, we know that $\Gamma(x) = \text{unit}$. From the **cons-ve** rule, we can conclude that VE contains a binding of the form $x{:}t \mapsto l$ for some t and l, $\Delta \vdash t \Downarrow \text{unit}$, and $\Psi(l) = \text{unit}$. From the **vh** rule, we know that VH must contain a binding $l \mapsto h$ for some h and that $\Phi; \Psi \vdash h : \text{unit}$. From the Canonical Forms lemma, we know that h must be $\langle\rangle$. □

Theorem 3.14 (Type Soundness) *If* $\vdash P : \text{unit}$*, then* $eval(P) \neq$ `*wrong*`.

Proof: If P diverges then $eval(P) = \bot$. If P does not diverge, then there exists some P' such that $P \stackrel{\mathbf{R}}{\longmapsto}{}^{*} P'$ and there is no P'' where $P' \stackrel{\mathbf{R}}{\longmapsto} P''$. By induction on the number of rewriting steps taking P to P' using the Preservation Lemma, we can show that $\vdash P' : \text{unit}$. By the Progress Lemma, P' must be an answer and since $\vdash P : \text{unit}$, P' is a well-formed answer by Lemma 3.13. Thus, $eval(P) = \top$. □

4 Heap Garbage

In this section, we consider a general definition of "garbage" as a heap object that is not needed by the program in order to produce the same result. (Notions of "garbage" for the stack and environment are considered in Section 6 below.)

Definition 4.1 (Heap Garbage) *Let* $P = (H \uplus H', S, E, e)$ *be a well-typed program and take* $P' = (H, S, E, e)$. *We say that* H' *is garbage with respect to* P *iff* $P \simeq P'$.

This definition of garbage allows us to eliminate any portion of the heap as long as we do not change the observable behaviour of the program. Notice that a heap object is not regarded as garbage if it is required in order for P to be well-typed, even if the computation could proceed to a final answer without referring to that object. It is possible to drop the well-formedness condition and consider a more semantic definition of garbage, at the expense of considerable technical complication[4]. We prefer the more restrictive definition because it is simpler and closer to practice.

Implementers use a variety of techniques to determine which portions of the heap can be collected. One of the most important techniques is based on the idea of accessibility. Formally, we can drop a heap binding if the resulting program has no free reference to the binding:

$$(\mathbf{GC})\quad \frac{FP(H,S,E,e)=\emptyset \qquad FL(H,S,E,e)=\emptyset}{(H \uplus H', S, E, e) \overset{\mathbf{GC}}{\longmapsto} (H, S, E, e)}$$

The idea is that $\overset{\mathbf{GC}}{\longmapsto}$ models a garbage collector that drops zero or more bindings from the heap, but ensures that none of the dropped bindings is accessible. For a well-typed program, the $\overset{\mathbf{GC}}{\longmapsto}$ rule is always enabled, since we can always drop an empty heap. Furthermore, the composition of two $\overset{\mathbf{GC}}{\longmapsto}$ steps can always be simulated by a single $\overset{\mathbf{GC}}{\longmapsto}$ step.

A key property of $\overset{\mathbf{GC}}{\longmapsto}$ is that it preserves typing in the same fashion as the other rewriting rules.

Lemma 4.2 *Suppose that* (H, S, E, e) *is closed.*

1. *If* $\vdash (H[p \mapsto \mu], S, E, e) : \text{unit}$, *then* $\vdash (H, S, E, e) : \text{unit}$.
2. *If* $\vdash (H[l \mapsto h], S, E, e) : \text{unit}$, *then* $\vdash (H, S, E, e) : \text{unit}$.

[4] In particular, if programs can have free locations or pointers, then we must worry about accidentally capturing these locations or pointers during allocation (Morrisett, Felleisen, and Harper 1995; Tofte and Talpin 1994)

Proof (sketch): We only argue the case for part 1, as the case for part 2 is similar. Suppose $H = (TH, VH)$ and $E = (TE, VE)$. Since $\vdash (H[p \mapsto \mu], S, E, e)$: unit, there exists Φ, σ_0, Ψ, σ', Δ, and Γ such that $\vdash TH[p \mapsto \mu] \Downarrow \Phi[p = \sigma_0]$, $\Phi[p = \sigma_0] \vdash VH : \Psi$, $\Phi[p = \sigma_0]; \Psi \vdash S : \sigma' \to \text{unit}$, $\Phi[p = \sigma_0] \vdash TE \Downarrow \Delta$, $\Psi; \Delta \vdash VE : \Gamma$, and $\Delta; \Gamma \vdash e : \sigma'$. Since $FP(H, S, E, e) = \emptyset$, $FP(H) = \emptyset$, $FP(S) \subseteq Dom(TH)$, $FP(E) \subseteq Dom(TH)$. Hence we may construct derivations of $\vdash TH \Downarrow \Phi$, $\Phi \vdash VH : \Psi$, $\Phi; \Psi \vdash S : \sigma' \to \text{unit}$, and $\Phi \vdash TE \Downarrow \Delta$. Therefore, $\vdash (H, S, E, e)$: unit. □

Lemma 4.3 (GC Preservation) *If* $\vdash P_1$: unit *and* $P_1 \overset{\mathbf{GC}}{\longmapsto} P_2$, *then* $\vdash P_2$: unit.

Proof: By induction on the number of bindings dropped, using Lemma 4.2.
□

From this lemma and our original Progress result (see 3.12), we can conclude that a well-typed program can never become stuck with respect to the $\overset{\mathbf{R}}{\longmapsto}$ rules, even if the program takes a $\overset{\mathbf{GC}}{\longmapsto}$ step.

Corollary 4.4 (GC Progress) *If* $\vdash P_1$: unit *and* $P_1 \overset{\mathbf{GC}}{\longmapsto} P_2$, *then either* P_2 *is an answer or else there exists a* P_3 *such that* $P_2 \overset{\mathbf{R}}{\longmapsto} P_3$.

Corollary 4.5 (GC Answer) *If* $\vdash A$: unit *and* $A \overset{\mathbf{GC}}{\longmapsto} A'$, *then* A' *is a well-formed answer.*

Consequently, no matter how we add $\overset{\mathbf{GC}}{\longmapsto}$ to our evaluation relation, a well-typed program will never become stuck.

We would like to add $\overset{\mathbf{GC}}{\longmapsto}$ to the rewriting rules for our abstract machine to model an implementation that interleaves evaluation with garbage collection. Since the null collection (in which no bindings are eliminated) is always possible, this introduces the potential for non-termination by infinite repetition of $\overset{\mathbf{GC}}{\longmapsto}$ steps. In practice garbage collection steps occur only after some number of standard evaluation steps have occurred (e.g., at the beginning of each basic block), ruling out infinite repetition of vacuous collection steps. We adopt this restriction by defining the $\overset{\mathbf{GCR}}{\longmapsto}$ relation to be the composition of the $\overset{\mathbf{GC}}{\longmapsto}$ and $\overset{\mathbf{R}}{\longmapsto}$ relations, and consider computation as a sequence of $\overset{\mathbf{GCR}}{\longmapsto}$ steps. Note that by GC Progress, the fact that $\overset{\mathbf{R}}{\longmapsto}$ is a partial function, and the fact that $\overset{\mathbf{GC}}{\longmapsto}$ does not affect the expression of a program, any $\overset{\mathbf{R}}{\longmapsto}$ step that can be taken before an arbitrary $\overset{\mathbf{GC}}{\longmapsto}$ step, can still be taken after the $\overset{\mathbf{GC}}{\longmapsto}$ step. We say a program P is stuck with respect to $\overset{\mathbf{GCR}}{\longmapsto}$ if either P is an answer but not well-formed, or else P is not an answer and there is no P' such that $P \overset{\mathbf{GCR}}{\longmapsto} P'$.

Definition 4.6 (GC Evaluation Relation)

1. $P \Downarrow_{\mathbf{GCR}} \top$ *iff there exists a well-formed* A *such that* $P \overset{\mathbf{GCR}}{\longmapsto}{}^{*} A$.

2. $P \Downarrow_{\mathbf{GCR}} \bot$ *iff* P *diverges with respect to* $\overset{\mathbf{GCR}}{\longmapsto}$.

3. $P \Downarrow_{\mathbf{GCR}}$ `*wrong*` *iff there exists a* P' *such that* $P \overset{\mathbf{GCR}}{\longmapsto}{}^{*} P'$, *and* P' *is stuck with respect to* $\overset{\mathbf{GCR}}{\longmapsto}$.

Theorem 4.7 (GC Type Soundness) *If* $\vdash P$: unit, *then it is not the case that* $P \Downarrow_{\mathbf{GCR}}$ `*wrong*`.

Proof: If P diverges then $P \Downarrow_{\mathbf{GCR}} \bot$. If P does not diverge, then there exists some P' such that $P \overset{\mathbf{GCR}}{\longmapsto}{}^{*} P'$ and there is no P'' where $P' \overset{\mathbf{GCR}}{\longmapsto} P''$. By induction on the number of rewriting steps taking P to P' using the Preservation and GC Preservation Lemmas, we can show that $\vdash P'$: unit. By the Progress Lemma, P' must be an answer. By Lemma 3.13, P' is a well-formed answer. Hence, it is not the case that $P \Downarrow_{\mathbf{GRCR}}$ `*wrong*`. □

We would like to show that the addition of the $\overset{\mathbf{GC}}{\longmapsto}$ steps to our evaluator does not affect the evaluation result of a given program. That is, we would like to show that $\Downarrow_{\mathbf{GCR}}$ is a total function mapping closed programs to results, and is in fact the same total function as our original *eval*. (Note that this result would fail if we allowed infinite repetition of garbage collection steps.)

We begin by showing that whenever a $\overset{\mathbf{GC}}{\longmapsto}$ step is followed by an $\overset{\mathbf{R}}{\longmapsto}$ step, we can postpone the garbage collection until after the $\overset{\mathbf{R}}{\longmapsto}$ step has been taken. From this, it follows that we can simulate any $\overset{\mathbf{GCR}}{\longmapsto}$ evaluation sequence with an $\overset{\mathbf{R}}{\longmapsto}$ evaluation sequence.

Lemma 4.8 (GC Postponement) *If* $\vdash P_1$: unit *and* $P_1 \overset{\mathbf{GC}}{\longmapsto} P_2 \overset{\mathbf{R}}{\longmapsto} P_3$, *then there exists a* P_2' *such that* $P_1 \overset{\mathbf{R}}{\longmapsto} P_2' \overset{\mathbf{GC}}{\longmapsto} P_3$.

Proof: Let $P_1 = (H_1 \uplus H_2, S, E, e)$, $P_2 = (H_1, S, E, e)$, and $P_3 = (H', S', E', e')$. We can show via case analysis on the rewriting rule taking P_2 to P_3, that $P_1 \overset{\mathbf{R}}{\longmapsto} (H' \uplus H_2, S', E', e')$. By Preservation and GC Preservation, we know that $\vdash P_3$: unit and thus P_3 is closed, and thus, $(H' \uplus H_2, S', E', e') \overset{\mathbf{GC}}{\longmapsto} (H', S', E', e')$. □

Corollary 4.9 *For all* $n \geq 0$, *if* $\vdash P_0$: unit *and* $P_0 \overset{\mathbf{GCR}}{\longmapsto}{}^{n} P_n$, *then there exists a* P_n' *such that* $P_0 \overset{\mathbf{R}}{\longmapsto}{}^{n} P_n'$ *and* $P_n' \overset{\mathbf{GC}}{\longmapsto} P_n$.

Proof: By induction on n using the GC Postponement lemma. □

Theorem 4.10 (GC Correctness) *If* $\vdash P : \text{unit}$, *then* $P \Downarrow r$ *iff* $P \Downarrow_{\mathbf{GCR}} r$.

Proof: We can simulate any $\overset{\mathbf{R}}{\longmapsto}$ step with a $\overset{\mathbf{GCR}}{\longmapsto}$ step by simply performing an empty garbage collection. That is, if $P \overset{\mathbf{R}}{\longmapsto} P'$, then $P \overset{\mathbf{GC}}{\longmapsto} P \overset{\mathbf{R}}{\longmapsto} P'$ and thus $P \overset{\mathbf{GCR}}{\longmapsto} P'$. Consequently, if $P \Downarrow r$, then $P \Downarrow_{\mathbf{GCR}} r$.

Suppose $P \Downarrow_{\mathbf{GCR}} r$. By GC Type Soundness, $r \neq \texttt{*wrong*}$. If $r = \top$, then there exists an n and A such that $P \overset{\mathbf{GCR}}{\longmapsto}{}^n A$. By Corollary 4.9, there exists an A' such that $P \overset{\mathbf{R}}{\longmapsto}{}^n A' \overset{\mathbf{GC}}{\longmapsto} A$. By Preservation, A' is well-formed and hence $P \Downarrow_\top$.

If $r = \bot$ then there exists an infinite sequence $P', P_1, P_1', P_2, P_2', \cdots$ such that

$$P \overset{\mathbf{GC}}{\longmapsto} P' \overset{\mathbf{R}}{\longmapsto} P_1 \overset{\mathbf{GC}}{\longmapsto} P_1' \overset{\mathbf{R}}{\longmapsto} P_2 \overset{\mathbf{GC}}{\longmapsto} P_2' \overset{\mathbf{R}}{\longmapsto} \cdots.$$

By Corollary 4.9, we can construct an infinite sequence $P'', P_1'', P_2'', \cdots$ such that

$$P \overset{\mathbf{R}}{\longmapsto} P'' \overset{\mathbf{R}}{\longmapsto} P_1'' \overset{\mathbf{R}}{\longmapsto} P_2'' \overset{\mathbf{R}}{\longmapsto} \cdots$$

Thus, $P \Downarrow \bot$. □

Of course, $\overset{\mathbf{GC}}{\longmapsto}$ is too high-level to be taken as a primitive instruction, because the side-conditions require a global constraint — no free references to pointers or locations — and checking this constraint requires examining every variable in the program's state. Some mechanism is needed to determine efficiently which pointers and locations can be safely garbage collected. The following section addresses this issue.

5 Type-Based Tag-Free Heap Collection

In this section, we formulate a garbage collection rewriting rule that models type-based, tag-free[5] copying collection in the style of Tolmach (Tolmach 1994) and the TIL/ML compiler (Tarditi, Morrisett, Cheng, Stone, Harper, and Lee 1996). The key idea is to preserve all heap objects that can be reached (either directly or indirectly) from the current environment and stack. We use the type information recorded in environments during evaluation[6] to determine the shape of heap objects. This allows us to extract locations (and their types) from heap objects without having to use any extra tags on the heap objects themselves.

[5]Strictly speaking, the algorithm is not "tag-free" since type information is maintained at run-time in order to support traversal of heap objects. However, the type "tags" remain separate from the data and hence the heap values are tag-free.

[6]For monomorphic languages, all type information can be pre-allocated in the type heap. Polymorphic languages require run-time allocation of type information.

We formalize the garbage collection process as a rewriting system. GC states are 4-tuples of the form (H_f, Q, L, H_t), where H_f and H_t are heaps, Q is a set of pointers, and L is a set of location and pointer pairs:

$$
\begin{array}{llll}
\text{(GC states)} & X & ::= & (H_f, Q, L, H_t) \\
\text{(type pointer sets)} & Q & ::= & \{p_1, \cdots, p_n\} \quad (n \geq 0) \\
\text{(typed location sets)} & L & ::= & \{l_1{:}p_1, \cdots, l_n{:}p_n\} \quad (n \geq 0)
\end{array}
$$

In the terminology of copying collectors, H_f is the "from-space", H_t is the "to-space", and L and Q together constitute the "scan-set" or "frontier". Throughout, Q and L contain those pointers and locations that are immediately accessible from the current environment, stack, or to-space but have not yet been forwarded from the from-space to the to-space. In addition, L tracks (pointers to) types of these accessible locations. From this extra type information, we can determine the "shape" of value objects referenced in the scan-set. For instance, if $l{:}p$ is in the scan-set and p is bound to a type heap value $p_1 \times p_2$, then we know that l must be bound to a heap value of the form $\langle l_1, l_2 \rangle$ and furthermore, l_i is described by p_i for $i = 1, 2$.

The basic rewriting rules of the GC algorithm are as follows. We use $S_1 \uplus S_2$ to denote the union of two disjoint sets. We also use $H_1 \uplus H_2$ to denote the union of two heaps whose domains are disjoint.

(gc-1) $$((TH_f[p \mapsto \mu], VH_f), Q \uplus \{p\}, L, (TH_t, VH_t)) \Longrightarrow ((TH_f, VH_f), Q \cup FP(\mu), L, (TH_t, VH_t[p \mapsto \mu]))$$

(gc-2) $$\frac{p \notin Dom(TH_f)}{((TH_f, VH_f), Q \uplus \{p\}, L, H_t) \Longrightarrow ((TH_f, VH_f), Q, L, H_t)}$$

(gc-3) $$\frac{\mathcal{F}[(TH_f \uplus TH_t)(p)](p, h) = (Q', L')}{((TH_f, VH_f[l \mapsto h]), Q, L \uplus \{l{:}p\}, (TH_t, VH_t)) \Longrightarrow ((TH_f, VH_f), Q \cup Q', L \cup L', (TH_t, VH_t[l \mapsto h]))}$$

(gc-4) $$\frac{l \notin Dom(VH_f)}{((TH_f, VH_f), Q, L \uplus \{l{:}p\}, H_t) \Longrightarrow ((TH_f, VH_f), Q, L, H_t)}$$

where

$$
\begin{array}{rcl}
\mathcal{F}[\text{unit}] & = & \lambda(p, \langle\rangle).(\emptyset, \emptyset) \\
\mathcal{F}[p_1 \times p_2] & = & \lambda(p, \langle l_1, l_2 \rangle).(\{p_1, p_2\}, \{l_1{:}p_1, l_2{:}p_2\}) \\
\mathcal{F}[p_1 \to p_2] & = & \lambda(p, \langle\!\langle E, \texttt{fix } x{:}t(x_1{:}t_1).e \rangle\!\rangle).\mathcal{F}_{\text{env}}(E) \\
\mathcal{F}[\text{list}[p']] & = & \lambda(p, h).\texttt{case } h \texttt{ of} \\
 & & \quad \texttt{nil} \Rightarrow (\emptyset, \emptyset) \\
 & & \quad \mid \texttt{cons}(l_1, l_2) \Rightarrow (\{p', p\}, \{l_1{:}p', l_2{:}p\}) \\
\mathcal{F}[\langle\!\langle TE, \forall t.\tau \rangle\!\rangle] & = & \lambda(p, \langle\!\langle E, \Lambda t.\, e \rangle\!\rangle).\mathcal{F}_{\text{env}}(E)
\end{array}
$$

and

$$\mathcal{F}_{\text{env}}(TE, VE) = (Rng(TE), \{l{:}TE(t) \mid x{:}t \mapsto l \in VE\})$$

The **gc-1** rule forwards a type binding $p \mapsto \mu$ from the from-space to the to-space when p is in the scan-set. All of the free pointers of the allocated type μ are added to the scan-set ensuring that these bindings are eventually forwarded to the to-space. Notice that calculating the free pointers of an allocated type requires tags on the allocated types so that we can tell, for instance, unit from $p_1 \to p_2$. The **gc-2** rule skips over a pointer in the scan-set when we determine that the pointer's binding has already been forwarded to the to-space.

The **gc-3** rule, like the **gc-1** rule, forwards a value binding $l \mapsto h$ from the from-space to the to-space when $l{:}p$ is in the scan-set. All of the free pointers and free locations of h, along with pointers to types describing these locations, are added to the scan-set. Unlike the first rule, we use the type information p recorded with a location to determine the shape of the corresponding heap value, and to extract the free pointers and locations. In particular, the function $\mathcal{F}$ takes an allocated type μ and returns a function which when given a pointer p to that allocated type and a heap value h of the appropriate type, returns appropriate Q and L sets for the heap value. In other words, $\mathcal{F}$ calculates the free pointers and locations of the heap value, as well as the types of those locations. Furthermore, $\mathcal{F}$ requires no run-time tags on h to distinguish, for instance, lists from pairs, or pairs from closures. We need some tag information in the case that $\mu = \text{list}[p]$ to determine whether the heap value is $\texttt{nil}$ or $\texttt{cons}(l_1, l_2)$. However, such a tag is needed anyway to support evaluation of `case` expressions.

The **gc-4** rule, like the **gc-2** rule, skips over a location/pointer pair in the scan-set when we determine that the location's binding has already been forwarded to the to-space.

The Tag-Free GC algorithm is initialized and terminated as follows:

$$\textbf{(tf-gc)}\quad \frac{\mathcal{F}_{\text{env}}(E) = (Q_1, L_1) \qquad \mathcal{F}_{\text{stack}}(S) = (Q_2, L_2) \qquad (H, Q_1 \cup Q_2, L_1 \cup L_2, \emptyset) \Longrightarrow^{*} (H_f, \emptyset, \emptyset, H_t)}{(H, S, E, e) \stackrel{\textbf{tf-gc}}{\longmapsto} (H_t, S, E, e)}$$

where

$$\begin{aligned}
&\mathcal{F}_{\text{stack}}([\,]) = (\emptyset, \emptyset)\\
&\mathcal{F}_{\text{stack}}(S \circ \langle\!\langle E, \lambda x{:}t.e\rangle\!\rangle) = (Q_a \cup Q_b, L_a \cup L_b)\\
&\qquad\qquad (\text{where } (Q_a, L_a) = \mathcal{F}_{\text{stack}}(S) \text{ and } (Q_b, L_b) = \mathcal{F}_{\text{env}}(E))
\end{aligned}$$

The algorithm begins by calculating the free pointers and free locations (along with their types) of the current environment and stack. This set of pointers and typed locations is taken as the initial scan-set, and the heap of the program is taken as the initial from-space. Then, the algorithm repeatedly applies the gc rewriting rules until the scan-set is empty. At this point, we take the to-space as the "new" heap of the program.

Two important properties of this GC algorithm are readily apparent. First, the GC algorithm only drops bindings from the heap — it does not introduce new bindings nor change existing bindings. Hence, at each stage of the computation, the original heap can be recovered by taking the union of the from- and to-spaces. Second, the rewriting system must terminate, since (a) each heap binding is moved at most once from the from-space to the to-space, and (b) at each step either an element is discarded from the scan-set, or else a binding is moved from the from-space to the to-space.

With these properties in mind, to prove the correctness of the collection algorithm it suffices to show that the Tag-Free GC algorithm does not get stuck (i.e., it is always possible to empty the scan-set), and the resulting program is closed. If the algorithm always results in a closed program, then the algorithm can be simulated by the original $\stackrel{\mathbf{GC}}{\longmapsto}$ rewriting rule, which we have already proved to be a correct specification of garbage collection.

The critical step in showing that the Tag-Free GC algorithm can run to completion is proving a variant of the Canonical Forms lemma. In particular, we must show that when we add a location/pointer pair $l{:}p$ to the scan-set, then p is bound to a type that describes the heap value to which l is bound. This ensures that the $\mathcal{F}$ function is in fact defined on this location/pointer pair. Furthermore, we must show that this property holds of any new bindings we add to the scan-set.

Lemma 5.1 (Unexpanded Canonical Forms) *If* $\vdash TH \Downarrow \Phi$, $\Phi \vdash VH : \Psi$, *and* $\Phi(p) = \Psi(l)$, *then:*

1. *if* $TH(p) = \text{unit}$, *then* $VH(l) = \langle\rangle$.
2. *if* $TH(p) = p_1 \times p_2$, *then* $VH(l) = \langle l_1, l_2\rangle$ *for some* l_1 *and* l_2. *Furthermore,* $\Phi(p_i) = \Psi(l_i)$ *for* $i = 1, 2$.
3. *if* $TH(p) = p_1 \to p_2$, *then* $VH(l) = \langle\!\langle (TE, VE), \texttt{fix } x_1{:}t_1(x_2{:}t_2).e\rangle\!\rangle$ *for some* TE, VE, x_1, t_1, x_2, t_2, *and* e. *Furthermore, for all* $x{:}t \mapsto l'$ *in* VE, $\Phi(TE(t)) = \Psi(l')$.
4. *if* $TH(p) = \text{list}[p']$, *then* $VH(l) = \texttt{nil}$ *or* $VH(l) = \texttt{cons}(l_1, l_2)$ *for some* l_1 *and* l_2. *Furthermore,* $\Phi(p') = \Psi(l_1)$ *and* $\Phi(p) = \Psi(l_2)$.
5. *if* $TH(p) = \langle\!\langle TE', \forall t.\tau\rangle\!\rangle$, *then* $VH(l) = \langle\!\langle (TE, VE), \Lambda t.\, e\rangle\!\rangle$ *for some* TE, VE, *and* e. *Furthermore, for all* $x{:}t \mapsto l'$ *in* VE, $\Phi(TE(t)) = \Psi(l')$.

Proof (sketch): Again, by inspection of the typing rules. For example, consider case 3: We know that $TH(p) = p_1 \to p_2$. So, by inspection of the type heap value reduction rules, only **th-arrow** applies. Thus, we know that there exist σ_1 and σ_2 such that $\Phi \vdash p_1 \to p_2 \Downarrow \sigma_1 \to \sigma_2$ by the **th-arrow** rule. Therefore, $\Phi(p) = \sigma_1 \to \sigma_2$, and by assumption, $\Psi(l) = \sigma_1 \to \sigma_2$. By inspection of the heap typing rules, $\Phi; \Psi \vdash VH(l) : \sigma_1 \to \sigma_2$ can only hold via the **vh-arrow** rule. Thus, $VH(l) = \langle\!\langle (TE, VE), \texttt{fix } x_1{:}t_1(x_2{:}t_2).e\rangle\!\rangle$ for some TE, VE, x_1, t_1, x_2, t_2, and e. Furthermore, we know there exists Δ and Γ such that $\Phi \vdash TE \Downarrow \Delta$ and

$\Delta; \Psi \vdash VE : \Gamma$. By the **cons-ve** rule, we can conclude that for all $x{:}t \mapsto l$ in VE, $\Phi(TE(t)) = \Psi(l)$. □

Lemma 5.2 *If $\Phi \vdash TE \Downarrow \Delta$ and $\Psi; \Delta \vdash VE : \Gamma$, then for some Q and L,*

1. $\mathcal{F}_{\text{env}}(TE, VE) = (Q, L)$,
2. $FP(TE, VE) = Q$,
3. $FL(TE, VE) = Dom(L)$,
4. *for all* $l{:}p \in L$, $\Phi(p) = \Psi(l)$.

Proof: From the definition of $\mathcal{F}_{\text{env}}$, it is clear that it is defined on all environments. Thus, $\mathcal{F}_{\text{env}}(TE, VE) = (Q, L)$ for some Q and L. Q must contain the free pointers of (TE, VE) since the only pointers that can occur must be in the range of TE. Similarly, the only locations that can occur in (TE, VE) are in the range of VE. Let $l{:}p$ be in L. Then from the definition of $\mathcal{F}_{\text{env}}$, there exists a VE', x and t such that $VE = VE'[x{:}t \mapsto l]$. Now $\Psi; \Delta \vdash VE : \Gamma$ can only hold via the **cons-ve** rule. Thus, $\Psi(l) = \sigma$ and $\Delta \vdash t \Downarrow \sigma$ for some σ. Hence, Δ must be of the form $\Delta'[t = \sigma]$ for some Δ'. Now $\Phi \vdash TE \Downarrow \Delta$ can only hold via the **cons-te** rule. Hence, there exists a TE' and p such that $TE = TE'[t \mapsto p]$ and $\Phi(p) = \sigma$. Therefore, $\Phi(p) = \Psi(l)$. □

Corollary 5.3 *If $\vdash TH \Downarrow \Phi$, $\Phi \vdash VH : \Psi$, and $\Phi(p) = \Psi(l)$, then for some Q and L:*

1. $\mathcal{F}[TH(p)](p, VH(l)) = (Q, L)$,
2. $FP(VH(l)) = Q$,
3. $FL(VH(l)) = Dom(L)$,
4. *for all* $l'{:}p' \in L$, $\Phi(p') = \Psi(l')$.

Proof: The result follows directly from the definition of $\mathcal{F}$, the Unexpanded Canonical Forms lemma, and Lemma 5.2. □

Corollary 5.4 *If $\vdash TH \Downarrow \Phi$, $\Phi \vdash VH : \Psi$, and $\Phi; \Psi \vdash S : \sigma_1 \to \sigma_2$, then for some Q and L,*

1. $\mathcal{F}_{\text{stack}}(S) = (Q, L)$,
2. $FP(S) = Q$,
3. $FL(S) = Dom(L)$,

4. *for all* $l':p' \in L$, $\Phi(p') = \Psi(l')$.

Proof: The result follows directly from the definition of $\mathcal{F}_{\text{stack}}$ and Lemma 5.2. □

Next, we formulate a set of invariants that a GC state has throughout the rewriting system.

Definition 5.5 (Well-Formed GC State) *Let* $P = ((TH, VH), S, E, e)$ *be a well-typed program, where* $\vdash TH \Downarrow \Phi$, *and* $\Phi \vdash VH : \Psi$ *are obtained from the proof that P is well-typed. We say a GC state* (H_f, Q, L, H_t) *is well-formed with respect to P iff:*

1. $(TH, VH) = H_f \uplus H_t$,
2. $FP(H_t, S, E, e) \subseteq Q$,
3. $FL(H_t, S, E, e) \subseteq Dom(L)$,
4. *for all* $l{:}p$ *in* L, $\Phi(p) = \Psi(l)$,
5. $Q \subseteq Dom(TH)$,
6. *for all* $l{:}p$ *in* L, $l \in Dom(VH)$ *and* $p \in Dom(TH)$.

The first requirement is that the from- and to-spaces, when taken together, constitute the original program's heap. Thus, no bindings are ever lost or created by the algorithm. The second and third invariants tell us that Q holds the free pointers of the to-space, while L holds the free locations of the to-space. The fourth invariant ensures that for all location/pointer pairs $l{:}p \in L$, p is bound to a type which, when normalized, is the same type assigned to the location l in the proof that the original program is well-formed. Finally, the fifth and sixth invariants ensure that all pointers and locations in the scan set are drawn from those pointers and locations bound in the program's heap.

Next, we show that the GC algorithm preserves well-formedness of GC states, and then show that well-formedness is sufficient to guarantee that a GC state is either terminal (i.e., the scan set is empty) or else there exists a transition to another well-formed GC state. These lemmas are the direct analogues of the Preservation and Progress Lemmas for the proof of type soundness for the abstract machine (see Section 3.4). Proofs of these Lemmas may be found in Appendix B.

Lemma 5.6 (GC State Preservation) *If* X *is well-formed with respect to* P *and* $X \Longrightarrow X'$, *then* X' *is well-formed with respect to* P.

Proof: See Appendix B. □

Lemma 5.7 (GC State Progress) *If $X = (H_f, Q, L, H_t)$ is well-formed with respect to P, then either Q and L are empty or else there exists a GC state X' such that $X \Longrightarrow X'$.*

Proof: See Appendix B. □

Finally, correctness of the GC algorithm is established by showing that the initial GC state is well-formed, and that well-formedness of a terminal state is a sufficient condition to guarantee that the to-space contains all bindings needed to keep the program closed.

Theorem 5.8 (Tag-Free GC Correctness) *If $\vdash P$: unit, then there exists a P' such that $P \overset{\textbf{tf-gc}}{\longmapsto} P'$. Furthermore, $P \overset{\textbf{GC}}{\longmapsto} P'$.*

Proof: Let $P = (H, S, E, e)$ where $H = (TH, VH)$ and $E = (TE, VE)$. Since $\vdash P$: unit, there exists Φ, Ψ, Δ, Γ, and σ' such that $\vdash TH \Downarrow \Phi$, $\Phi \vdash VH : \Psi$, $\Phi; \Psi \vdash S : \sigma' \rightarrow \text{unit}$, $\Phi \vdash TE \Downarrow \Delta$, and $\Psi; \Delta \vdash VE : \Gamma$.

By Lemma 5.2, we know that there exists Q_1 and L_1 such that $\mathcal{F}_{\text{env}}(E) = (Q_1, L_1)$, $FP(E) = Q_1$, $FL(E) = Dom(L_1)$, and for all $l{:}p$ in L_1, $\Phi(p) = \Psi(l)$. By Lemma 5.4, we know that there exists Q_2 and L_2 such that $\mathcal{F}_{\text{stack}}(S) = (Q_2, L_2)$, $FP(S) = Q_2$, $FL(S) = Dom(L_2)$, and for all $l{:}p$ in L_2, $\Phi(p) = \Psi(l)$. Therefore, taking $Q = Q_1 \cup Q_2$ and $L = L_1 \cup L_2$, we know that $FP(\emptyset, S, E, e) = Q$, $FL(\emptyset, S, E, e) = Dom(L)$, and for all $l{:}p$ in L, $\Phi(p) = \Psi(l)$.

Therefore, the initial GC state $X = (H, Q, L, \emptyset)$ is well-formed with respect to P. Since the GC rewriting system cannot diverge, there exists some GC state $X' = (H_f, Q', L', H_t)$ such that $X \Longrightarrow^* X'$ and no step can be taken from X'. By induction on the length of this rewriting sequence using the GC State Preservation Lemma, X' is well-formed with respect to P. Since no transition exists from X', we know via GC State Progress that both Q and L are empty. Hence, $P \overset{\textbf{tf-gc}}{\longmapsto} P'$ where $P' = (H_t, S, E, e)$.

Now, since X' is well-formed with respect to P, we know that $FP(P') \subseteq Q' = \emptyset$ and $FL(P') \subseteq Dom(L') = \emptyset$. Consequently, P' is closed and thus $P \overset{\textbf{GC}}{\longmapsto} P'$. □

6 Other Kinds of Garbage

In the previous sections, we showed how to specify a certain class of heap garbage and how to collect this garbage without changing the observational behaviour of programs. However, for our abstract machine, garbage is not limited to the heap. In this section, we consider two additional forms of garbage, *stack garbage* and *environment garbage*, each of which may be the source of "space leaks" in a program. We show how an implementation may avoid these leaks.

In the most general sense, a frame on the stack is garbage if removing that frame results in a Kleene-equivalent program (i.e., an observationally equivalent program). Likewise, a binding in an environment is garbage if removing that binding results in a Kleene-equivalent program. The following definitions make these notions of garbage precise.

Definition 6.1 (Stack Garbage) *Let $P = (H, S_1 \,\bar{\circ}\, S_2 \,\bar{\circ}\, S_3, E, e)$ be a well-typed program and take $P' = (H, S_1 \,\bar{\circ}\, S_3, E, e)$. We say that the sub-stack S_2 is garbage with respect to P iff $P \simeq P'$.*

Definition 6.2 (Environment Garbage) *Let P be a well-typed program with environment $E \cup E'$ occurring in P (i.e., either the program environment, or the environment of a closure), and let P' be the program obtained by replacing $E \cup E'$ with E. We say that the sub-environment E' is garbage with respect to P iff $P \simeq P'$.*

It may not be practical to re-claim space for stack frames or environment entries except at certain points during evaluation. Hence most implementations restrict their attention to a certain class of garbage stack frames or environment bindings. In the remainder of this section, we examine two specific approaches for collecting certain classes of stack and environment garbage, namely *tail-call elimination* for stack garbage collection, and *environment strengthening* (also known as "black-holing") for environment garbage collection.

6.1 Tail-Call Collection

Tail-call elimination is a space optimization used in many implementations to avoid unnecessary accumulation of control information[7]. The goal of tail-call elimination is to ensure that tail-recursive procedures execute in iterative fashion, with no further space than is required by the code itself. In our framework the tail-call optimization can be phrased as the elimination of *identity continuations* on the stack. The idea is formalized by the following transition rule:

$$\text{(ID)} \quad (H, S_1 \,\bar{\circ}\, \langle\!\langle E', \lambda x{:}t.x \rangle\!\rangle \,\bar{\circ}\, S_2, E, e) \overset{\textbf{ID}}{\longmapsto} (H, S_1 \,\bar{\circ}\, S_2, E, e)$$

The $\overset{\textbf{ID}}{\longmapsto}$ rule eliminates any stack frame if the code of the frame is syntactically equivalent to the identity function. The following lemmas show that $\overset{\textbf{ID}}{\longmapsto}$ preserves types and hence cannot cause a well-typed program to become stuck.

Lemma 6.3 (ID Preservation) *If* $\vdash P : \text{unit}$ *and* $P \overset{\textbf{ID}}{\longmapsto} P'$, *then* $\vdash P' : \text{unit}$.

[7] Tail-call elimination may also improve the running time of programs by avoiding unnecessary stack manipulations, and by decreasing the time taken to extract pointers and locations for heap garbage collection.

Proof: P must be of the form $(H, S_1 \bar{\circ} \langle\!\langle E_1, \lambda x{:}t.x \rangle\!\rangle \bar{\circ} S_2, E, e)$, where $H = (TH, VH)$, $E_1 = (TE_1, VE_1)$, and $E = (TE, VE)$. Since $\vdash P$: unit, there exists a Φ, Ψ, Δ, Γ, and σ' such that (a) $\vdash TH \Downarrow \Phi$, (b) $\Phi \vdash VH : \Psi$, (c) $\Phi; \Psi \vdash S_1 \bar{\circ} \langle\!\langle E_1, \lambda x{:}t.x \rangle\!\rangle \bar{\circ} S_2 : \sigma' \to \text{unit}$, (d) $\Phi \vdash TE \Downarrow \Delta$, (e) $\Psi; \Delta \vdash VE : \Gamma$, and (f) $\Delta; \Gamma \vdash e : \sigma'$. It suffices to show that $\Phi; \Psi \vdash S_1 \bar{\circ} S_2 : \sigma' \to \text{unit}$.

Now (c) can only hold via **cons-s**. Thus, by induction on the size of S_2, we can show that there exists a σ_1 such that (g) $\Phi; \Psi \vdash S_1 \bar{\circ} \langle\!\langle E_1, \lambda x{:}t.x \rangle\!\rangle : \sigma_1 \to \text{unit}$ and (h) $\Phi; \Psi \vdash S_2 : \sigma' \to \sigma_1$. It suffices to show that $\Phi; \Psi \vdash S_1 : \sigma_1 \to \text{unit}$, for then, by induction on the size of S_2 we may show that $\Phi; \Psi \vdash S_1 \bar{\circ} S_2 : \sigma' \to \text{unit}$.

Since (g) can only hold via **cons-s**, there must exist Δ_1, Γ_1, and σ_2 such that (i) $\Phi; \Psi \vdash S_1 : \sigma_2 \to \text{unit}$, (j) $\Phi \vdash TE_1 \Downarrow \Delta_1$, (k) $\Delta_1 \vdash t \Downarrow \sigma_1$, (l) $\Psi; \Delta_1 \vdash VE_1 : \Gamma_1$, and (m) $\Delta_1; \Gamma_1[x{:}\sigma_1] \vdash x : \sigma_2$. But (m) can only hold via the **var** rule and thus $\sigma_1 = \sigma_2$. Consequently, $\Phi; \Psi \vdash S_1 : \sigma_1 \to \text{unit}$. □

Corollary 6.4 (ID Progress) *If* $\vdash P_1$: unit *and* $P_1 \overset{\text{ID}}{\longmapsto} P_2$*, then either* P_2 *is a well-formed answer or else there exists a* P_3 *such that* $P_2 \overset{\text{R}}{\longmapsto} P_3$.

Proof: By ID Preservation, $\vdash P_2$: unit. By Progress and Lemma 3.13, P_2 is either a well-formed answer or else there exists a P_3 such that $P_2 \overset{\text{R}}{\longmapsto} P_3$. □

As with the $\overset{\text{GC}}{\longmapsto}$ rule of Section 4, we wish to show that adding $\overset{\text{ID}}{\longmapsto}$ to the rewriting rules for our abstract machine does not effect the observable behaviour of program evaluation. Let $\overset{\text{IDR}}{\longmapsto}$ be the union of the $\overset{\text{R}}{\longmapsto}$ and $\overset{\text{ID}}{\longmapsto}$ relations.

Definition 6.5 (ID Evaluation Relation)

1. $P \Downarrow_{\text{IDR}} r$ *iff there exists a well-formed* A *such that* $P \overset{\text{IDR}}{\longmapsto}{}^{*} A$.
2. $P \Downarrow_{\text{IDR}} \bot$ *iff* P *diverges with respect to* $\overset{\text{IDR}}{\longmapsto}$.
3. $P \Downarrow_{\text{IDR}}$ `*wrong*` *iff there exists a* P' *such that* $P \overset{\text{IDR}}{\longmapsto}{}^{*} P'$*, and* P' *is stuck with respect to* $\overset{\text{IDR}}{\longmapsto}$.

We would like to show that $\Downarrow_{\text{IDR}}$ is the same total function as our original *eval*. As with the $\Downarrow_{\text{GCR}}$ relation, we show that, whenever a $\overset{\text{ID}}{\longmapsto}$ step is followed by an $\overset{\text{R}}{\longmapsto}$ step, we can postpone the identity frame collection until after the $\overset{\text{R}}{\longmapsto}$ step has been taken. From this, it follows that we can simulate any $\overset{\text{IDR}}{\longmapsto}$ evaluation sequence with an $\overset{\text{R}}{\longmapsto}$ evaluation sequence.

Lemma 6.6 (ID Postponement) *If* $\vdash P_1$: unit, $P_1 \overset{\text{ID}}{\longmapsto} P_2 \overset{\text{R}}{\longmapsto} P_3$*, then there exists a* P_2' *such that* $P_1 \overset{\text{R}}{\longmapsto}{}^{*} P_2' \overset{\text{ID}}{\longmapsto}{}^{*} P_3$.

Proof (sketch): The argument proceeds by case analysis on the $\stackrel{\mathbf{R}}{\longmapsto}$ rewriting rule taking P_2 to P_3. The most interesting case is when P_2 steps to P_3 via the **return** rule. For this case, there are two sub-cases according to whether or not the identity frame eliminated by the $\stackrel{\mathbf{ID}}{\longmapsto}$ transition is the right-most stack frame.

Sub-case return-a: P_1 is of the form (H, S, E, x), where

$$S = S_1 \,\bar{\circ}\, \langle\!\langle E_1, \lambda x_1{:}t_1.e_1 \rangle\!\rangle \,\bar{\circ}\, \langle\!\langle E', \lambda x'{:}t'.x' \rangle\!\rangle,$$

and

$$P_1 \stackrel{\mathbf{ID}}{\longmapsto} (H, S_1 \,\bar{\circ}\, \langle\!\langle E_1, \lambda x_1{:}t_1.e_1 \rangle\!\rangle, E, x) \stackrel{\mathbf{return}}{\longmapsto} (H, S_1, E_1[x_1{:}t_1 \mapsto E(x)], e_1)$$

But then

$$\begin{array}{lll} P_1 & \stackrel{\mathbf{return}}{\longmapsto} & (H, S_1 \,\bar{\circ}\, \langle\!\langle E_1, \lambda x_1{:}t_1.e_1 \rangle\!\rangle, E'[x'{:}t' \mapsto E(x)], x') \\ & \stackrel{\mathbf{return}}{\longmapsto} & (H, S_1, E_1[x_1{:}t_1 \mapsto E'[x'{:}t' \mapsto E(x)](x')], e_1) \end{array}$$

Thus, $P_1 \stackrel{\mathbf{R}}{\longmapsto}^* P_3 \stackrel{\mathbf{ID}}{\longmapsto}^* P_3$.

Sub-case return-b: P_1 is of the form (H, S, E, x), where

$$S = S_1 \,\bar{\circ}\, \langle\!\langle E', \lambda x'{:}t'.x' \rangle\!\rangle \,\bar{\circ}\, S_2 \,\bar{\circ}\, \langle\!\langle E_1, \lambda x_1{:}t_1.e_1 \rangle\!\rangle$$

and

$$\begin{array}{lll} P_1 & \stackrel{\mathbf{ID}}{\longmapsto} & (H, S_1 \,\bar{\circ}\, S_2 \,\bar{\circ}\, \langle\!\langle E_1, \lambda x_1{:}t_1.e_1 \rangle\!\rangle, E, x) \\ & \stackrel{\mathbf{return}}{\longmapsto} & (H, S_1 \,\bar{\circ}\, S_2, E_1[x_1{:}t_1 \mapsto E(x)], e_1) \end{array}$$

But then

$$\begin{array}{lll} P_1 & \stackrel{\mathbf{return}}{\longmapsto} & (H, S_1 \,\bar{\circ}\, \langle\!\langle E', \lambda x'{:}t'.x' \rangle\!\rangle \,\bar{\circ}\, S_2, E_1[x_1{:}t_1 \mapsto E(x)], e_1) \\ & \stackrel{\mathbf{ID}}{\longmapsto} & (H, S_1 \,\bar{\circ}\, S_2, E_1[x_1{:}t_1 \mapsto E(x)], e_1) \end{array}$$

Thus, there exists a P_2' such that $P_1 \stackrel{\mathbf{R}}{\longmapsto}^* P_2' \stackrel{\mathbf{ID}}{\longmapsto}^* P_3$. □

Corollary 6.7 *For all $n \geq 0$, if* $\vdash P_0$: unit *and* $P_0 \stackrel{\mathbf{IDR}}{\longmapsto}^n P_n$, *then there exists a* P_n' *such that* $P_0 \stackrel{\mathbf{R}}{\longmapsto}^* P_n'$ *and* $P_n' \stackrel{\mathbf{ID}}{\longmapsto}^* P_n$.

Proof: By induction on n using the $\stackrel{\mathbf{ID}}{\longmapsto}$ Postponement lemma. □

Lemma 6.8 (ID Answer) *If* $\vdash P$: unit, *and* $P \stackrel{\mathbf{ID}}{\longmapsto}^* A$ *for some A, then* $P \stackrel{\mathbf{R}}{\longmapsto}^*$ *A.*

Proof (sketch): If $P \overset{\mathbf{ID}}{\longmapsto}^* A$, then P's stack must contain only identity frames, since an answer stack must be empty, and the **ID** rule only eliminates identity stack frames. It is thus easy to show by induction on the number of steps taking P to A that the same number of **return** steps can be taken to reach the same answer. □

Theorem 6.9 (ID Correctness) *If* $\vdash P : \text{unit}$, *then* $P \Downarrow r$ *iff* $P \Downarrow_{\mathbf{IDR}} r$.

Proof: We can simulate any $\overset{\mathbf{R}}{\longmapsto}$ step with a $\overset{\mathbf{IDR}}{\longmapsto}$ step by simply never performing an $\overset{\mathbf{ID}}{\longmapsto}$ transition. Consequently, if $P \Downarrow r$, then $P \Downarrow_{\mathbf{IDR}} r$.

Suppose $P \Downarrow_{\mathbf{IDR}} r$. By ID Soundness and ID Progress, $r \neq \texttt{*wrong*}$. If $r = \top$, then there exists an n and well-formed A such that $P \overset{\mathbf{IDR}}{\longmapsto}^n A$. By Corollary 6.7, there exists a P' such that $P \overset{\mathbf{R}}{\longmapsto}^* P' \overset{\mathbf{ID}}{\longmapsto}^* A$. By Lemma 6.8, $P' \overset{\mathbf{R}}{\longmapsto}^* A$. Therefore, $P \Downarrow \top$.

If $r = \bot$ then there exists an infinite sequence $P', P_1, P_1', P_2, P_2', \cdots$ such that

$$P \overset{\mathbf{ID}}{\longmapsto}^* P' \overset{\mathbf{R}}{\longmapsto} P_1 \overset{\mathbf{ID}}{\longmapsto}^* P_1' \overset{\mathbf{R}}{\longmapsto}^* P_2 \overset{\mathbf{ID}}{\longmapsto}^* P_2' \overset{\mathbf{R}}{\longmapsto} \cdots.$$

By Corollary 6.7, we can construct an infinite sequence $P'', P_1'', P_2'', \cdots$ such that

$$P \overset{\mathbf{R}}{\longmapsto} P'' \overset{\mathbf{R}}{\longmapsto} P_1'' \overset{\mathbf{R}}{\longmapsto} P_2'' \overset{\mathbf{R}}{\longmapsto} \cdots$$

Thus, $P \Downarrow \bot$. □

Whereas the proof of the $\overset{\mathbf{ID}}{\longmapsto}$ postponement lemma relies crucially upon the ability to throw away frames in the middle of the stack, real implementations avoid pushing identity frames onto the stack. In effect, every transition that can push a frame on the stack is split into two transitions. If the frame to be pushed on the stack is an identity frame, then the frame is simply discarded; otherwise it is pushed on the stack.

In our abstract machine, only the **c-zero**, **c-succ**, **app**, and **tapp** rules push frames on the stack. Composing these transitions with the $\overset{\mathbf{ID}}{\longmapsto}$ transition (applied to the right-most stack frame) yields the following new transition rules:

(tail-nil)
$$\frac{H(E(x')) = \texttt{nil}}{\begin{array}{l}(H, S, E, \texttt{let}\, x{:}t = \texttt{case}(x', e_0, \lambda[x_1{:}t_1, x_2{:}t_2].e_1)\, \texttt{in}\, x) \longmapsto \\ \quad (H, S, E, e_0)\end{array}}$$

(tail-cons)
$$\frac{H(E(x')) = \texttt{cons}(l_1, l_2)}{\begin{array}{l}(H, S, E, \texttt{let}\, x{:}t = \texttt{case}(x', e_0, \lambda[x_1{:}t_1, x_2{:}t_2].e_1)\, \texttt{in}\, x) \longmapsto \\ \quad (H, S, E[x_1{:}t_1 \mapsto l_1, x_2{:}t_2 \mapsto l_2], e_1)\end{array}}$$

$$\textbf{(tail-app)}\quad \frac{H(E(x_1)) = \langle\!\langle E', \texttt{fix}\ x_1'{:}t_1'(x_2'{:}t_2').e'\rangle\!\rangle}{\begin{array}{l}(H, S, E, \texttt{let}\,x{:}t = x_1\,x_2\,\texttt{in}\,x) \longmapsto \\ \qquad (H, S, E'[x_1'{:}t_1' \mapsto E(x_1), x_2'{:}t_2' \mapsto E(x_2)], e')\end{array}}$$

$$\textbf{(tail-tapp)}\quad \frac{H(E(x_1)) = \langle\!\langle E', \Lambda t_1'.\, e'\rangle\!\rangle}{\begin{array}{l}(H, S, E, \texttt{let}\,x{:}t = x_1\,[t_1]\,\texttt{in}\,x) \longmapsto \\ \qquad (H, S, E'[t_1' \mapsto E(t_1)], e')\end{array}}$$

It is easy to see that adding these new rules, and always choosing the appropriate **tail-** transition when possible, yields a computation without any identity stack frames. For certain classes of programs, this optimization is crucial in order to bound the amount of stack space needed to run programs. In particular, when programs are written in *continuation-passing style* (CPS) (Fischer 1993), then the **return** transition is never enabled until the end of the computation, assuming the computation terminates. Instead, each function is passed an extra argument function (the continuation), and the result of the function is passed to the continuation. In effect, all function applications turn into potential **tail-app** transitions. But if no tail-call elimination is performed, then this coding style delays all of the **return** transitions until the end of the computation (assuming the program terminates) and at worst results in unbounded stack-space requirements (assuming the program diverges). While this is reasonable behaviour in an observational sense, it is unreasonable behaviour in practice. Furthermore, a heap garbage collector must process and preserve all objects that are reachable from these unnecessary frames, so the total amount of garbage in the state of the abstract machine grows quickly.

Some languages, notably Scheme (Clinger and Rees 1991), require that all implementations faithfully implement tail-call elimination in order to address these practical concerns[8]. Yet, the standard models for Scheme make neither the control stack nor heap explicit (Clinger and Rees 1991), and thus the tail-call requirement is at best an informal contract between the language specification and its implementors. In contrast, the model we use here allows the language designer to specify the requirement precisely: asymptotically, an implementation should use no more space than our abstract machine requires with the **tail-** rules. Nevertheless, our model is sufficiently abstract that we can prove the correctness of such an implementation in the observational sense, without overly constraining implementations.

6.2 Environment Strengthening

Collecting garbage bindings in environments is much like collecting garbage bindings in the heap. In particular, a reasonable strategy for collecting bindings in an

[8]See Chase (Chase 1988) for a further discussion of practical space safety issues.

environment is to determine which bindings are inaccessible from the code associated with the environment, and to drop those bindings.

We formulate an environment garbage collector by specifying two inference rules that allow us to *strengthen* the environment of a type or value closure:

$$(\textbf{STE})\ \frac{FTV(\tau) \subseteq Dom(TE_1)}{\langle\!\langle TE_1 \uplus TE_2, \tau \rangle\!\rangle \overset{\textbf{STE}}{\longmapsto} \langle\!\langle TE_1, \tau \rangle\!\rangle}$$

$$(\textbf{SE})\ \frac{FV(e) \subseteq Dom(VE_1) \qquad FTV(VE_1) \cup FTV(e) \subseteq Dom(TE_1)}{\langle\!\langle (TE_1 \uplus TE_2,\ VE_1 \uplus VE_2), e \rangle\!\rangle \overset{\textbf{SE}}{\longmapsto} \langle\!\langle (TE_1,\ VE_1), e \rangle\!\rangle}$$

The $\overset{\textbf{STE}}{\longmapsto}$ rule allows us to strengthen the type environment of a type closure by discarding those bindings not referenced by the type. Similarly, the $\overset{\textbf{SE}}{\longmapsto}$ rule allows us to strengthen the type and value environment of a value closure, as long as all of the free variables of the code are in the domain of the resulting value environment, and all of the free type variables of both the code and the value environment are in the domain of the resulting type environment.

The rules $\overset{\textbf{STE}}{\longmapsto}$ and $\overset{\textbf{SE}}{\longmapsto}$ allow us to strengthen the various environments that may arise in an abstract machine state:

$$(\textbf{SE-th})\ \frac{\langle\!\langle TE_1, \tau \rangle\!\rangle \overset{\textbf{STE}}{\longmapsto} \langle\!\langle TE_2, \tau \rangle\!\rangle}{(H[p \mapsto \langle\!\langle TE_1, \tau \rangle\!\rangle], S, E, e) \overset{\textbf{SE-th}}{\longmapsto} (H[p \mapsto \langle\!\langle TE_2, \tau \rangle\!\rangle], S, E, e)}$$

$$(\textbf{SE-vh})\ \frac{\langle\!\langle E_1, e' \rangle\!\rangle \overset{\textbf{SE}}{\longmapsto} \langle\!\langle E_2, e' \rangle\!\rangle}{(H[l \mapsto \langle\!\langle E_1, e' \rangle\!\rangle], S, E, e) \overset{\textbf{SE-vh}}{\longmapsto} (H[l \mapsto \langle\!\langle E_2, e' \rangle\!\rangle], S, E, e)}$$

$$(\textbf{SE-stack})\ \frac{\langle\!\langle E_1, \lambda x'{:}t'.e' \rangle\!\rangle \overset{\textbf{SE}}{\longmapsto} \langle\!\langle E_2, \lambda x'{:}t'.e' \rangle\!\rangle}{\begin{array}{l}(H, S_1 \mathbin{\bar{\circ}} \langle\!\langle E_1, \lambda x'{:}t'.e' \rangle\!\rangle \mathbin{\bar{\circ}} S_2, E, e) \overset{\textbf{SE-stack}}{\longmapsto} \\ \qquad (H, S_1 \mathbin{\bar{\circ}} \langle\!\langle E_2, \lambda x'{:}t'.e' \rangle\!\rangle \mathbin{\bar{\circ}} S_2, E, e)\end{array}}$$

$$(\textbf{SE-env})\ \frac{\langle\!\langle E_1, e \rangle\!\rangle \overset{\textbf{SE}}{\longmapsto} \langle\!\langle E_2, e \rangle\!\rangle}{(H, S, E_1, e) \overset{\textbf{SE-env}}{\longmapsto} (H, S, E_2, e)}$$

Taken together, these rules allow us to trim the size of all the kinds of environments that may occur in a machine state. As with tail-call collection, trimming environments may also allow more heap garbage to be collected, since there are fewer references to heap allocated objects. Finally, proving that these rules preserve types and do not affect the observable behaviour of programs can be accomplished in the same way we argued these results for the $\overset{\textbf{GC}}{\longmapsto}$ and $\overset{\textbf{ID}}{\longmapsto}$ rules[9].

[9] Some care must be taken, as with the $\overset{\textbf{GC}}{\longmapsto}$ transition, to rule out infinite sequences of environment strengthening.

In practice, implementations only perform environment strengthening at certain points during evaluation, just as most implementations only perform tail-call elimination in conjunction with function application. In particular, Appel suggests that a *space-safe* implementation strategy for closures is to trim their environment only to those variables that occur free in the associated code (Appel 1992a); this is also the strategy used by Cardelli's FAM (Cardelli 1984). However, it is often impractical to trim the current environment (at every instruction), or to even trim the environments of closures as they are pushed on the stack. Instead, some implementations, including the TIL/ML compiler, delay trimming the current environment and the environments of stack frames until garbage collection is invoked.

Many implementations of functional languages perform a program transformation known as *closure conversion* (Appel and Jim 1989; Appel 1992a; Minamide, Morrisett, and Harper 1996) to eliminate nested, higher-order functions. As a result of the transformation, nested functions are replaced with a record, where the first component is a pointer to some code, and the second component is a pointer to a data structure containing bindings for the free variables of the original function. The code abstracts both the environment and the argument to the function. Application is replaced with operations to extract the code and environment, and to apply the code simultaneously to the environment and the argument. In this respect, closure conversion reifies the heap closures of our abstract machine as language constructs in the same fashion that CPS conversion reifies the stack closures of our abstract machine as functions.

During closure conversion, when emitting the operations to construct the environment for a particular closure, it is possible to strengthen the environment. It is also possible for different closures to share portions of the same environment. In particular, many implementations, such as the CAM (Cousineau, Curien, and Mauny 1985), allow closures in the same lexical scope to share an environment for that scope. However, care must be taken when two closures share an environment in order to avoid a class of space leaks (Shao and Appel 1994). In particular, the shared portion of the environment should only contain bindings for those variables that occur free in the code of both closures. Though the abstract machine presented here does not support shared environments, it is fairly straightforward to add environments to the set of heap-allocated values so that they may be shared.

7 Related Work

The ideas in this paper are derived from our previous work with Matthias Felleisen and Morrisett's dissertation (Morrisett, Felleisen, and Harper 1995; Morrisett 1995), where we presented a much simpler abstract machine that relied upon meta-level substitution and meta-level evaluation contexts to implicitly represent the control state and environment of a computation. In this paper, we make these details explicit so that issues like tail-call elimination and environment strengthening could be addressed. We further extended the previous work by addressing the issues of allocating and collecting type information, and by giving a full treatment of tag-free collection in the context of a polymorphic language.

The literature on garbage collection in sequential programming languages contains few papers that attempt to provide a compact characterization of algorithms or correctness proofs, and none of these papers covers heap, stack, and environment memory management.

Demers, Weiser, Hayes, Boehm, Bobrow, and Shenker (1990) give a model of memory parameterized by an abstract notion of a "points-to" relation. As a result, they can characterize *reachability*-based algorithms including mark-sweep, copying, generational, "conservative," and other sophisticated forms of garbage collection. However, their model is intentionally divorced from the programming language and cannot take advantage of any *semantic* properties of evaluation, such as type preservation. Consequently, their framework cannot model the type-based, tag-free collector of Section 5. Nettles (1992) provides a concrete specification of a copying garbage collection algorithm using the Larch specification language. Our $\stackrel{\mathbf{GC}}{\longmapsto}$ transition rule is essentially a high-level, one-line description of his specification, and the $\stackrel{\mathbf{tf\text{-}gc}}{\longmapsto}$ rule is a particular implementation.

Tofte and Talpin (1994) describe a memory management strategy for ML-like languages based on stack-allocated regions of memory and prove its correctness using operational techniques similar to the ones used here. The focus of the work is on using effects inference to determine in which region to allocate objects so that they may be collected as early as possible, given the last-in-first-out allocation strategy of regions. A later paper describes an implementation of a region-inference based compiler and runtime system (Birkedal, Tofte, and Vejlstrup 1996). It seems possible to accommodate a region-based collector within our operational framework. However, our typing rules preclude "dangling references", whereas Tofte and Talpin's typing does not. Failing to do so lead to considerable complications in the statements and proofs of the theorems.

Hudak (1986) gives a denotational model that tracks reference counts for a first-order language. He presents an abstraction of the model and gives an algorithm for computing approximations of reference counts statically. Chirimar, Gunter, and Riecke give a framework for proving invariants regarding memory management for a language with a *linear* type system (Chirimar, Gunter, and Riecke 1996; Chirimar, Gunter, and Riecke 1992). Their low-level semantics specifies explicit memory management based on reference counting. Furthermore, the typing they use for program states is based on an "unwinding lemma" that is similar to our rules for substituting the type heap for an allocated type. Both Hudak and Chirimar *et al.* assume a weak approximation of garbage (reference counts). Barendsen and Smetsers (1993) give a Curry-like type system for functional languages extended with *uniqueness* information that guarantees an object is only "locally accessible". This provides a compiler enough information to determine when certain objects may be garbage collected or over-written.

Tolmach (1994) built a type-recovery collector for a variant of SML that passes type information to polymorphic routines during execution, effectively implementing our $\lambda_{gc}^{\rightarrow\forall}$ language and the type-based, tag-free collector of Section 5. Aditya and Caro (1993) gave a type-recovery algorithm for an implementation of Id that uses a technique that appears to be equivalent to type passing; Aditya, Flood, and Hicks (1994) extended this work to garbage collection for Id.

A number of papers on inference-based, tag-free collection in monomorphic (Branquart and Lewi 1970; Wodon 1970; Britton 1975) and polymorphic languages have appeared in the literature. Appel (1989) argued informally that "tag-free" collection is possible for polymorphic languages, such as SML, by a combination of recording information statically and performing what amounts to type inference during the collection process, though the connections between inference and collection were not made clear. Baker (1990) recognized that Milner-style type inference can be used to prove that reachable objects can be safely collected, but did not give a formal account of this result. Goldberg and Gloger (1992) recognized that it is not possible to reconstruct the concrete types of all reachable values in an implementation of an ML-style language that does not pass types to polymorphic routines. They gave an informal argument based on traversal of stack frames to show that such values are *semantically* garbage. Fradet (1994) gave another argument based on Reynolds's abstraction/parametricity theorem (Reynolds 1983). None of these papers gives a complete formulation of the underlying dynamic and static semantics of the language.

Blelloch and Greiner (1996) give an abstract machine for evaluation of the parallel programming language NESL. The goal of their work was to provide provable space and time bounds for an implementation of NESL. Their machine is based directly on the CESK machine (Felleisen and Friedman 1987). However, some details in their formulation, such as the representation of control information, are left implicit.

8 Summary and Conclusions

We have presented an abstract machine for describing the evaluation of polymorphic functional programs. Unlike traditional models of functional languages, our abstract machine exposes many important details of memory management such as the heap, control stack, and environment. Nevertheless, our machine is sufficiently abstract that we are able to use conventional techniques to specify its static semantics, and to prove soundness of the static semantics with respect to the transitions of the abstract machine.

An important property of our abstract machine is that it "interprets" a relatively high-level language that is extremely close to a conventional language such as SML. Indeed, the only pre-processing required is to convert the original source code to named-form — a relatively simple, and easy to understand transformation. An alternative approach would be to specify a complete set of compile-time transformations that map source terms to low-level target terms. In particular, by applying CPS and closure-conversion transforms before evaluating the term, the abstract machine could be greatly simplified. However, this would make it more difficult to reason about the space and time requirements of the original program, and complicate the typing of the abstract machine. Furthermore, compiler-writers can still evaluate the space and time properties of various program transformations (e.g., FAM versus CAM-style environments) by using our abstract machine as a base-line for comparison.

Extending our abstract machine to support input/output, references and arrays, continuations, exceptions, and other computational effects appears to be straightforward. In particular, references and arrays are easy to support since we have a globally-scoped heap that supports cycles (Harper 1994). Similarly, mutually-recursive functions and values are also easy to support. Adding support for full recursive types also seems possible. However, there are some technical complications since the most convenient representation of allocated recursive types requires a cyclic type heap. This precludes an inductive definition for reducing an allocated type to a type, by simply substituting type heap bindings for type pointers. Nevertheless, it seems possible to scale our abstract machine to cover a full programming language such as Standard ML.

Since the abstract machine exposes memory management issues, we are able to precisely specify important classes of garbage that arise during the evaluation of programs, including unreachable heap values, tail-call stack frames, and unreferenced environment bindings. For each class of garbage, we presented an abstract specification of a collector which reclaims the garbage objects, and proved that these collectors do not affect the observable behaviour of well-formed programs. In addition, we gave a detailed specification of a Tolmach-style type-based, tag-free, garbage collector (Tolmach 1994) and proved its correctness. The techniques used to specify and prove correctness for all of the collectors were based on those used to establish type soundness for the abstract machine.

Admittedly, our machine abstracts many important low-level implementation details for memory management. In particular, we *a priori* consider programs equivalent up to α-conversion of bound variables and any re-ordering of heap or environment bindings; we also ignore representation and sharing issues for environments. However, abstracting these details greatly simplifies our reasoning and keeps us from over-constraining implementations. For example, the tag-free collector specified in Section 5 is compatible with either a copying or in-place mark/sweep collector. Hence, we claim that such a model provides an important intermediate step in establishing the correctness of a wide class of existing and future implementations.

Acknowledgments This paper is based on a preliminary version by Matthias Felleisen and the authors (Morrisett, Felleisen, and Harper 1995; Morrisett 1995). We very gratefully acknowledge the important contributions of Matthias Felleisen to the work described here. We are grateful to Chris Stone, Todd Wilson, Andrew Gordon, and the anonymous reviewers for their careful reading of this paper and for their many useful comments and suggestions. We are also grateful for our many discussions with Andrew Tolmach and Yasuhiko Minamide about tag-free garbage collection.

A Typing Rules for the Abstract Machine

5. $\Phi \vdash TE \Downarrow \Delta$

$$(\textbf{empty-te})\ \ \Phi \vdash \emptyset \Downarrow \emptyset$$

$$(\textbf{cons-te})\ \ \frac{\Phi \vdash TE \Downarrow \Delta \qquad \Phi(p) = \sigma}{\Phi \vdash TE[t \mapsto p] \Downarrow \Delta[t = \sigma]}$$

6. $\Phi \vdash \mu \Downarrow \sigma$

$$(\textbf{th-unit})\ \ \Phi \vdash \text{unit} \Downarrow \text{unit}$$

$$(\textbf{th-prod})\ \ \frac{\Phi(p_1) = \sigma_1 \quad \Phi(p_2) = \sigma_2}{\Phi \vdash p_1 \times p_2 \Downarrow \sigma_1 \times \sigma_2}$$

$$(\textbf{th-arrow})\ \ \frac{\Phi(p_1) = \sigma_1 \quad \Phi(p_2) = \sigma_2}{\Phi \vdash p_1 \to p_2 \Downarrow \sigma_1 \to \sigma_2}$$

$$(\textbf{th-list})\ \ \frac{\Phi(p) = \sigma}{\Phi \vdash \text{list}[p] \Downarrow \text{list}[\sigma]}$$

$$(\textbf{th-all})\ \ \frac{\Phi \vdash TE \Downarrow \Delta \qquad \Delta \vdash \forall t.\tau \Downarrow \forall t.\sigma}{\Phi \vdash \langle\!\langle TE, \forall t.\tau \rangle\!\rangle \Downarrow \forall t.\sigma}$$

7. $\vdash TH \Downarrow \Phi$

$$(\textbf{empty-th})\ \ \vdash \emptyset \Downarrow \emptyset$$

$$(\textbf{cons-th})\ \ \frac{\vdash TH \Downarrow \Phi \qquad \Phi \vdash \mu \Downarrow \sigma}{\vdash TH[p \mapsto \mu] \Downarrow \Phi[p = \sigma]}$$

Figure 10: Type Environment and Heap Reduction

8. $\Psi; \Delta \vdash VE : \Gamma$

$$\textbf{(empty-ve)}\quad \Psi; \Delta \vdash \emptyset : \emptyset \quad (Abstr(\Delta) = \emptyset)$$

$$\textbf{(cons-ve)}\quad \frac{\Psi; \Delta \vdash VE : \Gamma \qquad \Psi(l) = \sigma \qquad \Delta \vdash t \Downarrow \sigma}{\Psi; \Delta \vdash VE[x{:}t \mapsto l] : \Gamma[x{:}\sigma]}$$

9. $\Phi; \Psi \vdash h : \sigma$

$$\textbf{(vh-unit)}\quad \Phi; \Psi \vdash \langle\rangle : \text{unit}$$

$$\textbf{(vh-prod)}\quad \frac{\Psi(l_1) = \sigma_1 \quad \Psi(l_2) = \sigma_2}{\Phi; \Psi \vdash \langle l_1, l_2 \rangle : \sigma_1 \times \sigma_2}$$

$$\textbf{(vh-arrow)}\quad \frac{\Phi \vdash TE \Downarrow \Delta \qquad \Psi; \Delta \vdash VE : \Gamma \qquad \Delta; \Gamma \vdash \texttt{fix}\ \ x{:}t(x_1{:}t_1).e : \sigma_1 \to \sigma_2}{\Phi; \Psi \vdash \langle\!\langle (TE, VE), \texttt{fix}\ \ x{:}t(x_1{:}t_1).e \rangle\!\rangle : \sigma_1 \to \sigma_2}$$

$$\textbf{(vh-nil)}\quad \frac{FTV(\sigma) = \emptyset}{\Phi; \Psi \vdash \texttt{nil} : \text{list}[\sigma]} \qquad \textbf{(vh-cons)}\quad \frac{\Psi(l_1) = \sigma \quad \Psi(l_1) = \text{list}[\sigma]}{\Phi; \Psi \vdash \texttt{cons}(l_1, l_2) : \text{list}[\sigma]}$$

$$\textbf{(vh-all)}\quad \frac{\Phi \vdash TE \Downarrow \Delta \qquad \Psi; \Delta \vdash VE : \Gamma \qquad \Delta; \Gamma \vdash \Lambda t.\, e : \forall t.\sigma}{\Phi; \Psi \vdash \langle\!\langle (TE, VE), \Lambda t.\, e \rangle\!\rangle : \forall t.\sigma}$$

10. $\Phi \vdash VH : \Psi$

$$\textbf{(vh)}\quad \frac{Dom(\Psi) = Dom(VH) \qquad \forall l \in Dom(\Psi).\, \Phi; \Psi \vdash VH(l) : \Psi(l)}{\Phi \vdash VH : \Psi}$$

Figure 11: Value Environment and Heap Typing

11. $\Phi; \Psi \vdash S : \sigma_1 \rightarrow \sigma_2$

$$\textbf{(empty-s)}\quad \Phi; \Psi \vdash [] : \text{unit} \rightarrow \text{unit} \quad (FTV(\sigma) = \emptyset)$$

$$\textbf{(cons-s)}\quad \frac{\Phi; \Psi \vdash S : \sigma_3 \rightarrow \sigma_2 \qquad \Phi \vdash TE \Downarrow \Delta \qquad \Psi; \Delta \vdash VE : \Gamma \qquad \Delta \vdash t \Downarrow \sigma_1 \qquad \Delta; \Gamma[x{:}\sigma_1] \vdash e : \sigma_3}{\Phi; \Psi \vdash S \,\bar{\circ}\, \langle\!\langle (TE, VE), \lambda x{:}t.e \rangle\!\rangle : \sigma_1 \rightarrow \sigma_2}$$

12. $\vdash P : \sigma$

$$\textbf{(prog)}\quad \frac{\vdash TH \Downarrow \Phi \qquad \Phi \vdash VH : \Psi \qquad \Phi; \Psi \vdash S : \sigma' \rightarrow \text{unit} \qquad \Phi \vdash TE \Downarrow \Delta \qquad \Psi; \Delta \vdash VE : \Gamma \qquad \Delta; \Gamma \vdash e : \sigma'}{\vdash ((TH, VH), S, (TE, VE), e) : \text{unit}}$$

Figure 12: Stack and Program Typing

B Proofs of Main Lemmas

Lemma 3.10 (Preservation) *If* $\vdash P : \text{unit}$ *and* $P \stackrel{\mathbf{R}}{\longmapsto} P'$, *then* $\vdash P' : \text{unit}$.

Proof: Let $P = ((TH_0, VH_0), S_0, (TE_0, VE_0), e_0)$. The judgement $\vdash P : \sigma$ can only hold via the **prog** rule, so there must exist Φ_0, Ψ_0, Δ_0, Γ_0, and σ_0 such that:

(a) $\vdash TH_0 \Downarrow \Phi_0$,
(b) $\Phi_0 \vdash VH_0 : \Psi_0$,
(c) $\Phi_0; \Psi_0 \vdash S_0 : \sigma_0 \rightarrow \text{unit}$,
(d) $\Phi_0 \vdash TE_0 : \Delta_0$,
(e) $\Psi_0; \Delta_0 \vdash VE_0 : \Gamma_0$, and
(f) $\Delta_0; \Gamma_0 \vdash e_0 : \sigma_0$.

The proof proceeds by cases on the rewriting rule that takes P to P' (see Figure 8), using the syntax-directed nature of the typing rules.

case return: e_0 is x' and S_0 is $S \,\bar{\circ}\, \langle\!\langle (TE, VE), \lambda x{:}t.e \rangle\!\rangle$ for some x', S, TE, VE, x, t, and e, and

$$P' = ((TH_0, VH_0), S, (TE, VE[x{:}t \mapsto VE_0(x')]), e).$$

Hence, (c) must be derived from the **cons-s** rule and thus there exists a σ_1, Δ, and Γ such that $\Phi_0; \Psi_0 \vdash S : \sigma_1 \rightarrow \text{unit}$, $\Phi_0 \vdash TE \Downarrow \Delta$, $\Psi_0; \Delta \vdash VE : \Gamma$, $\Delta \vdash t \Downarrow \sigma_0$, and $\Delta;\Gamma[x{:}\sigma_0] \vdash e : \sigma_1$. Now, (f) must hold via the **var** rule and thus $\Gamma_0(x') = \sigma_0$. Therefore, (e) must hold via the **cons-ve** rule and thus $\Psi_0(VE_0(x')) = \sigma_0$. Hence, by the **cons-ve** rule, $\Psi_0;\Delta \vdash VE[x{:}t \mapsto l] : \Gamma[x{:}\sigma_0]$.

case talloc: e_0 is $\texttt{type}\, t = \nu\, \texttt{in}\, e$ for some t, ν, and e, and

$$P' = ((TH_0[p \mapsto \hat{TE}_0(\nu)], VH_0), S, (TE_0[t \mapsto p], VE_0), e).$$

Hence, (f) holds via the **type** rule, so there exists a σ' such that $\Delta_0 \vdash \nu \Downarrow \sigma'$, and $\Delta_0[t = \sigma']; \Gamma_0 \vdash e : \sigma_0$. Since (a) and (d) hold, Lemma 3.6 implies that $\Phi_0 \vdash \hat{TE}_0(\nu) \Downarrow \sigma'$. Therefore, by **cons-th,** $\vdash TH_0[p \mapsto \hat{TE}_0(\nu)] \Downarrow \Phi_0[p = \sigma']$. Hence, by **cons-te,** $\Phi_0[p = \sigma'] \vdash TE_0[t \mapsto p] : \Delta_0[t = \sigma']$.

For the remainder of the cases, e_0 must be of the form $\texttt{let}\, x{:}t = b\, \texttt{in}\, e$ for some x, t, b, and e. Therefore, (f) must hold via the **let** rule, and hence there exists some σ' such that:

(g) $\Delta_0 \vdash t \Downarrow \sigma'$,
(h) $\Delta_0; \Gamma_0 \vdash b : \sigma'$, and
(i) $\Delta_0; \Gamma_0[x{:}\sigma'] \vdash e : \sigma_0$.

The proof proceeds by cases on b. We present the interesting cases here.

case app: b is of the form $x_1\, x_2$ for some x_1 and x_2, and $VH_0(VE_0(x_1))$ is $\langle\!\langle (TE, VE), \texttt{fix}\ x_1'{:}t_1'(x_2'{:}t_2').e' \rangle\!\rangle$. Thus, P' is:

$$((TH_0, VH_0), S_0 \,\bar{\circ}\, \langle\!\langle (TE_0, VE_0), \lambda x{:}t.e \rangle\!\rangle,$$
$$(TE, VE[x_1'{:}t_1' \mapsto VE_0(x_1), x_2'{:}t_2' \mapsto VE_0(x_2)]), e').$$

By (c), (d), (e), (g), (i), and the **cons-s** rule,

$$\Phi_0; \Psi_0 \vdash S_0 \,\bar{\circ}\, \langle\!\langle (TE_0, VE_0), \lambda x{:}t.e \rangle\!\rangle : \sigma' \to \text{unit}.$$

Now (h) can only hold via the **arrow-E** rule and thus there exists a σ_1 such that $\Delta_0; \Gamma_0 \vdash x_1 : \sigma_1 \to \sigma'$ and $\Delta_0; \Gamma_0 \vdash x_2 : \sigma_1$. Therefore, $\Psi_0; \Delta_0 \vdash VE_0(x_1) : \sigma_1 \to \sigma'$ and $\Psi_0; \Delta_0 \vdash VE_0(x_2) : \sigma_1$. Consequently, $\Phi_0; \Psi_0 \vdash \langle\!\langle (TE, VE), \texttt{fix}\ x_1'{:}t_1'(x_2'{:}t_2').e' \rangle\!\rangle : \sigma_1 \to \sigma'$. Now this can only hold via the **vh-arrow** rule. Thus, there exists a Δ and Γ such that $\Phi_0 \vdash TE \Downarrow \Delta$, $\Delta \vdash t_1' \Downarrow \sigma_1 \to \sigma'$, $\Delta \vdash t_2' \Downarrow \sigma_1$, $\Psi_0; \Delta \vdash VE : \Gamma$, and $\Delta; \Gamma[x_1'{:}\sigma_1 \to \sigma', x_2'{:}\sigma_1] \vdash e' : \sigma'$. By **cons-ve,** $\Psi_0; \Delta_0 \vdash VE[x_1'{:}t_1' \mapsto VE_0(x_1), x_2'{:}t_2' \mapsto VE_0(x_2)] : \Gamma[x_1'{:}\sigma_1 \to \sigma', x_2'{:}\sigma_1]$.

case c-cons: b is $\texttt{case}(x', e_0', \lambda[x_1{:}t_1, x_2{:}t_2].e_1)$ for some x', e_0', x_1, t_1, x_2, t_2, and e_1. Furthermore, $VH_0(VE_0(x')) = \texttt{cons}(l_1, l_2)$ for some l_1 and l_2 and thus

$$\begin{aligned} P' \;=\; & ((TH_0, VH_0), S_0 \,\bar{\circ}\, \langle\!\langle (TE_0, VE_0), \lambda x{:}t.e \rangle\!\rangle, \\ & (TE_0, VE_0[x_1{:}t_1 \mapsto l_1, x_2{:}t_2 \mapsto l_2]), e_1). \end{aligned}$$

By (c), (d), (e), (g), (i) and the **cons-s** rule,

$$\Delta_0; \Gamma_0 \vdash S_0 \,\bar{\circ}\, \langle\!\langle (TE_0, VE_0), \lambda x{:}t.e \rangle\!\rangle : \sigma' \to \text{unit}.$$

Now (i) must hold via **list-E**, so we can conclude that for some σ_1, $\Delta_0; \Gamma_0 \vdash x' : \mathrm{list}[\sigma_1]$, $\Delta_0 \vdash t_1 \Downarrow \sigma_1$, $\Delta_0 \vdash t_2 \Downarrow \mathrm{list}[\sigma_1]$, and $\Delta_0; \Gamma_0[x_1{:}\sigma_1, x_2{:}\mathrm{list}[\sigma_1]] \vdash e_1 : \sigma'$. Therefore, through (e) and the **cons-ve** rule, we can conclude that $\Psi_0(VE_0(x')) = \mathrm{list}[\sigma_1]$. Thus, through (b) and the **vh** rule, $\Phi_0; \Psi_0 \vdash VH_0(VE_0(x')) : \mathrm{list}[\sigma_1]$ and consequently, $\Phi_0; \Psi_0 \vdash \mathtt{cons}(l_1, l_2) : \mathrm{list}[\sigma_1]$. Hence, working backwards from the **vh-cons** rule, $\Psi_0(l_1) = \sigma_1$ and $\Psi_0(l_2) = \mathrm{list}[\sigma_1]$. Therefore, $\Psi_0; \Delta_0 \vdash TE_0[x_1{:}t_1 \mapsto l_1, x_2{:}t_2 \mapsto l_2] : \Gamma_0[x_1{:}\sigma_1, x_2{:}\mathrm{list}[\sigma_1]]$.

case tapp: b is $x_1\,[t_2]$ for some x_1 and t_2, and $VH_0(VE_0(x_1)) = \langle\!\langle (TE, VE), \Lambda t'.\, e' \rangle\!\rangle$ for some (TE, VE), t', and e'. Thus,

$$P' = ((TH_0, VH_0), S_0 \,\overline{\circ}\, \langle\!\langle (TE_0, VE_0), \lambda x{:}t.e \rangle\!\rangle, (TE[t' \mapsto TE_0(t_2)], VE), e').$$

From (c), (d), (e), (g), (i), and the **cons-s** rule, we can conclude that $\Phi_0; \Psi_0 \vdash S_0 \,\overline{\circ}\, \langle\!\langle (TE_0, VE_0), \lambda x{:}t.e \rangle\!\rangle : \sigma' \to \mathrm{unit}$. Now (h) must hold via the **all-E** rule, and thus there exists σ_1 and σ_2 such that $\Delta_0; \Gamma_0 \vdash x_1 : \forall t'.\sigma_1$,$\Delta_0 \vdash t_2 \Downarrow \sigma_2$, and $\sigma' = \{\sigma_2/t'\}\sigma_1$. From this, we can conclude that $\Phi_0; \Psi_0 \vdash \langle\!\langle (TE, VE), \Lambda t'.\, e' \rangle\!\rangle : \forall t'.\sigma_1$. Now this can only hold through the **vh-all** rule, and thus there exists Δ and Γ such that $\Phi_0 \vdash TE \Downarrow \Delta$, $\Psi_0; \Delta \vdash VE : \Gamma$, and $\Delta[t']; \Gamma \vdash e' : \sigma_1$. Since $\Delta_0 \vdash t_2 \Downarrow \sigma_2$, we can conclude from the **cons-te** rule that $TE[t' \mapsto TE_0(t_2)] \Downarrow \Delta[t' = \sigma_2]$. Now, by Lemma 3.9, $\Delta[t' = \sigma_2]; \Gamma \vdash e' : \{\sigma_2/t'\}\sigma_1 = \sigma'$. □

Lemma 3.12 (Progress) *If* $\vdash P : \mathrm{unit}$, *then either* P *is an answer or else there exists a* P' *such that* $P \overset{\mathbf{R}}{\longmapsto} P'$.

Proof: Let $P = (H_0, S_0, E_0, e_0)$, $H_0 = (TH_0, VH_0)$ and $E_0 = (TE_0, VE_0)$. Since $\vdash P : \mathrm{unit}$ must be derived from the **prog** rule, there exists Φ_0, Ψ_0, Δ_0, Γ_0, and σ_0 such that:

(a) $\vdash TH_0 \Downarrow \Phi_0$,
(b) $\Phi_0 \vdash VH_0 : \Psi_0$,
(c) $\Phi_0; \Psi_0 \vdash S_0 : \sigma_0 \to \mathrm{unit}$,
(d) $\Phi_0 \vdash TE_0 : \Delta_0$,
(e) $\Psi_0; \Delta_0 \vdash VE_0 : \Gamma_0$, and
(f) $\Delta_0; \Gamma_0 \vdash e_0 : \sigma_0$.

The proof proceeds by cases on e.

case: $e_0 = x'$. If $S_0 = []$, then P is an answer. Suppose S_0 is equal to $S \,\overline{\circ}\, \langle\!\langle E, \lambda x{:}t.e \rangle\!\rangle$. Since (f) holds, it must be the case that $x' \in Dom(\Gamma_0)$. By (e), this implies that $x' \in Dom(VE_0)$. Consequently, $P \longmapsto (H_0, S, E[x{:}t \mapsto VE_0(x')], e)$ by the **return** rule.

case: $e_0 = \mathtt{type}\, t = \nu\ \mathtt{in}\, e$. Thus (f) must hold via the **type** rule and we can conclude that, since $\Delta_0 \vdash \nu \Downarrow \sigma'$ for some σ', $FTV(\nu) \subseteq Dom(\Delta_0)$. Since $\Phi_0 \vdash TE_0 : \Delta_0$, we know that $Abstr(\Delta_0) = \emptyset$. Thus, $FTV(\nu) \subseteq Dom(TE_0)$. Consequently, $\hat{TE}_0(\nu)$ is defined. Thus $P \longmapsto (H_0[p \mapsto \hat{TE}_0(\nu)], S_0, E_0[t \mapsto p], e)$ by the **talloc** rule.

For the remainder of the cases, e_0 must be of the form $\mathtt{let}\, x{:}t = b\ \mathtt{in}\, e$ for some x, t, b, and e. Therefore, (f) must hold via the **let** rule, and hence there exists some σ' such that:

(g) $\Delta_0 \vdash t \Downarrow \sigma'$,
(h) $\Delta_0; \Gamma_0 \vdash b : \sigma'$, and
(i) $\Delta_0; \Gamma_0[x{:}\sigma'] \vdash e : \sigma_0$.

The proof proceeds by cases on b. We show some representative cases here.

case: $b = \pi_i\, x'$. Now (h) must hold via the **prod-E** rule. Thus, $\Delta_0; \Gamma_0 \vdash x' : \sigma_1 \times \sigma_2$ for some σ_1 and σ_2 such that $\sigma_i = \sigma'$. Since (e) holds, $x' \in \mathit{Dom}(\mathit{VE}_0)$. Therefore, $\mathit{VE}_0(x') \in \mathit{Dom}(\Psi_0)$ and thus $\mathit{VE}_0(x') \in \mathit{Dom}(\mathit{VH}_0)$. Since (b) holds, $\Phi_0; \Psi_0 \vdash \mathit{VH}_0(\mathit{VE}_0(x')) : \sigma_1 \times \sigma_2$. By the Canonical Forms lemma, $\mathit{VH}_0(\mathit{VE}_0(x'))$ must be of the form $\langle l_1, l_2 \rangle$ for some l_1 and l_2. Thus, $P \longmapsto (H_0, S_0, E_0[x{:}t \mapsto l_i], e)$ by the **proj** rule.

case: $b = x_1\, x_2$. Now (h) must hold via the **arrow-E** rule. Thus, $\Delta_0; \Gamma_0 \vdash x_1 : \sigma_1 \to \sigma'$ and $\Delta_0; \Gamma_0 \vdash x_2 : \sigma_1$ for some σ_1. Thus, x_1 and x_2 are in $\mathit{Dom}(\Gamma_0)$ and since (e) holds, x_1 and x_2 are in $\mathit{Dom}(\mathit{VE}_0)$. Furthermore, $\mathit{VE}_0(x_1) \in \mathit{Dom}(\Psi_0)$ and since (b) holds, $\mathit{VE}_0(x_1) \in \mathit{Dom}(\mathit{VH}_0)$ and $\Phi_0; \Psi_0 \vdash \mathit{VH}_0(\mathit{VE}_0(x_1)) : \sigma_1 \to \sigma'$. By the Canonical Forms lemma, $\mathit{VH}_0(\mathit{VE}_0(x_1))$ must be of the form $\langle\!\langle E, \mathtt{fix}\ x_1'{:}t_1'(x_2'{:}t_2').e' \rangle\!\rangle$ for some E, x_1', t_1', x_2', t_2', and e'. Thus,

$$P \longmapsto (H_0, S_0 \,\overline{\circ}\, \langle\!\langle E_0, \lambda x{:}t.e \rangle\!\rangle, E[x_1'{:}t_1' \mapsto \mathit{VE}_0(x_1), x_2'{:}t_2' \mapsto \mathit{VE}_0(x_2)], e')$$

by the **app** rule.

case:

$b = \mathtt{case}(x', e_0', \lambda[x_1'{:}t_1', x_2'{:}t_2'].e_1')$. Now (h) must hold through the **list -E** rule. Thus, $\Delta_0; \Gamma_0 \vdash x' : \mathrm{list}[\sigma_1]$ for some σ_1. Since (h) holds, $FV(b) \subseteq \mathit{Dom}(\Gamma_0)$ and thus $x' \in \mathit{Dom}(\Gamma_0)$. But then (e) implies $x' \in \mathit{Dom}(\mathit{VE}_0)$. In turn, this implies that $\Psi_0(\mathit{VE}_0(x')) = \mathrm{list}[\sigma_1]$. Since (b) holds, this implies that $\Phi_0; \Psi_0 \vdash \mathit{VH}_0(\mathit{VE}_0(x')) : \mathrm{list}[\sigma_1]$. By the Canonical Forms lemma, $\mathit{VH}_0(\mathit{VE}_0(x'))$ is either $\mathtt{nil}$ or $\mathtt{cons}(l_1, l_2)$ for some l_1 and l_2. Thus,

$$P \longmapsto (H_0, S_0 \,\overline{\circ}\, \langle\!\langle E_0, \lambda x{:}t.e \rangle\!\rangle, E', e')$$

where either $E' = E_0$ and $e' = e_0'$, or else $E' = E_0[x_1'{:}t_1' \mapsto l_1, x_2'{:}t_2' \mapsto l_2]$ and $e' = e_1'$, by either the **c-nil** or **c-cons** rule respectively.

□

Lemma 5.6 (GC State Preservation) *If X is well-formed with respect to P and $X \Longrightarrow X'$, then X' is well-formed with respect to P.*

Proof: Let $P = (H, S, E, e)$, $H = (\mathit{TH}, \mathit{VH})$, $\vdash \mathit{TH} \Downarrow \Phi$, $\Phi \vdash \mathit{VH} : \Psi$, and let $X = (H_f, Q, L, H_t)$ be well-formed with respect to P and $X \Longrightarrow X'$. Since X is well-formed, we know that:

(a) $H_f \uplus H_t = H$,
(b) $\mathit{FP}(H_t, S, E, e) \subseteq Q$,
(c) $\mathit{FL}(H_t, S, E, e) \subseteq \mathit{Dom}(L)$,
(d) for all $l{:}p \in L$, $\Phi(p) = \Psi(l)$,
(e) $Q \subseteq \mathit{Dom}(\mathit{TH})$, and
(f) for all $l{:}p$ in L, $l \in \mathit{Dom}(\mathit{VH})$ and $p \in \mathit{Dom}(\mathit{TH})$.

The argument continues by cases on the rule taking X to X'. Throughout, it is clear that any free pointers or locations entered into the scan-set must be bound in the original heap.

case gc-1:

$H_f = H'_f[p \mapsto \mu]$, $Q = Q' \uplus \{p\}$, and $X' = (H'_f, Q' \cup FP(\mu), L, H_t[p \mapsto \mu])$. By (a), we know that $H'_f \uplus H_t[p \mapsto \mu] = H$. Suppose $H_t = (TH_t, VH_t)$. Then from (b), we know that $FP(H_t) \subseteq Q' \uplus \{p\}$. Therefore,

$$\begin{array}{rcl} FP(H_t[p \mapsto \mu]) & = & (FP(H_t) \setminus \{p\}) \cup (FP(\mu) \setminus (Dom(TH_t) \cup \{p\})) \\ & \subseteq & ((Q' \uplus \{p\}) \setminus \{p\}) \cup (FP(\mu) \setminus (Dom(TH_t) \cup \{p\})) \\ & = & Q' \cup (FP(\mu) \setminus (Dom(TH_t) \cup \{p\})) \\ & \subseteq & Q' \cup FP(\mu). \end{array}$$

Thus, $FP(H_t[p \mapsto \mu], S, E, e) \subseteq Q' \cup FP(\mu)$. Hence, from (c) and (d) we can conclude that X' is well-formed with respect to P.

case gc-2: $Q = Q' \uplus \{p\}$, $p \notin Dom(H_f)$, and $X' = (H_f, Q', L, H_t)$. By (a) and the fact that H is well-formed, we can conclude that p must be bound in either H_f or H_t. Since p is not bound in H_f, it must be bound in H_t. Thus, $p \notin FP(H_t, S, E, e)$ and from (b) we can conclude that $FP(H_t, S, E, e) \subseteq Q'$. Hence from (d) and (e), we can conclude that X' is well-formed with respect to P.

case gc-3: $H_f = H'_f[l \mapsto h]$, $L = L' \uplus \{l{:}p\}$, and $X' = (H'_f, Q \cup Q_1, L \cup L_2, H_t[l \mapsto h])$ where $\mathcal{F}[(H_f \cup H_t)(p)](p, h) = (Q_1, L_1)$. Since X is well-formed, we know that $\Phi(p) = \Psi(l)$ and thus $FP(h) \subseteq Q_1$ and $FL(h) \subseteq Dom(L_1)$. Thus, from (b), (c), (d) and Corollary 5.3, we know that $FP(H_t[l \mapsto h], S, E, e) \subseteq Q \cup Q_1$ and $FL(H_t[l \mapsto h], S, E, e) \subseteq Dom(L \cup L_1)$, and for all $l'{:}p' \in L \cup L_1$, $\Phi(p') = \Psi(l')$. Therefore, X' is well-formed with respect to P.

case gc-4: $L = L' \uplus \{l{:}p\}$, $l \notin Dom(H_f)$, and $X' = (H_f, Q, L', H_t)$. By (a) and the fact that H is well-formed, we can conclude that l must be bound in either H_f or H_t. Since l is not bound in H_f, it must be bound in H_t. Thus, $l \notin FL(H_t, S, E, e)$ and from (c) we can conclude that $FL(H_t, S, E, e) \subseteq L'$. Hence from (b) and (e), we can conclude that X' is well-formed with respect to P.

□

Lemma 5.7 (GC State Progress) *If $X = (H_f, Q, L, H_t)$ is well-formed with respect to P, then either Q and L are empty or else there exists a GC state X' such that $X \Longrightarrow X'$.*

Proof: Let $X = (H_f, Q, L, H_t)$ be a GC state such that Q or L is non-empty and assume X is well-formed with respect to the program $P = (H, S, E, e)$, where $H = (TH, VH)$. Since P is well-formed, there exists a Φ and Ψ such that $\vdash TH \Downarrow \Phi$ and $\Phi \vdash VH : \Psi$. Since X is well-formed with respect to P:

(a) $H_f \uplus H_t = H$,
(b) $FP(H_t, S, E, e) \subseteq Q$,
(c) $FL(H_t, S, E, e) \subseteq Dom(L)$,
(d) for all $l{:}p \in L$, $\Phi(p) = \Psi(l)$,
(e) $Q \subseteq Dom(TH)$, and
(f) for all $l{:}p$ in L, $l \in Dom(VH)$ and $p \in Dom(TH)$.

If Q is non-empty, then $Q = Q' \uplus \{p\}$ for some Q' and p. By conditions (a) and (e), we know that p is either bound in H_f or H_t. If p is bound in H_t then **gc-2** applies. If p is bound in H_f, then **gc-1** applies.

If L is non-empty, then $L = L' \uplus \{l{:}p\}$ for some L', l, and p. By condition (a) and (f), l must be bound in either H_f or H_t. If l is bound in H_t, then the **gc-4** rule applies. If l is bound in H_f, then there exists an H'_f and h such that $H_f = H'_f[l \mapsto h]$. By condition (a) and (f), p is bound in $H_f \uplus H_t$. By conditions (e) and (d), the well-formedness of P, and Corollary 5.3, we know that $\mathcal{F}[(H_f \uplus H_t)(p)](p, h) = (Q', L')$ for some Q' and L'. Consequently, **gc-3** applies. □

References

Aditya, S. and A. Caro (1993, June). Compiler-directed type reconstruction for polymorphic languages. In *ACM Conference on Functional Programming and Computer Architecture*, Copenhagen, pp. 74–82.

Aditya, S., C. Flood, and J. Hicks (1994, June). Garbage collection for strongly-typed languages using run-time type reconstruction. In *ACM Conference on Lisp and Functional Programming*, Orlando, pp. 12–23.

Appel, A. W. (1989). Run-time tags aren't necessary. *LISP and Symbolic Computation 2*, 153–162.

Appel, A. W. (1992a). *Compiling with Continuations*. Cambridge University Press.

Appel, A. W. (1992b, February). A critique of Standard ML. Technical Report CS–TR–364–92, Princeton University, Princeton, NJ.

Appel, A. W. and T. Jim (1989, January). Continuation-passing, closure-passing style. In *Sixteenth ACM Symposium on Principles of Programming Languages*, Austin, TX, pp. 293–302.

Appel, A. W. and D. B. MacQueen (1991, August). Standard ML of New Jersey. In J. Maluszynski and M. Wirsing (Eds.), *Third Int'l Symp. on Prog. Lang. Implementation and Logic Programming*, New York, pp. 1–13. Springer-Verlag.

Baker, H. (1990). Unify and conquer (garbage, updating, aliasing ...) in functional languages. In *ACM Conference on Lisp and Functional Programming*, Nice, pp. 218–226.

Barendsen, E. and S. Smetsers (1993). Conventional and uniqueness typing in graph rewrite systems. In *Proceedings of the 13th Conference on the Foundations of Software Technology and Theoretical Computer Science 1993, Bombay*, New York. Springer-Verlag. Extended abstract.

Birkedal, L., M. Tofte, and M. Vejlstrup (1996, January). From region inference to von Neumann machines via region representation inference. In *Twenty-Third ACM Symposium on Principles of Programming Languages*, St. Petersburg, FL, pp. 171–183.

Blelloch, G. E. and J. Greiner (1996, May). A provable time and space efficient implementation of NESL. In *ACM Conference on Functional Programming and Computer Architecture*, Philadelphia, PA, pp. 213–225.

Branquart, P. and J. Lewi (1970). A scheme for storage allocation and garbage collection for Algol-68. In *Algol-68 Implementation*. North-Holland Publishing Company, Amsterdam.

Britton, D. E. (1975). Heap storage management for the programming language Pascal. Master's thesis, University of Arizona.

Cardelli, L. (1984). Compiling a functional language. In *ACM Symposium on LISP and Functional Programming*, pp. 208–217.

Cardelli, L. (1989). Typeful programming. Technical Report 45, DEC Systems Research Center.

Chase, D. (1988, June). Safety considerations for storage allocation optimizations. In *ACM SIGPLAN Conference on Programming Language Design and Implementation*, Atlanta, GA.

Chirimar, J., C. A. Gunter, and J. G. Riecke (1992, June). Proving memory management invariants for a language based on linear logic. In *ACM Conference on Lisp and Functional Programming*, San Francisco, CA, pp. 139–150.

Chirimar, J., C. A. Gunter, and J. G. Riecke (1996). Reference counting as a computational interpretation of linear logic. *Journal of Functional Programming 6*(2), 195–244.

Clément, D., J. Despeyroux, T. Despeyroux, L. Hascoet, and G. Kahn (1985, June). Natural semantics on the computer. Technical Report RR 416, INRIA, Sophia–Antipolis, France.

Clinger, W. and J. Rees (1991, July-Sep.). Revised^4 report on the algorithmic language Scheme. *LISP Pointers IV*(3), 1–55.

Cousineau, G., P.-L. Curien, and M. Mauny (1985). The categorical abstract machine. In J. P. Jouannaud (Ed.), *1985 Conference on Functional Programming and Computer Architecture*, Volume 201 of *Lecture Notes in Computer Science*. Springer-Verlag.

Demers, A., M. Weiser, B. Hayes, H. Boehm, D. Bobrow, and S. Shenker (1990, January). Combining generational and conservative garbage collection: Framework and implementations. In *Seventeenth ACM Symposium on Principles of Programming Languages*, San Francisco, pp. 261–269.

Felleisen, M. and D. P. Friedman (1987, January). A calculus for assignments in higher-order languages. In *Thirteenth ACM Symposium on Principles of Programming Languages*.

Felleisen, M. and R. Hieb (1992). The revised report on the syntactic theories of sequential control and state. *Theoretical Computer Science 10*(2), 235–271.

Fischer, M. J. (1993, November). Lambda-calculus schemata. *LISP and Symbolic Computation 6*(3/4), 259–288.

Fradet, P. (1994, June). Collecting more garbage. In *ACM Conference on Functional Programming and Computer Architecture*, Orlando, pp. 24–33.

Girard, J.-Y. (1972). *Interprétation Fonctionnelle et Élimination des Coupures dans l'Arithmétique d'Ordre Supérieure*. Ph. D. thesis, Université Paris VII.

Goldberg, B. and M. Gloger (1992, June). Polymorphic type reconstruction for garbage collection without tags. In *ACM Conference on Lisp and Functional Programming*, San Francisco, pp. 53–65.

Harper, R. (1994). A simplified account of polymorphic references. *Information Processing Letters 51*, 201–206.

Harper, R. and G. Morrisett (1995, January). Compiling polymorphism using intensional type analysis. In *Twenty-Second ACM Symposium on Principles of Programming Languages*, San Francisco, CA, pp. 130–141.

Hudak, P. (1986, August). A semantic model of reference counting and its abstraction. In *ACM Conference on Lisp and Functional Programming*, pp. 351–363.

Milner, R., M. Tofte, and R. Harper (1990). *The Definition of Standard ML*. MIT Press.

Minamide, Y., G. Morrisett, and R. Harper (1996, January). Typed closure conversion. In *Twenty-Third ACM Symposium on Principles of Programming Languages*, St. Petersburg, FL, pp. 271–283.

Morrisett, G. (1995, December). *Compiling with Types*. Ph. D. thesis, School of Computer Science, Carnegie Mellon University, Pittsburgh, PA. (Available as Carnegie Mellon University School of Computer Science technical report CMU–CS–95–226.).

Morrisett, G., M. Felleisen, and R. Harper (1995, June). Abstract models of memory management. In *Functional Programming and Computer Architecture*, La Jolla, CA, pp. 66–77. ACM.

Nettles, S. (1992, December). A Larch specification of copying garbage collection. Technical Report CMU–CS–92–219, School of Computer Science, Carnegie Mellon University.

Plotkin, G. (1981). A structural approach to operational semantics. Technical Report DAIMI–FN–19, Computer Science Department, Aarhus University.

Reynolds, J. C. (1974). Towards a theory of type structure. In *Colloq. sur la Programmation*, Volume 19 of *Lecture Notes in Computer Science*, pp. 408–423. Springer-Verlag.

Reynolds, J. C. (1983). Types, abstraction, and parametric polymorphism. In R. E. A. Mason (Ed.), *Information Processing '83*, pp. 513–523. Elsevier Science Publishers B. V.

Sabry, A. and M. Felleisen (1992, June). Reasoning about programs in continuation-passing style. In *1992 ACM Conference on LISP and Functional Programming*, San Francisco, CA, pp. 288–298. ACM.

Shao, Z. and A. W. Appel (1994, June). Space-efficient closure representations. In *ACM Conference on Lisp and Functional Programming*, Orlando, pp. 150–161.

Tarditi, D., G. Morrisett, P. Cheng, C. Stone, R. Harper, and P. Lee (1996, May). TIL: A type-directed optimizing compiler for ML. In *ACM SIGPLAN Conference on Programming Language Design and Implementation*, Philadelphia, PA, pp. 181–192.

Tofte, M. (1990, November). Type inference for polymorphic references. *Information and Computation 89*, 1–34.

Tofte, M. and J.-P. Talpin (1994, January). Implementing the call-by-value lambda-calculus using a stack of regions. In *Twenty-First ACM Symposium on Principles of Programming Languages*, Portland, OR, pp. 188–201.

Tolmach, A. (1994, June). Tag-free garbage collection using explicit type parameters. In *Proc. 1994 ACM Conference on LISP and Functional Programming*, Orlando, FL, pp. 1–11. ACM.

Wilson, P. R. (1992, September). Uniprocessor garbage collection techniques. In Y. Bekkers and J. Cohen (Eds.), *International Workshop on Memory Management*, Number 637 in Lecture Notes in Computer Science, St. Malo, pp. 1–42. Springer-Verlag.

Wilson, P. R. (1995). Garbage collection. *Computing Surveys*. Expanded version of (Wilson 1992). Draft available via anonymous internet FTP from `cs.utexas.edu` as `pub/garbage/bigsurv.ps`. In revision, to appear.

Wodon, P. (1970). Methods of garbage collection for Algol-68. In *Algol-68 Implementation*. North-Holland Publishing Company, Amsterdam.

Wright, A. K. and M. Felleisen (1994, November). A syntactic approach to type soundness. *Information and Computation 115*(1), 38–94.

Operational reasoning for functions with local state

Andrew Pitts and Ian Stark

Abstract

Languages such as ML or Lisp permit the use of recursively defined function expressions with locally declared storage locations. Although this can be very convenient from a programming point of view it severely complicates the properties of program equivalence even for relatively simple fragments of such languages—such as the simply typed fragment of Standard ML with integer-valued references considered here. This paper presents a method for reasoning about *contextual equivalence* of programs involving this combination of functional and procedural features. The method is based upon the use of a certain kind of *logical relation* parameterised by relations between program states. The form of this logical relation is novel, in as much as it involves relations not only between program expressions, but also between program continuations (also known as *evaluation contexts*). The authors found this approach necessary in order to establish the 'Fundamental Property of logical relations' in the presence of both dynamically allocated local state and recursion. The logical relation characterises contextual equivalence and yields a proof of the best known context lemma for this kind of language—the Mason-Talcott 'ciu' theorem. Moreover, it is shown that the method can prove examples where such a context lemma is not much help and which involve representation independence, higher order memoising functions, and profiling functions.

1 Introduction

Lisp and ML are *functional* programming languages because they treat functions as values on a par with more concrete forms of data: functions can be passed as arguments, can be returned as the result of computation, can be recursively defined, and so on. They are also *procedural* languages because they permit the use of references (or 'cells', or 'locations') for storing values: references can be created dynamically and their contents read and updated as expressions are evaluated. This paper presents a method for reasoning about the equivalence of programs involving this combination of functional and procedural features. What emerges is an operationally-based form of reasoning about functions with local state that seems to be both intuitive and theoretically powerful. Throughout we assume a passing familiarity with the language Standard ML (Milner, Tofte, and Harper 1990) and its associated terminology. If in difficulty, see (Paulson 1991).

Some motivation

The combination of functional and procedural features in Standard ML is very expressive. For example, it permits the programmer to exploit the modularity of the functional idiom (Hughes 1989) in defining high-level control structures for manipulating program state. The combination is also useful from the point of view of efficiency, since the use of local storage permits the efficient implementation of some functions and data structures with purely functional observable behaviour. As a simple example, consider the following 'memoised' version of the factorial function in Standard ML.

Example 1.1.

$$\begin{array}{lll} \mathtt{val\,f} & = & \mathtt{let\,val\,a = ref\,0\,and\,r = ref\,1} \\ & & \quad \mathtt{fun\,f'\,x = (if\,x = 0\,then\,1\,else\,x * f'(x-1))} \\ & & \mathtt{in} \\ & & \quad \mathtt{fn\,x \Rightarrow ((if\,x = !a\,then\,()\,else\,(a := x; r := f'\,x)); !r)} \\ & & \mathtt{end} \end{array} \qquad (dec_1)$$

The local references a and r are used to store the argument and the result of the most recent invocation of the function; and the function acts like the purely functional factorial

$$\mathtt{fun\,f\,x} \;=\; \mathtt{(if\,x = 0\,then\,1\,else\,x * f(x-1))} \qquad (dec_2)$$

except that when called with the same argument twice in succession it uses the cached result !r, saving recomputation. So evaluating

$$\mathtt{let}\ dec_1\ \mathtt{in\,(f\,1000 + f\,1000)\,end}$$

will yield the same integer result as evaluating

$$\mathtt{let}\ dec_2\ \mathtt{in\,(f\,1000 + f\,1000)\,end}$$

but will only involve computing the factorial of 1000 once. Of course in this simple example a similar saving can easily be achieved without leaving the purely functional part of the language, for example with

$$\mathtt{let}\ dec_2\,;\ \mathtt{val\,x = (f\,1000)\,in\,(x + x)\,end}.$$

The point is that in general such functional transformations may require complicated static analysis of the context, whereas the transformation involving the memoised version is simply one of replacing occurrences of dec_2 with dec_1 uniformly in any context. The correctness of this optimisation amounts to the assertion that dec_1 and dec_2 are contextually equivalent. In general one says that two phrases e_1 and e_2 in a programming language are *contextually equivalent*, and writes $e_1 \cong e_2$, if for all contexts $C[-]$, *i.e.* for all expressions which become complete programs when the hole '$-$' is filled with e_1 or e_2, executing the program $C[e_1]$ yields exactly the same observable results as executing $C[e_2]$.

Why are dec_1 and dec_2 contextually equivalent? While it may be easy to see for some particular context such as `let` $[-]$ `in` (`f 1000` + `f 1000`), that $C[dec_1]$ and $C[dec_2]$ evaluate to the same result, it is quite a different matter to prove that this is so for *all* contexts. Nevertheless there are reasons for believing that $dec_1 \cong dec_2$ holds, based upon the 'privacy' of locally declared references and properties of the state that remain invariant during evaluation. Here is how the argument goes.

Informal 'proof' of $dec_1 \cong dec_2$. Consider the following property:

$$\text{the integer stored in } \mathtt{r} \text{ is the factorial of that stored in } \mathtt{a}. \tag{1.1}$$

Note that if dec_1 is evaluated then the two references created satisfy (1.1) (since 1 is the factorial of 0). Moreover, the function value bound to `f` as a result of that evaluation is such that if (1.1) holds before evaluating an application `f(n)`, then it continues to hold afterwards and the value returned agrees with what we would have obtained using dec_2 instead of dec_1 (namely the factorial of `n`).

Given any context $C[-]$, since `a` and `r` are bound identifiers in dec_1 and evaluation of expressions respects α-conversion, we may assume that `a` and `r` do not occur in $C[-]$; so, *the only way that the contents of the created references* `a` *and* `r` *could be mutated during evaluation of* $C[dec_1]$ *is through applications of the function value bound to* `f`. It follows from the previous paragraph both that the property (1.1) is invariant throughout the evaluation of $C[dec_1]$ and that any result returned is the same as for $C[dec_2]$. Since $C[-]$ was arbitrary, dec_1 and dec_2 are contextually equivalent. □?

The reason why this is only an informal proof resides mainly in the statement in italics about how a context can make use of its 'hole', which certainly needs further justification. To emphasise this point, we tease the reader with a similar informal 'proof' of contextual equivalence that turns out to be false. Recall that `int ref` is the Standard ML type of integer references: its values are addresses of integer storage locations, and those values can be tested for equality—meaning equality of the reference addresses rather than equality of their contents. Consider the following declarations of functions of type `int ref` $\to$ `int ref`.

Example 1.2.

```
val f = let val a = ref 0 and b = ref 0                (dec3)
        in
            fn c => (if c = a then b else a)
        end

val f = let val a = ref 0 and b = ref 0                (dec4)
        in
            fn c => (if c = b then b else a)
        end
```

False 'proof' of $dec_3 \cong dec_4$. Given any context $C[-]$, since a and b are bound identifiers in dec_i ($i = 3, 4$) and evaluation of expressions respects α-conversion, we may assume that a and b do not occur in $C[-]$. Thus in evaluating $C[dec_i]$ *any value of type* `int ref` *which is supplied by* $C[-]$ *to the function declared by* dec_i *cannot be either* a *or* b. Therefore any such application will always use the second branch of the conditional and return a. So evaluation of $C[dec_3]$ will produce the same result as evaluating $C[dec_4]$. Since $C[-]$ was arbitrary, dec_3 and dec_4 are contextually equivalent. □?

The italicised part of this 'proof' is of the same kind as in the previous case, but this time it is false. Indeed dec_3 and dec_4 are not contextually equivalent. As with any contextual inequivalence, this can be demonstrated rigorously by exhibiting a context $C[-]$ for which $C[dec_3]$ and $C[dec_4]$ produce different results. Such a context is

$$\texttt{let}\,[-];\ \texttt{val c} = \texttt{ref 0 in (f(f c)} = \texttt{f c) end}$$

since in this case $C[dec_3]$ evaluates to `false` whereas $C[dec_4]$ evaluates to `true`. For in the environment created by evaluating the local declarations in $C[dec_3]$ (respectively $C[dec_4]$), `f c` evaluates to a (respectively a), hence `f(f c)` evaluates to b (respectively a) and therefore the test `f(f c) = f c` yields `false` (respectively `true`). Note that contrary to the expectation in the false 'proof' given above, even though $C[-]$ does not know about the local references a and b, it is able to feed them as arguments to `f` after one application of `f` to some external reference c.

Incidentally, Example 1.2 demonstrates that the following naïve *extensionality principle* fails for Standard ML functions:

> Two expressions F and F' of function type $\sigma \to \sigma'$ are contextually equivalent if for all values V of type σ, $F\,V$ and $F'\,V$ are contextually equivalent expressions of type σ'.

We have just seen that if F_3 and F_4 are the expressions of type `int ref` $\to$ `int ref` that occur on the right-hand sides of the declarations dec_3 and dec_4 respectively, then $F_3 \not\cong F_4$. On the other hand, one can show for all values c : `int ref` that F_3 c and F_4 c are contextually equivalent. So F_3 and F_4 do not satisfy the above extensionality principle.

This failure of extensionality is not merely a result of mixing higher order functions with imperative features. For in Reynolds' Idealised Algol (1981, 1982) with its call-by-name function application and restriction of local state just to commands (*i.e.* expressions of type `unit`, in ML terminology), such an extensionality principle *does* hold: see (Pitts 1997). Rather, it is the fact that in ML access to local references can be passed out of their original scope during evaluation which complicates the properties of contextual equivalence. We saw this when demonstrating $dec_3 \not\cong dec_4$ in Example 1.2. Incidentally, it is worth noting that although this example makes use of equality testing on references, the failure of extensionality in ML does not depend upon this feature. (Indeed, in the fragment of ML we use in this paper this equality test is definable from more primitive ones: see Remark 2.1.) The operationally-based parametric logical relation we present in this paper provides a characterisation of contextual equivalence that yields a rigorous underpinning for the kind of informal argument used in Example 1.1, while avoiding the pitfalls illustrated by Example 1.2.

Some background

The methods presented here for reasoning about recursive functions and local storage are rooted in the work of O'Hearn and Tennent (1995) and Seiber (1995). These authors use relational parametricity (Reynolds 1983) and logical relations (Plotkin, 1973, 1980) to give denotational models of Algol-like languages which match the operational behaviour of local variables better than previous models did. Since our goal is not to produce 'fully abstract' models, but rather to identify practically useful proof methods for contextual equivalence, there is some advantage to concentrating on operationally-based versions of these relational techniques. This was done for Algol-like languages in (Pitts 1997). Here we carry out a similar program for an ML-like language. For the reasons given in the previous subsection, the difficulties which have to be overcome to produce useful proof methods for ML contextual equivalence are greater than those for Algol. Nevertheless, we obtain a fairly light-weight tool compared with the mathematical structures involved in the denotational models, and one which relates directly to the syntax and structural operational semantics of the language. But of course these operationally-based techniques would not have arisen without the previous, denotational insights. Furthermore, the method we use to establish the fundamental properties of the operationally-based logical relation with respect to recursive program constructs relies on operational analogues of familiar denotational methods (*viz.* fixed point induction and admissibility properties).

Mason and Talcott have developed a number of operational methods for reasoning about Lisp programs with destructive update (Mason and Talcott 1991a; Mason and Talcott 1992a; Honsell, Mason, Smith, and Talcott 1995). Like us, they highlight the issue of functions with local state, which they call 'objects' (1991b, 1992b). Notions of 'constraint' and 'equivalence under constraints' are used, which can be loosely identified with the use we make in this paper of relations between states. These lead to a set of reasoning principles that match certain aspects of our operational logical relation. Their **(inv)** expresses the fact that properties of local store are preserved; while their **(abstract)** and **(abstractable)** say that if two functions preserve some property of store, and whenever it holds they give the same result, then they are equivalent. Proofs based on these principles are similar in some ways to those given in Section 5. There are however limitations to these methods, which our work removes. For example, the validity of **(inv)**, **(abstract)** and **(abstractable)** is restricted to first-order functions over atoms, as a consequence of their 'hands-on' proof through direct consideration of reduction in certain contexts. Our logical relation has no such restriction (witness the higher order profiler of Example 5.8). Our techniques then can be seen as a certain generalisation to higher types of the results of Mason *et al*, through the powerful machinery of parameterised logical relations.

Overview of the paper

In Section 2 we introduce a language of Recursive Functions with local State, called ReFS, which is the vehicle for the formal development in the rest of this paper. Syntactically, it is a simply typed lambda calculus: there are ground types for booleans, integers, the unit value, and integer references; higher types are built up over these using product and function type constructors. We give the structural operational semantics of ReFS in terms of an inductively defined evaluation relation

$$s, M \Downarrow V, s' \,. \tag{1.2}$$

This and the associated definition of contextual equivalence are quite standard, and make ReFS equivalent to a fragment of SML according to its definition in (Milner, Tofte, and Harper 1990). Harper and Stone (1996) reformulate the operational semantics of SML in terms of transitions between configurations containing a component for the current program continuation, or evaluation context. (See also Harper, Duba, and MacQueen 1993.) The advantage of this approach is that it can give a *structurally inductive* characterisation of the termination predicate, $\exists V, s' \, (s, M \Downarrow V, s')$ used to define contextual equivalence. Accordingly, in Section 3 we introduce a new termination relation

$$\langle s, K, M \rangle{\downarrow} \tag{1.3}$$

where the component K formalises the ReFS evaluation contexts. The relation (1.3) is defined by induction on the structure of M and K, and contains the original termination relation for $\Downarrow$ as a retract. We are able to exploit the structural nature of our formulation of termination to streamline the induction proofs that arise when proving properties of contextual equivalence. A case in point is the proof of the Unwinding Theorem 3.2 that completes this section. It expresses a compactness property of recursive function values with respect to termination which we need later to prove a crucial preservation property of our parametric logical relation (Proposition 4.8(xv)).

The logical relation itself is introduced in Section 4 and its fundamental properties established. It is parameterised by binary relations between states. Apart from being operationally- rather than denotationally-based, we are able to make a pleasing simplification of (O'Hearn and Tennent 1993, Section 6), in that our parameters are just *arbitrary* (non-empty) state-relations without any extra structure of a partial bijection on the underlying address names. In fact the definition of the logical relation is rather different from previous such definitions for languages with local state, because it involves binary relations between evaluation contexts K as well as binary relations between expressions M.

We found this approach unavoidable in order to establish the Fundamental Property of the logical relation (Theorem 4.9) and hence its connection with contextual equivalence (Theorem 4.10). The reason has to do with the interaction between recursion and the fact that the 'size' of the state (measured by the number of storage locations allocated) may grow in a non-trivial fashion during evaluation in a language like ReFS. Thus in (1.2), the number of locations in the final state s' may be strictly greater than the number in the initial state s and we cannot 'garbage collect' that part of s' involving these extra locations, because the value V may be a function closure using those locations. Now in defining a logical relation parameterised by state-relations and based upon the evaluation relation (1.2), it is natural to use existential quantification over relations on the dynamically created part of s': this is what the authors did for their nu-calculus in (Pitts and Stark 1993), for example. However, such an existential quantification destroys the (operational analogue of the) admissibility property needed to show that recursive program constructs respect the logical relation—without which there would be no connection between contextual equivalence and the logical relation.[1]

By contrast, the logical relation we give here takes account of evaluation contexts rather than final states and uses the termination relation (1.3), which makes no explicit mention of final states. This allows us to avoid any use of existential quantification over state relations in the definition and renders the proof of the Fundamental Property relatively straightforward. The price we pay is that the definition of the logical relation between expressions is intertwined with the definition of a 'dual' relation between evaluation contexts (program continuations). However, it is a price worth paying, since not only does it allow us to prove the crucial Fundamental Property of the logical relation, but also we are able to characterise contextual equivalence in terms of the logical relation[2] and deduce the Mason-Talcott 'closed instantiations of uses' theorem for ReFS as a corollary (see Theorem 4.10). Moreover, we show in Section 5 that we can recover a technique for proving ReFS contextual equivalence involving existential quantification over 'locally invariant' state relations which is reminiscent of the methods of (Pitts and Stark 1993; Pitts 1997). This Principle of Local Invariants (Proposition 5.1) is put to work in Section 5 to prove examples of contextual equivalence involving the notion of representation independence, higher-order memoising functions, and higher-order profiling functions. We also examine the limitations of this method, giving an example (Example 5.9) of two contextually equivalent ReFS expressions that are not easily seen to be logically related.

In the final Section 6 we discuss some desirable extensions of the ReFS language

[1] This problem did not surface in (Pitts and Stark 1993) because the nu-calculus does not contain any recursive features.

[2] A similar characterisation for the nu-calculus definitely fails for the logical relation of (Pitts and Stark 1993).

and how our techniques might be extended to cope with them.

2 Recursive functions with local state

The examples discussed in the Introduction involved the interaction between recursively declared functions and dynamically created, mutable references for storing integer values. They were phrased in a simply typed fragment of Standard ML with ground types `bool` (booleans), `int` (integers), `unit` (one-element type), and `int ref` (integer storage locations). In this section we introduce a typed lambda calculus called ReFS—a language of Recursive Functions with local State. It is essentially equivalent to the fragment of Standard ML we have in mind and will be the vehicle for the formal development in the rest of this paper.

The ReFS language

The syntax of ReFS is given in Figure 1. It takes an unusually reduced form, in that most operators may take only values as arguments. This is essentially a technical convenience: it means that all the sequential aspects of the language devolve onto the *let* construct, and can therefore be treated uniformly. Unrestricted forms are easily defined in terms of *let* as shown in Figure 2, and we shall use them freely. Note that the ReFS *let* is much simpler than that of ML, being neither recursive nor polymorphic.

ReFS has two kinds of identifier, variables $(x, y, f, g, \dots)$ and location constants $(\ell, \ell', \dots)$. The latter occur explicitly in ReFS expressions because we prefer to avoid the use of environments in the ReFS operational semantics. Variables may be free or bound, while locations are always free. The form $rec\, f(x).\, M$ binds free occurrences of the variables f and x in expression M, and $let\, x = M\, in\, M'$ binds any free occurrences of x in M'. We identify expressions and values up to α-conversion of bound variables. The finite sets of free variables and locations of an expression M are denoted $fv(M)$ and $loc(M)$ respectively. We substitute values for free variables $M[V/x]$ in the usual capture-avoiding way; the restriction to values V arises from the choice of reduced syntax and is appropriate for a call-by-value language.

We only consider expressions that are well-typed. The ReFS types are given in Figure 1: *bool* and *int* are the types of booleans and integers respectively; *unit* is a one-value type; *loc* is the type of names of integer storage locations, corresponding to the Standard ML type `int ref`; $\sigma \to \sigma'$ and $\sigma \times \sigma$ are function and product types, corresponding to the Standard ML types σ `->` σ' and $\sigma * \sigma'$. For simplicity, we assume that the set *Var* of variables is partitioned into a family of countably infinite subsets, one for each type: thus each variable x comes with a type σ, and we write $x : \sigma$ to indicate this. The rules for assigning types to expressions are given in Figure 3 and are quite standard. They inductively define a judgement of

$$
\begin{array}{lrl}
\textit{Expressions} & M ::= & V \mid \textit{if } V \textit{ then } M \textit{ else } M \mid V \textit{ op } V \mid \textit{fst}(V) \mid \textit{snd}(V) \\
& \mid & \textit{ref}(V) \mid !V \mid V := V \mid VV \mid \textit{let } x = M \textit{ in } M \\
\textit{Values} & V ::= & x \mid \textit{true} \mid \textit{false} \mid n \mid () \mid \ell \mid \textit{rec}\, x(x).\, M \mid (V, V) \\
\textit{Types} & \sigma ::= & \textit{bool} \mid \textit{int} \mid \textit{unit} \mid \textit{loc} \mid \sigma \to \sigma \mid \sigma \times \sigma
\end{array}
$$

where

$x \in \mathit{Var}$ an infinite set of *variables*,
$\ell \in \mathit{Loc}$ an infinite set of *locations*,
$n \in \mathbb{Z} = \{\ldots, -2, -1, 0, 1, 2, \ldots\}$ the set of integers,
$op \in \{+, -, =, \leq, \ldots\}$ a finite set of arithmetic operations and relations.

Figure 1: ReFS syntax

$$
\textit{if } M_1 \textit{ then } M_2 \textit{ else } M_3 \stackrel{\text{def}}{=} \textit{let } x = M_1 \textit{ in } (\textit{if } x \textit{ then } M_2 \textit{ else } M_3) \quad \text{where } x \notin \textit{fv}(M_2, M_3)
$$

and similar clauses for M_1 *op* M_2, (M_1, M_2), $\textit{fst}(M)$, $\textit{snd}(M)$, $M_1 M_2$, $\textit{ref}(M)$, $!M$, and $M_1 := M_2$.

$$
\begin{array}{rcl}
\lambda x.\, M & \stackrel{\text{def}}{=} & \textit{rec}\, f(x).\, M \quad \text{where } f \notin \textit{fv}(M) \\
M; M' & \stackrel{\text{def}}{=} & \textit{let } x = M \textit{ in } M' \quad \text{where } x \notin \textit{fv}(M') \\
Y_{cbv} & \stackrel{\text{def}}{=} & \textit{rec}\, y(f).\, \lambda x.\, f(yf)x \\
\textit{while } B \textit{ do } M & \stackrel{\text{def}}{=} & (\textit{rec}\, f(x).\, \textit{if } B \textit{ then } (M; f()) \textit{ else } ())() \\
& & \quad \text{where } f, x \notin \textit{fv}(B, M) \\
\textit{let } x = M_1; x' = M_2 \textit{ in } M_3 & \stackrel{\text{def}}{=} & \textit{let } x = M_1 \textit{ in } (\textit{let } x' = M_2 \textit{ in } M_3) \\
\textit{let } (x_1, x_2) = M_1 \textit{ in } M_2 & \stackrel{\text{def}}{=} & \textit{let } x = M_1 \textit{ in let } x_1 = \textit{fst}(x) \textit{ in} \\
& & \quad \textit{let } x_2 = \textit{snd}(x) \textit{ in } M_2 \quad \text{where } x \notin \textit{fv}(M_2) \\
\textit{let } f(x) = M_1 \textit{ in } M_2 & \stackrel{\text{def}}{=} & \textit{let } f' = \textit{rec}\, f(x).\, M_1 \textit{ in } M_2[f'/f] \\
& & \quad \text{where } f' \notin \textit{fv}(M_2)
\end{array}
$$

Figure 2: Sugar for the ReFS syntax

$$\Gamma, x : \sigma \vdash x : \sigma \qquad \Gamma \vdash \mathit{true} : \mathit{bool} \qquad \Gamma \vdash \mathit{false} : \mathit{bool}$$

$$\Gamma \vdash n : \mathit{int} \quad (n \in \mathbb{Z}) \qquad \Gamma \vdash () : \mathit{unit} \qquad \Gamma \vdash \ell : \mathit{loc} \quad (\ell \in \mathit{Loc})$$

$$\frac{\Gamma, f : \sigma \to \sigma', x : \sigma \vdash M : \sigma'}{\Gamma \vdash \mathit{rec}\, f(x).\, M : \sigma \to \sigma'}\ (f, x \notin \Gamma) \qquad \frac{\Gamma \vdash V : \sigma \quad \Gamma \vdash V' : \sigma'}{\Gamma \vdash (V, V') : \sigma \times \sigma'}$$

$$\frac{\Gamma \vdash V : \mathit{bool} \quad \Gamma \vdash M : \sigma \quad \Gamma \vdash M' : \sigma}{\Gamma \vdash \mathit{if}\ V\ \mathit{then}\ M\ \mathit{else}\ M' : \sigma}$$

$$\frac{\Gamma \vdash V : \mathit{int} \quad \Gamma \vdash V' : \mathit{int}}{\Gamma \vdash V\ \mathit{op}\ V' : \gamma}\ (\gamma \in \{\mathit{bool}, \mathit{int}\} \text{ is the result type of } \mathit{op})$$

$$\frac{\Gamma \vdash V : \sigma \times \sigma'}{\Gamma \vdash \mathit{fst}(V) : \sigma} \qquad \frac{\Gamma \vdash V : \sigma \times \sigma'}{\Gamma \vdash \mathit{snd}(V) : \sigma'}$$

$$\frac{\Gamma \vdash V : \mathit{int}}{\Gamma \vdash \mathit{ref}(V) : \mathit{loc}} \qquad \frac{\Gamma \vdash V : \mathit{loc}}{\Gamma \vdash\ !V : \mathit{int}} \qquad \frac{\Gamma \vdash V : \mathit{loc} \quad \Gamma \vdash V' : \mathit{int}}{\Gamma \vdash V := V' : \mathit{unit}}$$

$$\frac{\Gamma \vdash V : \sigma \to \sigma' \quad \Gamma \vdash V' : \sigma}{\Gamma \vdash V V' : \sigma'} \qquad \frac{\Gamma \vdash M : \sigma \quad \Gamma, x : \sigma \vdash M' : \sigma'}{\Gamma \vdash \mathit{let}\ x = M\ \mathit{in}\ M' : \sigma'}\ (x \notin \Gamma)$$

Notation. We use the following notation for various collections of well-typed expressions and values.

$$\begin{aligned} \mathit{Exp}_\sigma(\Gamma) &\stackrel{\text{def}}{=} \{M \mid \Gamma \vdash M : \sigma\} & \mathit{Val}_\sigma(\Gamma) &\stackrel{\text{def}}{=} \{V \in \mathit{Exp}_\sigma(\Gamma) \mid V \text{ a value}\} \\ \mathit{Exp}_\sigma &\stackrel{\text{def}}{=} \mathit{Exp}_\sigma(\emptyset) & \mathit{Val}_\sigma &\stackrel{\text{def}}{=} \mathit{Val}_\sigma(\emptyset) \\ \mathit{Exp} &\stackrel{\text{def}}{=} \bigcup\{\mathit{Exp}_\sigma \mid \sigma \text{ a type}\} & \mathit{Val} &\stackrel{\text{def}}{=} \bigcup\{\mathit{Val}_\sigma \mid \sigma \text{ a type}\}. \end{aligned}$$

Figure 3: ReFS type assignment

the form $\Gamma \vdash M : \sigma$, where Γ is a finite subset of *Var*, M is a ReFS expression, and σ is a ReFS type. The role of Γ in the judgement is to indicate explicitly a set of variables free for substitution in M. Indeed, it is not hard to prove that if $\Gamma \vdash M : \sigma$ is derivable then $fv(M) \subseteq \Gamma$. Most of the time we will be dealing with *closed* expressions, by which we mean expressions with no free variables, but quite possibly involving location constants $\ell \in Loc$.

To further simplify the operational semantics of ReFS we have rolled function abstraction and recursive function declaration into the one form $rec\, f(x).\, M$ which corresponds to the Standard ML value

$$\texttt{fn x} \Rightarrow \texttt{(let fun f x = M in M end)}.$$

Figure 2 shows how ordinary lambda abstraction, the call-by-value Y combinator, local recursive function definitions and *while* loops are all special cases of this construct.

The ReFS operations for manipulating store are exactly as in Standard ML, but restricted to storage of *integer* values. Expression $ref(V)$ allocates local store, placing the integer denoted by V at some fresh location, which is then returned as the value of the expression; operation $!V$ fetches the value stored at the location denoted by V; and $V := V'$ updates it with the integer denoted by V', returning the unit value ().

Remark 2.1 (Testing equality of locations). ReFS does not contain a primitive operation $eq : loc \to loc \to bool$ for testing equality of locations (as opposed to equality of their contents). Nevertheless such an operation is definable. For example

$$eq \stackrel{\text{def}}{=} \lambda\, x.\, \lambda\, x'.\, let\; v = {!x}\; in\; (x := {!x'} + 1;\, let\; b = ({!x} = {!x'})\; in\; (x := v;\, b))$$

has the required evaluation properties with respect to the operational semantics of ReFS introduced below.

Evaluation of expressions

The meaning of ReFS expressions clearly depends on the current contents of memory or *state*. We represent states as finite partial functions from locations to integers $s : Loc \rightharpoonup_{\text{fin}} \mathbb{Z}$, with $dom(s)$ being the locations actually occupied. The empty state is denoted (), and for any state s, location ℓ and integer n we write $(s; \ell := n)$ for the updated state defined by

$$\begin{aligned} dom(s; \ell := n) &= dom(s) \cup \{\ell\} \\ (s; \ell := n)(\ell') &= \begin{cases} s(\ell') & \text{if } \ell' \neq \ell, \\ n & \text{if } \ell' = \ell. \end{cases} \end{aligned}$$

$$s, V \Downarrow V, s \qquad (\Downarrow\text{val})$$

$$\frac{s, M_b \Downarrow V, s'}{s, \mathit{if}\ b\ \mathit{then}\ M_{\mathit{true}}\ \mathit{else}\ M_{\mathit{false}} \Downarrow V, s'} \qquad (\Downarrow\text{if})$$

$$s, n\ \mathit{op}\ n' \Downarrow c, s \quad \text{if } c = n\ \mathit{op}\ n' \qquad (\Downarrow\text{op})$$

$$s, \mathit{fst}((V, V')) \Downarrow V, s \qquad (\Downarrow\text{fst})$$

$$s, \mathit{snd}((V, V')) \Downarrow V', s \qquad (\Downarrow\text{snd})$$

$$\frac{s, M[\,(\mathit{rec}\ f(x).\ M)/f,\ V/x\,] \Downarrow V', s'}{s, (\mathit{rec}\ f(x).\ M)V \Downarrow V', s'} \qquad (\Downarrow\text{app})$$

$$s, \mathit{ref}(n) \Downarrow \ell, s \otimes (\ell := n) \quad \text{any } \ell \notin \mathit{dom}(s) \qquad (\Downarrow\text{ref})$$

$$s, !\ell \Downarrow n, s \quad \text{if } n = s(\ell) \qquad (\Downarrow\text{get})$$

$$s, \ell := n \Downarrow (), (s; \ell := n) \qquad (\Downarrow\text{set})$$

$$\frac{s, M \Downarrow V, s' \qquad s', M'[V/x] \Downarrow V', s''}{s, \mathit{let}\ x = M\ \mathit{in}\ M' \Downarrow V', s''} \qquad (\Downarrow\text{let})$$

Figure 4: ReFS evaluation rules

In the case that $\ell \notin dom(s)$, we write $s \otimes (\ell := n)$ for $(s; \ell := n)$. More generally, given states s and s' with disjoint domains their *smash product* $s \otimes s'$ is the state with

$$dom(s \otimes s') = dom(s) \cup dom(s')$$
$$(s \otimes s')(\ell) = \begin{cases} s(\ell) & \text{if } \ell \in dom(s), \\ s'(\ell) & \text{if } \ell \in dom(s'). \end{cases}$$

We write Sta for the set of all states; and if $\omega \subseteq Loc$ is a finite set of location constants, we write $Sta(\omega)$ for the subset of Sta consisting of all states s with $dom(s) = \omega$.

Much as in the Definition of Standard ML (Milner, Tofte, and Harper 1990), we give the operational semantics of ReFS via an inductively defined evaluation relation of the form

$$s, M \Downarrow V, s' \tag{2.1}$$

where $s, s' \in Sta$, $M \in Exp$, and $V \in Val$. We consider only *well-formed* judgements, where M and V may be given some common type σ, and all locations used are properly defined: $loc(M) \subseteq dom(s)$ and $loc(V) \subseteq dom(s')$. The rules defining the relation are given in Figure 4 and are all quite standard. We write $s, M \Downarrow$ to indicate termination, i.e. that $s, M \Downarrow V, s'$ holds for some s', V (and hence in particular that $loc(M) \subseteq dom(s)$).

Even taking into account differences in syntax, there are some differences between this operational semantics and the corresponding fragment of the Standard ML definition (Milner, Tofte, and Harper 1990). For one thing, we have eliminated the use of environments in the evaluation relation at the expense of introducing the syntactic operation of substitution. Thus in rule ($\Downarrow$app), $M[(rec\, f(x). M)/f,\ V/x]$ denotes the result, well-defined up to α-conversion, of simultaneously substituting $rec\, f(x). M$ for all free occurrences of f and V for all free occurrences of x, in M. The small price to pay for this approach is the explicit appearance of locations in the syntax of expressions.

More significantly, the reduced syntax has concentrated the sequencing of evaluation in the language down to just one rule: only ($\Downarrow$let) has more than one hypothesis, and most have none.

Contextual equivalence

We regard two expressions of ReFS as equivalent if they can be used interchangeably in any program without affecting the observable results of program execution. This is formalised by the standard notion of *contextual equivalence*, suitably adapted for the language in hand.

As usual, a *context* $C[-]$ is a ReFS expression in which some subexpressions have been replaced by occurrences of a parameter, or *hole*, '$-$'. The expression resulting from filling the holes with an expression M is denoted by $C[M]$. Since the holes may occur within the scope of *let*- and *rec*-binders, free variables of M may become bound in $C[M]$. This 'capture' of variables means that although the operation of substituting M for '$-$' in $C[-]$ respects α-conversion of M, it does not necessarily respect α-conversion of $C[-]$. Therefore we do not identify contexts up to α-conversion.

In the following definitions of contextual preorder and equivalence, we take convergence at arbitrary type as our basic observable. As it happens, the expressiveness of contexts means that we could have chosen other observations without changing the relations that result: convergence at unit type, or to a specified integer value, would do just as well.

Definition 2.2 (Contextual preorder, contextual equivalence).
Suppose that $M_1, M_2 \in Exp_\sigma(\Gamma)$ are ReFS expressions. We write

$$\Gamma \vdash M_1 \leq M_2 : \sigma \qquad \textit{(contextual preorder)}$$

if for all contexts $C[-]$ such that $C[M_1]$ and $C[M_2]$ are closed terms of the same type it is the case that

$$s, C[M_1] \Downarrow \Rightarrow s, C[M_2] \Downarrow$$

holds for all states s with $loc(C[M_1], C[M_2]) \subseteq dom(s)$. We define

$$\Gamma \vdash M_1 \cong M_2 : \sigma \qquad \textit{(contextual equivalence)}$$

to mean that $\Gamma \vdash M_1 \leq M_2 : \sigma$ and $\Gamma \vdash M_2 \leq M_1 : \sigma$.

It is an easy consequence of these definitions that $\leq$ is reflexive and transitive, and hence that $\cong$ is an equivalence relation; moreover both relations are preserved by all the expression-forming operations of the language (including those that bind free variables).

3 A structurally inductive definition of termination

Before describing the logical relation for ReFS which is the main contribution of this paper, we need to describe the continuation-based termination relation upon which it depends. As mentioned on page 233, the reformulation of termination which we present in this section seems necessary in order to formulate a notion of logical relation that respects both dynamically allocated local state and recursively defined higher-order functions. Apart from this, the structurally inductive definition of termination we give here is very convenient for formalising inductive proofs about contextual equivalence, for the following reason.

Developing properties of ReFS contextual equivalence directly from its definition is not so easy. This is due to the quantification over all possible contexts that occurs in Definition 2.2 together with the nature of the termination relation, $s, M \Downarrow$. Although it is an inductive (*i.e.* recursively enumerable) subset of $\mathit{Sta} \times \mathit{Exp}$, its definition is not *structurally* inductive. For example, we can derive the rule

$$\frac{s', M'[V/x] \Downarrow}{s, \mathit{let}\, x = M\, \mathit{in}\, M' \Downarrow} \quad \text{if } s, M \Downarrow V, s'$$

but the value expression V used in the substitution $M'[V/x]$ is not a primitive recursive function of the syntax of $\mathit{let}\, x = M\, \mathit{in}\, M'$. As a consequence, the proof methods for contextual equivalence which naturally suggest themselves—induction over the structure of contexts and induction on the derivation of termination from the rules in Figure 4—very often founder for want of a sufficiently strong induction hypothesis. We shall fill this need for stronger induction hypotheses by considering a larger set than $\mathit{Sta} \times \mathit{Exp}$, carving out a subset by structural induction, and exhibiting the termination relation $\{(s, M) \mid s, M \Downarrow\}$ as a retract of this subset. The key ingredient in this strategy is a formal version of continuations.

Continuations

The concept of continuation that we extract from ReFS evaluation is fairly standard. However, our continuations are typed at both argument and result; and we have no need here of continuation *passing*. Continuations take the form of finite lists of expression abstractions $(x)M$, with $\mathcal{I}d$ for the empty list and '$\circ$' for concatenation:

$$K ::= \mathcal{I}d \mid K \circ (x)M\,.$$

Free variables and locations are defined by

$$\begin{aligned} fv(\mathcal{I}d) &= \emptyset & \qquad fv(K \circ (x)M) &= fv(K) \cup (fv(M) \setminus \{x\}) \\ loc(\mathcal{I}d) &= \emptyset & \qquad loc(K \circ (x)M) &= loc(K) \cup loc(M). \end{aligned}$$

We identify continuations up to α-conversion of bound variables (free occurrences of x in M are bound in $(x)M$).

The *application* $K@M$ of a continuation to an expression is defined by

$$\begin{aligned} \mathcal{I}d@M &\stackrel{\text{def}}{=} M \\ (K \circ (x)M')@M &\stackrel{\text{def}}{=} K@(\mathit{let}\, x = M\, \mathit{in}\, M') \end{aligned}$$

and is an expression (well-defined up to α-conversion). This notion of application gives a tie-up with *evaluation contexts*. For ReFS, with its reduced form of syntax, these are simply the subset of expression contexts given by

$$E[-] ::= [-] \mid \mathit{let}\, x = E[-]\, \mathit{in}\, M.$$

For any such $E[-]$, there is a continuation K such that $E[M] \equiv K@M$ for all expressions M, and conversely every continuation has a matching evaluation context. Evaluation contexts were originally derived (as 'unlabelled sk-contexts') from continuations in (Felleisen and Friedman 1986).

To each continuation we assign a type $\sigma \multimap \sigma'$, where the notation is meant to suggest the fact that evaluation contexts would give rise to *strict* (continuous) functions in a denotational semantics. The rules for types are as follows:

$$\Gamma \vdash \mathcal{I}d : \sigma \multimap \sigma \qquad \frac{\Gamma \vdash K : \sigma_2 \multimap \sigma_3}{\Gamma \vdash K \circ (x)M : \sigma_1 \multimap \sigma_3} \text{ if } \Gamma, x : \sigma_1 \vdash M : \sigma_2$$

Note that if $\Gamma \vdash K : \sigma \multimap \sigma'$ and $\Gamma \vdash M : \sigma$, then $\Gamma \vdash K@M : \sigma'$. We collect typed continuations into a range of indexed sets.

$$\mathit{Cont}_{\sigma,\sigma'}(\Gamma) \stackrel{\text{def}}{=} \{K \mid \Gamma \vdash K : \sigma \multimap \sigma'\} \quad \mathit{Cont}_{\sigma}(\Gamma) \stackrel{\text{def}}{=} \bigcup\{\mathit{Cont}_{\sigma,\sigma'}(\Gamma) \mid \sigma' \text{ a type}\}$$
$$\mathit{Cont}_{\sigma} \stackrel{\text{def}}{=} \mathit{Cont}_{\sigma}(\emptyset) \qquad \mathit{Cont} \stackrel{\text{def}}{=} \bigcup\{\mathit{Cont}_{\sigma} \mid \sigma \text{ a type}\}.$$

Termination

We are now ready to give our *structurally* defined termination relation. This will be an inductively defined subset of $\mathit{Sta} \times \mathit{Cont} \times \mathit{Exp}$ and we write

$$\langle s, K, M \rangle\!\downarrow$$

to indicate that (s, K, M) is in the subset. As usual we consider only well-formed judgements, here requiring that $M \in \mathit{Exp}_{\sigma}$ and $K \in \mathit{Cont}_{\sigma}$ for some type σ, and that $\mathit{loc}(K, M) \subseteq \mathit{dom}(s)$. Figure 5 gives the rules defining the relation. Notice that these are now properly structurally inductive, with a simple syntactic connection between the conclusion and hypothesis of each rule.

Theorem 3.1 (Termination). *The two termination relations correspond in the sense that*

$$\langle s, K, M \rangle\!\downarrow \;\Leftrightarrow\; s, K@M \Downarrow . \tag{3.1}$$

In particular, one has

$$\langle s, \mathcal{I}d, M \rangle\!\downarrow \;\Leftrightarrow\; s, M \Downarrow \tag{3.2}$$
$$\langle s, K, M \rangle\!\downarrow \;\Leftrightarrow\; \exists V, s' \,(s, M \Downarrow V, s' \;\&\; \langle s', K, V \rangle\!\downarrow). \tag{3.3}$$

Proof. One way to prove these properties is to note that

$$\langle s, K, M \rangle\!\downarrow \Leftrightarrow \exists s', V\,(\langle s, K, M \rangle \to^* \langle s', \mathcal{I}d, V \rangle).$$

where $\to^*$ is the reflexive-transitive closure of a suitable transition relation $\to$ between configurations. One can then establish (3.1)–(3.3) via a series of inductions involving $\Downarrow$ and $\to$. We omit the details. $\square$

$$\langle s, \mathcal{I}d, V\rangle\downarrow \qquad (\downarrow\text{val}_1)$$

$$\frac{\langle s, K, M[V/x]\rangle\downarrow}{\langle s, K \circ (x)M, V\rangle\downarrow} \qquad (\downarrow\text{val}_2)$$

$$\frac{\langle s, K, M_b\rangle\downarrow}{\langle s, K, \mathit{if}\ b\ \mathit{then}\ M_{\mathit{true}}\ \mathit{else}\ M_{\mathit{false}}\rangle\downarrow} \qquad (\downarrow\text{if})$$

$$\frac{\langle s, K, c\rangle\downarrow}{\langle s, K, n\ \mathit{op}\ n'\rangle\downarrow}\ \text{if } c = n\ \mathit{op}\ n' \qquad (\downarrow\text{op})$$

$$\frac{\langle s, K, V\rangle\downarrow}{\langle s, K, \mathit{fst}((V, V'))\rangle\downarrow} \qquad (\downarrow\text{fst})$$

$$\frac{\langle s, K, V'\rangle\downarrow}{\langle s, K, \mathit{snd}((V, V'))\rangle\downarrow} \qquad (\downarrow\text{snd})$$

$$\frac{\langle s, K, M[\,(\mathit{rec}\,f(x).\,M)/f,\ V/x\,]\rangle\downarrow}{\langle s, K, (\mathit{rec}\,f(x).\,M)V\rangle\downarrow} \qquad (\downarrow\text{app})$$

$$\frac{\langle s \otimes (\ell := n), K, \ell\rangle\downarrow}{\langle s, K, \mathit{ref}(n)\rangle\downarrow}\ \text{if } \ell \notin \mathit{dom}(s) \cup \mathit{loc}(K) \qquad (\downarrow\text{ref})$$

$$\frac{\langle s, K, n\rangle\downarrow}{\langle s, K, !\ell\rangle\downarrow}\ \text{if } n = s(\ell) \qquad (\downarrow\text{get})$$

$$\frac{\langle s; \ell := n, K, ()\rangle\downarrow}{\langle s, K, \ell := n\rangle\downarrow} \qquad (\downarrow\text{set})$$

$$\frac{\langle s, K \circ (x)M', M\rangle\downarrow}{\langle s, K, \mathit{let}\ x = M\ \mathit{in}\ M'\rangle\downarrow} \qquad (\downarrow\text{let})$$

Figure 5: Continuation-based termination relation

The unwinding theorem

In contrast to $\Downarrow$, the *structural* nature of the termination relation $\downarrow$ enables many properties of the contextual preorder and equivalence relations to be proved in a rather straightforward way, via an induction on the derivation of $\langle s, K, M\rangle\downarrow$. As an illustration, we give such a proof for the 'unwinding theorem' for recursive function values in ReFS, which provides a syntactic analogue of Dana Scott's induction principle for least fixed points and which is needed in the proof of the Fundamental Property of the logical relation introduced in the next section. Such theorems have been proved by several different people in various contexts: see for example (Mason, Smith, and Talcott 1996).

We fix some closed recursively defined function value $\mathit{rec}\, f(x).\, F \in \mathit{Val}_{\sigma\to\sigma'}$ and define the following abbreviations:

$$\begin{aligned}
\Omega &\stackrel{\text{def}}{=} (\mathit{rec}\, f(x).\, fx)() \\
F_0 &\stackrel{\text{def}}{=} \lambda x.\, \Omega \\
F_{n+1} &\stackrel{\text{def}}{=} \lambda x.\, F[F_n/f] \\
F_\omega &\stackrel{\text{def}}{=} \mathit{rec}\, f(x).\, F\,.
\end{aligned}$$

Each F_n is a finite unwinding of the full function F_ω. The essence of the following theorem is that these finite approximations provide all the observable behaviour of F_ω itself.

Theorem 3.2 (Unwinding). *For any* $M \in \mathit{Exp}_{\sigma''}(f{:}\sigma\to\sigma')$ *we have*

$$s, M[F_\omega/f]\Downarrow \Leftrightarrow \exists n \in \mathbb{N}\,(s, M[F_n/f]\Downarrow).$$

Equivalently, for any $K \in \mathit{Cont}_{\sigma\to\sigma'}$

$$\langle s, K, F_\omega\rangle\downarrow \Leftrightarrow \exists n \in \mathbb{N}\,\langle s, K, F_n\rangle\downarrow.$$

Proof. The two statements in the theorem are equivalent by Theorem 3.1, noting that for any K and F, $K@F$ is of the form $M[F/f]$ for some M, and conversely that when F is a value then $s, M[F/f]\Downarrow$ holds if and only if $\langle s, \mathcal{I}d \circ (x)M, F\rangle\downarrow$. The theorem (in its second formulation) follows from parts (iii) and (iv) of the following lemma, by taking $K' = K$ and $M' = g$. □

Lemma 3.3. *For all* $M' \in \mathit{Exp}_{\sigma_1}(g{:}\sigma\to\sigma')$, $K' \in \mathit{Cont}_{\sigma_1}(g{:}\sigma\to\sigma')$, *and* $s \in \mathit{Sta}$, *if* $\mathit{loc}(M', K', F) \subseteq \mathit{dom}(s)$ *then*

(i) *for all* $G \in \mathit{Val}_{\sigma\to\sigma'}$ *with* $\mathit{loc}(G) \subseteq \mathit{dom}(s)$

$$\langle s, K'[F_0/g], M'[F_0/g]\rangle\downarrow \;\Rightarrow\; \langle s, K'[G/g], M'[G/g]\rangle\downarrow$$

(ii) *for all* $n \in \mathbb{N}$

$$\langle s, K'[F_n/g], M'[F_n/g]\rangle\downarrow \;\Rightarrow\; \langle s, K'[F_{n+1}/g], M'[F_{n+1}/g]\rangle\downarrow$$

(iii) $\langle s, K'[F_\omega/g], M'[F_\omega/g]\rangle\!\downarrow \;\Rightarrow\; \exists n \in \mathbb{N}.\langle s, K'[F_n/g], M'[F_n/g]\rangle\!\downarrow$

(iv) *for all* $n \in \mathbb{N}$

$$\langle s, K'[F_n/g], M'[F_n/g]\rangle\!\downarrow \;\Rightarrow\; \langle s, K'[F_\omega/g], M'[F_\omega/g]\rangle\!\downarrow.$$

Proof. (i) is proved by induction on the derivation of $\langle s, K'[F_0/g], M'[F_0/g]\rangle\!\downarrow$ from the rules in Figure 5. More precisely, one shows that the set of machine states

$$\{\, \langle s, K, M\rangle \mid \forall K', M' \,(K = K'[F_0/g] \;\&\; M = M'[F_0/g] \\ \Rightarrow \forall G\, \langle s, K'[G/g], M'[G/g]\rangle\!\downarrow)\,\}$$

is closed under those rules. The only non-straightforward case is ($\downarrow$app), where one uses the easily verified fact that $\langle s, K, \Omega\rangle\!\downarrow$ cannot hold for any s and K. We omit the details.

(ii) is proved by induction on n, with part (i) providing the base case of $n = 0$.

For (iii), again one works by induction on the proof of termination, showing that the set of machine states

$$\mathbb{T} = \{\, \langle s, K, M\rangle \mid \forall K', M' \,(K = K'[F_\omega/g] \;\&\; M = M'[F_\omega/g] \\ \Rightarrow \exists n \in \mathbb{N}\,\langle s, K'[F_n/g], M'[F_n/g]\rangle\!\downarrow)\,\}$$

is closed under the rules of Figure 5 generating $\downarrow$. As for part (i), the only difficult case is closure under the application rule ($\downarrow$app). For that, suppose we have

$$\langle s, K, M[\,(\mathit{rec}\, f(x).\, M)/f,\, V/x\,]\rangle \in \mathbb{T}. \tag{3.4}$$

Then we have to show that $\langle s, K, (\mathit{rec}\, f(x).\, M)V\rangle \in \mathbb{T}$, i.e. that if

$$K = K'[F_\omega/g] \quad \text{and} \quad (\mathit{rec}\, f(x).\, M)V = M'[F_\omega/g] \tag{3.5}$$

then $\langle s, K'[F_n/g], M'[F_n/g]\rangle\!\downarrow$ holds for some finite n. Now (3.5) must hold because $M' = V_1V_2$ for some values V_1 and V_2 such that

$$\mathit{rec}\, f(x).\, M = V_1[F_\omega/g] \quad \text{and} \quad V = V_2[F_\omega/g].$$

The first of these can occur in two situations:

(a) $V_1 = g$ and $\mathit{rec}\, f(x).\, M = F_\omega$, thus $M = F$.

(b) $V_1 = \mathit{rec}\, f(x).\, M_1$ for some M_1 with $M = M_1[F_\omega/g]$.

The proof in case (b) is straightforward and we omit it. In case (a) we now have $M[\,(\mathit{rec}\, f(x).\, M)/f, V/x\,] = F[\,g/f,\, V_2/x\,][F_\omega/g]$ and so by (3.4) there is some finite m with $\langle s, K'[F_m/g], F[\,g/f,\, V_2/x\,][F_m/g]\rangle\!\downarrow$. Using the definition of F_{m+1}

and rule ($\downarrow$app) gives $\langle s, K'[F_m/g], F_{m+1}(V_2[F_m/g])\rangle\downarrow$ and hence by part (ii) also $\langle s, K'[F_{m+1}/g], F_{m+1}(V_2[F_{m+1}/g])\rangle\downarrow$. But

$$F_{m+1}(V_2[F_{m+1}/g]) = (V_1V_2)[F_{m+1}/g] = M'[F_{m+1}/g]$$

and so we have the desired conclusion that $\langle s, K'[F_n/g], M'[F_n/g]\rangle\downarrow$ holds for some n (namely $n = m + 1$).

The closure of $\mathbb{T}$ under the other rules of Figure 5 requires the same straightforward reasoning as for case (b), and we omit the details.

Finally, part (iv) of the lemma is once again proved by an induction over $\downarrow$: one shows that the set of machine states

$$\{\, \langle s, K, M\rangle \mid \forall K', M', n\, (K = K'[F_n/g] \;\&\; M = M'[F_n/g] \Rightarrow \langle s, K'[F_\omega/g], M'[F_\omega/g]\rangle\downarrow)\,\}$$

is closed under the rules generating $\downarrow$. Again, the only non-routine case is for ($\downarrow$app) and for that the proof is very much as for part (iii), with two distinct cases (a) and (b). We omit the details. □

Note that the imperative features of ReFS have little rôle in the proof of unwinding. If we had storage of non-ground data, these features would play a greater part, but the same proof methods would still work.

4 A parametric logical relation

In this section we define a family of binary relations between ReFS expressions (of equal type) parameterised by relations between states and establish its relationship to contextual equivalence. We prove a 'Fundamental Property' typical of logical relations (Theorem 4.9). This is the main technical result of the paper and it draws heavily upon the work of the previous section. From the Fundamental Property we easily deduce an extensionality result for ReFS contextual equivalence (Theorem 4.10) that includes the 'ciu' theorem of Mason and Talcott (1992b). So we get proofs for a range of basic contextual equivalences that are the usual consequences of the 'ciu' theorem. However, our extensionality theorem also characterises contextual equivalence in terms of the logical relation (with the state-relation parameter instantiated to the identity). In the next section we shall show that this characterisation can be used to give quite straightforward proofs for some examples of contextual equivalence which are not easily seen to be direct consequences of the 'ciu' theorem.

Definitions

We begin by defining a variety of relations between elements of our ReFS language, starting with states.

Definition 4.1 (State relations). Given finite subsets $\omega_1, \omega_2 \subseteq Loc$, a *state relation* from ω_1 to ω_2 is a non-empty subset $r \subseteq Sta(\omega_1) \times Sta(\omega_2)$. (Recall from page 239 that $Sta(\omega)$ denotes the set of all states with domain of definition equal to ω.) We write

$$Rel(\omega_1, \omega_2)$$

for the set of all such relations. Given $r \in Rel(\omega_1, \omega_2)$, we refer to ω_1 and ω_2 as the domain and codomain of r respectively. (Note that since we are assuming that any state relation r is in particular non-empty,[3] its domain and codomain are uniquely determined.)

For any finite subset $\omega \subseteq Loc$, the *identity state relation* on ω is

$$id_\omega \stackrel{\text{def}}{=} \{(s, s) \mid dom(s) = \omega\}.$$

Given two state relations relations $r \in Rel(\omega_1, \omega_2)$ and $r' \in Rel(\omega_1', \omega_2')$ with $\omega_i \cap \omega_i' = \emptyset$ $(i = 1, 2)$, their *smash product* $r \otimes r' \in Rel(w_1 \cup \omega_1', \omega_2 \cup \omega_2')$ is defined using the smash product of states defined in Section 2:

$$r \otimes r' \stackrel{\text{def}}{=} \{(s_1 \otimes s_1', s_2 \otimes s_2') \mid (s_1, s_2) \in r \;\&\; (s_1', s_2') \in r'\}.$$

It is straightforward to show that

$$\begin{array}{ll} id_\omega \otimes id_{\omega'} = id_{\omega \cup \omega'} \quad (w \cap w' = \emptyset) & r \otimes r' = r' \otimes r \\ id_\emptyset \otimes r = r & r \otimes (r' \otimes r'') = (r \otimes r') \otimes r'' \end{array}$$

with the last three in particular following from the corresponding property of $\otimes$ on states.

We say that a state relation r' *extends* another one r, and write $r' \rhd r$, if $r' = r \otimes r''$ for some r''. It follows from the above properties of the smash product $\otimes$ that the extension relation $\rhd$ is a partial order.

Suppose we have two configurations $\langle s, K, M\rangle$ and $\langle s', K', M'\rangle$ of the abstract machine described in Section 3. We say that they are *convergence equivalent*, written

$$\langle s, K, M\rangle \updownarrow \langle s', K', M'\rangle$$

if they are both well formed, *i.e.* $loc(KM) \subseteq dom(s)$ and $loc(K'M') \subseteq dom(s')$, and they converge or diverge together:

$$\langle s, K, M\rangle{\downarrow} \Leftrightarrow \langle s', K', M'\rangle{\downarrow}.$$

[3] This is merely a technical convenience which, amongst other things, simplifies the definition of the logical relation at ground types.

Definition 4.2 (A parametric logical relation for ReFS).
For each state relation $r \in Rel(\omega_1, \omega_2)$ and each type σ we define three binary relations:

$$\begin{aligned}\mathcal{E}_\sigma(r) &\subseteq \mathit{Exp}_\sigma(\omega_1) \times \mathit{Exp}_\sigma(\omega_2)\\ \mathcal{K}_\sigma(r) &\subseteq \mathit{Cont}_\sigma(\omega_1) \times \mathit{Cont}_\sigma(\omega_2)\\ \mathcal{V}_\sigma(r) &\subseteq \mathit{Val}_\sigma(\omega_1) \times \mathit{Val}_\sigma(\omega_2).\end{aligned}$$

Here $\mathit{Exp}_\sigma(\omega)$ denotes the set of closed ReFS expressions of type σ involving location constants in the finite set ω; similarly for continuations $\mathit{Cont}_\sigma(\omega)$ and values $\mathit{Val}_\sigma(\omega)$. We make the definitions of these relations for all r simultaneously. The first relation, between expressions, is defined in terms of the second:

$$(M_1, M_2) \in \mathcal{E}_\sigma(r) \overset{\text{def}}{\Leftrightarrow} \forall r' \rhd r, (s_1, s_2) \in r', (K_1, K_2) \in \mathcal{K}_\sigma(r') \,.\\ \langle s_1, K_1, M_1\rangle \updownarrow \langle s_2, K_2, M_2\rangle. \quad (4.1)$$

The second relation, on continuations, is defined in terms of the third:

$$(K_1, K_2) \in \mathcal{K}_\sigma(r) \overset{\text{def}}{\Leftrightarrow} \forall r' \rhd r, (s_1, s_2) \in r', (V_1, V_2) \in \mathcal{V}_\sigma(r') \,.\\ \langle s_1, K_1, V_1\rangle \updownarrow \langle s_2, K_2, V_2\rangle. \quad (4.2)$$

The final relation, between values, is defined by induction on the structure of the type σ:

$$(c_1, c_2) \in \mathcal{V}_\sigma(r) \overset{\text{def}}{\Leftrightarrow} c_1 = c_2 \quad \text{for } \sigma \in \{\mathit{unit}, \mathit{bool}, \mathit{int}\} \quad (4.3)$$

$$(\ell_1, \ell_2) \in \mathcal{V}_{\mathit{loc}}(r) \overset{\text{def}}{\Leftrightarrow} (!\ell_1, !\ell_2) \in \mathcal{E}_{\mathit{int}}(r)\\ \& \ \forall n \in \mathbb{Z} \,.\, (\ell_1 := n, \ell_2 := n) \in \mathcal{E}_{\mathit{unit}}(r) \quad (4.4)$$

$$(V_1, V_2) \in \mathcal{V}_{\sigma \times \sigma'}(r) \overset{\text{def}}{\Leftrightarrow} (\mathit{fst}(V_1), \mathit{fst}(V_2)) \in \mathcal{E}_\sigma(r)\\ \& \ (\mathit{snd}(V_1), \mathit{snd}(V_2)) \in \mathcal{E}_{\sigma'}(r) \quad (4.5)$$

$$(V_1, V_2) \in \mathcal{V}_{\sigma \to \sigma'}(r) \overset{\text{def}}{\Leftrightarrow} \forall r' \rhd r, (W_1, W_2) \in \mathcal{V}_\sigma(r') \,.\\ (V_1 W_1, V_2 W_2) \in \mathcal{E}_{\sigma'}(r'). \quad (4.6)$$

We call this family of relations 'logical' simply because it relates function values if, roughly speaking, they map related arguments to related results. This is the characteristic feature of a wide range of relations used in connection with the lambda calculus which ever since (Plotkin 1973, 1980) have been called 'logical relations'.

Note. It is possible to simplify Definition 4.2 by replacing the use of an arbitrary extension $r' \rhd r$ by r itself in the defining clauses for $\mathcal{E}_\sigma(r)$ and $\mathcal{K}_\sigma(r)$ (but not $\mathcal{V}_{\sigma \to \sigma'}(r)$). This simplification depends partly upon the 'flat' nature of state in ReFS and since we have an eye to generalisations of ReFS (see Section 6), we chose not to build it into the definition. Furthermore, this simplification would complicate the proof of the following property.

Lemma 4.3 (Weakening). *Extending a state relation preserves existing relations between expressions, continuations and values: if $r' \rhd r$ then*

$$(M_1, M_2) \in \mathcal{E}_\sigma(r) \Rightarrow (M_1, M_2) \in \mathcal{E}_\sigma(r')$$
$$(K_1, K_2) \in \mathcal{K}_\sigma(r) \Rightarrow (K_1, K_2) \in \mathcal{K}_\sigma(r')$$
$$(V_1, V_2) \in \mathcal{V}_\sigma(r) \Rightarrow (V_1, V_2) \in \mathcal{V}_\sigma(r')$$

Proof. Clauses (4.1) and (4.2) of Definition 4.2 specify $\mathcal{E}_\sigma(r)$ and $\mathcal{K}_\sigma(r)$ by quantifying over all extensions $r' \rhd r$ and so the first two parts are immediate (since $\rhd$ is a preorder). The third part concerning values then follows from the first, matching the way clauses (4.3) to (4.6) define $\mathcal{V}_\sigma(r)$ in terms of $\mathcal{E}_\sigma(r)$. □

The definition of the relations $\mathcal{E}_\sigma(r)$ on expressions and $\mathcal{V}_\sigma(r)$ on values are quite different; nevertheless they agree in that values can be considered as expressions without changing their relations, as the following lemma shows.

Lemma 4.4 (Coincidence). *Relations $\mathcal{E}_\sigma(r)$ and $\mathcal{V}_\sigma(r)$ coincide on values: for $V_1, V_2 \in Val_\sigma$*

$$(V_1, V_2) \in \mathcal{E}_\sigma(r) \Leftrightarrow (V_1, V_2) \in \mathcal{V}_\sigma(r).$$

Proof. The direction from right to left follows at once from the definition of $\mathcal{E}_\sigma(r)$ and $\mathcal{K}_\sigma(r)$ given in clauses (4.1) and (4.2), together with Lemma 4.3. From left to right, we proceed by cases on the structure of type σ.

Case $\sigma = unit$ is trivial, as the only unit value is () and $((), ()) \in \mathcal{V}_{unit}(r)$ for any r.

Case $\sigma = bool$. Consider the continuation

$$K = \mathcal{I}d \circ (x)(if\ x\ then\ ()\ else\ \Omega)$$

where Ω is the non-terminating expression used in the Unwinding Theorem 3.2. From the definition of $\mathcal{V}_{bool}$ and $\mathcal{K}_{bool}$ it is not hard to show that $(K, K) \in \mathcal{K}_{bool}(r)$. Suppose then that $b_1, b_2 \in \{true, false\}$ with $(b_1, b_2) \in \mathcal{E}_{bool}(r)$. Since state relations are by definition non-empty, we can choose some $(s_1, s_2) \in r$. Then we have $\langle s_1, K, b_1\rangle \updownarrow \langle s_2, K, b_2\rangle$ and hence

$$\langle s_1, \mathcal{I}d, if\ b_1\ then\ ()\ else\ \Omega\rangle \updownarrow \langle s_2, \mathcal{I}d, if\ b_2\ then\ ()\ else\ \Omega\rangle.$$

Since $\langle s_i, \mathcal{I}d, \Omega\rangle\not\downarrow$ and $\langle s_i, \mathcal{I}d, ()\rangle\downarrow$ it follows that $b_1 = b_2$, and thus $(b_1, b_2) \in \mathcal{V}_{bool}(r)$ as required.

Case $\sigma = int$ is similar to the previous case, using the continuation

$$K = \mathcal{I}d \circ (x)(let\ y = (V_1 = x)\ in\ if\ y\ then\ ()\ else\ \Omega)$$

where V_1 is one of the integer values involved.

Case $\sigma = loc$. Suppose that $(\ell_1, \ell_2) \in \mathcal{E}_{loc}(r)$. We need to prove that $(!\ell_1, !\ell_2) \in \mathcal{E}_{int}(r)$ and also $((\ell_1 := n), (\ell_2 := n)) \in \mathcal{E}_{unit}(r)$ for every $n \in \mathbb{Z}$. Suppose that at some extension $r' \rhd r$ we have $(s_1, s_2) \in r'$ and $(K_1, K_2) \in \mathcal{K}_{int}(r')$. For the first property, we have to show that $\langle s_1, K_1, !\ell_1\rangle \updownarrow \langle s_2, K_2, !\ell_2\rangle$. But it is not hard to verify that $((K_1 \circ (x)!x), (K_2 \circ (x)!x)) \in \mathcal{K}_{loc}(r')$, and then because $(\ell_1, \ell_2) \in \mathcal{E}_{loc}(r)$ we obtain

$$\langle s_1, (K_1 \circ (x)!x), \ell_1\rangle \updownarrow \langle s_2, (K_2 \circ (x)!x), \ell_2\rangle$$

and hence also $\langle s_1, K_1, !\ell_1\rangle \updownarrow \langle s_2, K_2, !\ell_2\rangle$, as required. The argument that $(\ell_1 := n, \ell_2 := n) \in \mathcal{E}_{unit}(r)$ is similar.

Case $\sigma = \sigma_1 \times \sigma_2$. The proof is as in the previous case, this time taking $(K_1, K_2) \in \mathcal{K}_{\sigma_1}(r')$ to $(K_1 \circ (x)\,\mathit{fst}(x), K_2 \circ (x)\,\mathit{fst}(x)) \in \mathcal{K}_\sigma(r')$ and similarly with *snd*.

Case $\sigma = \sigma_1 \to \sigma_2$. The proof takes the same form again, based on the observation that if $r'' \rhd r' \rhd r$ and $(K_1, K_2) \in \mathcal{K}_{\sigma_2}(r'')$ then

$$(\,(K_1 \circ (x)xW_1),\ (K_2 \circ (x)xW_2)\,) \in \mathcal{K}_{\sigma_1 \to \sigma_2}(r'')$$

for all $(W_1, W_2) \in \mathcal{V}_{\sigma_1}(r')$.

These last three cases all use the weakening results of Lemma 4.3. □

Definition 4.5 (Extension of the logical relation to open expressions). Given two open expressions $M_1, M_2 \in \mathit{Exp}_\sigma(\Gamma)$ with $loc(M_i) \subseteq \omega_i$ $(i = 1, 2)$ and a state relation $r \in \mathit{Rel}(\omega_1, \omega_2)$ we write

$$\Gamma \vdash M_1 \; \{r\} \; M_2 : \sigma$$

to mean that for all extensions $r' \rhd r$ and values $\{V_{1x}, V_{2x} \in \mathit{Val}_{\sigma'} \mid x : \sigma' \in \Gamma\}$ we have

$$(\forall x : \sigma' \in \Gamma \,.\, (V_{1x}, V_{2x}) \in \mathcal{V}_{\sigma'}(r')) \Rightarrow (M_1[\vec{V_1}/\vec{x}], M_2[\vec{V_2}/\vec{x}]) \in \mathcal{E}_\sigma(r').$$

In particular $\emptyset \vdash M_1 \{r\} M_2 : \sigma$ holds if and only if $(M_1, M_2) \in \mathcal{E}_\sigma(r)$, thanks to Lemma 4.3: so this is indeed an extension of the original logical relation.

The following structural properties of this relation are automatic from the above definition.

$$\Gamma \vdash M_1 \{r\} M_2 : \sigma \Rightarrow \Gamma\Gamma' \vdash M_1 \{r\} M_2 : \sigma$$
$$\Gamma \vdash M_1 \{r\} M_2 : \sigma \Rightarrow \Gamma \vdash M_1 \{r \otimes r'\} M_2 : \sigma$$

$$(\Gamma \vdash V_1 \{r\} V_2 : \sigma) \;\&\; (\Gamma, x : \sigma \vdash M_1 \{r\} M_2 : \sigma') \Rightarrow$$
$$\Gamma \vdash M_1[V_1/x] \{r\} M_2[V_2/x] : \sigma' \qquad (V_1, V_2 \in \mathit{Val}_\sigma(\Gamma)).$$

In addition to the logical relation, we shall use the following equivalence between expressions.

Definition 4.6 ('ciu' equivalence). Given $M_1, M_2 \in \mathit{Exp}_\sigma$ we write

$$M_1 \cong^{ciu} M_2 : \sigma$$

to mean that for all $s \in \mathit{Sta}$ and $K \in \mathit{Cont}_\sigma$ with $\mathit{loc}(K, M_1, M_2) \subseteq \mathit{dom}(s)$,

$$\langle s, K, M_1 \rangle \updownarrow \langle s, K, M_2 \rangle.$$

We extend this to open expressions by value substitution: for $M_1, M_2 \in \mathit{Exp}_\sigma(\Gamma)$,

$$\Gamma \vdash M_1 \cong^{ciu} M_2 : \sigma$$

means that for all $\{V_x \in \mathit{Val}_{\sigma'} \mid x : \sigma' \in \Gamma\}$ we have $M_1[\vec{V}/\vec{x}] \cong^{ciu} M_2[\vec{V}/\vec{x}] : \sigma$. (Note that the V_x may use locations not mentioned in M_1 or M_2.)

This relation '$\cong^{ciu}$' coincides with the ciu-equivalence of (Mason and Talcott 1991a; Talcott 1997). This is because the results of Section 3 imply that $\Gamma \vdash M_1 \cong^{ciu} M_2 : \sigma$ holds if and only if for all suitable value substitutions $\{V_x \mid x \in \Gamma\}$, evaluation contexts $E[-]$ and states s:

$$s, E[M_1[\vec{V}/\vec{x}]] \Downarrow \Leftrightarrow s, E[M_2[\vec{V}/\vec{x}]] \Downarrow.$$

These are the appropriate 'closed instantiations of uses' for ReFS expressions. The next result shows that the logical relations respect ciu-equivalence.

Lemma 4.7 (Composition). *The logical relation is closed under composition with ciu-equivalence. For closed terms we have*

$$(M_1' \cong^{ciu} M_1 \;\&\; (M_1, M_2) \in \mathcal{E}_\sigma(r) \;\&\; M_2 \cong^{ciu} M_2') \Rightarrow (M_1', M_2') \in \mathcal{E}_\sigma(r)$$

and more generally for open ones

$$(\Gamma \vdash M_1' \cong^{ciu} M_1 \;\&\; \Gamma \vdash M_1 \,\{r\}\, M_2 \;\&\; \Gamma \vdash M_2 \cong^{ciu} M_2') \Rightarrow \Gamma \vdash M_1' \,\{r\}\, M_2'.$$

Proof. For the first property, suppose that $r' \rhd r$ and that we have states $(s_1, s_2) \in r'$ and continuations $(K_1, K_2) \in \mathcal{K}_\sigma(r')$. Then

$$\langle s_1, K_1, M_1' \rangle \updownarrow \langle s_1, K_1, M_1 \rangle \updownarrow \langle s_2, K_2, M_2 \rangle \updownarrow \langle s_2, K_2, M_2' \rangle$$

and the result follows by transitivity of '$\updownarrow$'. For open expressions, we consider values $\{V_{1x}, V_{2x} \in \mathit{Val}_{\sigma'} \mid x : \sigma' \in \Gamma\}$ with each $(V_{1x}, V_{2x}) \in \mathcal{V}_{\sigma'}(r')$ and deduce that

$$M_1'[\vec{V_1}/\vec{x}] \cong^{ciu} M_1[\vec{V_1}/\vec{x}] \;\&\; M_2[\vec{V_2}/\vec{x}] \cong^{ciu} M_2'[\vec{V_2}/\vec{x}]$$
$$\&\; (M_1[\vec{V_1}/\vec{x}], M_2[\vec{V_2}/\vec{x}]) \in \mathcal{E}_\sigma(r').$$

The first part now gives $(M_1'[\vec{V_1}/\vec{x}], M_2'[\vec{V_2}/\vec{x}]) \in \mathcal{E}_\sigma(r')$ and so $\Gamma \vdash M_1' \,\{r\}\, M_2'$ as desired. □

Fundamental property of the relation

We aim to prove the 'Fundamental Property' of the logical relation introduced in Definition 4.2. Roughly speaking, this says that the relations $Exp_\sigma(r)$ are preserved by the various operations in the ReFS language; the precise statement is given below in Theorem 4.9.

The reader familiar with previous work on relational parametricity for languages with storage locations may be surprised that such a property holds without some restriction on the parameterising relations r. O'Hearn and Tennent (1993, Section 6) sketch a construction for a language like ReFS in which the parameter is a binary relation between states equipped with a partial bijection between the underlying sets of locations, which together must satisfy some simple conditions to do with assignment and look-up. The reason given for the use of the extra information of a partial bijection is to ensure that the operation for location-equality testing preserves the parametric logical relation. But in fact use of partial bijections is superfluous. We will establish the preservation property for all expressions in ReFS with respect to the logical relation simply parameterised by state relations; and we noted in Remark 2.1 that location-equality testing is definable in ReFS—so in particular it preserves the logical relation. In this respect ReFS is simpler than the 'nu-calculus' studied in (Pitts and Stark 1993) where location-equality testing is not definable in terms of the rest of the language and use of partial bijections between locations is unavoidable.

Proposition 4.8. *The logical relation is preserved by all the expression-forming operations of the ReFS language.*

(i) $\Gamma, x : \sigma \vdash x \, \{r\} \, x : \sigma$.

(ii) $\Gamma \vdash () \, \{r\} \, () : unit$.

(iii) $\Gamma \vdash b \, \{r\} \, b : bool$, *for each* $b \in \{true, false\}$.

(iv) $\Gamma \vdash n \, \{r\} \, n : int$, *for any* $n \in \mathbb{Z}$.

(v) $\Gamma \vdash \ell \, \{r \otimes id_{\{\ell\}}\} \, \ell : loc$, *where* $\ell \notin dom(r) \cup cod(r)$.

(vi) *If* $\Gamma \vdash V_1 \, \{r\} \, V_2 : \sigma$ *and* $\Gamma \vdash V_1' \, \{r\} \, V_2' : \sigma'$ *then*
$\Gamma \vdash (V_1, V_1') \, \{r\} \, (V_2, V_2') : \sigma \times \sigma'$.

(vii) *If* $\Gamma \vdash V_1 \, \{r\} \, V_2 : bool$, $\Gamma \vdash M_1 \, \{r\} \, M_2 : \sigma$ *and* $\Gamma \vdash M_1' \, \{r\} \, M_2' : \sigma$ *then*
$\Gamma \vdash (if\ V_1\ then\ M_1\ else\ M_1') \, \{r\} \, (if\ V_2\ then\ M_2\ else\ M_2') : \sigma$.

(viii) *If* $\Gamma \vdash V_1 \, \{r\} \, V_2 : int$ *and* $\Gamma \vdash V_1' \, \{r\} \, V_2' : int$ *then*
$\Gamma \vdash (V_1\ op\ V_1') \, \{r\} \, (V_2\ op\ V_2') : \gamma$, *where* γ *is the result type of op.*

(ix) *If* $\Gamma \vdash V_1 \, \{r\} \, V_2 : \sigma \times \sigma'$ *then* $\Gamma \vdash fst(V_1) \, \{r\} \, fst(V_2) : \sigma$ *and*
$\Gamma \vdash snd(V_1) \, \{r\} \, snd(V_2) : \sigma'$.

(x) *If* $\Gamma \vdash V_1 \{r\} V_2 : int$ *then* $\Gamma \vdash ref(V_1) \{r\} ref(V_2) : loc$.

(xi) *If* $\Gamma \vdash V_1 \{r\} V_2 : loc$ *then* $\Gamma \vdash !V_1 \{r\} !V_2 : int$.

(xii) *If* $\Gamma \vdash V_1 \{r\} V_2 : loc$ *and* $\Gamma \vdash V_1' \{r\} V_2' : int$ *then* $\Gamma \vdash (V_1 := V_1') \{r\} (V_2 := V_2') : unit$.

(xiii) *If* $\Gamma \vdash V_1 \{r\} V_2 : \sigma \to \sigma'$ *and* $\Gamma \vdash V_1' \{r\} V_2' : \sigma$ *then* $\Gamma \vdash (V_1 V_1') \{r\} (V_2 V_2') : \sigma'$.

(xiv) *If* $\Gamma \vdash M_1 \{r\} M_2 : \sigma$ *and* $\Gamma, x : \sigma \vdash M_1' \{r\} M_2' : \sigma'$ *then* $\Gamma \vdash (let\ x = M_1\ in\ M_1') \{r\} (let\ x = M_2\ in\ M_2') : \sigma'$.

(xv) *If* $\Gamma, f : \sigma \to \sigma', x : \sigma \vdash M_1 \{r\} M_2 : \sigma'$ *then* $\Gamma \vdash (rec\ f(x).\ M_1) \{r\} (rec\ f(x).\ M_2) : \sigma \to \sigma'$.

Proof. As might be expected, many of the clauses here have similar proofs, with only four of them ((v), (x), (xiv) and (xv)) requiring individual attention. Moreover, there is no hard work: essentially all the proofs are compositions of properties proved earlier. First though we note some general points. Because each clause preserves Γ and makes no use of it, we may assume without loss of generality that all of its variables have already been substituted by $\{r\}$-related values, and so take $\Gamma = \emptyset$. We may similarly take just r rather than an extension $r' \rhd r$ in all clauses where Γ is the only source of free variables (*i.e.* (ii)–(xiii)). Lemma 4.4, which says that $\mathcal{V}_\sigma(r)$ and $\mathcal{E}_\sigma(r)$ coincide on values, allows us to move between the two relations and we do this silently throughout.

Cases (i)–(iv) all follow immediately from the definition of $\{r\}$ and $\mathcal{V}_\sigma(r)$. In case (v) we need to show that

$$(!\ell, !\ell) \in \mathcal{E}_{int}(r \otimes id_{\{\ell\}}) \quad \text{and} \quad \forall n \in \mathbb{Z}\,.\,(\ell := n, \ell := n) \in \mathcal{E}_{unit}(r \otimes id_{\{\ell\}})$$

for a given location ℓ not mentioned by r. We look at the first of these: the second is treated similarly. Suppose that $(s_1, s_2) \in (r \otimes id_{\{\ell\}} \otimes r')$ and $(K_1, K_2) \in \mathcal{K}_{int}(r \otimes id_{\{\ell\}} \otimes r')$ for some r'. We have to show

$$\langle s_1, K_1, !\ell \rangle \updownarrow \langle s_2, K_2, !\ell \rangle. \tag{4.7}$$

As $(s_1, s_2) \in (r \otimes id_{\{\ell\}} \otimes r')$ we know that $s_1(\ell) = s_2(\ell) = n$ for some integer n. Then

$$\langle s_i, K_i, !\ell \rangle \updownarrow \langle s_i, K_i, n \rangle \quad \text{for } i = 1, 2. \tag{4.8}$$

But $(n, n) \in \mathcal{V}_{int}(r \otimes id_{\{\ell\}} \otimes r')$ and as $(K_1, K_2) \in \mathcal{K}_{int}(r \otimes id_{\{\ell\}} \otimes r')$,

$$\langle s_1, K_1, n \rangle \updownarrow \langle s_2, K_2, n \rangle. \tag{4.9}$$

Combining (4.8) and (4.9) gives (4.7) as required.

Cases (vi), (vii) and (viii) are all alike and we look only at the first. We have

$$(V_1, V_2) \in \mathcal{E}_\sigma(r) \quad \text{and} \quad (V_1', V_2') \in \mathcal{E}_{\sigma'}(r), \tag{4.10}$$

and need to show $((V_1, V_1'), (V_2, V_2')) \in \mathcal{V}_{\sigma\times\sigma'}(r)$. This requires

$$\begin{aligned} (\,fst(V_1, V_1'),\, fst(V_2, V_2')\,) &\in \mathcal{E}_\sigma(r) \\ (\,snd(V_1, V_1'),\, snd(V_2, V_2')\,) &\in \mathcal{E}_{\sigma'}(r). \end{aligned} \tag{4.11}$$

The following ciu-equivalences are all straightforward:

$$\begin{aligned} fst(V_1, V_2) &\cong^{ciu} V_1 \qquad & fst(V_1', V_2') &\cong^{ciu} V_1' \\ snd(V_1, V_2) &\cong^{ciu} V_2 \qquad & snd(V_1', V_2') &\cong^{ciu} V_2' \end{aligned} \tag{4.12}$$

and by Lemma 4.7 we can combine these with the logical relations of (4.10) to give (4.11) as required. Such use of ciu-equivalence is also the key to cases (vii) and (viii).

In case (ix) we are given $(V_1, V_2) \in \mathcal{V}_{\sigma\times\sigma'}(r)$ and need to show that $(fst(V_1), fst(V_2)) \in \mathcal{E}_\sigma(r)$ and $(snd(V_1), snd(V_2)) \in \mathcal{E}_{\sigma'}(r)$—but this is exactly the definition of $\mathcal{V}_{\sigma\times\sigma'}(r)$ on page 248. Cases (xi), (xii) and (xiii) use the definition of $\mathcal{V}(r)$ at locations and function types in exactly the same way.

For case (x) we again need to consider actual continuations. Suppose that $(V_1, V_2) \in \mathcal{V}_{int}(r)$, *i.e.* $V_1 = V_2 = n$ for some $n \in \mathbb{Z}$. For any $r' \rhd r$, $(s_1, s_2) \in r'$, and $(K_1, K_2) \in \mathcal{K}_{loc}(r')$ we need to show that

$$\langle s_1, K_1, ref(n)\rangle \updownarrow \langle s_2, K_2, ref(n)\rangle. \tag{4.13}$$

By considering a single reduction step[4] we have that

$$\langle s_i, K_i, ref(n)\rangle \updownarrow \langle s_i \otimes (\ell := n), K_i, \ell\rangle \quad \text{for } i = 1, 2 \text{ and } \ell \text{ fresh.} \tag{4.14}$$

Now $(s_1\otimes(\ell{:=}n), s_2\otimes(\ell{:=}n)) \in r'\otimes id_{\{\ell\}}$, by the weakening Lemma 4.3 we have $(K_1, K_2) \in \mathcal{K}_{loc}(r' \otimes id_{\{\ell\}})$, and from part (v) we know $(\ell, \ell) \in \mathcal{V}_{loc}(r' \otimes id_{\{\ell\}})$. Thus

$$\langle s_1 \otimes (\ell := n), K_1, \ell\rangle \updownarrow \langle s_2 \otimes (\ell := n), K_2, \ell\rangle \tag{4.15}$$

and this in combination with (4.14) gives (4.13) as required.

In part (xiv) we have the hypothesis that

$$(M_1, M_2) \in \mathcal{E}_\sigma(r) \quad \text{and} \quad x : \sigma \vdash M_1' \,\{r\}\, M_2' : \sigma'.$$

Consider $r' \rhd r$, $(s_1, s_2) \in r'$, and $(K_1, K_2) \in \mathcal{K}_{\sigma'}(r')$: we need to show

$$\langle s_1, K_1, let\ x = M_1\ in\ M_1'\rangle \updownarrow \langle s_2, K_2, let\ x = M_2\ in\ M_2'\rangle.$$

[4] Strictly speaking, the left-to-right implication in (4.14) relies upon the easily verified fact that the termination relation $\downarrow$ is invariant under bijective renamings of location constants.

Again, taking one reduction step gives

$$\langle s_i, K_i, let\ x = M_i\ in\ M_i' \rangle \updownarrow \langle s_i, K_i \circ (x)M_i', M_i \rangle \quad \text{for } i = 1, 2,$$

and as $(M_1, M_2) \in \mathcal{E}_\sigma(r)$ it is sufficient to prove that

$$(\, K_1 \circ (x)M_1',\ K_2 \circ (x)M_2' \,) \in \mathcal{K}_\sigma(r'). \tag{4.16}$$

Suppose that $r'' \rhd r'$, $(s_1', s_2') \in r''$, and $(V_1, V_2) \in \mathcal{V}_\sigma(r'')$; we now need

$$\langle s_1', K_1 \circ (x)M_1', V_1 \rangle \updownarrow \langle s_2', K_2 \circ (x)M_2', V_2 \rangle. \tag{4.17}$$

A single reduction step gives

$$\langle s_i', K_i \circ (x)M_i', V_i \rangle \updownarrow \langle s_i', K_i, M_i'[V_i/x] \rangle \quad \text{for } i = 1, 2. \tag{4.18}$$

Finally the hypothesis on M_i' and choice of V_i gives $(M_1'[V_1/x], M_2'[V_2/x]) \in \mathcal{E}_\sigma(r'')$, from which we get

$$\langle s_1', K_1, M_1'[V_1/x] \rangle \updownarrow \langle s_2', K_2, M_2'[V_2/x] \rangle. \tag{4.19}$$

Combining this with (4.18) gives (4.17) and hence (4.16) as required.

For case (xv), concerning recursively defined function values, it is no surprise that we turn to the Unwinding Theorem 3.2. The first step is to show that for non-recursive functions

$$x : \sigma \vdash M_1 \{r\} M_2 : \sigma' \;\Rightarrow\; \vdash (\lambda\, x.\, M_1) \{r\} (\lambda\, x.\, M_2) \tag{4.20}$$

which is done through the ciu-equivalence

$$(\lambda\, x.\, M)V \cong^{ciu} M[V/x]$$

in much the same way as case (vi). Now suppose more generally that we have

$$f : \sigma \to \sigma', x : \sigma \vdash M_1 \{r\} M_2 : \sigma'. \tag{4.21}$$

As in Section 3, consider the following progressive unwindings:

$$\Omega \stackrel{\text{def}}{=} (rec\, f(x).\, fx)() \qquad F_{i,n+1} \stackrel{\text{def}}{=} \lambda\, x.\, M_i[F_{i,n}/f]$$

$$F_{i,0} \stackrel{\text{def}}{=} \lambda\, x.\, \Omega \qquad F_{i,\omega} \stackrel{\text{def}}{=} rec\, f(x).\, M_i\,.$$

for $i = 1, 2$. We then prove in turn

$$(\Omega, \Omega) \in \mathcal{E}_{\sigma \to \sigma'}(r) \tag{4.22}$$

$$(F_{1,n}, F_{2,n}) \in \mathcal{E}_{\sigma \to \sigma'}(r) \tag{4.23}$$

$$(F_{1,\omega}, F_{2,\omega}) \in \mathcal{E}_{\sigma \to \sigma'}(r). \tag{4.24}$$

The first of these is straightforward as Ω never terminates in any context; this provides the base case to prove (4.23) by induction on n, using (4.20) and (4.21) at each step; and finally the Unwinding Theorem 3.2 allows us to deduce (4.24), which is exactly the desired result:

$$\vdash (rec\, f(x).\, M_1)\ \{r\}\ (rec\, f(x).\, M_2) : \sigma \to \sigma'.$$

What we are using here is that the $\mathcal{E}_\sigma(r)$ relations are *admissible*, in an appropriate syntactic variant of the usual notion on domains: if every finite approximation of some (M_1, M_2) is in $\mathcal{E}_\sigma(r)$, then so is (M_1, M_2) itself. □

Theorem 4.9 (Fundamental Property of the Logical Relation).

(i) *Contexts preserve the identity logical relation: if* $\Gamma \vdash M_1\ \{id_\omega\}\ M_2 : \sigma$, *then for any context* $C[-]$ *with* $fv(C) \subseteq \Gamma' \subseteq \Gamma$, $loc(C[-]) \subseteq \omega$, *and* $\Gamma' \vdash C[M_i] : \sigma'$ *for* $i = 1, 2$ *(so that the hole '$-$' occurs in* $C[-]$ *within the scope of binding occurrences of the variables in* $\Gamma \setminus \Gamma'$*), it is the case that* $\Gamma' \vdash C[M_1]\ \{id_\omega\}\ C[M_2] : \sigma'$.

(ii) *The identity logical relation is reflexive: if* $M \in Exp_\sigma(\Gamma)$ *with* $loc(M) \subseteq \omega$, *then* $\Gamma \vdash M\ \{id_\omega\}\ M : \sigma$.

Proof. Part (i) is proved by induction on the structure of $C[-]$, using Proposition 4.8. Part (ii) is then the special case when $C[-]$ has no occurrences of the hole '$-$' at all, and is just an ordinary expression M. □

The following result draws together all the relations we have defined between ReFS expressions. It includes the 'ciu' theorem of Mason and Talcott (1992b).

Theorem 4.10 (Operational Extensionality). *The logical relation* $\{id_\omega\}$, *contextual equivalence* $\cong$, *and ciu-equivalence* $\cong^{ciu}$ *all coincide: for any* $M_1, M_2 \in Exp_\sigma(\Gamma)$

$$\Gamma \vdash M_1\ \{id_\omega\}\ M_2 \Leftrightarrow \Gamma \vdash M_1 \cong M_2 \Leftrightarrow \Gamma \vdash M_1 \cong^{ciu} M_2\,.$$

Proof. We show that each of the three relations entails the next, in rotation. First, that

$$\Gamma \vdash M_1\ \{id_\omega\}\ M_2 \Rightarrow \Gamma \vdash M_1 \cong M_2\,.$$

Suppose that M_1 and M_2 are identity related as shown and that $C[-]$ is some context with $\emptyset \vdash C[M_i] : \sigma'$ $(i = 1, 2)$. Using the weakening Lemma 4.3 on $\Gamma \vdash M_1\ \{id_\omega\}\ M_2$ if necessary, we can assume without loss of generality that $loc(C[-]) \subseteq \omega$. Then by Theorem 4.9(i) we have $\emptyset \vdash C[M_1]\ \{id_\omega\}\ C[M_2]$, that is $(C[M_1], C[M_2]) \in \mathcal{E}_{\sigma'}(id_\omega)$. Given any state s with $dom(s) = \omega$ we know that $(s, s) \in id_\omega$; and $(\mathcal{I}d, \mathcal{I}d) \in \mathcal{K}_{\sigma'}(id_\omega)$ holds by definition of $\mathcal{K}_{\sigma'}(id_\omega)$. Therefore from the definition of $\mathcal{E}_{\sigma'}(id_\omega)$ we have

$$\langle s, \mathcal{I}d, C[M_1]\rangle \updownarrow \langle s, \mathcal{I}d, C[M_2]\rangle.$$

Equivalently (by Theorem 3.1),

$$s, C[M_1] \Downarrow \;\Leftrightarrow\; s, C[M_2] \Downarrow .$$

Since this holds for any suitable $C[-]$ and s, we have contextual equivalence of M_1 and M_2, as required.

Now for

$$\Gamma \vdash M_1 \cong M_2 \;\Rightarrow\; \Gamma \vdash M_1 \cong^{ciu} M_2 .$$

Consulting the note after Definition 4.6, we recall that ciu-equivalence for an expression M is entirely determined by the set of terminations

$$s, E[M[\vec{V}/\vec{x}]] \Downarrow$$

for states s, evaluation contexts $E[-]$ and values $\vec{V}$ to instantiate the free variables of M. This however corresponds exactly to termination in the context $E[(\lambda\,\vec{x}.\,(-))\vec{V}]$. As ciu-equivalence thus requires correspondence only in a subset of all contexts, it is clear that it is entailed by contextual equivalence, which requires agreement on all of them.

Finally,

$$\Gamma \vdash M_1 \cong^{ciu} M_2 \;\Rightarrow\; \Gamma \vdash M_1 \;\{id_\omega\}\; M_2 .$$

By Theorem 4.9(ii) we have $\Gamma \vdash M_1 \;\{id_\omega\}\; M_1$, and Lemma 4.7 lets us compose this with $\Gamma \vdash M_1 \cong^{ciu} M_2$ to obtain the logical relation $\Gamma \vdash M_1 \;\{id_\omega\}\; M_2$ that we desire. □

5 Examples

In this section we look at some practical applications of the parametric logical relation to proving ReFS contextual equivalences, via the Operational Extensionality Theorem 4.10.

Before giving applications that make overt use of the logical relation, let us recall (from Mason and Talcott 1992b, for example) that the coincidence of contextual equivalence with ciu-equivalence gives sufficient leverage to prove a range of basic contextual equivalences. This includes those ciu-equivalences that hold by virtue of the immediate evaluation behaviour of the terms involved, such as

$$(\mathit{rec}\, f(x).\, M)V \;\cong\; M[\,(\mathit{rec}\, f(x).\, M)/f,\; V/x\,].$$

It also includes equivalences incorporating 'garbage collection', in the manner of Mason's 'strong isomorphism' (Mason 1986; Mason and Talcott 1991a), allowing us to ignore parts of the store that are unreachable.

Using logical relations

To prove specific contextual equivalences via the logical relation, we need to be able to show that pairs of expressions are indeed related. The next result gives a general technique for demonstrating $(M_1, M_2) \in \mathcal{E}_\sigma(r)$: if their evaluation preserves r and we can exhibit some 'local invariant' r'' that correctly captures the way M_1 and M_2 treat their local variables, then they are logically related.

Proposition 5.1 (Principle of Local Invariants). *Given a state relation r and expressions M_1, M_2, suppose that for all $(s_1, s_2) \in r$,*

$$s_1, M_1 \Downarrow V_1, s_1' \Rightarrow \exists r', s_2', V_2 \,.\, (s_1', s_2') \in (r \otimes r') \\ \& \; s_2, M_2 \Downarrow V_2, s_2' \;\&\; (V_1, V_2) \in \mathcal{E}_\sigma(r \otimes r')$$

and

$$s_2, M_2 \Downarrow V_2, s_2' \Rightarrow \exists r'', s_1', V_1 \,.\, (s_1', s_2') \in (r \otimes r'') \\ \& \; s_1, M_1 \Downarrow V_1, s_1' \;\&\; (V_1, V_2) \in \mathcal{E}_\sigma(r \otimes r'').$$

Then $(M_1, M_2) \in \mathcal{E}_\sigma(r)$. (We call the state relations r', r'' local invariants.*)*

Proof. To prove $(M_1, M_2) \in \mathcal{E}_\sigma(r)$ it suffices to show for all $(s_1, s_2) \in r$ and $(K_1, K_2) \in \mathcal{K}_\sigma(r)$ that $\langle s_1, K_1, M_1 \rangle\!\downarrow$ if and only if $\langle s_2, K_2, M_2 \rangle\!\downarrow$ (cf. the *Note* on page 248). By the symmetry of the assumptions, it suffices to prove just the forward direction of this bi-implication. So suppose $\langle s_1, K_1, M_1 \rangle\!\downarrow$. Then by (3.3) for some s_1' and V,

$$s_1, M_1 \Downarrow V_1, s_1' \quad \text{and} \quad \langle s_1', K_1, V_1 \rangle\!\downarrow.$$

So by hypothesis there are r', s_2' and V_2 such that $s_2, M_2 \Downarrow V_2, s_2'$, $(s_1', s_2') \in (r \otimes r')$, and $(V_1, V_2) \in \mathcal{E}_\sigma(r \otimes r')$. From Lemma 4.3 we have $(K_1, K_2) \in \mathcal{K}_\sigma(r \otimes r')$ and so $\langle s_1', K_1, V_1 \rangle \updownarrow \langle s_2', K_2, V_2 \rangle$. Hence $\langle s_2', K_2, V_2 \rangle\!\downarrow$ and then the other direction of (3.3) gives $\langle s_2, K_2, M_2 \rangle\!\downarrow$ as desired. Similarly, the second hypothesis implies that $\langle s_2, K_2, M_2 \rangle\!\downarrow \Rightarrow \langle s_1, K_1, M_1 \rangle\!\downarrow$ and so we have $(M_1, M_2) \in \mathcal{E}_\sigma(r)$ as required. □

This gives us a tool for proving instances of the logical relation. Conversely, if we have that two expressions are related, what can we deduce about them? To answer this requires a mild restriction on the state relations considered.

Definition 5.2. A state relation $r \in Rel(\omega_1, \omega_2)$ is *closed* if every non-element can be detected as such. That is, for each pair of states $(s_1, s_2) \in (Sta(\omega_1) \times Sta(\omega_2)) \setminus r$ there are continuations $(K_1, K_2) \in \mathcal{K}_{unit}(r)$ such that

$$\langle s_1, K_1, () \rangle \not\updownarrow \langle s_2, K_2, () \rangle$$

with one converging and the other diverging.

All the state relations we shall encounter are closed. In particular we have the following result.

Lemma 5.3. *If a state relation* $r \in Rel(\omega_1, \omega_2)$ *is bijective where defined*

$$(s_1, s_2) \in r \ \& \ (s_1, s_2') \in r \Rightarrow s_2 = s_2'$$
$$(s_1, s_2) \in r \ \& \ (s_1', s_2) \in r \Rightarrow s_1 = s_1'$$

then it is closed.

Proof. First we note that all states have finite domain, so for any state s we can write an expression $test_s$ such that $s', test_s \Downarrow$ precisely when s' is of the form $s \otimes s''$.

Now suppose $(s_1, s_2) \in (Sta(\omega_1) \times Sta(\omega_2)) \setminus r$. We seek r-related continuations that distinguish between the two. If there is no s_2' such that $(s_1, s_2') \in r$, then we choose

$$K_1 \stackrel{\text{def}}{=} \mathcal{I}d \circ (x)\, test_{s_1} \quad \text{and} \quad K_2 \stackrel{\text{def}}{=} \mathcal{I}d \circ (x)\Omega.$$

If on the other hand $(s_1, s_2') \in r$ holds for some s_2', then by assumption on r we must have $s_2' \neq s_2$ (since $(s_1, s_2) \notin r$) and we take

$$K_1 \stackrel{\text{def}}{=} \mathcal{I}d \circ (x)\, test_{s_1} \quad \text{and} \quad K_2 \stackrel{\text{def}}{=} \mathcal{I}d \circ (x)\, test_{s_2'} .$$

In either case we have $\langle s_1, K_1, ()\rangle{\downarrow}$ and $\langle s_2, K_2, ()\rangle{\not\downarrow}$, while these continuations agree on all state pairs in any $r \otimes r'$ and so $(K_1, K_2) \in \mathcal{K}_{unit}(r)$ as required. □

Proposition 5.4. *If* $(M_1, M_2) \in \mathcal{E}_\sigma(r)$ *and* $(s_1, s_2) \in r$ *then*

$$s_1, M_1 \Downarrow \Leftrightarrow s_2, M_2 \Downarrow .$$

If r is closed, then related expressions also preserve the state relation:

$$s_1, M_1 \Downarrow V_1, s_1' \quad \textit{and} \quad s_2, M_2 \Downarrow V_2, s_2'$$

implies there is r' *such that* $(s_1', s_2') \in (r \otimes r')$.

Proof. For the first part, consider the continuation $K = \mathcal{I}d \circ (x)()$ of type $(\sigma \multimap unit)$. Clearly $(K, K) \in \mathcal{K}_\sigma(r)$ and so using (3.3) we can deduce

$$s_1, M_1 \Downarrow \Leftrightarrow \langle s_1, K, M_1\rangle{\downarrow} \Leftrightarrow \langle s_2, K, M_2\rangle{\downarrow} \Leftrightarrow s_2, M_2 \Downarrow$$

as required. For the second part, suppose that r is closed and that M_1 and M_2 evaluate as given. Taking $r' = \omega_1' \times \omega_2'$, where $\omega_i' = dom(s_i') \setminus dom(s_i)$ $(i = 1, 2)$, we need only show that $(s_1'|_{dom(r)}, s_2'|_{cod(r)}) \in r$. Since r is closed, if these states are not so related, then there is some $(K_1, K_2) \in \mathcal{K}_{unit}(r)$ that can detect this and hence for which

$$\langle s_1, K_1 \circ (x)(), M_1\rangle \not\updownarrow \langle s_2, K_2 \circ (x)(), M_2\rangle.$$

This however would contradict the assumption that $(M_1, M_2) \in \mathcal{E}_\sigma(r)$, and instead we must have $(s_1'|_{dom(r)}, s_2'|_{cod(r)}) \in r$ and hence $(s_1', s_2') \in (r \otimes r')$ as required. □

This provides a partial converse to Proposition 5.1 (at least as regards termination and treatment of store) which we will use in the higher-order profiling Example 5.8. At ground types we can do better and show that the resulting values will also be related. However, the converse of Proposition 5.1 does not hold in general. Example 5.9 gives a pair of logically related expressions where no choice of r'' will make V_1 and V_2 related. Thus as a method for demonstrating instances of the logical relation and hence contextual equivalence, the Principle of Local Invariants of Proposition 5.1 is not complete. Nevertheless, it does provide a powerful method for proving equivalences, as the examples in the following subsections show. We consider various idioms for using functions with local state and prove that they behave correctly, interacting properly with surrounding code that may itself use state and higher order functions. The general approach is that we present contextual equivalences which express the desired behaviour of a program fragment, and then prove that these hold by using the logical relation. In all cases the crucial step is to choose the right local invariant that captures the way an expression is expected to use its local store.

Representation independence

Informally, it is clear that if two functions in ReFS have private local store that they use in different ways to compute the same result, then they should be contextually equivalent. One can use coincidence of contextual equivalence with ciu-equivalence to show that this is true for expressions which use local store only for temporary variables. However in ReFS it is also possible to write functions that rely on store remaining private from one invocation to the next. Logical relations can capture this notion of privacy through local invariants, and we give here two examples of how this can lead to proofs of contextual equivalence.

Consider the following expressions of Standard ML:

```
let val c = ref 1                  ≅ let
    fun inc ()  = (c:=!c + 1)              fun skip () = ()
    fun test () = (!c > 0)                 fun test' () = true
in                                     in
    (inc, test)                            (skip, test')
end                                    end.
```

The first of these evaluates to a pair of functions sharing a common storage cell c; one function to increment c, and one to test its contents. However the test always returns true and the increment cannot be observed; so this expression has an equivalent simpler version which doesn't bother with the cell c. A corresponding example in ReFS is this:

Example 5.5.

$$(let\ c = ref(1)\ in\ (inc\ c, test\ c)) \cong (skip, test') \quad : (unit \to unit) \times (unit \to bool) \tag{5.1}$$

where

$$inc \stackrel{\text{def}}{=} \lambda c.\,\lambda x.\,(c := (!c + 1)) \qquad skip \stackrel{\text{def}}{=} \lambda x.\,()$$

$$test \stackrel{\text{def}}{=} \lambda c.\,\lambda x.\,(!c > 0) \qquad test' \stackrel{\text{def}}{=} \lambda x.\,true.$$

Proof. Although the internal action of these expressions is quite different, they are contextually equivalent because the value stored in cell c is always positive. This invariance property is expressed by the state relation

$$r \stackrel{\text{def}}{=} \{(s, ()) \mid s(\ell) > 0\} \in Rel(\{\ell\}, \emptyset).$$

Looking at the bodies of the functions *inc* and *skip* we can show by Proposition 5.1 that

$$(\,(\ell := !\ell + 1),\ ()\,) \in \mathcal{E}_{unit}(r)$$

because both preserve r. Similarly for the *test* functions

$$(\,(!\ell > 0),\ true\,) \in \mathcal{E}_{bool}(r)$$

because they give equal results provided that r holds. By Proposition 4.8(xv) lambda abstraction preserves these relations and we can then derive

$$(inc\ \ell, skip) \in \mathcal{E}_{unit\to unit}(r) \quad \text{and} \quad (test\ \ell, test') \in \mathcal{E}_{unit\to bool}(r).$$

Proposition 4.8(vi) now gives

$$(\,(inc\ \ell, test\ \ell),\ (skip, test')\,) \in \mathcal{E}_{(unit\to unit)\times(unit\to bool)}(r)$$

which are the results of evaluating either side of (5.1). Since $((\ell := 1), ()) \in r$, the corresponding states resulting from this evaluation are also related and so by the Principle of Local Invariants (Proposition 5.1)

$$(\,(let\ c = ref(1)\ in\ (inc\ c, test\ c)),\ (skip, test')\,) \in \mathcal{E}_{(unit\to unit)\times(unit\to bool)}(id_{\emptyset}).$$

The contextual equivalence (5.1) then follows by Operational Extensionality Theorem 4.10. □

The next example considers not private shared state, but more visible store used in two different but equivalent ways. Consider these two counters in Standard ML:

```
let val c = ref 0                  ≅  let val c = ref 0
     fun up x = (c := !c + x; !c)          fun down x = (c := !c − x; 0 − !c)
in                                     in
     up                                     down
end                                    end
```

which can be written in ReFS thus:

Example 5.6.

$$(\textit{let } c = \textit{ref}(0) \textit{ in up } c) \cong (\textit{let } c = \textit{ref}(0) \textit{ in down } c)$$

where

$$\textit{up} \stackrel{\text{def}}{=} \lambda c.\, \lambda x.\, (c := (!c + x); !c) \qquad \textit{down} \stackrel{\text{def}}{=} \lambda c.\, \lambda x.\, (c := (!c - x); 0 - !c).$$

Proof. Both of these functions maintain an accumulator, summing the arguments to successive calls and returning a running total. Internally though, the second function reverses signs throughout. The appropriate local invariant is the relation $r \stackrel{\text{def}}{=} \{(s_1, s_2) \mid s_1(\ell) = -s_2(\ell)\} \in \textit{Rel}(\{\ell\}, \{\ell\})$. For this we have $(\textit{up } \ell, \textit{down } \ell) \in \mathcal{E}_{\textit{int}\to\textit{int}}(r)$ and the proof of contextual equivalence proceeds as in the previous example. □

In both of these examples, the local store is not in fact private: the functions do export a certain limited access to it, both for reading and writing. What is important though is that this access is certain to preserve the relevant invariant, no matter how a surrounding program uses it; and as long as the invariant holds, the results returned by the given functions always agree.

Memoisation

One practical use for local state is in the implementation of a *memo function*. This is a function that retains a cache of past results in order to assist future computations. Logical relations provide a means to show that the consistency of this cache is maintained, whatever the surrounding program.

Here we consider a higher-order memoisation function, that transforms any 'repeatable' function into a memo function. For simplicity, we only record a single argument/result pair, and take both to be integers. In Standard ML one might define this by:

```
fun memoise f  =  let val a = ref 0 and r = ref(f 0);
                      fun f' x =
                          ((if x = !a then () else (a := x; r := f x)); !r)
                  in
                      f'
                  end

        memoise : (int → int) → (int → int)
```

The idea here is that `memoise` modifies function `f` by attaching two private cells, `a` and `r`, to hold the argument and result of its most recent invocation. The resulting function `f'` acts like `f`, except that when called with the same argument twice in succession it uses the cached result `!r`, saving recomputation. This can be written in ReFS as follows.

Example 5.7. Let

$$memoise \stackrel{\text{def}}{=} \lambda f.\, let\ a = ref(0); r = ref(f\,0)\ in\ \lambda x.\,((if\ x = !a\ then\ ()\ else\ (a := x; r := f x)); !r)$$

We say that $F \in Val_{int \to int}$ *computes* some total function $\phi : \mathbb{Z} \to \mathbb{Z}$ if for each state s with $loc(F) \subseteq dom(s)$ and every $n \in \mathbb{Z}$,

$$s, Fn \Downarrow \phi(n), (s \otimes s_n)$$

for some s_n. Thus F may make use of local or global store, but its results are 'repeatable' in the sense that they do not depend on the global state s and s is unchanged at the end of evaluating the application of F to a numeral. We claim that such an F is suitable for memoisation:

$$memoise\,F \cong F. \tag{5.2}$$

In particular for each $n \in \mathbb{Z}$, $(memoise\,F)n$ computes the same integer as Fn, namely $\phi(n)$.

Proof. First note that

$$s, memoise\,F \Downarrow F', (s \otimes (\ell_a := 0) \otimes s_0 \otimes (\ell_r := \phi(0))) \tag{5.3}$$

where

$$F' \stackrel{\text{def}}{=} \lambda x.\,((if\ x = !\ell_a\ then\ ()\ else\ \ell_a := x; \ell_r := Fx); !\ell_r)$$

is the 'memoised' version of F. A suitable local invariant is that locations ℓ_a and ℓ_r always hold a valid argument/result pair; which we express with the relation

$$r \stackrel{\text{def}}{=} \{(s, ()) \mid \phi(s(\ell_a)) = s(\ell_r)\} \in Rel(\omega_0 \ell_a \ell_r, \emptyset).$$

where $\omega_0 = dom(s_0)$ (which by α-conversion we can assume is disjoint from $\{\ell_a, \ell_r\}$). As before the Principle of Local Invariants (Proposition 5.1) shows that the bodies of F and F' are r-related, so we can use Proposition 4.8(xv) to obtain

$$(F', F) \in \mathcal{V}_{int \to int}(id_\omega \otimes r)$$

where $loc(F) \subseteq \omega$. Since the states $(\ell_a := 0; s_0; \ell_r := \phi(0))$ and $()$ are related by r, taking (5.3) we can apply Proposition 5.1 again to give

$$((memoise\,F), F) \in \mathcal{E}_{int \to int}(id_\omega).$$

The Operational Extensionality Theorem 4.10 then provides the desired contextual equivalence (5.2). □

We considered total functions $\phi : \mathbb{Z} \to \mathbb{Z}$ in this example only to simplify matters. Extending the definition of 'F computes ϕ in a repeatable fashion' to partial functions (when $\phi(n)$ is undefined Fn must diverge, and *vice versa*), (5.2) still holds *provided* we restrict attention to those ϕ for which $\phi(0)$ is defined, since $memoise$ initialises the cache using this value.

Note that this same memoisation function can be used repeatedly in a program, to give several memo functions each with their own local store. One memo function can even be used within another without interference. For example, if F and G are function abstractions computing ϕ and ψ, then the composition $F \circ G$ (definable in ReFS in the usual way) computes the composition of ϕ with ψ; and (5.2) together with the congruence properties of contextual equivalence imply

$$memoise((memoise\, F) \circ (memoise\, G)) \cong F \circ G$$

(although one of the memoisations is redundant).

Higher-order profiling

Next we consider the use of local state for *profiling* function use, *i.e.* recording the calls to a particular function as it is used within a larger program. We use contextual equivalence to express two important properties of the profiled function:

- it correctly counts the number of times it is called;
- the overall program is otherwise unaffected.

Both of these assertions are then proved using logical relations, although in this case we need to use Proposition 5.4 in addition to the Principle of Local Invariants (Proposition 5.1).

As with memoisation, a single higher order function can capture the whole operation of profiling. In Standard ML:

```
fun profile f  =  let val c = ref 0;
                      fun f' x = (c:=!c + 1; f x);
                      fun r () = !c
                  in
                      (f', r)
                  end
```

$$\texttt{profile} : (\sigma \to \sigma') \to ((\sigma \to \sigma') \times (\texttt{unit} \to \texttt{int}))$$

This `profile` takes any function `f` and returns an instrumented version `f'` together with a read operation `r`. Both `f'` and `r` share a private local counter `c`, incremented by each call to `f'` and read by means of `r()`. Otherwise `f'` behaves exactly as the original function `f`; which may include further side-effects on global or local store. The profiling operation is truly higher order, working with functions of all types; we could for example safely apply it to the `memoise` function described earlier.

In ReFS one can write this profiling functional as follows.

Example 5.8.

$$\textit{profile} \stackrel{\text{def}}{=} \lambda f.\,(\textit{let } c = \textit{ref}(0) \textit{ in } (f', r)) \quad \text{where} \quad \begin{aligned} f' &\stackrel{\text{def}}{=} \lambda x.\,(c := !c + 1; f x) \\ r &\stackrel{\text{def}}{=} \lambda x.\,!c. \end{aligned}$$

The fact the profiling correctly records function calls means that the following contextual equivalence between integer expressions:

$$\begin{array}{ll} \textit{let } (f', r) = \textit{profile } F \cong & \textit{let } (f', r) = \textit{profile } F \\ \textit{in} & \textit{in} \\ \quad P f'; F V; Q f'; & \quad P f'; f' V; Q f'; \\ \quad r() + 1 & \quad r() \end{array} \tag{5.4}$$

holds for *any* $F \in \mathit{Val}_{\sigma \to \sigma'}$, $P, Q \in \mathit{Val}_{(\sigma \to \sigma') \to \mathit{unit}}$, and $V \in \mathit{Val}_{\sigma}$.

Here the context $(P f'; [-]V; Q f')$ represents a program using the instrumented function f'. Depending on whether its hole is filled with F or f', the final total $r()$ alters by 1. It is significant that the values P and Q have access only to f' in this context and cannot use r to read the current contents of the counter. More generally, the function f' on its own is indistinguishable from the original F:

$$\textit{fst}(\textit{profile } F) \cong F : \sigma \to \sigma' \tag{5.5}$$

In this contextual equivalence the read operator is thrown away, with *fst* selecting just the profiled function f'.

Proof. To demonstrate (5.4) and (5.5), look first at the evaluation of the expressions in (5.4). The computation is in three parts, followed by examination of the counter c using the read operation $r()$. Assume that the counter is bound to location ℓ and set

$$F' \stackrel{\text{def}}{=} \lambda x.\,(\ell := !\ell + 1; F x). \tag{5.6}$$

Both sides of (5.4) begin with the same evaluation:

$$s \otimes (\ell := 0), P F' \Downarrow (), s' \otimes (\ell := n) \otimes s_1$$

for some $n \in \mathbb{Z}$. Thanks to the 'garbage collection' properties of contextual equivalence mentioned at the beginning of this section, the unreachable extra store s_1 need not concern us. The next step is the evaluation of a call to F or F':

$$\begin{aligned} s' \otimes (\ell := n), F V &\Downarrow V', s'' \otimes (\ell := n) \otimes s_2 \\ s' \otimes (\ell := n), F' V &\Downarrow V', s'' \otimes (\ell := (n+1)) \otimes s_2 \end{aligned}$$

The only difference so far is the value stored at location ℓ. What is important now is that $Q F'$ preserves this but is otherwise unaffected. The appropriate local invariant is the relation

$$r \stackrel{\text{def}}{=} \{(s, s') \mid s'(\ell) = s(\ell) + 1\} \in \mathit{Rel}(\{\ell\}, \{\ell\}),$$

which is closed, by Lemma 5.3.

By the Fundamental Property of the logical relation (Theorem 4.9(ii)) we have that both F and Q are id_ω-related to themselves. Using Proposition 5.1 we can show directly that increment preserves r:

$$((\ell := !\ell + 1),\ (\ell := !\ell + 1)) \in \mathcal{E}_{unit}(r).$$

Applying Proposition 4.8, we combine all these with the definition (5.6) of F' to deduce that the application QF' satisfies

$$(QF', QF') \in \mathcal{E}_{unit}(id_\omega \otimes r).$$

We know that the closed relation $(id_\omega \otimes r)$ holds before this application, and Proposition 5.4 now tells us that it also holds after it. Thus

$$s'' \otimes (\ell := n), QF' \Downarrow (), s''' \otimes (\ell := n') \otimes s_3$$
$$s'' \otimes (\ell := n+1), QF' \Downarrow (), s''' \otimes (\ell := n'+1) \otimes s_3$$

for some $n' \geq n$, s''', and s_3. The last computation for each alternative is then

$$s''' \otimes (\ell := n'), (r() + 1) \Downarrow (n'+1), s''' \otimes (\ell := n')$$
$$s''' \otimes (\ell := n'+1), r() \Downarrow (n'+1), s''' \otimes (\ell := n'+1).$$

The final states are $(id_\omega \otimes r)$-related and the returned values are equal; thus by the Principle of Local Invariants, the two original expressions are id_ω-related and the equivalence (5.4) follows.

The second equivalence (5.5), that F' on its own is indistinguishable from F, is more straightforward. We need to show that

$$((let\ c = ref(0)\ in\ \lambda x. (c := !c + 1; f x)),\ F) \in \mathcal{E}_{\sigma \to \sigma'}(id_\omega)$$

and this follows by Proposition 5.1 from

$$(F', F) \in \mathcal{V}_{\sigma \to \sigma'}(id_\omega \otimes r)$$

where $r \stackrel{\text{def}}{=} \{(s, ()) \mid s \in Sta(\{\ell\})\}$. Thus the operation *profile* has exactly the behaviour we would expect. □

As with memoisation, we can apply *profile* many times to give several profiled functions, each with its own private counter. So when we write *profile* F, the function F may have subprocedures within it that are already recording profiles, without causing interference. The procedure can also be adapted to profile the recursive calls a function makes to itself. The proof in this case is no more complicated than before, thanks to the fact that logical relations are preserved by recursive function abstractions (Proposition 4.8(xv)).

A more intricate situation with shared store arises if we use a profiler that keeps the same global counter for each function that it modifies:

```
val(g_profile, g_read) = let val c = ref 0;
                                 fun prof f x = (c := !c + 1; f x);
                                 fun read ()  = !c
                             in
                                 (prof, read)
                             end.
```

Analogues of the equivalences (5.4) and (5.5) can be given for this global profiler, and proved using logical relations.

Limitations of the Principle of Local Invariants

We give an example to show that the existence of a local state relation, as asserted in the hypotheses of the Principle of Local Invariants (Proposition 5.1), although sufficient, is not necessary in order for two expressions to be $\{id_w\}$-related and hence to be contextually equivalent.

Consider the following two second-order functions in Standard ML:

```
          val awkward = let val c = ref 0;
                            fun upto_one f = (c := 1; f(); !c)
                        in
                            upto_one
                        end
        val const_one = fn f => (f(); 1)
awkward, const_one : (unit -> unit) -> int.
```

Both of these evaluate to functions that take a command `f` as an argument, execute it and then return the value 1. The second achieves this in a straightforward manner, whereas the first achieves it in an awkward manner—through the function `upto_one` which fetches the return value 1 from private cell `c`. One expects `awkward` and `const_one` to be contextually equivalent because this cell, although it initially holds 0, is set to 1 before every inspection, and during the execution of `upto_one` in any context the function `f()` cannot reset `c` to 0. We shall turn this into a formal proof of equivalence below. First, let us express these functions in ReFS:

Example 5.9.

$$awkward \cong const\_one : (unit \to unit) \to int \tag{5.7}$$

where

$$awkward \stackrel{\text{def}}{=} let\ c = ref(0)\ in\ \lambda f.\,(c := 1;\, f();\, !c)$$

$$const\_one \stackrel{\text{def}}{=} \lambda f.\,(f();\, 1).$$

To show (5.7) using Proposition 5.1 we would need $r \in Rel(\{\ell\}, \emptyset)$ satisfying

$$((\ell := 0),\ ()) \in r \qquad (5.8)$$

$$\text{and} \quad (upto\_one,\ const\_one) \in \mathcal{E}(r). \qquad (5.9)$$

where $upto\_one \stackrel{\text{def}}{=} \lambda f. (\ell := 1; f(); !\ell)$. From (5.8) we can deduce that $((\lambda x. (\ell := 0)),\ \lambda x. ()) \in \mathcal{V}_{unit \to unit}(r)$. Using Proposition 4.8(xiii) to combine this with (5.9), we deduce

$$(\, upto\_one(\lambda x. (\ell := 0)),\ const\_one(\lambda x. ())\,) \in \mathcal{E}_{int}(r).$$

But these expressions evaluate to give different results

$$(\ell := 0), upto\_one(\lambda x. (\ell := 0)) \Downarrow 0, (\ell := 0)$$
$$(), const\_one(\lambda x. ()) \Downarrow 1, ().$$

and this is easily seen to be impossible for expressions related by $\mathcal{E}$ at a ground type. Thus we cannot have both (5.8) and (5.9) at the same time, and there is no way to prove contextual equivalence (5.7) through Proposition 5.1.

We are left in the situation that although (5.7) does hold, and by Theorem 4.10 the two expressions are therefore related by $\mathcal{E}(id_\emptyset)$, it seems hard to demonstrate this relation directly. The root of the problem is that the argument $(\lambda x. (\ell := 0))$, which causes $upto\_one$ to return the surprise value 0, cannot in fact be provided by any surrounding context. Note that the location ℓ is not entirely private, since its contents can be changed (from 0 to 1) by a use of $upto\_one$ in a context which knows nothing of ℓ (such as $[-](\lambda x. ())$). (See Stark 1994, §5.4, Example 14 for a related example, this time of contextual inequivalence.)

This problem with $(\lambda x. (\ell := 0))$ resembles known subtleties of contextual equivalence in Algol due to the undefinability of so-called 'snapback' operations in the language (see Pitts 1997, Example 4.1—an example due to O'Hearn). However this particular example has no direct Algol equivalent, because it relies on the fact that $upto\_one$ can both change the state and return a value — such 'active integers' are intentionally excluded from Algol.

We conjecture that a more general form of logical relation can be used to demonstrate the equivalence (5.7) via a result like Proposition 5.1, if we use parameterising relations r with Kripke-style indexing to capture the one-way nature of state change. Here this would allow the following relation with two components:

$$r_1 \supset r_2 \qquad \text{where} \quad r_1 = \{(s, ()) \mid s(\ell) = 0 \text{ or } 1\}$$
$$r_2 = \{(s, ()) \mid s(\ell) = 1\}.$$

This is meant to express the fact that the value stored at location ℓ may progress from 0 to 1, but is then fixed. More complex examples of progressing state would require a more complex index structure.

Without such generalised logical relations, we can proceed only by brute force.

Proof of (5.7). By completeness of ciu-equivalence (Theorem 4.10) it is enough to consider evaluation in any continuation. In this case we derive the requirement that for any state s and continuation K with $\ell \notin dom(s) \supseteq loc(K)$

$$\langle s \otimes (\ell := 0), K, upto\_one\rangle \updownarrow \langle s, K, const\_one\rangle .$$

This is equivalent to showing that for any state s and expression M with $\ell \notin dom(s) \supseteq loc(M)$ and $fv(M) \subseteq \{g : (unit \to unit) \to int\}$

$$s \otimes (\ell := 0), M[upto\_one\,/g] \Downarrow \;\Leftrightarrow\; s, M[const\_one\,/g] \Downarrow . \tag{5.10}$$

This can be proved by computation induction, but we first need a suitably strong induction hypothesis. Define the predicate $\mathbb{P}(s, M)$ for states s and expressions M with $\ell \notin dom(s) \supseteq loc(M)$ according to

$$\begin{aligned}
\mathbb{P}(s, M) \overset{\text{def}}{\Leftrightarrow}\ & \text{There is a state } s' \text{ and a value } V \text{ with free variable } g \text{ such that} \\
& 1. \qquad s, M[const_one\,/g] \Downarrow V[const_one\,/g], s' \\
& \text{and 2a.} \quad \forall n \in \mathbb{Z}.\ s \otimes (\ell := n), M[upto_one\,/g] \\
& \qquad\qquad \Downarrow V[upto_one\,/g], s' \otimes (\ell := 1) \\
& \text{or 2b.} \quad \forall n \in \mathbb{Z}.\ s \otimes (\ell := n), M[upto_one\,/g] \\
& \qquad\qquad \Downarrow V[upto_one\,/g], s' \otimes (\ell := n) \\
& \qquad\qquad \&\ \ s, M[\lambda f.\,\Omega/g] \Downarrow V[\lambda f.\,\Omega/g], s'.
\end{aligned}$$

This rather complex expression captures exactly the way that evaluations of *upto_one* and *const_one* correspond to each other in appropriate contexts. In particular, whenever $M[-/g]$ is evaluated, it either applies the function replacing g (case 2a), or it does not (case 2b).

The following properties hold of $\mathbb{P}(s, M)$:

$$\forall n \in \mathbb{Z}.\ (\mathbb{P}(s, M) \;\Leftrightarrow\; s \otimes (\ell := n), M[upto\_one\,/g] \Downarrow) \tag{5.11}$$

$$\mathbb{P}(s, M) \;\Leftrightarrow\; s, M[const\_one\,/g] \Downarrow . \tag{5.12}$$

The forward implications simply expand the definition of $\mathbb{P}(s, M)$. The reverse directions can be proved by induction on the height of proofs of the evaluations $s \otimes (\ell := 0), M[upto\_one\,/g] \Downarrow V', s'$ and $s, M[const\_one\,/g] \Downarrow V', s'$ respectively. All the details are routine: in particular every evaluation rule either creates one of the situations (2a) or (2b), or preserves an existing one.

These equivalences (5.11) and (5.12) immediately give (5.10), from which the original contextual equivalence (5.7) follows as indicated. □

6 Further topics

We have seen that for each type σ, two ReFS expressions are contextually equivalent if and only if they are $\{id_\omega\}$-related. Moreover, this characterisation of contextual equivalence not only implies the Mason-Talcott 'ciu' theorem for ReFS, but also allows one to formalise various intuitive arguments about contextual equivalence based on invariant state relations. The examples in the previous section demonstrate that the logical relation provides a powerful method for establishing ReFS contextual equivalences. Clearly it is of interest to extend the techniques introduced here to larger fragments of Standard ML than that represented by the ReFS language. In particular we would like to be able to treat:

(a) recursively defined types (rather than the simple types of ReFS),

(b) references to data of any type (rather than the integer-valued references of ReFS), and

(c) no types at all!

(a) would enable one to tackle proofs of equivalence involving efficient implementation with pointers and arrays of data structures with purely functional behaviour. (One would probably want to consider abstract types at the same time.) (b) is of interest because of the connections between object-based programming and the use of storage for function and procedure values. By (c) we mean the kind of untyped imperative lambda calculus considered by Mason and Talcott (1991a) and others; its dynamics includes the phenomena that (a) and (b) introduce in a more disciplined way, and more besides.

Extension (a) takes us beyond the techniques used in this paper because we relied on the simple nature of ReFS types to define the relations $\mathcal{E}_\sigma(r)$, $\mathcal{K}_\sigma(r)$, and $\mathcal{V}_\sigma(r)$ *by induction on the structure of the type* σ (see Definition 4.2). In the non-simply typed case one could instead attempt to define these relations for all types simultaneously by solving a fixed point equation for a suitable operator on (families of) relations. The addition of algebraic data types (lists, trees, *etc.*) to ReFS could be accommodated in this way. However, general forms of data type declaration may have negative or mixed-variance occurrences of the type being defined. The property required of the logical relation at such a type takes the form of a fixed point equation for an operator that is non-monotone; so it is not immediately clear that it can be satisfied. For denotationally-based logical relations there are ways of overcoming this problem using the 'minimal invariance' property of recursively defined domains: see (Pitts 1994; Pitts 1996). Operational versions of the techniques in *loc. cit.* are possible and can be used to extend the results presented here to cover (a). (This suggestion has been taken up for a pure functional language in Birkedal and Harper 1997.)

Regarding (b), it is well known that the ability to store function values gives rise to more complex behaviour than storing only values of ground types. For example, it becomes possible to encode recursive function definitions. This is reflected in the denotational semantics of such storage by the need to solve a mixed-variance domain equation. In this respect the difficulties which must be overcome to define a suitable logical relation might seem to be similar to those in case (a). However, there are further complications. In ReFS any dynamically created state has 'support' disjoint from the existing global state: the definition of the logical relation exploits this fact in the use it makes of the smash product $r \otimes r'$ of state-relations. This disjointness of support breaks down with (b), since a global location can get updated with a function value involving a freshly created location. (Consider for example `let val b = ref(fn x => 0) in a := (fn x => (!b)0) end`, where `a` is some previously declared identifier of type `(int → int) ref`.) Therefore the way the parameterisation of the logical relation treats dynamic allocation is more complicated in the presence of (b) and it remains to be seen if the techniques of this paper extend to cover this case.

Even for ReFS itself, it is possible to consider more refined versions of the parameterisation. For example one can consider relations on the flat complete partial order of states rather than on the set of states. Building on work of O'Hearn and Reynolds (1996), Pitts (1997, Example 4.1) shows how this small alteration helps with operational reasoning about divergence in Idealised Algol. It seems likely that it would be similarly useful for ReFS.

Of course the above list of enhancements is hardly complete: one might well want to consider I/O effects, or exception mechanisms, for example. When adding language features, we also need to keep in mind the feasibility of the proof method. The strength of the technique presented here lies as much in its usability as in its theoretical power. Although one may need to develop operationally-based analogues of some rather sophisticated methods from domain theory in order to define a logical relation (and establish its Fundamental Property) for function references and recursive datatypes, these technicalities do not necessarily complicate the *use* of logical relations to prove contextual equivalence. We can already see this in the treatment of recursion. The proof of Proposition 4.8(xv) is not straightforward, but its statement is simple and its use unrestricted: the logical relation is preserved by any recursive function abstraction. Our aim is to further increase the power of operationally-based logical relations without compromising their ease of use.

The operationally based logical relation we have presented here seems to provide a convenient and reasonably powerful method for proving contextual equivalences between functions with local store. Once a correct relation between states has been identified, verifying equivalence involves routine calculations with the structural operational semantics of the language. However, the examples we have given are all small-scale. It would be interesting to investigate machine-assistance for proofs using our methods. Note that we do not necessarily have to implement the proof that logical relations imply contextual equivalence; what might benefit from machine-assistance is the demonstration, in the case of large programs, that two expressions are $\{id_\omega\}$-related.

References

Birkedal, L. and R. Harper (1997). Relational interpretation of recursive types in an operational setting (Summary). In *Proc. TACS'97*, Lecture Notes in Computer Science. Springer-Verlag, Berlin. To appear.

Felleisen, M. and D. P. Friedman (1986). Control operators, the SECD-machine and the λ-calculus. In *Formal Description of Programming Concepts III*, pp. 193–217. North Holland.

Harper, R., B. F. Duba, and D. MacQueen (1993). Typing first-class continuations in ML. *Journal of Functional Programming 3*(4), 465–484.

Harper, R. and C. Stone (1996). A type-theoretic account of Standard ML 1996 (version 2). Technical Report CMU–CS–96–136R, Carnegie Mellon University, Pittsburgh, PA.

Honsell, F., I. A. Mason, S. F. Smith, and C. L. Talcott (1995). A variable typed logic of effects. *Information and Computation 119*(1), 55–90.

Hughes, R. J. M. (1989). Why functional programming matters. *The Computer Journal 32*(2), 98–107.

Mason, I. A. (1986). *The Semantics of Destructive Lisp*. Ph. D. thesis, Stanford University. Also published as CSLI Lecture Notes Number 5, Center for the Study of Language and Information, Stanford University.

Mason, I. A., S. F. Smith, and C. L. Talcott (1996). From operational semantics to domain theory. *Information and Computation 128*(1), 26–47.

Mason, I. A. and C. L. Talcott (1991a). Equivalence in functional languages with effects. *Journal of Functional Programming 1*, 287–327.

Mason, I. A. and C. L. Talcott (1991b). Program transformations for configuring components. In *PEPM '91: Proceedings of the ACM/IFIP Symposium on Partial Evaluation and Semantics-based Program Manipulation*, ACM SIGPLAN Notices 26(9), pp. 297–308.

Mason, I. A. and C. L. Talcott (1992a). Inferring the equivalence of functional programs that mutate data. *Theoretical Computer Science 105*, 167–215.

Mason, I. A. and C. L. Talcott (1992b). References, local variables and operational reasoning. In *Proceedings of the 7th Annual Symposium on Logic in Computer Science*, pp. 186–197. IEEE Computer Society Press.

Milner, R., M. Tofte, and R. Harper (1990). *The Definition of Standard ML*. MIT Press.

O'Hearn, P. W. and J. C. Reynolds (1996, April). From Algol to polymorphic linear lambda-calculus. Draft version, 46 pp.

O'Hearn, P. W. and R. D. Tennent (1993). Relational parametricity and local variables. In *20th SIGPLAN-SIGACT Symposium on Principles of Programming Languages*, pp. 171–184. ACM Press.

O'Hearn, P. W. and R. D. Tennent (1995). Parametricity and local variables. *Journal of the ACM 42*(3), 658–709.

Paulson, L. C. (1991). *ML for the Working Programmer*. Cambridge University Press.

Pitts, A. M. (1994). Computational adequacy via 'mixed' inductive definitions. In *Proc. MFPS'93, New Orleans, LA, USA, April 1993*, Volume 802 of *Lecture Notes in Computer Science*, pp. 72–82. Springer-Verlag, Berlin.

Pitts, A. M. (1996). Relational properties of domains. *Information and Computation 127*, 66–90.

Pitts, A. M. (1997). Reasoning about local variables with operationally-based logical relations. In P. W. O'Hearn and R. D. Tennent (Eds.), *Algol-Like Languages*, Volume 2, Chapter 17, pp. 173–193. Birkhauser. First appeared in *Proc. LICS'96*, pp 152–163, IEEE Computer Society Press, 1996.

Pitts, A. M. and I. D. B. Stark (1993). Observable properties of higher order functions that dynamically create local names, or: What's new? In *Proc. MFCS'93, Gdańsk, 1993*, Volume 711 of *Lecture Notes in Computer Science*, pp. 122–141. Springer-Verlag, Berlin.

Plotkin, G. D. (1973). Lambda-definability and logical relations. Memorandum SAI-RM-4, School of Artificial Intelligence, University of Edinburgh.

Plotkin, G. D. (1980). Lambda-definability in the full type hierarchy. In J. P. Seldin and J. R. Hindley (Eds.), *To H. B. Curry: Essays on Combinatory Logic, Lambda Calculus and Formalism*, pp. 363–373. Academic Press.

Reynolds, J. C. (1981). The essence of Algol. In J. W. de Bakker and J. C. van Vliet (Eds.), *Algorithmic Languages. Proceedings of the International Symposium on Algorithmic Languages*, pp. 345–372. North-Holland, Amsterdam.

Reynolds, J. C. (1982). Idealized Algol and its specification logic. In D. Néel (Ed.), *Tools and Notions for Program Construction*, pp. 121–161. Cambridge University Press.

Reynolds, J. C. (1983). Types, abstraction and parametric polymorphism. In R. E. A. Mason (Ed.), *Information Processing 83*, pp. 513–523. North-Holland, Amsterdam.

Seiber, K. (1995). Full abstraction for the second order subset of an ALGOL-like language. Technical Report A 04/95, Fach. Informatik, Univ. des Saarlandes, Saarbrücken, Germany.

Stark, I. D. B. (1994). *Names and Higher-Order Functions*. Ph. D. thesis, University of Cambridge. Also published as Technical Report 363, University of Cambridge Computer Laboratory, April 1995.

Talcott, C. (1997). Reasoning about functions with effects. In this volume, pp. 347–390.

Improvement theory and its applications

David Sands

Abstract

An *improvement theory* is a variant of the standard theories of observational approximation (or equivalence) in which the basic observations made of a functional program's execution include some intensional information about, for example, the program's computational cost. One program is an improvement of another if its execution is more efficient in any program context. In this article we give an overview of our work on the theory and applications of improvement. Applications include reasoning about time properties of functional programs, and proving the correctness of program transformation methods. We also introduce a new application, in the form of some bisimulation-like proof techniques for equivalence, with something of the flavour of Sangiorgi's "bisimulation up to expansion and context".

1 Introduction

An *improvement theory* is a variant of the standard theories of observational approximation (or equivalence) in which the basic observations made of a program's execution include some intensional information about, for example, the program's computational cost. One program is an improvement of another if its execution is more efficient in any program context.

In this article we survey a number of applications of a particular improvement theory developed for a small untyped functional language.

The initial motivation for considering such relations was to support a simple calculus for reasoning about time behaviour of non-strict functional programs (Sands 1993). From this work it was a natural step to consider a more general class of improvement theories for functional languages, providing contextually robust theories of optimisation (Sands 1991).

However, the real pay-off for this study is not in reasoning about efficiency properties *per se*, but in reasoning about equivalence: *The Improvement Theorem* (Sands 1995b) provides a condition for the total correctness of transformations on recursive programs. Roughly speaking, the Improvement Theorem says that if the local steps of a transformation are contained in a particular improvement theory, then correctness of the transformation follows. This result has furnished:

- an equivalence-preserving variant of the classic *Unfold-Fold* transformation in a higher-order functional languages (Sands 1995b), and

- the first correctness proofs for a number of well-known transformation methods(Sands 1996a) (see also (Sands 1995a)).

New work reported in this article is the development of some proof techniques for equivalence based on the improvement theory, with something of the flavour of Sangiorgi's "bisimulation up-to expansion and context".

Overview

In the next section we introduce the syntax and semantics of the language used in the remainder of the article. **Section 3** introduces a simple improvement theory for the language based on observing the number of recursive calls made during evaluation. We introduce proof techniques for establishing improvement, and introduce the *tick algebra* which facilitates the calculation of simple improvement properties. **Section 4** considers the application which originally motivated the study of improvement relations, namely the problem of *time analysis* of functional programs. **Section 5** describes a correctness problem in program transformation. We present The Improvement Theorem, which shows, in principle, how the problem can be solved by using improvement. **Section 6** illustrates this application by considering a particular program transformation method. Finally, **Section 7** introduces and illustrates some proof techniques for the equivalence of programs which can be derived from the Improvement Theorem.

2 Preliminaries

We summarise some of the notation used in specifying the language and its operational semantics. The subject of this study will be an untyped higher-order non-strict functional language with lazy data-constructors.

We assume a flat collection of mutually recursive definitions of constants, each of the form $\mathsf{f} \triangleq e_{\mathsf{f}}$, where e_{f} is a closed expression. Symbols f, g, h ..., range over the constants, $f, h, x, y, z \ldots$ over variables and $e, e_1, e_2 \ldots$ over expressions. The syntax of expressions is as follows:

$$
\begin{array}{rcll}
e & = & x \mid \mathsf{f} \mid e_1\, e_2 & \text{(Variable; Recursive constant; Application)} \\
 & \mid & \lambda x.e & \text{(Lambda-abstraction)} \\
 & \mid & \mathsf{case}\ e\ \mathsf{of} & \text{(Case expressions)} \\
 & & \quad pat_1 \Rightarrow e_1 \ldots pat_n \Rightarrow e_n & \\
 & \mid & c(\bar{e}) & \text{(Constructor expressions and constants)} \\
 & \mid & p(\bar{e}) & \text{(Strict primitive functions)} \\
 & & & \\
pat & = & c(\bar{x}) & \text{(Patterns)}
\end{array}
$$

Somewhat improperly we will refer to the constants f, g, etc., as function names, or function calls. In general they need not be functions however.

We assume that each constructor c and each primitive function p has a fixed arity, and that the constructors include constants (i.e. constructors of arity zero). Constants will be written as c rather than $c()$. The primitives and constructors are not curried – they cannot be written without their full complement of operands. We assume that the primitive functions map constants to constants.

We can assume that the case expressions are defined for any subset of patterns $\{pat_1 \ldots pat_n\}$ such that the constructors of the patterns are distinct. A variable can occur at most once in a given pattern; the number of variables must match the arity of the constructor, and these variables are considered to be bound in the corresponding branch of the case-expression.

A list of zero or more expressions $e_1, \ldots e_n$ will often be denoted $\bar{e}$. Application, as is usual, associates to the left, so $((\cdots(e_0 e_1)\ldots)e_n)$ may be written as $e_0\ e_1 \ldots e_n$, and further abbreviated to $e_0\ \bar{e}$.

The expression written $e\{\bar{x} := \bar{e}'\}$ will denote simultaneous (capture-free) substitution of a sequence of expressions $\bar{e}'$ for free occurrences of a sequence of variables $\bar{x}$, respectively, in the expression e. We will use σ, σ', ϕ etc. to range over substitutions. The term $\mathrm{FV}(e)$ will denote the set of free variables of expression e, and $\vec{\mathrm{FV}}(e)$ will be used to denote a (canonical) list of the free variables of e. Sometimes we will informally write "substitutions" of the form $\{\bar{\mathrm{g}} := \bar{e}\}$ to represent the replacement of occurrences of function symbols $\bar{\mathrm{g}}$ by expressions $\bar{e}$. This is not a proper substitution since the function symbols are not variables. Care must be taken with such substitutions since the notion of equivalence between expressions is not closed under these kind of replacements.

A *context*, ranged over by C, C_1, etc. is an expression with zero or more "holes", [ ], in the place of some subexpressions; $C[e]$ is the expression produced by replacing the holes with expression e. Contrasting with substitution, occurrences of free variables in e may become bound in $C[e]$; if $C[e]$ is closed then we say it is a *closing context* (for e).

We write $e \equiv e'$ to mean that e and e' are identical up to renaming of bound variables. Contexts are identified up to renaming of those bound variables which are not in scope at the positions of the holes.

2.1 Operational Semantics, Approximation and Equivalence

The operational semantics is used to define an evaluation relation $\Downarrow$ (a partial function) between closed expressions and the "values" of computations. The set of values, following the standard terminology (see e.g. (Peyton Jones 1987)), are called *weak head normal forms*. The weak head normal forms, $w, w_1, w_2, \ldots \in$ WHNF are just the constructor-expressions $c(\bar{e})$, and the *Closures* (lambda expressions), as given by

$$w \;=\; c(\bar{e}) \;\mid\; \lambda x.e$$

The operational semantics is call-by-name, and $\Downarrow$ is defined in terms of a one-step evaluation relation using the notion of a *reduction context* (Felleisen, Friedman, and Kohlbecker 1987). If $e{\Downarrow}w$ for some closed expression e then we say that e *evaluates to* w. We say that e *converges*, and sometimes write $e{\Downarrow}$ if there exists a w such that $e{\Downarrow}w$. Otherwise we say that e *diverges*. We make no finer distinctions between divergent expressions, so that run-time errors and infinite loops are identified.

Reduction contexts, ranged over by $\mathbb{R}$, are contexts containing a single hole which is used to identify the next expression to be evaluated (reduced).

Definition 1 *A reduction context $\mathbb{R}$ is given inductively by the following grammar*

$$\mathbb{R} = [\,] \mid \mathbb{R}\; e \mid \mathsf{case}\; \mathbb{R}\; \mathsf{of}\; pat_1 \Rightarrow e_1 \ldots pat_n \Rightarrow e_n \;\mid p(\bar{c}, \mathbb{R}, \bar{e})$$

The reduction context for primitive functions forces left-to-right evaluation of the arguments. This is just a matter of convenience to make the one-step evaluation relation deterministic.

Now we define the one step reduction relation. We assume that each primitive function p is given meaning by a partial function $[\![p]\!]$ from vectors of constants (according to the arity of p) to the constants (nullary constructors). We do not need to specify the exact set of primitive functions; it will suffice to note that they are strict—all operands must evaluate to constants before the result of an application, if any, can be returned— and are only defined over constants, not over arbitrary weak head normal forms.

Definition 2 *One-step reduction $\mapsto$ is the least relation on closed expressions satisfying the rules given in Figure 1.*

$$\begin{array}{rcll}
\mathbb{R}[\mathsf{f}] & \mapsto & \mathbb{R}[e_{\mathsf{f}}] & \textbf{(fun)} \\
 & & (\text{if } \mathsf{f} \text{ is defined by } \mathsf{f} \triangleq e_{\mathsf{f}}) & \\
\mathbb{R}[(\lambda x.e)\, e'] & \mapsto & \mathbb{R}[e\{x := e'\}] & (\beta) \\
\mathbb{R}[\mathsf{case}\; c_i(\bar{e})\; \mathsf{of} \ldots c_i(\bar{x}_i) \Rightarrow e_i \ldots] & \mapsto & \mathbb{R}[e_i\{\bar{x}_i := \bar{e}\}] & \textbf{(case)} \\
\mathbb{R}[p(\bar{c})] & \mapsto & \mathbb{R}[c'] & \textbf{(prim)} \\
 & & (\text{if } [\![p]\!]\bar{c} = c') &
\end{array}$$

Figure 1: One-step reduction rules

In each rule of the form $\mathbb{R}[e] \mapsto \mathbb{R}[e']$ in Figure 1, the expression e is referred to as a *redex*. The one step evaluation relation is deterministic; this relies on the fact that if $e_1 \mapsto e_2$ then e_1 can be uniquely factored into a reduction context $\mathbb{R}$ and a redex e' such that $e_1 = \mathbb{R}[e']$. Let $\mapsto^*$ denote the transitive reflexive closure of $\mapsto$.

Definition 3 *Closed expression e converges to weak head normal form w, $e{\Downarrow}w$, if and only if $e \mapsto^* w$.*

Using this notion of convergence we now define the standard notions of operational approximation and equivalence. We use is the standard Morris-style contextual ordering, or *observational approximation* see e.g. (Plotkin 1975).The notion of "observation" we take is just the fact of convergence, as in the lazy lambda calculus (Abramsky 1990). Operational equivalence equates two expressions if and only if in all closing contexts they give rise to the same observation – i.e. either they both converge, or they both diverge.

Definition 4 *1.* e operationally approximates e', $e \lesssim e'$, *if for all contexts* C *such that* $C[e]$, $C[e']$ *are closed, if* $C[e]\Downarrow$ *then* $C[e']\Downarrow$.

2. e *is* operationally equivalent *to* e', $e \cong e'$, *if* $e \lesssim e'$ *and* $e' \lesssim e$.

Choosing to observe, say, only computations which produce constants would give rise to slightly weaker versions of operational approximation and equivalence - but the above versions would still be *sound* for reasoning about the weaker variants of the relation.

3 A Theory of Improvement

In this section we introduce a theory of improvement, as a refinement of the theory of operational approximation. Roughly speaking, *improvement* is a refinement of operational approximation which expression e is improved by e' if, in all closing contexts, computation using e' is no less efficient than when using e, measured in terms of the number of function calls (f, g, etc.) made. From the point of view of applications of the theory to program transformation and analysis, the important property of improvement is that it is a contextual congruence—an expression can be improved by improving a sub-expression. For reasoning about improvement a more tractable formulation of the improvement relation is introduced and some proof techniques related to this formulation are used.

Variations on the Definition of Improvement There are a number of variations that we can make in the definition of improvement. We could, for example, additionally count the number of primitive functions called. Such variations might be used to give additional information about transformations. However, the fact that we count the number of recursive function calls in the definition of improvement will be *essential* to the Improvement Theorem presented in the next section; the Theorem does not hold if we use an improvement metric which does not count these function calls.

We begin by defining a variation of the evaluation relation which includes the number of applications of the **(fun)** rule.

Definition 5 *Define* $e \overset{\bullet}{\mapsto} e'$ *if* $e \mapsto e'$ *by application of the* **(fun)***rule; define* $e \overset{\circ}{\mapsto} e'$ *if* $e \mapsto e'$ *by application of any other rule.*

Define the family of binary relations on expressions $\{\mapsto_n\}_{n\geq 0}$ *inductively as follows:*

$$e \mapsto_0 e' \quad \text{if} \quad e \overset{\circ}{\mapsto}{}^{*} e'$$
$$e \mapsto_{k+1} e' \quad \text{if} \quad e \overset{\circ}{\mapsto}{}^{*} e_1 \overset{\bullet}{\mapsto} e_2 \mapsto_k e' \text{ for some } e_1, e_2.$$

We say that a closed expression e *converges in* n **(fun)**-*steps to weak head normal form* w*, written* $e{\Downarrow}^n w$ *if* $e \mapsto_n w$.

The determinacy of the one-step evaluation relation guarantees that if $e{\Downarrow}^n w$ and $e{\Downarrow}^{n'} w'$ then $w \equiv w'$ and moreover $n = n'$. It will be convenient to adopt the following abbreviations:

- $e{\Downarrow}^n \stackrel{\text{def}}{=} \exists w.\, e{\Downarrow}^n w$
- $e{\Downarrow}^{n\leq m} \stackrel{\text{def}}{=} e{\Downarrow}^n \;\&\; n \leq m$
- $e{\Downarrow}^{\leq m} \stackrel{\text{def}}{=} \exists n.\, e{\Downarrow}^{n\leq m}$

Now improvement is defined in a way analogous to observational approximation:

Definition 6 (Improvement) e is improved by e', $e \trianglerighteq e'$, *if for all contexts* C *such that* $C[e]$, $C[e']$ *are closed, if* $C[e]{\Downarrow}^n$ *then* $C[e']{\Downarrow}^{\leq n}$.

It can be seen from the definition that $\trianglerighteq$ is a *precongruence* (transitive, reflexive, closed under contexts, i.e. $e \trianglerighteq e' \Rightarrow C[e] \trianglerighteq C[e']$) and is a refinement of operational approximation, i.e. $e \trianglerighteq e' \Rightarrow e \sqsubseteq e'$.

We also define a strong version of improvement which contains (by definition) operational equivalence:

Definition 7 (Strong Improvement, Cost-Equivalence) *The strong improvement relation* $\trianglerighteq_s$ *is defined by:* $e \trianglerighteq_s e'$ *if and only if* $e \trianglerighteq e'$ *and* $e \cong e'$.

The cost equivalence relation, $\trianglelefteq\!\trianglerighteq$*, is defined by:* $e \trianglelefteq\!\trianglerighteq e'$ *if and only if* $e \trianglerighteq e'$ *and* $e' \trianglerighteq e$.

If R is a relation, then let R^{-1} denote the inverse of the relation, so that $a \; R \; b \iff b \; R^{-1} \; a$. It is not difficult to see that $\trianglerighteq_s = (\trianglerighteq) \cap (\sqsupseteq)$. This fact, and other relationships between the various preorders and equivalence relations we have considered so far, are summarised in the Hasse diagram of Figure 2. In this lattice, the binary meet (greatest lower bound) corresponds to the set-intersection of the relations, and the top element, $\top$, relates any two expressions.

3.1 Proving Improvement

Finding a more tractable characterisation of improvement (than that provided by Def. 6) is desirable in order to establish improvement laws (and the Improvement Theorem itself). The characterisation we use says that two expressions are in the improvement relation if and only if they are contained in a certain kind of *simulation* relation. This is a form of *context lemma* eg. (Milner 1977; Abramsky

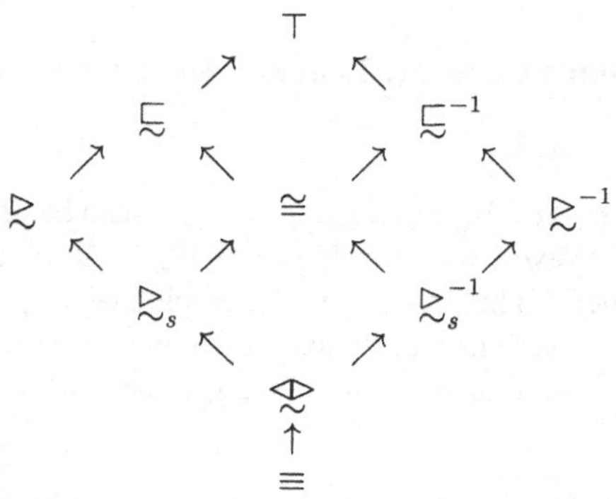

Figure 2: A $\sqcap$-semi-sub-lattice of preorders

1990; Howe 1989), and the proof of the characterisation uses previous technical results concerning a more general class of improvement relations (Sands 1991). In (Sands 1991), we abstracted over the way improvement is defined in terms of the operational semantics, and following Howe (1989), we gave some conditions which guarantee that the simulation relations are sound for reasoning about improvement.

Definition 8 *A relation* $\mathcal{IR}$ *on closed expressions is an* improvement simulation *if for all e, e′, whenever* $e \ \mathcal{IR}\ e'$, *if* $e{\Downarrow}^n w_1$ *then* $e'{\Downarrow}^{\leq n} w_2$ *for some* w_2 *such that either:*

1. $w_1 \equiv c(e_1 \ldots e_n)$, $w_2 \equiv c(e'_1 \ldots e'_n)$, *and* $e_i \ \mathcal{IR}\ e'_i$, $(i \in 1 \ldots n)$, or
2. $w_1, w_2 \in$ *Closures, and for all closed* e_0, $(w_1\, e_0)\ \mathcal{IR}\ (w_2\, e_0)$

For a given relation $\mathcal{IR}$ *and weak head normal forms* w_1 *and* w_2 *we will abbreviate the property "(1) or (2)" in the above by* $w_1\ \mathcal{IR}^{\dagger}\ w_2$.

So, intuitively, if an improvement simulation relates e to e', then if e converges, e' does so at least as efficiently, and yields a "similar" result, whose "components" are related by that improvement simulation.

The key to reasoning about the improvement relation is the fact that $\trianglerighteq$, restricted to closed expressions, is itself an improvement simulation, and is in fact the *largest* improvement simulation. Furthermore, improvement on open expressions can be characterised in terms of improvement on all closed instances. This is summarised in the following.

Let $\mathrel{\underset{\approx}{\triangleright}}$ denote the largest improvement simulation. It is easy to verify that this exists, and is given by the union of all simulation relations. Let $\mathrel{\underset{\approx}{\triangleright}}^{\circ}$ denote its extension to open terms specified by $e \gtrsim^{\circ} e'$ if and only if $e\sigma \gtrsim e'\sigma$ for all closing substitutions σ.

Lemma 1 (Improvement Context-Lemma) *For all e, e', $e \gtrsim e'$ if and only if $e \gtrsim^{\circ} e'$.*

The most important part of the lemma, that $\gtrsim^{\circ} \subseteq \gtrsim$, can be proved by a straightforward application of Howe's method (Howe 1989), as illustrated in (Sands 1991). We omit the proof here. The proof of the "completeness" part of the lemma, that $e \gtrsim e'$ implies $e \gtrsim^{\circ} e'$, is rather more involved than the proof of the corresponding property for operational approximation. We give an outline of the main ingredients:

- Characterise $\gtrsim$ inductively in the form $\bigcap_{i<\omega} \gtrsim_i$ (where $\gtrsim_i$ is "simulation up to a depth i"). Then $e \not\gtrsim e'$ implies that there exists a smallest $m > 0$ such that $e \not\gtrsim_m e'$.
- It is sufficient to assume e and e' closed, and to show that $e \not\gtrsim e'$ implies $e \not\gtrsim e'$. By induction on the minimal m above, this can be done by building a context which distinguishes e and e'. This in turn depends on the existence of contexts which can magnify any non-zero computational cost by an arbitrary degree.

The lemma provides a basic proof technique:

> to show that $e \gtrsim e'$ it is sufficient to find an improvement-simulation containing each closed instance of the pair.

An alternative presentation of the definition of improvement simulation is in terms of the maximal fixed point of a certain monotonic function on relations. In that case the above proof technique is called *co-induction*. This proof technique is crucial to the proof of the Improvement Theorem which follows in the next section. It can also be useful in proving that specific transformation rules are improvements. Here is an illustrative example; it also turns out to be a useful transformation rule:

Proposition 9 *If the free variables of $I\!\!R$ are distinct from the variables in the patterns $pat_1, \ldots, pat_n$, then*

$$\begin{aligned} &I\!\!R[\mathsf{case}\ x\ \mathsf{of}\ pat_1 \Rightarrow e_1 \cdots pat_n \Rightarrow e_n\ ] \\ \lesssim\!\!\!\gtrsim\ \ &\mathsf{case}\ x\ \mathsf{of}\ pat_1 \Rightarrow I\!\!R[e_1] \cdots pat_n \Rightarrow I\!\!R[e_n] \end{aligned}$$

PROOF. We illustrate just the $\gtrsim$-half. The other half is similar. Let R be the relation containing $\equiv$, together with all pairs of closed expressions of the form:

$$\begin{aligned} (\ &I\!\!R[\mathsf{case}\ e_0\ \mathsf{of}\ c_1(\bar{x}_1) \Rightarrow e_1 \ldots c_n(\bar{x}_n) \Rightarrow e_n\ ], \\ &\mathsf{case}\ e_0\ \mathsf{of}\ c_1(\bar{x}_1) : I\!\!R[e_1] \ldots c_n(\bar{x}_n) : I\!\!R[e_n]\ ) \end{aligned} \tag{3.1}$$

It is sufficient to show that R is an improvement simulation. Suppose $e \ R \ e'$, and suppose further that $e{\Downarrow}^n w$. We need to show that $e'{\Downarrow}^{\leq n} w'$ for some w' such that $w \ R^\dagger \ w'$. If $e \equiv e'$ then this follows easily. Otherwise e and e' have the form of (3.1). Now since $I\!R[\mathsf{case}\ [\,]\ \mathsf{of}\ c_1(\bar{x}_1) \Rightarrow e_1 \ldots c_n(\bar{x}_n) \Rightarrow e_n\ ]$ is a reduction context, then we must have

$$\begin{array}{l} I\!R[\mathsf{case}\ e_0\ \mathsf{of}\ c_1(\bar{x}_1) \Rightarrow e_1 \ldots c_n(\bar{x}_n) \Rightarrow e_n\ ] \\ \mapsto^k \ I\!R[\mathsf{case}\ c_i(\bar{e}'')\ \mathsf{of}\ c_1(\bar{x}_1) \Rightarrow e_1 \ldots c_n(\bar{x}_n) \Rightarrow e_n\ ] \end{array}$$

for some expression $c_i(\bar{e}'')$, and some $k \leq n$ and since each of these reductions is "in" e_0, we have matching reduction steps

$$\begin{array}{l} \mathsf{case}\ e_0\ \mathsf{of}\ c_1(\bar{x}_1) : I\!R[e_1] \ldots c_n(\bar{x}_n) : I\!R[e_n] \\ \mapsto^k \ \mathsf{case}\ c_i(\bar{e}'')\ \mathsf{of}\ c_1(\bar{x}_1) : I\!R[e_1] \ldots c_n(\bar{x}_n) : I\!R[e_n] \end{array}$$

Now the former derivative reduces in one more step to $I\!R[e_i\{\bar{x}_i := \bar{e}''\}]$, whilst the latter reduces to $I\!R[e_i]\{\bar{x}_i := \bar{e}''\}$. Since reduction contexts do not bind variables, and since by assumption the free variables of the patterns are disjoint from the free variables of $I\!R$, then these are syntactically equivalent, and so we conclude that

$$\mathsf{case}\ e_0\ \mathsf{of}\ c_1(\bar{x}_1) \Rightarrow I\!R[e_1] \ldots c_n(\bar{x}_n) \Rightarrow I\!R[e_n] \ {\Downarrow}^n w.$$

The remaining conditions for improvement simulation (recall Def. 8 and the $\cdot^\dagger$ operator) are trivially satisfied, since $w \equiv^\dagger w$, which implies $w \ R^\dagger \ w$ as required. □

3.2 The Tick Algebra

A particularly useful method for reasoning about improvement is to make use of certain *identity functions*, i.e., functions f such that for all e, $f\ e \cong e$. Sometimes it is useful to consider functions which are the identity for expressions e of a certain type (e.g., lists). The point of such functions is that they take time to do nothing; in other words $f\ e \mathrel{\underset{\sim_s}{\vartriangleright}} e$. Such functions facilitate the simple calculation of improvements, and are used extensively in applications of the theory. Here we consider the simplest form of identity function, which we call the *tick* function.

$$\checkmark e \equiv \mathsf{tick}\ e$$

where tick is an identity function, given by the definition

$$\mathsf{tick} \triangleq \lambda x.x$$

The tick function will be our canonical syntactic representation of a single computation step. From the point of view of observational equivalence we can safely regard it as an annotation, since $\checkmark e \cong e$; but from the point of view of improvement it is more significant. In particular, since the tick is a function call, from the operational semantics it should be clear that

$$e{\Downarrow}^n h \iff \checkmark e{\Downarrow}^{n+1} h$$

In terms of improvement, observe that $\checkmark e \gtrsim e$ but $e \not\gtrsim \checkmark e$ (except if all closed instances of e diverge).

A key property regarding the tick function is that if function f is defined by $\mathsf{f} \triangleq e$, then

$$\mathsf{f} \;\triangleleft\!\!\!\triangleright\!\!\!\!\!\sim\; \checkmark e$$

In Figure 3 gives some simple laws for $\checkmark$, *the tick algebra*, which we state without proof. In the laws, $\mathbb{R}$ ranges over reduction contexts, possibly containing free variables. There is a related rule for propagation of ticks over contexts. If we define an open context C to be *strict* if for all closing substitutions ϕ, $C[\bot]\phi\Uparrow$, where $\bot$ is any closed expression such that $\bot \Uparrow$. Then we claim that for all expressions e, $C[\checkmark e] \gtrsim_s \checkmark C[e]$. The improvement is not reversible since the expression in the hole may get duplicated.

We will see see more of the tick functions when we come to consider applications of the theory.

$$\frac{e \overset{\bullet}{\mapsto} e'}{e \;\triangleleft\!\!\!\triangleright\!\!\!\!\!\sim\; \checkmark e'} \qquad \frac{e \overset{\circ}{\mapsto}{}^{*} e'}{e \;\triangleleft\!\!\!\triangleright\!\!\!\!\!\sim\; e'}$$

$$\checkmark e \gtrsim e \qquad \frac{\checkmark e_1 \gtrsim \checkmark e_2}{e_1 \gtrsim e_2}\text{(similarly for } \gtrsim_s \text{ and } \triangleleft\!\!\!\triangleright\!\!\!\!\!\sim\text{)}$$

$$\mathbb{R}[\checkmark e] \;\triangleleft\!\!\!\triangleright\!\!\!\!\!\sim\; \checkmark \mathbb{R}[e] \qquad \checkmark p(e_1 \ldots e_n) \;\triangleleft\!\!\!\triangleright\!\!\!\!\!\sim\; p(e_1 \ldots \checkmark e_i \ldots e_n)$$

$$\checkmark \begin{array}{l}\mathsf{case}\ e\ \mathsf{of} \\ c_1(\vec{x}_1) \Rightarrow e_1 \ldots c_n(\vec{x}_n) \Rightarrow e_n\end{array} \;\triangleleft\!\!\!\triangleright\!\!\!\!\!\sim\; \begin{array}{l}\mathsf{case}\ e\ \mathsf{of} \\ c_1(\vec{x}_1) \Rightarrow \checkmark e_1 \ldots c_n(\vec{x}_n) \Rightarrow \checkmark e_n\end{array}$$

Figure 3: Tick laws

4 Time Analysis using Cost Equivalence

In this section we consider the application of the theory of improvement — and in particular the theory of cost equivalence — to the problem of reasoning about the running-time properties of programs. This section summarises some of the work developed in Sands (1993).

Prominent in the study of algorithms in general, and central to formal activities such as program transformation and parallelisation, are questions of efficiency, i.e., the running-time and space requirements of programs. These are *intensional* properties of a program—properties of *how* the program computes, rather that *what* it computes. In this section we illustrate how improvement can be used as a tool for reasoning about the running time of lazy functional programs.

In Sands (1990) we introduced a simple set of "naïve" *time rules*, derived directly from the operational semantics. These concern equations on $\langle e \rangle$, the "time" to evaluate expression e to (weak) head normal form, and $\langle e \rangle^N$, the time to evaluate e to normal form. One of the principal limitations of the direct operational approach to reasoning is the fact that the usual meanings of "equality" for programs do not provide equational reasoning in the context of the time rules. This problem motivated the development of a nonstandard theory of operational equivalence in which the number of computation steps are viewed as an "observable" component of the evaluation process. The resulting theory is the cost equivalence relation defined in the previous section.

4.1 Motivation

As a motivating example for developing techniques to support reasoning about running time, consider the following defining equations for insertion sort (written in a Haskell-like syntax)

```
isort [ ]         =  [ ]
isort (h:t)       =  insert h (isort t)

insert x [ ]      =  [x]
insert x (h:t)    =  x:(h:t)          if x ≤ h
                  =  h:(insert x t)   otherwise
```

As expected, isort requires $\mathcal{O}(n^2)$ time to sort a list of length n. However, under lazy evaluation, isort enjoys a rather nice modularity property with respect to time: if we specify a program which computes the minimum of a list of numbers, by taking the head of the sorted list[1],

$$\text{minimum} = \text{head} \circ \text{isort}$$

then the time to compute minimum is only $\mathcal{O}(n)$. This rather pleasing property of insertion-sort is a well-used example in the context of reasoning about running time of lazy evaluation.

By contrast, the following time property of lazy "quicksort" is seldom reported. A typical definition of a functional quicksort over lists might be:

```
qsort [ ]    =  [ ]
qsort (h:t)  =  qsort (below h t) ++(h:qsort (above h t))
```

where below and above return lists of elements from t which are no bigger, and strictly smaller than h, respectively, and ++ is infix list-append. Functional accounts of quicksort are also quadratic time algorithms, but conventional wisdom

[1] The example is originally due to D. Turner; it appears as an exercise in informal reasoning about lazy evaluation in (Bird and Wadler 1988)[Ch. 6], and in the majority(!) of papers on time analysis of non-strict evaluation.

would label quicksort as a better algorithm than insertion sort because of its better average-case behaviour. A rather less pleasing property of lazy evaluation is that by replacing "better" sorting algorithm qsort for isort in the definition of minimum, we obtain an *asymptotically worse* algorithm, namely one which is $\Omega(n^2)$ in the length of the input. We will return to these examples.

4.2 Reasoning with Time

We outline how cost-equivalence can be used to help reason about the running time of some simple lazy programs.

Time Equations The basic questions we wish to ask are of the form "How many function-calls are required to compute the weak head normal form of expression e". Typically e will not be a simple closed expression, but will contain a meta-variable ranging over some first-order input values (normal forms). As is usual, the kind of answer we would like is a (closed form) function of the size of the input value, representing the exact, or asymptotic, cost. We will not be particularly formal about the treatment of meta-variables, so most of our reasoning is as if we are dealing with (families of) closed expressions.

The basic idea is that we will use the instrumented evaluation $e{\Downarrow}^n w$ as our cost-model. In order to abstract away from the result of a computation it is convenient to introduce phrases of the form $\langle e \rangle$: the time to compute expression e to weak head normal form. In Sands (1993) we used rules along the lines of the following:

$$\langle w \rangle = 0 \qquad \langle e \rangle = \begin{cases} \langle e' \rangle & \text{if } e \overset{\circ}{\mapsto} e' \\ 1 + \langle e' \rangle & \text{if } e \overset{\bullet}{\mapsto} e' \end{cases}$$

This has an obvious shortcoming that it does not model the usual implementation mechanism. namely *call-by-need*, but proves to be adequate for many purposes. An approach to call-by-need is investigated in Sands (1993) also, but we will not consider it here. Here we will mainly work with the cost-equivalence relation, and only employ the time equations when it is notationally convenient to abstract away from the result computed by the "top-level" expression.

Notation For $n \geq 0$, let ${}^{n}\!\surd e$ denote the application of n ticks to expression e.

The following property follows easily from the tick algebra:

Proposition 10 *For all closed expressions e,*

1. $e{\Downarrow}^n w$ *implies* $e \mathrel{\underset{\sim}{\lhd\!\rhd}} {}^{n}\!\surd w$

2. $e \mathrel{\underset{\sim}{\lhd\!\rhd}} {}^{n}\!\surd w' \in \text{WHNF}$ *implies* $e{\Downarrow}^n w$ *for some* w *such that* $w \mathrel{\underset{\sim}{\lhd\!\rhd}} w'$.

$$
\begin{array}{lll}
\mathsf{isort} & \triangleq & \lambda xs.\ \mathsf{case}\ xs\ \mathsf{of} \\
& & \qquad nil \Rightarrow \mathsf{nil} \\
& & \qquad h : t \Rightarrow \mathsf{insert}\ h\ (\mathsf{isort}\ t) \\
\\
\mathsf{insert} & \triangleq & \lambda x.\lambda ys.\ \mathsf{case}\ ys\ \mathsf{of} \\
& & \qquad \mathsf{nil} \Rightarrow x : \mathsf{nil} \\
& & \qquad h : t \Rightarrow \mathsf{if}\ x \leq h\ \mathsf{then}\ x : (h : t) \\
& & \qquad\qquad\qquad\qquad \mathsf{else}\ h : (\mathsf{insert}\ x\ t)
\end{array}
$$

Figure 4: Insertion Sort

In terms of the time equations, we note that if $e \underset{\sim}{\lhd\rhd} {}^{n}\!\surd e'$ then $\langle e \rangle = n + \langle e' \rangle$. The point of the proposition is that we can use $\underset{\sim}{\lhd\rhd}$ as a basis for reasoning about evaluation steps. Moreover, because $\underset{\sim}{\lhd\rhd}$ is a congruence, we can use it to simplify subexpressions.

Insertion Sort Returning to the example given earlier, Figure 4 presents the insertion sort function, this time in the syntax of the language introduced earlier, but retaining the infix ":" list constructor.

The time to compute the head-normal form of insertion sort is relatively simple to determine. We consider computing the head normal form of insertion sort applied to some arbitrary (evaluated) list of integers $v_n : \ldots : v_1 :$ nil where $n \geq 1$. Let V_0 denote the list nil and, for each $i < n$, let V_{i+1} denote the list $v_{i+1} : V_i$. The following shows that the time needed to compute the first element of insertion sort is always linear in the length of the argument.

Proposition 11 *For all* $i > 0$, *there exist an expression* e' *and some value* v *in the set* $\{v_1, \ldots, v_i\}$ *such that*

$$\mathsf{isort}\ V_i \underset{\sim}{\lhd\rhd} {}^{(2i+1)}\!\surd v : e'$$

PROOF. By induction on i, and calculating using the tick algebra. In the base case $(i = 1)$ we have $\mathsf{isort}\ V_1 \underset{\sim}{\lhd\rhd} \surd \mathsf{insert}\ v_1\ (\mathsf{isort}\ V_0) \underset{\sim}{\lhd\rhd} {}^{3}\!\surd v_1 : \mathsf{nil}$.

In the induction case $(i = k + 1)$ we calculate:

$$
\begin{array}{lll}
\mathsf{isort}\ V_{k+1} & \underset{\sim}{\lhd\rhd} & \surd \mathsf{insert}\ v_{k+1}\ (\mathsf{isort}\ V_k) \\
& \underset{\sim}{\lhd\rhd} & \surd \mathsf{insert}\ v_{k+1}\ {}^{(2k+1)}\!\surd(v : e') \qquad \text{(Hypothesis)} \\
& & \textit{for some } e' \textit{ and some } v' \in \{v_1, \ldots v_k\} \\
& \underset{\sim}{\lhd\rhd} & {}^{2}\!\surd \mathsf{case}\ {}^{(2k+1)}\!\surd(v : e')\ \mathsf{of} \ldots \\
& \underset{\sim}{\lhd\rhd} & {}^{(2(k+1)+1)}\!\surd \mathsf{if}\ v_{k+1} \leq v\ \mathsf{then}\ v_{k+1} : v : e' \\
& & \qquad\qquad\qquad \mathsf{else}\ v : (\mathsf{insert}\ v_{k+1}\ e') \\
& \underset{\sim}{\lhd\rhd} & \begin{cases} {}^{(2(k+1)+1)}\!\surd v_{k+1} : v : e' & \textit{if } v_{k+1} \leq v \\ {}^{(2(k+1)+1)}\!\surd v : (\mathsf{insert}\ v_{k+1}\ e') & \textit{otherwise} \end{cases}
\end{array}
$$

$$
\begin{array}{rcl}
\mathsf{qs} & \triangleq & \lambda xs.\ \mathsf{case}\ xs\ \mathsf{of} \\
& & \quad \mathsf{nil} \Rightarrow \mathsf{nil} \\
& & \quad h : t \Rightarrow \mathsf{qs}(\mathsf{below}\ h\ t) +\!\!+ (h : \mathsf{qs}(\mathsf{above}\ h\ t)) \\
\\
\mathsf{below} & \triangleq & \lambda x.\lambda ys.\ \mathsf{case}\ ys\ \mathsf{of} \\
& & \quad \mathsf{nil} \Rightarrow \mathsf{nil} \\
& & \quad h : t \Rightarrow \mathsf{if}\ h \leq x\ \mathsf{then}\ h : \mathsf{below}\ x\ t \\
& & \qquad\qquad\qquad\qquad \mathsf{else}\ \mathsf{below}\ x\ t \\
xs +\!\!+ ys & \triangleq & \mathsf{case}\ xs\ \mathsf{of} \\
& & \quad \mathsf{nil} \Rightarrow ys \\
& & \quad h : t \Rightarrow h : (t +\!\!+ ys)
\end{array}
$$

Figure 5: Functional Quicksort

□

As a direct corollary we have $\langle \mathsf{isort}\ V_i \rangle = 2i + 1$.

Quicksort Now we consider a more involved example. The equations in Figure 5 define a simple functional version of quicksort (qs) using auxiliary functions below and above, and append written here as an infix function ++. Primitive functions for integer comparison have also been written infix to aid readability. The definition for above has been omitted, but is like that of below with the comparison ">" in place of "≤".

The aim will be fairly modest: to show that quicksort exhibits its worst-case $\mathcal{O}(n^2)$ behaviour even when we only require the first element of the list to be computed, in contrast to the earlier insertion sort example which always takes linear time to compute the first element of the result. First consider the general case:

$$
\langle \mathsf{qs}\, e \rangle = 1 + k + \begin{cases} 0 & \textit{if}\ e \mathrel{\underset{\sim}{\diamondsuit}} {}^{k}\!\surd\mathsf{nil} \\ \left\langle \begin{array}{l} \mathsf{qs}(\mathsf{below}\, h\, t) \\ +\!\!+ (y : \mathsf{qs}(\mathsf{above}\, h\, t)) \end{array} \right\rangle & \textit{if}\ e \mathrel{\underset{\sim}{\diamondsuit}} {}^{k}\!\surd(h : t) \end{cases}
$$

From the time rules and the definition of append, this simplifies to

$$
\langle \mathsf{qs}\, e \rangle = 1 + k + \begin{cases} 0 & \textit{if}\ e \mathrel{\underset{\sim}{\diamondsuit}} {}^{k}\!\surd\mathsf{nil} \\ 1 + \langle \mathsf{qs}(\mathsf{below}\, y\, z) \rangle & \textit{if}\ e \mathrel{\underset{\sim}{\diamondsuit}} {}^{k}\!\surd(h : t) \end{cases} \tag{4.1}
$$

Proceeding to the particular problem, it is not too surprising that we will use non-increasing lists v to show that $\langle \mathsf{qs}\, v \rangle = \Omega(n^2)$. Towards this goal, fix an arbitrary family of integer values $\{v_i\}_{i>0}$ such that $v_i \leq v_j$ whenever $i \leq j$. Now define the set of non-increasing lists $\{A_i\}_{i\geq 0}$ by induction on i: let A_0 denote the list nil, and, for each $k > 0$ let A_{k+1} denote the list $v_{k+1} : A_k$.

The goal is now to show that $\langle \mathsf{qs}(A_n) \rangle$ is quadratic in n. It is easy to see, instantiating (4.1) that

$$\langle \mathsf{qs}(A_{k+1}) \rangle = 2 + \langle \mathsf{qs}(\mathsf{below}\ v_{k+1}\ A_k) \rangle$$

but continuing with this simple style of reasoning we quickly see the limitations of the "naive" operational approach to reasoning. Unlike the insertion-sort example where basic operational reasoning is sufficient (see (Sands 1993), where cost equivalence is not used for the isort example), the successive calls to qs become increasingly complex. The key to showing that $\langle \mathsf{qs}\ A_n \rangle$ is quadratic in n is the identification of a cost equivalence which allows us to simplify (a generalised version of) the call to below. To do this we will need another form of identity function.

Identity Functions on Lists We introduce another identity function, this time on the domain of list-valued expressions. Let T be the identity function on lists given by

$$\begin{aligned} \mathsf{T} \triangleq \lambda x.\ & \mathsf{case}\ x\ \mathsf{of} \\ & \quad \mathsf{nil} \Rightarrow \mathsf{nil} \\ & \quad h : t \Rightarrow (h : \mathsf{T}t) \end{aligned}$$

As with the tick function, let T^n denote the n-fold composition of T, where $\mathsf{T}^0 e$ is just e. It follows from this definition that

$$\begin{aligned} \mathsf{T}^n\,\mathsf{nil} &\mathrel{\triangleleft\!\triangleright\!\!\!\!\sim} {}^{n}\!\surd\mathsf{nil} \\ \mathsf{T}^n\,(h : t) &\mathrel{\triangleleft\!\triangleright\!\!\!\!\sim} {}^{n}\!\surd(h : \mathsf{T}^n\,t) \end{aligned}$$

So T^n is an identity function for lists which increases the cost of producing each constructor in the list's structure by n ticks. We use T to characterise a key property of a certain call to below:

Proposition 12 *For all* $a \geq 0$, *and* i, j *such that* $0 \leq j \leq i$,

$$\mathsf{below}(v_i, \mathsf{T}^a A_j) \mathrel{\triangleleft\!\triangleright\!\!\!\!\sim} \mathsf{T}^{a+1} A_j.$$

PROOF. By induction on j, using the tick algebra (it can also be proved straightforwardly by coinduction).

Base: $(j = 0)$ $\mathsf{below}(v_i, \mathsf{T}^a A_0) \mathrel{\underset{\sim}{\lhd\!\rhd}} \sqrt{}\mathsf{case}\ \mathsf{T}^a A_0\ \mathsf{of} \ldots)$

$$\begin{aligned} &\mathrel{\underset{\sim}{\lhd\!\rhd}} \sqrt{}(\mathsf{case}\ {}^{n}\!\sqrt{}\mathsf{nil}\ \mathsf{of}\ \ldots)) \\ &\mathrel{\underset{\sim}{\lhd\!\rhd}} {}^{a+1}\!\sqrt{}(\mathsf{nil}) \\ &\mathrel{\underset{\sim}{\lhd\!\rhd}} \mathsf{T}^{a+1} A_0 \end{aligned}$$

Induction: $(j = k{+}1)$ $\mathsf{below}(v_i, \mathsf{T}^a A_{k+1})$

$$\begin{aligned} &\mathrel{\underset{\sim}{\lhd\!\rhd}} \sqrt{}(\mathsf{case}\ \mathsf{T}^a A_{k+1}\ \mathsf{of} \ldots) \\ &\mathrel{\underset{\sim}{\lhd\!\rhd}} {}^{a+1}\!\sqrt{}(\mathsf{case}\ v_{k+1} : \mathsf{T}^a A_k\ \mathsf{of} \ldots) \\ &\mathrel{\underset{\sim}{\lhd\!\rhd}} {}^{a+1}\!\sqrt{}(\mathsf{if}\ v_{k+1} \le v_i\ \mathsf{then}\ v_{k+1} : \mathsf{below}(v_i, \mathsf{T}^a A_k) \\ &\qquad\qquad \mathsf{else}\ \mathsf{below}(v_i, \mathsf{T}^a A_k)) \\ &\mathrel{\underset{\sim}{\lhd\!\rhd}} {}^{a+1}\!\sqrt{}(v_{k+1} : \mathsf{below}(v_i, \mathsf{T}^a A_k)) \\ &\mathrel{\underset{\sim}{\lhd\!\rhd}} {}^{a+1}\!\sqrt{}(v_{k+1} : \mathsf{T}^{a+1} A_k) \qquad \text{(Hypothesis)} \\ &\mathrel{\underset{\sim}{\lhd\!\rhd}} \mathsf{T}^{a+1} A_{k+1} \end{aligned}$$

□

Now we can make use of the proposition in the analysis of quicksort. We consider the more general case of $\langle \mathsf{qs}\ \mathsf{T}^a A_j \rangle$. Considering the cases when $j = 0$ and $j = k + 1$, and instantiating the general time equation gives:

$$\begin{aligned} \langle \mathsf{qs}(\mathsf{T}^a A_0) \rangle &= 1 + a \\ \langle \mathsf{qs}(\mathsf{T}^a A_{k+1}) \rangle &= 2 + a + \langle \mathsf{qs}(\mathsf{below}\ v_{k+1}\ \mathsf{T}^a A_k) \rangle \\ &= 2 + a + \langle \mathsf{qs}(\mathsf{T}^{a+1} A_k) \rangle \end{aligned}$$

Thus we have derived a recurrence equation which is easily solved; a simple induction is sufficient to check that

$$\langle \mathsf{qs}\ \mathsf{T}^a A_n \rangle = \frac{n(n+5)}{2} + a(n+1) + 1.$$

Finally, since the A_n are just $\mathsf{T}^0 A_n$, we have that the time to compute the weak head normal form of qs A_n is quadratic in n:

$$\langle \mathsf{qs}\ A_n \rangle = \frac{n(n+5)}{2} + 1.$$

Further Work Under a call-by-need computation model some computations are shared, so we would expect that, for example, $(\lambda x.x + x) \sqrt{}0 \mathrel{\underset{\sim}{\lhd\!\rhd}} \sqrt{}0$ where $+$ is a primitive function. Instead, we get $(\lambda x.x + x) \sqrt{}0 \mathrel{\underset{\sim}{\lhd\!\rhd}} {}^{2}\!\sqrt{}0$ which can make cost equivalence unreliable for reasoning about non-linear functions. As we mentioned earlier, the problems of reasoning about call-by-need are addressed in Sands (1993)— but not via a call-by-need theory of cost equivalence. Defining call-by-need improvement is not problematic. The problem is to find an appropriate context lemma, and this is a topic we plan to address in future work. The applications of the Improvement Theorem introduced in the next section depend less critically on the intentional qualities of improvement theorem. For these applications the call-by-name origin of our improvement theory is often advantageous, since for example unrestricted beta-reduction is an improvement for call-by-name. We do not yet know whether the development of the next section will go through for a call-by-need theory.

5 The Improvement Theorem

In this section we motivate and introduce the Improvement Theorem. The Improvement Theorem employs the improvement relation to prove the correctness of program transformations. The interesting point of this application is that the goal is not to prove that program transformations improve programs *per se*, but simply to prove that they produce operationally equivalent programs.

5.1 The Correctness Problem

The goal of program transformation is to improve efficiency while preserving meaning. Source-to-source transformation methods such as *unfold-fold transformation*, *partial evaluation* (specialisation) and *deforestation* (Burstall and Darlington 1977; Jones, Gomard, and Sestoft 1993; Wadler 1990), are some well-known examples. These kind of transformations are characterised by the fact that

- they utilise a small number of relatively simple transformation steps, and
- in order to compound the effect of these relatively simple local optimisations, the transformations have the ability to introduce new recursive calls.

Transformations such as deforestation (Wadler 1990) (a functional form of loop-fusion) and program specialisation (and analogous transformations on logic programs) are able to introduce new recursive structures via a process of selectively memoising previously encountered expressions, and introducing recursion according to a "*déjà vu*" principle (Jones, Gomard, and Sestoft 1993). In the classic unfold-fold transformation, it is the *fold* step which introduces recursion. See Pettorossi and Proietti (1995) for an overview of transformation strategies which fit this style.

The problem is that for many transformation methods which deal with recursive programs (including those methods mentioned above), correctness cannot be argued by simply showing that the basic transformation steps are meaning preserving.[2] Yet this problem (exemplified below) runs contrary to many informal—and some "formal"—arguments which are used in attempts to justify correctness of particular transformation methods. This is the problem for which the Improvement Theorem was designed to address.

[2]One might say that there are two problems with correctness – the other problem is that it has not been widely recognised as a problem!

To take a simple example to illustrate the problem, consider the following "transformation by equivalence-preserving steps". Start with the function repeat which produces the "infinite" list of its argument:

$$\mathsf{repeat}\, x \triangleq x : (\mathsf{repeat}\, x)$$

Suppose the function tail computes the tail of a list. The following property can be easily deduced: $\mathsf{repeat}\, x \cong \mathsf{tail}(\mathsf{repeat}\, x)$. Now suppose that we use this "local equivalence" to transform the body of the function to obtain a new version of the function:

$$\mathsf{repeat}'\, x \triangleq x : (\mathsf{tail}(\mathsf{repeat}'\, x))$$

The problem is that this function is not equivalent to the original, since it can never produce more than first element in the list.

One might be tempted to suggest that this is "just a problem of name-capture", and to conclude that the problem can be solved by

- not allowing transformations on the body which depend on the function being transformed; in the example above, this means that if we transform the body, repeat must be treated as a free variable, or
- making the new function non-recursive, so that e.g., we would obtain:

$$\mathsf{repeat}'\, x \triangleq x : (\mathsf{tail}(\mathsf{repeat}\, x))$$

Unfortunately these "solutions", while preventing us from performing incorrect transformations, also prevent us from performing any interesting correct ones!

5.2 A Solution: Local Improvement

To obtain total correctness without losing the local, stepwise character of program transformation, it is clear that a stronger condition than extensional equivalence for the local transformation steps is needed. In Sands (1995b) we presented such a condition, namely *improvement*.

In the remainder of this section we outline the main technical result from Sands (1995b), which says that if transformation steps are guided by certain natural optimisation concerns, then correctness of the transformation follows. We also present "local" version of the Improvement Theorem which is stated at expression-level recursion using a simple "letrec" construct.

More precisely, the *Improvement Theorem* says that if e is improved by e', in addition to e being operationally equivalent to e', then a transformation which replaces e by e' (potentially introducing recursion) is totally correct; in addition this guarantees that the transformed program is a formal improvement over the original.

Notice that in the problematic example above, replacement of $\mathsf{repeat}\,x$ by the equivalent term $\mathsf{tail}(\mathsf{repeat}\,x)$ is not an improvement since the latter requires evaluation of an additional call to repeat in order to reach weak head normal form.

The fact that the theorem, in addition to establishing correctness, also guarantees that the transformed program is an improvement over the original is an added bonus. It can also allow us to apply the theorem iteratively. It also gives us an indication of the limits of the method. Transformations which do not improve a program cannot be justified using the Improvement Theorem alone. However, in combination with some other more basic methods for establishing correctness, the Improvement Theorem can still be effective. We refer the reader to Sands (1996b) for examples of other more basic methods and how they can be used together with the Improvement Theorem.

For the purposes of the formal statement of the Improvement Theorem, transformation is viewed as the introduction of some *new* functions from a given set of definitions, so the transformation from a program consisting of a single function $\mathsf{f} \triangleq e$ to a new version $\mathsf{f} \triangleq e'$ will be represented by the derivation of a new function $\mathsf{g} \triangleq e'\{\mathsf{f} := \mathsf{g}\}$. In this way we do not need to explicitly parameterise operational equivalence and improvement by the intended set of function definitions.

In the following (Theorem 1 – Proposition 14) let $\{\mathsf{f}_i\}_{i \in I}$ be a set of functions indexed by some set I, given by some definitions:

$$\{\mathsf{f}_i \triangleq e_i\}_{i \in I}$$

Let $\{e'_i\}_{i \in I}$ be a set of expressions. The following results relate to the transformation of the functions f_i using the expressions e'_i: let $\{\mathsf{g}_i\}_{i \in I}$ be a set of new functions (i.e. the definitions of the f_i do not depend upon them) given by definitions

$$\{\mathsf{g}_i \triangleq e'_i\{\bar{\mathsf{f}} := \bar{\mathsf{g}}\}\}_{i \in I}$$

We begin with the standard partial correctness property associated with "transformation by equivalence":

Theorem 1 (Partial Correctness) *If* $e_i \cong e'_i$ *for all* $i \in I$, *then* $\mathsf{g}_i \precsim \mathsf{f}_i$, $i \in I$.

This is the "standard" partial correctness result (see eg. (Kott 1978)(Courcelle 1979)) associated with e.g. unfold-fold transformations. It follows easily from a least fixed-point theorem for $\precsim$ (the full details for this language can be found in Sands (1996b)) since the $\bar{\mathsf{f}}$ are easily shown to be fixed points of the defining equations for functions $\bar{\mathsf{g}}$.

Partial correctness is clearly not adequate for transformations, since it allows the resulting programs to loop in cases where the original program terminated. We obtain a guarantee of total correctness by combining the partial correctness result with the following:

Theorem 2 (The Improvement Theorem (Sands 1995b)) *If we have* $e_i \trianglerighteq\!\!\!\sim e'_i$ *for all* $i \in I$, *then* $\mathsf{f}_i \trianglerighteq\!\!\!\sim \mathsf{g}_i$, $i \in I$.

The proof of the Theorem, given in detail in (Sands 1996b), makes use of the alternative characterisation of the improvement relation given later.

Putting the two theorems together, we get:

Corollary 13 *If we have* $e_i \trianglerighteq_s e'_i$ *for all* $i \in I$, *then* $\mathsf{f}_i \trianglerighteq_s \mathsf{g}_i$, $i \in I$.

Informally, this implies that:

> if a program transformation proceeds by repeatedly applying some set of transformation rules to a program, providing that the basic rules of the transformation are equivalence-preserving, and also contained in the improvement relation (with respect to the original definitions), then the resulting transformation will be correct. Moreover, the resulting program will be an improvement over the original.

There is also a third variation, a "cost-equivalence" theorem, which is also useful:

Proposition 14 *If* $e_i \trianglelefteq\!\trianglerighteq e'_i$ *for all* $i \in I$, *then* $\mathsf{f}_i \trianglelefteq\!\trianglerighteq \mathsf{g}_i$, $i \in I$.

5.3 An Improvement Theorem for Local Recursion

In this section we introduce a form of the improvement theorem which deals with local expression-level recursion, expressed with a fixed point combinator or with a simple "letrec" definition.

Definition 15 *Let* fix *be a recursion combinator defined by* $\mathsf{fix} \triangleq \lambda h.h(\mathsf{fix}\,h)$. *Now define a letrec expression* $\mathsf{letrec}\ h = e\ \mathsf{in}\ e'$ *as a syntactic abbreviation for the term* $(\lambda h.e')(\mathsf{fix}\,\lambda h.e)$.

Using these definitions we can present an expression-level version of the Improvement Theorem, analogous to Corollary 13:

Theorem 3 (Sands 1996a) *If* $\lambda h.e_0$ *and* $\lambda h.e_1$ *are closed expressions, then if*

$$\mathsf{letrec}\ h = e_0\ \mathsf{in}\ e_0 \trianglerighteq_s \mathsf{letrec}\ h = e_0\ \mathsf{in}\ e_1$$

then for all expressions e

$$\mathsf{letrec}\ h = e_0\ \mathsf{in}\ e \trianglerighteq_s \mathsf{letrec}\ h = e_1\ \mathsf{in}\ e$$

There is a more primitive variant of this theorem expressed in terms of fix which nicely illustrates the reciprocity between the least fixed-point property and the Improvement Theorem[3].

[3]This variant was suggested by Søren Lassen.

Theorem 4

$$
\begin{array}{lll}
(i) & e_0(\mathsf{fix}\, e_0) \underset{\sim}{\sqsupset} e_1(\mathsf{fix}\, e_0) \implies & \mathsf{fix}\, e_0 \underset{\sim}{\sqsupset} \mathsf{fix}\, e_1 \\
(ii) & e_0(\mathsf{fix}\, e_0) \underset{\sim}{\trianglerighteq} e_1(\mathsf{fix}\, e_0) \implies & \mathsf{fix}\, e_0 \underset{\sim}{\trianglerighteq} \mathsf{fix}\, e_1
\end{array}
$$

PROOF. Parts (i) and (ii) can be established easily from Theorem 1 and Theorem 2 respectively. Here we just sketch how part (ii) can be derived, since part (i) is standard. Assume that $e_0(\mathsf{fix}\, e_0) \underset{\sim}{\trianglerighteq} e_1(\mathsf{fix}\, e_0)$. Define $\mathsf{g} \triangleq e_0(\mathsf{fix}\, e_0)$; it follows from this definition that $\mathsf{g} \underset{\sim}{\trianglelefteq\!\trianglerighteq} {}^{\surd}e_0(\mathsf{fix}\, e_0) \underset{\sim}{\trianglelefteq\!\trianglerighteq} \mathsf{fix}\, e_0$. From the initial assumption we can use this to show that $e_0(\mathsf{fix}\, e_0) \underset{\sim}{\trianglerighteq} e_1\, \mathsf{g}$. By Theorem 2 we have $\mathsf{g} \underset{\sim}{\trianglerighteq} \mathsf{h}$ where $\mathsf{h} \triangleq e_1\, \mathsf{h}$. But $\mathsf{h} \underset{\sim}{\trianglelefteq\!\trianglerighteq} \mathsf{fix}\, e_1$, and hence we can conclude $\mathsf{fix}\, e_0 \underset{\sim}{\trianglerighteq} \mathsf{fix}\, e_1$ are required. □

6 Example Application to the Correctness of Program Transformations

In this section we illustrate the application of the Improvement Theorem to the verification of the correctness of a small program transformation. The example is taken from Sands (1996b), and concerns a transformation described in Wadler (1989). More extensive examples are found in Sands (1996a), where the Improvement Theorem is used to provide a total correctness proof for an automatic transformation based on a higher-order variant of the deforestation method (Wadler 1990).

The main application studied in Sands (1996b) is the classic unfold-fold method. The problem is different from the task of verifying specific transformation methods (such as the one in this section) because, in general, unfold-fold transformations are not correct. Task is to design, with the help of the Improvement Theorem, a simple syntactic method for constraining the transformation process such that correctness is ensured.

6.1 Concatenate Vanishes

We consider a simple mechanizable transformation which aims to eliminate calls to the concatenate (or *append*) function. The effects of the transformation are well known, such as the transformation of a naive quadratic-time reverse function into a linear-time equivalent.

The systematic definition of the transformation used here is due to Wadler (Wadler 1989) (with one small modification). Wadler's formulation of this well-known transformation is completely mechanizable, and the transformation "algorithm" always terminates. Unlike many other mechanizable transformations (such as deforestation and partial evaluation), it can improve the asymptotic complexity of some programs.

The basic idea is to eliminate an occurrence of concatenate (defined in Fig. 5) of the form $\mathsf{f}\, e_1 \ldots e_n \mathbin{+\!\!+} e'$, by finding a function f^+ which satisfies

$$\mathsf{f}^+\, x_1 \ldots x_n\, y \cong (\mathsf{f}\, x_1 \ldots x_n) \mathbin{+\!\!+} y.$$

Definition 1 ("Concatenate Vanishes") The transformation has two phases: *initialization*, which introduces an initial definition for f^+, and *transformation*, which applies a set of rewrites to the right-hand sides of all definitions.

Initialization For some function $\mathsf{f}\, x_1 \ldots x_n \triangleq e$, for which there is an occurrence of a term $(\mathsf{f}\, e_1 \ldots e_n) \mathbin{+\!\!+} e'$ in the program, define a *new* function

$$\mathsf{f}^+ x_1 \ldots x_n\, y \triangleq e \mathbin{+\!\!+} y.$$

Transformation Apply the following rewrite rules, in any order, to all the right-hand sides of the definitions in the program:

$$
\begin{array}{llcl}
(1) & \mathsf{nil} \mathbin{+\!\!+} x & \rightarrow & x \\
(2) & (x : y) \mathbin{+\!\!+} z & \rightarrow & x : (y \mathbin{+\!\!+} z) \\
(3) & (x \mathbin{+\!\!+} y) \mathbin{+\!\!+} z & \rightarrow & x \mathbin{+\!\!+} (y \mathbin{+\!\!+} z) \\
(4) & (\,\mathsf{case}\ x\ \mathsf{of} & \rightarrow & \mathsf{case}\ x\ \mathsf{of} \\
 & \quad c_1(\vec{y}_1) \Rightarrow e_1 & & \quad c_1(\vec{y}_1) \Rightarrow (e_1 \mathbin{+\!\!+} z) \\
 & \quad \ldots & & \quad \ldots \\
 & \quad c_n(\vec{y}_n) \Rightarrow e_n) \mathbin{+\!\!+} z & & \quad c_n(\vec{y}_n) \Rightarrow (e_n \mathbin{+\!\!+} z) \\
(5) & (\mathsf{f}\, x_1 \ldots x_n) \mathbin{+\!\!+} y & \rightarrow & \mathsf{f}^+\, x_1 \ldots x_n\, y \\
(6) & (\mathsf{f}^+\, x_1 \ldots x_n\, y) \mathbin{+\!\!+} z & \rightarrow & \mathsf{f}^+\, x_1 \ldots x_n\, (y \mathbin{+\!\!+} z)
\end{array}
$$

In rule (4) (strictly speaking it is a rule *schema*, since we assume an instance for each vector of expressions $e_1 \ldots e_n$) it is assumed that z is distinct from the pattern variables $\vec{y}_i$.

Henceforth, let $\rightarrow$ be the rewrite relation generated by the above rules (i.e., the compatible closure) and $\rightarrow^+$ be its transitive closure.

It should be clear that the rewrites can only be applied a finite number of times, so the transformation always terminates—and the rewrite system is Church-Rosser (although this property is not needed for the correctness proof).

Example 16 *The following example illustrates the effect of the transformation:* itrav *computes the* inorder *traversal of a binary tree. Trees are assumed to be built from a nullary* leaf *constructor, and a ternary* node, *comprising a left subtree, a node-element, and a right subtree.*

$$
\begin{array}{lcl}
\mathsf{itrav}\ t & \triangleq & \mathsf{case}\ t\ \mathsf{of} \\
 & & \quad \mathsf{leaf} \Rightarrow \mathsf{nil} \\
 & & \quad \mathsf{node}(l, n, r) \Rightarrow (\mathsf{itrav}\ l) \mathbin{+\!\!+} (n : \mathsf{itrav}\ r).
\end{array}
$$

The second branch of the case expression is a candidate for the transformation, so we define:

$$\begin{array}{ll}\mathsf{itrav}^{+}\, t\, y \triangleq (\mathsf{case}\ t\ \mathsf{of} & \\ \qquad\qquad \mathsf{leaf} \Rightarrow \mathsf{nil} & \\ \qquad\qquad \mathsf{node}(l,n,r) \Rightarrow (\mathsf{itrav}\, l){+\!\!+}(n : \mathsf{itrav}\, r) & \\ \qquad)\,{+\!\!+}\,y & \end{array}$$

Now we transform the right-hand sides of these two definitions, respectively:

$$\begin{array}{l}\mathsf{case}\ t\ \mathsf{of}\ \ \mathsf{leaf} \Rightarrow \mathsf{nil}\\ \quad \mathsf{node}(l,n,r) \Rightarrow (\mathsf{itrav}\, l){+\!\!+}(n : \mathsf{itrav}\, r)\\ \rightarrow \begin{array}{l}\mathsf{case}\ t\ \mathsf{of}\ \ \mathsf{leaf} \Rightarrow \mathsf{nil}\\ \quad \mathsf{node}(l,n,r) \Rightarrow \mathsf{itrav}^{+}\, l\, (n : \mathsf{itrav}\, r)\end{array}\end{array}$$

$$\begin{array}{ll} & (\mathsf{case}\ t\ \mathsf{of}\ \ \mathsf{leaf} \Rightarrow \mathsf{nil}\\ & \quad \mathsf{node}(l,n,r) \Rightarrow (\mathsf{itrav}\, l){+\!\!+}(n : \mathsf{itrav}\, r)){+\!\!+}y\\ \rightarrow & \mathsf{case}\ t\ \mathsf{of}\ \ \mathsf{leaf} \Rightarrow \mathsf{nil}{+\!\!+}y\\ & \quad \mathsf{node}(l,n,r) \Rightarrow ((\mathsf{itrav}\, l){+\!\!+}(n : \mathsf{itrav}\, r)){+\!\!+}y\\ \rightarrow^{+} & \mathsf{case}\ t\ \mathsf{of}\ \ \mathsf{leaf} \Rightarrow y\\ & \quad \mathsf{node}(l,n,r) \Rightarrow \mathsf{itrav}^{+}\, l\, (n : \mathsf{itrav}^{+}\, r\, y)\end{array}$$

The resulting expressions are taken as the right-hand sides of new versions of itrav *and* itrav^{+} *respectively (where we elide the renaming):*

$$\begin{array}{lll}\mathsf{itrav}\, t & \triangleq & \mathsf{case}\ t\ \mathsf{of}\ \ \mathsf{leaf} \Rightarrow \mathsf{nil}\\ & & \quad \mathsf{node}(l,n,r) \Rightarrow \mathsf{itrav}^{+}\, l\, (n : \mathsf{itrav}\, r)\\ & & \\ \mathsf{itrav}^{+}\, t\, y & \triangleq & \mathsf{case}\ t\ \mathsf{of}\ \ \mathsf{leaf} \Rightarrow y\\ & & \quad \mathsf{node}(l,n,r) \Rightarrow \mathsf{itrav}^{+}\, l\, (n : \mathsf{itrav}^{+}\, r\, y)\end{array}$$

The running time of the original version is quadratic (worst case) in the size of the tree, while the new version is linear (when the entire result is computed).

The following correctness result for *any* transformation using this method shows that the new version must be an *improvement* over the original, which implies that the new version never leads to more function calls, regardless of the context in which it is used.

6.2 Correctness

It is intuitively clear that each rewrite of the transformation is an equivalence; the first two rules comprise the definition of concatenate; the third is the well-known associativity law; the fourth is a consequence of distribution law for case expressions; and the last two follow easily from the preceding rules and the initial definitions. This is sufficient (by Theorem 1) to show that the new versions of functions are less in the operational order than the originals, but does not guarantee equivalence. In particular note that rule (5) gives the transformation the ability to introduce recursion into the definition of the new auxiliary functions. To prove total correctness we apply the Improvement Theorem; it is sufficient to verify that the transformation rewrites are all contained in the strong improvement relation.

Proposition 17 *The transformations rules* (1)–(6) *are strong improvements.*

PROOF. [Outline] Using the context lemma for improvement it is sufficient to consider only closed instances of the rewrites. Rules (1) and (2) are essentially just unfoldings of the standard definition of concatenate and thus are improvements. Rule (3) can be proved from the operational semantics by showing that its reflexive closure is an improvement simulation (it is also proved using a new proof technique in the next section). Rule (4) can be proved with the help of Proposition 9, observing that the context $[\ ]\mathbin{+\!\!+} z$ unfolds to a reduction context. Rule (5) follows directly from the definition of f^+ provided by the initialization, since after two reduction steps on each side of the laws the left and right-hand sides are identical. Furthermore, this law is a "cost equivalence" — it is also an improvement in the other direction, and so for (6) we have that:

$$\begin{array}{llll} (\mathsf{f}^+\,x_1\ldots x_n\,y)\mathbin{+\!\!+}z & \mathrel{\underset{\sim}{\lhd\!\rhd}} & ((\mathsf{f}\,x_1\ldots x_n)\mathbin{+\!\!+}y)\mathbin{+\!\!+}z & (\text{since } (5) \subset (\mathrel{\underset{\sim}{\lhd\!\rhd}})) \\ & \mathrel{\underset{\sim}{\rhd}}_s & (\mathsf{f}\,x_1\ldots x_n)\mathbin{+\!\!+}(y\mathbin{+\!\!+}z) & (\text{by } (3)) \\ & \mathrel{\underset{\sim}{\rhd}}_s & \mathsf{f}^+\,x_1\ldots x_n\,(y\mathbin{+\!\!+}z) & (\text{by } (5)) \end{array}$$

□

Then we get the following from the Improvement Theorem (Corollary 13).

Proposition 18 *The transformation is correct, and the resulting functions are improvements over the originals.*

7 Proof Techniques Based on Improvement

In this section we consider a new application: the construction of proof techniques for $\cong$ which make use of the improvement relation.

7.1 Equivalence by Transformation

A method for correctly transforming programs provides us with a natural method for proving the equivalence of expressions. For example, let e and e' be two arbitrary expressions, and let the sequence of variables $\vec{x}$ contain all their free variables. Then e and e' can be proved equivalent by showing that the new (nonrecursive) functions f and f′ defined by

$$\begin{array}{lll} \mathsf{f} & \triangleq & \lambda\vec{x}.e \\ \mathsf{f}' & \triangleq & \lambda\vec{x}.e' \end{array}$$

can be transformed into a common third function.

This approach to equivalence proofs was suggested by Kott (1982). Kott used a variant of the unfold-fold transformation method [4] to transform functions f and f′ into functions g and g′ respectively, such that g and g′ are syntactically identical up to renaming. Kott called this "the Mc Carthy method" after McCarthy's recursion induction principal (McCarthy 1967).

In this section we present a proof technique for equivalence which is derived from this transformational viewpoint, using the improvement theorem. However, our method will abstract away from the transformational origins of the approach. The method will not explicitly construct functions like f and f′ above—except in the correctness proof of the method itself.

7.2 Strong Improvement Up To Context

We introduce some notation to simplify the presentation. Let $\rhd$ denote a refinement of strong improvement given by

$$e \rhd e' \iff e \underset{\sim_s}{\rhd} \checkmark e'.$$

Definition 19 *If R is a binary relation on expressions, let R^{C} denote the* closure under substitution and context *of R, given by*

$$\{(C[e_1\sigma_1, \ldots, e_n\sigma_n], C[e'_1\sigma_1, \ldots, e'_n\sigma_n] \mid e_i\ R\ e'_i, i \in 1 \ldots n\},$$

where C denotes an arbitrary n-holed context, and the σ_i are arbitrary substitutions.

Definition 20 (bisimulation up to improvement and context) *A binary relation on expressions R is a* bisimulation up to improvement and context *if*

whenever $e_1\ R\ e_2$, then there exists expressions e'_1 and e'_2 such that

$$e_1 \rhd e'_1,\ e_2 \rhd e'_2,\ \textit{and}\ e'_1 R^{\mathrm{C}} e'_2.$$

Theorem 5 *If R is a bisimulation up to improvement and context, then $R \subseteq \cong$.*

PROOF. Let $R = \{(e_i, e'_i)\}_{i \in I}$. Then by definition of improvement context simulation, for each $i \in I$ there exist contexts C_i, $i \in I$ such that $e_i \rhd C_i[\vec{e}]$ and $e'_i \rhd C_i[\vec{e}\,']$ where where the respective pairs of expressions from $\vec{e}$ and $\vec{e}\,'$ are substitution instances of pairs in R. To simplify the exposition, assume that the C_i

[4]Unfortunately, in (Kott 1982) the proposed method of ensuring that the unfold-fold transformations are correct is unsound. Kott states (Proposition 1, *loc. cit.*) that unfold-fold transformations for a first-order call-by-value language are correct whenever the number of folds does not exceed the number of unfolds. A counterexample can be found in Sands (1996b)(Section 1). Kott's oversight is that the language in question contains a non-strict operator—the conditional. Without this operator the Proposition is sound, but is not useful.

have only one distinct type of hole. The generalisation of the proof to the case of "polyadic" contexts is completely straightforward, but notationally cumbersome.

So for each $(e_i, e'_i) \in R$ we have a substitution σ_i such that $e_i \rhd C_i[e_j\sigma_i]$ and $e'_i \rhd C_i[e'_j\sigma_i]$ for some $j \in I$. Thus we define the following set of functions:

$$\left\{ \begin{array}{lll|l} \mathsf{f}_i & \triangleq & \lambda\vec{x}_i.C_i[e_j\sigma_i], & e_i \rhd C_i[e_j\sigma_i], \quad \vec{x}_i = \mathrm{FV}(e_i\ C_i[e_j\sigma_i]\ e'_i\ C_i[e'_j\sigma_i]) \\ \mathsf{g}_i & \triangleq & \lambda\vec{x}_i.C_i[e'_j\sigma_i] & e'_i \rhd C_i[e'_j\sigma_i] \end{array} \right\}$$

Since $\rhd \subseteq \cong$, we have that $e_i \cong C_i[e_j\sigma_i]$ and $e'_i \cong C_i[e'_j\sigma_i]$. Hence it is sufficient to prove that $\mathsf{f}_i \cong \mathsf{g}_i$, $i \in I$. We will do this by showing that the f_i and the g_i can be correctly transformed, respectively, into functions f'_i and g'_i such that f'_i and g'_i are syntactically identical.

From the above definitions is easy to see that, for each $k \in I$

$$\begin{array}{lll} e_k & \underset{\sim}{\trianglerighteq}_s & \surd C_k[e_l\sigma_k] \text{ for some } l \in I \\ & \underset{\sim}{\lhd\!\rhd} & \mathsf{f}_k\,\vec{x}_k \end{array}$$

Thus we have $C_i[e_j\sigma_i] \underset{\sim}{\trianglerighteq}_s C_i[(\mathsf{f}_j\,\vec{x}_j)\sigma_i]$. Using this fact together with The Improvement Theorem (viz. Corollary 13) we have that $\mathsf{f}_i \underset{\sim}{\trianglerighteq}_s \mathsf{f}'_i$ where

$$\mathsf{f}'_i \triangleq \lambda\vec{x}_i.C_i[(\mathsf{f}'_j\,\vec{x}_j)\sigma_i].$$

Following the same lines we can show that $\mathsf{g}_i \underset{\sim}{\trianglerighteq}_s \mathsf{g}'_i$ where

$$\mathsf{g}'_i \triangleq \lambda\vec{x}_i.C_i[(\mathsf{g}'_j\,\vec{x}_j)\sigma_i].$$

Since these function definitions are identical modulo naming, clearly we have $\mathsf{f}_i \underset{\sim}{\trianglerighteq}_s \mathsf{f}'_i \underset{\sim}{\lhd\!\rhd} \mathsf{g}'_i$ and $\mathsf{g}_i \underset{\sim}{\trianglerighteq}_s \mathsf{g}'_i$. Since operational equivalence is contained in strict improvement, this concludes the proof. □

Taking the special case of bisimulation up to improvement and contextwhich contains just a single pair of expressions (and where the context is unary), we obtain:

Corollary 21 *Expressions e and e′ are operationally equivalent if there exists some context C, and some substitution σ such that*

$$e \rhd C[e\sigma] \quad \textit{and} \quad e' \rhd C[e'\sigma]$$

We mention this special case because it turns out to be sufficient for many examples. The following variation of the above Theorem enables us to prove strong improvement properties:

Definition 22 (strong improvement up to improvement and context) *A binary relation on expressions R is a* strong improvement up to improvement and context *if whenever* $\mathrm{e}_1\ R\ \mathrm{e}_2$*, then there exists expressions* e'_1 *and* e'_2 *such that*

$$\mathrm{e}_1 \rhd \mathrm{e}'_1, \quad \mathrm{e}_2 \underset{\sim}{\lhd\!\rhd} \surd\mathrm{e}'_2, \quad \textit{and } \mathrm{e}'_1 R^{\mathrm{C}} \mathrm{e}'_2.$$

Proposition 23 *If R is a strong improvement up to improvement and context then* $R \subseteq \underset{\sim}{\triangleright}_s$.

PROOF. (Sketch) As in the proof of Theorem 5, except that we obtain $e'_i \underset{\sim}{\triangleleft\!\triangleright} g_i \underset{\sim}{\triangleleft\!\triangleright} g'_i$, by making use of Proposition 14. □

There are many other obvious variations of these proof methods along similar lines; for example for proving weaker properties like operational approximation ($\underset{\sim}{\sqsubset}$) and improvement ($\underset{\sim}{\triangleright}$).

7.3 Examples

Here we consider a few simple examples to illustrate the application of the proof techniques given above. Corollary 21 will in fact be sufficient for current purposes. We will routinely omit simple calculations where they only employ the rules of the tick algebra.

Definition 2 *A context C is a* pseudo reduction context *if it is a single-holed context which does not capture variables, and which satisfies the following properties:*

1. $C[\checkmark e] \underset{\sim}{\triangleleft\!\triangleright} \checkmark C[e]$
2. $C[\mathsf{case}\ e_0\ \mathsf{of}\ pat_1 \Rightarrow e_1 \ldots pat_n \Rightarrow e_n\ ] \underset{\sim}{\triangleleft\!\triangleright}$
   $\mathsf{case}\ e_0\ \mathsf{of}\ pat_1 \Rightarrow C[e_1] \ldots pat_n \Rightarrow C[e_n],\quad \mathrm{FV}(C)$ *distinct from* $\mathrm{FV}(pat_i)$

In what follows, we state that certain contexts are pseudo reduction contexts by way of a proof hint. To establish this property in all cases below requires nothing more than the tick algebra, together with Proposition 9 (the propagation-rule for reduction contexts).

Associativity of Append We can prove the well-known associativity property of append by simply showing that $R = \{((x{+\!\!+}y){+\!\!+}z, x{+\!\!+}(y{+\!\!+}z))\}$ is a bisimulation up to improvement and context. In fact, in Section 6 we used a stronger property of the pair above, namely that it is contained in strong improvement. This is shown by proving that R is a strong improvement up to improvement and context. Contexts of the form $[\,]{+\!\!+}e$ are pseudo reduction context, and using this fact the following calculations are routine:

$$
\begin{array}{lll}
(x{+\!\!+}y){+\!\!+}z & \underset{\sim}{\triangleright}_s & \checkmark\,\mathsf{case}\ x\ \mathsf{of} \\
& & \quad \mathsf{nil} \Rightarrow y{+\!\!+}z \\
& & \quad h : t \Rightarrow h : (\boxed{(t{+\!\!+}y){+\!\!+}z})
\end{array}
$$

$$
\begin{array}{lll}
x{+\!\!+}(y{+\!\!+}z) & \underset{\sim}{\triangleleft\!\triangleright} & \checkmark\,\mathsf{case}\ x\ \mathsf{of} \\
& & \quad \mathsf{nil} \Rightarrow y{+\!\!+}z \\
& & \quad h : t \Rightarrow h : (\boxed{t{+\!\!+}(y{+\!\!+}z)})
\end{array}
$$

The subexpressions are boxed to highlight the common context. The two boxed subexpressions are just renamings of the respective expressions on the left-hand sides. This is sufficient to show that R is a strong improvement up to improvement and context, and hence that $(x{+\!\!+}y){+\!\!+}z \trianglerighteq\!\!\!\sim_s x{+\!\!+}(y{+\!\!+}z)$.

The example can, of course, be proved by considering all closed instances, and using coinduction. The points to note are that the proof works directly on open expressions, and that the "commmon context" (the expression "outside" the boxes above) does indeed capture variables.

A Filter Example Continuing with standard examples, consider map and filter defined by:

$$\begin{array}{ll}
\mathsf{filter} \triangleq & \mathsf{map} \triangleq \lambda m.\lambda xs.\ \mathsf{case}\ xs\ \mathsf{of} \\
\quad \lambda p.\lambda xs.\ \mathsf{case}\ xs\ \mathsf{of} & \qquad \mathsf{nil} \Rightarrow \mathsf{nil} \\
\qquad \mathsf{nil} \Rightarrow \mathsf{nil} & \qquad y : ys \Rightarrow (f\ y) : \mathsf{map}\ f\ ys \\
\qquad y : ys \Rightarrow & \\
\qquad \mathsf{if}\ p\,y\ \mathsf{then}\ y : \mathsf{filter}\ p\ ys & \\
\qquad\qquad \mathsf{else}\ \mathsf{filter}\ p\ ys &
\end{array}$$

Now we wish to prove that

$$e = \mathsf{map}\,f(\mathsf{filter}\,(p \circ f)\,xs) \cong (\mathsf{filter}\,p\,(\mathsf{map}\,f\,xs) = e'$$

where $(p \circ f)$ is just shorthand for $\lambda a.(p\,(f\,a))$, (and where the conditional expression in the definition of filter represents the obvious case-expression on booleans). We can do this by finding a context C, and a substitution σ such that $e \rhd C[e\sigma]$ and $e' \rhd C[e'\sigma]$. Observing that filter z [ ] and map f [ ] are pseudo reduction contexts, two simple calculations are sufficient to derive a suitable C and σ, namely:

$$\sigma = \{xs := ys\} \text{ and } C = \begin{array}{l}\mathsf{case}\ xs\ \mathsf{of} \\ \quad \mathsf{nil} \Rightarrow \mathsf{nil} \\ \quad y : ys \Rightarrow \mathsf{if}\ p\,(f\,y)\ \mathsf{then}\ f\,y : [\ ] \\ \qquad\qquad\qquad\qquad\quad \mathsf{else}\ [\ ].\end{array}$$

Equivalence of Fixed Point Combinators The previous examples can also be proved using more standard variations of "applicative bisimulation" (e.g., see Gordon (1995)). The following example proves a property for which the usual bisimulation techniques are rather ineffective. The problem is to prove the equivalence of two different fixed point combinators. Define the following:

$$\begin{array}{rcl}
\mathsf{Y} & \triangleq & \lambda h.h(\mathsf{D}\,h\,(\mathsf{D}\,h)) \\
\mathsf{D} & \triangleq & \lambda h.\lambda x.h(x\,x)
\end{array}$$

$$\text{and as before, } \mathsf{fix} \triangleq \lambda h.h(\mathsf{fix}\,h)$$

We can prove that $\mathsf{Y} \cong \mathsf{fix}$ by constructing a bisimulation up to improvement and context which contains the above pair of expressions. As in the previous examples, a relation which contains *only* this pair is sufficient. We begin with Y:

$$\begin{aligned} \mathsf{Y} &\mathrel{\underset{\sim}{\lhd\!\rhd}} {}^{\surd}\lambda h.h\,(\mathsf{D}\,h\,(\mathsf{D}\,h)) \\ &\mathrel{\underset{\sim}{\lhd\!\rhd}} {}^{\surd}\lambda h.h\,{}^{\surd}(h\,(\mathsf{D}\,h\,(\mathsf{D}\,h))) \\ &\mathrel{\underset{\sim}{\lhd\!\rhd}} {}^{\surd}\lambda h.h\,(\boxed{\mathsf{Y}}\,h) \end{aligned}$$

From the definition of fix we have immediately that $\mathsf{fix} \mathrel{\underset{\sim}{\lhd\!\rhd}} {}^{\surd}\lambda h.h(\boxed{\mathsf{fix}}\,h)$, and we are done. By two applications of Proposition 23 we also have that $\mathsf{Y} \mathrel{\underset{\sim}{\lhd\!\rhd}} \mathsf{fix}$. Note that if we had started with $\mathsf{Y}' \triangleq \lambda h.\mathsf{D}\,h\,(\mathsf{D}\,h)$ we would not have been able to proceed as above; but in this case $\mathsf{Y}' \mathrel{\underset{\sim_s}{\rhd}} \mathsf{Y}$ follows by just unfolding D once.

7.4 Related Proof Techniques

We have used the terminology of "bisimulation up to" from CCS (see e.g., (Milner 1989)). The closest proof technique to that presented here is Sangiorgi's "weak bisimulation up-to context and up to expansion" which we discuss below.

Functional Proof Methods In the setting of functional languages Gordon (1995) has considered a number of variations on the basic Abramsky-style applicative bisimulation, including some "small step" versions. The method of bisimulation up to improvement and context introduced here is sufficiently strong to prove all the examples from (Gordon 1995) which hold in an untyped language[5], and many of the proofs become simpler, and are certainly more calculational in style. Although Gordon's methods are "complete" in theory, in practice one must be able to write down *representations* of the bisimulations in question; it does not seem possible to write down an appropriate bisimulation to prove $\mathsf{fix} \cong \mathsf{Y}$ without judicious quantification over contexts.

Pitts (Pitts 1995) has considered a variation of "bisimulation up to context" where two expressions are bisimilar up to context if they both evaluate to weak head normal forms with the same outermost constructor (or they both diverge), and the respective terms under the constructor can be obtained by substituting bisimilar terms into a common subexpression. The weakness of Pitt's method is that the "context" in question cannot capture variables.

Process Calculus Proof Methods The proof methods described in this section were derived from the improvement theorem. However, there turns out to be a very closely related proof technique developed by Sangiorgi for the pi-calculus. This relationship has influenced the terminology we have chosen.

In Sands (1991) we noted the similarity between the definition of improvement, and the efficiency preorder for CCS investigated by Arun-Kumar and Hennessy

[5]The operational equivalence in this paper is different from Gordon's because his language is statically typed, and because we observe termination of functions. The only example equivalence from (Gordon 1995) which does not hold here is the "Take Lemma".

(Arun-Kumar and Hennessy 1991). The efficiency preorder is based on the number of internal (silent) actions performed by a process, and expressed as a refinement of weak bisimulation. As with improvement, the application of the efficiency preorder to the problem of reasoning about "ordinary" equivalence (in the case of CCS, weak bisimulation) seems to have come later; in (Sangiorgi and Milner 1992) the efficiency preorder, also dubbed *expansion*, is used to provide a "bisimulation up to" proof technique for weak bisimulation.

In the setting of the pi-calculus, Sangiorgi (1995, 1994) has used a refinement of these earlier proof techniques to great effect in studying the relationships between various calculi. The proof technique in question is called "bisimulation up to context and up to $\gtrsim$", where $\gtrsim$ is the expansion relation. We will not go into the details of this proof technique here, but it contains similar ingredients to our bisimulation up to improvement and context. There are also some important differences. We use the $\triangleright$ relation as an abstract alternative to using the one-step evaluation relation. This enables us to handle open expressions, but the proof technique fails to be complete (for example, it cannot prove that any pair of weak head normal forms are equivalent).

We summarise some informal correspondences between the notions in process calculus and the relations defined in this article in Table 1. Our attempts to complete this picture find a more exact correspondence between the proof techniques relating to bisimulation up to improvement and contexthave so far been unsuccessful.

Proces Calc.	Functional
silent transition ($\xrightarrow{\tau}$)	$\overset{\circ}{\mapsto}{}^* \overset{\bullet}{\mapsto} \overset{\circ}{\mapsto}{}^*$
strong bisimulation	cost equivalence $\underset{\sim}{\triangleleft\!\triangleright}$
weak bisimulation	operational equivalence ($\cong$) (see Gordon (1995))
expansion ($\gtrsim$)	strong improvement ($\underset{\sim}{\triangleright}_s$)
($\xrightarrow{\tau}\gtrsim$)	strict improvement ($\triangleright$)

Table 1: Informal relationships to Notions in Process Algebra

Another notion in concurrency which appears to have some connection to the Improvement Theorem, but which we have not yet investigated, is the metric-space semantics in the context of timed systems (e.g., Reed and Roscoe (1986)).

Acknowledgements Alan Jeffrey and Søren Lassen provided feedback on an earlier draft and made a number of valuable suggestions. The connections between proof techniques using the Improvement Theorem and Sangiorgi's work which have been sketched in this article where discovered in collaboration with Davide Sangiorgi. Thanks to Davide for numerous interesting discussions on the subject.

References

Abramsky, S. (1990). The lazy lambda calculus. In D. Turner (Ed.), *Research Topics in Functional Programming*, pp. 65–116. Reading, Mass.: Addison-Wesley.

Arun-Kumar, S. and M. Hennessy (1991). An efficiency preorder for processes. In *TACS*. LNCS 526.

Bird, R. and P. Wadler (1988). *Introduction to Functional Programming*. Prentice Hall.

Burstall, R. and J. Darlington (1977). A transformation system for developing recursive programs. *J. ACM 24*(1), 44–67.

Courcelle, B. (1979). Infinite trees in normal form and recursive equations having a unique solution. *Mathematical Systems Theory 13*(1), 131–180.

Felleisen, M., D. Friedman, and E. Kohlbecker (1987). A syntactic theory of sequential control. *Theoretical Computer Science 52*(1), 205–237.

Gordon, A. D. (1995). Bisimilarity as a theory of functional programming. Technical Report BRICS NS-95-3, BRICS, Aarhus University, Denmark. Preliminary version in MFPS'95.

Howe, D. J. (1989). Equality in lazy computation systems. In *The 4th Annual Symposium on Logic in Computer Science*, New York, pp. 198–203. IEEE.

Jones, N. D., C. Gomard, and P. Sestoft (1993). *Partial Evaluation and Automatic Program Generation*. Englewood Cliffs, N.J.: Prentice-Hall.

Kott, L. (1978). About transformation system: A theoretical study. In B. Robinet (Ed.), *Program Transformations*, Paris, pp. 232–247. Dunod.

Kott, L. (1982). The Mc Carthy's recursion induction principle: "oldy" but "goody". *Calcolo 19*(1), 59–69.

McCarthy, J. (1967). *A Basis for a Mathematical Theory of Computation*. Amsterdam: North-Holland.

Milner, R. (1977). Fully abstract models of the typed lambda-calculus. *Theoretical Computer Science 4*(1), 1–22.

Milner, R. (1989). *Communication and Concurrency*. Englewwood Cliffs, N.J.: Prentice-Hall.

Pettorossi, A. and M. Proietti (1995). Rules and strategies for transforming functional and logic programs. To appear ACM Computing Surveys. (Preliminary version in *Formal Program Development*, LNCS 755, Springer-Verlag).

Peyton Jones, S. L. (1987). *The Implementation of Functional Programming Languages*. Prentice-Hall International Ltd. London.

Pitts, A. M. (1995, March). An extension of Howe's "$(-)^*$" construction to yield simulation-up-to-context results. Unpublished Manuscript, Cambridge.

Plotkin, G. D. (1975). Call-by-name, Call-by-value and the λ-calculus. *Theoretical Computer Science 1*(1), 125–159.

Reed, G. and A. Roscoe (1986). Metric space models for real-time concurrency. In *ICALP'86*, Volume 298 of *LNCS*. Springer-Verlag.

Sands, D. (1990). *Calculi for Time Analysis of Functional Programs*. Ph. D. thesis, Dept. of Computing, Imperial College, Univ. of London, London.

Sands, D. (1991). Operational theories of improvement in functional languages (extended abstract). In *Proceedings of the 4th Glasgow Workshop on Functional Programming* (Skye, Scotland), pp. 298–311. Springer-Verlag.

Sands, D. (1993). A naïve time analysis and its theory of cost equivalence. TOPPS Rep. D-173, DIKU. Also in *Logic and Comput.*, *5*, 4, pp. 495-541, 1995.

Sands, D. (1995a). Higher-order expression procedures. In *Proceeding of the ACM SIGPLAN Syposium on Partial Evaluation and Semantics-Based Program Manipulation, PEPM'95*, New York, pp. 190–201. ACM.

Sands, D. (1995b). Total correctness by local improvement in program transformation. In *POPL'95*. ACM Press. Extended version in (Sands 1996b).

Sands, D. (1996a). Proving the correctness of recursion-based automatic program transformations. *Theoretical Computer Science A*(167), 193–233. Preliminary version in TAPSOFT'95, LNCS 915.

Sands, D. (1996b). Total correctness by local improvement in the transformation of functional programs. *ACM Transactions on Programming Languages and Systems (TOPLAS) 18*(2), 175–234.

Sangiorgi, D. (1994). Locality and non-interleaving semantics in calculi for mobile processes. Technical report, LFCS, University of Edinburgh, Edinburgh, U.K.

Sangiorgi, D. (1995). Lazy functions and mobile processes. Rapport de recherche 2515, INRIA Sophia Antipolis.

Sangiorgi, D. and R. Milner (1992). The problem of "weak bisimulation up to". In *Proceedings of CONCUR '92*, Number 789 in Lecture Notes in Computer Science. Springer-Verlag.

Wadler, P. (1989). The concatenate vanishes. Univ. of Glasgow, Glasgow, Scotland. Preliminary version circulated on the fp mailing list, 1987.

Wadler, P. (1990). Deforestation: Transforming programs to eliminate trees. *Theoretical Computer Science 73*(1), 231–248. Preliminary version in ESOP 88, Lecture Notes in Computer Science, vol. 300.

The coverage of operational semantics

Scott F. Smith

Abstract

Techniques of operational semantics do not apply universally to all language varieties: techniques that work for simple functional languages may not apply to more realistic languages with features such as objects and memory effects. We focus mainly on the characterization of the so-called finite elements. The presence of finite elements in a semantics allows for an additional powerful induction mechanism. We show that in some languages a reasonable notion of finite element may be defined, but for other languages this is problematic, and we analyse the reasons for these difficulties.

We develop a formal theory of language embeddings and establish a number of properties of embeddings. More complex languages are given semantics by embedding them into simpler languages. Embeddings may be used to establish more general results and avoid reproving some results. It also gives us a formal metric to describe the gap between different languages. Dimensions of the untyped programming language design space addressed here include functions, injections, pairs, objects, and memories.

1 Introduction

This paper is an exploration of a space of (untyped, deterministic) languages to determine what fundamental operational notions may be fruitfully defined.

A full and faithful notion of equivalence may be defined over an operational semantics via the Morris/Plotkin notion of operational/observational equivalence between program expressions, $\cong$. Operational equivalence has also been shown to yield good notions of equivalence for languages with memories (Mason and Talcott 1991), explicit control operators (Talcott 1989), types and objects (Gordon and Rees 1996), and distributed objects (Agha, Mason, Smith, and Talcott 1992).

It is important to characterize what "full and faithful" means: it is full in the sense that as many programs are equivalent as is possible, and it is faithful in the sense that we do not go overboard and equate programs that have differing behaviours. Operational equivalence $a \cong b$ is defined to precisely capture this notion: two program fragments are equivalent unless some use inside a larger program text can distinguish the two. This program text can be viewed as a particular "test" of a. Letting C denote a program text and $C[a]$ the result of placing a in some "hole" in this text, we then may define $a \cong b$ as $C[a]$ and $C[b]$ having the same testing outcome. For many languages, termination suffices as the observation. Thus, to prove operational equivalence $a \cong b$, one supposes for arbitrary context C that $C[a]$ terminates and establishes that $C[b]$ also terminates, by induction on the size of $C[a]$'s computation (and, vice-versa).

It is a difficult question how operational equivalences $a \cong b$ may be established in practice (see (Talcott 1997) in this volume for more on this topic). Using computational induction as outlined above to directly establish operational equivalences is in fact very difficult. Even proving $1 + 1 \cong 2$ is difficult since a context could make many copies of $1 + 1$ (if for instance $1 + 1$ occurred in a function which was being passed to another function) before evaluating it. However, proofs are possible. A number of alternate characterizations of $\cong$ have been developed to make proofs of equivalence much simpler, including bisimulation (Abramsky 1990), applicative orderings (Bloom 1990), and **ciu** equivalence (Mason and Talcott 1991). These alternate characterizations may be shown to be the same as $\cong$ (a so-called *fully abstract* alternate equivalence). Bisimulation equivalences give rise to a coinduction principle which makes establishing equivalences easier; **ciu** equivalences still often must be established by computational induction, but the inductions are considerably simpler. Applicative orderings are very close in spirit to bisimulation orderings; in many settings the difference between the two could be called trivial.

The focus of this paper is the search for additional proof techniques for establishing fully abstract equivalences and other properties of programs. The main focus is the additional inductive structure of the finite or ω-algebraic elements in a domain. To review very briefly, the finite elements of a domain are the elements that are the lub of no infinite $\sqsubseteq$-directed set.

$$d \text{ is finite iff for all } \sqsubseteq\text{-directed sets } D \text{ with } d \sqsubseteq \bigsqcup D, d \sqsubseteq d_0 \text{ for some } d_0 \in D$$

Then, ω-algebraicity is the property that any domain element d can be decomposed into its finite elements:

$$\text{for all } d, d = \bigsqcup\{d_0 \mid d_0 \text{ is finite and } d_0 \sqsubseteq d\}$$

This equivalence allows a property of d to be proved by instead proving the property for each $d_0 \sqsubseteq d$ (assuming continuity also holds). If the finite elements also may be stratified into finite ranks $1, 2, \ldots, n, \ldots$, this gives rise to the possibility of proving properties of d by proving it for all $d_0 \sqsubseteq d$ by induction on the finite rank of d_0. This is very important because it gives a new, and often powerful, induction principle.

A closely related property is fixed point induction (Scott 1976). The greatest utility of the finite elements lies in the proof principle of rank induction, as just mentioned. For special cases of d it is possible to consider special forms of $\sqsubseteq$-ordered chain. One such example is fixed point induction, which is based on the finite approximation set

$$\mathit{fix}(d) = \bigsqcup\{d(\bot), d(d(\bot)), \ldots, \overbrace{d(d(\ldots d(}^{n}\bot)\ldots), \ldots\}$$

for fixed point $fix(d)$. As in the case of finite elements, it is then possible to prove a property of the fixed point by proving a property of the finite approximants, by induction on n. So, even if ω-algebraicity cannot be established, there still may be particular finitary decompositions that lead to useful proof principles. Another example of the use of rank induction is found in the ideal model construction (MacQueen, Plotkin, and Sethi 1984), where it is used to give semantics to recursive types.

The obvious solution for defining finite elements is to work in a domain that models the language. The inductive structure is usually present in a domain directly by its manner of definition (Scott 1976). However, it is well-known that for many languages it is difficult to define a domain which has a notion of equivalence that is fully abstract. In fact, none of the languages studied in this paper have such a model extant in the literature. Our alternate approach here is to build finite elements out of the program syntax. This approach has proved successful for a particular simple functional language (Mason, Smith, and Talcott 1996). Syntactic projection functions $\pi^n(e)$ are defined within the programming language to project expression e to be a finite expression of level n. In this operational theory an additional powerful induction principle is thus obtained: induction on the rank of the finite elements.

Since memory-based languages often contain cyclical structures formed by memory self-references (for instance a function is in a cell and the function body contains a reference to the cell it is in), the idea of applying this technique to memory-based languages is particularly appealing. One problem in particular it could address is the question of a semantic definition of types in the presence of memory, a problem that is currently open.

So, the main goal of this paper is to address how the concept of finite elements generalizes to a broader class of languages. We will show that in some cases an effective finite element structure may be defined, and in other cases this cannot be established in a fully abstract manner (*i.e.*, finiteness may only be established with respect to an equivalence which is not operational equivalence $\cong$), showing the semantic tools which may be brought to bear on certain varieties of language are currently limited in this regard.

We want to consider a range of languages rather than addressing a single programming language. A series of (untyped) programming languages $\mathbb{L}$ is studied. $\mathbb{L}_{\mathrm{inj}}$ contains only the call-by-value λ-calculus and injections. $\mathbb{L}_{\mathrm{bpn}}$ adds booleans, numbers, and pairs. $\mathbb{L}_{\mathrm{obj}}$ has simple objects, and $\mathbb{L}_{\mathrm{m}}$ has a memory. We will not explicitly address control operators, typed languages, or concurrent or distributed computation. All languages we study follow the evaluation order most common in programming languages today, namely function application is call-by-value, pairing and injection are strict, and evaluation never takes place inside a λ.

Rather than presenting multiple semantic definitions, we give semantics to languages by defining language embeddings that map high-level languages down to low-level languages that lack many of the high-level features. In particular, all languages are mapped down to languages with injections only, $\mathbb{L}_{\text{inj}}$. This approach makes clear what the "difference" between languages is, and helps us focus on the particular difficulties that arise in some languages. A theory of embeddings is developed and a number of theorems proved to better characterize what can be embedded in what and how well. The mappings also allow us to define some hybrid forms of language quite easily, and in certain cases allows the "lifting" of theorems from low-level to high-level languages. The approach of defining language features by embeddings has a long history going back to Strachey (Milne and Strachey 1976). We obtain some interesting results about these mappings, and the mappings themselves are an additional topic of the paper.

An outline of the paper is as follows. A language-independent framework for operational semantics and language embeddings is defined in Section 2. Next, in Section 3 the injection language $\mathbb{L}_{\text{inj}}$ is studied in detail and its finite element theory developed. Then, in Sections 4 and 5 a wider space of languages is explored via embeddings into $\mathbb{L}_{\text{inj}}$. Section 5 presents a memory language $\mathbb{L}_{\text{m}}$ in full detail. Conclusions regarding what succeeds and what fails are found in Section 6.

2 A Framework for Operational Semantics

Before studying particular languages we define a simple semantic framework for languages with an operational evaluation relation, and for embeddings between languages. It is general enough to encompass all languages studied herein, but is not intended as a general framework along the lines of (Mosses 1992). In particular it will not fully capture nondeterministic or concurrent languages. It will allow for a general notion of language embedding to be defined. We will give definitions and properties that hold over an arbitrary operational structure; these definitions will then not have to be repeated for each language studied.

2.1 Operational Structures

We begin with an official definition of a language structure, called an *operational structure*. Languages are taken to come with an operational evaluation relation. Some of the language mappings need to be based on the grammatical structure of the language, so a general notation for operators op is also defined in the tradition of a theory of arities (Harper, Honsell, and Plotkin 1993). All languages are defined with respect to a single shared set of program variables $\mathbb{X}$ for simplicity.

DEFINITION 2.1 A Language $\mathbb{L}$ has structure $\langle \mathbb{E}, \mathbb{V}, \mathbb{O}, \mapsto \rangle$ where

$\mathbb{E}$ is the set of expressions of the language

$\mathbb{V} \subseteq \mathbb{E}$ are the value expressions

$\mathbb{O}$ are the operators. Each operator op $\in \mathbb{O}$ can be viewed as a map from $(\mathbb{X}^{m_1} \times \mathbb{E}) \times \ldots \times (\mathbb{X}^{m_n} \times \mathbb{E})$ to $\mathbb{E}$ for some values of n and m_i, $1 \leq i \leq n$ associated with op.

$\mapsto \in \mathbb{E} \times \mathbb{E}$ is the evaluation relation, mapping expressions to final computation results. It is reflexive on values.

Our notion of operational evaluation relation maps expressions to expressions; although this may seem restrictive, it is possible to define evaluation relations for languages with control primitives and effects in a purely syntactic fashion (Mason and Talcott 1991; Felleisen and Hieb 1992). We impose some informal regularity on the notation used for languages. $\mathbb{L}$ is implicitly $\langle \mathbb{E}, \mathbb{V}, \mathbb{O}, \mapsto \rangle$, $\mathbb{L}_{\mathsf{inj}(i)}$ taken to be $\langle \mathbb{E}_{\mathsf{inj}(i)}, \mathbb{V}_{\mathsf{inj}(i)}, \mathbb{O}_{\mathsf{inj}(i)}, \mapsto_{\mathsf{inj}(i)} \rangle$, $\mathbb{L}'$ taken to be $\langle \mathbb{E}', \mathbb{V}', \mathbb{O}', \mapsto' \rangle$, etc. We let x, y, z range over $\mathbb{X}$, v range over $\mathbb{V}$, a, b, c, d, e range over $\mathbb{E}$, and op range over $\mathbb{O}$. For the remainder of this section we develop results for an arbitrary fixed language $\mathbb{L}$. Each definition of this section, *e.g.* $\cong$, is applied to a particular language by subscripting: $\cong_{\mathrm{m}}$ indicates the $\cong$ relation for language $\mathbb{L}_{\mathrm{m}}$.

The operators are a general notation which allows each field to bind some number of variables. In each product $(\mathbb{X}^{m_i} \times \mathbb{E})$, the variables bind free occurrences in the expression. An example operator is

$$\texttt{sample} - \mathsf{op}(x.y.e_1, e_2, z.e_3)$$

—free x and y in e_1 and free z in e_3 are bound, and no other free variables in e_1, e_2, e_3 are bound. We will use this informal notation of writing out an example to define the arity of an operator.

The set of expressions $\mathbb{E}$ is constrained to be the least superset of $\mathbb{X}$ closed under the operators in $\mathbb{O}$. We will implicitly coerce between operators of one language and operators of another language, provided the arities of the two operators are the same. Furthermore, if an expression $e \in \mathbb{L}_1$ is constructed with operators which are all in $\mathbb{O}_2$ for some $\mathbb{L}_2$, then e may be implicitly coerced to be in $\mathbb{E}_2$ by the obvious pointwise operator mapping.

A *closed expression* is an expression with no free variables; $\mathbb{E}^{\emptyset}$ is the set of all closed expressions. $a[b/x]$ is the result of substituting b for the free occurrences of x in a taking care not to trap free variables of b. *Contexts* $C \in \mathbb{C}$ are expressions with holes "•" punched in them, and $C[e]$ denotes placing e in the hole(s) in C, possibly incurring the capture of some free variables in e.

A *value substitution* is a finite map from variables to values. We let σ range over value substitutions. $a[\sigma]$ is the result of simultaneous substitution of free occurrences of $x \in \mathrm{Dom}(\sigma)$ in a by $\sigma(x)$, again taking care not to trap variables.

2.2 Operational Ordering and Equivalence

In this section we give basic definitions of orderings and equivalence that are uniform with respect to the language studied.

DEFINITION 2.2 ($\precsim$, $\cong$)

$$a \precsim b \text{ iff for all } C \in \mathbb{C} \text{ such that } C[a], C[b] \in \mathbb{E}^{\emptyset}, C[a]\downarrow \text{ implies } C[b]\downarrow$$
$$a \cong b \text{ iff } a \precsim b \text{ and } b \precsim a$$

Note, a is *defined* (written $a\downarrow$) if it evaluates to a result: $a \mapsto b$ for some b. And, $a\uparrow$ if $a\downarrow$ fails to hold. In this definition of observational equivalence we are implicitly taking termination as the single observable property because it is a proper notion of observation for the languages studied herein. A more complete treatment would allow for a more general notion of observation than just termination.

LEMMA 2.3 (ELEMENTARY $\precsim$ / $\cong$ PROPERTIES) (i) $\precsim$ is transitive and reflexive (a pre-order).

(ii) $\cong$ is an equivalence relation.

(iii) $\precsim$ is a pre-congruence, i.e. $a \precsim b$ implies $C[a] \precsim C[b]$.

(iv) $\cong$ is a congruence, i.e. $a \cong b$ implies $C[a] \cong C[b]$.

Over any operational structure, it is also possible to define an operational notion of directed set. This is simply a $\precsim$-directed set of expressions in place of a $\sqsubseteq$-directed set of domain elements.

DEFINITION 2.4 ($\precsim$-DIRECTED SETS) A set A is *directed* iff for all a, b, if $a, b \in A$, then there is some $c \in A$ where $a \precsim c$ and $b \precsim c$.

We let A, B range over directed sets with finitely many free variables[1], and V range over directed sets with $V \subseteq \mathbb{V}$. We allow directed sets of expressions to be used as subexpressions with the convention $C[A] = \{C[a] \mid a \in A\}$. Value substitutions σ extend pointwise to sets of expressions: $A[\sigma] = \{a[\sigma] \mid a \in A\}$.

The first hurdle encountered is the lack of an operational analogue of a lub operator $\sqcup$. Some chains may not even have an upper bound because each element of the chain could be a function with a finite domain, but the lub could have an infinite domain and be uncomputable. Thus, $\precsim$ is not complete.

A number of solutions to this problem are possible. For one, we could restrict the directed sets A to be recursively enumerable (r.e.) sets. The lub will also be r.e. since A is r.e. This approach may be effectively applied to the simply typed λ-calculus (Freyd, Mulry, Rosolini, and Scott 1990).

A variation would be to further require that the directed set A is *internally* represented by a function f in $\mathbb{L}$ such that `f (n)` for natural number n produces the n-th element of the directed set, and to have an expression `lub (f)` in the language

[1]For technical reasons, we only allow directed sets with finitely many free variables, otherwise a directed set may contain all the variables $\mathbb{X}$ free and problems may arise in obtaining fresh variables.

which internally computes the lub of f (this argument assumes the language $\mathbb{L}$ has functions and numbers). Unfortunately, `lub` must then have the ability to dovetail computations in the directed set, and this will require new syntax in the language and change the underlying equivalence. So, this approach may be of limited value.

It thus does not appear to be feasible to construct structures isomorphic to domains directly on expressions. It is however possible to make progress by using $\precsim$-directed sets of expressions as a space over which an ordering is defined (Smith 1992). A simple pre-ordering on directed sets of expressions, $\{\cdot\} \precsim \{\cdot\}$, is defined for this purpose. This pre-ordering has the property that $a \precsim b$ iff $\{a\} \precsim \{b\}$, meaning that it fully and faithfully generalizes $\precsim$.

DEFINITION 2.5 (SET RELATIONS $\{\cdot\} \precsim \{\cdot\}$, $\{\cdot\} \cong \{\cdot\}$) For A, B directed, define

$$\begin{array}{lll} A \precsim B & \text{iff} & \text{for all } a \in A \text{ and for all } C \in \mathbb{C} \text{ such that } C[A], C[B] \subseteq \mathbb{E}^{\emptyset}, \\ & & \text{if } C[a]\downarrow \text{ then there exists a } b \in B \text{ such that } C[b]\downarrow. \\ A \cong B & \text{iff} & A \precsim B \text{ and } B \precsim A \end{array}$$

This ordering is not quite what one might initially expect, as the $b \in B$ may be chosen depending on the particular testing context C which exercises $a \in A$. Therein lies the power of the ordering. From the context of use it will be possible to disambiguate between $\precsim$ and $\{\cdot\} \precsim \{\cdot\}$. Some elementary properties of $\{\cdot\} \precsim \{\cdot\}$ include the following.

LEMMA 2.6 (ELEMENTARY $\{\cdot\} \precsim \{\cdot\}/\{\cdot\} \cong \{\cdot\}$ PROPERTIES) (i) $\{\cdot\} \precsim \{\cdot\}$ is a pre-congruence: $A \precsim B$ implies $C[A] \precsim C[B]$.

(ii) $\{\cdot\} \cong \{\cdot\}$ is a congruence: $A \cong B$ implies $C[A] \cong C[B]$.

(iii) $\{a\} \precsim \{b\}$ iff $a \precsim b$.

(iv) $A \precsim \{b\}$ iff for all $a \in A$, $a \precsim b$.

(v) $a \in A$ implies $\{a\} \precsim A$.

This ordering will be used to characterize the finite expressions.

DEFINITION 2.7 (FINITE EXPRESSIONS $\mathbb{E}^{\omega}$) The set of finite expressions $\mathbb{E}^{\omega}$ is defined by

$$\mathbb{E}^{\omega} = \{b \in \mathbb{E}^{\emptyset} \mid \text{for all closed } A, \text{ if } \{b\} \precsim A \text{ then } b \precsim a \text{ for some } a \in A\}$$

Note that the previous development was language-independent: the ordering $\{\cdot\} \precsim \{\cdot\}$ was successfully defined over any language $\mathbb{L}$. Much of the power of this relation is derived from its generality. This completes the brief general theory of languages. We next define a theory of embeddings between languages.

2.3 Language Embeddings

For the purpose of embedding one programming language in another, a general theory of language embeddings is now defined. Other closely related notions of language embedding have been previously defined (Felleisen 1991; Mitchell 1993; Riecke 1993). Our definitions combine ideas from these approaches. The embeddings will be used to give semantics to a number of languages in Section 4, and will enable a number of properties to be proved concerning the relation between equivalences in one language and equivalences in a similar language.

DEFINITION 2.8 (EMBEDDING) Given high- and low-level languages $\mathbb{L}_h$ and $\mathbb{L}_l$, a sound embedding $[\![\cdot]\!] \in \mathbb{L}_h \to \mathbb{L}_l$ is defined as maps $[\![\cdot]\!] \in \mathbb{E}_h \to \mathbb{E}_l$ $[\![\cdot]\!] \in \mathbb{C}_h \to \mathbb{C}_l$ and an initial context $C_{\text{init}} \in \mathbb{C}_l$ such that

(i) For $C \in \mathbb{C}_h, e \in \mathbb{E}_h$, $[\![C[e]]\!] = [\![C]\!][[\![e]\!]]$

(ii) For closed $e \in \mathbb{E}_h$, $e \downarrow_h$ iff $C_{\text{init}}[[\![e]\!]] \downarrow_l$

C_{init} is not $\bullet$ for embeddings that require a special initial context; for most embeddings, C_{init} will just be $\bullet$. Our (i) is Mitchell's (R1) condition, and (ii) is similar to Felleisen's condition 2 of his Eliminability notion (Felleisen 1991).

For brevity in this presentation, we will generally not define $\downarrow_h$ and $\mapsto_h$ for the high-level languages. We will often leave $\mapsto_h$ undefined and take (ii) above as a *definition* of $\downarrow_h$. Since operational equivalence needs only to have termination defined, termination alone is a sufficient operational characterization for our purposes. Sound embeddings will thus only need to satisfy (i). Value set definitions $\mathbb{V}_h$ will similarly not be needed. We take $[\![A]\!]$ to abbreviate $\{[\![a]\!] \mid a \in A\}$.

It is useful to consider the induced ordering $[\![a]\!] \lessapprox_l [\![b]\!]$. Since programs in $\mathbb{L}_h$ will be able to be tested by contexts that are not in the codomain of the translation, this equivalence may be more fine-grained than $\lessapprox_h$.

LEMMA 2.9 If $[\![a]\!] \lessapprox_l [\![b]\!]$ then $a \lessapprox_h b$; and, if $[\![A]\!] \lessapprox_l [\![B]\!]$ then $A \lessapprox_h B$.

PROOF: For arbitrary C, suppose $C[a] \downarrow_h$, show $C[b] \downarrow_h$, assuming $[\![a]\!] \lessapprox_l [\![b]\!]$. Since the embedding is sound, $[\![C[a]]\!] = [\![C]\!][[\![a]\!]]$ and $C_{\text{init}}[[\![C]\!][[\![a]\!]]] \downarrow_l$ and thus by assumption $C_{\text{init}}[[\![C]\!][[\![b]\!]]] \downarrow_l$, allowing us to conclude $C[b] \downarrow_h$. The proof for the set-based ordering is similar, noting that if $[\![A]\!]$ is directed, A also is. □

An even more desirable property of embeddings is *full abstraction*, Mitchell's (R2). This is the case when the $\mathbb{L}_l$ contexts cannot expose any more structure than the $\mathbb{L}_h$ contexts already had exposed.

DEFINITION 2.10 An embedding $[\![\cdot]\!] \in \mathbb{L}_h \to \mathbb{L}_l$ is *fully abstract* if $a \lessapprox_h b$ iff $[\![a]\!] \lessapprox_l [\![b]\!]$. It is *set fully abstract* if $A \lessapprox_h B$ iff $[\![A]\!] \lessapprox_l [\![B]\!]$.

Set full abstraction trivially implies full abstraction by the definitions, but not the converse. (It is an open question whether the converse holds).

Full abstraction imposes a strong global structure on the embedding, one that many embeddings will fail to satisfy. It is also useful to consider imposing local structure on the embedding. The first additional constraint we impose is the notion of a *parametric* embedding.

DEFINITION 2.11 (PARAMETRIC EMBEDDING) Given a sound embedding $[\![\cdot]\!] \in \mathbb{L}_h \rightarrow \mathbb{L}_l$, it is *parametric* if for each op $\in \mathbb{O}_h$, there exists an expression e_{op} with $\text{FreeVars}(e_{\text{op}}) = \{y_1, \ldots, y_n\}$ such that

$$[\![\text{op}(\overline{x_1}.e_1, \ldots, \overline{x_n}.e_n)]\!] = e_{\text{op}}\,\{[\![e_1]\!]/y_1, \ldots, [\![e_n]\!]/y_n\}$$

where $a\,\{b/x\}$ indicates a substitution of all free occurrences of variable x by b, *allowing* the free variables of b to be captured in a. Furthermore, there is a $\mathbb{L}_l$ context C_{var} such that

$$[\![x]\!] = C_{\text{var}}[x]$$

C_{var} interprets variables; in more complex embeddings such as state and control, variables cannot just map to themselves. The reader may now want to look ahead to Definitions 4.3, 4.18, and 5.3, which contain examples of parametric embeddings. Parametric embeddings are closely related to Felleisen's condition 3, so-called "Macro Eliminability" (Felleisen 1991).

One other important property of an embedding is the syntax of some high-level operators may be preserved by the embedding.

DEFINITION 2.12 (HOMOMORPHIC EMBEDDING) A parametric embedding $[\![\cdot]\!] \in \mathbb{L}_h \rightarrow \mathbb{L}_l$ is a *homomorphic embedding* with respect to operators $\mathbb{O}$ if

(i) $C_{\text{init}} = \bullet$

(ii) $\mathbb{O} \subseteq \mathbb{O}_h \cap \mathbb{O}_l$, and the arity of operators in $\mathbb{O}$ is the same in $\mathbb{O}_l$ and $\mathbb{O}_h$

(iii) for each op $\in \mathbb{O}$, the embedding is homomorphic:

$$[\![\text{op}(\overline{x_1}.e_1, \ldots, \overline{x_m}.e_n)]\!] = \text{op}(\overline{x_1}.[\![e_1]\!], \ldots, \overline{x_m}.[\![e_n]\!])$$

(iv) $C_{\text{var}} = \bullet$

In terms of equivalence, homomorphic embeddings preserve equations that only use operators in $\mathbb{O}$. This allows equations in the low-level language to be lifted to the higher language, avoiding the need to re-prove them.

LEMMA 2.13 (LIFTING) If $a \precsim_l b$ and a and b only use operators in $\mathbb{O}$, and $[\![\cdot]\!] \in \mathbb{L}_h \rightarrow \mathbb{L}_l$ is a homomorphic embedding with respect to $\mathbb{O}$, then $a \precsim_h b$. Similarly, $A \precsim_l B$ implies $A \precsim_h B$ when A and B only use operators in $\mathbb{O}$.

PROOF: $[\![a]\!] = a$ and $[\![b]\!] = b$ in this case; the result then follows from the fact that all testing contexts $C \in \mathbb{C}_h$ can be mapped to $[\![C]\!] \in \mathbb{C}_l$. □

The main advantage of homomorphic embeddings is the ability to use the Lifting Lemma. Our notion of homomorphic embedding is closely related to Felleisen's eliminability definition, condition 1 (Felleisen 1991). Definitions 4.3 and 4.18 below are examples of homomorphic embeddings.

Embeddings compose in the obvious fashion.

LEMMA 2.14 Define $[\![\cdot]\!] \in \mathbb{L}_1 \to \mathbb{L}_3$ as the composition of $[\![\cdot]\!]_1 \in \mathbb{L}_1 \to \mathbb{L}_2$ and $[\![\cdot]\!]_2 \in \mathbb{L}_2 \to \mathbb{L}_3$ formed by defining $[\![\cdot]\!] \in \mathbb{E}_1 \to \mathbb{E}_3$ as $[\![\cdot]\!]_2 \circ [\![\cdot]\!]_1$.

(i) $[\![\cdot]\!] \in \mathbb{L}_1 \to \mathbb{L}_3$ is a sound embedding.

(ii) If $[\![\cdot]\!]_1$ and $[\![\cdot]\!]_2$ are both parametric (resp., homomorphic with respect to $\mathbb{O}_1$ and $\mathbb{O}_2$) embeddings, then $[\![\cdot]\!]$ is also a parametric (resp., homomorphic with respect to $\mathbb{O}_1 \cap \mathbb{O}_2$) embedding.

3 The Injection Languages $\mathbb{L}_{\mathsf{inj}(k)}$

The development up to this point has been independent of a particular language. We now study a particular family of languages in-depth, the family of injection languages $\mathbb{L}_{\mathsf{inj}(1)}, \mathbb{L}_{\mathsf{inj}(2)}, \ldots$. Following this section, we define a series of languages via embeddings into $\mathbb{L}_{\mathsf{inj}(k)}$. Pure λ-expressions plus injections provide just enough syntax to allow a wide range of programming languages to be faithfully embedded. The injections $\mathtt{inj}_i(a)$ serve to wrap high-level expressions a to distinguish different sorts; Lemma 4.5 below shows why the pure λ-calculus will not suffice as an embedding target language. The injection languages consist of the untyped call-by-value λ-calculus augmented with a finite number of injections. The language $\mathbb{L}_{\mathsf{inj}(k)}$ has injections $\mathtt{inj}_1(a), \ldots, \mathtt{inj}_k(a)$.

DEFINITION 3.1 ($\mathbb{L}_{\mathsf{inj}(k)}$) For $k \in \mathbb{N}$, define

$$\mathbb{L}_{\mathsf{inj}(k)} = \langle \mathbb{E}_{\mathsf{inj}(k)}, \mathbb{V}_{\mathsf{inj}(k)}, \mathbb{O}_{\mathsf{inj}(k)}, \mapsto_{\mathsf{inj}(k)} \rangle$$

as follows.

$$\mathbb{O}_{\mathsf{inj}(k)} = \{\mathtt{app}(a, b), \mathtt{lambda}(x.a)\} \cup \bigcup_{1 \leq i \leq k} \{\mathtt{inj}_i(a), \mathtt{out}_i(a), \mathtt{is}_i(a)\}$$

$$\mathbb{V}_{\mathsf{inj}(k)} = \mathbb{X} \cup \{\mathtt{lambda}(x.a) \mid a \in \mathbb{E}_{\mathsf{inj}(k)}\} \cup \bigcup_{1 \leq i \leq k} \{\mathtt{inj}_i(v) \mid v \in \mathbb{V}_{\mathsf{inj}(k)}\}$$

$\mapsto_{\mathsf{inj}(k)}$ is defined below.

For the remainder of this section, the k in $\mathbb{L}_{\mathsf{inj}(k)}$ is taken to be some arbitrary fixed value and we write $\mathbb{L}_{\mathsf{inj}}$, $\mathbb{E}_{\mathsf{inj}}$, etc. Several syntactic abbreviations will be made to aid in readability of programs through the use of more conventional notation. These include

$$\begin{array}{rcl}
\lambda x.a & = & \texttt{lambda}(x.a) \\
a\,\texttt{(}b\texttt{)} & = & \texttt{app}(a,b) \\
\texttt{let}\ x = a\ \texttt{in}\ b & = & (\lambda x.b)\,\texttt{(}a\texttt{)} \\
\texttt{bot} & = & (\lambda x.x\,\texttt{(}x\texttt{)}\,)\,\texttt{(}\lambda x.x\,\texttt{(}x\texttt{)}\,\texttt{)} \\
\texttt{etrue} & = & \lambda x.\lambda y.x\,\texttt{(}x\texttt{)} \\
\texttt{efalse} & = & \lambda x.\lambda y.y\,\texttt{(}y\texttt{)} \\
\texttt{eif}(a,b,c) & = & a\,\texttt{(}\lambda x.b\texttt{)}\ \texttt{(}\lambda x.c\texttt{)}\ \text{for fresh } x \\
\texttt{fix} & = & \lambda y.(\lambda x.\lambda z.y\,\texttt{(}x\,\texttt{(}x\texttt{)}\,\texttt{)}\,\texttt{(}z\texttt{)}\,)\,\texttt{(}\lambda x.\lambda z.y\,\texttt{(}x\,\texttt{(}x\texttt{)}\,\texttt{)}\,\texttt{(}z\texttt{)}\,\texttt{)} \\
a \circ b & = & \lambda x.a\,\texttt{(}b\,\texttt{(}x\texttt{)}\,\texttt{)}
\end{array}$$

Booleans and conditional are encoded via the standard method. The "e" prefixing `etrue`, `efalse`, `eif` indicates that these are encoded notions of these constructs and not primitives. Observe typewriter font parentheses $a\,\texttt{(}b\texttt{)}$ abbreviate function application. `fix` is a call-by-value version of the standard fixed-point combinator for functionals.

3.1 Operational Semantics

The operational semantics of expressions is given by a single-step evaluation relation $\mapsto_{\text{inj}}$, using the convenient notion of a reduction context (a.k.a. evaluation context) from (Felleisen, Friedman, and Kohlbecker 1987). The *redices* are expressions of the form $v\,\texttt{(}a\texttt{)}$, $\texttt{is}_i(v)$, or $\texttt{out}_i(v)$. Redices are either immediately available for execution, $\texttt{out}_i(\texttt{inj}_i(a))$, or are *stuck*, $\texttt{out}_i(\lambda x.x)$. In this presentation stuck computations are treated as divergent for simplicity. Reduction contexts $\mathbb{R}_{\text{inj}}$ determine the subexpression that is to be reduced next.

DEFINITION 3.2 (REDUCTION CONTEXTS $\mathbb{R}_{\text{inj}}$) The set of reduction contexts, $R \in \mathbb{R}_{\text{inj}}$, is the least subset of $\mathbb{C}_{\text{inj}}$ that includes

$$\bullet,\ R\,\texttt{(}e\texttt{)}\,,\ v\,\texttt{(}R\texttt{)}\,,\ \texttt{inj}_i(R),\ \texttt{out}_i(R),\ \texttt{is}_i(R)$$

for all $e \in \mathbb{E}_{\text{inj}}$, $v \in \mathbb{V}_{\text{inj}}$, $R \in \mathbb{R}_{\text{inj}}$, and $1 \le i \le k$.

In an expression $R[a]$, R denotes the continuation for the computation a. Reduction contexts are used in evaluation as follows. In order to perform one step of computation of some non-value expression a, it is uniquely decomposed into $a = R[b]$ for some R and redex b by the following Lemma. Uniqueness of decomposition implies evaluation is deterministic.

LEMMA 3.3 (DECOMPOSITION) Either $a \in \mathbb{V}_{\text{inj}}$ or a can be written uniquely as $R[b]$ where b is a redex.

Definition 3.4 (Evaluation $\mapsto_{\text{inj}}$) The evaluation relation $\mapsto_{\text{inj}}$ for $\mathbb{L}_{\text{inj}(k)}$ is the transitive, reflexive closure of the single-step evaluation relation $\mapsto^1_{\text{inj}}$, which is generated by the following clauses:

$$\begin{array}{lrcl}
\text{(beta)} & R[(\lambda x.a)\,(v)\,] & \mapsto^1_{\text{inj}} & R[a\,[v/x]] \\
\text{(out)} & R[\mathtt{out}_i(\mathtt{inj}_i(v))] & \mapsto^1_{\text{inj}} & R[v] \\
\text{(is-t)} & R[\mathtt{is}_i(\mathtt{inj}_i(v))] & \mapsto^1_{\text{inj}} & R[\mathtt{etrue}] \\
\text{(is-f)} & R[\mathtt{is}_i(\mathtt{inj}_j(v))] & \mapsto^1_{\text{inj}} & R[\mathtt{efalse}] \text{ where } i \neq j \\
\text{(is-lam)} & R[\mathtt{is}_i(\lambda x.a)] & \mapsto^1_{\text{inj}} & R[\mathtt{efalse}]
\end{array}$$

Note it is possible to compute with open expressions using the above definition. A few simple properties concerning computation are the following.

Lemma 3.5 (Uniformity of evaluation) (i) $b_0 = b_1$ if $a \mapsto^1_{\text{inj}} b_0$ and $a \mapsto^1_{\text{inj}} b_1$

(ii) $a \mapsto^1_{\text{inj}} b$ implies $a\,[\sigma] \mapsto^1_{\text{inj}} b\,[\sigma]$

(iii) $a \mapsto^1_{\text{inj}} b$ implies $R[a] \mapsto^1_{\text{inj}} R[b]$

We now define an alternative but equivalent notion of $\sqsubseteq_{\text{inj}}$, restricting the space of contexts to be **c**losed **i**nstances of all **u**ses of an expression. This equivalence is thus called **ciu** equivalence, $\cong^{\text{ciu}}_{\text{inj}}$, following (Mason and Talcott 1991). $a \cong^{\text{ciu}}_{\text{inj}} b$ means a and b behave identically when closed (the *closed instances* part) and placed in any reduction context R (the *uses* part).

Definition 3.6 (ciu ordering, $\sqsubseteq^{\text{ciu}}_{\text{inj}}$)

$a \sqsubseteq^{\text{ciu}}_{\text{inj}} b$ iff for all R, σ such that $R[a\,[\sigma]], R[b\,[\sigma]]$ closed, $R[a\,[\sigma]]\downarrow$ implies $R[b\,[\sigma]]\downarrow$

Theorem 3.7 (ciu) $a \sqsubseteq_{\text{inj}} b$ iff $a \sqsubseteq^{\text{ciu}}_{\text{inj}} b$.

For a proof, see (Mason, Smith, and Talcott 1996). For this simple language it is even possible to characterize $\sqsubseteq_{\text{inj}}$ via a bisimulation ordering (Howe 1996). We now list a collection of basic $\cong_{\text{inj}}$ / $\sqsubseteq_{\text{inj}}$ properties, all easily provable from Theorem 3.7.

Lemma 3.8 (Basic $\sqsubseteq_{\text{inj}}$ / $\cong_{\text{inj}}$ properties) (i) If $a \sqsubseteq_{\text{inj}} b$, then for $v \in \mathbb{V}^{\emptyset}_{\text{inj}}$, $a\,[v/x] \sqsubseteq_{\text{inj}} b\,[v/x]$.

(ii) $\mathtt{bot} \sqsubseteq_{\text{inj}} a$.

(iii) For closed a, $a\uparrow$ iff $a \cong_{\text{inj}} \mathtt{bot}$.

(iv) $R[\mathtt{bot}] \cong_{\text{inj}} \mathtt{bot}$.

(v) $\cong_{\text{inj}}$ respects computation, i.e. $a \cong_{\text{inj}} b$ if $a \mapsto_{\text{inj}} b$.

(vi) If $a \mapsto_{\mathrm{inj}} \lambda x.b$ and $a \cong_{\mathrm{inj}} a'$ then $a' \cong_{\mathrm{inj}} \lambda x.b'$ for some $b' \cong_{\mathrm{inj}} b$.

(vii) If $a \mapsto_{\mathrm{inj}} \mathtt{inj}_i(b)$ and $a \cong_{\mathrm{inj}} a'$ then $a' \cong_{\mathrm{inj}} \mathtt{inj}_i(b')$ for some $b' \cong_{\mathrm{inj}} b$.

(viii) $a \cong_{\mathrm{inj}} \mathtt{out}_i(\mathtt{inj}_i(a))$.

(ix) If $y \notin \mathrm{FreeVars}(\lambda x.b)$, then $\lambda x.b \cong_{\mathrm{inj}} \lambda y.(\lambda x.b)\,(y)$.

(x) Extensionality: $\lambda x.a_0 \sqsubseteq_{\mathrm{inj}} \lambda x.a_1$ if and only if $(\lambda x.a_0)\,(v) \sqsubseteq_{\mathrm{inj}} (\lambda x.a_1)\,(v)$ for all values v.

Properties of the above general form may be proved across a wide range of languages (Mason and Talcott 1991; Gordon and Rees 1996; Talcott 1989). They may in theory be proved directly by induction on computation length (Talcott 1989), but it is far more effective to prove them via first establishing an alternate characterization of $\sqsubseteq_{\mathrm{inj}}$ via $\sqsubseteq^{\mathrm{ciu}}_{\mathrm{inj}}$ or a bisimulation ordering. For all of the above properties except extensionality, either **ciu** or bisimulation characterizations allow for direct proofs; extensionality is trivial to establish via a bisimulation characterization but requires some work when proved via **ciu**.

As was the case for $\sqsubseteq_{\mathrm{inj}}$, an alternate characterization of $\{\cdot\} \sqsubseteq_{\mathrm{inj}} \{\cdot\}$ is needed to facilitate proofs. An analogue of **ciu** ordering may be defined for $\{\cdot\} \sqsubseteq_{\mathrm{inj}} \{\cdot\}$. Bisimulation characterizations of $\{\cdot\} \sqsubseteq_{\mathrm{inj}} \{\cdot\}$ are also possible.

DEFINITION 3.9 (CIU SET ORDERING $\sqsubseteq^{\mathrm{ciu}}_{\mathrm{inj}}$) $A \sqsubseteq^{\mathrm{ciu}}_{\mathrm{inj}} B$ for $\sqsubseteq_{\mathrm{inj}}$-directed A and B if and only if for all $a \in A$ and for all σ, R such that $R[A[\sigma]]$ and $R[B[\sigma]]$ are sets of closed expressions, if $R[a[\sigma]]\downarrow$ then there exists $b \in B$ such that $R[b[\sigma]]\downarrow$.

The main characterization theorem is

THEOREM 3.10 (SET ORDERING CIU) $A \sqsubseteq_{\mathrm{inj}} B$ iff $A \sqsubseteq^{\mathrm{ciu}}_{\mathrm{inj}} B$.

This is Theorem 4.6 of (Mason, Smith, and Talcott 1996).

$\{\cdot\} \sqsubseteq_{\mathrm{inj}} \{\cdot\}$ has the important property of allowing fixed points to be approximated. Fixed points may be shown equivalent to their set of finite unrollings. This breaks the cycle of a fixed point and gives an induction principle for reasoning about recursive functions. We make the following abbreviation: for a functional $f = \lambda x.\lambda y.a$, define $f^0 = \lambda x.\mathtt{bot}$ and $f^{n+1} = f\,(f^n)$.

LEMMA 3.11 (FIXED POINT) For a functional f,

(i) $\{\mathtt{fix}\,(f)\} \cong_{\mathrm{inj}} \{f^n \mid n \in \mathbb{N}\}$,

(ii) $\mathtt{fix}\,(f) \cong_{\mathrm{inj}} f\,(\mathtt{fix}\,(f))$, and

(iii) for all a, $\lambda x.a \cong_{\mathrm{inj}} f\,(\lambda x.a)$ implies $\mathtt{fix}\,(f) \sqsubseteq_{\mathrm{inj}} \lambda x.a$.

3.2 Finite Elements

The problem we focus on in this paper is obtaining additional proof principles using the finite algebraic structure of the language. As mentioned in the introduction, this allows reasoning about infinite elements in terms of their finite elements since each infinite element is the lub of all smaller finite elements.

We show in this section how finite elements may be defined in an operational semantics. This material is taken from (Mason, Smith, and Talcott 1996), where complete proofs are also to be found.

With the fixed point property we saw how recursive functions could be decomposed into finite components for inductive reasoning. Similar properties could be proved for other particular structures, such as lists formed via iterative pairing. However, what would be even more desirable would be a general principle for decomposing *all* programs into finite components. The finite decomposition of functions above still does not decompose the argument or return value of the function, which may still be infinite.

The finite expressions accomplish precisely this goal: any expression may be decomposed into a set of finite approximations stratified by level k that are finite in the sense that there are only finitely many distinct approximations up to operational equivalence at any level k. The finite decomposition of expressions is critical to constructions that define self-referential structures (MacQueen, Plotkin, and Sethi 1984; Pitts 1996), for it gives an inductive structure by which self-referentiality may be avoided.

We construct finite expressions "top-down", by syntactically projecting arbitrary expressions to produce finite expressions. This is the opposite of domain construction, which starts with only finite elements. In order for projections to be performed, the presence of recognizer operators `is`... in the language is critical: each sort in a multi-sorted language is projected in a different manner, and recognizers allow a run-time projection operation to be defined.

DEFINITION 3.12 (FINITE PROJECTIONS π^n_{inj}) The projection functional π_{inj}, finite projections π^n_{inj}, and infinite projection π^∞_{inj} are defined as follows.

$$
\begin{aligned}
\pi_{\text{inj}} &= \lambda y.\lambda x.\\
&\qquad \texttt{eif}(\texttt{is}_1(x), \texttt{inj}_1(y\,(\texttt{out}_1(x))),\\
&\qquad \texttt{eif}(\texttt{is}_2(x), \texttt{inj}_2(y\,(\texttt{out}_2(x))), \ldots,\\
&\qquad \texttt{eif}(\texttt{is}_k(x), \texttt{inj}_k(y\,(\texttt{out}_k(x))),\\
&\qquad y \circ x \circ y) \ldots))\\
\pi^0_{\text{inj}} &= \lambda x.\texttt{bot}\\
\pi^{n+1}_{\text{inj}} &= \pi_{\text{inj}}\,(\pi^n_{\text{inj}})\\
\pi^\infty_{\text{inj}} &= \texttt{fix}\,(\pi_{\text{inj}})
\end{aligned}
$$

It is interesting to observe that for $k = 0$, $\mathbb{L}_{\text{inj}(0)}$ is the pure call-by-value λ-calculus, so the above defines projection operations on the pure λ-calculus. This approach to finite expressions is not found in Barendregt (Barendregt 1984). Barendregt Chapter 14 does review another similar approach which is worth contrasting: Hyland and Wadsworth's labelled λ-calculus. Rather than defining a syntactic projection $\pi^n_{\text{inj}}\,(e)$, the expression e is labelled with constant n, producing the *labelled λ-term* e^n. evaluation then projects: $(\lambda x.a^{n+1})\,(b) \to (a[b^n/x])^n$. This is identical to how $\pi^{n+1}\,(\lambda x.e)$ projects the function argument and result both to be at level n. Other researchers have also studied labelled λ-reduction (Egidi, Honsell, and della Rocca 1992). We do not pursue labelled reduction because the addition of labels changes the language and thus changes operational equivalence (see Lemma 4.16 below). Since the projections π^n_{inj} are definable *within* the language, they are guaranteed not to change the underlying equivalence.

Note that for expressions in a simply-typed λ-calculus, there is no need for run-time projection operations: given the type of an expression e, $\pi^k\,(e)$ can be partially evaluated to remove all cases on the sort, as the type itself reveals the sort This is one way to characterize Milner's construction (Milner 1977).

The following lemma establishes elementary properties of the syntactic projections. For brevity henceforward we drop the subscript inj from the projections π^n.

LEMMA 3.13 (ELEMENTARY π^n/π^∞ PROPERTIES)

$$
\begin{array}{rl}
\text{(fix)} & \pi^\infty \cong_{\text{inj}} \{\pi^n \mid n \in \mathbb{N}\} \\
\text{(idemp)} & \pi^n \circ \pi^n \cong_{\text{inj}} \pi^n, \quad \pi^\infty \circ \pi^\infty \cong_{\text{inj}} \pi^\infty \\
\text{(compose)} & \pi^m \circ \pi^n \cong_{\text{inj}} \pi^{\min(m,n)} \\
\text{(order)} & \pi^n \sqsubseteq_{\text{inj}} \pi^{n+1} \sqsubseteq_{\text{inj}} \pi^\infty \\
\text{(inject)} & \pi^{n+1}\,(\mathtt{inj}_i(v)) \cong_{\text{inj}} \mathtt{inj}_i(\pi^n\,(v)), \pi^\infty\,(\mathtt{inj}_i(v)) \cong_{\text{inj}} \mathtt{inj}_i(\pi^\infty\,(v)) \\
\text{(fun.0)} & \pi^1\,(\lambda x.e) \cong_{\text{inj}} \lambda x.\mathtt{bot} \\
\text{(fun.+)} & \pi^{n+1}\,(\lambda x.a) \cong_{\text{inj}} \pi^n \circ \lambda x.a \circ \pi^n, \quad \pi^\infty\,(\lambda x.a) \cong_{\text{inj}} \pi^\infty \circ \lambda x.a \circ \pi^\infty \\
\text{(prune)} & \pi^n\,(a) \sqsubseteq_{\text{inj}} a, \quad \pi^\infty\,(a) \sqsubseteq_{\text{inj}} a \\
\text{(value)} & \pi^\infty\,(v)\downarrow \text{ for all closed values } v
\end{array}
$$

The Finite Approximation Theorem is a key result: any expression is equivalent to its set of finite projections, yielding an inductive decomposition of every expression into its finite counterparts. This property is a close analogue of the ω-algebraicity property of domains.

THEOREM 3.14 (FINITE APPROXIMATION) $\{\pi^n\,(a) \mid n \in \mathbb{N}\} \cong_{\text{inj}} \{a\}$.

To prove this, we show that for any particular computation, a large enough projection n will suffice. However, a direct proof of this property is a bookkeeping nightmare as different projection values π^k may percolate throughout the expression during evaluation. A simpler proof is to characterize the limit of the projection function. π^∞ may be characterized as an identity function.

LEMMA 3.15 (IDENTITY OF π^∞) $\pi^\infty \cong_{\text{inj}} \lambda x.x$

To prove this, we characterize how the projections π^∞ may percolate throughout expressions during evaluation. Inductively define $\tau(a)$ and $\tau(R)$ as follows:

$$\begin{aligned}
&\tau(x) = x\\
&\tau(\mathtt{op}^-(a_0, \ldots, a_n)) = \pi^\infty\,(\mathtt{op}^-(\tau(a_0), \ldots, \tau(a_n)))\\
&\tau(\mathtt{inj}_i(a)) = \mathtt{inj}_i(\tau(a))\\
&\tau(\lambda x.a) = \pi^\infty \circ \lambda x.\tau(a) \circ \pi^\infty\\
&\tau(R) = \tau(R[x])[\bullet/x]
\end{aligned}$$

where operator $\mathtt{op}^-$ is either app, $\mathtt{out}_i$, or $\mathtt{is}_i$. This definition is carefully chosen to have properties corresponding to how π^∞ percolates through evaluation; notice for instance $\tau(v)$ is a value for any value v. The identity of π^∞ may be proved by establishing that $a\downarrow$ implies $\tau(a)\downarrow$; this then establishes the Finite Approximation Theorem. In Section 5.2 below, analogous results are established for a language with state; more complete proofs are given there.

The syntactic projections may rightfully be called "finite expressions": all expressions that are finite in the classical sense of Definition 2.7 are equivalent to some syntactically projected expression, and the cardinality of each level is finite.

THEOREM 3.16 (FINITENESS CHARACTERIZATION) (i) For all $n \in \mathbb{N}$,

$$\{a \mid a \in \mathbb{E}^{\emptyset}_{\text{inj}} \text{ and } a \cong_{\text{inj}} \pi^n\,(a)\,\}$$

contains finitely many $\cong_{\text{inj}}$-distinct expressions.

(ii) For all $a \in \mathbb{E}^{\emptyset}_{\text{inj}}$ and $n \in \mathbb{N}$, $\pi^n\,(a)$ is finite in the sense of Definition 2.7.

(iii) $\mathbb{E}^{\omega}_{\text{inj}} = \bigcup_{n\in\mathbb{N}}\{a \mid a \in \mathbb{E}^{\emptyset}_{\text{inj}} \text{ and } a \cong_{\text{inj}} \pi^n\,(a)\,\}$

Furthermore, $\{\cdot\} \sqsubseteq_{\text{inj}} \{\cdot\}$-directed sets all may be shown to have least upper bounds, and $\sqsubseteq_{\text{inj}}$ is ω-algebraic; see (Mason, Smith, and Talcott 1996) for these properties and a proof of the previous Theorem.

4 A Space Of Languages

In the previous section a very simple language family $\mathbb{L}_{\text{inj}(k)}$ was studied. In this section we study progressively more complex languages and consider what results still hold from the development for $\mathbb{L}_{\text{inj}(k)}$, and what results fail. High-level languages $\mathbb{L}_h$ are studied by defining embeddings of $\mathbb{L}_h$ into the injection languages $\mathbb{L}_{\text{inj}(k)}$. This allows for us to quickly present a sequence of languages, and also helps highlight how small (or large) the gap is between different languages.

Notions of operational ordering $\sqsubseteq$ and operational set ordering $\{\cdot\} \sqsubseteq \{\cdot\}$ were defined on arbitrary operational structures in Section 2, so there is no question of the generality of those definitions. Our main goal here is to study how well the finite elements may be characterized, and in particular if Theorems 3.14 and 3.16 stated above for $\mathbb{L}_{\text{inj}(k)}$ may be proved for these more complex languages.

4.1 Booleans, Pairs, and Numbers

We now define a language $\mathbb{L}_{\mathsf{bpn}(k)}$ which adds booleans, pairs, and numbers to $\mathbb{L}_{\mathsf{inj}(k)}$. We preserve the $\mathtt{inj}_k/\mathtt{out}_k/\mathtt{is}_k$ operators to allow this language to be extended in turn. The case $k = 0$ yields a language with no injections, and $k = 2$ yields the standard left/right injections.

DEFINITION 4.1 $\mathbb{L}_{\mathsf{bpn}(k)}$ has structure $\langle \mathbb{E}, \mathbb{V}, \mathbb{O}, \mapsto \rangle$ where

$$\begin{aligned} \mathbb{O} \;=\; & \mathbb{O}_{\mathsf{inj}(k)} \cup \{\mathtt{true}, \mathtt{false}, \mathtt{isbool}(e), 0, 1, 2, \ldots, \mathtt{succ}(e), \mathtt{pred}(e), \\ & \mathtt{iszero}(e), \mathtt{isnat}(e), \mathtt{pr}(e, e'), \mathtt{fst}(e), \mathtt{snd}(e), \mathtt{ispr}(e), \mathtt{if}(e, e', e'')\} \end{aligned}$$

We include recognizer operators $\mathtt{isbool}$, $\mathtt{isnat}$, $\mathtt{ispr}$ in $\mathbb{L}_{\mathsf{bpn}(k)}$. In Section 4.2 below we consider the alternative case when there are no recognizers. We will very briefly outline the evaluator for $\mathbb{L}_{\mathsf{bpn}(k)}$ (and, will not define explicit evaluators for most of the languages that follow). For brevity we will define some notions as extensions of the notions defined in the presentation of $\mathbb{L}_{\mathsf{inj}(k)}$ of Section 3, reading those definitions with $\mathbb{E}_{\mathsf{bpn}(k)}$ in place of $\mathbb{E}_{\mathsf{inj}(k)}$. The values $\mathbb{V}_{\mathsf{bpn}(k)}$ include the cases as $\mathbb{L}_{\mathsf{inj}(k)}$ plus numbers, booleans, and $\mathtt{pr}(v, v)$. The reduction contexts $\mathbb{R}_{\mathsf{bpn}(k)}$ include the same cases plus $\mathtt{if}(R[\bullet], e, e)$, $\mathtt{pred}(R[\bullet])$, $\mathtt{succ}(R[\bullet])$, $\mathtt{iszero}(R[\bullet])$, $\mathtt{fst}(R[\bullet])$, $\mathtt{snd}(R[\bullet])$, $\mathtt{pr}(R[\bullet], e)$, $\mathtt{pr}(v, R[\bullet])$, $\mathtt{isbool}(R[\bullet])$, and $\mathtt{isnat}(R[\bullet])$ and $\mathtt{ispr}(R[\bullet])$.

DEFINITION 4.2 ($\mapsto^1_{\mathsf{bpn}(k)}, \mapsto_{\mathsf{bpn}(k)}$) $\mapsto_{\mathsf{bpn}(k)}$ is the transitive, reflexive closure of $\mapsto^1_{\mathsf{bpn}(k)}$:

$$\begin{array}{rcl} R[e] & \mapsto^1_{\mathsf{bpn}(k)} & R[e'] \\ & & \text{where } R[e] \mapsto^1_{\mathsf{inj}(k)} R[e'] \text{ is a case of Definition 3.4} \\ R[\mathtt{if}(\mathtt{true}, a, b)] & \mapsto^1_{\mathsf{bpn}(k)} & R[a] \text{ and } \mapsto^1_{\mathsf{bpn}(k)} R[b] \text{ for } \mathtt{false} \text{ case} \\ R[\mathtt{fst}(\mathtt{pr}(v, v'))] & \mapsto^1_{\mathsf{bpn}(k)} & R[v] \text{ and } \mapsto^1 R[v'] \text{ for } \mathtt{snd} \\ R[\mathtt{succ}(v)] & \mapsto^1_{\mathsf{bpn}(k)} & R[v+1] \text{ for } v \in \mathbb{N} \\ R[\mathtt{pred}(v+1)] & \mapsto^1_{\mathsf{bpn}(k)} & R[v] \text{ for } v \in \mathbb{N} \\ R[\mathtt{iszero}(v)] & \mapsto^1_{\mathsf{bpn}(k)} & R[b] \\ & & \text{for } v \in \mathbb{N}, b \text{ a boolean, and } b = \mathtt{true} \text{ iff } v = 0 \\ R[\mathtt{is}\{\mathtt{bool/pr/num}\}(v)] & \mapsto^1_{\mathsf{bpn}(k)} & R[b] \\ & & \text{where } v \notin \mathbb{X} \text{ and boolean } b \text{ is } \mathtt{true} \text{ iff } v \text{ is a } \mathtt{bool/pr/num} \end{array}$$

$\mathbb{L}_{\mathsf{bpn}(k)}$ is mapped to low-level language $\mathbb{L}_{\mathsf{inj}(k+3)}$ by the following homomorphic embedding.

DEFINITION 4.3 $[\![\cdot]\!] \in \mathbb{L}_{\mathrm{bpn}(k)} \to \mathbb{L}_{\mathrm{inj}(k+3)}$ is defined as $C_{\mathrm{init}} = \bullet$ and an embedding of expressions as follows.

$$\begin{aligned}
[\![\mathtt{true}]\!] &= \mathtt{inj}_{k+3}(\mathtt{etrue})\\
[\![\mathtt{false}]\!] &= \mathtt{inj}_{k+3}(\mathtt{efalse})\\
[\![\mathtt{if}(e,e',e'')]\!] &= \mathtt{out}_{k+3}([\![e]\!])\;(\lambda x.[\![e']\!])\;(\lambda x.[\![e'']\!]) \text{ for fresh } x\\
[\![\mathtt{isbool}(a)]\!] &= \mathtt{eif}(\mathtt{is}_{k+3}([\![a]\!]), [\![\mathtt{true}]\!], [\![\mathtt{false}]\!])\\
[\![\mathtt{pr}(a,b)]\!] &= \mathtt{inj}_{k+2}((\lambda x.\lambda y.\lambda p.p\;(x)\;(y))\;([\![a]\!])\;([\![b]\!]))\\
[\![\mathtt{fst}(a)]\!] &= \mathtt{out}_{k+2}([\![a]\!])\;(\lambda x.\lambda y.x)\\
[\![\mathtt{snd}(a)]\!] &= \mathtt{out}_{k+2}([\![a]\!])\;(\lambda x.\lambda y.y)\\
[\![\mathtt{ispr}(a)]\!] &= \mathtt{eif}(\mathtt{is}_{k+2}([\![a]\!]), [\![\mathtt{true}]\!], [\![\mathtt{false}]\!])\\
[\![n]\!] &= \mathtt{inj}_{k+1}([\![\overbrace{\mathtt{pr}(\mathtt{true},\ldots\mathtt{pr}(\mathtt{true}}^{n},\mathtt{pr}(\mathtt{false},\mathtt{false}))\ldots)]\!])\\
[\![\mathtt{succ}(e)]\!] &= \mathtt{let}\; x = \mathtt{out}_{k+1}([\![e]\!])\;\mathtt{in}\;\mathtt{inj}_{k+1}([\![\mathtt{pr}(\mathtt{true},x)]\!])\\
[\![\mathtt{pred}(e)]\!] &= \mathtt{let}\; x = \mathtt{out}_{k+1}([\![e]\!])\;\mathtt{in}\;\mathtt{inj}_{k+1}(\mathtt{inj}_{k+2}(\mathtt{out}_{k+2}([\![\mathtt{snd}(x)]\!])))\\
[\![\mathtt{iszero}(e)]\!] &= \mathtt{let}\; x = \mathtt{out}_{k+1}([\![e]\!])\;\mathtt{in}\\
&\qquad \mathtt{eif}(\mathtt{out}_{k+3}([\![\mathtt{fst}(x)]\!]), [\![\mathtt{false}]\!], [\![\mathtt{true}]\!])\\
[\![\mathtt{isnat}(a)]\!] &= \mathtt{eif}(\mathtt{is}_{k+1}([\![a]\!]), [\![\mathtt{true}]\!], [\![\mathtt{false}]\!])\\
[\![e]\!] &= \text{homomorphic for all other } e \in \mathbb{E}_{\mathrm{bpn}(k)}
\end{aligned}$$

The mapping for contexts extends the above with the case $[\![\bullet]\!] = \bullet$. Observe how operator $\mathtt{inj}_{k+3}$ wraps booleans, $\mathtt{inj}_{k+2}$ wraps pairs, and $\mathtt{inj}_{k+1}$ wraps numerals, keeping these datatypes disjoint. Boolean and pair encodings are the classic Church encodings; we then use the booleans and pairs to encode numerals.

LEMMA 4.4 $[\![\cdot]\!] \in \mathbb{L}_{\mathrm{bpn}(k)} \to \mathbb{L}_{\mathrm{inj}(k+3)}$ is a sound embedding homomorphic in $\mathbb{O}_{\mathrm{inj}(k)}$.

PROOF: Show $a \downarrow_{\mathrm{bpn}(k)}$ iff $[\![a]\!] \downarrow_{\mathrm{inj}(k+3)}$. We may show $a \mapsto^1_{\mathrm{bpn}(k)} b$ implies $[\![a]\!] \cong_{\mathrm{inj}(k+3)} [\![b]\!]$ by inspection of the cases of $\mapsto^1_{\mathrm{inj}(k+3)}$. Also, we may show that if $a \not\mapsto^1_{\mathrm{bpn}(k)}$, *i.e.*, it is stuck, then $[\![a]\!] \not\downarrow_{\mathrm{inj}(k+3)}$. And, from the fact that for all values $v \in \mathbb{V}_{\mathrm{bpn}(k)}$, $[\![v]\!] \downarrow_{\mathrm{inj}(k+3)}$, the result follows.

The embedding can easily be seen to be homomorphic in $\mathbb{O}_{\mathrm{inj}(k)}$. □

Additional abbreviations for $\mathbb{E}_{\mathrm{bpn}(k)}$ include

$$\begin{aligned}
\mathtt{nateq}(e,e') &= \mathtt{fix}(\lambda f.\lambda x.\lambda y.\mathtt{if}(\mathtt{iszero}(x), \mathtt{iszero}(y),\\
&\qquad \mathtt{if}(\mathtt{iszero}(y), \mathtt{false}, f\;(\mathtt{pred}(x))\;(\mathtt{pred}(y)))))\;(e)\;(e')\\
\mathtt{let}\;\mathtt{pr}(x_1,x_2) = e\;\mathtt{in}\;e' &= \mathtt{let}\; x = e\;\mathtt{in}\\
&\qquad \mathtt{let}\; x_1 = \mathtt{fst}(x)\;\mathtt{in}\\
&\qquad\quad \mathtt{let}\; x_2 = \mathtt{snd}(x)\;\mathtt{in}\; e', \text{ for } x \text{ fresh}
\end{aligned}$$

If the embedding did not use injections, numbers and functions would be of the same sort, and $\mathbb{L}_{\mathrm{bpn}}$ computations such as $0\;(\lambda x.x)$ would terminate when they should be stuck. This fact is expressed in the following Lemma, which shows the pure λ-calculus is too weak to serve as an embedding target.

LEMMA 4.5 There is no sound embedding $[\![\cdot]\!] \in \mathbb{L}_{\mathsf{bpn}(0)} \to \mathbb{L}_{\mathsf{inj}(0)}$ homomorphic in $\mathbb{O}_{\mathsf{inj}(0)}$.

PROOF: Suppose there was. $[\![0]\!] \cong_{\mathsf{inj}(0)} \lambda x.e_0$ and $[\![1]\!] \cong_{\mathsf{inj}(0)} \lambda x.e_1$ since $[\![0]\!]\downarrow_{\mathsf{inj}(0)}$ and $[\![1]\!]\downarrow_{\mathsf{inj}(0)}$. Consider $[\![\mathtt{iszero}(e)]\!]$; since $[\![\mathtt{true}]\!]$ and $[\![\mathtt{false}]\!]$ must be non-equivalent, and $[\![0]\!]$ and $[\![1]\!]$ must be non-equivalent, this $\mathbb{L}_{\mathsf{inj}}$ computation must touch expression e, so for e being $[\![0]\!]$ it will compute to $R[[\![0]\!]\,(\lambda x.e')]$ for some $\lambda x.e'$ (this being the first place where $[\![0]\!]$ is touched), and go on to terminate. Thus $[\![0]\!]\,(\lambda x.e')\downarrow_{\mathsf{inj}(0)}$. Since the embedding is homomorphic, $[\![\lambda x.e']\!] = \lambda x.e'$, and so $[\![0\,(\lambda x.e')]\!]\downarrow_{\mathsf{inj}(0)}$, a contradiction. □

LEMMA 4.6 $[\![\cdot]\!] \in \mathbb{L}_{\mathsf{bpn}(k)} \to \mathbb{L}_{\mathsf{inj}(k+3)}$ is not fully abstract.

PROOF: $\lambda x.\mathtt{if}(\mathtt{ispr}(x), (\lambda x.0)\,(\mathtt{fst}(x)), 0) \cong_{\mathsf{bpn}(k)} \lambda x.0$ but the $\mathbb{L}_{\mathsf{inj}(k+3)}$ context $(\bullet)\,(\mathtt{inj}_{k+2}(\lambda x.\mathtt{bot}))$ distinguishes the embedded forms. □

Still, since the embedding is homomorphic, equations from $\mathbb{L}_{\mathsf{inj}(k+3)}$ can be directly lifted to $\mathbb{L}_{\mathsf{bpn}(k)}$. One concrete example is the fixed point lemma.

LEMMA 4.7 $\{\mathtt{fix}\,(\lambda x.\lambda z.f\,(x)\,(z))\} \cong_{\mathsf{bpn}(k)} \{\lambda x.\lambda z.f^n\,(x)\,(z) \mid n \in \mathbb{N}\}$.

PROOF: This property is proved for $\mathbb{L}_{\mathsf{inj}(k)}$ as Lemma 3.11, and since the expressions only involve operators homomorphic in the embedding $[\![\cdot]\!] \in \mathbb{L}_{\mathsf{bpn}(k)} \to \mathbb{L}_{\mathsf{inj}(k+3)}$ (taking f to be a variable and not a metavariable), the result follows by Lemma 2.13. □

The finite approximation theorem (3.14) can also be "lifted" from $\mathbb{L}_{\mathsf{inj}}$, but the syntactic projection functions π will not project pairs or numbers and will thus be incomplete; in particular 3.16 will not be provable. To obtain complete projection functions, fuller forms may be directly defined in $\mathbb{L}_{\mathsf{bpn}(k)}$.

DEFINITION 4.8 (FINITE PROJECTIONS π^n_{bpn})

$$
\begin{aligned}
\pi_{\mathsf{bpn}} = {} & \lambda y.\lambda x.\\
& \quad \mathtt{eif}(\mathtt{is}_1(x), \mathtt{inj}_1(y\,(\mathtt{out}_1(x))),\\
& \quad \mathtt{eif}(\mathtt{is}_2(x), \mathtt{inj}_2(y\,(\mathtt{out}_2(x))), \ldots,\\
& \quad \mathtt{eif}(\mathtt{is}_k(x), \mathtt{inj}_k(y\,(\mathtt{out}_k(x))),\\
& \quad \mathtt{if}(\mathtt{isbool}(x), x,\\
& \quad \mathtt{if}(\mathtt{ispr}(x), \mathtt{pr}(y\,(\mathtt{fst}(x)), y\,(\mathtt{snd}(x))),\\
& \quad \mathtt{if}(\mathtt{isnat}(x), \mathtt{if}(\mathtt{iszero}(x), 0, \mathtt{succ}(y\,(\mathtt{pred}(x)))),\\
& \quad y \circ x \circ y)) \ldots))\\
\pi^0_{\mathsf{bpn}} = {} & \lambda x.\mathtt{bot}\\
\pi^{n+1}_{\mathsf{bpn}} = {} & \pi_{\mathsf{bpn}(k)}\,(\pi^n_{\mathsf{bpn}(k)})\\
\pi^\infty_{\mathsf{bpn}(k)} = {} & \mathtt{fix}\,(\pi_{\mathsf{bpn}})
\end{aligned}
$$

These finite projections in turn allow the finite elements of $\mathbb{L}_{\mathsf{bpn}}$ to be characterized.

THEOREM 4.9 Theorems 3.14 and 3.16 hold for $\mathbb{L}_{\mathrm{bpn}(k)}$ with projections π^n_{bpn}.

Proofs of these theorems are found in (Mason, Smith, and Talcott 1996). The principle of induction on the finite rank n is thus successfully obtained for this language.

4.2 Booleans, Pairs, and Numbers Without Recognizers

It is interesting to consider ramifications of languages without recognizers `isnat`, `ispr`, `isbool`, and $\mathtt{is}_k$. In such languages the case analysis programmed into the syntactic projection functions π^n_{bpn} cannot be programmed, and thus the approach of Section 3.2 is not directly possible. We show there still is some capability of reasoning using finite projections, but at the cost of fully abstract reasoning.

DEFINITION 4.10 (i) $\mathbb{L}_{\mathrm{inj}-(k)}$ is defined to be $\mathbb{L}_{\mathrm{inj}(k)}$ with recognizer operators $\mathtt{is}_i$, $1 \leq i \leq k$, removed from $\mathbb{O}_{\mathrm{inj}(k)}$ and the $\mathtt{is}_i$ cases removed from $\mapsto_{\mathrm{inj}(k)}$.

(ii) $\mathbb{L}_{\mathrm{bpn}-(k)}$ is defined to be $\mathbb{L}_{\mathrm{bpn}(k)}$ without recognizer operators `isnat`, `ispr`, `isbool`, or $\mathtt{is}_k$ for any k.

(iii) $[\![\cdot]\!] \in \mathbb{L}_{\mathrm{bpn}-(k)} \to \mathbb{L}_{\mathrm{inj}-(k+3)}$ is then the obvious restriction of the above embedding (Definition 4.3) that removes the recognizer cases. (Notice that $\mathtt{is}_k$ is not used in any non-recognizer cases).

This embedding is getting closer to being fully abstract than the mapping with recognizers, but there are some subtle cases where parametricity is observable in $\mathbb{L}_{\mathrm{inj}-(k)}$ but masked in $\mathbb{L}_{\mathrm{bpn}-(k)}$.

LEMMA 4.11 $[\![\cdot]\!] \in \mathbb{L}_{\mathrm{bpn}-(k)} \to \mathbb{L}_{\mathrm{inj}-(k+3)}$ is not fully abstract.

PROOF:

$$\lambda x.\mathtt{let}\ y = \mathtt{fst}(x)\ \mathtt{in}\ \mathtt{let}\ z = \mathtt{snd}(x)\ \mathtt{in}\ x \cong_{\mathrm{bpn}-(k)}$$
$$\lambda x.\mathtt{let}\ y = \mathtt{fst}(x)\ \mathtt{in}\ \mathtt{let}\ z = \mathtt{snd}(x)\ \mathtt{in}\ \mathtt{pr}(y, z)$$

but the $\mathbb{L}_{\mathrm{inj}-(k+3)}$ context $\mathtt{out}_{k+2}((\bullet)\,(\mathtt{inj}_{k+2}(\lambda p.p\,(\lambda x.\mathtt{bot}))))\,(\lambda x.x)\,(\lambda x.x)$ distinguishes the embedded forms. □

A similar problem arises with booleans, so neither pairing nor booleans and conditional can be encoded in a full and faithful manner. Numbers however can probably be encoded faithfully in a language with only pairs and booleans.

We now establish that removal of recognizers causes the equivalence to change. This means we are not completely free to add or remove recognizers from languages as tools (*e.g.*, to use them to define the finite projections), because the underlying equivalence will be altered and full abstraction will then fail.

LEMMA 4.12 For all g, if $\mathtt{iszero}(g\,(0))\downarrow_{\mathrm{bpn}-(k)}$ and $\mathtt{if}(g\,(\mathtt{true}), 0, 0)\downarrow_{\mathrm{bpn}-(k)}$, then $g \cong \lambda x.x$.

PROOF: First observe that this requires $g\,\mathtt{(0/true)} \downarrow_{\mathrm{bpn}-(k)}$. g must then never touch its argument, for suppose it did: then g must compute to $R[0/\mathtt{true}]$ for some R. Since $\mathbb{E}_{\mathrm{bpn}-(k)}$ contains no recognizers, this state will get stuck on at least one of 0 or true filling the hole (note that iszero(true) is stuck), contradiction. So, since g does not touch its argument, the result of $g\,\mathtt{(0/true)}$ must be a parametric value of the form $C[0/\mathtt{true}]$. The only case then for which both $\mathtt{iszero}(C[0])$ and $\mathtt{if}(C[\mathtt{true}], 0, 0)$ do not get stuck is then when $C[x] \mapsto_{\mathrm{bpn}-(k)} x$. Thus, $g\,(v) \cong v$ for any v, and the result follows by extensionality. □

LEMMA 4.13 $\precsim_{\mathrm{bpn}(k)} \subsetneq \precsim_{\mathrm{bpn}-(k)}$ when these relations are restricted to expressions of $\mathbb{E}_{\mathrm{bpn}-(k)}$.

PROOF: Consider the $\mathbb{L}_{\mathrm{bpn}-(k)}$ context

$$C \;=\; \lambda z.\mathtt{if}(z\,\mathtt{(true)}, \mathtt{if}(\mathtt{nateq}(z\,\mathtt{(0)}, 0), \bullet, 0), 0)$$

Then, $C[\mathtt{pr}(0,0)] \precsim_{\mathrm{bpn}-(k)} C[z\,(\mathtt{pr}(0,0))]$: if $C[\mathtt{pr}(0,0)]\,(g) \downarrow_{\mathrm{bpn}-(k)}$, then by Lemma 4.12, $g \cong_{\mathrm{bpn}-(k)} \lambda x.x$, and so $C[z\,(\mathtt{pr}(0,0))]\,(g) \downarrow_{\mathrm{bpn}-(k)}$ as well. However, the $\mathbb{L}_{\mathrm{bpn}(k)}$ context $\bullet\,(\lambda x.\mathtt{if}(\mathtt{ispr}(x, \mathtt{bot}, x)))$ distinguishes the two expressions. □

4.2.1 Finite Projections Without Recognizers

Since $\mathbb{L}_{\mathrm{bpn}-(k)}$ contains no recognizers, the syntactic projection operations π^n_{bpn} are not definable within the language as was possible in the presence of recognizers. Without some other approach, no finite element structure can be developed for such a language.

It is possible to use $\precsim_{\mathrm{bpn}(k)}$ to directly prove instances of $\precsim_{\mathrm{bpn}-(k)}$ via Lemma 4.13, and in the former language the syntactic projection functions may be directly expressed. However, ordering $\precsim_{\mathrm{bpn}(k)}$ is far too fine-grained, as Lemma 4.13 shows.

One solution is to add the projections π^n_{bpn} of $\mathbb{L}_{\mathrm{bpn}(k)}$ to $\mathbb{L}_{\mathrm{bpn}-(k)}$ as primitive operations $\mathtt{proj}^n$. This means we will not allow all recognizers in testing contexts of $\mathbb{L}_{\mathrm{bpn}-(k)}$; they will only be used in the restricted way the projections use them. We define this language in abbreviated form via a mapping to $\mathbb{L}_{\mathrm{bpn}(k)}$.

DEFINITION 4.14 (i) $\mathbb{E}_{\mathrm{bpn}\pi-(k)}$ is $\mathbb{E}_{\mathrm{bpn}-(k)}$ with additional 0-ary operators $\mathtt{proj}^n$ for each $n \in \mathbb{N}$.

(ii) $[\![\cdot]\!] \in \mathbb{L}_{\mathrm{bpn}\pi-(k)} \to \mathbb{L}_{\mathrm{bpn}(k)}$ is homomorphic in all operators $\mathrm{op} \in \mathbb{O}_{\mathrm{bpn}\pi-(k)}$ except

$$[\![\mathtt{proj}^n]\!] \;=\; \pi^n_{\mathrm{bpn}}$$

THEOREM 4.15 Finite Approximation, Theorem 3.14, is provable for the projections $\mathtt{proj}^n(e)$ of $\mathbb{L}_{\mathrm{bpn}\pi-(k)}$: $\{\mathtt{proj}^n(a) \mid n \in \mathbb{N}\} \cong_{\mathrm{bpn}\pi-(k)} \{a\}$.

PROOF: The results from Theorem 4.9 may directly be applied to $\mathbb{L}_{\text{bpn}\pi-}$ by Lemma 2.9. □

Since $\mathbb{L}_{\text{bpn}\pi-(k)}$ in addition contains operators $\texttt{proj}^n$, $\sqsubseteq\!\!\!\!\sim_{\text{bpn}\pi-(k)}$ restricted to expressions of $\mathbb{L}_{\text{bpn}-(k)}$ has more testing contexts than $\sqsubseteq\!\!\!\!\sim_{\text{bpn}-(k)}$. These extra contexts can distinguish more expressions, so adding atomic projection operations has an undesirable effect on equivalence.

LEMMA 4.16 $\sqsubseteq\!\!\!\!\sim_{\text{bpn}\pi-(k)} \subsetneq \sqsubseteq\!\!\!\!\sim_{\text{bpn}-(k)}$ when the relations are restricted to $\mathbb{E}_{\text{bpn}-(k)}$.

PROOF: $\subset$ follows from the fact that $\mathbb{E}_{\text{bpn}-(k)} \subseteq \mathbb{E}_{\text{bpn}\pi-(k)}$. They are unequal by the following. The proof of Lemma 4.13 defines a C such that $C[\texttt{pr}(0,0)] \sqsubseteq\!\!\!\!\sim_{\text{bpn}-(k)} C[z\,(\texttt{pr}(0,0))]$. But $C[\texttt{pr}(0,0)] \not\sqsubseteq\!\!\!\!\sim_{\text{bpn}\pi-(k)} C[z\,(\texttt{pr}(0,0))]$, because the context $\bullet\,(\texttt{proj}^1)$ distinguishes the two: $C[\texttt{pr}(0,0)]\,(\texttt{proj}^1)$ converges, and

$$C[z\,(\texttt{pr}(0,0))]\,(\texttt{proj}^1)$$

diverges because $\texttt{proj}^1\,(\texttt{pr}(0,0))$ diverges. □

A similar problem would likely arise if an explicit expression labelling scheme were attempted in analogy with labelled λ-expressions (Barendregt 1984; Egidi, Honsell, and della Rocca 1992): presence of the labels will cause operational equivalence to change. This shows it is very difficult to characterize the finite structure of untyped languages in a fully abstract manner if the language does not already have recognizer operators as primitives.

4.3 Simple Objects

We briefly study a language with simple functional objects. Simple objects may be defined via a homomorphic embedding. We conjecture here that they may be embedded in $\mathbb{L}_{\text{bpn}}$ in a fully abstract manner.

Our simple objects contain methods that may refer to the object itself. Since they are functional, they do not contain mutable instances, and there is also no notion of class or of method override. Classes (Eifrig, Smith, Trifonov, and Zwarico 1995) and method override (Abadi, Cardelli, and Viswanathan 1996) may also be interpreted via homomorphic embeddings; for brevity we leave them out of this presentation.

DEFINITION 4.17 $\mathbb{L}_{\text{obj}(k)}$ has structure $\langle \mathbb{E}_{\text{obj}(k)}, \mathbb{V}_{\text{obj}(k)}, \mathbb{O}_{\text{obj}(k)}, \mapsto_{\text{obj}(k)} \rangle$ where

$$\begin{aligned}\mathbb{O}_{\text{obj}(k)} &= \mathbb{O}_{\text{bpn}(k)} \cup \{\texttt{isobj}(e)\} \cup \{\texttt{send}_m(e) \mid m \in \mathbb{M}\} \\ &\quad \cup \{\texttt{obj}_{m_1,\dots,m_n}(x_1.e_1,\dots,x_n.e_n) \mid m_1,\dots,m_n \in \mathbb{M}\}\end{aligned}$$

for some countable set of messages $\mathbb{M}$; $count(m)$ for $m \in \mathbb{M}$ is a bijection from $\mathbb{M}$ to $\mathbb{N}$.

This notation for objects uses a different operator for each object message form to allow objects to fit the operator arity syntax convention. $\mathbb{L}_{\mathsf{obj}(k)}$ is mapped to lower-level language $\mathbb{L}_{\mathsf{bpn}(k+1)}$ by the following embedding homomorphic in $\mathbb{O}_{\mathsf{bpn}(k)}$ (a composition with $[\![\cdot]\!] \in \mathbb{L}_{\mathsf{bpn}(k)} \to \mathbb{L}_{\mathsf{inj}(k+3)}$ would then yield an embedding into $\mathbb{L}_{\mathsf{inj}(k+4)}$).

DEFINITION 4.18 $[\![\cdot]\!] \in \mathbb{L}_{\mathsf{obj}(k)} \to \mathbb{L}_{\mathsf{bpn}(k+1)}$ is defined as $C_{\mathrm{init}} = \bullet$ and an embedding of expressions as follows.

$$\begin{array}{rcl} [\![\mathtt{obj}_{m_1,\ldots,m_n}(x_1.e_1,\ldots,x_n.e_n)]\!] & = & \mathtt{inj}_{k+1}(\mathtt{fix}(\lambda ob.\lambda y. \\ & & \mathtt{if}(\mathtt{nateq}(y, \mathit{count}(m_1)), (\lambda x.[\![e_1]\!])\,(ob), \\ & & \mathtt{if}(\ldots, \\ & & \mathtt{if}(\mathtt{nateq}(y, \mathit{count}(m_n)), (\lambda x.[\![e_n]\!])\,(ob), \\ & & \mathtt{bot})\ldots)))) \\ [\![\mathtt{send}_m(e)]\!] & = & \mathtt{out}_{k+1}([\![e]\!])\,(\mathit{count}(m)) \\ [\![\mathtt{isobj}(e)]\!] & = & \mathtt{eif}(\mathtt{is}_{k+1}([\![e]\!]), \mathtt{true}, \mathtt{false}) \\ [\![e]\!] & = & \text{homomorphic for all other } e \end{array}$$

This encoding does not expose the self $(x_1, \ldots, x_n)$ since a fixed point is taken (Kamin and Reddy 1994). We conjecture this encoding is fully abstract.

CONJECTURE 4.19 $[\![\cdot]\!] \in \mathbb{L}_{\mathsf{obj}(k)} \to \mathbb{L}_{\mathsf{bpn}(k+1)}$ is set fully abstract.

If the encoding were not fully abstract, there would be two $\mathbb{L}_{\mathsf{obj}(k)}$ expression sets $A \lesssim_{\mathsf{obj}(k)} B$ but a $\mathbb{L}_{\mathsf{bpn}(k+1)}$ context could distinguish $[\![A]\!]$ and $[\![B]\!]$. However, $\mathbb{L}_{\mathsf{bpn}(k+1)}$ contexts cannot access internal details of object implementations given the representation used. Thus the conjecture is that functional objects are not very complex additions to a language. Establishing this conjecture appears difficult.

A fixed-point principle for reasoning about objects may be easily derived by mapping objects into $\mathbb{L}_{\mathsf{bpn}(k+1)}$ via the above embedding, and lifting the fixed point principle of that language.

DEFINITION 4.20 Given fixed object $\mathtt{obj}_{m_1,\ldots,m_n}(x_1.e_1,\ldots,x_n.e_n)$, define $\mathtt{obj}^j$ inductively as

$$\begin{array}{l} \mathtt{obj}^0 = \mathtt{obj}_{m_1,\ldots,m_n}(x_1.\mathtt{bot},\ldots,x_n.\mathtt{bot}) \\ \mathtt{obj}^{j+1} = \mathtt{obj}_{m_1,\ldots,m_n}(x_1.e_1\,[\mathtt{obj}^j/x_1],\ldots,x_n.e_n\,[\mathtt{obj}^j/x_n]) \end{array}$$

LEMMA 4.21 Given object $\mathtt{obj}_{m_1,\ldots,m_n}(x_1.e_1,\ldots,x_n.e_n)$,

$$\{\mathtt{obj}_{m_1,\ldots,m_n}(x_1.e_1,\ldots,x_n.e_n)\} \cong_{\mathsf{obj}(k)} \{\mathtt{obj}^j \mid j \in \mathbb{N}\}.$$

PROOF: It suffices to show

$$[\![\{\mathtt{obj}_{m_1,\ldots,m_n}(x_1.e_1,\ldots,x_n.e_n)\}]\!] \cong_{\mathsf{bpn}(k+1)} [\![\{\mathtt{obj}^j \mid j \in \mathbb{N}\}]\!],$$

and this follows from Lemmas 4.7 and 2.13. □

The simple objects under study are little more than mutually recursive function definitions, so this principle is not much of a generalization over the fixed point property for functions. But, this lifting approach should apply to mappings of more general notions of object.

4.3.1 Finite Projections for Objects

Consider how the syntactic projection operations for objects might be defined, in analogy with the syntactic projections for $\mathbb{L}_{\text{inj}(k)}$ and $\mathbb{L}_{\text{bpn}(k)}$.

$$\begin{aligned}\pi_{\text{obj}} = \lambda y.\lambda x.&\\ &\texttt{if}(\texttt{isbool}(x), \ldots,\\ &\texttt{if}(\texttt{isobj}(x), ???, \ldots))\end{aligned}$$

At the "???" point, each method of the object x must be projected, but it is not possible inside $\mathbb{L}_{\text{obj}(k)}$ to detect which methods an arbitrary object has at run-time, so it appears the object projection operation cannot be syntactically expressed. We could at this point fruitfully pursue an alternate theory of objects in which message names had enough of a first-class status so that the projections could be defined. It could indeed be argued that the "proper" notion of an untyped object would allow for first-class message operations (an assertion supported by their presence in the Smalltalk language). But, we elect instead to continue with the current object constructs.

4.4 Simple Objects With Atomic Projections

An alternative is to proceed as we did for $\mathbb{L}_{\text{bpn}-(k)}$ in Section 4.2: extend the language with atomic projection operations $\texttt{proj}^n_{\text{obj}}$ at the expense of possibly changing the operational equivalence.

DEFINITION 4.22 (i) $\mathbb{O}_{\text{obj}\pi(k)}$ is $\mathbb{O}_{\text{obj}(k)}$ with additional 0-ary operators $\texttt{proj}^n_{\text{obj}}$ added for each $n \in \mathbb{N}$.

(ii) $[\![\cdot]\!] \in \mathbb{L}_{\text{obj}\pi(k)} \to \mathbb{L}_{\text{bpn}(k+1)}$ extends $[\![\cdot]\!] \in \mathbb{L}_{\text{obj}(k)} \to \mathbb{L}_{\text{bpn}(k+1)}$ of Definition 4.18 by adding the following clause

$$[\![\texttt{proj}^n_{\text{obj}}]\!] = \pi^n_{\text{bpn}}$$

THEOREM 4.23 Finite Approximation, Theorem 3.14, is provable for the projections $\texttt{proj}^n(e)$ of $\mathbb{L}_{\text{obj}\pi}$: $\{\texttt{proj}^n(a) \mid n \in \mathbb{N}\} \cong_{\text{obj}\pi} \{a\}$.

PROOF: The results from Theorem 4.9 may directly be applied to $\mathbb{L}_{\text{obj}\pi}$ by Lemma 2.9. □

If the embedding $[\![\cdot]\!] \in \mathbb{L}_{\text{obj}(k)} \to \mathbb{L}_{\text{bpn}(k+1)}$ is set fully abstract as conjectured, addition of these projections would fortunately *not* change the underlying equivalence: $[\![\cdot]\!] \in \mathbb{L}_{\text{obj}\pi(k)} \to \mathbb{L}_{\text{bpn}(k+1)}$ would also clearly be set fully abstract. A full and faithful theory of finite objects could then be developed. Thus, there is some potential for developing a full and faithful finite expression theory for objects via this route.

More serious difficulties with finite expressions arise in the presence of effects. We will consider memory effects in the next section.

5 Global effects: Memories

In this section we study a simple memory-based language, $\mathbb{L}_{\mathrm{m}(k)}$. The languages studied in the previous section all could be defined by homomorphic embeddings, because there were no global effects. The addition of global effects thus represents a significant change. We first present an embedding into $\mathbb{L}_{\mathrm{bpn}(k+1)}$. Strachey's memory-threading transformation is used (Milne and Strachey 1976). After establishing some results about this embedding, we define an equivalent direct operational semantics: proving facts via the embedding is cumbersome. We then develop a series of results which characterize the finite elements for a memory-based language.

For simplicity we will define $\mathbb{L}_{\mathrm{m}(k)}$ which has k injections, but no booleans, numbers, or pairs.

DEFINITION 5.1 $\mathbb{L}_{\mathrm{m}(k)}$ has structure $\langle \mathbb{E}_{\mathrm{m}(k)}, \mathbb{V}_{\mathrm{m}(k)}, \mathbb{O}_{\mathrm{m}(k)}, \mapsto_{\mathrm{m}(k)} \rangle$, where

$$\mathbb{O} = \mathbb{O}_{\mathrm{inj}(k)} \cup \{\mathtt{ref}(e), \mathtt{set}(e, e'), \mathtt{get}(e), \mathtt{iscell}(e)\}$$

$\mathtt{ref}(e)$ creates a new memory cell with e as the initial value, $\mathtt{set}(e, e')$ sets a cell e with new value e', and $\mathtt{get}(e)$ gets the value from cell e. We let $a; b$ abbreviate sequencing, $(\lambda x.b)\,(a)$ for x fresh.

We hereafter take k to be an arbitrary fixed value and refer to this language as $\mathbb{L}_{\mathrm{m}}$. The previous section gives evidence that a family of injections captures the complexity of other simple features such as booleans, numbers, pairs, and objects. In our embedding of objects into $\mathbb{L}_{\mathrm{bpn}(k)}$ we preserved these features because the embedding was homomorphic. In the memory case, no homomorphic embedding can be defined.

LEMMA 5.2 There is no embedding $[\![\cdot]\!] \in \mathbb{L}_{\mathrm{m}(k)} \to \mathbb{L}_{\mathrm{bpn}(k+j+1)}$ for any j, k that is homomorphic in $\mathbb{O}_{\mathrm{inj}(k)}$.

PROOF: The basic idea of the proof is the observation that a homomorphic embedding would force functions in the memory language to have no side-effects. $(\lambda x.y\,(0))\,(y\,(0)) \cong_{\mathrm{bpn}(k+j+1)} y\,(0)$, so if a homomorphic map existed, by lifting we would have $(\lambda x.y\,(0))\,(y\,(0)) \cong_{\mathrm{m}} y\,(0)$ but $y = \lambda x.\mathtt{set}(z, \mathtt{inj}_i(\mathtt{get}(z)))$ causes this to fail. □

$\mathbb{L}_{\mathrm{m}}$ is embedded into $\mathbb{L}_{\mathrm{bpn}(k+1)}$ by the following parametric embedding, which passes the memory to all computations and computes (value, memory)-pairs as result. $\mathtt{inj}_{k+1}$ is used to label cell numbers. The memory is a function from cell numbers to values; memory location 0 holds the next free cell address.

DEFINITION 5.3 Parametric embedding $[\![\cdot]\!] \in \mathbb{L}_{\mathrm{m}} \to \mathbb{L}_{\mathrm{bpn}(k+1)}$ is defined as $C_{\mathrm{init}} = \bullet\,(\lambda x.0)$ and an embedding of expressions as follows.

$$\begin{array}{rcl}
[\![x]\!] & = & \lambda m.\mathtt{pr}(x,m) = C_{\mathrm{var}}[x] \\
[\![\mathtt{ref}(e)]\!] & = & \lambda m.\mathtt{let}\;\mathtt{pr}(v,m_1) = [\![e]\!]\,(m)\;\mathtt{in} \\
& & \quad \mathtt{pr}(\mathtt{inj}_{k+1}(m_1\,(0)), \lambda c'.\mathtt{if}(\mathtt{iszero}(c'), \mathtt{succ}(m_1(0)), \\
& & \qquad \mathtt{if}(\mathtt{nateq}(c', m_1(0)), v, m_1(c')))) \\
[\![\mathtt{set}(e,e')]\!] & = & \lambda m.\mathtt{let}\;\mathtt{pr}(c,m_1) = [\![e]\!]\,(m)\;\mathtt{in} \\
& & \quad \mathtt{let}\;\mathtt{pr}(v,m_2) = [\![e']\!]\,(m_1)\;\mathtt{in} \\
& & \quad \mathtt{pr}(v, \lambda c'.\mathtt{if}(\mathtt{nateq}(c', \mathtt{out}_{k+1}(c)), v, m_2(c'))) \\
[\![\mathtt{get}(e)]\!] & = & \lambda m.\mathtt{let}\;\mathtt{pr}(c,m_1) = [\![e]\!]\,(m)\;\mathtt{in}\;\mathtt{pr}(m_1(\mathtt{out}_{k+1}(c)), m_1) \\
[\![\mathtt{iscell}(e)]\!] & = & \lambda m.\mathtt{let}\;\mathtt{pr}(v,m_1) = [\![e]\!]\,(m)\;\mathtt{in}\;\mathtt{pr}(\mathtt{is}_{k+1}(v), m_1) \\
[\![\lambda x.e]\!] & = & \lambda m.\mathtt{pr}(\lambda x.[\![e]\!], m) \\
[\![\mathtt{op}(e)]\!] & = & \lambda m.\mathtt{let}\;\mathtt{pr}(v,m_1) = [\![e]\!]\,(m)\;\mathtt{in}\;\mathtt{pr}(\mathtt{op}(v), m_1) \\
& & \text{for all other unary operators op} \in \mathbb{O}_{\mathrm{m}} \\
[\![e\,(e')]\!] & = & \lambda m.\mathtt{let}\;\mathtt{pr}(f,m_1) = [\![e]\!]\,(m)\;\mathtt{in} \\
& & \quad \mathtt{let}\;\mathtt{pr}(v,m_2) = [\![e']\!]\,(m_1)\;\mathtt{in}\;f\,(v)\,(m_2)
\end{array}$$

This encoding is clearly not fully abstract: $\mathbb{L}_{\mathrm{bpn}(k+1)}$ contexts will be able to inspect and alter the contents of arbitrary memory cells.

LEMMA 5.4 $[\![\cdot]\!] \in \mathbb{L}_{\mathrm{m}} \to \mathbb{L}_{\mathrm{bpn}(k+1)}$ is not fully abstract.

PROOF: $\lambda x.e\,(e) \cong_{\mathrm{bpn}(k+1)} e$ for x not free in e, but if e has a cumulative effect (such as $e = \mathtt{set}(y, \mathtt{inj}_i(\mathtt{get}(y))))$ the equation will fail to be $\cong_{\mathrm{m}}$. □

This parametric embedding is only sometimes useful for establishing equivalences $\cong_{\mathrm{m}}$: since it is not homomorphic, there is no lifting of equations possible. The one tool it provides is the ability to prove $a \cong_{\mathrm{m}} b$ by showing $[\![a]\!] \cong_{\mathrm{bpn}(k+1)} [\![b]\!]$. This technique is useful for principles that do not require memory locality, the source of lack of full abstraction in the translation.

5.1 Direct Memory Semantics

Since working in memory-passing style is difficult, hereafter we will work over a direct evaluation semantics for $\mathbb{L}_{\mathrm{m}}$, using notation close to (Honsell, Mason, Smith, and Talcott 1995; Mason and Talcott 1991). Most of the proofs in this section are direct generalizations of the functional proofs from (Mason, Smith, and Talcott 1996) to a language with memories. Very little extra reasoning is needed to handle the memory. The projection functions, defined in the following section, do require considerable extra work in the memory case.

A memory context Γ is defined as a context

$\mathtt{let}\;c_1 = \mathtt{ref}(\mathtt{etrue})\ldots\mathtt{let}\;c_n = \mathtt{ref}(\mathtt{etrue})\;\mathtt{in}\;\mathtt{set}(c_1, v_1)\ldots;\mathtt{set}(c_n, v_n);\;\bullet$

for distinct $c_1, \ldots, c_n$. Γ may equivalently be viewed as a finite map from variables to values; here $\mathrm{Dom}(\Gamma) = c_1, \ldots, c_n$. To distinguish variables used as cell names from other variables, we define $\mathbb{X}_{\mathrm{cell}} \subseteq \mathbb{X}$ such that $\mathbb{X}_{\mathrm{cell}}$ and $\mathbb{X}_\lambda = \mathbb{X} - \mathbb{X}_{\mathrm{cell}}$ are both countably infinite. Invariably, $\mathrm{Dom}(\Gamma) \subseteq \mathbb{X}_{\mathrm{cell}}$, and λ-bound variables are in $\mathbb{X}_\lambda$. α-conversion of cell variables is not allowed. We use shorthand $\Gamma\{c = v\}$ to indicate an extension to Γ mapping cell c to value v.

For brevity we will define some notions as extensions of the notions defined in the presentation of $\mathbb{L}_{\mathrm{inj}(k)}$ of Section 3, reading those definitions with $\mathbb{E}_{\mathrm{m}}$ in place of $\mathbb{E}_{\mathrm{inj}(k)}$. The values $\mathbb{V}_{\mathrm{m}}$ are the same cases as for $\mathbb{L}_{\mathrm{inj}(k)}$, and the reduction contexts $\mathbb{R}_{\mathrm{m}}$ include the same cases plus $\mathtt{ref}(\bullet) \cup \mathtt{set}(\bullet, \mathbb{E}_{\mathrm{m}}) \cup \mathtt{set}(\mathbb{V}_{\mathrm{m}}, \bullet) \cup \mathtt{get}(\bullet) \cup \mathtt{iscell}(\bullet)$. Single-step evaluation is a map $\Gamma[\![R[e]]\!] \mapsto^1_{\mathrm{m}} \Gamma'[\![R[e']]\!]$ for $R \in \mathbb{R}_{\mathrm{m}}$, e a redex and e' its contractum.

DEFINITION 5.5 ($\mapsto^1_{\mathrm{m}}, \mapsto_{\mathrm{m}}$) $\mapsto_{\mathrm{m}}$ is the transitive, reflexive closure $\mapsto^1$:

(fun)	$\Gamma[a]$	$\mapsto^1$	$\Gamma[b]$
	where $a \mapsto^1_{\mathrm{inj}(k)} b$ is a case of Definition 3.4		
(ref)	$\Gamma[\![R[\mathtt{ref}(v)]]\!]$	$\mapsto^1$	$\Gamma\{c = v\}[\![R[c]]\!]$ for fresh $c \in \mathbb{X}_{\mathrm{cell}}$
(set)	$\Gamma\{c = v_0\}[\![R[\mathtt{set}(c, v)]]\!]$	$\mapsto^1$	$\Gamma\{c = v\}[\![R[v]]\!]$
(get)	$\Gamma\{c = v\}[\![R[\mathtt{get}(c)]]\!]$	$\mapsto^1$	$\Gamma\{c = v\}[\![R[v]]\!]$
(iscell-t)	$\Gamma[\![R[\mathtt{iscell}(c)]]\!]$	$\mapsto^1$	$\Gamma[\![R[\mathtt{etrue}]]\!]$ where $c \in \mathbb{X}_{\mathrm{cell}}$
(iscell-f)	$\Gamma[\![R[\mathtt{iscell}(v)]]\!]$	$\mapsto^1$	$\Gamma[\![R[\mathtt{efalse}]]\!]$ where $v \notin \mathbb{X}$

The **ciu** ordering is defined for $\mathbb{L}_{\mathrm{m}}$ as follows.

DEFINITION 5.6 (CIU ORDERING, $\lesssim^{\mathrm{ciu}}_{\mathrm{m}}$) For all a and b, $a \lesssim^{\mathrm{ciu}}_{\mathrm{m}} b$ iff for all Γ, σ, R such that $\Gamma[\![R[a^{[\sigma]}]]\!]$ and $\Gamma[\![R[b^{[\sigma]}]]\!]$ are closed, if $\Gamma[\![R[a^{[\sigma]}]]\!]\downarrow$ then $\Gamma[\![R[b^{[\sigma]}]]\!]\downarrow$.

THEOREM 5.7 (CIU) $a \lesssim_{\mathrm{m}} b$ iff $a \lesssim^{\mathrm{ciu}}_{\mathrm{m}} b$.

For a proof, see (Honsell, Mason, Smith, and Talcott 1995). The theorem also follows from set ordering **ciu**, proved below as Theorem 5.10, by Lemma 2.6 (iii). Applicative bisimulation equivalences may be defined for languages with memories (Ritter and Pitts 1995) and may be effectively used to directly establish equivalences. They (to lesser degree) suffer the same problem of lack of locality as does $[\![a]\!] \cong_{\mathrm{bpn}(k+1)} [\![b]\!]$, and so are not fully abstract.

An important property that holds for $\lesssim_{\mathrm{m}}$ is extensionality. It seems not to have been stated or proved before in the literature so we give a proof.

THEOREM 5.8 ($\lesssim_{\mathrm{m}}$ EXTENSIONALITY) For all a_0 and a_1, $\lambda x.a_0 \lesssim_{\mathrm{m}} \lambda x.a_1$ if and only if $(\lambda x.a_0)\,(v) \lesssim_{\mathrm{m}} (\lambda x.a_1)\,(v)$ for all values v.

PROOF: $\Rightarrow$ is direct from the pre-congruence of $\lesssim_{\mathrm{m}}$. For $\Leftarrow$, assume for all v that $\lambda x.a_0\,(v) \lesssim_{\mathrm{m}} \lambda x.a_1\,(v)$ and show $\lambda x.a_0 \lesssim_{\mathrm{m}} \lambda x.a_1$. It suffices to fix v to be x; then by β-value, $a_0 \lesssim_{\mathrm{m}} a_1$ and so by congruence, $\lambda x.a_0 \lesssim_{\mathrm{m}} \lambda x.a_1$. □

It is perhaps surprising that extensionality holds, because extensionality shows that it suffices to test a function without iterative application. If the function is a closure with local state it will not have the same value when executed a second time. However, since the theorem is proved for λ-values only, these cannot have any local state. Extensionality fails for imperative objects (closures), because they may allocate their own local store. Consider the simple object defined as follows.

$$o = \mathtt{let}\ c = \mathtt{ref(etrue)}\ \mathtt{in}\ \lambda z.\mathtt{set}(c, \mathtt{inj}_1(\mathtt{get}(c)))$$

$o(v) \cong_{\mathrm{m}} \mathtt{inj}_1(\mathtt{etrue})$ for any v by computing, so if o was an extensional object, $o \cong_{\mathrm{m}} \lambda z.\mathtt{inj}_1(\mathtt{etrue})$ should hold but it clearly does not.

As was the case for $\mathbb{L}_{\mathrm{inj}(k)}$, the $\sqsubseteq_{\mathrm{m}}$-directed set ordering $\{\cdot\} \sqsubseteq_{\mathrm{m}} \{\cdot\}$ also has a **ciu** characterization which is critical for proving facts about $\{\cdot\} \sqsubseteq_{\mathrm{m}} \{\cdot\}$.

Definition 5.9 (ciu Set Ordering, $\sqsubseteq^{\mathrm{ciu}}_{\mathrm{m}}$) For $\sqsubseteq_{\mathrm{m}}$-directed sets of expressions A and B, $A \sqsubseteq^{\mathrm{ciu}}_{\mathrm{m}} B$ if and only if for all $a \in A$ and for all Γ, σ, R such that $\Gamma[R[A[\sigma]]]$ and $\Gamma[R[B[\sigma]]]$ are sets of closed expressions, if $\Gamma[R[a[\sigma]]]\downarrow$ then there exists a $b \in B$ such that $\Gamma[R[b[\sigma]]]\downarrow$.

The **ciu** theorem is

Theorem 5.10 ($\sqsubseteq^{\mathrm{ciu}}_{\mathrm{m}}$ ciu) $A \sqsubseteq_{\mathrm{m}} B$ iff $A \sqsubseteq^{\mathrm{ciu}}_{\mathrm{m}} B$.

This proof does not appear in previous papers and so is given here. The proof here is a direct combination of the proof of $\{\cdot\} \sqsubseteq \{\cdot\}$ **ciu** for a functional call-by-value language in (Mason, Smith, and Talcott 1996) and **ciu** for a memory-based language in (Honsell, Mason, Smith, and Talcott 1995). The proof may be factored into three Lemmas. The ($\Rightarrow$) direction is not difficult, since $\sqsubseteq^{\mathrm{ciu}}_{\mathrm{m}}$ has a smaller collection of contexts to distinguish expressions than $\{\cdot\} \sqsubseteq_{\mathrm{m}} \{\cdot\}$ has. ($\Leftarrow$) is the difficult direction. This proof uses the observation that it suffices to show $\sqsubseteq^{\mathrm{ciu}}_{\mathrm{m}}$ is a pre-congruence. To establish this, we prove lemmas that establish pre-congruence for single constructors: non-λ operators $\mathbb{O}_{\mathrm{m}}$ (Lemma 5.11) and λx (Lemma 5.12) may be placed around sets of expressions while preserving $\sqsubseteq^{\mathrm{ciu}}_{\mathrm{m}}$.

Lemma 5.11 ($\sqsubseteq^{\mathrm{ciu}}_{\mathrm{m}}$ Operator ciu) If $A \sqsubseteq^{\mathrm{ciu}}_{\mathrm{m}} B$ holds, then

$$\mathsf{op}(\bar{c}, A, \bar{d}) \sqsubseteq^{\mathrm{ciu}}_{\mathrm{m}} \mathsf{op}(\bar{c}, B, \bar{d})$$

for any $\mathsf{op} \in \mathbb{O}_{\mathrm{m}}$ that is not `lambda`.

Proof: We consider the case of an arbitrary binary operator op; the simpler unary case should be uniformly apparent from this case. It suffices to show the two cases

$\Gamma[R[\mathsf{op}(a[\sigma], c))]]\downarrow$ implies there exists a $b \in B$ such that $\Gamma[R[\mathsf{op}(b[\sigma], c)]]\downarrow$

and

$$\Gamma[R[\mathtt{op}(c, a_{[\sigma]})]] \downarrow \text{ implies there exists a } b \in B \text{ such that } \Gamma[R[\mathtt{op}(c, b_{[\sigma]})]] \downarrow$$

We proceed by induction on the length of the computation of the assumption. Assume the statements are true for all shorter computations. In the first case above define $R_0 = R[\mathtt{op}(\bullet, c)]$, and in the second case when c is a value, define $R_0 = R[\mathtt{op}(c, \bullet)]$, and the conclusion follows directly by assumption. So, we may concentrate on the second case when c is not a value. In this case we have a reduction context

$$R_0 = R[\mathtt{op}(\bullet, a_{[\sigma]})],$$

so by computing

$$\Gamma[R[\mathtt{op}(c, a_{[\sigma]})]] \mapsto^1 \Gamma'[R[\mathtt{op}(c', a_{[\sigma]})]],$$

which is an instance of the induction hypothesis since this computation will terminate in one fewer steps. □

LEMMA 5.12 ($\lesssim^{\text{ciu}}_{\text{m}}$ LAMBDA CIU) If $A \lesssim^{\text{ciu}}_{\text{m}} B$, then $\lambda x.A \lesssim^{\text{ciu}}_{\text{m}} \lambda x.B$.

PROOF: It suffices to assume expressions in A and B contain at most x free, the conclusion then follows by definition of $\lesssim^{\text{ciu}}_{\text{m}}$. For arbitrary R and Γ, show for fixed $a \in A$

$$\Gamma[R[\lambda x.a]] \downarrow \text{ implies there exists a } b \in B \text{ such that } \Gamma[R[\lambda x.b]] \downarrow.$$

We may generalize this statement to

$$\Gamma[e]_{[\lambda x.a/z]} \downarrow \text{ implies there exists a } b \in B \text{ such that } \Gamma[e]_{[\lambda x.b/z]} \downarrow,$$

for free variables of e coming only from $\mathrm{Dom}(\Gamma) \cup \{z\}$. The original goal follows by letting $e = R[z]$. Proceed by induction on the length of the computation of the assumption. Consider whether $\Gamma[e]$ is uniform in z, i.e. whether

$$\Gamma[e] \mapsto^1 \Gamma'[e']$$

for some $\Gamma'[e']$. If it is uniform, then

$$\Gamma[e]_{[\lambda x.e''/z]} \mapsto^1 \Gamma'[e']_{[\lambda x.e''/z]}, \text{ for all } e'',$$

and the result follows by the induction hypothesis.

Consider the case where $\Gamma[e]$ is stuck, i.e. does not reduce. Since $\Gamma[e]_{[\lambda x.a/z]} \downarrow$, it does not get stuck when a λ-value is substituted for z. By the evaluation rules, replacing z with a λ-value causes a stuck computation to become un-stuck in two cases. The first is if the redex is $\mathtt{is}_i(z)$ or $\mathtt{iscell}(z)$; but these cases are still uniform for any λ-value and reasoning analogous to the previous uniform case applies. The only other non-uniform case is where $e = R[z\,(v)]$ for some R, v which have free variables from $\mathrm{Dom}(\Gamma) \cup \{z\}$. By the form of the β-value reduction rule, we then have the following:

$$\Gamma[R[(\lambda x.e')\,(v)\,]] \mapsto^1 \Gamma[R[e'\,[v/x]]],$$

for all expressions e', v, R. In particular, it holds for e' being a or any $b \in B$. It thus suffices to show

$$\text{there exists a } b \in B \text{ such that } \Gamma[R[b\,[v/x]]]\,[\lambda x.b/z]\downarrow.$$

By the induction hypothesis,

$$\text{there exists a } b' \in B \text{ such that } \Gamma[(R[a\,[v/x]])]\,[\lambda x.b'/z]\downarrow.$$

Then by the assumption $A \lesssim_m^{\mathrm{ciu}} B$, a above may be replaced by some $b'' \in B$ (take the substitution in the definition of $\lesssim_m^{\mathrm{ciu}}$ to be $[v\,[\lambda x.b'/z]/x]$), giving

$$\text{there exists a } b'' \in B \text{ such that } \Gamma[(R[b''\,[v/x]])]\,[\lambda x.b'/z]\downarrow.$$

By the directedness of B, we can find a b such that $b', b'' \lesssim_m b$, and this means first that

$$\Gamma[(R[b''\,[v/x]])]\,[\lambda x.b/z]\downarrow.$$

Now by the simple fact that $\lesssim_m$ respects value substitution, $b''\,[v'/x] \lesssim_m b\,[v'/x]$ for $v' = v\,[\lambda x.b/z]$, so

$$\Gamma[(R[b\,[v/x]])]\,[\lambda x.b/z]\downarrow.$$

□

Iteratively applying the two previous lemmas then allows an arbitrary context to be constructed around sets A and B one operator at a time:

LEMMA 5.13 ($\lesssim_m^{\mathrm{ciu}}$ PRE-CONGRUENCE) $\lesssim_m^{\mathrm{ciu}}$ is a pre-congruence, $A \lesssim_m^{\mathrm{ciu}} B$ implies $C[A] \lesssim_m^{\mathrm{ciu}} C[B]$.

And, from $\lesssim_m^{\mathrm{ciu}}$ pre-congruence, Theorem 5.10 directly follows.

LEMMA 5.14 (FIXED POINT) For a functional f, $\{\mathtt{fix}\,(f)\,\} \cong_m \{f^n \mid n \in \mathbb{N}\}$.

PROOF: Without loss of generality assume the free variables of f are cell variables only, for from this case the result follows for arbitrary f by Theorem 5.10. The $\gtrsim_m$ direction follows by induction on n; consider then proving $\lesssim_m$. First note $\mathtt{fix}\,(f)\,\cong_m u\,(u)$ where $u = \lambda x.\lambda z.f\,(x\,(x)\,)\,(z)$, so it suffices to show $\{u\,(u)\,\} \lesssim_m \{f^k \mid k \in \mathbb{N}\}$. Expanding definitions, the desired result is to show for all a with free variables from $\{x\} \cup \mathrm{Dom}(\Gamma)$, $\Gamma[a]\,[u\,(u)\,/x]\downarrow$ implies $\Gamma[a]\,[f^k/x]\downarrow$ for some k. Assume $\Gamma[a]\,[u\,(u)\,/x]\downarrow$, proceed by induction on the length of this computation to show the above statement. Consider the next step of computation performed on $\Gamma[a]\,[u\,(u)\,/x]$. If the step is uniform in $u\,(u)$, the conclusion follows directly by induction hypothesis. Then, consider non-uniform steps; all such cases can easily be seen to be of the form

$$\Gamma[a]_{[u\,(u)/x]} = \Gamma[R[u\,(u)\,]]_{[u\,(u)/x]} \mapsto_1 \Gamma[R[\lambda z.f(u\,(u)\,)(z)]]_{[u\,(u)/x]},$$

we show $\Gamma[R[f^k]]_{[f^k/x]}\downarrow$ for some k. By the induction hypothesis,

$$\Gamma[R[\lambda z.f(f^{k_0})(z)]]_{[f^{k_0}/x]}\downarrow$$

for some k_0, so since $f^{k_0} \precsim_{\mathrm{m}} f^{k_0+1}$ and $\lambda z.f(f^{k_0})(z) \cong_{\mathrm{m}} f^{k_0+1}$ by extensionality, $\Gamma[R[f^{k_0+1}]]_{[f^{k_0+1}/x]}\downarrow$, and letting k be $k_0 + 1$, the desired conclusion has been reached. □

5.2 Memory Projections

We will hereafter informally use numbers, pairs, and lists as $\mathbb{L}_{\mathrm{m}}$ syntax, taking numbers and pairs to be encoded as in the embedding of $\mathbb{L}_{\mathrm{bpn}}$ of Definition 4.3, and (functional) lists and list operations, `nil`/`cons`/`carcdr`/`isnil`/`mapcar`, encoded via the standard pair-based encoding. We will define `member` for lists of cells below. Syntactic projections π^n_{m} may be defined as follows.

DEFINITION 5.15 (PROJECTIONS π^n_{m})

```
πm = λy.λz.λx.
        eif(is1(x), inj1(y(z) (out1(x))),
        eif(is2(x), inj2(y(z) (out2(x))),... ,
        eif(isk(x), injk(y(z) (outk(x))),
        eif(iscell(x), set(w, cons(x, get(w)));
            eif(member(x, z), x, set(x, y(cons(x, z)) (get(x))))),
        λx0.mapcar(λx.y(nil) (x), get(w));
            let r = y(nil) (x(y(nil) (x0))) in
            mapcar(λx.y(nil) (x), get(w)); r)...))

member(x, l) = fix(λf.λl.eif(isnil(l), efalse,
        eif(celleq(x, car(l)), etrue, f(cdr(l)))(l)
celleq(x, y) = let x0 = get(x) in let y0 = get(y) in
        set(x, efalse); set(y, etrue);
        let r = get(x) in set(x, x0); set(y, y0); r
πm^0 = λx.bot
πm^(n+1) = let w = ref(nil) in πm(πm^n) (nil)
πm^∞ = let w = ref(nil) in fix(πm) (nil)
```

The difficult question is what the projection operation should do with a memory cell. The above projections will project the contents of any memory cell encountered. If there is cyclic data in the memory, such as a cell x containing $\mathtt{inj}_2(x)$, we must not repeatedly project x, for this process will loop forever. The extra z parameter here, not found in the functional projection functions, serves the purpose of accumulating cells already encountered, and preventing such cells from being projected again. Note that projection of cell x containing $\lambda y.x$ causes no looping problem because the projection operation will halt at the λ. For this reason, at this point z is reset.

The global cell list in reference w serves to close a "back-door" communication channel. Note that w is free in π_{m} and becomes bound in π^{n+1}_{m} and $\pi^{\infty}_{\mathrm{m}}$ definitions. The cells in this list are cells that "entered" or "exited" this projection at some point in the computation history. Subexpression

$$\texttt{mapcar}(\lambda x.y\,(x)\,(z)\,,\texttt{get}(w))$$

above serves to project all the cells accumulated thus far in w. Without w and these additional projections, cells would only be projected when they are explicitly passed to or returned from a function, and thus a cell passed to a projected function could on successive calls to the function serve as a "back-door" communication channel if the function remembers this cell name locally. We give an example to clarify this point. A wrapper around a function f of the form

$$\begin{array}{rcl} z & = & \texttt{let}\ c = \texttt{ref}(\texttt{inj}_1(\lambda x.x))\ \texttt{in} \\ & & \lambda y.\texttt{eif}(\texttt{is}_1(\texttt{get}(c)), \texttt{set}(c, y), \texttt{set}(\texttt{get}(c), f\,(\texttt{get}(\texttt{get}(c))))) \end{array}$$

would then allow f to be computed even when z is projected: first a cell could be passed in to z which serves as a communication channel to the context that would not be subsequently projected. Consider

$$\begin{array}{rcl} f' & = & \lambda x.\texttt{let}\ z = \pi^3_{\mathrm{m}}\,(z)\ \texttt{in} \\ & & \texttt{let}\ y = \texttt{ref}(\lambda x.\texttt{bot})\ \texttt{in}\ z\,(y);\ \texttt{set}(y, x);\ z\,(\lambda x.x);\ \texttt{get}(y) \end{array}$$

—$f \cong_{\mathrm{m}} f'$ would hold if nonlocal cell projection were not a component of the definition of π_{m} above.

We may prove π^n_{m} possesses the finite approximation property:

THEOREM 5.16 Finite Approximation, Theorem 3.14, is provable for the projections π^n_{m}: $\{\pi^n_{\mathrm{m}}\,(a) \mid n \in \mathbb{N}\} \cong_{\mathrm{m}} \{a\}$.

The proof of this Theorem parallels the proof for $\mathbb{L}_{\mathrm{inj}(k)}$ of Section 3.2. More details of proofs are provided here since the memory changes some aspects of the proof in a nontrivial way. Hereafter the m subscript on projections π is implicit.

LEMMA 5.17 (ELEMENTARY $\pi^n_{\mathrm{m}}/\pi^{\infty}_{\mathrm{m}}$ PROPERTIES) The elementary π^n/π^{∞} properties of Lemma 3.13 all hold when lifted to $\mathbb{L}_{\mathrm{m}}$.

Following $\mathbb{L}_{\mathrm{inj}(k)}$, we define $\tau(a)$ and $\tau(R)$ to characterize how the projections percolate into expressions. The only addition is the projections may percolate into the memory Γ and so $\tau(\Gamma)$ also needs to be defined. The definitions of $\tau(a)$ and $\tau(R)$ may be directly lifted from $\mathbb{L}_{\mathsf{inj}(k)}$ (cells are in fact variables, so no extra case is needed there). $\tau(\Gamma)$ is defined as replacing each cell value v in Γ with $\tau(v)$. Observe that $\tau(\Gamma)$ is always a legal memory context since it stores only values. Basic properties of $\tau(e)$ sets include the following.

LEMMA 5.18 (i) For a with all free variables bound by memory context Γ, $\tau(\Gamma)[\tau(R)[\pi^\infty(\tau(a))]]\downarrow \Leftrightarrow \tau(\Gamma)[\tau(R)[\tau(a)]]\downarrow$.

(ii) $\tau(a) \lessapprox_{\mathrm{m}} a$, $\tau(R[x]) \lessapprox_{\mathrm{m}} R[x]$, and $\tau(\Gamma[a])\downarrow \Rightarrow \Gamma[a]\downarrow$.

(iii) $\tau(R[b]) = \tau(R)[\tau(b)]$, and $\tau(a[v/x]) = \tau(a)[\tau(v)/x]$.

PROOF: (i), $\Rightarrow$ follows from Lemma 5.17, (prune). For $\Leftarrow$, first observe it suffices to consider the case of a being a value by computing. The structure of values in this language can be viewed as a chain of chains terminating in a λ, described as follows: outermost, the value is $\mathtt{inj}_{i_1}(\ldots\mathtt{inj}_{i_n}(v)\ldots)$ where v is a λ or a cell; if it is a cell, the contents of the cell, $\tau(\Gamma)(v)$, in turn must have a similar chain structure. This chain of chains must eventually terminate in a λ, or in a cell already encountered previously on the chain. An induction on the structure of this chain establishes that the π^∞ operation here has no effect.

(ii) follows from Lemma 5.17 (prune), and (iii) is direct from the definition of τ. □

LEMMA 5.19 (IDENTITY OF π^∞_{m}) $\pi^\infty \cong_{\mathrm{m}} \lambda x.x$

PROOF: The $\lessapprox_{\mathrm{m}}$ direction follows from Lemma 5.17 (prune) and extensionality. For the $\gtrapprox_{\mathrm{m}}$ direction, we successively rephrase the statement five times. It suffices to show for all a with only cell variables free that $\Gamma[R[a]]]\downarrow \Rightarrow \Gamma[R[\pi^\infty(a)]]]\downarrow$ by the **ciu** and extensionality theorems. For this it then suffices to show $\Gamma[R[a]]\downarrow \Rightarrow \tau(\Gamma)[\tau(R)[\pi^\infty(\tau(a))]])]\downarrow$ by Lemma 5.18 (ii). And, by Lemma 5.18 (i) it then suffices to show $\Gamma[R[a]]\downarrow \Rightarrow \tau(\Gamma)[\tau(R)[\tau(a)]])]\downarrow$ So, it suffices to show $\Gamma[a_0]\downarrow \Rightarrow \tau(\Gamma)[\tau(a_0)]\downarrow$ by Lemma 5.18 (iii). And lastly, to show this it suffices to show $\Gamma_0[a_0] \mapsto^1 \Gamma_1[a_1] \Rightarrow \tau(\Gamma_0)[\tau(a_0)]\downarrow \Leftrightarrow \tau(\Gamma_1)[\tau(a_1)]\downarrow$, for the conclusion then follows by induction on computation length and the observation that $\tau(v)$ is a value for any value v.

So, assume $\Gamma_0[a_0] \mapsto^1 \Gamma_1[a_1]$, show $\tau(\Gamma_0)[\tau(a_0)]\downarrow \Leftrightarrow \tau(\Gamma_1)[\tau(a_1)]\downarrow$. Consider this step of computation; $a_0 = R[a]$ for some redex a; proceed by cases on the form of a.

If $a = \mathsf{app}(\lambda x.c, v)$, then $a_1 = R[c[v/x]]$. By inspection of the definitions of $\tau(a)$ and $\tau(R)$, $\tau(\Gamma_0)[\tau(a_0)]$ must be of the form

$$\tau(\Gamma_0)[\tau(R)[\pi^\infty(\mathsf{app}(\pi^\infty \circ \lambda x.\tau(c) \circ \pi^\infty, \tau(v)))]].$$

Computing from this point yields

$$
\begin{array}{ll}
& \tau(\Gamma_0)[\tau(R)[\pi^\infty(\mathrm{app}(\pi^\infty \circ \lambda x.\tau(c) \circ \pi^\infty, \tau(v)))]]\downarrow \\
\Leftrightarrow & \tau(\Gamma_0)[\tau(R)[\pi^\infty(\pi^\infty(\mathrm{app}(\lambda x.\tau(c), \pi^\infty(\tau(v)))))]]\downarrow \\
\Leftrightarrow & \tau(\Gamma_0)[\tau(R)[\pi^\infty(\mathrm{app}(\lambda x.\tau(c), \tau(v)))]]\downarrow \text{ by Lemmas 5.17 (idemp), 5.18 (i)} \\
\Leftrightarrow & \tau(\Gamma_0)[\tau(R)[\pi^\infty(\tau(c)[\tau(v)/x])]]\downarrow \\
\Leftrightarrow & \tau(\Gamma_0)[\tau(R)[\tau(c)[\tau(v)/x]]]\downarrow \text{ by Lemma 5.18 (i) and (iii)} \\
\Leftrightarrow & \tau(\Gamma_0)[\tau(R[c[v/x]])]\downarrow \text{ by Lemma 5.18 (iii).}
\end{array}
$$

If a is any other redex except a memory operation, the proof is similar to the previous case. For the memory operations, the proof is somewhat similar but requires a bit of extra reasoning; consider redex $\mathtt{set}(x, v)$. The memory cell x in Γ_1 will then have value v, whereas $\mathtt{set}(x, \tau(v))$ will place $\tau(v)$ as x's value, precisely what $\tau(\Gamma_1)$ should be by its definition. □

Unfortunately these projections do not produce finite elements. The projection operations π can force the domain and range of a function to be statically finite, but there are still infinitely many different histories this function can have on successive invocations.

LEMMA 5.20 (π_m FINITENESS FAILURE) $\{a \mid a \text{ is closed and } a \cong_m \pi^3(a)\}$ contains infinitely many $\cong_m$-distinct expressions.

PROOF: For each n,

$$\mathtt{let}\ x = \mathtt{ref}(n)\ \mathtt{in}\ \lambda x.\mathtt{if}(\mathtt{iszero}(\mathtt{set}(x, \mathtt{pred}(\mathtt{get}(x)))), \mathtt{bot}, 0)$$

is a distinct constant function which only may be used up to n times before diverging. □

This suggests that some aspect of history must be included in a finite characterization of memory-based languages. There is one additional incompleteness. These projected expressions are also not finite in the operational sense, namely a computation of $\pi^n(a)$ could compute forever without attempting to compute $\pi^0(v)$ for some v. In particular, a memory-based fixed point (defined as a function in a cell c which in its body retrieves the function in c, *i.e.* itself, and invokes it) could compute forever even if every subexpression is projected. Consider for example the evaluation of

$$\Gamma\{c = \pi^n_m \circ \lambda y.\pi^n_m(\mathtt{get}(\pi^{n+1}_m(c))(0))\}[\pi^n_m(\mathtt{get}(\pi^{n+1}_m(c))(0))].$$

This computation will compute infinitely along the sequence of states

$$\Gamma\{c = \pi^n_m \circ \lambda y.\pi^n_m(\mathtt{get}(\pi^{n+1}_m(c))(0))\}[\pi^n_m(\ldots\pi^n_m(\mathtt{get}(\pi^{n+1}_m(c))(0))\ldots)].$$

Any functional fixed point which uses the projected fixed point combinator $\pi^n(\mathtt{fix})$ will not suffer from this problem: the bound n will be the maximum number of recursive calls of $\pi^n(\mathtt{fix})(f)$ for any functional f.

5.3 Toward Finite Memory Projections

We now outline a potential solution to the above problems. The number of times a projected function can be successively invoked is limited to a fixed number, removing the infinitude uncovered in Lemma 5.20. This is implemented by modifying projections at level n to use a unique counter cell for each function that counts the number of calls, and diverges after n calls. We conjecture that finiteness holds for these modified projections, $\pi^n_{\mathrm{m}+}$.

DEFINITION 5.21 (FINITE PROJECTIONS $\pi^n_{\mathrm{m}+}$)

$$
\begin{array}{l}
\pi^0_{\mathrm{m}-} = \lambda z.\lambda x.\mathtt{bot} \\
\pi^{n+1}_{\mathrm{m}-} = \lambda z.\lambda x. \\
\qquad \mathtt{eif}(\mathtt{is}_1(x), \mathtt{inj}_1(\pi^n_{\mathrm{m}-}\,(z)\,(\mathtt{out}_1(x))), \\
\qquad \mathtt{eif}(\mathtt{is}_2(x), \mathtt{inj}_2(\pi^n_{\mathrm{m}-}\,(z)\,(\mathtt{out}_2(x))), \ldots, \\
\qquad \mathtt{eif}(\mathtt{is}_k(x), \mathtt{inj}_k(\pi^n_{\mathrm{m}-}\,(z)\,(\mathtt{out}_k(x))), \\
\qquad \mathtt{eif}(\mathtt{iscell}(x), \mathtt{set}(w, \mathtt{cons}(x, \mathtt{get}(w))); \\
\qquad\qquad \mathtt{eif}(\mathtt{member}(x, z), x, \mathtt{set}(x, \pi^n_{\mathrm{m}-}\,(\mathtt{cons}(x, z))\,(\mathtt{get}(x))))), \\
\qquad \mathtt{let}\ c = \mathtt{ref}(n)\ \mathtt{in}\ \lambda x_0. \\
\qquad\qquad \mathtt{eif}(\mathtt{iszero}(\mathtt{get}(c)), \mathtt{bot}, \mathtt{set}(c, \mathtt{pred}(\mathtt{get}(c)))); \\
\qquad\qquad \mathtt{mapcar}(\lambda x.\pi^n_{\mathrm{m}-}\,(\mathtt{nil})\,(x), \mathtt{get}(w)); \\
\qquad\qquad \mathtt{let}\ r = \pi^n_{\mathrm{m}-}\,(\mathtt{nil})\,(x\,(\pi^n_{\mathrm{m}-}\,(\mathtt{nil})\,(x_0)))\ \mathtt{in} \\
\qquad\qquad \mathtt{mapcar}(\lambda x.\pi^n_{\mathrm{m}-}\,(\mathtt{nil})\,(x), \mathtt{get}(w));\ r)\ldots)) \\
\pi^n_{\mathrm{m}+} = \mathtt{let}\ w = \mathtt{ref}(\mathtt{nil})\ \mathtt{in}\ \pi^n_{\mathrm{m}-}\,(\mathtt{nil})
\end{array}
$$

Variable c above is a counter, freshly created for each function projected, to count the number of calls. Besides this one change, these projections are the same as the π^n_{m}.

THEOREM 5.22 Finite Approximation, Theorem 3.14, is provable for the projections $\pi^n_{\mathrm{m}+}$: $\{\pi^n_{\mathrm{m}+}\,(a) \mid n \in \mathbb{N}\} \cong_{\mathrm{m}} \{a\}$.

PROOF: By Lemma 5.16, it suffices to show

$$\{\pi^n_{\mathrm{m}+}\,(a) \mid n \in \mathbb{N}\} \cong_{\mathrm{m}} \{\pi^n_{\mathrm{m}}\,(a) \mid n \in \mathbb{N}\}.$$

Since $\pi^n_{\mathrm{m}+}$ only adds additional possibilities for divergence to π^n_{m}, the $\precsim$ direction is not difficult. For $\succsim$, suppose $C[\pi^n_{\mathrm{m}}\,(a)]\downarrow$, in m steps; we show $C[\pi^{m+n+1}_{\mathrm{m}}\,(a)]\downarrow$: in the $C[\pi^n_{\mathrm{m}}\,(a)]$ computation there can be no more than m application steps, so no single function is applied more than m times, so if the counters for all projected functions are initially set to be larger than m, no counter will ever reach 0. And, π^{m+n+1}_{m} indeed will assure every counter is initially larger than m since termination of $C[\pi^n_{\mathrm{m}}\,(a)]$ guarantees the minimum projection must be more than π^{m+1}_{m}. □

We conjecture that these finite projections do indeed "project enough" to produce only finitely many programs at each rank.

CONJECTURE 5.23 (FINITENESS) The set

$$\{a \mid a \text{ is closed and } a \cong_{\mathrm{m}} \pi^n_+ (a)\}$$

contains finitely many $\cong_{\mathrm{m}}$-distinct expressions for each $n \in \mathbb{N}$.

In the functional case, extensionality is critical to prove this property: there are finitely many functions at a certain level because by induction, the functions have a finite domain and finite range of elements of the next lowest level, and thus by extensionality there can be only finitely many such functions. In the memory case, the failure of extensionality for closures causes this proof technique to fail. A proof of the conjecture thus appears difficult.

We can at least conclude that there is some hope of developing finite projections in the memory case.

It is also possible to develop a theory of projections for $\mathbb{L}_{\mathrm{m}}$ by adding new, atomic projection operators, following the idea of the $\mathbb{L}_{\mathrm{bpn}\pi-(k)}$ and $\mathbb{L}_{\mathrm{obj}\pi(k)}$ constructions. The atomic projections can be interpreted as the $\mathbb{L}_{\mathrm{bpn}}$ projections via the embedding of Definition 5.3. These atomic projections will have the effect of projecting local memory cells, thus destroying full abstraction.

6 Conclusions

We have studied a fairly broad family of languages, and return with mixed results on whether fully abstract finite element theories may be developed. For functional languages with recognizer operators ($\mathbb{L}_{\mathrm{inj}(k)}$ of Section 3 and $\mathbb{L}_{\mathrm{bpn}(k)}$ of Section 4.1), the prospects are excellent. Without recognizers present ($\mathbb{L}_{\mathrm{bpn}-(k)}$ of Section 4.2), prospects do not look as promising. Simple objects ($\mathbb{L}_{\mathrm{obj}(k)}$ of Section 4.3) apparently have no elegant projection operations π^n definable. For memories, we conjecture that the projection functions π^n_+ yield finitely many expressions at each rank, so the problem is open but there is some possibility of a solution.

We showed it is always possible to develop a theory of projections by adding new, atomic projection operators ($\mathbb{L}_{\mathrm{bpn}\pi-(k)}$ of Section 4.2.1, and $\mathbb{L}_{\mathrm{obj}\pi(k)}$ of Section 4.4). This however may expose internal details and thus lose full abstraction. Lemma 4.16 shows in some cases it is provable that addition of atomic projections changes the equivalence. Many explicit λ-labelling methods will also suffer from the same problem. For some applications, on the other hand, projections of this form may be adequate.

On a positive note, an inductive characterization of fixed points was possible for all languages studied, so for the particular ranked sequence of successively larger approximations to a fixed point, an additional induction principle was gained. For $\mathbb{L}_{\mathrm{obj}}$, an inductive characterization of the self-reference found in objects was also possible. One of the reasons why this characterization was possible across such a wide range of languages is the set ordering $\{\cdot\} \sqsubseteq \{\cdot\}$ applies across the whole spectrum of languages. This generality is one of the major benefits of using this ordering. Its main weakness is that it does not directly generalize to the nondeterministic case.

Does full abstraction matter? It depends on the problem. In some cases it does not matter, and other times it might be critical. Negative uses of $\sqsubseteq$ are the major source of problems when an equivalence that is too fine-grained, $\cong_{\text{too-fine}} \subsetneq \cong$, is used. For instance, extensionality (Theorem 5.8) is one such property. For this reason, extensionality of a more fine-grained equivalence will not imply extensionality of $\cong$. The notion of a faithful ideal (Abadi, Pierce, and Plotkin 1991) also has a negative instance of $\cong$: "if $a \in I$ and $a \cong b$, then $b \in I$". The secondary source of problems is that a more fine-grained equivalence will mean some operational equivalences will not be provable via the too-fine-grained characterization.

Language embeddings also are of interest in their own right. The embeddings studied here give precise lemmas which characterize concepts that informally are well-known, but were without rigorous characterization. The fact that a language with injections alone allowed many other language features to be homomorphically embedded in them gives a case for studying untyped languages of that form. The inability of the pure λ-calculus to serve as the target of any homomorphic embedding defining $\mathbb{L}_{\text{bpn}}$ (Lemma 4.5) justifies why it is often inadequate to study the pure λ-calculus alone as a model of functional programming. The largest divide in language semantics lies between languages which can be homomorphically embedded into simple languages $\mathbb{L}_{\text{inj}(k)}$, and those which have only non-homomorphic embeddings into $\mathbb{L}_{\text{inj}(k)}$. This gap serves as one means to formally separate the functional from non-functional languages. Global effects such as memories lack a homomorphic embedding and are semantically difficult to deal with. Functional objects are homomorphic and justifiably semantically simpler than memories, and in fact the addition of objects may not modify operational equivalence (Conjecture 4.19).

6.1 Other Language Features

It is at least worth a brief mention of how other language features not discussed may be handled; greater exploration of this topic is a subject for future work. Objects were only partially addressed here. Imperative objects will pose additional difficulties beyond the problems exposed here.

Two features not touched on here are control effects and types. Control effects such as exceptions and `call/cc` are probably manageable, but values that escape to the top will cause complications because values that are not finite may escape: π^4 `(abort(1000))` would abort the projection operation and return 1000. If these values are "observable", values of any rank could escape.

Simply-typed higher order functional languages such as PCF are not particularly difficult because type membership may be inductively defined, and given the type of an expression e, its finite projection may be defined statically. More complex types such as polymorphic, recursive, and parameterized types greatly complicate matters by removing this possibility. In this case, recognizers must exist in the language, but recognizers are difficult to type. So, a `typecase` construct is probably required to preserve full abstraction.

The real question we seek an answer to is whether finite element characterizations are possible for real languages such as Standard ML that combine all of these features, and whether the characterizations may be used to prove deep properties of programs. We are still not quite able to answer that question. One particular challenge is whether it is possible to give a semantics to Standard ML that defines types "semantically," without recourse to type proof systems.

Acknowledgements The original research on finite projections (Mason, Smith, and Talcott 1996) was done in collaboration with Ian Mason and Carolyn Talcott. The author would like to also thank Carolyn Talcott for a careful reading of an early version of this paper that caught a number of errors; Lemma 5.20 is hers. Laurent Dami and Andy Pitts also gave careful readings of the paper which the author is thankful for. The author would like to acknowledge support for this work from NSF grants CCR-9301340 and CCR-9312433.

References

Abadi, M., L. Cardelli, and R. Viswanathan (1996). An interpretation of objects and object types. In *Conference Record of the Twenty-Third Annual ACM Symposium on Principles of Programming Languages*. ACM.

Abadi, M., B. Pierce, and G. Plotkin (1991). Faithful ideal models for recursive polymorphic types. *International Journal of Foundations of Computer Science* 2(1), 1–21.

Abramsky, S. (1990). The lazy lambda calculus. In *Research Topics in Functional Programming*, pp. 65–116. Addison-Wesley.

Agha, G., I. Mason, S. F. Smith, and C. Talcott (1992). Towards a theory of actor computation. In *CONCUR*, Volume 630 of *Lecture notes in Computer Science*, pp. 565–579. Springer-Verlag.

Barendregt, H. P. (1984). *The Lambda Calculus: Its Syntax and Semantics* (Revised ed.), Volume 103 of *Studies in Logic and the Foundations of Mathematics*. Amsterdam: North-Holland.

Bloom, B. (1990). Can LCF be topped? *Information and Computation 87*, 264–301.

Egidi, L., F. Honsell, and S. R. della Rocca (1992). Operational, denotational and logical descriptions: a case study. *Fundamenta Informaticae 16*(2), 149–170.

Eifrig, J., S. Smith, V. Trifonov, and A. Zwarico (1995). An interpretation of typed OOP in a language with state. *Lisp and Symbolic Computation 8*(4), 357–397.

Felleisen, M. (1991). On the expressive power of programming languages. *Science of Computer Programming 17*, 35–75.

Felleisen, M., D. Friedman, and E. Kohlbecker (1987). A syntactic theory of sequential control. *Theoretical Computer Science 52*, 205–237.

Felleisen, M. and R. Hieb (1992). The revised report on the syntactic theories of sequential control and state. *Theoretical Computer Science 103*, 235–271.

Freyd, P., P. Mulry, G. Rosolini, and D. Scott (1990). Extensional PERs. In *Proceedings of the Fifth Annual Symposium on Logic in Computer Science*, pp. 346–354.

Gordon, A. D. and G. D. Rees (1996). Bisimilarity for a first-order calculus of objects with subtyping. In *Conference Record of the Twenty-Third Annual ACM Symposium on Principles of Programming Languages.*

Harper, R., F. Honsell, and G. Plotkin (1993). A framework for defining logics. *Journal of the Association of Computing Machinery*, 143–184.

Honsell, F., I. A. Mason, S. F. Smith, and C. L. Talcott (1995). A variable typed logic of effects. *Information and Computation 119*(1), 55–90.

Howe, D. J. (1996, February). Proving congruence of bisimulation in functional programming languages. *Information and Computation 124*(2), 103–112.

Kamin, S. N. and U. S. Reddy (1994). Two semantic models of object-oriented languages. In C. A. Gunter and J. C. Mitchell (Eds.), *Theoretical Aspects of Object-Oriented Programming*, Chapter 13, pp. 464–495. MIT Press.

MacQueen, D. B., G. Plotkin, and R. Sethi (1984). An ideal model of types. In *Conference Record of the Eleventh Annual ACM Symposium on Principles of Programming Languages.*

Mason, I. A., S. F. Smith, and C. L. Talcott (1996). From operational semantics to domain theory. *Information and Computation 128*(1).

Mason, I. A. and C. L. Talcott (1991). Equivalence in functional languages with effects. *Journal of Functional Programming 1*, 287–327.

Milne, R. E. and C. Strachey (1976). *A theory of programming language semantics.* Chapman and Hall, London, and Wiley, New York.

Milner, R. (1977). Fully abstract models of typed λ-calculi. *Theoretical Computer Science 4*, 1–22.

Mitchell, J. (1993). On abstraction and the expressive power of programming languages. *Science of Computer Programming 21.*

Mosses, P. D. (1992). *Action Semantics.* Cambridge.

Pitts, A. M. (1996, 15 June). Relational properties of domains. *Information and Computation 127*(2), 66–90.

Riecke, J. G. (1993). Fully abstract translations between functional languages. *Mathematical Structures in Computer Science 3*, 387–415.

Ritter, E. and A. M. Pitts (1995). A fully abstract translation between a λ-calculus with reference types and standard ml. In *2nd Int. Conf. on Typed Lambda Calculus and Applications, Edinburgh, 1995*, Volume 902 of *Lecture Notes in Computer Science*, pp. 397–413. Springer-Verlag, Berlin.

Scott, D. (1976). Data types as lattices. *SIAM J. Computing 5*, 522–587.

Smith, S. F. (1992). From operational to denotational semantics. In *MFPS 1991*, Volume 598 of *Lecture notes in Computer Science*, pp. 54–76. Springer-Verlag.

Talcott, C. L. (1989). Programming and proving with function and control abstractions. Technical Report STAN-CS-89-1288, Stanford University, Stanford, CA 94305.

Talcott, C. L. (1997). Reasoning about functions with effects. In this volume, pp. 347–390.

Reasoning about functions with effects

Carolyn Talcott

1 Introduction

An important advantage claimed for functional programming is the elegant equational theory and the ability to reason about programs by simply replacing equals by equals. Also higher-order functions provide the ability to define high-level abstractions that simplify programming. On the other hand, real programs have effects, and it is often more concise to express a computation using effects. We would like to have the best of both worlds: functions with effects. The methods described in this paper allow one to have the expressive power of functions with effects and to develop rich equational theories for such languages. We extend our previous work on semantics of imperative functional languages (Talcott 1985, 1992; Mason and Talcott 1991a, 1992; Honsell, Mason, Smith, and Talcott 1995) by treating the combination of control and memory effects, and developing the semantic theory in a more abstract setting to better capture the essential features of program equivalence.

We adopt the view proposed in (Landin 1966) that a programming language consists of expressions of the lambda calculus augmented with primitive operations. We call such languages λ-languages. The primitive operations that we have in mind include not only basic constants, branching, and algebraic operations such as arithmetic and pairing, but also operations that manipulate the computation state (store, continuation), and the environment (sending messages, creating processes). The presence of higher-order objects in λ-languages makes defining and reasoning about program equivalence more complicated than in the first-order case, with or without effects. The methods and results described in this paper arose from a desire to treat a wide range of λ-languages in a unified manner. Although we only consider sequential languages here, the key ideas seem to extend to primitives for concurrency as well (Agha, Mason, Smith, and Talcott 1997).

Overview

We take an operational approach to defining the semantics of λ-languages. We begin with a small step semantics in which computation state is represented using syntactic entities such as expressions and contexts. There is a single reduction rule for each operation. Care is taken so that the reduction rule for an operation is not changed when new operations or new pieces of state are added. Computation is uniform is the sense that reduction steps can be performed on states with missing parts and the missing information can be filled in later. Such a syntactic reduction system has the combined advantages of a simple transition system semantics and the symbolic reasoning of a reduction calculus.

We then abstract from the details of computations by defining the notions of operational approximation and equivalence on expressions. Intuitively, two expressions are operationally equivalent (also called contextually equivalent in the literature) if no program context can distinguish them. More precisely, operational equivalence is the equivalence naturally associated with the operational approximation pre-order. One expression operationally approximates another expression if when placed in any closing program context either the resulting first program is undefined or both resulting programs are defined.

Some laws of program equivalence, including laws that axiomatize operations with effects, hold because of the general nature of the languages we are considering. These laws are robust in the sense that they are not invalidated by addition of new primitive operations to the language (subject to minimal constraints on the semantics). They include the laws of computational lambda calculus (Moggi 1988), and the program calculi developed in (Felleisen 1987; Felleisen and Hieb 1992) for Scheme-like languages. These laws typically have simple computational justifications. For example, two expressions are equivalent if they reduce to a common expression (while having the same effect on the computation state). As another example, two expressions are equivalent if they correspond to placing a third expression in computationally equivalent contexts. Other laws, such as those that change the order of evaluation, need more careful formulation as they are sensitive to the particular choice of primitive operations. In order to get a better understanding of these observations, we identify properties of the operational semantics of a λ-language — structure of computation states and reduction rules — which allow us to establish computational laws in a quite general setting. If these properties hold we say that the language has *uniform semantics*. This allows us to build an equational core that holds for all λ-languages with uniform semantics, as well as to investigate more specialized laws in the same framework.

A key result for λ-languages with uniform semantics is an alternate characterization of the operational approximation relation that reduces the number of contexts that must be considered to establish laws of approximation and equivalence. In particular we show that we only need to consider contexts which correspond to computation states in which the hole corresponds to the program counter (the expression to be evaluated next). We call this the **ciu** theorem since the contexts considered correspond to all Closed Instantiations of Uses of the expressions to be tested. Although rudimentary, this characterization turns out to be quite useful. Our method for establishing the correctness of this alternative characterization relies on the notion of uniform computation, which underlies the definition of uniform semantics. Uniform computation allows computation steps to be carried out on states with missing information. It has the property that computing commutes with filling in of missing information. Using **ciu** and other consequences of uniform semantics we then establish some general principles for proving program equivalence that capture the computational intuitions. To make these ideas concrete, we give uniform semantics and derive equivalence laws for algebraic, control, and memory operations which combined form the kernel of a Scheme- or (untyped) ML- like language.

Related Work

Previous work of Talcott, Mason, Felleisen, and Moggi establishes a mathematical foundation for studying notions of program equivalence for programming languages with function and control abstractions operating on objects with memory. This work builds on work of Landin, Reynolds, Morris and Plotkin. Landin (1964) and Reynolds (1972) describe high-level abstract machines for defining language semantics. Morris (1968) defines an extensional equivalence relation for the classical lambda calculus. Plotkin (1975) extends these ideas to the call-by-value lambda calculus and introduces the operational equivalence relation.

Talcott (1985); Mason (1986, 1988); Talcott (1989); Mason and Talcott (1991a, 1992) develop various operational methods for the studying operational approximation and equivalence for subsets of a language with function and control abstractions and objects with memory. Agha, Mason, Smith, and Talcott (1992, 1997) extend these methods to develop an operational semantics of a λ-language with primitives for actor computation (distributed object-based computation). Felleisen (1987) studies reduction calculi extending the call-by-value lambda calculus to languages with control and assignment abstractions. These calculi are simplified and extended in (Felleisen and Hieb 1989). The notion of computational monad as a framework for axiomatizing features of programming languages is introduced in (Moggi 1989, 1990). Reduction calculi and operational equivalence both provide a sound basis for purely equational reasoning about programs. Calculi have the advantage that the reduction relations are inductively generated from primitive reductions (such as beta-conversion) by closure operations (such as transitive closure or congruence closure). Equations proved in a calculus continue to hold when the calculus is extended to treat additional language constructs. Operational equivalence is, by definition, sensitive to the set of language constructs and basic data available. However, pure reduction calculi are not adequate to prove many basic equivalences in languages with effects. For example, Felleisen found it is necessary to extend his reduction calculus by meta principles (cf. the **safety rule** of Felleisen (1987), thm 5.27, p.149). Using operational approximation we can express and prove properties such as non-termination, computation induction and existence of least fixed points which cannot even be expressed in reduction calculi. The uniform semantics framework presented in this paper provides the extensibility of reduction calculi for a wide range of λ-languages. Operations are given semantics by reduction rules that are not modified when new features are added to the language. This kind of modularity is in the spirit of action semantics (Mosses 1992). The objective of action semantics is to support modular (compositional) specification of the semantics of a language allowing each feature to be specified independently, and allowing new features to be added without modifying the specification of the original language. This is accomplished by splitting computation state into orthogonal facets and defining a set of action combinators to be used as denotations. Action semantics treats a wider range of languages, and provides a number of generic tools. However, development of equational theories derived from action semantics has only recently begun (Lassen 199X) (see below).

The fact that one can present a syntactic reduction system for imperative λ-calculi was discovered independently in 1986-1987: by Talcott (Mason and Talcott 1991a), and by Felleisen and Hieb (1992). As well as being conceptually elegant, it has also provided the necessary tools for several key results and proofs. In addition to eliminating messy isomorphism considerations, to deal with arbitrary choice of names of newly allocated structures, it also was a key step leading to the formulation of the **ciu** theorem, first presented in (Mason and Talcott 1989). In 1987, Mason realized that it provided the ideal notion of a normal form and symbolic evaluation needed in the completeness result presented in (Mason and Talcott 1992). Syntactic reduction systems provided the basis for the elegant revision of the imperative calculi of Felleisen (1987) that was published in (Felleisen and Hieb 1992). Other successful uses of the technique include: the type soundness proof, via subject reduction, for the imperative ML type system (Felleisen and Wright 1991); the analysis of parameter passing in Algol (Crank and Felleisen 1991; Weeks and Felleisen 1993); and the analysis of reduction calculi for Scheme-like languages (Sabry and Felleisen 1993; Fields and Sabry 1993).

Much work has been done to develop methods for reasoning about operational approximation and equivalence: Abramsky (1990, 1991); Bloom (1990); Egidi, Honsell, and Ronchi della Rocca (1992); Howe (1989, 1996); Gordon (1995); Lassen (199X); Mason (1986); Mason and Talcott (1991a); Jim and Meyer (1991); Milner (1977); Ong (1988); Pitts and Stark (1993, 1996); Ritter and Pitts (1995); Pitts (1996); Smith (1992); Sullivan (1996); Talcott (1985). Methods developed for reasoning about operational approximation and equivalence include: general schemes for establishing equivalence; context lemmas (alternative characterizations that reduce the number of contexts to be considered); and (bi)simulation relations (alternative characterizations or approximations based on co-inductively defined relations). An early example is Milner's context lemma (Milner 1977) which greatly simplifies the proof of operational equivalence in the case of the typed lambda calculus by reducing the contexts to be considered to a simple chain of applications. Talcott (1985) studies general notions of equivalence for languages based on the call-by-value lambda calculus, and develops several schemes for establishing properties of such relations. Howe (1989) develops a schema for proving congruence for a class of languages with a particular style of operational semantics. This schema succeeds in capturing many simple functional programming language features. Building on this work, Howe (1996) uses an approach similar to the idea of uniform computation to define structured evaluation systems in which the form of the evaluation rules guarantees that (bi)simulation relations are congruences. The form of the rules is specified using meta variables with arities and higher-order substitutions. This syntax enrichment is very similar to the notions of place-holder and filling used here to specify uniform semantics. The idea of using such meta terms to specify classes of rules giving rise to reduction relations with special properties was used in (Aczel 1978) to prove a general Church-Rosser theorem and in (Klop 1980) to develop the theory of Combinatory Reduction Systems. Meta terms are also used in describing a unification procedure for higher-order patterns in (Nipkow 1991). As discussed above, Mason and Talcott (1989, 1991a) introduced the **ciu** characterization of operational equivalence which is a form of context lemma for imperative languages. The uniform computation method used to first prove **ciu** was adapted to develop computational path transformation methods for proving equivalence of actor programs in (Agha, Mason, Smith, and Talcott 1997). Ritter and Pitts (1995) use operational techniques to establish the correctness of a translation between an imperative subset of standard ML and a simply typed lambda calculus with reference types. An applicative bisimulation is defined and shown to be sound for operational equivalence. This relation is adequate for establishing the correctness of the translations in question, but is weaker that operational equivalence. Finding a bisimulation relation that coincides with operational equivalence in the case of imperative higher-order languages such as Scheme or ML remains an open problem (to this author's knowledge). Pitts (1996) proves a context lemma for a higher-order language with assignable variables that only store first-order values. The proof uses logical relations that are defined in terms of the operational semantics. The logical relation mechanism combined with the context lemma provide a useful method for establishing program equivalence. Pitts and Stark (1996) extend these ideas to a language with richer types. A challenging problem is to apply the logical relations approach to untyped languages. Sullivan (1996) also takes a mixed operational-denotational approach. A metalanguage based on PCF extended with I/O and dynamic store primitives is defined operationally. A context lemma for this language is proved by proving that an applicative simulation relation is a pre-congruence. One can reason about programs with imperative features by giving them compositional denotations in this metalanguage. This is promising blend of operational and denotational semantics, providing a better approximation to operational equivalence than most existing denotational approaches. Gordon (1995) uses standard process algebra techniques to derive bisimulation relations from labelled transition systems based on operational semantics. In the case of typed functional languages (PCF+streams) bisimulations can found that coincide with operational equivalence. It will be interesting to see if this approach to defining bisimulations can be extended to imperative λ-languages, to develop useful if not complete reasoning tools. Lassen (199X) presents an approach to developing a general framework for reasoning about program equivalence based on action semantics (Mosses 1992). Several operational pre-orderings are defined for a portion of action notation adequate for functional languages. Although there are no imperative effects, the action semantics allows for non-deterministic primitives, thus the interest in multiple pre-orders. Simulation relations that are essentially complete are defined for each of the pre-orders and used to verify properties of an (untyped)

PCF-like language by giving the language an action semantics. A next stage in this effort is to consider actions that support imperative primitives. A co-induction rule for establishing operational equivalence in a λ-language with reference cells that captures much of the reasoning in the Mason-Talcott papers based on computation induction and the **ciu** theorem has been suggested by S. Lassen (1995).

Plan

The remainder of the paper is organized as follows. In §2. we develop the general framework for studying equivalence of programs in λ-languages. The basic syntactic notions are introduced, the semantic notions of definedness and equivalence are defined (relative to details to be filled in for specific languages), the notion of uniform semantics is introduced and the key properties of languages with uniform semantics are stated. In §3. we give the semantics for a representative collection of functional primitives, and discuss equational laws for the functional primitives valid in any λ-language with uniform semantics. We also consider some properties specific to the functional language. In §4. we give the semantics for a typical control primitive and discuss its equational theory. In §5. we give the semantics for a collection of primitives for allocating, accessing and updating ML-like reference cells and discuss the equational theory for these operations. In §6. we combine the primitives of the previous section into a full Scheme-like language and discuss the ramifications to the individual equational theories. In §7. we introduce the placeholder machinery needed to fill in the details in the definition of uniform semantics for λ-languages. We then show that the languages defined in the previous sections have uniform semantics. In §8. we use uniform computation techniques to establish the **ciu** theorem for λ-languages with uniform semantics. We then establish several other results that provide a basis for developing a core equational theory valid for all such languages. §9. contains some concluding remarks.

Along the way we give some very simple programming and proving examples to provide basic intuitions about the various program primitives and reasoning principles. Many more examples of programming and proving with functions, control, and memory can be found in (Burge 1975); (Talcott 1985 1989, 1992); (Felleisen 1987, 1988); (Mason 1986); (Mason and Talcott 1990, 1991a, 1991b, 1992, 1994a, 1994b). Examples include: higher-order functionals as generic program modules; manipulating mutable lists; stream processing; co-routines; and objects as functions (lambda abstractions) with state.

Notation

We conclude the introduction with a summary of our notation conventions. Let X, X_0, X_1 be sets. We specify meta-variable conventions in the form: 'let x range over X', which should be read as: 'the meta-variable x and decorated variants such as x', x_0, ..., range over the set X'. $\text{Fmap}[X_0, X_1]$ is the set of finite maps from X_0 to X_1. We write $\mathrm{Dom}(f)$ for the domain of a function and $\mathrm{Rng}(f)$ for its range. For any function f, $f\{x \mapsto x'\}$ is the function f' such that $\mathrm{Dom}(f') = \mathrm{Dom}(f) \cup \{x\}$, $f'(x) = x'$, and $f'(z) = f(z)$ for $z \neq x, z \in \mathrm{Dom}(f)$. Also $f\lceil X$ is the restriction of f to X: the function f' such that $\mathrm{Dom}(f') = \mathrm{Dom}(f) \cap X$ and $f'(x) = f(x)$ for $x \in \mathrm{Dom}(f')$. $\mathbf{N} = \{0, 1, 2, \ldots\}$ is the set of natural numbers and $i, j, n, n_0, \ldots$ range over $\mathbf{N}$. In the defining equations for various syntactic classes we use two notational conventions: pointwise lifting of syntax operations to syntax classes; and the Einstein summation convention that a phrase of the form $F_n(Z^n)$ abbreviates $\bigcup_{n\in\mathbf{N}} F_n(Z^n)$. For example if Ω is a ranked set of operator symbols, then the terms over Ω can be defined inductively by (as the least solution to) the equation: $T_\Omega = \Omega_n(T_\Omega^n)$. Unabbreviated, this equation reads:

$$T_\Omega = \bigcup_{n\in\mathbf{N}} \{\omega(t_1, \ldots, t_n) \mid \omega \in \Omega_n \wedge t_i \in T_\Omega \quad \text{for} \quad 1 \leq i \leq n\}.$$

2 The General Framework

In this section a general framework for studying the semantics of λ-languages is set up. The syntactic entities and semantic notions of λ-languages are defined and the properties required for a uniform semantics are stated. Then several results, including the **ciu** theorem, valid in any λ-language with uniform semantics are presented. To simplify reasoning about effects we restrict attention to call-by-value semantics, but we see no problem is adapting the basic ideas to other evaluation strategies.

2.1 Expression Syntax of a λ-language

Fix a countably infinite set of variables, $\mathbf{X}$. The basic syntax of a λ-language is then determined by giving a countable set of atoms, $\mathbf{A}$, and a family of operation symbols $\mathbf{O} = \{\mathbf{O}_n \mid n \in \mathbf{N}\}$ ($\mathbf{O}_n$ is a set of n-ary operation symbols) such that the sets $\mathbf{X}$, $\mathbf{A}$, $\mathbf{O}_n$ for $n \in \mathbf{N}$ are pairwise disjoint. We assume that $\mathbf{O}$ contains at least the binary operation app (lambda application). For example, taking $\mathbf{A} = \{\ \}$ and $\mathbf{O} = \{\mathsf{app}\}$ we obtain the expressions of the pure call-by-value lambda calculus, Λ_v.

Definition (E, L): The set of expressions, $\mathbf{E}$, and the set of λ-abstractions, $\mathbf{L}$, are defined as the least sets satisfying the following equations:

$$\mathbf{E} = \mathbf{X} \cup \mathbf{A} \cup \mathbf{L} \cup \mathbf{O}_n(\mathbf{E}^n)$$

$$\mathbf{L} = \lambda\mathbf{X}.\mathbf{E}$$

We let a range over $\mathbf{A}$, x, y, z range over $\mathbf{X}$, e range over $\mathbf{E}$, and φ range over $\mathbf{L}$. Elements of $\mathbf{L}$ are called *lambda abstractions* or more briefly *lambdas*. λ is a binding operator with free and bound variables of expressions defined as usual.

Two expressions are considered equal if they are the same up to renaming of bound variables. $\mathrm{FV}(e)$ is the set of free variables of e, and we write $\mathrm{FV}(e_1, \ldots, e_n)$ for $\mathrm{FV}(e_1) \cup \ldots \cup \mathrm{FV}(e_n)$. A *closed expression* is an expression with no free variables. Substitution $e^{\{x \mapsto e_0\}}$ of e_0 for free occurrences of x in e is defined as usual, renaming bound variables of e where needed to avoid capture of free variables of e_0. We will make use of the following common abbreviations and notation conventions.

$$\lambda x_1, \ldots, x_n.e \triangleq \lambda x_1.\ldots\lambda x_n.e$$

$$\mathtt{app}(e_0, e_1, \ldots, e_n) \triangleq \mathtt{app}(\ldots\mathtt{app}(e_0, e_1), \ldots e_n)$$

$$e_0(e_1, \ldots, e_n) \triangleq \mathtt{app}(e_0, e_1, \ldots, e_n)$$

$$\mathtt{let}\ x = e_0\ \mathtt{in}\ e_1 \triangleq \mathtt{app}(\lambda x.e_1, e_0)$$

$$v_0 \circ v_1 \triangleq \lambda x.v_0(v_1(x)) \quad \text{if} \quad x \notin \mathrm{FV}(v_0, v_1)$$

$$e_0; e_1 \triangleq \mathtt{let}\ d = e_0\ \mathtt{in}\ e_1 \qquad \text{sequencing} \quad \text{where} \quad d \notin \mathrm{FV}(e_0, e_1)$$

$$\mathtt{Yv} \triangleq \lambda f.\mathtt{let}\ h = \lambda h.\lambda x.\mathtt{app}(\mathtt{app}(f, \mathtt{app}(h, h)), x)\ \mathtt{in}\ \mathtt{app}(h, h)$$

call-by-value recursion combinator

2.2 Operational Semantics – Overview

A small-step operational semantics is obtained by defining a notion of state and a single step reduction relation on states. States consist of an expression and a state context. A state context often describes dynamically created entities such as memory cells, arrays, files, etc. The form of state contexts needed depends on the choice of primitive operations. There is an empty state context, and for each state there is an associated expression representing that state. Value expressions are a subset of the set of expressions used to represent semantic values. These include variables, atoms, and lambdas. If the expression component of a state is a value, then the state is a value state and no reduction steps are possible. Otherwise, the expression decomposes uniquely into a redex placed in a reduction context. A (call-by-value) redex is a primitive operator applied to a list of values. There is one reduction rule for each primitive operator, and the single-step reduction relation on states is determined by the reduction rule for the redex operator. Of course it may happen that a redex is ill-formed (a runtime error) and no reduction step is possible. A state is defined just if it reduces (in a finite number of steps) to a value state. Using these basic notions we define the operational approximation and equivalence relations in the usual way. This is the basic semantic framework, independent of the choice of primitive operations. Within this framework we define the notion of uniform semantics and develop tools for proving laws of approximation and equivalence in λ-languages with uniform semantics. For a particular choice of operations what remains is to define

- the structure of state contexts, including specifying
  - the empty state context
  - the map giving the expression associated to a state
- the reduction rule for each primitive operation

2.3 Operational Semantics – Details

We now make precise the concepts discussed above. As pointed out above, some features are fully defined (relative to others), while others must obey certain constraints, but may vary depending on the particular choice of language. To distinguish these situations, we use the header **Definition** to signal definitions of uniformly defined features and the header **Specification** to signal constraints on language dependent features.

We begin with the concepts of context, value expression, and value substitution needed to state the definitions of definedness and operational equivalence. These are also sufficient to state the first requirement for uniform semantics, **g-unif** (global uniformity). We then introduce additional notions of reduction context and redex. This allows us to describe the form of computation rules and to state informally the second requirement for uniform semantics, **s-unif** (stepwise uniformity). Finally we state the **ciu** theorem and some consequences that formalize the principles underlying the computational laws of equivalence.

Definition (Contexts (C)): Contexts are expressions with holes. We use • to denote a hole. The set of contexts, **C**, is defined by

$$\mathbf{C} = \{\bullet\} \cup \mathbf{X} \cup \mathbf{A} \cup \lambda\mathbf{X}.\mathbf{C} \cup \mathbf{O}_n(\mathbf{C}^n)$$

We let C range over **C**. $C[e]$ denotes the result of replacing each hole in C by e. Free variables of e may become bound in this process. For example free occurrences of x will become bound when an expression is placed in the hole in $\lambda x.\bullet$, as in $(\lambda x.\bullet)[x] = \lambda x.x$. We let Traps($C$) be the set of lambda variables of C with a hole in their scope – the variables that can be trapped when the holes are filled. For example, Traps$(\lambda x.\bullet) = \{x\}$. Note that renaming of bound variables in a context is not allowed since it changes the meaning of the context. For example, $(\lambda z.\bullet)[x] = \lambda z.x \neq \lambda x.x$. Many contexts of interest have the property that there are no holes in the scope of a λ, and for such contexts, renaming of bound variables is still valid, and we extend the application of substitutions to such contexts by defining $\bullet^{\{x \mapsto e\}} = \bullet$.

Specification (Value Expressions (V), Value Substitutions (S)):
The set of value expressions, **V**, contains all variables, atoms, and lambdas. It may in addition contain expressions of the form $\vartheta(v^n)$. Value substitutions, **S**, are finite maps from variables to value expressions. **V** must be closed under application of

value substitutions. More precisely, we require:

$$\mathbf{X} \cup \mathbf{A} \cup \mathbf{L} \subseteq \mathbf{V} \subseteq \mathbf{X} \cup \mathbf{A} \cup \mathbf{L} \cup \mathbf{O}_n(\mathbf{V}^n)$$

$$\mathbf{S} = \mathrm{Fmap}[\mathbf{X}, \mathbf{V}]$$

$$\mathbf{V}^{\mathbf{S}} = \mathbf{V}$$

We let v range over $\mathbf{V}$ and σ range over $\mathbf{S}$. e^σ is the result of simultaneous substitution of free occurrences of $x \in \mathrm{Dom}(\sigma)$ in e by $\sigma(x)$, taking care not to trap variables. We write $\{x_i \mapsto v_i \mid i < n\}$ for the value substitution, σ, with domain $\{x_i \mid i < n\}$ such that $\sigma(x_i) = v_i$ for $i < n$. Operators, ϑ, that produce value expressions, are called constructors. In the languages considered here the binary pairing operation, `pr`, will serve as the prototypical constructor.

Specification (State contexts (Z)): $\mathbf{Z}$ is the subset of $\mathbf{C}$ consisting of the set of state contexts, ζ ranges over $\mathbf{Z}$ and $\diamond \in \mathbf{Z}$ is the empty state context. ζ^σ is the result of 'replacing' free occurrences of $x \in \mathrm{Dom}(\sigma) - \mathrm{Traps}(\zeta)$ by $\sigma(x)$. Variables in $\mathrm{FV}(\sigma) \cap \mathrm{Traps}(\zeta)$ may become bound in the process.

The full determination of $\mathbf{Z}$, $\diamond$, and ζ^σ must be made for each λ-language as a part of defining its semantics. In the languages considered here, the state context will be a context with a single hole. The context surrounding the hole can be thought of as a canonical form describing the state in which an expression placed in that hole is to be evaluated. The variables trapped at the hole in a state context provide a means of naming dynamically created values. For example, if there are no operators with effects, as in Λ_v, then $\diamond = \bullet$ and $\mathbf{Z} = \{\diamond\}$. In a language with a primitive operation, `aref`, that constructs reference cells for atoms, $\zeta^{\mathrm{aref}} =$ $\mathtt{let}\ z_1 = \mathtt{aref}(a_1)\ \mathtt{in}\ \mathtt{let}\ z_2 = \mathtt{aref}(a_2)\ \mathtt{in}\ \bullet$ would be a state context representing a state with two reference cells that can be referred to as z_1 and z_2. z_1 initially contains a_1 and z_2 initially contains a_2. As we will see in §5. slightly more complex contexts are needed to represent memory that may contain cycles. The states of languages considered here can be decomposed as $\zeta = \zeta_a[\![\zeta_e]\!]$ where all trapping is done in ζ_a (a for allocation) and ζ_e describes the state of the allocated structures (e for effects). In this case we define $\zeta^\sigma = \zeta_a[\![\zeta_e^\sigma]\!]$ for $\mathrm{Dom}(\sigma) \cap \mathrm{Traps}(\zeta) = \emptyset$. Continuing the example of reference cells for atoms, assume there is an atom `nil`, and an assignment operation $z := v$ that assigns v to the cell z when v is an atom. Then we refine state contexts so that ζ^{aref} becomes $\zeta_a^{\mathrm{aref}}[\![\zeta_e^{\mathrm{aref}}]\!]$ where $\zeta_a^{\mathrm{aref}} = \mathtt{let}\ z_1 = \mathtt{aref(nil)}\ \mathtt{in}\ \mathtt{let}\ z_2 = \mathtt{aref(nil)}\ \mathtt{in}\ \bullet$ and $\zeta_e^{\mathrm{aref}} = z_1 := a_1; z_2 := a_2; \bullet$.

Specification (Computation States (CS)): $\mathbf{CS} = \mathbf{Z} : \mathbf{E}$ is the set computation states. We let S range over $\mathbf{CS}$ and let $\zeta : e$ be the state with state context ζ and expression e. s2e(_) is the map associating to each state a representing expression. We will restrict attention to the case when the mapping is defined by hole filling: $\mathrm{s2e}(\zeta : e) = \zeta[\![e]\!]$. A state is *closed* just if its corresponding expression is closed. Application of value substitutions to states is defined by: $(\zeta : e)^\sigma = \zeta^\sigma : e^\sigma$ for $\mathrm{Dom}(\sigma) \cap \mathrm{Traps}(\zeta) = \emptyset$.

Specification (Reduction ($\longrightarrow$, $\longrightarrow\!\!\!\!\!\!\!\twoheadrightarrow$)): $\longrightarrow$ is the single step reduction relation on states and $\twoheadrightarrow$ is the reflexive transitive closure of $\longrightarrow$.

As an example the single step reduction relation in Λ_v is the least relation such that

$$\bullet : \mathtt{app}(\lambda x.e, v) \longrightarrow \bullet : e^{\{x \mapsto v\}}$$

$$\bullet : e \longrightarrow \bullet : e' \Rightarrow \bullet : \mathtt{app}(e, e_1) \longrightarrow \bullet : \mathtt{app}(e', e_1)$$

$$\bullet : e \longrightarrow \bullet : e' \Rightarrow \bullet : \mathtt{app}(v, e) \longrightarrow \bullet : \mathtt{app}(v, e')$$

We will see below how to define the rule for app for an arbitrary λ-language. Notice that we do not restrict the reduction relation to closed states.

Definition (Definedness): For states S, S_0, S_1, definedness, $S\downarrow$, approximation, $S_0 \preceq S_1$, equi-definedness, $S_0 \updownarrow S_1$, and computation length of defined states, $|S|$, are defined by

$$S\downarrow \Leftrightarrow (\exists v \in \mathbf{V}, \zeta \in \mathbf{Z})(S \twoheadrightarrow \zeta : v)$$

$$S_0 \preceq S_1 \Leftrightarrow (S_0\downarrow \Rightarrow S_1\downarrow)$$

$$S_0 \updownarrow S_1 \Leftrightarrow (S_0\downarrow \Leftrightarrow S_1\downarrow)$$

$|S|$ is the least $n \in \mathbf{N}$ such that S reduces to a value state in n steps, if $S\downarrow$.

The first set of requirements for uniform semantics can now be stated. We require that: single step reduction is essentially deterministic; reduction is preserved by value substitution; a state, and its associated expression started in the empty state context, are equi-defined; and if one state reduces to another then the two states are equi-defined and the reduct has shorter computation length, if defined.

Definition (Global uniformity (g-unif)): A λ-language satisfies **g-unif** if the following hold.

(unicity) $S \longrightarrow S_0 \wedge S \longrightarrow S_1 \Rightarrow \mathrm{s2e}(S_0) = \mathrm{s2e}(S_1)$

(vsub) $\zeta : e \longrightarrow \zeta' : e' \Rightarrow \zeta : e^{\sigma} \longrightarrow \zeta' : e'^{\sigma}$

if $\mathrm{Dom}(\sigma) \cap (\mathrm{Traps}(\zeta) \cup \mathrm{Traps}(\zeta')) = \emptyset$

(rep) $\diamond : \mathrm{s2e}(S) \updownarrow S$

(red) $S \longrightarrow S' \wedge S\downarrow \Rightarrow S'\downarrow \wedge |S'| < |S|$

In the languages we consider (**unicity**) holds because the only non-determinism in a reduction step is the choice of names used in the state context. (**rep**) holds because reduction of $\diamond : \mathrm{s2e}(\zeta : e)$ essentially recreates the state context ζ. (**red**) says that if a state is defined, then any reduction makes progress. Clearly if the reduct state is defined, then the original state is defined. It is easy to see that Λ_v satisfies these properties. The only hard part is to show that value substitution and beta-v reduction commute, which is a standard result.

2.4 Approximation and Equivalence

Now we define operational approximation and equivalence and lay the ground work for studying properties of these relations.

Definition (Approximation $e_0 \sqsubseteq e_1$**, Equivalence** $e_0 \cong e_1$**):**

$$e_0 \sqsubseteq e_1 \;\Leftrightarrow\; (\forall C \mid \mathrm{FV}(C[e_0], C[e_1]) = \emptyset)(\diamond : C[e_0] \;\preceq\; \diamond : C[e_1])$$

$$e_0 \cong e_1 \;\Leftrightarrow\; e_0 \sqsubseteq e_1 \wedge e_1 \sqsubseteq e_0$$

It is easy to see that operational approximation is a congruence: if $e_0 \sqsubseteq e_1$, then $C[e_0] \sqsubseteq C[e_1]$. Similarly for operational equivalence.

Two simple examples which can be stated in Λ_v are

(lv.1) $\mathtt{let}\ x = (\mathtt{let}\ y = e_y\ \mathtt{in}\ e_x)\ \mathtt{in}\ e \cong \mathtt{let}\ y = e_y\ \mathtt{in}\ \mathtt{let}\ x = e_x\ \mathtt{in}\ e$

if $y \notin \mathrm{FV}(e)$

(lv.2) $\mathsf{app}(\lambda x.\mathsf{app}(x, x), \lambda x.\mathsf{app}(x, x)) \sqsubseteq e$

(**lv.1**) is an example of an expression, e_y, placed in two computationally equivalent contexts. This will be made precise below. (**lv.2**) holds because an expression that is not defined in any context, approximates any other expression. We will see below how to establish these results for an arbitrary λ-language with uniform semantics.

To define reduction rules and to state additional properties of reduction and equivalence, we introduce the notions of redex and reduction context. Since evaluation is call-by-value, a redex is simply an non-constructor operator applied to the appropriate number of value expressions. Redexes and value expressions must be disjoint, thus we must account for the fact that some expressions of the form $\vartheta(v_1, \ldots, v_n)$ may be value expressions. For example, $\mathsf{app}(\lambda x.e, v)$ is a redex in any λ-language, while $\mathtt{pr}(v_0, v_1)$ is not a redex in any λ-language whose operations contain the binary pairing constructor, $\mathtt{pr}$.

Definition (Redexes ($\mathbf{E}_\mathrm{r}$)): The set of redexes, $\mathbf{E}_\mathrm{r}$, is defined by:

$$\mathbf{E}_\mathrm{r} = \mathbf{O}_n(\mathbf{V}^n) - \mathbf{V}$$

Reduction contexts (also called evaluation contexts in the literature) identify the subexpression of an expression in which reduction to a value must occur next. They correspond to the left-first, call-by-value reduction strategy of Plotkin (1975) and were first introduced by Felleisen and Friedman (1986).

Definition (Reduction Contexts (R)): The set of reduction contexts, $\mathbf{R}$, is the subset of $\mathbf{C}$ defined by

$$\mathbf{R} = \{\bullet\} \cup \mathbf{O}_{m+n+1}(\mathbf{V}^m, \mathbf{R}, \mathbf{E}^n)$$

We let R range over $\mathbf{R}$. $\mathsf{app}(\bullet, e)$ is a reduction context for any e, and $\mathsf{app}(v, \bullet)$ is a reduction context for any v, but neither $\mathsf{app}(\mathsf{app}(v_0, v_1), \bullet)$ nor $\lambda x.\mathsf{app}(\bullet, e)$

are reduction contexts. Since the hole of a reduction context is not in the scope of any bound variables, no free variables are trapped when filling the hole of a reduction context. In particular the application of value substitutions extends to reduction contexts.

It is easy to check that an expression is either a value expression or decomposes uniquely into a redex placed in a reduction context (a proof can be found in (Mason and Talcott 1991a)).

Lemma (Decomposition): If $e \in \mathbf{E}$ then either $e \in \mathbf{V}$ or e can be written uniquely as $R[r]$ where R is a reduction context and $r \in \mathbf{E}_r$.

For the languages considered here, the single step reduction relation is defined by giving a reduction rule for each operation. Ideally, we would like to give the rule for an operation, independent of the language, subject to constraints ensuring that state contexts are adequate to support the operation. This is a difficult task. Our approximate solution is to define the reduction rules using minimal information about the context $\zeta : R$ surrounding a redex. More detail is given in §3. As a first simple example, the rule for the application operation app can be expressed in a language independent way as follows:

$$\zeta : R[\mathtt{app}(\lambda x.e, v)] \longrightarrow \zeta : R[e^{\{x \mapsto v\}}].$$

Now we consider the remaining requirements for a uniform semantics, **s-unif**. The objective is to formalize the requirement that each reduction rule is uniform in the form of its parameters. A reduction step may depend on the kind of construction of a redex argument, but not on any information about subparts. We do this by enriching the syntax of λ-languages to include place-holders for various syntactic sorts. In §7. we give the details of the syntax enrichment, and show how the reduction rules can be lifted to states of the enriched syntax. Here we introduce just enough notation to aide in reading the stepwise requirement. We decorate metavariables with $\star$ to signify the enriched forms. Thus $^{\star}e$ is an expression of the enriched syntax. $^{\star}e[\star \mapsto e_0]$ is the result of filling expression place-holders in $^{\star}e$ with e_0. Similar notation is used for filling place-holders of other sorts in entities of other sorts.

Definition (Uniform reduction (s-unif)):
A λ-language satisfies **s-unif** if the single step reduction relation can be lifted to states of the enriched syntax so that:

1. If $^{\star}\zeta : {}^{\star}e \longrightarrow {}^{\star}\zeta_1 : {}^{\star}e_1$, then $({}^{\star}\zeta : {}^{\star}e)[\star \mapsto x] \longrightarrow ({}^{\star}\zeta_1 : {}^{\star}e_1)[\star \mapsto x]$ for any x of a sort for which there are place-holders.

2. If $({}^{\star}\zeta : {}^{\star}e)[\star \mapsto x] \longrightarrow {}^{\star}\zeta' : {}^{\star}e'$ then either ${}^{\star}\zeta : {}^{\star}e$ touches a hole (${}^{\star}e$ has the form ${}^{\star}R[P]$ for some place-holder P), or ${}^{\star}\zeta : {}^{\star}e \longrightarrow {}^{\star}\zeta_1 : {}^{\star}e_1$, for some ${}^{\star}\zeta_1 : {}^{\star}e_1$ such that ${}^{\star}\zeta' : {}^{\star}e' = ({}^{\star}\zeta_1 : {}^{\star}e_1)[\star \mapsto x]$.

Definition (Uniform semantics): A λ-language has *uniform semantics* if it satisfies **g-unif** and **s-unif**.

A key result for λ-languages with uniform semantics is the **ciu** theorem. This theorem reduces the number of contexts that need to be considered when establishing operational approximation and equivalence. **ciu** is a form of context lemma (Milner 1977). Typically context lemmas characterize equivalence using only applicative contexts – contexts A of the form $A = \bullet$ or $A = \mathtt{app}(A', v)$ – observing termination and equality of observable values (booleans, numbers, etc.). Our context lemma uses arbitrary reduction contexts, observing termination only. To state the **ciu** theorem we introduce the **ciu**-approximation relation which holds just if each Closed Instantiation of a Use of the first expression approximates (as a state) the same Closed Instantiation of a Use of the second expression.

Definition (ciu-approximation $e_0 \sqsubseteq^{\mathrm{ciu}} e_1$):

$$e_0 \sqsubseteq^{\mathrm{ciu}} e_1 \Leftrightarrow (\forall \zeta, R, \sigma \mid \bigwedge_{j<2} \zeta : R[\![e_j^{\sigma}]\!] \text{ closed})(\zeta : R[\![e_0^{\sigma}]\!] \preceq \zeta : R[\![e_1^{\sigma}]\!])$$

Theorem (ciu): For a λ-language with uniform semantics operational approximation and **ciu**-approximation coincide:

$$e_0 \sqsubseteq e_1 \Leftrightarrow e_0 \sqsubseteq^{\mathrm{ciu}} e_1$$

The proof of this theorem will be given in §8 using the uniform computation machinery developed in §7. The approximation (**lv.2**) above is an easy consequence of **ciu**. Another consequence is the following.

Corollary (substitutivity): In a λ-language with uniform semantics operational approximation is preserved by substitution: if $e_0 \sqsubseteq e_1$, then $e_0^{\sigma} \sqsubseteq e_1^{\sigma}$. Similarly for operational equivalence.

To state the theorems underlying computational equivalences in this general setting we introduce the notion of a context independent (CI) redex.

Definition (Context independent reduction ($\xrightarrow{\mathrm{ci}}\!\!\twoheadrightarrow$)):
A redex $\vartheta(v_1, \ldots, v_n)$ is CI if the interpretation is independent of the context: either there is no reduction possible in any state, or the redex is replaced by the same reduct expression in any state. That is, exactly one of the following holds:

1. For any ζ, R there is no S' such that $\zeta : R[\![\vartheta(v_1, \ldots, v_n)]\!] \longrightarrow S'$.

2. There is some e such that $\zeta : R[\![\vartheta(v_1, \ldots, v_n)]\!] \longrightarrow \zeta : R[\![e]\!]$ for any ζ, R.

A CI redex neither examines nor modifies its context (state or reduction). For example, any redex with operator $\mathtt{app}$ is CI. We write $e \xrightarrow{\mathrm{ci}}\!\!\twoheadrightarrow e'$ if $\zeta : R[\![e]\!] \longrightarrow\!\!\twoheadrightarrow \zeta : R[\![e']\!]$ by a sequence of CI steps for any ζ and R.

The intuition that two expressions are equivalent if they have a common reduct, is justified by (**equi-reduct**). Similarly reasoning that two expressions are equivalent if the result from placing a third expression computationally equivalent reduction contexts is justified by (**equi-rcx**).

Theorem (Equi-reduct): In a λ-language with uniform semantics, if there is some e such that $e_j \stackrel{\text{ci}}{\twoheadrightarrow} e$ for $j < 2$ then $e_0 \cong e_1$.

Proof : Assume $e_j \stackrel{\text{ci}}{\twoheadrightarrow} e$ for $j < 2$. By **ciu** (and symmetry), to show that $e_0 \cong e_1$ we need only show $e_0 \sqsubseteq^{\text{ciu}} e_1$. Pick some closing ζ, R, σ and assume $\zeta : R[e_0^\sigma] \downarrow$. By assumption and **g-unif** $\zeta : R[e_j^\sigma] \stackrel{\text{ci}}{\twoheadrightarrow} \zeta : R[e^\sigma]$. Thus, by **g-unif**, $\zeta : R[e^\sigma] \downarrow$, and hence $\zeta : R[e_1^\sigma] \downarrow$.

$\Box_{\text{Equi-reduct}}$

Theorem (Equi-rcx): In a λ-language with uniform semantics, if for z fresh there are $e_0 \cong e_1$ such that $R_j[z] \stackrel{\text{ci}}{\twoheadrightarrow} e_j$ for $j < 2$, then $R_0[e] \cong R_1[e]$ for any e.

The proof of this theorem is given in §8, since to establish the result in our general setting we use the uniform computation machinery. In fact we prove a stronger version that is most conveniently stated using the enriched syntax. The equivalence (**lv.1**) given above is a direct consequence of (**equi-rcx**).

A global variant of (**equi-reduct**) that applies to any reduction holds if we strengthen the final clause of **g-unif**.

Definition (Strongly Uniform Semantics): A λ-language has *strongly uniform semantics* if it satisfies the properties **g-unif**† and **s-unif**, where **g-unif**† is the specification obtained by adding the clause (**sred**)

$$\text{(sred)} \quad S_0 \longrightarrow S_1 \quad \text{implies} \quad \zeta : R[\text{s2e}(S_0)^\sigma] \updownarrow \zeta : R[\text{s2e}(S_1)^\sigma]$$
$$\text{for all closing } \zeta, R, \sigma$$

Although the requirement seems strong, it is in fact easy to show for the languages considered here.

Corollary (redeq): In a λ-language with strongly uniform semantics, reduction preserves operational equivalence: $S_0 \longrightarrow S_1 \Rightarrow \text{s2e}(S_0) \cong \text{s2e}(S_1)$.

If λ-language has uniform semantics, then reduction steps on states with a free variable p are uniform in the assumption that $p \in \mathbf{L}$. This is made precise in (**L-unif**).

Theorem (Lambda uniformity (L-unif)): Working in a λ-language with uniform semantics, let $\zeta : e$ be a state with a most one free variable, p. If

$$(\zeta : e)^{\{p \mapsto \lambda x.e_0\}} \longrightarrow \zeta_1 : e_1,$$

then either e has the form $R[\mathtt{app}(p, v)]$ or there is some $\zeta_2 : e_2$ such that

$$(\zeta : e)^{\{p \mapsto \lambda x.e_0'\}} \longrightarrow (\zeta_2 : e_2)^{\{p \mapsto \lambda x.e_0'\}}$$

for any $\lambda x.e_0' \in \mathbf{L}$. Similarly for multiple free variables assumed to be lambdas.

It is easy to verify (**L-unif**) once the place-holder and uniform computation machinery is in place. (**L-unif**) gives us a simulation-like method for establishing equivalence of lambdas. Intuitively, we can see that one lambda approximates another if any terminating computation containing occurrences of substitution instances of the first can be transformed into a terminating computation containing corresponding occurrences of substitution instances of the second. We use states with variables to mark the corresponding occurrences of lambda instances. Lambda uniformity lets us reduce the work of establishing the correspondence to considering the case when a marked lambda occurrence is applied.

Corollary (L-unif-sim): In a λ-language with uniform semantics, to show that $\varphi_0 \sqsubseteq \varphi_1$, for $\varphi_0, \varphi_1 \in \mathbf{L}$, it suffices to show that for each list of instantiations of the free variables of φ_0, φ_1, $[\varphi_{j,i} = \varphi_j^{\sigma_i} \mid 0 \leq i \leq n]$, $j < 2$, and each ζ, R, v that closes the instantiated lambdas but may have free variables $\{p_0 \ldots p_n\}$ we can find ζ', e' and a list of additional instantiations $[\varphi_{j,i} = \varphi_j^{\sigma_i} \mid n+1 \leq i \leq n+k]$, $j < 2$, such that for any i

1. $\zeta : R\,[\mathtt{app}(\varphi_{0,i}, v)] \twoheadrightarrow (\zeta' : e')^{\{p_{n+j} \mapsto \varphi_{0,n+j} \mid 1 \leq j \leq k\}}$ in one or more steps, and
2. $(\zeta' : e')^{\{p_i \mapsto \varphi_{1,i} \mid 0 \leq i \leq n+k\}} \preceq (\zeta : R\,[\mathtt{app}(p_i, v)\,])^{\{p_i \mapsto \varphi_{1,i} \mid 0 \leq i \leq n\}}$

Proof : Assume the conditions above hold. By **ciu**, to show $\varphi_0 \sqsubseteq \varphi_1$ it suffices to show that

$$(\zeta : e)^{\{p_i \mapsto \varphi_{0,i} \mid 0 \leq i \leq n\}} \preceq (\zeta : e)^{\{p_i \mapsto \varphi_{1,i} \mid 0 \leq i \leq n\}}$$

for each list of instantiations $\varphi_{j,i}$ as above, and each closing $\zeta : e$ with free variables among $\{p_i \mid 0 \leq i \leq n\}$. Assume the left-hand state is defined, then we show by induction on the computation length that the right-hand state is also define. By (**L-unif**) we have three cases to consider.

(v) $e^{\{p_i \mapsto \varphi_{j,i} \mid 0 \leq i \leq n\}}$ is a value for $j < 2$ and we are done.

(r) $\zeta : e \longrightarrow \zeta' : e'$ assuming $\{p_i \mid 0 \leq i \leq n\}$ are lambdas. By **g-unif** $\zeta' : e'$ has a smaller computation length, thus by computation induction we are done.

(p) e has the form $R\,[\mathtt{app}(p_i, v)\,]$. By assumption 1. we can find and e' and extend the list of instantiations so that

$$\zeta : R\,[\mathtt{app}(p_i, v)\,]^{\{p_i \mapsto \varphi_{0,i} \mid 0 \leq i \leq n\}} \twoheadrightarrow \zeta : e'^{\{p_i \mapsto \varphi_{0,i} \mid 0 \leq i \leq n+k\}}$$

in one or more steps, thus $(\zeta : e'^{\{p_i \mapsto \varphi_{1,i} \mid 0 \leq i \leq n+k\}})\downarrow$ by computation induction, and by assumption 2. we are done.

$\square_{\mathbf{L-unif-sim}}$

To illustrate the use of (**L-unif-sim**) we prove that $\mathtt{Yv}$ is a least-fixed-point combinator.

Theorem (Least Fix): For F of the form $\lambda f.\lambda x.e$ $\mathtt{Yv}(F)$ is the $\sqsubseteq$-least fixed point of F:

(fix) $\mathtt{Yv}(F) \cong F(\mathtt{Yv}(F))$

(least) $F(\varphi) \sqsubseteq \varphi \Rightarrow \mathtt{Yv}(F) \sqsubseteq \varphi$

Proof: Let $F = \lambda f.\lambda x.e$, $H = \lambda h.\lambda x.F(h(h))(x)$, $\mathtt{Yv}[F] = \lambda x.F(H(H))(x)$, and $F[\mathtt{Yv}[F]] = \lambda x.(e^{\{f \mapsto \mathtt{Yv}[F]\}})$. Here we are using the notation convention that when $\psi(v)$ reduces to a lambda then we write $\psi[v]$ for that lambda. In particular by the rule for app we have $\mathtt{Yv}(F) \longrightarrow\!\!\!\!\!\!\!\!\succ \mathtt{Yv}[F]$, and $F(\mathtt{Yv}[F]) \longrightarrow\!\!\!\!\!\!\!\!\succ F[\mathtt{Yv}[F]]$. With this convention we have $\psi(v) \cong \psi[v]$ by (**Equi-red**). Also, by the rule for app we have $\mathtt{Yv}[F](v) \longrightarrow\!\!\!\!\!\!\!\!\succ F[\mathtt{Yv}[F]](v)$. To prove (**fix**), using the notation of (**L-unif-sim**), we take $e' = R[\, e^{\{f \mapsto \mathtt{Yv}[F], x \mapsto v\}}\,]$ and it is easy to see that the conditions 1,2 hold for both directions of the approximation. To prove (**least**), assume that $F(\varphi) \sqsubseteq \varphi$. Let $e' = R[\, F(p')(v)\,]$, with p' fresh. Then $R[\, \mathtt{Yv}[F](v)\,] \longrightarrow\!\!\!\!\!\!\!\!\succ e'^{\{p' \mapsto \mathtt{Yv}[F]\}}$ and using $F(\varphi)(v) \sqsubseteq \varphi(v)$ we see that conditions 1 and 2 of (**L-unif-sim**) hold and we are done.

3 Functional Primitives

In the example languages considered here, we assume $\mathbf{A}$ contains two distinct atoms playing the role of booleans, `t` for *true* and `nil` for *false*, and atoms playing the role of the natural numbers, which we denote by $0, 1, \ldots$.

The functional language, Λ_{f}, has operations $\mathbf{O}^{\mathrm{f}}$ where $\mathbf{O}^{\mathrm{f}}$ includes lambda application (`app` – arity 2), branching (`br` – arity 3), equality on atoms (`eq` – arity 2), pairing (`pr`, `fst`, `snd`, `ispr` – arities 2,1,1,1), and arithmetic operations (`+1`, `-1`, `isnat`, `iszero`, ... – arities 1,1,1,1, ...). The definition of value expressions of Λ_{f} is completed by specifying

$$\mathbf{V} = \mathbf{X} \cup \mathbf{A} \cup \mathbf{L} \cup \mathbf{P}$$

$$\mathbf{P} = \mathtt{pr}(\mathbf{V}, \mathbf{V})$$

The branching primitive is strict, due to the call-by-value semantics. However the usual if-then-else conditional, `if`, can be defined as follows.

$$\mathtt{if}(e_0, e_1, e_2) \triangleq \mathtt{app}(\mathtt{br}(e_0, \lambda d.e_1, \lambda d.e_2), \mathtt{nil}) \quad \text{where} \quad d \notin \mathrm{FV}(e_1, e_2)$$

In the functional case, there is no state information and hence only one state context, the initial context, which we represent as the empty context: $\diamond = \bullet$. We write e for $\bullet : e$. Thus, in Λ_{f}, states are not notationally distinguished from expressions and are self representing – the expression representing a state is $\mathrm{s2e}(e) = \bullet[\, e\,] = e$.

We want to specify the rules for the functional primitives in a manner that will work for any λ-language containing these primitives. Because we allow free variables in redexes, to reduce testing operations such as `br`, `eq`, or `ispr`, with a variable argument, it is necessary to know whether or not the variable is bound in the state context, and in complex states more information about the binding may be needed. Thus we define the reduction rules in terms of a satisfaction relation, $\zeta \models \Phi$, between state contexts, ζ, and assertions Φ. This allows us to specialize the reduction rule for an operation to a particular language by completing the specification of the satisfaction relation for state contexts of that language. For the languages considered here, we use assertions about membership and non-membership in sets of values and binary relations on values.

Definition (Assertions): Let W_1 range over sets of values such as $\{\texttt{nil}\}$, $\mathbf{A}$, $\mathbf{L}$, $\mathbf{P}$, etc. and let W_2 range over binary relations on values. In Λ_{f} assertions are of one of the following forms: $v \in W_1$; $v \notin W_1$; $(v_0, v_1) \in W_2$; $(v_0, v_1) \notin W_2$.

We first define satisfaction for the empty context (of any language). We then state some further constraints on satisfaction.

Definition (Satisfaction $\diamond \models \Phi$):

$$\mathbf{AtEq} = \{(v, v) \mid v \in \mathbf{A}\}$$

$$\diamond \models v \in W \quad \text{iff} \quad v \in W \qquad \text{for } W \in \{\mathbf{A}, \mathbf{P}, \mathbf{L}, \{\texttt{nil}\}\}$$

$$\diamond \models (v_0, v_1) \in \mathbf{AtEq} \quad \text{iff} \quad (v_0, v_1) \in \mathbf{AtEq}$$

$$\diamond \models v \notin W \quad \text{iff} \quad v \in (\mathbf{A} \cup \mathbf{P} \cup \mathbf{L}) - W \qquad \text{for } W \in \{\mathbf{A}, \mathbf{P}, \mathbf{L}, \{\texttt{nil}\}\}$$

$$\diamond \models (v_0, v_1) \notin \mathbf{AtEq} \quad \text{iff} \quad (v_0, v_1) \in ((\mathbf{A} \cup \mathbf{P} \cup \mathbf{L}) \times (\mathbf{A} \cup \mathbf{P} \cup \mathbf{L})) - \mathbf{AtEq}$$

Note that in general a state context provides only partial information and thus need not satisfy either a membership assertion or its corresponding non-membership assertion. For example neither $\diamond \models x \in \mathbf{A}$ nor $\diamond \models x \notin \mathbf{A}$ holds for a variable x. We require that if an assertion holds in the empty context, then it holds in any context. Also satisfaction must be preserved by value substitution.

Specification (Satisfaction $\zeta \models \Phi$):

$$\diamond \models \Phi \Rightarrow \zeta \models \Phi$$

$$\zeta \models \Phi \Rightarrow \zeta^{\sigma} \models \Phi^{\sigma} \quad \text{if} \quad \mathrm{Dom}(\sigma) \cap \mathrm{Traps}(\zeta) = \emptyset$$

For static assertions such as those defined above, it will be the case that $\zeta \models \Phi$ and $\zeta : e \longrightarrow \zeta' : e'$ implies $\zeta' \models \Phi$, but we don't make this an official requirement.

Since neither the state context nor the reduction context is changed by reducing a functional redex, we define a local reduction relation $r \hookrightarrow_{\zeta} e$, then lift this to states in the obvious manner. As examples of local functional reduction rules we give the rule for application (aka beta-v) rule, and the rules for branching, projection, and the tests for pairs, and equality.

Definition (Functional rules):

(app) $\texttt{app}(\lambda x.e, v) \hookrightarrow_{\zeta} e^{\{x \mapsto v\}}$

(br) $\texttt{br}(v_0, v_1, v_2) \hookrightarrow_{\zeta} \begin{cases} v_1 & \text{if } \zeta \models v \notin \{\texttt{nil}\} \\ v_2 & \text{if } \zeta \models v \in \{\texttt{nil}\} \end{cases}$

(fst) $\texttt{fst}(\texttt{pr}(v_0, v_1)) \hookrightarrow_{\zeta} v_0$

(ispr) $\texttt{ispr}(v) \hookrightarrow_{\zeta} \begin{cases} \texttt{t} & \text{if } \zeta \models v \in \mathbf{P} \\ \texttt{nil} & \text{if } \zeta \models v \notin \mathbf{P} \end{cases}$

$$\text{(eq)} \qquad \mathtt{eq}(v_0, v_1) \hookrightarrow_\zeta \begin{cases} \mathtt{t} & \text{if } \zeta \models (v_0, v_1) \in \mathbf{AtEq} \\ \mathtt{nil} & \text{if } \zeta \models (v_0, v_1) \notin \mathbf{AtEq} \end{cases}$$

$$\text{(rdx)} \qquad \zeta : R\,[\,r\,] \longrightarrow \zeta : R\,[\,e\,] \quad \text{if} \quad r \hookrightarrow_\zeta e$$

It is easy to see from the form of the rules that **g-unif** holds in Λ_{f}. In addition we have the following properties of computation in Λ_{f}.

Lemma (fred): In Λ_{f}

$$\text{(R-unif)} \quad R\,[\,e_0\,] \longrightarrow R\,[\,e_1\,] \;\Rightarrow\; R'\,[\,e_0\,] \longrightarrow R'\,[\,e_1\,] \qquad \text{for any } R, R', e_0 \notin \mathbf{V}$$

$$\text{(isdef)} \quad R\,[\,e\,]\downarrow \;\Rightarrow\; (\exists v')R\,[\,e\,] \longrightarrow\!\!\!\!\!\!\!\succ R\,[\,v'\,]$$

The following is a sampling of the equational laws for the functional operations. The first two laws correspond to the laws of the computational lambda calculus (Moggi 1988).

Theorem (Functional laws): In any λ-language with uniform semantics extending Λ_{f} we have

$$\text{(betav)} \quad \mathtt{app}(\lambda x.e, v) \cong e^{\{x \mapsto v\}}$$

$$\text{(dist)} \quad (\mathtt{let}\ x = e\ \mathtt{in}\ R\,[\,x\,]\,) \cong R\,[\,e\,] \quad \text{if} \quad x \notin \mathrm{FV}(R)$$

$$\text{(if.dist)} \quad R\,[\,\mathtt{if}(e, e_1, e_2)\,] \cong \mathtt{if}(e, R\,[\,e_1\,], R\,[\,e_2\,]\,)$$

$$\text{(proj)} \quad \mathtt{fst}(\mathtt{pr}(x, y)) \cong x \quad \text{and} \quad \mathtt{snd}(\mathtt{pr}(x, y)) \cong y$$

$$\text{(if)} \quad \mathtt{if}(\mathtt{t}, e_1, e_2) \cong e_1 \quad \text{and} \quad \mathtt{if}(\mathtt{nil}, e_1, e_2) \cong e_2$$

Proof : **(betav,if,proj)** follow from **(equi-red)** since the equated expressions have a common reduct. **(dist,if.dist)** follow from **(equi-rcx)** (the stronger form is needed for **(if.dist)**) since the equated expressions are the result of placing a common expression, e in equivalent reduction contexts.

□**Functional laws**

Since functional computation has no effects, two computations that do not use each other's results can be permuted.

Lemma (perm): In Λ_{f}, if $x \notin \mathrm{FV}(e_1)$ and $y \notin \mathrm{FV}(e_0)$, then

$$(\mathtt{let}\ x = e_0\ \mathtt{in}\ \mathtt{let}\ y = e_1\ \mathtt{in}\ e) \cong (\mathtt{let}\ y = e_1\ \mathtt{in}\ \mathtt{let}\ x = e_0\ \mathtt{in}\ e)$$

This law relies strongly on the **(fred.isdef)** property, and fails in various ways, as we shall see, in the presence of effects.

3.1 Programming Examples

Everywhere Undefined Functions

By **(ciu)** it is easy to see that any two undefined expressions are equivalent. Abstracting and using **(L-unif)** we have that any two lambdas that are everywhere undefined are equivalent. The classic example of an everywhere undefined lambda is

$$\texttt{Bot} \triangleq \lambda x.\mathrm{app}(\lambda x.\mathrm{app}(x,x), \lambda x.\mathrm{app}(x,x))$$

In Λ_{f}, another example of an everywhere undefined lambda is the "do-forever" loop.

$$\texttt{Do} \triangleq \lambda f.\texttt{Yv}(\lambda \texttt{Do}\lambda x.\texttt{Do}(f(x))$$

By the recursive definition, for any lambda φ and value v

$$\texttt{Do}(\varphi)(v) \longrightarrow\!\!\!\!\!\!\!\succ \texttt{Do}(\varphi)(\varphi(v))$$

In Λ_{f}, either $\varphi(v) \longrightarrow\!\!\!\!\!\!\!\succ v'$ for some v' or $\varphi(v)$ is undefined. In the latter case the computation is undefined since the redex is undefined. In the former case, the computation reduces to $\texttt{Do}(\varphi)(v')$ and on we go. The argument for undefinedness of `Bot` relies only on the **(app)** rule and will be valid in any uniform semantics. In contrast the argument for undefinedness of $\texttt{Do}(\varphi)$ relies on the **(fred.isdef)** property of Λ_{f}.

Functional Streams

We now illustrate the use of **(L-unif-sim)** computation to reason about streams represented as functions which when accessed (applied) return a pair consisting of the next stream element and the function representing the remainder of the stream. As Gordon (1995) and others have shown, bisimulation methods are also well suited to reasoning about equivalence of functional streams. We will see later that **(L-unif-sim)** generalizes nicely for reasoning about objects with private memory. $\texttt{NumS}(k)$ is the stream of numbers in increasing order beginning with k, and $\texttt{OddS}(k)$ is the stream of odd numbers starting with $2k+1$. $\texttt{Alt}(s)$ is the stream obtained by removing every other element of s.

$$\texttt{NumS} \triangleq \texttt{Yv}(\lambda\texttt{NumS}.\lambda k.\lambda d.\mathrm{pr}(k, \texttt{NumS}(k+1))$$

$$\begin{aligned}\texttt{Alt} \triangleq \texttt{Yv}(\lambda\texttt{Alt}.\lambda s.\lambda d.\ &\texttt{let}\, xs = s(\texttt{nil})\ \texttt{in}\\ &\quad\texttt{let}\, ys = \texttt{snd}(xs)(\texttt{nil})\ \texttt{in}\\ &\qquad\texttt{pr}(\texttt{fst}(xs), \texttt{Alt}(\texttt{snd}(ys))))\end{aligned}$$

$$\texttt{OddS} \triangleq \texttt{Yv}(\lambda\texttt{OddS}.\lambda k.\lambda d.\mathrm{pr}(2k+1, \texttt{OddS}(k+1)))$$

Lemma (odds): $\texttt{OddS}(k) \cong \texttt{Alt}(\texttt{NumS}(2k+1))$.

Proof : Let $\varphi_{0,k} = \texttt{OddS}(k)$ and $\varphi_{1,k} = \texttt{Alt}(\texttt{NumS}(2k+1))$. By the computation rules for `OddS`, `Alt`, `NumS`, for any ζ, R, $k \in \mathbf{N}$,

$$\zeta : R\,[\varphi_{j,k}(v)] \longrightarrow\!\!\!\!\!\!\!\succ (\zeta : R\,[\texttt{pr}(2k+1, p_{k+1})])^{\{p_{k+1} \mapsto \varphi_{j,k+1}\}}$$

and it is easy to see that the **(L-unif-sim)** conditions hold in both directions of approximation.

$\Box_{\mathbf{odds}}$

4 Control Effects

Now we introduce control effects, adding a new primitive operator ncc (for Note Current Continuation). The language with control facilities, Λ_c, has operations $O^c = O^f \cup \{\texttt{ncc}\}$.

Roughly speaking, $\texttt{ncc}(v)$ captures the current reduction context as a continuation, and applies v to this continuation at the top level. ncc is called $\mathcal{C}$ in (Felleisen and Friedman 1986; Felleisen 1987). ncc differs from the Scheme call/cc primitive (Steele and Sussman 1975; Rees and Clinger 1986) in that call/cc evaluates the application of v to the captured continuation in the context of that continuation rather than discarding it. call/cc can be defined using ncc as follows.

$$\texttt{call/cc} \triangleq \lambda f.\texttt{ncc}(\lambda c.c(f(c)))$$

ncc can also be used to define an abort primitive. We call this top and we use it to represent the top level of a computation. top, simply returns its argument to the top level.

$$\texttt{top} \triangleq \lambda x.\texttt{ncc}(\lambda k.x)$$

As in the functional case, Λ_c has only one state context, the initial context, $\diamond_c = \texttt{top}(\bullet)$. Thus, a Λ_c state has the form $\diamond_c : e$ and the expression associated to a Λ_c state is defined by $\mathrm{s2e}(\diamond_c : e) = \texttt{top}(e)$. Even though there is only one state context, we keep it explicit in our notation to emphasize the distinction between top level in the presence of control primitives and the simple functional case. Reduction rules for functional operations apply directly to Λ_c states since satisfaction for $\diamond$ is the same in any language. Thus, we need only supply a reduction rule for ncc.

Definition (Ncc reduction):

(ncc) $\quad \zeta : R\,[\texttt{ncc}(v)] \longrightarrow \zeta : \texttt{app}(v, \texttt{top} \circ R)$

We use the convention that R used where a lambda should appear abbreviates $\lambda x.R\,[x]$ for some $x \notin \mathrm{FV}(R)$. As for the functional primitives, we have specified the rule for ncc in a manner that defines the rule for any λ-language containing the ncc operation. We say a λ-language has ncc *control*, if ncc is among the operations of that λ-language, the reduction rule for ncc in that λ-language is that given above, and no other reduction rules manipulate the reduction context. In particular rules for primitives other than ncc will have the form $\zeta : R\,[\vartheta(v_1, \ldots, v_n)] \longrightarrow \zeta' : R\,[e]$. We introduce the notion of λ-languagewith ncc control to characterize a class of languages for which the basic ncc laws hold. As we will see below, permitting other control primitives can invalidate these laws.

Lemma (top rule): The derived reduction rule for top is

(top) $\quad \zeta : R\,[\texttt{top}(v)] \twoheadrightarrow \zeta : v$

Proof : Using the Λ_c computation rules we have

$$\begin{aligned}\zeta : R\,[\mathtt{top}(v)] &\triangleq \zeta : R\,[(\lambda x.\mathtt{ncc}(\lambda c.x))(v)]\\ &\longrightarrow \zeta : R\,[\mathtt{ncc}(\lambda c.v)] \qquad c \notin \mathrm{FV}(v)\\ &\longrightarrow \zeta : \mathtt{app}(\lambda c.v, \mathtt{top} \circ R)\\ &\longrightarrow \zeta : v\end{aligned}$$

$\square_{\mathbf{top\ rule}}$

To provide further intuition about computation with ncc, we introduce a useful abbreviation, note$(c)e$, and derive its computation rule. note$(c)e$ binds c in e to the current continuation and arranges for e to be evaluated without discarding the current continuation. note is to call/cc what let is to λ.

$$\mathtt{note}(c)e \triangleq \mathtt{ncc}(\lambda c.\mathtt{app}(c, e))$$

Lemma (note rule):

(note) $\zeta : R\,[\mathtt{note}(c)e] \twoheadrightarrow \zeta : \mathtt{app}(\mathtt{top} \circ R, e^{\{c \mapsto \mathtt{top} \circ R\}})$

Proof :

$$\begin{aligned}\zeta : R\,[\mathtt{note}(c)e] &\triangleq \zeta : R\,[\mathtt{ncc}(\lambda c.c(e))]\\ &\longrightarrow \zeta : \mathtt{app}(\lambda c.c(e), \mathtt{top} \circ R)\\ &\longrightarrow \zeta : \mathtt{app}(\mathtt{top} \circ R, e^{\{c \mapsto \mathtt{top} \circ R\}})\end{aligned}$$

$\square_{\mathbf{note\ rule}}$

It is again easy to see that **g-unif** holds in Λ_c. However, the functional reduction properties (**fred**) fail. To see this, note that $\zeta : R\,[\mathtt{top}(0)] \downarrow$ but for non-empty R, there is no value v such that $\zeta : R\,[\mathtt{top}(0)]$ reduces to $\zeta : R\,[v]$.

A lemma that is useful in dealing with the top-level is the following.

Lemma (top.elim): In a λ-language with uniform semantics and ncc control

(1) $\mathtt{top} \cong R \circ \mathtt{top}$

(2) $\zeta : R\,[\mathtt{top}(e)] \updownarrow \zeta : e$ for ζ closed R, e

Proof : To show **(1)** we use **(L-unif)** noting that by the top rule, $\zeta : R'\,[\mathtt{app}(\varphi, v)] \twoheadrightarrow \zeta : v$ for $\varphi \in \{\mathtt{top}, R \circ \mathtt{top}\}$. For **(2)** if $e \in \mathbf{V}$ we are done (by the top rule). Also if the computation leading from $\zeta : e$ does not invoke the ncc rule, then (by the ncc control assumption) either both states are undefined, or both lead to the same value state. Otherwise suppose $\zeta : e \twoheadrightarrow \zeta' : R\,[\mathtt{ncc}(v)]$ by steps not involving ncc. Then $\zeta : e \twoheadrightarrow \zeta' : \mathtt{app}(v, \mathtt{top} \circ R)$, and $\zeta : \mathtt{top}(e) \twoheadrightarrow \zeta' : \mathtt{app}(v, \mathtt{top} \circ \mathtt{top} \circ R)$. By **(1)** and the functional laws, $\mathtt{top} \cong \mathtt{top} \circ \mathtt{top}$ and we are done. $\square_{\mathbf{top.elim}}$

(**top.elim**) is used in establishing a number of basic $\mathtt{ncc}$ laws. To see how this can fail in the presence of other control primitives, consider adding $\mathtt{fcc}$ defined by the rule $\zeta : R\,[\mathtt{fcc}(v)] \longrightarrow \zeta : \mathtt{app}(v, R)$. The continuation captured by $\mathtt{fcc}$ composes with rather than escaping from any surrounding context when it is applied. Let $e = \mathtt{fcc}(\lambda k.\,\mathtt{let}\ x = k(v)\ \mathtt{in}\ \mathtt{Bot}$. Then $\zeta : \mathtt{top}(e) \twoheadrightarrow \zeta : v$ while $\zeta : e \twoheadrightarrow \zeta : \mathtt{Bot}$ and hence is undefined.

The following is a sampling of the laws axiomatizing $\mathtt{ncc}$.

Theorem (Ncc laws (ncc)): In any λ-language with uniform semantics and $\mathtt{ncc}$ control

(1) $\mathtt{ncc}(\lambda c.\mathtt{ncc}(e)) \cong \mathtt{ncc}(\lambda c.\mathtt{app}(e, \mathtt{top}))$

(2) $R\,[\mathtt{ncc}(e)] \cong \mathtt{ncc}(\lambda c.\mathtt{app}(e, c \circ R)) \qquad c \notin \mathrm{FV}(e, R)$
$\mathtt{ncc}(f) \cong \mathtt{ncc}(\mathtt{top} \circ f)$

(3) $\mathtt{ncc}(\lambda c.C\,[c]) \cong \mathtt{ncc}(\lambda c.C\,[\mathtt{top} \circ c])$

(4) $\mathtt{note}(c)e \cong e \quad \text{if} \quad c \notin \mathrm{FV}(e)$

(5) $\mathtt{note}(c)R\,[e] \cong \mathtt{let}\ x = e\ \mathtt{in}\ \mathtt{note}(c)R\,[x] \quad \text{if} \quad c \notin \mathrm{FV}(e), x \notin \mathrm{FV}(R)$

(6) $\mathtt{note}(c)\mathtt{if}(e_0, e_1, e_2) \cong \mathtt{if}(e_0, \mathtt{note}(c)e_1, \mathtt{note}(c)e_2) \quad \text{if} \quad c \notin \mathrm{FV}(e_0)$

Proof : The general idea for establishing (**ncc**) is the following. To show $e_0 \cong e_1$, by **ciu** it suffices to show that

$$\zeta : R^*\,[e_0^\sigma] \updownarrow \zeta : R^*\,[e_1^\sigma]$$

for any closing ζ, R^*, σ. To do this we proceed as follows (except for (3) which follows by direct calculation).

1. Find R_0, R_1, e_{01} such that $\zeta : R^*\,[e_j^\sigma] \twoheadrightarrow \zeta : R_j\,[e_{01}]$ for $j < 2$
2. Show that $\mathtt{top} \circ R_0 \cong \mathtt{top} \circ R_1$

Then for $j < 2$

$\zeta : R^*\,[e_j^\sigma] \updownarrow \zeta : R_j\,[e_{01}]$ by 1.

$\zeta : R_j\,[e_{01}] \updownarrow \zeta : \mathtt{top}(R_j\,[e_{01}])$ by (**top.elim**)

$\zeta : \mathtt{top}(R_j\,[e_{01}]) \updownarrow \zeta : (\mathtt{top} \circ R_j)(e_{01})$ by (**dist**)

and by condition 2. we are done.

As an example we carry out this process for (**ncc.5**). In this case we have $e_0 = \mathtt{note}(c)R\,[e]$ and $e_1 = \mathtt{let}\ x = e\ \mathtt{in}\ \mathtt{note}(c)R\,[x]$ where $c \notin \mathrm{FV}(e)$ and $x \notin \mathrm{FV}(R)$. Pick some closing ζ, R^*, σ, and let

$R_0 = (\mathtt{top} \circ R^*)(R^{\{c \mapsto \mathtt{top} \circ R^*\}})$

$R_1 = R^*\,[\mathtt{let}\ x = \bullet\ \mathtt{in}\ \mathtt{note}(c)R\,[x]\,]$

$e_{01} = e$

Then using the $\texttt{note}$ rule and (**L-unif**) it is easy to check that conditions 1. and 2. hold.

□**Ncc laws**

A somewhat non-intuitive equivalence that holds in λ-languages with $\texttt{ncc}$ control is $\texttt{top}(v) \cong \texttt{top}(v')$ for any v and v'. This simply expresses the fact that values returned by $\texttt{top}$ can not be observed by any program. A refined notion of equivalence for which this equation holds only when the value expressions are equivalent, but for which the (**Ncc laws**) are valid was studied in (Talcott 1989).

Note that $\texttt{Do}(f) \cong \texttt{Bot}$ fails in Λ_c. The reason is the ability to escape from a loop. A distinguishing context is $\texttt{note}(c)\ \texttt{let}\ f = \lambda x.\texttt{if}(\texttt{iszero}(x), c(0), x - 1)\ \texttt{in}\ \texttt{app}(\bullet, 0)$.

(**perm**) also fails in Λ_c, since permutation of the order of expression evaluation can change termination properties. As a counterexample let $e_0 = \texttt{ncc}(\lambda k.0)$ and $e_1 = \texttt{Bot}(0)$, then

$$\zeta : \texttt{let}\ x_0 = \texttt{ncc}(\lambda k.0)\ \texttt{in}\ \texttt{let}\ x_1 = \texttt{Bot}(0)\ \texttt{in}\ e \twoheadrightarrow \zeta : 0$$

$$\zeta : \texttt{let}\ x_1 = \texttt{Bot}(0)\ \texttt{in}\ \texttt{let}\ x_0 = \texttt{ncc}(\lambda k.0)\ \texttt{in}\ e$$

$$\twoheadrightarrow \zeta : \texttt{let}\ x_1 = \texttt{app}(\lambda x.x(x), \lambda x.x(x))\ \texttt{in}\ \texttt{let}\ x_0 = \texttt{ncc}(\lambda k.0)\ \texttt{in}\ e$$

$$\twoheadrightarrow \ldots \qquad \text{forever}$$

The following lemma shows that $\texttt{call/cc}$ and $\texttt{note}$ are inter-definable, and $\texttt{ncc}$ is definable from $\texttt{call/cc}$ and $\texttt{top}$.

Lemma (control):

(1) $\texttt{call/cc} \cong \lambda f.\texttt{note}(c) f(c)$

(2) $\texttt{note}(c) e \cong \texttt{call/cc}(\lambda c.e)$

(3) $\texttt{ncc} \cong \lambda f.\texttt{call/cc}(\lambda c.\texttt{top}(f(c)))$

Proof : (**1,2**) follow by expanding the definitions, possibly using (**betav**). (**3**) requires an application of (**ncc.2**) as well. □

5 Memory Effects

Now we consider memory effects. The language Λ_m has operations

$$\mathbf{O}^m = \{\texttt{mk}, \texttt{get}, \texttt{set}, \texttt{iscell}\} \cup \mathbf{O}^f.$$

Intuitively, $\texttt{mk}(v)$ allocates a new cell containing v and returns that cell, $\texttt{get}(z)$ returns the contents of the cell z, $\texttt{set}(z, v)$ sets the contents of the cell z to be v, and $\texttt{iscell}(v)$ tests whether v is a cell.

A state context of Λ_m is a memory context, M, of the form

$$M = \texttt{let}\ z_1 = \text{mk}(\texttt{nil})\ \texttt{in}$$
$$\dots$$
$$\texttt{let}\ z_k = \text{mk}(\texttt{nil})\ \texttt{in}$$
$$\texttt{set}(z_1, v_1); \dots \texttt{set}(z_k, v_k); \bullet$$

The `let`s of M allocate new cells, named z_i, and the `set`s assign the contents. If the value put in a cell does not refer to any newly created cell then that `set` could be omitted and the value expression used as argument to the corresponding mk. However in general, separation of allocation and assignment is needed in order to represent stores with cycles. For example, consider creating a cell that contains itself. This is described by the memory context $\texttt{let}\ z = \text{mk}(\texttt{nil})\ \texttt{in}\ \texttt{set}(z, z); \bullet$. This is not the same as the context $\texttt{let}\ z = \text{mk}(z)\ \texttt{in}\ \bullet$, since in the latter case the z in the argument to mk is bound outside the context and is distinct from the created z. Memory contexts are a syntactic representation of the stores of more traditional semantics (finite maps from locations to storable values). Thus, we define analogues of finite map operations on memory contexts. For M as above, $\text{Dom}(M) = \{z_1, \dots z_k\}$, $M(z_i) = v_i$ for $1 \leq i \leq k$, and we write $\{z_i \mapsto \text{mk}(v_i) \mid 1 \leq i \leq k\}$ for M. This notation is intentionally ambiguous about the order of allocation of cells and assigning values to cells. When we only care about the finite map represented by M the ambiguity makes no difference. The empty state context of Λ_m is the empty context, $\bullet$, and the map associating Λ_m states to expressions is defined by $\text{s2e}(M : e) = M\,[\,e\,]$.

To define the reduction relation for the new Λ_m operations two new assertions – $v \in \text{Cell}$ and $v \notin \text{Cell}$ – are needed. The definition of satisfaction for Λ_m state contexts is completed as follows.

Definition (Satisfaction for memory contexts):

$$M \models v \in \text{Cell} \quad \text{iff} \quad v \in \text{Dom}(M)$$
$$M \models v \notin \text{Cell} \quad \text{iff} \quad v \notin \text{Dom}(M)$$
$$M \models v \notin W \quad \text{if} \quad v \in \text{Dom}(M) \quad \text{for} \quad W \in \{\mathbf{A}, \mathbf{L}, \mathbf{P}, \{\texttt{nil}\}\}$$

Definition (Memory Rules):

$$\text{(iscell)} \quad \texttt{iscell}(v) \hookrightarrow_M \begin{cases} \texttt{t} & \text{if } M \models v \in \text{Cell} \\ \texttt{nil} & \text{if } M \models v \notin \text{Cell} \end{cases}$$

$$\text{(mk)} \quad M : R\,[\,\text{mk}(v)\,] \longrightarrow M\{z \mapsto \text{mk}(v)\} : R\,[\,z\,]$$
$$z \notin (\text{Dom}(M) \cup \text{FV}(M\,[\,R\,[\,v\,]\,]))$$

$$\text{(get)} \quad M : R\,[\,\texttt{get}(z)\,] \longrightarrow M : R\,[\,v\,] \quad \text{if} \quad M(z) = v$$

$$\text{(set)} \quad M : R\,[\,\texttt{set}(z, v)\,] \longrightarrow M\{z \mapsto \text{mk}(v)\} : R\,[\,\texttt{nil}\,] \quad \text{if} \quad z \in \text{Dom}(M)$$

Recall from §3. that local reduction lifts according to the **(rdx)** rule: $M : R\,[\,r\,] \longrightarrow M : R\,[\,e\,]$ if $r \hookrightarrow_M e$. Note that the rule for `get` could also have been expressed as a local rule: $\mathtt{get}(v) \hookrightarrow_M v'$ if $v \in \mathrm{Dom}(M)$ and $Mv = v'$. On the other hand, the rules for mk and set can not be formulated as local rules.

It is again easy to verify that **g-unif** holds in Λ_{m}. The unicity property makes explicit the fact that, in our model, arbitrary choice in cell allocation is the same phenomenon as arbitrary choice of names of bound variables. The following analogue of **(fred)** holds in Λ_{m}.

Lemma (mred): In Λ_{m}

(R-unif) $M : R[e] \longrightarrow M' : R[e'] \Rightarrow M : R'[e] \longrightarrow M' : R'[e']$

if $e \notin \mathbf{V}$, $(\mathrm{Dom}(M') \cap \mathrm{FV}(R')) \subseteq \mathrm{Dom}(M)$

(isdef) $M : R[e] \downarrow \Rightarrow (\exists M', v)(M : R[e] \longrightarrow\!\!\!\!\!\rightarrow M' : R[v])$

Some further simple consequences of the computation rules are that memory contexts may be pulled out of reduction contexts, and that computation is uniform in unreferenced memory.

Lemma (umem): In Λ_{m}

(1) $\bullet : R[M[e]] \longrightarrow\!\!\!\!\!\rightarrow M : R[e]$ if $\mathrm{FV}(R) \cap \mathrm{Dom}(M) = \emptyset$.

(2) $M : e \longrightarrow M' : e' \Rightarrow (M_0 \cup M) : e \longrightarrow (M_0 \cup M') : e'$

if $\mathrm{Dom}(M_0) \cap \mathrm{Dom}(M') = \emptyset$

(2a) $(M_0 \cup M) : e \longrightarrow (M_0 \cup M') : e' \Rightarrow M : e \longrightarrow M' : e'$

if $(\mathrm{Dom}(M') \cup \mathrm{FV}(M[e])) \cap \mathrm{Dom}(M_0) = \emptyset$

Note that in **(umem.2)** the if clause implies that $\mathrm{Dom}(M) \cap \mathrm{Dom}(M_0) = \emptyset$.

An example computation

NumO is the mutable analogue of NumS. The value of $\mathtt{NumO}(k)$ is the 'object' with script $\mathtt{NumOa}(z)$ where z is a private cell (accessible only from within $\mathtt{NumOa}(z)$) whose initial contents is k. When queried, $\mathtt{NumOa}(z)$ returns the contents of z and increments that contents by 1, thus generating the stream of numbers.

$$\mathtt{NumO} \triangleq \lambda x.\mathtt{NumOa}(\mathtt{mk}(x))$$

$$\mathtt{NumOa} \triangleq \lambda z.\lambda d.\,\mathtt{let}\ x = \mathtt{get}(z)\ \mathtt{in}\ \mathtt{set}(z, x+1); x$$

The computation rules for NumO and NumOa are given by the following lemma.

Lemma (NumO rules): For $z \notin (\mathrm{Dom}(M) \cup \mathrm{FV}(R)$, $k \in \mathbf{N}$

(numo) $M : R[\mathtt{NumO}(k)] \longrightarrow\!\!\!\!\!\rightarrow M\{z \mapsto \mathtt{mk}(k)\} : R[\mathtt{NumOa}(z)]$

(numa) $M\{z \mapsto \mathtt{mk}(k)\} : R[\mathtt{NumOa}(z)(v)] \longrightarrow\!\!\!\!\!\rightarrow M\{z \mapsto \mathtt{mk}(k+1)\} : R[k]$

Proof :

$$\bullet : \texttt{NumO}(k) = \bullet : \lambda x.\texttt{NumOa}(\texttt{mk}(x))(k) \qquad \text{by definition}$$
$$\longrightarrow \bullet : \texttt{NumOa}(\texttt{mk}(k)) \qquad \textbf{(app)}$$
$$\longrightarrow \{z \mapsto \texttt{mk}(k)\} : \texttt{NumOa}(z) \qquad \textbf{(mk,app)}$$

and

$$\{z \mapsto \texttt{mk}(k)\} : \texttt{NumOa}(z)(v)$$
$$\longrightarrow \{z \mapsto \texttt{mk}(k)\} : \texttt{let } x = \texttt{get}(z) \texttt{ in set}(z, x+1); x \qquad \textbf{(app)}$$
$$\twoheadrightarrow \{z \mapsto \texttt{mk}(k)\} : \texttt{set}(z, k+1); k \qquad \textbf{(get,app)}$$
$$\twoheadrightarrow \{z \mapsto \texttt{mk}(k+1)\} : k \qquad \textbf{(set,app)}$$

Thus using **(mred.R-unif,umem.2)** we are done.

□**NumOrules**

The following equivalences are a sampling of the laws axiomatizing memory operations. Here eqc extends the definition of eq to reference cells. This can be taken as primitive, or defined as shown in Mason (1986). The (derived) computation rule for eqc is given by

$$\mathbf{CEq}[M] = \{(v, v) \mid v \in \mathrm{Dom}(M)\} \cup \mathbf{AtEq}$$
$$M \models (v_0, v_1) \in \mathbf{CEq} \quad \text{iff} \quad (v_0, v_1) \in \mathbf{CEq}[M]$$
$$\diamond \models (v_0, v_1) \notin \mathbf{CEq} \quad \text{iff} \quad (v_0, v_1) \in (\mathbf{A} \cup \mathbf{P} \cup \mathbf{L} \cup \mathrm{Dom}(M))^2 - \mathbf{CEq}[M]$$
$$\texttt{eqc}(v_0, v_1) \hookrightarrow_M \begin{cases} \texttt{t} & \text{if } M \models (v_0, v_1) \in \mathbf{CEq} \\ \texttt{nil} & \text{if } M \models (v_0, v_1) \notin \mathbf{CEq} \end{cases}$$

Theorem (Memory laws (mem)): In Λ_{m}

(1) $\texttt{get}(\texttt{mk}(x)) \cong x$

(2) $\texttt{let } x = \texttt{mk}(v) \texttt{ in } R\,[\texttt{eqc}(x, y)] \cong \texttt{let } x = \texttt{mk}(v) \texttt{ in } R\,[\texttt{nil}]$

(3) $\texttt{let } x = \texttt{mk}(v) \texttt{ in set}(x, v'); e \cong \texttt{let } x = \texttt{mk}(v') \texttt{ in } e \quad \text{if} \quad x \notin \mathrm{FV}(v')$

(4) $\texttt{set}(x, v); \texttt{get}(x) \cong \texttt{set}(x, v); v$

(5) $\texttt{set}(x, v); \texttt{set}(y, v') \cong \texttt{if}(\texttt{eqc}(x, y), \texttt{set}(x, v'), \texttt{set}(y, v'); \texttt{set}(x, v))$

(6) $M\,[\,e\,] \cong e \qquad \text{if } \mathrm{FV}(e) \cap \mathrm{Dom}(M) = \emptyset$

Proof : The memory laws are all established by the following general argument, which formalizes the intuition that two expressions are equivalent if they reduce to the same expression, with the same effects on memory ignoring inaccessible memory (garbage). To show that $e_0 \cong e_1$ by **(ciu)** pick an arbitrary closing M^*, R^*, σ and show that $M^* : R^*\,[\,e_0^\sigma\,]$ and $M^* : R^*\,[\,e_1^\sigma\,]$ are equidefined. To do this, we show that there are e' (the common reduct), M' (the result of the common effects on M), and M_j (the garbage) such that $\mathrm{Dom}(M_j) \cap (\mathrm{Dom}(M') \cup \mathrm{FV}(M'[e'])) = \emptyset$ and

$$M^* : e_j^{\sigma^*} \longrightarrow M_j \cup M' : e'$$

Then by **(mred.R-unif)**

$$M^* : R^*[e_j^{\sigma}] \longrightarrow M_j \cup M' : R[e']$$

and by **(umem.2)** the two states $M_j \cup M' : R[e']$ are equidefined. Thus we are done. As an example of this argument, consider memory law (1), with M^*, R^*, σ as above. Thus $e_0 = \mathtt{get}(\mathtt{mk}(x))$ and $e_1 = x$. We let $M_0 = \{z \mapsto \mathtt{mk}(\sigma(x))\}$, $M_1 = \bullet$, $M' = M^*$, and $e' = \sigma(x)$.

□MemoryLaws

To simplify the presentation, we have given the rules and equational theory for the memory operations only for Λ_{m}. This can be generalized to a wide class of λ-languages by identifying conditions that prevent interference with the memory operations as was done for the theory of ncc.

The **(perm)** law fails in Λ_{m}. A simple counterexample is obtained by taking $e_0 = \mathtt{set}(z, 0)$, $e_1 = \mathtt{set}(z, 1)$, and $e = \mathtt{get}(z)$. Then by **(mem.4,5)**

$$\mathtt{let}\ x = e_0\ \mathtt{in}\ \mathtt{let}\ y = e_1\ \mathtt{in}\ e \cong \mathtt{let}\ y = e_1\ \mathtt{in}\ 1$$

$$\mathtt{let}\ y = e_1\ \mathtt{in}\ \mathtt{let}\ x = e_0\ \mathtt{in}\ e \cong \mathtt{let}\ x = e_0\ \mathtt{in}\ 0$$

However, allocation of memory can be permuted with evaluation of expressions that have no access to that memory. This is a key law for reasoning about programs that manipulate memory (see Mason and Talcott (1990, 1992, 1994a) for some examples).

Lemma (delay): In Λ_{m}, if $x \notin \mathrm{FV}(e_1)$ and $y \notin \mathrm{FV}(v)$, then

$$(\mathtt{let}\ x = \mathtt{mk}(v)\ \mathtt{in}\ \mathtt{let}\ y = e_1\ \mathtt{in}\ e)$$
$$\cong (\mathtt{let}\ y = e_1\ \mathtt{in}\ \mathtt{let}\ x = \mathtt{mk}(v)\ \mathtt{in}\ e)$$

In Λ_{m}, **(delay)** is a fairly easy consequence of **(ciu)** and **(mred.isdef)**. A proof appears in (Mason and Talcott 1991a). As an example of the use of the memory and delay laws we show that $\mathtt{eqc}(\mathtt{mk}(0), \mathtt{mk}(0)) \cong \mathtt{nil}$

$\mathtt{eqc}(\mathtt{mk}(0), \mathtt{mk}(0))$

$\cong \mathtt{let}\ x = \mathtt{mk}(0)\ \mathtt{in}\ \mathtt{let}\ y = \mathtt{mk}(0)\ \mathtt{in}\ \mathtt{eqc}(x, y)$ **(dist)** twice

$\cong \mathtt{let}\ y = \mathtt{mk}(0)\ \mathtt{in}\ \mathtt{let}\ x = \mathtt{mk}(0)\ \mathtt{in}\ \mathtt{eqc}(x, y)$ **(delay)**

$\cong \mathtt{let}\ y = \mathtt{mk}(0)\ \mathtt{in}\ \mathtt{let}\ x = \mathtt{mk}(0)\ \mathtt{in}\ \mathtt{nil}$ **(mem.2)**

$\cong \mathtt{nil}$ **(mem.6)**

Stream Object equivalence

As a further example of using uniform computation techniques we show the equivalence of two stream objects built using the mutable analogues `NumO`, `AltO`, and `OddO` of `NumS`, `Alt`, and `OddS`. `NumO` was defined above.

$$\texttt{OddO} \triangleq \lambda k.\texttt{OddOa}(\texttt{mk}(k))$$

$$\texttt{OddOa} \triangleq \lambda z.\lambda d.\,\texttt{let}\ x = \texttt{get}(z)\ \texttt{in}\ \texttt{set}(z, x+1); 2x+1$$

$$\texttt{AltO} \triangleq \lambda s.\lambda d.\,\texttt{let}\ x = \texttt{app}(s, \texttt{nil})\ \texttt{in}\ \texttt{app}(s, \texttt{nil}); x$$

Lemma (mutable stream): $\texttt{OddO}(k) \cong \texttt{AltO}(\texttt{NumO}(2k+1))$

Proof : The proof indicates how to generalize **(L-unif-sim)** to objects. Since objects have private memory, this has to be done with a bit of care. By **ciu** we need only show that

$$M : R\,[\texttt{OddO}(k)] \updownarrow M : R\,[\texttt{AltO}(\texttt{NumO}(2k+1)].$$

By **g-unif** and the derived computation rules for the defined objects, we need only show that

$$M\{z \mapsto \texttt{mk}(k)\} : R\,[\texttt{OddOa}(z)] \updownarrow M\{z \mapsto \texttt{mk}(2k{+}1)\} : R\,[\texttt{AltO}(\texttt{NumOa}(z)]$$

for $k \in \mathbf{N}$. We do this by defining a notion of similar states and showing by computation induction that similar states are equi-defined. Similar states are states of the form

$$S_o = (M\{z \mapsto \texttt{mk}(k)\} : e)^{\{o \mapsto \texttt{OddOa}(z)\}}$$

and

$$S_a = (M\{z \mapsto \texttt{mk}(2k+1)\} : e)^{\{o \mapsto \texttt{AltO}(\texttt{NumOa}(z))\}}$$

for $M : e$ such that $z \notin \mathrm{Dom}(M) \cup \mathrm{FV}(e)$ and $\mathrm{FV}(M\,[e]) = \{o\}$. To show equi-definedness, assume $S_o\!\downarrow$ or $S_a\!\downarrow$. If $e \in \mathbf{V}$ then we are done. Otherwise, by **(L-unif)** either $M : e \longrightarrow M' : e'$ assuming $o \in \mathbf{L}$ (and we are done since we have smaller computations of the same form), or e has the form $R\,[\texttt{app}(o, v)]$. In this case

$$S_o \longrightarrow\!\!\!\!\!\!\succ (M\{z \mapsto \texttt{mk}(k+1) : R\,[2k+1])^{\{o \mapsto \texttt{OddOa}(z)\}}$$

and

$$S_a \longrightarrow\!\!\!\!\!\!\succ (M\{z \mapsto \texttt{mk}(2k+3) : R\,[2k+1])^{\{o \mapsto \texttt{AltO}(\texttt{NumOa}(z))\}}$$

and again we have the desired smaller computations of the same form.

$\Box_{\mathbf{mutablestream}}$

More examples of proof principles (and proofs) for reasoning about mutable streams and other forms of object, including a simulation induction principle that abstracts and generalizes the above argument, can be found in Mason and Talcott (1994a, 1994b).

6 Control + Memory Effects

We combine the control and memory operations to obtain a Scheme-like language, Λ_s. The operations of Λ_s, $\mathbf{O}^s = \mathbf{O}^c \cup \mathbf{O}^m$, are the union of the operations of Λ_m and Λ_c. State contexts of Λ_s combine the memory context of Λ_m and the top marker of Λ_c, and are of the form $M\,[\mathtt{top}(\bullet)]$. We write $M_T : e$ for the Λ_s state with expression e and state context $M\,[\mathtt{top}(\bullet)]$. As usual, the expression associated to such a state is defined by $\mathrm{s2e}(M_T : e) = M\,[\mathtt{top}(e)]$.

The reduction relation in Λ_s is obtained by combining the rules for operations of Λ_m and Λ_c. This works, because adding the top marker does not change satisfaction, and the operation ncc is uniform in the state context.

Definition (Λ_s reduction rules):

$$M_T : e \longrightarrow M_T : e' \quad \text{if} \quad \diamond_c : e \longrightarrow \diamond_c : e'$$

$$M_T : e \longrightarrow M'_T : e' \quad \text{if} \quad M : e \longrightarrow M' : e'$$

Note that $M\,[\mathtt{top}(e)] \cong \mathtt{top}(M\,[\,e\,])$, thus we could have used state contexts of the form $\mathtt{top}(M)$ without changing the induced approximation and equivalence relations.

The properties of memory computation (**umem.1,2,2a**) persist, and the semantics of Λ_s is uniform. Thus, the functional, ncc, and memory laws hold in Λ_s. Also, the (**top.elim**) property of Λ_c holds in Λ_s. but (**mred**) fail in Λ_s for the same reasons that (**fred**) fails in Λ_c.

As pointed out by Felleisen (1993), (**delay**) fails in Λ_s if the expression whose evaluation is permuted with memory allocation has control effects. An example of this failure is obtained by taking $e_1 = \mathtt{ncc}(\lambda k.k(k))$ and $e = \mathtt{set}(x, \mathtt{get}(x) + 1); y(\theta(x))$ where $\theta = \lambda x.\lambda d.\mathtt{get}(x)$. To see the problem, let

$$R_0 = \mathtt{let}\ y = \bullet\ \mathtt{in}\ \mathtt{set}(x, \mathtt{get}(x) + 1); y(\theta(x))$$

$$e_l = \mathtt{let}\ x = \mathrm{mk}(0)\ \mathtt{in}\ R_0\,[\mathtt{ncc}(\lambda k.k(k))]$$

$$R_1 = \mathtt{let}\ y = \bullet\ \mathtt{in}\ \mathtt{let}\ x = \mathrm{mk}(0)\ \mathtt{in}\ \mathtt{set}(x, \mathtt{get}(x) + 1); y(\theta(x))$$

$$e_r = R_1\,[\mathtt{ncc}(\lambda k.k(k))]$$

$$R = \mathtt{if}(\mathtt{eq}(\bullet, 1), 1, \mathtt{Bot}(1))$$

then $(\diamond : R\,[\,e_r\,])\downarrow$ but $\neg((\diamond : R\,[\,e_l\,])\downarrow)$.

Semantically, an expression is control-free if in any computation context, evaluation of (any instance of) the expression uses no control rules. Syntactically, we can ensure this in Λ_s by requiring that ncc does not appear in the expression (or any imported definitions), that get does not appear (thus control effects can not be dynamically imported), and that all applications are of the form $\mathtt{app}(\lambda x.e, e')$ (so no functions with control effects can be imported from the environment). For example, $\mathtt{app}(\mathtt{get}(y), x)$ could import control effects from the contents of y and

$\mathtt{app}(w, x)$ could import control effects from the value of w, which is determined by the program context.

Lemma (delay.s): In Λ_s, if $x \notin \mathrm{FV}(e_1)$, $y \notin \mathrm{FV}(v)$, and e_1 is control free, then

$$(\mathtt{let}\ x = \mathtt{mk}(v)\ \mathtt{in}\ \mathtt{let}\ y = e_1\ \mathtt{in}\ e)$$
$$\cong (\mathtt{let}\ y = e_1\ \mathtt{in}\ \mathtt{let}\ x = \mathtt{mk}(v)\ \mathtt{in}\ e)$$

Note that the argument used to establish **(delay)** in Λ_m now works, since **(mred)** holds for computations of allowed e_1.

7 Uniform Computation

In this section we develop the machinery necessary to state precisely the **s-unif** property of uniform semantics. We first enrich λ-language syntax to include place-holders for expressions and reduction contexts. After stating the **s-unif** requirement, we show that Λ_s (and hence the contained languages) has uniform semantics by lifting the reduction rules for Λ_s to enriched states in a manner the meets the **s-unif** requirements.

To motivate our definition of enriched syntax, we first consider adding place-holders for closed expressions in the case where state contexts are trivial and states are simply expressions. The holes of traditional contexts (such as those we defined in §2) are a kind of place-holder for expressions. To keep the two uses separate we introduce $\odot$ for place-holders. We add $\odot$ to the clause defining expressions, just as we added $\bullet$ to obtain standard contexts. Enriched versions of the remaining syntactic sorts are generated by replacing expressions by enriched expressions in the definitions. We signify entities of enriched syntax sorts by decorating metavariables with $\star$. Since $\odot$ will only be replaced by closed expressions, we extend substitution to the enriched syntax, by defining $\odot^{\star\sigma} = \odot$. Since filling of place-holders by closed expression, e is the same as substitution of e for $\odot$, this simple enrichment is adequate for closed expressions. However, it doesn't provide an adequate notion of uniform reduction for arbitrary expressions. To see this consider ${}^\star e = \mathtt{app}(\lambda y.\mathtt{app}(\lambda x.\lambda y.\odot, \lambda x.\odot), \lambda x.x)$. If we lift the reduction rules using the above definition of substitution, we have ${}^\star e \longrightarrow\!\!\!\!\!\!\succ \lambda y.\odot$ while ${}^\star e[\odot \mapsto \mathtt{app}(x, y)] \longrightarrow\!\!\!\!\!\!\succ \lambda y.\mathtt{app}(\lambda x.\mathtt{app}(x, \lambda x.x), y)$. Clearly we need to keep track of substitutions at occurrences of $\odot$. Thus we might try decorating $\odot$ with a substitution to be carried out when the place-holder is filled and extend substitution to the enriched syntax by composing at place-holders. Starting with empty substitution decorating the occurrences of $\odot$ in ${}^\star e$ we have

$$\mathtt{app}(\lambda y.\mathtt{app}(\lambda x.\lambda y.\odot^{\emptyset}, \lambda x.\odot^{\emptyset}), \lambda x.x) \longrightarrow \mathtt{app}(\lambda x.\lambda y.\odot^{\emptyset}, \lambda x.\odot^{\{y \mapsto \lambda x.x\}})$$

and now we notice that to continue the computation, the decorating substitutions must be allowed to have values in the enriched syntax in their range.

Our solution to the problem of an appropriate notion of place-holder is based on idea of decorating holes with substitutions and it accomplishes several things. It provides a means of defining substitution on expressions enriched with place-holders in such a way that filling and substitution commute. This is the key to lifting the computation rules to enriched states. It also separates the mechanism for trapping free variables of the filling expression from the mechanism for binding of free variables in the filled expression. The former is the province of the decorating substitution, trapped variables are those in its domain. The latter is the province of λ as usual, and is propagated to the filling expression via binding of free variables in the range of the decorating substitution. A consequence of the separation is that alpha conversion is valid even for lambda variables with place-holders in their scope.

The presentation below is adapted from Agha, Mason, Smith, and Talcott (1997) where uniform computation methods are developed to establish equational laws for actor computations. This in turn was based on the theory of binding structures (Talcott 1991, 1993). We add E-holes (to be filled with expressions) to the summands of the defining equation for expressions, and R-holes (to be filled with reduction contexts) to the summands in the defining equation for reduction contexts. We also add R-holes with the redex hole filled to the summands of the defining equation for expressions. The specifications of the remaining syntactic classes are correspondingly modified to refer to the enriched syntax. We adopt the convention that an extended syntactic class is indicated by the mark $\star$. Metavariables ranging over these classes are indicated by the same mark, and we prefix the names of these classes by ER-. Thus, we have ER-expressions where $^\star e$ ranges over $^\star\mathbf{E}$, ER-reduction contexts where $^\star R$ ranges over $^\star\mathbf{R}$, etc. Mostly we consider syntactic entities enriched with only on kind of place-holder. Thus one can read ER as E or R rather than E and R. We use the prefix E- and the mark $^\circ$ for E-hole enriched syntax and we use the prefix R- and the mark $^\diamond$ for R-hole enriched syntax. Thus we speak of E-expressions where $^\circ e$ ranges over $^\circ\mathbf{E}$ or R-expressions where $^\diamond e$ ranges over $^\diamond\mathbf{E}$.

For simplicity, we give the definitions for λ-languages in which the only additional values are pairs.

Definition (*E, *V, *S, *R, $^\star\mathbf{E}_{\mathrm{rdx}}$):

$$^\star\mathbf{E} = \mathbf{A} \cup \mathbf{X} \cup \lambda\mathbf{X}.{}^\star\mathbf{E} \cup \mathbf{O}_n({}^\star\mathbf{E}^n) \cup \circ^{{}^\star\mathbf{S}} \cup \diamond^{{}^\star\mathbf{S}}\,[{}^\star\mathbf{E}]$$

$$^\star\mathbf{V} = \mathbf{A} \cup \mathbf{X} \cup \lambda\mathbf{X}.{}^\star\mathbf{E} \cup \mathtt{pr}({}^\star\mathbf{V}, {}^\star\mathbf{V})$$

$$^\star\mathbf{S} = \mathrm{Fmap}[\mathbf{X}, {}^\star\mathbf{V}]$$

$$^\star\mathbf{R} = \{\,\bullet\,\} \cup \mathbf{O}_{m+n+1}({}^\star\mathbf{V}^m, {}^\star\mathbf{R}, {}^\star\mathbf{E}^n) \cup \diamond^{{}^\star\mathbf{S}}\,[{}^\star\mathbf{R}]$$

$$^\star\mathbf{E}_{\mathrm{rdx}} = \mathbf{O}_n({}^\star\mathbf{V}^n) - {}^\star\mathbf{V}$$

As before, λ is the only binding operator, and free variables of ER-expressions are defined as follows:

Definition (Free variables – $\mathrm{FV}({}^{\star}e)$, $\mathrm{FV}({}^{\star}\sigma)$**):**

$$\mathrm{FV}(\circ^{{}^{\star}\sigma}) = \mathrm{FV}({}^{\star}\sigma)$$
$$\mathrm{FV}(\diamond^{{}^{\star}\sigma}[{}^{\star}e]) = \mathrm{FV}({}^{\star}\sigma) \cup \mathrm{FV}({}^{\star}e)$$
$$\mathrm{FV}(x) = \{x\}$$
$$\mathrm{FV}(\lambda z.{}^{\star}e) = \mathrm{FV}({}^{\star}e) - \{z\}$$
$$\mathrm{FV}(\vartheta({}^{\star}e_1, \ldots, {}^{\star}e_n)) = \mathrm{FV}({}^{\star}e_1) \cup \ldots \cup \mathrm{FV}({}^{\star}e_n) \qquad \vartheta \in \mathbf{O}_n$$
$$\mathrm{FV}({}^{\star}\sigma) = \bigcup_{x \in \mathrm{Dom}({}^{\star}\sigma)} \mathrm{FV}({}^{\star}\sigma(x))$$

The variables in the domain of an occurrence of ${}^{\star}\sigma$ are neither free nor bound. Renaming of bound variables and substitution for free variables only act on the range of a substitution associated with a hole, not on its domain.

Definition (Substitution – ${}^{\star}e^{{}^{\star}\sigma}$, ${}^{\star}R^{{}^{\star}\sigma}$, ${}^{\star}\sigma \odot {}^{\star}\sigma'$**):** Substitution is extended to ER-expressions as follows:

$$(\circ^{{}^{\star}\sigma'})^{{}^{\star}\sigma} = \circ^{{}^{\star}\sigma \odot {}^{\star}\sigma'}$$
$$(\diamond^{{}^{\star}\sigma'}[{}^{\star}e])^{{}^{\star}\sigma} = \diamond^{{}^{\star}\sigma \odot {}^{\star}\sigma'}[{}^{\star}e^{{}^{\star}\sigma}]$$
$$x^{{}^{\star}\sigma} = \begin{cases} x & \text{if } x \notin \mathrm{Dom}({}^{\star}\sigma) \\ {}^{\star}\sigma(x) & \text{if } {}^{\star}e \in \mathrm{Dom}({}^{\star}\sigma) \end{cases}$$
$$(\lambda z.{}^{\star}e)^{{}^{\star}\sigma} = \lambda z.({}^{\star}e^{{}^{\star}\sigma\lceil(\mathrm{Dom}({}^{\star}\sigma)-\{z\})}) \quad \text{if} \quad z \notin \mathrm{FV}({}^{\star}\sigma\lceil(\mathrm{Dom}({}^{\star}\sigma) - \{z\}))$$
$$\vartheta({}^{\star}e_1, \ldots, {}^{\star}e_n)^{{}^{\star}\sigma} = \vartheta({}^{\star}e_1^{{}^{\star}\sigma}, \ldots, {}^{\star}e_n^{{}^{\star}\sigma})$$
$$\bullet^{{}^{\star}\sigma} = \bullet$$
$$\diamond^{{}^{\star}\sigma'}[{}^{\star}R]^{{}^{\star}\sigma} = \diamond^{{}^{\star}\sigma \odot {}^{\star}\sigma'}[{}^{\star}R^{{}^{\star}\sigma}]$$
$${}^{\star}\sigma \odot {}^{\star}\sigma' = \lambda x \in \mathrm{Dom}({}^{\star}\sigma').{}^{\star}\sigma'(x)^{{}^{\star}\sigma}$$

As defined here substitution is a partial operation. Using renaming substitutions (bijections on variables) we can rename bound variables in the usual way. We consider ER-expressions (and entities containing them) to be equal if they differ only by renaming of bound variables. Thus, for any substitution we can always choose a variant such that substitution is defined. Recall (§2) that such renaming is not possible in the case of traditional contexts.

The operations of filling E-holes in ${}^{\star}e$ with e, ${}^{\star}e[\circ \mapsto e]$, and filling R-holes in ${}^{\star}e$ with R, ${}^{\star}e[\diamond \mapsto R]$, are defined by induction on the structure of ${}^{\star}e$. As for substitution, we rename bound variables of ${}^{\star}e$ to avoid capture of free variables in e or R by lambda binding. When an expression is placed in an E-hole or a reduction context is place in an R-hole the filled decorating substitution is applied to the filler. Similarly for filling of E- or R- holes in ER-reduction contexts.

Definition (${}^{\star}e[\circ \mapsto e]$**):**

$$\circ^{{}^{\star}\sigma}[\circ \mapsto e] = e^{{}^{\star}\sigma[\circ \mapsto e]}$$

$$\diamond^{\star\sigma}\,[{}^\star e\,]\,[\circ \mapsto e] = \diamond^{\star\sigma[\circ\mapsto e]}\,[{}^\star e[\circ \mapsto e]\,]$$
$$\vartheta({}^\star e_1, \ldots, {}^\star e_n)[\circ \mapsto e] = \vartheta({}^\star e_1[\circ \mapsto e], \ldots, {}^\star e_n[\circ \mapsto e])$$
$${}^\star v[\circ \mapsto e] = {}^\star v \quad \text{if} \quad {}^\star v \in \mathbf{A} \cup \mathbf{X}$$
$$(\lambda x.{}^\star e')[\circ \mapsto e] = \lambda x.({}^\star e'[\circ \mapsto e]) \quad \text{if} \quad x \notin \mathrm{FV}(e)$$
$${}^\star\sigma[\circ \mapsto e] = \lambda x \in \mathrm{Dom}({}^\star\sigma).({}^\star\sigma(x)[\circ \mapsto e])$$

Consider the following simple example.

$$(\lambda x.\circ^{\emptyset})[\circ \mapsto x] = (\lambda z.\circ^{\emptyset})[\circ \mapsto x] = \lambda z.(\circ^{\emptyset}[\circ \mapsto x]) = \lambda z.x$$
$$(\lambda x.\circ^{x\mapsto x})[\circ \mapsto x] = (\lambda z.\circ^{x\mapsto z})[\circ \mapsto x] = \lambda z.z = \lambda x.x$$

This example shows, among other things, that the precise domain of the substitution decorating a hole is important. This is in contrast to substitutions viewed as maps on expressions, where σ is the same map as $\sigma\{x \mapsto x\}$ for $x \notin \mathrm{Dom}(\sigma)$.

Definition (${}^\star e[\diamond \mapsto R]$)**:**

$$\circ^{\star\sigma}[\diamond \mapsto R] = \circ^{\star\sigma[\diamond\mapsto R]}$$
$$\diamond^{\star\sigma}\,[{}^\star e\,]\,[\diamond \mapsto R] = R^{\star\sigma[\diamond\mapsto R]}\,[{}^\star e[\diamond \mapsto R]\,]$$
$$\vartheta({}^\star e_1, \ldots, {}^\star e_n)[\diamond \mapsto R] = \vartheta({}^\star e_1[\diamond \mapsto R], \ldots, {}^\star e_n[\diamond \mapsto R])$$
$${}^\star v[\diamond \mapsto R] = {}^\star v \quad \text{if} \quad {}^\star v \in \mathbf{A} \cup \mathbf{X}$$
$$(\lambda x.{}^\star e')[\diamond \mapsto R] = \lambda x.({}^\star e'[\diamond \mapsto R]) \quad \text{if} \quad x \notin \mathrm{FV}(R)$$
$${}^\star\sigma[\diamond \mapsto R] = \lambda x \in \mathrm{Dom}({}^\star\sigma).({}^\star\sigma(x)[\diamond \mapsto R])$$

As an example of R-hole filling we have

$$\diamond^{\{x\mapsto\lambda x.x\}}\,[\,2\,]\,[\diamond \mapsto \mathtt{app}(x, \bullet)] = \mathtt{app}(\lambda x.x, 2)$$

It is easy (but tedious) to check that E-hole and R-hole filling commute.

Lemma (ER-hole filling):

$${}^\star e[\circ \mapsto e][\diamond \mapsto R] = {}^\star e[\diamond \mapsto R][\circ \mapsto e]$$

The following lemma is the key to developing a notion of uniform computation. A proof can be found in (Agha, Mason, Smith, and Talcott 1997).

Lemma (fil-subst): Hole filling and substitution commute.

$${}^\circ e^{\circ\sigma}[\circ \mapsto e'] = {}^\circ e[\circ \mapsto e']^{\circ\sigma[\circ\mapsto e']} \quad \text{if} \quad \mathrm{Dom}({}^\circ\sigma) \cap \mathrm{FV}(e') = \emptyset$$
$${}^\diamond e^{\circ\sigma}[\diamond \mapsto R] = {}^\diamond e[\diamond \mapsto R]^{\circ\sigma[\diamond\mapsto R]} \quad \text{if} \quad \mathrm{Dom}({}^\circ\sigma) \cap \mathrm{FV}(R) = \emptyset$$

Note that ER-reduction contexts possess two types of holes: decorated holes, and traditional, undecorated holes. The process of filling the redex hole, $\bullet$, with an E-expression, ${}^\circ e$, remains unchanged, and we continue to denote it by ${}^\circ R\,[{}^\circ e\,]$.

Defining $\bullet[\circ \mapsto e] = \bullet[\diamond \mapsto R] = \bullet$ we see that filling of decorated and undecorated holes commutes.

Lemma (ER- C- hole fill):

$$^\star R[\circ \mapsto e_0]\,[\,e\,] = {}^\star R\,[\,e\,]\,[\circ \mapsto e_0] \quad \text{and} \quad {}^\star R[\diamond \mapsto e_0]\,[\,e\,] = {}^\star R\,[\,e\,]\,[\diamond \mapsto e_0]$$

As an example of this commuting we have

$$\begin{aligned}&(\diamond^{\{x \mapsto \lambda x.x\}}\,[\,\bullet\,])\,[\,2\,]\,[\diamond \mapsto \mathtt{app}(x, \bullet)] \\ &\quad = (\diamond^{\{x \mapsto \lambda x.x\}}\,[\,\bullet\,])[\diamond \mapsto \mathtt{app}(x, \bullet)]\,[\,2\,] = \mathtt{app}(\lambda x.x, 2)\end{aligned}$$

For each ordinary context C there is a corresponding E-expression, $\widehat{C}$ such that

$$C\,[\,e\,] = \widehat{C}[\circ \mapsto e].$$

$\widehat{C}$ is obtained by decorating each hole occurrence in C with a binding substitution $\{x_i \mapsto x_i \mid x_i \in X\}$ where X is the set of lambda variables having the hole occurrence in their scope. For example, the E-expression corresponding to $\lambda x.\bullet$ is $\lambda x.\circ^{x \mapsto x}$.

The decomposition lemma for ER-expressions has two new cases: when an E-hole or an R-hole appears in the redex position. As before, the proofs are an easy induction on the syntax structure.

Lemma (E-expression decomposition): For any ER-expression, $^\star e$, exactly one of the following holds:

(0) $\quad {}^\star e \in {}^\star\mathbf{V}$, or

(1) $\quad (\exists! {}^\star R, {}^\star r)({}^\star e = {}^\star R\,[\,{}^\star r\,])$, or

(2e) $\quad (\exists! {}^\star R, {}^\star\sigma)({}^\star e = {}^\star R\,[\,\circ^{{}^\star\sigma}\,])$, or

(2r) $\quad (\exists! {}^\star R, {}^\star\sigma, {}^\star v)({}^\star e = {}^\star R\,[\,\diamond^{{}^\star\sigma}[\bullet \mapsto {}^\star v]\,])$

ER-states are composed of an ER-state context, and an ER-expression. ER-state contexts are formed just like state contexts replacing (value) expressions by ER-(value) expressions in the constructions. In particular, we continue to use ordinary holes and hole filling to represent state contexts and their conversion to expressions. Thus $\mathrm{s2e}({}^\star\zeta : {}^\star e) = {}^\star\zeta\,[\,{}^\star e\,]$. An ER-state whose expression decomposes according to case (2e) or (2r) is said to *touch a hole*. E-hole filling of ER-states is defined by $({}^\star\zeta : {}^\star e)[\circ \mapsto e] = {}^\star\zeta[\circ \mapsto e]) : ({}^\star e[\circ \mapsto e]$. In the cases we have considered, E-hole filling of ER-state contexts is defined using the decomposition of states into a constant allocation part and an effects part. For example is the case of memory contexts we have

$$(\{z_i \mapsto \mathtt{mk}({}^\circ v_i) \mid 1 \le i \le n\})[\circ \mapsto e] = \{z_i \mapsto \mathtt{mk}({}^\circ v_i[\circ \mapsto e]) \mid 1 \le i \le n\}.$$

Similarly for R-hole filling.

The property required of ER-computation for uniform semantics can now be stated: an ER-state either reduces uniformly, hangs uniformly, or touches a hole.

Definition (Uniform reduction (s-unif)): A λ-language satisfies the **s-unif** property if the reduction rules can be extended to E-states and R-states such that:

1. If ${}^{\star}\zeta : {}^{\star}e \longrightarrow {}^{\star}\zeta_1 : {}^{\star}e_1$, then $({}^{\star}\zeta : {}^{\star}e)[\circ \mapsto e] \longrightarrow ({}^{\star}\zeta_1 : {}^{\star}e_1)[\circ \mapsto e]$ for any e and $({}^{\star}\zeta : {}^{\star}e)[\diamond \mapsto R] \longrightarrow ({}^{\star}\zeta_1 : {}^{\star}e_1)[\diamond \mapsto R]$ for any R.
2. If $({}^{\star}\zeta : {}^{\star}e)[\circ \mapsto e] \longrightarrow {}^{\star}\zeta' : {}^{\star}e'$ or $({}^{\star}\zeta : {}^{\star}e)[\diamond \mapsto R] \longrightarrow {}^{\star}\zeta' : {}^{\star}e'$, then either ${}^{\star}\zeta : {}^{\star}e$ touches a hole (${}^{\star}e$ has the form ${}^{\star}R\,\texttt{[}P\texttt{]}$ where P is of the form $\circ^{{}^{\star}\sigma}$ or $\diamond^{{}^{\star}\sigma}\,\texttt{[}{}^{\star}v\texttt{]}$) or there is some ${}^{\star}\zeta_1, {}^{\star}e_1$ such that ${}^{\star}\zeta : {}^{\star}e \longrightarrow {}^{\star}\zeta_1 : {}^{\star}e_1$.

We now show how to lift the reduction rules for the languages considered in the previous sections. Since place-holders can only occur in value expressions inside a lambda, their presence does not change the definition of the satisfaction relation for state contexts. Thus, the reduction rules for the various operations can be extended to the ER-redexes and ER-states simply by annotating metavariables with *'s. As examples, we give the local rules for `app`, `br`, and `eq`. the local lifting rule, and rules for `ncc` and `set`.

Definition (Reduction rules lifted):

(app) $\quad \texttt{app}(\lambda x.{}^{\star}e, {}^{\star}v) \hookrightarrow_{{}^{\star}\zeta} {}^{\star}e^{\{x \mapsto {}^{\star}v\}}$

(br) $\quad \texttt{br}({}^{\star}v_0, {}^{\star}v_1, {}^{\star}v_2) \hookrightarrow_{{}^{\star}\zeta} \begin{cases} {}^{\star}v_1 & \text{if } {}^{\star}\zeta \models {}^{\star}v \notin \{\texttt{nil}\} \\ {}^{\star}v_2 & \text{if } {}^{\star}\zeta \models {}^{\star}v \in \{\texttt{nil}\} \end{cases}$

(eq) $\quad \texttt{eq}({}^{\star}v_0, {}^{\star}v_1) \hookrightarrow_{{}^{\star}\zeta} \begin{cases} \texttt{t} & \text{if } {}^{\star}\zeta \models ({}^{\star}v_0, {}^{\star}v_1) \in \mathbf{AtEq} \\ \texttt{nil} & \text{if } {}^{\star}\zeta \models ({}^{\star}v_0, {}^{\star}v_1) \notin \mathbf{AtEq} \end{cases}$

(rdx) $\quad {}^{\star}\zeta : {}^{\star}R\,\texttt{[}{}^{\star}r\texttt{]} \longrightarrow {}^{\star}\zeta : {}^{\star}R\,\texttt{[}{}^{\star}e\texttt{]} \quad \text{if} \quad {}^{\star}r \hookrightarrow_{{}^{\star}\zeta} {}^{\star}e$

(ncc) $\quad {}^{\star}\zeta : {}^{\star}R\,\texttt{[ncc(}{}^{\star}v\texttt{)]} \longrightarrow {}^{\star}\zeta : \texttt{app}({}^{\star}v, \texttt{top} \circ {}^{\star}R)$

(set) $\quad {}^{\star}M_T : {}^{\star}R\,\texttt{[set(}z, {}^{\star}v\texttt{)]} \longrightarrow {}^{\star}M\{z \mapsto \mathrm{mk}({}^{\star}v)\}_T : {}^{\star}R\,\texttt{[nil]}$

$\qquad\qquad \text{if} \quad z \in \mathrm{Dom}({}^{\star}M)$

Theorem (Uniformity): The languages Λ_f, Λ_c, Λ_m, and Λ_s all have uniform semantics.

8 Proof of the ciu theorem and consequences

8.1 Proof of ciu

There are several proofs of the **ciu** theorem for Λ_m in the literature. The first proof (Mason and Talcott 1991a) uses the uniform computation technique, but the details are not fully spelled out. In a more recent paper (Honsell, Mason, Smith, and Talcott 1995) a proof is given based on the observation that it suffices to show that $\sqsubseteq^{\text{ciu}}$ is a congruence.

First we recall the statement of the theorem. The **ciu**-approximation relation is defined by

$$e_0 \sqsubseteq^{\text{ciu}} e_1 \Leftrightarrow (\forall \zeta, R, \sigma \mid \bigwedge_{j<2} \zeta : R\,[\,e_j^\sigma\,] \text{ closed})(\zeta : R\,[\,e_0^\sigma\,] \preceq \zeta : R\,[\,e_1^\sigma\,])$$

We want to show that for any λ-language with uniform semantics, $e_0 \sqsubseteq^{\text{ciu}} e_1$ iff $e_0 \sqsubseteq e_1$. That $e_0 \sqsubseteq e_1$ implies $e_0 \sqsubseteq^{\text{ciu}} e_1$ is (almost) direct from the definitions. It relies on the fact that

$$\zeta : R\,[\,e^\sigma\,] \updownarrow \circ : \zeta\,[\,R\,[\,e^\sigma\,]\,] \updownarrow \circ : \zeta\,[\,R\,[\,\mathtt{let}\,\sigma\,\mathtt{in}\,e\,]\,]$$

where $\mathtt{let}\ \sigma\ \mathtt{in}\ e$ expands the parallel substitution σ to a suitable sequence of $\mathtt{let}$ s, taking care that the sequentialization does not cause substitution into the range of σ. This fact follows from **g-unif**. Thus, we need only show that $e_0 \sqsubseteq e_1$ under the assumption that $e_0 \sqsubseteq^{\text{ciu}} e_1$. Using the representation of contexts as E-expressions it suffices to show that

$$({}^\circ\zeta : {}^\circ e)[\circ \mapsto e_0] \preceq ({}^\circ\zeta : {}^\circ e)[\circ \mapsto e_1]$$

for any E-state ${}^\circ\zeta : {}^\circ e$ such that both sides are closed. We use induction on the computation length. Assume $({}^\circ\zeta : {}^\circ e)[\circ \mapsto e_0]\downarrow$. First we consider the case in which e_0 is not a value expression. If ${}^\circ e \in {}^\circ\mathbf{V}$ then $({}^\circ\zeta : {}^\circ e)[\circ \mapsto e']\downarrow$ for any e' since it is a value state. Otherwise, to show $({}^\circ\zeta : {}^\circ e)[\circ \mapsto e_1]\downarrow$, we need only find ${}^\circ\zeta' : {}^\circ e'$ such that

1. $({}^\circ\zeta : {}^\circ e)[\circ \mapsto e_0] \twoheadrightarrow ({}^\circ\zeta' : {}^\circ e')[\circ \mapsto e_0]$ (in one or more steps)
2. $({}^\circ\zeta' : {}^\circ e')[\circ \mapsto e_1]\downarrow$ implies $({}^\circ\zeta : {}^\circ e)[\circ \mapsto e_1]\downarrow$.

since 1. together with the induction hypothesis imply $({}^\circ\zeta' : {}^\circ e')[\circ \mapsto e_1]\downarrow$.

If ${}^\circ\zeta : {}^\circ e \longrightarrow {}^\circ\zeta' : {}^\circ e'$ then we are done. Otherwise by **s-unif**, ${}^\circ e$ has the form ${}^\circ R\,[\,\circ^{{}^\circ\sigma}\,]$. Since e_0 is not a value, and holes in ${}^\circ\sigma$ appear only inside lambdas it must be the case that $e_0^{{}^\circ\sigma}$ has the form ${}^\circ R_0\,[\,{}^\circ r\,]$. Thus by **s-unif** there is some ${}^\circ\zeta' : {}^\circ e'$ such that ${}^\circ\zeta : {}^\circ R\,[\,e_0^{{}^\circ\sigma}\,] \longrightarrow {}^\circ\zeta' : {}^\circ e'$. Clearly ${}^\circ\zeta' : {}^\circ e'$ satisfies condition 1. To see that it satisfies condition 2. note that

$$({}^\circ\zeta : {}^\circ R\,[\,e_0^{{}^\circ\sigma}\,])[\circ \mapsto e_1] \longrightarrow ({}^\circ\zeta' : {}^\circ e')[\circ \mapsto e_1]$$

and by the **ciu**-hypothesis

$$({}^\circ\zeta : {}^\circ R\,[\,e_0^{{}^\circ\sigma}\,])[\circ \mapsto e_1] \preceq ({}^\circ\zeta : {}^\circ R\,[\,e_1^{{}^\circ\sigma}\,])[\circ \mapsto e_1].$$

For the case in which e_0 is a value expression, we prove a lemma (**uval**) that shows that by filling a finite number of holes in ${}^\circ e$ with e_0 we obtain an E-expression ${}^\circ e_k$

such that either ${}^{\circ}e_k$ is an E-value, or ${}^{\circ}\!\varsigma : {}^{\circ}e_k$ reduces, thus giving ${}^{\circ}\!\varsigma' : {}^{\circ}e'$ satisfying condition 1. Since the holes filled by e_0 appear in redex positions, we may apply the **ciu** assumption to show that 2. holds. We begin with the lemma.

Lemma (uval): If $({}^{\circ}\!\varsigma : {}^{\circ}e)[\circ \mapsto v]\!\downarrow$, then we can find $k \in \mathbf{N}$, ${}^{\circ}r$, ${}^{\circ}e_j$, ${}^{\circ}R_j$, ${}^{\circ}\sigma_j$ for $j \leq k$ such that

$${}^{\circ}e = {}^{\circ}e_0$$

$${}^{\circ}e_j = {}^{\circ}R_j\,[\,\circ^{{}^{\circ}\sigma_j}\,] \quad \text{for} \quad j < k$$

$${}^{\circ}e_{j+1} = {}^{\circ}R_j\,[\,v^{{}^{\circ}\sigma_j}\,]$$

And either ${}^{\circ}e_k$ is an E-value or there is some ${}^{\circ}r$ such that ${}^{\circ}e_k = {}^{\circ}R_k\,[\,{}^{\circ}r\,]$ and ${}^{\circ}\!\varsigma : {}^{\circ}e_k$ reduces.

Proof (uval): Let ${}^{\circ}e_0 = {}^{\circ}e$ as required. By the decomposition lemma and **s-unif** either $k = 0$ or ${}^{\circ}e$ has the form ${}^{\circ}R_0\,[\,\circ^{{}^{\circ}\sigma_0}\,]$. In the latter case, let ${}^{\circ}e_1 = {}^{\circ}R_0\,[\,v^{{}^{\circ}\sigma_0}\,]$ and continue the process. Each step reduces the number of E-holes not in the scope of a lambda, and hence must terminate.

$\Box_{\mathbf{uval}}$

Now let $k \in \mathbf{N}$, ${}^{\circ}r$, ${}^{\circ}e_j$, ${}^{\circ}R_j$, ${}^{\circ}\sigma_j$ for $j \leq k$ be as given by (**uval**) with $v = e_0$. Note that ${}^{\circ}e_j[\circ \mapsto e_0] = {}^{\circ}e[\circ \mapsto e_0]$ for $j \leq k$. Now we prove by induction on $k - j$ that $({}^{\circ}\!\varsigma : {}^{\circ}e_j)[\circ \mapsto e_1]\!\downarrow$ for $0 \leq j \leq k$. For $k = j$ we use the same argument as for the case in which e_0 is a non-value. Assume $({}^{\circ}\!\varsigma : {}^{\circ}e_{j+1})[\circ \mapsto e_1]\!\downarrow$ for some $j + 1 \leq k$. By construction

$${}^{\circ}e_{j+1}[\circ \mapsto e_1] = ({}^{\circ}R_j\,[\,e_0^{{}^{\circ}\sigma_j}\,])[\circ \mapsto e_1]$$

so by the **ciu** hypothesis

$$({}^{\circ}\!\varsigma : {}^{\circ}R_j\,[\,e_1^{{}^{\circ}\sigma_j}\,])[\circ \mapsto e_1]\!\downarrow$$

which completes the e_0 is a value case.

$\Box_{\mathbf{ciu}}$

We leave the proof of (**L-unif**) to the reader, but we note that 'reduces assuming $p \in \mathbf{L}$' can be reformulated by replacing free occurrences of p by $\lambda x.\circ^{\{x \mapsto x\}}$.

8.2 Proof of Equi-rcx

Now we use **ciu** combined with R-uniform computation to establish (**equi-rcx**). For the readers convenience we first recall the statement of the theorem.

Theorem (Equi-rcx): For any λ-language with uniform semantics, if for z fresh there is $e_0 \cong e_1$ such that $R_j\,[\,z\,] \xrightarrow{\text{ci}}\!\!\!\twoheadrightarrow e_j$ for $j < 2$, then $R_0\,[\,e\,] \cong R_1\,[\,e\,]$ for any e.

Remark In Λ_{f} or Λ_{m} establishing (**equi-rcx**) is a fairly straightforward application of **ciu** in combination with (**fred.isdef**) or (**mred.isdef**). In Λ_{c} it is still fairly easy. However, to establish the result in a more general setting requires a bit more work. We use the R-hole uniformity of uniform semantics.

We prove a more general result.

Theorem (Equi-rcx!): For any λ-language with uniform semantics, to show $R_0\,[\,e\,] \cong R_1\,[\,e\,]$ for any e it suffices to show that for any ${}^{\circ}\zeta$, ${}^{\circ}R$, ${}^{\circ}\sigma$, z fresh such that ${}^{\circ}\zeta$ closes ${}^{\circ}R\,[\,R_j\,[\,z\,]^{{}^{\circ}\sigma}\,]$ we can find an ${}^{\circ}e$ such that ${}^{\circ}\zeta : {}^{\circ}R\,[\,R_j\,[\,z\,]^{{}^{\circ}\sigma}\,] \twoheadrightarrow {}^{\circ}\zeta : {}^{\circ}e$.

It is easy to see by uniformity properties that **(Equi-rcx!)** implies **(Equi-rcx)**. So we proceed with the proof of the more general result.

Proof (equi-rcx!): Assume the **(equi-rcx)** hypothesis. By **ciu**, we need only show that

$$\zeta : R\,[\,R_0\,[\,e\,]^{\sigma}\,] \updownarrow \zeta : R\,[\,R_1\,[\,e\,]^{\sigma}\,]$$

for any closing ζ, R, σ. We claim that for any closing ${}^{\circ}\zeta, {}^{\circ}e$ if $({}^{\circ}\zeta : {}^{\circ}e)[\diamond \mapsto R_0]\downarrow$, then $({}^{\circ}\zeta : {}^{\circ}e)[\diamond \mapsto R_1]\downarrow$. Then taking ${}^{\circ}\zeta = \zeta$ and ${}^{\circ}e = R\,[\,\diamond^{\sigma}\,[\,e^{\sigma}\,]\,]$ we are done.

To prove the claim, pick some closing ${}^{\circ}\zeta, {}^{\circ}e$ such that $({}^{\circ}\zeta : {}^{\circ}e)[\diamond \mapsto R_0]\downarrow$. If ${}^{\circ}e$ is an R-value or if ${}^{\circ}\zeta : {}^{\circ}e$ steps uniformly, then we are done. Otherwise, by the R-decomposition property ${}^{\circ}e$ has the form ${}^{\circ}R\,[\,\diamond^{{}^{\circ}\sigma}\,[\,{}^{\circ}v\,]\,]$. By assumption we can find ${}^{\circ}e'$ such that

$${}^{\circ}\zeta : {}^{\circ}R\,[\,R_j^{{}^{\circ}\sigma}\,[\,{}^{\circ}v\,]\,] \twoheadrightarrow {}^{\circ}\zeta : {}^{\circ}e' \quad \text{for} \quad j < 2$$

and hence

$$({}^{\circ}\zeta : {}^{\circ}e)[\diamond \mapsto R_j] \twoheadrightarrow ({}^{\circ}\zeta : {}^{\circ}e')[\diamond \mapsto R_j] \quad \text{for} \quad j < 2$$

If $\twoheadrightarrow$ is one or more steps for $j = 0$ or if ${}^{\circ}\zeta : {}^{\circ}e'$ steps uniformly, then

$$({}^{\circ}\zeta : {}^{\circ}e')[\diamond \mapsto R_1]\downarrow \qquad \text{by computation induction}$$

and we are done. Similarly, if ${}^{\circ}e' \in {}^{\circ}\mathbf{V}$ we are done. Thus by uniformity we may assume ${}^{\circ}e' = {}^{\circ}R\,[\,R_0^{{}^{\circ}\sigma}\,[\,{}^{\circ}v\,]\,]$ has the form ${}^{\circ}R'\,[\,\diamond^{{}^{\circ}\sigma'}\,[\,{}^{\circ}v'\,]\,]$ and we apply the above argument to ${}^{\circ}\zeta : {}^{\circ}e'$. Since ${}^{\circ}e'$ has one fewer $\diamond$ not in the scope of a lambda this process must terminate and, as in the proof of **ciu**, we are done.

$\Box_{\mathbf{Equi-rcx!}}$

9 Conclusion

In this paper we have unified our earlier work on semantics of imperative functional programs in a more abstract and general setting. We defined a notion of uniform semantics for λ-languages, and developed general principles for reasoning about program equivalence in any λ-languages with uniform semantics. In particular we have shown that the **ciu** theorem holds in any λ-language with uniform semantics. For such languages we have the combined benefits of reduction calculi (modular axiomatization), and operational equivalence (more equations).

This is a small step towards a usable methodology for developing equational semantics of higher-order languages with effects, and there are a number of directions for future work. A useful refinement would be to identify a form of rules that guarantees uniform semantics, generalizing the ideas of Howe (1996) to functional languages with effects. Another extension would be to develop denotational tools in this setting generalizing Mason, Smith, and Talcott (1996).

Another direction is to treat a wider range of languages. Of particular interest is extending the uniform framework to incorporate actor and other concurrency primitives. As mentioned earlier, the notion of uniform computation was key to developing methods for reasoning about program equivalence in a λ-language with actor primitives. In the actor world termination is not an interesting property: it is the infinite (fair) computations that are of interest. Thus, rather than appealing to computation induction, we use uniform computation to transform computation paths, preserving fairness.

This more general setting should also facilitate extending the VTLoE programming logic (Honsell, Mason, Smith, and Talcott 1995) to a wider range of program primitives.

Acknowledgements Most of the work that this paper builds on was done in collaboration with Ian Mason who contributed many important ideas and insights. The author would like to thank Ian Mason, Soeren Lassen, Scott Smith, José Meseguer, and Ian Stark for numerous helpful criticisms and pointing out errors in an earlier draft. She would also like to thank the editors of this volume, Andrew Gordon and Andrew Pitts, for their encouragement and patience during the writing of the paper. This research was partially supported by ARPA grant NAVY N00014-94-1-0775, ONR grant N00014-94-1-0857, NSF grant CCR-9302923, and NSF grant CCR-9312580.

References

Abramsky, S. (1990). The lazy lambda calculus. In D. Turner (Ed.), *Research Topics in Functional Programming*. Addison-Wesley.

Abramsky, S. (1991). Domain theory in logical form. *Annals of Pure and Applied Logic 51*(1), 1–77.

Aczel, P. (1978, July). A generalized church-rosser theorem.

Agha, G., I. A. Mason, S. F. Smith, and C. L. Talcott (1992, August). Towards a theory of actor computation. In *The Third International Conference on Concurrency Theory (CONCUR '92)*, Volume 630 of *Lecture Notes in Computer Science*, pp. 565–579. Springer Verlag.

Agha, G., I. A. Mason, S. F. Smith, and C. L. Talcott (1997). A foundation for actor computation. *Journal of Functional Programming*. to appear.

Bloom, B. (1990). Can LCF be topped? *Information and Computation 87*, 264–301.

Burge, W. H. (1975). Stream processing functions. *IBM Journal of Research and Development 19*, 12–25.

Crank, E. and M. Felleisen (1991). Parameter-passing and the lambda-calculus. In *Proceedings of the 18th ACM Symposium on Principles of Programming Languages*, pp. 233–245.

Egidi, L., F. Honsell, and S. Ronchi della Rocca (1992). Operational, denotational and logical descriptions: a case study. *Fundamenta Informaticae 16*(2), 149–170.

Felleisen, M. (1987). *The Calculi of Lambda-v-cs Conversion: A Syntactic Theory of Control and State in Imperative Higher-Order Programming Languages*. Ph. D. thesis, Indiana University.

Felleisen, M. (1988). λ-v-cs: An extended λ-calculus for Scheme,. In *1988 ACM conference on Lisp and functional programming*, Volume 52, pp. 72–85.

Felleisen, M. (1993). Personal communication.

Felleisen, M. and D. Friedman (1986). Control operators, the SECD-machine, and the λ-calculus. In M. Wirsing (Ed.), *Formal Description of Programming Concepts III*, pp. 193–217. North-Holland.

Felleisen, M. and R. Hieb (1989). The revised report on the syntactic theories of sequential control and state. Technical Report COMP TR89-100, Rice University.

Felleisen, M. and R. Hieb (1992). The revised report on the syntactic theories of sequential control and state. *Theoretical Computer Science 103*, 235–271.

Felleisen, M. and A. K. Wright (1991). A syntactic approach to type soundness. Technical Report Rice COMP TR91-160, Rice University Computer Science Department. To appear, *Information and Computation*.

Fields, J. and A. Sabry (1993). Reasoning about explicit and implicit representations of state. In *ACM Sigplan Workshop on State in Programming Languages*. YaleU/DCS/RR-968.

Gordon, A. D. (1995, July). Bisimilarity as a theory of functional programming (minicourse). Technical Report NS-95-3, BRICS, Department of Computer Science, Aarhus University.

Honsell, F., I. A. Mason, S. F. Smith, and C. L. Talcott (1995). A Variable Typed Logic of Effects. *Information and Computation 119*(1), 55–90.

Howe, D. (1989). Equality in the lazy lambda calculus. In *Fourth Annual Symposium on Logic in Computer Science*. IEEE.

Howe, D. J. (1996). Proving congruence of bisimulation in functional programming languages. *Information and Computation 124*(2), 103–112.

Jim, T. and A. Meyer (1991). Full abstraction and the context lemma. In *Theoretical Aspects of Computer Science*, Volume 526 of *Lecture Notes in Computer Science*, pp. 131–151. Springer-Verlag.

Klop, J. (1980). *Combinatory Reduction Systems*. Number 127 in Mathematical Centre Tracts. Mathematisch Centrum, Amsterdam.

Landin, P. J. (1964). The mechanical evaluation of expressions. *Computer Journal 6*, 308–320.

Landin, P. J. (1966). The next 700 programming languages. *Comm. ACM 9*, 157–166.

Lassen, S. B. (1995). private communication, Oct 1995.

Lassen, S. B. (199X). Action semantics reasoning about functional programs. *Mathematical Structures in Computer Science*. Special issue dedicated to the Workshop on Logic, Domains, and Programming Languages (Darmstadt, May 1995). To appear.

Mason, I. A. (1986). *The Semantics of Destructive Lisp*. Ph. D. thesis, Stanford University. Also available as CSLI Lecture Notes No. 5, Center for the Study of Language and Information, Stanford University.

Mason, I. A. (1988). Verification of programs that destructively manipulate data. *Science of Computer Programming 10*, 177–210.

Mason, I. A., S. F. Smith, and C. L. Talcott (1996). From Operational Semantics to Domain Theory. *Information and Computation to appear*.

Mason, I. A. and C. L. Talcott (1989). Programming, transforming, and proving with function abstractions and memories. In *Proceedings of the 16th EATCS Colloquium on Automata, Languages, and Programming, Stresa*, Volume 372 of *Lecture Notes in Computer Science*, pp. 574–588. Springer-Verlag.

Mason, I. A. and C. L. Talcott (1990). Reasoning about programs with effects. In *Programming Language Implementation and Logic Programming, PLILP'90*, Volume 456 of *Lecture Notes in Computer Science*, pp. 189–203. Springer-Verlag.

Mason, I. A. and C. L. Talcott (1991a). Equivalence in functional languages with effects. *Journal of Functional Programming 1*, 287–327.

Mason, I. A. and C. L. Talcott (1991b). Program transformation for configuring components. In *ACM/IFIP Symposium on Partial Evaluation and Semantics-based Program Manipulation*.

Mason, I. A. and C. L. Talcott (1992). Inferring the equivalence of functional programs that mutate data. *Theoretical Computer Science 105*(2), 167–215.

Mason, I. A. and C. L. Talcott (1994a). Program transformation via contextual assertions. In N. D. Jones, M. Hagiya, and M. Sato (Eds.), *Logic, Language, and Computation: Festschrift in Honor of Satoru Takasu*, Number 792 in Lecture Notes in Computer Science, pp. 225–254. Springer-Verlag.

Mason, I. A. and C. L. Talcott (1994b). Reasoning about object systems in vtloe. submitted to International Journal of Foundations of Computer Science.

Milner, R. (1977). Fully abstract models of typed λ-calculi. *Theoretical Computer Science 4*, 1–22.

Moggi, E. (1988). Computational lambda-calculus and monads. Technical Report ECS-LFCS-88-86, University of Edinburgh.

Moggi, E. (1989). Computational lambda-calculus and monads. In *Fourth Annual Symposium on Logic in Computer Science*. IEEE.

Moggi, E. (1990). An abstract view of programming languages. Technical Report ECS-LFCS-90-113, Laboratory for Foundations of Computer Science, University of Edinburgh.

Morris, J. H. (1968). *Lambda calculus models of programming languages*. Ph. D. thesis, Massachusetts Institute of Technology.

Mosses, P. D. (1992). *Action Semantics*. Number 26 in Cambridge Tracts in Theoretical Computer Science. Cambridge University Press.

Nipkow, T. (1991). Higher-order critical pairs. In *Sixth Annual Symposium on Logic in Computer Science*. IEEE.

Ong, C.-H. (1988). *The Lazy Lambda Calculus: An investigation into the Foundations of Functional Programming*. Ph. D. thesis, Imperial College, University of London.

Pitts, A. M. (1996). Reasoning about local variables with operationally-based logical relations. In *Eleventh Annual Symposium on Logic in Computer Science*. IEEE.

Pitts, A. M. and I. Stark (1993). On the observable properties of higher order functions that dynamically create local names. In *ACM Sigplan Workshop on State in Programming Languages*. YaleU/DCS/RR-968.

Pitts, A. M. and I. Stark (1996). Operational reasoning for functions with local state. In this volume, pp. 227–273.

Plotkin, G. (1975). Call-by-name, call-by-value and the lambda calculus. *Theoretical Computer Science 1*, 125–159.

Rees, J. and W. e. Clinger (1986). The revised^3 report on the algorithmic language scheme. *Sigplan Notices 21*(12), 37–79.

Reynolds, J. C. (1972). Definitional interpreters for higher-order programming languages. In *Proceedings, ACM National Convention*, pp. 717–740.

Ritter, E. and A. M. Pitts (1995). A fully abstract translation between a λ-calculus with reference types and standard ML. In *Proceedings TLCA'95, Edinburgh*.

Sabry, A. and M. Felleisen (1993). Reasoning about programs in continuation-passing style. *Lisp and Symbolic Computation 6*(3/4), 287–358.

Smith, S. F. (1992). From operational to denotational semantics. In *MFPS 1991*, Volume 598 of *Lecture Notes in Computer Science*, pp. 54–76. Springer-Verlag.

Steele, G. L. and G. J. Sussman (1975). Scheme, an interpreter for extended lambda calculus. Technical Report Technical Report 349, Massachusetts Institute of Technology, Artificial Intelligence Laboratory.

Sullivan, G. T. (1996). *An Extensional MetaLanguage with I/O and a Dynamic Store*. Ph. D. thesis, Northeastern University. in preparation.

Talcott, C. L. (1985). *The essence of Rum: A theory of the intensional and extensional aspects of Lisp-type computation*. Ph. D. thesis, Stanford University.

Talcott, C. L. (1989). Programming and proving with function and control abstractions. Technical Report STAN-CS-89-1288, Stanford University Computer Science Department.

Talcott, C. L. (1991). Binding structures. In V. Lifschitz (Ed.), *Artificial Intelligence and Mathematical Theory of Computation*. Academic Press.

Talcott, C. L. (1992). A theory for program and data type specification. *Theoretical Computer Science 104*, 129–159.

Talcott, C. L. (1993). A theory of binding structures and its applications to rewriting. *Theoretical Computer Science 112*, 99–143.

Weeks, S. and M. Felleisen (1993). On the orthogonality of assignments and procedures in Algol. In *Proceedings 20th ACM Symposium on Principles of Programming Languages*, pp. 57–70.

Printed in the United States
By Bookmasters